Plain Papers Relating to the Excise Branch of the Inland Revenue Department, from 1621 to 1878, Or, a History of the Excise

John Owens

PLAIN PAPERS.

A HISTORY OF THE EXCISE.

PLAIN PAPERS.

A HISTORY OF THE EXCISE.

PLAIN PAPERS

RELATING TO THE

EXCISE BRANCH

OF THE

INLAND REVENUE DEPARTMENT

From 1621 to 1878:

OR

A HISTORY OF THE EXCISE.

BY

JOHN OWENS,

SUPERVISOR OF INLAND REVENUE.

Experience is by industry achieved
And perfected by the swift course of Time."—*Shakespeare.*

LINLITHGOW.

1879.

PREFACE.

THESE Papers have been written to afford a glance into the Excise, as it was, as it is: its duties, its discipline. Those to which an asterisk is prefixed, in the index, are long papers, in which from the nature of the subject treated, it seemed desirable to trace the history with some detail for the benefit of the inquirer, that in the case of fiscal duties he might be informed of their origin, continuance, commutation, reduction, repeal, revival, and, in the case of discipline, he might not be uninformed of the trials, triumphs and tributes of his predecessors, while, in the language of Pope, "The learn'd reflect on what before they knew."

To obtain the necessary facts I have had recourse to that incomparable store-house of written human wisdom, the British Museum Library, where, during a period of three years and several subsequent visits, I have made a systematic research, which has included every volume of Cobbett's Parliamentary History, Hansard, Parliamentary Papers, bearing on my subject, London Gazette, State Papers, Statutes, many local histories, besides hundreds of miscellaneous issues. I have gleaned numerous important facts from the Commissioners' Reports and Orders, the Civil Service Gazette, the Civilian, and other sources: I have communicated with every grade in the department, to whom I now present my best thanks: I have gone into grave-yards in search of epitaphs, and into "back slums" in quest of songs: while, during the past six years, to economise sufficient time to complete my self-imposed task, I have to acknowledge my large indebtedness to an efficient and ever-obliging staff.

Neither exertion nor outlay has been spared in collecting, collating, and narrating these widely-scattered facts, which, now that they are brought within the compass of two covers, form a History of the Excise, which, I fondly hope, will be found at once comprehensive and reliable, be found acceptable to the members of my department, and be found a not-unworthy book of general departmental reference.

JOHN OWENS.

LINLITHGOW, 1879.

CONTENTS.

THE order of the alphabet having been adopted, with the exception of the first paper; see the Index.

ABBREVIATIONS.

H. L., House of Lords; H. C., House of Commons; P. Ret., P. Rep., P. P., P. O., Parliamentary Return, Report, Paper, Ordinance, respectively; T. W., Treasury Warrant; C. 1 R., Commissioners' First Report; L. G., London Gazette; G. I., General Instructions; E., England; S. Scotland; I., Ireland; C. S. G., Civil Service Gazette; C., Civilian.

CORRECTIONS AND ADDITIONS.

See page 558.

EXCISE.

AS A WORD: AS A BRANCH OF REVENUE.

The earliest forms of the word are these:

EXSYIS.
EXCYSE (S. Act, Aug. 4, 1621).
EXYSE (S. Act, Jan. 4, 1644).
EXCISE (Parl. Ord., 1643).
EXCYSIS (S. Act, June 4, 1650).
EXCISSE (S. Act, Oct. 8, 1663).
EXCIZE (I. 14 Caroli 2, c. 1).
EXIZE (29 Car. 2, c. 4).
ESSISE (1 Gule. and M., c. 24).
EXCISUM, "The excisum or part to be cut out and laid aside for public uses." (A Treatise of Tax and Contribution, 1662.) As used in an epitaph—
X I S (*Chambers' Journal*, 1873).
EXCISE is also found in the Bible, in the Book of Ezra as translated by Dr Benisch, and first in the Index to the Journal of the House of Commons in 1643; in the *London Gazette*, Sept. 10, 1666. (See Acts of Parliament).

Its synonym was "new impost" (12 Car. 2, c. 24). "An excise is only a word for a tax raised in a particular manner" (Warner's "History of the Rebellion and Civil war in Ireland," 1767). In France it was early called—

GABELLE (Smith's "Excises in France," 1733).

It was formerly used in the plural

EXCIZES ("Parliamentary Remonstrance," 1642).
EXCISES (Act of Union, 1707). Its equivalent—
IMPOSITIONS.
EXCISEMAN, a name borne by a race-horse (*Daily News*, Aug. 5, 1870). The functionaries were termed—
EXCISERS ("Dutch Devill Excise," 1653). Their technical language—
EXCISEISMS ("Excise Life as It Is," 1878). Their functions—

PLAIN PAPERS.

A HISTORY OF THE EXCISE.

The word excise is not used. The commission was then carried to the House of Commons, where, having been read, Sir Edward Cook observed, "The end of it was Excises for they are Impositions, and to be sure he would have the word (otherwise) wherefore his advice was to go up to the Lords, and desire a Conference, to complain of the Commission and desire it may be cancelled, and if there be any inrolment of it, to cancel that also, and that the projector may be found out and punished." He denounced the scheme as "monstrum, horrendum, informe, ingens."[1]

Rushworth then continues, that the Lord Keeper reported to the House of Lords, from his Majesty, "That their Lordships had reason to be satisfied with what was truly and rightly told them by the Lords of the Council, that this Commission was no more but a warrant of advice, which his Majesty knew to be agreeable at the time, and the manifold occasions then in hand, but now having a supply from the loves of his people, he esteems the Commission useless; and therefore though he knows no cause why any jealousie should have arised thereby, yet at their desires he is content it be cancelled, and he had commanded me to bring both the Commission and the Warrant to him, and it shall be cancelled in his own presence. The day following the Lord Keeper reported that his Majesty had cancelled the Commission and the Warrant for putting the Seal thereunto; and did there openly show it, and a Message was sent to the Commons to shew them the said cancelled Commission and Warrant."—June 16, 1628. It would seem that this act of his Majesty was quite unconstitutional; for John Pym, afterwards referred to, pointed out that "The Soveraigne power . . . . cannot lay any Tax, or Imposition upon his people without their consent in Parliament, made in a full and free House by the Lords and Commons, with the Kings Royall assent thereto, as the Statutes of 25 Edw. I. c. 5, 6; 34 Ed. I. c. 1, the Petition of Right, 3 Caroli and other Acts resolve."[1]

Though the project was now withdrawn, there was still a secret desire to see it re-introduced and adopted, but the mere utterance of it "neer fourteen years after its fatall doom"[1] again aroused the people and induced the House of Commons to issue the following declaration:—

"Die Sabbati, October 8, 1642.—The Commons House of Parliament receiving information that divers publick rumours and asper-

[1] Dutch Devill Excise," 1653.

sions are by Malignant Persons cast upon this House, that they intend assesse every mans Pewter, and Lay Excizes Upon That And Other Commodities. The said House for their Vindication therein do declare, That Those Rumours Are False And Scandalous; and forasmuch as those false rumours and scandalls are raised by Ill-Affected Persons, And Tend Much to the Disservice of the Parliament, it is therefore ordered, that the Authors of those false, scandalous rumours shall be searched and inquired after, and apprehended and brought to this House to receive their Condigne Punishment. Ordered by the Commons in Parliament that this be forthwith printed and published. Henry Elsing, Cler. Parl. D. Conv."[1]

And though this declaration was soon succeeded by a second, to the same effect, by both the Lords and the Commons,[2] the troubles of the times so increased, and with them a greater demand for means, that a Parliamentary Ordinance was issued at Westminster on May 13, 1643,[3] to establish the system, which had been previously, by twenty-two years, partially adopted in Scotland by an Act dated Aug. 4, 1621, and generally by a subsequent Act dated January 31, 1644; the Royalists at Oxford following by an Order dated Oct. 11, 1645. It commenced in Ireland in 1643.[4]

This mode of charge then having been established both in England and Scotland, under a promise in the former country that it should continue only during the war, month by month,[3] and in the latter country "bot for ane yeere;"[5] those entrusted with its management experienced many difficulties, more particularly when the people found, at the expiration of those periods, that the promises remained unobserved, and that the duties were to be continued on a plan proposed by John "Pym, who seems to have been the father of the Excise," and who stated in a letter to Sir John Hotham "that they had proceeded in the Excise to many particulars and intended to go further, but that it would be necessary to use the people to it by little and little."[6]

The repugnance and resistance of the people rose so high in 1646 that the House of Commons appointed a Committee to remove the obstructions with which the Commissioners of Excise were beset: to prepare reasons for first laying on the Excise, and the necessity

[1] "Dutch Devill Excise," 1653. [2] Jan. 12, 1642.

[3] Cobbett's "Parliamentary History.

[4] Warner's "Hist. of Rebellion and Civil War in Ireland," 1767.

[5] Act, Jan. 31, 1644. [6] "Encyclopædia Brittanica," 1834.

for its continuance: and to restrain the arbitrary power of the Sub-Commissioners.

About this time too the public uneasiness had become so general that the Excise Office in Smithfield was burnt down in a riot. Even the Lord Mayor himself was desired to suppress the tumult and proceed against the offenders.[1] Hume observes, in 1647, "The Excise was an odious tax formerly unknown to the nation, and was now extended on provisions and the common necessaries of life." He is scarcely right with regard to the incidence of the tax, but certainly so with respect to its character. The records in the Royal Library in the British Museum prove this in its collection of pamphlets and sheets:—

EXCISE—A Panegyrick on the Proceedings in Parliament.[2]
EXCISE—A New Ballad called a Review of the Rebellion.[2]
EXCISE—A Ditty of eighteen verses.[2]
EXCIZE—The Penitent Traytor.[2]
EXCISE-MEN—A Quarterne of Quearies.[2]
EXCISE—The poore Committee-man's Accompt.[2]
EXCISE—The true Protestants humble Desires.[2]
EXCISE—Ireland's Complaint of the Armies Hypocrisie.
EXCISES—The Cryes of Westminster, Or a Whole Pack of Parliamentary Knavery opened and set to Sale.
EXCISE—Hard Times—A New Song.

The resistance continued, and to such an extent, that the House of Commons found it necessary, in 1649, to prepare a "Model for better ordering and improving the Excise," and the "Speaker to sign Letters to the Judges of the Circuits to prevent Tumult by reason of the Excise."[3] Other fly-sheets and pamphlets were issued, as—

The Excise-Men's Lamentation; or Their Strange Creed and Letany: a parody on a portion of the Litany.[3]
A Dialogue betwixt an Excise-Man and Death.[3]
Dutch Devill Excise—The Judiciall Arraignment, Condemnation, Execution, and Interment of the late pernicious, endenizened Dutch Devil Excise, and its infernal Imps Excize-Men, England's grand Pests.

[1] Index to Journal of House of Commons.
[2] 1647.
[3] 1652: "Bagford Ballads," 1652.

This is a document of some historical value, and concludes with a general denunciation, of which the following is an extract:—"What infinite intolerable, oppressions, corruptions, abuses, are daily exercised by viperous Excizers, the Pollers and Caterpillers of the Nation in all places, would require a large volume to display and are so well known to most, that it would be expense of paper to record them, which have exasperated the people in some places to oppose and beat some, and cut off the ears of others of them, to stone and knock out the brains, and geld and cut out the stones of others of them, that they might have none of the generation of Vipers thereafter to infest them. . . . ."[1]

The sheets which appeared after this date were mere laments—

Excise Anotomized and Trade Epitomized.[2]

Excise Decryed, Trades Destruction is England's Ruine.[2]

Cromwell and his Council on obtaining possession of Parliament found it necessary to pass an Ordinance "for enforcing the Acts and Ordinances made before the meeting of the last Parliament touching the Collection of the Excise,"—Jan. 22, 16$\frac{54}{55}$;[3] and shortly afterwards, on the union of Scotland with England in one Commonwealth, to pass another "Ordinance and Declaration" to extend the levy of most of the excise duties, than chargeable in England, to Scotland,[12] and, not long before the close of his daring deeds, to proclaim, in a print of handsome black letter, that a yearly sum had been settled for "the support of the Government and defence of these nations by sea and land," and that "It being found that the Imposition of the Excise is the most easie and indifferent levy that can be laid upon the People," it shall continue to be collected. "Protector Olivaris Dei Gra: Reipub: Angliæ, Scotiæ et Hiberniæ. Given at our Palace at Westminster."[4]

Under this authority the excise continued to be enforced until his death, and very probably until the Restoration of Charles II.—12 Caroli II., cc. 5, 8. His Majesty Charles II. having arrived in England on May 29, 1660, little time was lost before revenue matters were considered, and on July 30, 1660, a m mittee was appointed to settle the excise on the king for life. This was voted on Nov. 27, 1660. Alexander Pringle offered to procure an Act for settling on His Majesty and his successors upwards of two millions

[1] Royal Library, British Museum.
[2] 1659.
[3] May 22, 1655.
[4] March 10, 1657.

a year by way of subsidy, which, with the revenue of Excise and other duties, would make His Majesty very rich. The King was well pleased with the proposition, but on conferring with Chancellor Hyde, that minister told his Majesty "That the best revenue he could have would be the gaining the hearts of his Subjects; that if he would trust to them, he would find such Supplies as should never fail in Time of Need."[1] The committee having concluded their deliberations and made a proposition to double the duties, and to thus settle one moiety of the excise on the King and his successors, in perpetuity, Sir Heneage Finch brought in the bill which was twice read, and then referred to a "Grand Committee" who sat de die in diem until the business was despatched.[2]

The celebrated Andrew Marvell, who was the M.P. for Kingston-upon-Hull, both before and after the Restoration, wrote: "The Excise Bill for longer continuance (I wish it prove not too long) will come in next week. And I foresee we shall be called upon fully to effect our vote made the former sitting of raising his Majesty's revenue to £1,200,000 per ann. I do not love to write so much of the money news, but I think that you have observed that Parliaments have been always made use of to that purpose; and though we may buy gold too dear, yet we must at any rate be glad of peace, freedom, and a good conscience."[3]

The Crown, down to the date of the later enactment, enjoyed certain prerogatives in the "Court of Wards and Liveries, and Tenures in Capite, and by Knights Service and Purveyance,"[4] which were now discontinued in exchange for a moiety of the duties arising from beer, cider, aqua vitæ, and other liquors, which in turn have been commuted into an annual sum, which is, of course, not obligatory on a royal successor, seeing that the moiety of the previously stated duties is settled in perpetuity on the Crown.

The first half of the excise duties was continued by Parliament to several of Charles's successors,[5] but the hereditary moiety, with respect to commutation, has always awaited the pleasure of the Crown: thus George IV. stated in his speech on opening Parliament, "I have entirely at your disposal my interest in the hereditary

[1] Convention Parliament, Nov. 6, 1660. [2] Dec. 14, 1660.

[3] Cobbett's "Parliamentary History."

[4] 12 Caroli 2 c. 24; Hume: Justyne, C. S. G., 1864.

[5] H. C., May 22, 1685: 1 W. & M., c. 14; 1 Anne, c. 1.: H. C., July 4, 1727.

revenue."[1] On the accession of Her Majesty Queen Victoria, the duties on beer and cider were ordered to be charged, but the Lords of the Treasury countermanded those directions in anticipation of Her Majesty surrendering her right for an annual sum. This she did by 1 & 2 Vict., c. 2. The excise, as a branch of revenue, then, is in part a Royal Revenue in abeyance.

The opinions of a few of those who, at different dates, were able to judge of the merits of this department, will close this paper.

1644. Scotland. The Convention of Estates "Thinks that the most just and equall way of lifting of the same is be way of Excyse." (Jan. 4, 1644.) This opinion was confirmed by a declaration to that effect on July 29, 1644.

1647. "For as this Duty is by Experience found to be the most easie and equal Way both in relation to the People and to the Publick; as the Lords and Commons are resolved through all Opposition, whatsoever to insist upon the due Collection thereof.[2]

1662. An author of very considerable pen-power who wrote, as previously referred to, "A Treatise on Tax and Contributions," gave five reasons for its continuance.

1666. Samuel Pepys—"The true reason why the country gentlemen are for a land tax and against a general excise, is because they are fearful that if the latter be granted they shall never get it down again."[3]

1678. Mr Poole, in speaking on a demand made by his Majesty for £300,000, "I know not how this revenue can be granted but upon a Home Excise."[4]

1731. Board of Trade proposed to transfer the duty on wool.[5]

1733. Sir R. Walpole, Chancellor of the Exchequer, proposed, to prevent the great frauds on the Customs duties on wines and tobacco, to place those duties conjointly under the Customs and Excise. *See* Excise Scheme.[6]

1763. Wm. Pitt, in speaking on the cider duty, indirectly admitted the efficiency of the force when he stated that the mode of levy was "intolerable to the private person."[7]

1781. Lord North—"The excise was the best managed branch of the public revenue."[8]

1786. Wm. Pitt, Chancellor of the Exchequer, "the excise . . . .

[1] H. L., April 27, 1820. [2] P. O., Aug. 30, 1647. [3] Nov. 6, 1666.
[4] H. C., June 18, 1678. [5] Feb. 25, 1731. [6] H. C., 1733.
[7] H. C., March 8, 1763. [8] H. C., May 10, 1781.

had been found by experience to be the most effectual and the least expensive method."[1]

1790. Mr Sheridan, "the business of the excise was better conducted than that of the Customs."[2]

1796. Wm. Pitt, Chancellor of the Exchequer, "the taxes drawn from this quarter give us confidence with respect to any new experiments."[3]

1797. Select-Committee of House of Commons reported—"This department appears to have been conducted with the same regularity and vigilance as then."[4]—1780.

1809. Mr Huskisson—"A system of collection hitherto remarkable for its regularity and purity."[5]

1819. Adam Smith—"The duties are more unpopular than those of the Customs."[6]

1824. Jos. Hume—"No part of the public business was so attentively and laboriously performed as that done by the officers of excise."[7]

1846. Earl Dalhousie—". . . . if anyone could be called well-managed," it "deserved that commendation—the excise department."[8]

1851. C. Wood, Chancellor of the Exchequer—"The best test of the condition of the people—I mean the Excise."[9]

1866. J. S. Mill—"Customs duties are *cæteris paribus* much less objectionable than excise; but they must be laid only on things which either cannot or at least will not be produced in the country itself, or else their production there must be prohibited (as in England is the case with tobacco) or subjected to an excise duty of equivalent amount."[10]

1869. R. Lowe, Chancellor of the Exchequer—"The change has been attended with a remarkable result. . . . . I mean the result of bringing under taxation in one year 600,000 dogs which previously wholly evaded the tax." The financier should have added—less sheep dogs.[11]

1870. R. Lowe, in the same capacity—"We are so satisfied with

[1] H. C., May 5, 1786.
[2] H. C., April 16, 1790.
[3] H. C., Dec. 7, 1796.
[4] P. Rep., July 19, 1797.
[5] H. C., June 9, 1809.
[6] "Wealth of Nations."
[7] H. C., March 15, 1824.
[8] H. L., April 6, 1846.
[9] H. C., Feb. 17, 1851.
[10] "Principles of Political Economy."
[11] H. C., April 18, 1869.

the result of the experiment, that we are determined to carry the matter further (laughter); and to take the opinion of the House whether the time has not arrived when we can put an end to this system of collecting taxes through parochial officers, not merely in those licences which are substituted for the assessed taxes, but in the income-tax, the land tax, and the house tax."[1]

See Parnell Committee.

ABSENCE.

In earlier times absence from duty, even without pay, seems to have been scarcely permitted under any conditions. In 1743 the supervisor had to ask the Honourable Commissioners for leave for both himself and his officers, for even the shortest period of absence. In the London stations in 1781 no officer was allowed to be absent more than one course without the sanction of the Board, and if he required further leave it was obtained through his surveyor or supervisor.

Absence is occasioned by special duty or request, by pecuniary or other embarrassment, by sickness, by private business.

Special duty usually implies employment on account of special official aptitude; and request, such as the attendance in Court under subpœna, at examination, &c., &c. Salary, in these cases, is allowed.

Pecuniary embarrassment or imprisonment for debt implied supercession in 1830, unless business were resumed within fourteen days, and in 1831, within twenty-eight days. The difficulties of debt, however, had become so frequent in 1839, that the Board decided not to restore any official unless he produced the schedule under the Insolvent Debtors Act, and clearly proved that his insolvency had arisen through unavoidable misfortune. A still more severe decision was announced in 1841, by which every case was ordered to be specially reported, the debtor not to be allowed to resume his duties, nor be paid salary for the absent time, without special order.

Sickness. Salary appears to have been paid either in whole or in part for variable periods by the respective Boards, to those who through indisposition had not been able to perform their duties.

[1] H. C., April 11, 1870.

Robert Burns, while absent on sick leave, proves this. In writing to a friend in 1796 he states, "The deuce of the matter is this: when an exciseman is off duty his salary is reduced. What way, in the name of thrift, shall I maintain myself and keep a horse in country quarters on £35?" Absence on this account from both duty and station in 1787 was granted for a period of six weeks without the Board's leave, but at the expiration of that period a special application was made by the supervisor in whose district the invalid resided, in the case of an officer, to which was added in 1821, and strictly enforced in 1831, the periods of sickness within the two preceding years. In 1830, on the completion of the six weeks, the application was restricted to a period of one month, and repeated until an absence of thirty-six weeks was completed by a collector, and twenty-four by an inferior officer, when the absentee was required to relinquish: salary was paid, on the production of the Board's authority, to the former for a period of twenty-four weeks, and to the latter for a period of fifteen weeks, in 1860 extended to sixteen. Liberty to leave the station, without special sanction, was withdrawn in 1856. In England in 1811, and in Scotland in 1833, a collector paid his representative, when on the round, at the rate of four shillings per station, and a supervisor two shillings. The limit of the supervisor's permission of six weeks was reduced to fourteen days in 1836, and the collector's to the same in 1860. The production of a medical certificate, customary at the Chief Office, was now—1860—required of those whose illness extended beyond the first grant of fourteen days. It was also required, in 1865, of the examiner who remained away from the Chief Office, four days. In 1820 the examiner was also required to underwrite the sick supervisor's application. Absence caused by accident while on duty is usually treated with special liberality.

Private Leave. These regulations have varied in a similar manner to those of sick leave. In England in 1738 the supernumerary was required to perform the duties of an absent officer: in 1759 the Board's permission seems to have been necessary for even the shortest absence; salary, however, was paid to both supervisor and officer for the first fourteen days. In Scotland in 1804 a collector was permitted to grant not more than three days to a supervisor or an officer, but in any case in which this period was insufficient, he made an application to the Commissioners for periods of not more than fourteen days each; the absentee was not paid salary, and, in the case of an officer, he had to pay the person who performed his duties: a supervisor was also authorized to grant an officer three days' absence, and when he—supervisor—was on leave, the "neighbouring supervisors" made "interfering surveys." Not more than one supervisor in the same collection was allowed to be absent at the same time. It was not until 1830, when the three Boards were consolidated, that uniformity of practice was ordered. A collector was not allowed to be absent during the collecting round, nor more than three days at any other time without special permission: a supervisor was required to ask the Commissioners, through the collector, for length of absence greater than three days, and to request, on that being granted, the other supervisors to interfere, but this was not granted if a supervisor were already on leave, except under peculiar circumstances: an officer was required to make arrangements for the due performance of his duties, to the satisfaction of the supervisor, petition the Board, through his supervisor, for permission, and pay his officiator at the rate of £30 per annum, with any extra expense incurred by him, while in charge, through incapacity, but this payment was made for only the first fourteen days. Absence, within a year of the date of the period requested, was stated in the application. Salary was paid for fourteen days. In 1851 the regulations applicable to a collector were applied to a collecting supervisor: the officiator was paid by the Commissioners instead of by the officer: a ride officer was required to lend his representative his horse: a collector was authorized to grant a supervisor fourteen days' leave, and a supervisor an officer the same. In 1858 Sundays and official holidays were excluded in computing the permitted period. In 1867 an examiner was granted, when unemployed, twenty-eight days, and in 1874, if the whole of this grant were not taken on his appointment to a district, he was allowed to complete it. In 1870 the principle of cumulation was yielded to supervisors, clerks, and officers, by which they were allowed to defer the whole or a portion of the leave of one year until the next, and to thus take a prolonged absence of double duration, or of such as with that previously taken would make up that period. In 1872 a supervisor who required leave to commence on removal was allowed to apply for special permission through his collector, an officer through his supervisor.

No record of absence of any kind appears to have been enjoined to be kept until 1831[1], when it was required to be noted in the first

[1] Treasury Minute, June 21, 1831.

column of the diary, and an abstract of the whole inserted at the end: in 1851 the collector made a roundly return: in 1854 it was entered in the roundly diary abstract: in 1859 it was recorded in the General Store Register: in 1870 it was returned annually in the first round diary abstract.

The termination of the absence year was—in 1830, "the particular time" of request; in 1851, January 5; in 1856, December 31.

Glancing through my written annals of the outside movement for an extension of private leave, the earliest expressed desire was made in 1853. In 1854 exception was taken to the inclusion of Sundays and official holidays, because they were excluded by the Customs' authorities. Then running rapidly down a quiet period of two years to 1858, petitions from Aberdeen and Campbelton were presented to their Honours for twenty-eight days, and, remarkable to relate, about the same time a petition from Port Ellen, signed by two officers, and styled "An Anti-Four-Weeks-Leave Memorial," against the application. But these were unsuccessful, except in so far as, previously noted, the exclusion of Sundays and official holidays. These were followed by one in 1859 from Tullibody District, thirty-two in 1860, and two in 1861, which of course were Pro-Four-Weeks-Leave Memorials. No direct appeal was afterwards made until 1867, when the Central Committee included it in the Address presented by them, and the outcome of this may be stated to have been the concession of cumulation previously noticed. The comparative silence of the next three years was terminated by the embodiment of the request in a draft address prepared, but not presented, by the Inverness Committee in 1871. It was ultimately laid before the Civil Service Commission in 1874. *Vide* Holidays.

ACCOUNTS.

The earliest reference to a periodical account is in a black letter Parliamentary Ordinance, dated Aug. 31, 1644, by which a quarterly account of receipts and disbursements was required to be sent in. These quarter days were fixed the same year[1] for the four usual Feast Terms—Dec. 25, March 25, June 24, September 29. The accounts were also audited, examined, and "pricked over" with the

[1] P.O. Oct. 4, 1644.

vouchers, entries and books of account in the several offices throughout the Kingdom, but it appears to have taken about a year and nine months to have done so.[1]

General directions were issued under the same form of authority in 1654. These quarterly accounts were required to be sent in within ten days of the end of the quarter, and with them an "Abstract and Accompt Current" of all the duties received "for the better method and ease of the Accomptant at the "Grand Office." A separate return of fines was made. An arrear list was sent up with the books quarterly. And as to the local accountancy a transcript of all "Tickets"—paytickets—was made in a book, and no payment of duty or drawback was made until a certificate, like that given in the "President," was produced. The names of the books were "Journal, Entry Book, Cash Book, and Ledger," and the system of keeping them very similar to that by double entry. These instructions were issued to the sub-commissioners.[2]

The first general system of accounts for the United Kingdom commenced in 1826, when the financial year was fixed to include from April 6 to April 5, this was continued until 1855, when two supplementary "rounds" were added, and the period was changed to include from April 1 to March 31.

The inaccuracy of revenue accounts in 1702, but not of excise in particular, appears to have been such as to induce Her Majesty Queen Anne to state in Her first Royal Speech to Parliament—"That my subjects may the more cheerfully bear the necessary taxes, I desire you to inspect the accounts of the public receipt and expenditure, and if there have been any abuses or mismanagements, I hope you will detect them, that the offenders may be punished."[3]

On the Union of England and Scotland, John Downer, "Gentleman," an A1 officer of that day, was sent down to Scotland as "Methodizer of Excise."[4] The Irish accounts were incorporated with those of England, *i.e.*, in so far as stated by the Chancellor of the Exchequer—in 1817[5], though in the annual statement of the Honourable Commissioners, a separate account is rendered for each country, and in the estimates, too, for effective services a separate demand is made.

The excise system of accounts has been examined by Select Committees of the House of Commons in 1797, 1809 I., 1834, and

[1] P.O. July 30, 1646. [2] P.O. May 30, 1654. [3] Oct. 20, 1702.
[4] Royal Gauger. [5] H. C. June 20, 1817.

1862. In 1834 the keeping, controlling, and auditing, were examined by a Mr Abbott, an accountant, whose labours extended over a period of four months, and resulted in his reporting that there were no fewer than 826 books of account, and 107,434 forms of document. He suggested the introduction of book-keeping by double entry, and the discontinuance of 54,578 forms. This blue book contains a report of 58 pages, and an appendix of forms of 166 pages.[1]

The methods of account applicable to the out-door section are explained in Johnston's Manual, section 43.

ACETOMETER.

This densimeter, used to ascertain the strength of vinegar, was preceded, in England in 1743, by a "viol," a bottle lowered into a cask to ascertain by its clear or "foul" appearance, when drawn out, if the contents were the same throughout, and in Scotland in 1804 by a "sinking phial." In ascertaining the strength, a "glass measure" of vinegar, and another of rain or river water were emptied into the "assay glass," and lime added until it precipitated in flakes, and left the sample quite clear. The mixture which, during the commotion, had become considerably raised in temperature, was then reduced to a heat of 70°F., the degree at which the acetometer was constructed to act, and the indication taken. The weights were marked 10, 20, 30, 40, 50, 60, 70, and 80, respectively; the "intermediate" ones 1, 2, 4, 8, and the "fractional" one ½. But when the instrument was applied to undistilled vinegar a weight mark "M" was "used as a counterbalance of the mucilage." In estimating the proof gallons, the number of bulk gallons was multiplied by the number on the weight on the instrument, and the last figure struck off thus—150 × 30 = 4500—final figure 450. As a slide rule accompanied each instrument, it was not compulsory to work out the proofs by pen. The acetometer and its accompaniments required a large box, while a small one, containing a quantity of "hydral of lime," a thermometer, two glass beads, and a spoon, was provided that it might be "conveniently carried in the pocket." The spoon was used for stirring up the mixture, and in taking out the beads. A

[1] Parnell Report, No. 11. [2] Jan. 14, 1840 [3] Ret.
[4] Leadbetter's Royal Gauger, p. 284. [5] Instructions, Scotland, p. 151.

"glass hydrometer, made to work at a temperature of 70° only, was used to test the water.[1] Discontinued in 1844.[2]

ACTS OF PARLIAMENT.

England, Scotland, and Ireland, of course, had each its own Acts of Parliament, until the respective Unions in 1707 and 1800, afterwards, each act, unless otherwise enacted, applied, respectively, to both or all three countries. In England, prior to the Restoration of Charles II., the Parliamentary Ordinance took the place of the regal act. About thirty of these were issued, and the earliest, in matters excise, is dated May 13, 1643. The first act in which the word excise occurs, is in England, 12 Charles II., c. 5; in Scotland, an act, dated Aug. 4, 1621—peculiar to Edinburgh—and in Ireland, 14 Charles II., c. 1. In Scotland, during a period of 61 years—1644 to 1705—about 30 acts were passed, but much was done by "warrand:" in Ireland, during a period of 133 years, about 104 applied. To return to England and its Unions, from 1660 to 1876, nearly 1100. The length of an Act has varied from one to upwards of two hundred sections. The largest number passed in one regnal year appears to have been in that of 55 George III., when about thirty received the Royal Assent. An abstract of an important act was formerly[3] inserted in the London Gazette, and the acts supplied to the various stations were obtained through the collector,[4] for many years, but latterly, through the supervisor. The first issue of a code or collection of statutes for the use of officers was made in 1874, to supervisors, of course, very much earlier.

General publicity, however, of the Excise acts in a collected form or code was not given, for Lord Colchester's Committee on Finance in 1797, has recorded in its Fifth Report—"It appears no collection of Excise Laws is published or sold for public use, but a collection, from all the statutes down to 33 George III., printed for the use of the office. By the usage of the Excise Office, this collection has been confined to the officers, but your committee see no reason for imposing any restriction upon its unreserved publication." This exclusiveness appears to have been followed by a general move in

[1] Vinegar Instructions, 1820.
[2] 7 & 8 Vict. c. 25.
[3] 1731.
[4] 1823.

the Houses of Parliament. In the House of Lords, in 1816, Earl Stanhope complained of the voluminous, defective, confused state of the laws; in the House of Commons, in 1821, Mr Calcraft made a similar statement; in 1828, Mr Bright thought a great reform necessary, and suggested consolidation; in 1833, a Parliamentary Committee—the Parnel—was appointed to examine the excise laws, &c., and the time it occupied in doing so extended over a period of three years; it reported—"Notwithstanding this strong declaration"—Colchester Committee's—"the Commissioners did not then alter the usage of the office, nor has it since been altered:" it concluded by recommending a consolidation. Although this committee effected many repeals, yet in 1838 a petition was forwarded for further alteration, and the then Chancellor of the Exchequer admitted that the state of the law was "open to much objection." "It is complicated and embarrassed with provisions which it is impossible to act upon." In 1847, it transpired that the head of the department, with some of the most experienced officials, had been deliberating on the alteration and amendment; in 1848, thirty-two petitions were presented for an inquiry, and in 1849, no fewer than forty-five, containing 5023 signatures. But during the period included in this Parliamentary outline the laws were codified and issued to the public, as will appear in the list of publications which follow:—

1676. "A Collection of all the Statutes relating to the Excise, with notes in the margin, &c." Printed by the "Assigns of His Majestie's Printers." This was announced in the London Gazette.

1683. "An Abridgement of the Excise Laws now in Force," given in Hunt's Practical Gauging.

1717. "A Collection of all the Statutes now in Force, relating to the Excise upon Beer, Ale, and other Liquors; and the Duties upon Candles, &c. . . . . printed together in volume, in 12mo, and sold by Robert Vincent and Robert Vincent, jun., at the Crown and Sceptre, in Fleet Street, London." Announced in London Gazette.

1724. "A Collection of All the Statutes now in Force, relating to the Excise upon Beer, Ale, and other Liquors. And the Duties upon Malt, Brandy and Hops, with abridgment of Statutes and Table of Rates." Printed by Watson, Edinburgh, in small 8vo, black letter.

1735. A folio edition published.

1737. "The Excise Statutes upon Beer, Ale, and other Licences," "edited by Robert Eyre, of the Excise Office." This edition is printed black letter, and contains about fifty acts, and parts of acts, with marginal notes. Pages 800, post 8vo. The editor was probably Commissioner Robert Eyre.

1742. "An Exact Abridgment of all the Acts of Parliament relating to the Excise." "Sold at the Cross Keys, Fleet Street, London." Pages 214, 8vo. The promise in the title was not fulfilled, as only those on "liquors" were given.

1764. "A Collection of all the Statutes now in Force, relating to the Duties of Excise in England." 124 acts quoted. Pages 896, folio. The compiler's name is not given. Printed by M. Bassett, Printer to the King's Most Excellent Majesty, for J. & R. Tonson, in the Strand, London.

1796. "A Practical Arrangement of the Laws relating to the Excise, by Anthony Highmore, Jun., Solicitor. In 2 vols., pp. 512 and 862, 8vo., London.

1797. An Abridgment of Excise Statutes, by James Huie, first edition. Edinburgh.

1803. A Complete Abridgment of all Excise and Customs, Duties . . . . and Laws, by Peter Jonas, late Supervisor of Excise. Pages about 800, 8vo, Hartnel, London.

1804. Huie Do., second edition, Edinburgh.

1818. Do., third edition. Great Britain, J. Huie, Collector, pp. 900, 8vo.

1823. Do., fourth edition. Acts cited more than 700.

1840. "The General Laws of Excise." by J. Bateman. A small 8vo of 172 pages. Second edition, 3s. 6d.

1843. "The Laws of Excise, being a Collection of all the existing Statutes, relating to the Revenue of Excise," &c., by Jos. Bateman, LL.D. 401 acts and parts of acts quoted. Pages 983. Price £1, 4s.

1865. "An Abridgment of the Laws," by "James Bell, Surveying General Examiner," published with the third edition of the Excise Officer's Manual, by J. Bateman, LL.D.

1873. "The Laws of Excise." A compact volume of 1100 pages, after the arrangement of 1843, by James Bell and John H. Dwelly, of the Inland Revenue. 409 acts and parts of acts are included in this issue. Maxwell & Son. Price £1, 4s., to the department 18s.

"From the first establishment of the Excise till the year 1801," wrote the Commissioners to the Parnel Committee, "the number of Acts of Parliament amounted to 220, and since that period upwards of 400 Acts have been passed affecting the revenue." The number cited in the respective collections is—1823, 700; 1836, 621; 1843, 401; 1873, 409.

ADDRESS OF CONDOLENCE.

This department joined the other departments in an Address of Condolence to Her Majesty the Queen on the death of His Royal Highness the Prince Consort in 1862.

ADULTERATION.

The adulteration of commodities liable to excise duties is nearly as old as the excise itself. Beer and malt have each in their turn called for special legislation in this respect, but no systematic chemical effort to detect and suppress the adulteration of articles was made with a view to the protection of the revenue until 1832, when the adulteration of coffee came under general notice, and the Board ordered samples to be forwarded for examination. In 1835 numerous complaints were made of the addition of sugar and treacle to tobacco, and these adulterants with others formed the bases of research, which afterwards resulted in the establishment of the excise laboratory. In the second report by the Parnell Committee on wine, in 1833, it is stated that the excise have nothing to do with adulteration: but this was clearly disproved with regard to tobacco in 1844, in a Parliamentary Report in which it is reported that the Board had found out a mode of detection by chemical analysis. From this date to the present the laboratory has held a high position: so high, indeed, that in 1871 Mr Bruce proposed in his Exciseable Liquors (Licences) Bill to entrust the suppression of adulteration to this chemical staff; and in 1875 Mr Sclater Booth to support, in speaking on the Sale of Food and Drugs Bill, the Inland Revenue Laboratory as a Court of Final Appeal.

Various returns of adulteration, which will be referred to under their respective heads, have been made to Parliament: notably so in 1850, No. 301, and in 1853, No. 472. Printed adulteration notices were first issued in 1844: the Storekeeper General issued no fewer than 91,032 in 1872.[1]

Punch received a letter from "Mrs Grundy on the Adulteration of Food," in which she noted the adulterants in tea, coffee, cocoa, pepper, ale, &c., &c.—1855[2]; and Dr Hassall, in his "Adulterations Detected," published in 1857,[3] having considered "how far the Excise has hitherto protected the revenue from loss through adulteration," states, "The Excise, then, has most signally failed in its principal duty." Frequent reference is made to the First Principal of the Laboratory by Dr Hassall, who wrote, it should be borne in mind, in 1857.

AGRICULTURAL STATISTICS,

Collected first in Ireland, then in England, and afterwards in Scotland.

These annual statistics were first obtained in Ireland in 1847,[4] through the agency of the county constabulary, at an expense of about £3000,[5] and have been continued to be collected by the same or the police.[6]

An effort was made the same year to pass a Bill to collect them in England and Wales, but as this was not successful, no further attempt was made to collect them until 1852, when the machinery of the Poor Law Board was employed in the counties of Norfolk and

[1] P. Ret. No. 378. [2] Vol. 29, p. 54. [3] Longman.
[4] H. L., March 11, 1856. [5] H. C., Feb. 24, 1859. [6] H. L., Feb. 9, 1860.

Hants. The result in Norfolk was satisfactory, but in Hants not so.[1] Mr. William Meikle, an officer of this department, suggested to the Chancellor of the Exchequer that his department should be employed to collect: this, however, was not then acted upon.[2] Another attempt on a larger scale was made in 1853. Eleven counties were selected and collected under a plan devised by Sir J. Walsham,[3] whose staff failed to an extent of only 7 per cent.[1] £13,000 were voted for these and those collected in Scotland and Ireland, with a promise that if the experiment were satisfactory it would be further extended.[4] Punch reviewed these proceedings under the title of "The Agricultural Inquisition."[5] In 1855 Mr Bouverie stated, in the House of Commons on June 11, "the English returns generally are not satisfactory. With the exception of the West Riding of Yorkshire the attempt has proved a failure. Of the eleven counties fixed upon, ten had not given returns to a sufficient extent to justify the Government in following up the plan which had been adopted. The returns which had been received did not amount to 16 per cent. of the whole. . . . . As the experiment had not succeeded, his noble friend the President of the Board of Trade had given notice of his intention to move for the appointment of a select committee in the other House to ascertain the best mode of procuring agricultural statistics." This motion was acted upon,[6] and a Bill[7] was prepared by the Upper House. The leading provisions were these—that the overseer in the month of February should hand a return of every occupier of land to the Poor Law Board; that the schedules should be issued in May, to be filled up and returned on the first of June; that they should contain the acreage, and number of live stock; that a penalty not exceeding two pounds should be imposed on those who refused to make the return; and a penalty of not more than five pounds on the officers for neglect of duty. This Bill was read the second time,[8] but in committee the agency of the Board of Trade was substituted for that of the Poor Law Board by a majority of 5 votes—con. 18, noncon. 13,[9] and with this amendment was sent down to the House of Commons, where Viscount Palmerston, seeing that great difference of opinion prevailed upon the measure, proposed that it should be considered by a committee in the coming

[1] See No. 1. [2] C. S. G. 1869, p. 84. [3] P. P. 263, 1854.
[4] H. C., Dec. 15, 1854. [5] Vol. 25, p. 207. [6] P. Rep. 501, 1855.
[7] No. 97, 1856. [8] H. L., Mar. 11, 1856. [9] April 8.

session.[1] This promise was twice alluded to in 1857:[2] a Bill was brought in on July 21, but this also shared the fate of the two which had preceded it.[3] The following year Mr Caird moved the collection and publication of the "acres under the several crops of corn, vegetables, and grass," but in this he was not successful by 11 votes —ayes 152, noes 163.[4] In 1858 the fourth Bill, which, similar to the others, related to only England and Wales, was also rejected.[5] The next endeavour, made in 1861, assumed the form of an application to the Magistrates of the different Quarter Sessions for permission to employ the police,[6] this, too, was unsuccessful.[7] An application was then made to the Registrar-General to suggest a plan, to which he replied that a grant of £15,000 would be required, and authority to enforce the return of the schedule.[8] The Inland Revenue Department was suggested by Mr Heygate on June 11, 1863.[9] No further steps appear to have been taken until 1865, when Mr M. Gibson announced to the irrepressible Mr Caird that a plan had been suggested, and, if practicable, the Government would propose a vote.[10] They were first collected by this department and transmitted to the Board of Trade in 1866, and so efficiently and promptly that the subject has seldom since been mentioned in Parliament.[11]

"In Scotland," said Lord Stanley of Alderly, "attention was first directed to the subject in the year 1853, and an effort was made by the Highland Society, in connection with the Board of Trade, to collect the statistics in the counties Haddington, Roxburgh, and Sutherland.[12] That effort proved most successful, and in consequence the attention of the Board of Trade having been drawn by the Society to the project, it was determined to extend the inquiry to the whole of Scotland, which had been attended with complete success."[13] It was stated that only one-fifth of one per cent. had failed to give in returns in 1855.[14] These statistics were also first collected by this department in 1866.

In the Isle of Man and the Channel Islands similar statistics are collected under the direction of the local authority.[15]

[1] H. C., June 28, 1856. [2] Feb. 19; May 12. [3] No. 146, 1857.
[4] Feb. 24, 1859. [5] March 12, 1858. [6] April 22, 1861.
[7] April 10, 1862. [8] June 22, 1862. [9] H. C.
[10] March 31, 1863. [11] Feb. 15, 1867; Aug. 8, 1867.
[12] P. P. 56, 1854; 343, 1855; Report, v. 47, 637, 1855.
[13] H. L., March 11, 1856. [14] H. C., June 11, 1855. [15] P. Ret., 1873.

The first Parliamentary Return appears to have been made in 1856, and consisted of the estimated average produce: then in 1859 the returns for Scotland and Ireland; the latter, probably, having been previously printed annually: and then in 1866, those for Great Britain. Since that date the returns have been made more comprehensive, and the annual Parliamentary Return has included comparative tables of the British Possessions and Foreign Countries.

The remuneration, £3000 as previously stated, was granted for the collection in Ireland: in 1854 £13,000 to cover the cost in Ireland, Scotland, and the eleven counties in England: in 1865 £10,000 in England and Scotland,[1] in 1866[2] and 1867[3] the same: in 1868 the same, with a supplementary estimate of £8000:[4] in 1875 £15,490,—remuneration to officers of Inland Revenue, £11,750; collection in Channel Islands, £190; postage, £3300; incidental expenses, £250.[5]

ALEXANDER'S POEMS.

The full title is "Life's Phantoms and Other Poems:" author, one Alexander, late "exciseman": publisher, Collins, Glasgow, about 1856.

"The author may not lay claim to a poetic genius of the highest order, but he undoubtedly possesses the gift of writing harmonious verses filled with bright thoughts, and glowing with a lofty inspiration."[6]

ALLOWANCES

Include contingent, special, sitting, officiating, subsistence, travelling, horse, compensation, charity, superannuation, and commutation allowances; also fees, perquisites, and rewards. Each will be separately treated after division horse.

In point of time "riding charges"—horse hire on the round—perhaps took precedence, and these were equivalent to travelling

[1] H. C., June 8, 1865. [2] July 22, 1866. [3] March 16, 1867.
[4] March 16, 1868. [5] Estimates. [6] C. S. G., 1856.

allowances; the officiating allowance was long paid by the officer in whose station the officiator was employed, before it was paid by the Commissioners; the horse allowance, although it was given earlier in Scotland than in England, may be stated to have been granted in consequence of the repeal of fiscal duties, and the discontinuance of purely official protective duties, which of course tended to enlarge the areas of stations generally; the travelling allowance of later times by reason of the great net-work of railways. The members of the out-door department have, whenever a new allowance was needed, or an increase to an existing one required, respectfully sought and obtained, in the majority of cases, the grant requested, although, it must be added, in some instances not until persistence in appeal had been shown. These efforts will be narrated.

Contingent Allowances.—This designation appears to have included riding charges, sitting expenses, officiating, officiating and periodical allowances, extra salary to those employed on the hop survey, paid by the Commissioners, and the payment per station made by sick collectors and supervisors to those who performed their duties on the round. It may be considered to have stood in the precise position now assigned to allowances. As payments or allowances upon different contingencies arose and increased in number, so the expression was gradually dropped, a specific one employed, and all included under the general one-word term which heads this paper.

Special Allowance.—A payment made under peculiar circumstances, such as salary in case of injury, extra outlay incurred on unusual duty, &c.

Sitting Allowance.—The Board, in 1811, contemplated making some allowance to collectors when on the round out of residence for "Entertainment at an Inn," to enable them to see that "the Supervisors and Officers performed the Business entrusted to their care in such a Manner as the Safety of the Revenue require." This appears to have been granted, but owing to the extra expense incurred, disallowed in 1830, when the first scale of allowances for absence on the round appears to have been authorised. A sitting allowance to supervisors, who met the collector and remained out of residence more than eight hours, was first granted in 1854.

A desire for such a concession was shown, but not directly to the authorities, in 1853. This became a grievance to the officer who reiterated his claim until it was acceded in 1857. The line of demarcation, however, by which it was allowed or withheld, in 1862, became a matter for consideration with those whose official deeds did not carry them over to the receiving side. "Othos" was one of these, and probably induced "Quill" and another, themselves supposed sufferers, to suggest that an absence of four hours from home, or of eight hours, or a journey of five miles, should entitle the traveller to the subsistence. It was suggested in 1863 that a half should be given on being absent four hours. Little official interest has since been taken in the matter.

THE OFFICIATING ALLOWANCE.—The examiner who, in 1801 and 1811, had his salary made equal, when officiating, to that of a supervisor, and whose allowance in 1807 was claimed as an incident on the duty which bore the salary of the supervisor for whom he officiated, made no marked effort to obtain an improvement in his position until 1862, when it was discussed, and, 1863, when decisive steps were taken. Gleaning from the *Civil Service Gazette*—Fiat, Orientalis, Archimedes, and Justicia were the first in the field of discussion. Orientalis sought the addition of the amount of £30 to the annual horse allowance, while another agitant, after the failure of the application, subsequently narrated, would ask for an allowance of £1 per week. The first mode of preparing a memorial was given by Fiat, who proposed that a petition should be drafted and left with the editor, who would announce the fact in the columns of his paper, that the examiners might affix their names in the order of seniority; and when completed, a printed copy of the document might be transmitted to the Commissioners. It is not recorded if this timid suggestion were acted upon; but it appears on the authority of Fiat, Justicia, Ruat, Cœlum, that a meeting of the examiners was held, at which it was resolved to ask for "a more just and equitable scale of allowance;" and that after the application had been laid before their Honours a few days, the chairman of the examiners was informed by a first-class surveying general examiner that the Board had declined to entertain the petition without entering into any details or assigning any reason. Their old and tried friend the editor could not regard the refusal "in any other light than that of cruelty." He urged "their next step should be to carry their case, without any loss of time, before the Treasury. Failing in this, it should go before Parliament, and for this reason there ought to be the more expedition in pushing the case on." To argue on the brevity of the "examiner's tenure of office," he said, "is not sound policy." The failure of the appeal and the incentive words of the editor, just quoted and subsequently given—"That such a system can exist which has no analogy in the regulation of any private firm or public company in the kingdom . . . . seems to be almost beyond belief," *i.e.*, excess of outlay over income occasioned a somewhat long correspondence, in which a desire was expressed that the riding supervisor should join them in an appeal to the Treasury, but that the examiners should assume the directorate, while an examiner wrote in woeful terms of his small allowance of 1s. 7½d. per day. 1864, the year of triumph. It was not until the department had read that the officiating allowance for a footwalk district should be doubled for that of a riding district, and that Orientalis had indirectly purchased his supervisorship at a cost of £50, that the editor announced the presentation of a second memorial from the examiners for their "actual expenses," nor was it before Saturday, December 10, that he could editorially congratulate them on the issue of the Treasury Minute, dated November 29, 1864, by which they and their successors would enjoy the receipt of an increased annual allowance of £50. This, however, while it gave immediate satisfaction, did not prove ultimately satisfactory, inasmuch as an uniform grant was made, whether the exertion and outlay were great or small. In 1867, the Central Committee stated the fact in their able Address: in 1870 the Commissioners made a discriminative grant by which the person in charge of a footwalk received £40 per annum, in a riding district £60 per annum. In 1842 the allowance was not paid during illness, nor, in 1876, after one week's illness, without the sanction of the Commissioners.

THE SUPERNUMERARY, ASSISTANT, EXPECTANT. In Scotland, in 1804, the supernumerary or assistant who acted for an officer was paid "such extra allowance on incidents as will give them on the whole the same rate of salary which an established officer has for the like duty," while an expectant does not appear to have been paid except employed to officiate, and then at a salary which varied from £55 to £65; in 1829 the supernumerary received an extra £38, the expectant an extra £30, on salaries of £52 and £50 respectively. In England, in 1811, an officiator was allowed £80 per annum, and a supernumerary £38, which with his salary of £52 = £80; in 1828, the regulations issued by Treasury Warrant, dated Nov. 8, 1815, were revoked, and an expectant was allowed, in addition to his salary of £50, an employment pay of £30. These allowances, with an exception of three years, seem to have been continued to, and received without question or dissatisfaction by, the recipients until 1857, when a larger sum was desired and discussed: and, notwithstanding an increase of salary to £60 in 1858, still desired and discussed until 1860, when the propriety of addressing the Honourable Board was considered, if not acted upon. "The hot springs of zeal" of these youthful agitants subsided with the stream, "palpably unjust and unreasonable," in 1862. They were replayed to the suggestive force of three shillings per day for a division, and four shillings per day for a ride, in 1866, supported by the Central Committee in 1867, and acknowledged at a force of two shillings and three shillings respectively in 1870: zeal rewarded by extra pay awarded.

SUBSISTENCE ALLOWANCE. The origin of this form of allowance may be traced, in so far as the outdoor section is concerned, to special employment from residence and station. The earliest record the writer has found is dated 1820, when officers below the rank of supervisor or surveyor were granted subsistence at the rate of 12s. per diem on attending legal proceedings in town; next came, in 1843, an extension of the principle to supervisors and officers at the rate of 7s. 6d. and 6s. per day, respectively, while proceeding to, and under, examination for promotion: after that, in 1854, a general extension. Coming to the desires of the department, in 1854, 4s. per day was suggested for officers who perform double duty; in 1858, a grant to both supervisor and officer when absent from residence. The later efforts have been included with those for an increased horse allowance, which will be subsequently given.

Travelling allowance may be stated to include the old form of riding charges, the actual outlay and mileage. Riding charges were paid in England as early as 1743, and very likely earlier; in 1780, to a collector at the rate of 5s. per station, and varied in the total from £88 to £112 per annum; in Scotland, in 1779, as a fixed sum, to a collector from £30 to £50, to a collecting supervisor £20, to a clerk £10 to £30; in 1804, the total to a collector was restricted to £50, and a supervisor received £14; in Ireland, very probably included under that indefinite term "Incidents." The actual outlay—long made to superior officers—granted in 1843, when a more rapid mode of travelling was becoming general, superseded the daily travelling allowance, *i.e.*, for travel alone; in 1848, second class railway fare was allowed to examiners and officers; in

1854, revised regulations were issued; and in 1857, other regulations ordered. These comparatively rapid revisions gave general satisfaction. Mileage has been paid on different principles—go so far, go beyond so far, and, only go—thus, by so much per thirty miles, in 1796, by so much per mile over fifty miles, in 1829, by so much per mile, in Scotland, in 1804; the rates per *mile* have varied—in Scotland, in 1804, an uniform 4d.; in England, from 4d., 6d., and 7d., in 1829, to 3d. in 1857, according, in the earlier instance, to the rank of the traveller. The use of the rail was allowed in 1861, 6d. per day was allowed, in 1874, to officers in London who could not reside within the limits of their stations. See the following—

HORSE ALLOWANCE, &c. 1760: in Tom Paine's time no allowance was made, but he states in his justly celebrated "Case of the Officers of Excise," that "the Expense of Horse-Keeping cannot be brought under Fourteen Pounds a Year." In Robert Burns's time, on his entering the department, in 1788, one condition of entry was "that he has sufficient at the Time to purchase a Horse for his Business," and it is quite clear that the supervisor in Scotland, in 1804, was allowed £16 per annum, and the general supervisors the necessary expenses incurred in keeping "two able horses." The Border officer, too, in 1834, was allowed 5s. per day for this purpose. It was not generally paid until January 1, 1856. An advance towards the purchase of a horse, but repayable by instalments, was first made by the Commissioners in 1868, and an increased allowance was made in 1869. Digressing awhile to tell the tale of tolls, assessed taxes on horses and carriages, and the use of the officer's horse by the officiator. Tolls were at first allowed for only a horse: in 1834 the use of a vehicle became general, and with it the claim for the tolls paid, these, however, were not then allowed. Supervisors and officers who "travel for their own accommodation otherwise than on horseback must not burden the public with the additional charges;" they were allowed in 1854. Assessed taxes were paid on horses by the equestrian excise, in 1815, and to insure that they did so, although the taxes were repaid, surveyors of taxes were supplied in 1831, with their names. It remained for Sir Henry Parnel and his two coadjutors to suggest its discontinuance—"Duty is not charged for yeomanry, cavalry horses, and there seems to be no good reason why the duty on the exciseman's horse should be paid into the revenue with one hand to be taken out with the other. . . . We recommend that the horses of officers, for which the excise now pay, should in future be exempted from payment of the tax." This recommendation was adopted by Treasury Warrant, dated February 1842. A gig each was exempted from assessed tax by Treasury Warrant, dated April 29, 1853: the exemption has since been extended to a vehicle each. In 1830 a ride officer was required to lend his horse to his officiator, and in 1834, if he did not do so, pay him—genus homo—horse-hire; this regulation was replaced by one granting the officiator an allowance of £10 for horse-hire per annum.

To resume: the action of the out-door applicants. The initial effort on the first publication of the Civil Service Gazette in 1853 pointed out the hardship of having to provide and keep a horse. In 1854 the editor appears to have been the first impression maker—£10 for horse-hire, £30 where a horse is kept, £10 for an outfit. The preparation of a memorial to the Treasury quickly followed the suggestion, but without success. One of the interested equestrians supplied the particulars of the expenses of 263 supervisors at so early a date as 1842, these ran up to £120 per annum: another suffering horseman suggested an allowance of fourteen shillings per week. Mr Henderson of Edinburgh, of Periodical Removes celebrity, now came to the rescue, and addressed their Lordships for an allowance of £30 per annum: he was informed—"as you are unconnected with the Public Service, and as their Lordships cannot recognise you in any way as an advocate of the officers of the Inland Revenue Department, they must decline to enter into correspondence with you on the subject in question." Mr Henderson replied by announcing his right to do so if he thought fit.

In 1855. It is stated in a letter that an allowance of £40 to the supervisor and £20 to the officer, had been submitted for the approval of the Board, but that the chairman had, in his wisdom, thought fit to cancel those amounts, and substitute £20 and £10 in lieu of them. However, this "dash of the pen" appears to have gone for something in this case, for if it did not appraise the extent of the allowance, it acknowledged the justice of the claim. The Lords of the Treasury granted on December 12, an allowance of £30 to a riding supervisor, and £20 to a ride officer, to commence on January 1, 1856. The credit of this concession was given to Mr John Barwise, supervisor of Boston district, in consequence of his having appealed to the chairman of the Board to support an application which he addressed to the Lords of the Treasury on November

19, 1855. It was suggested that the allowances should be paid to those who could utilise the rail.

In 1856. The re-scheming of the stations, which followed the grant of last year, was written of in terms niggardliness. The grant, however, prompted a spirit of gratitude, which it was suggested should be expressed by a contribution of two and sixpence, or five shillings to the proprietors of the Civil Service Gazette, or by a contribution of the odd shillings of the first allowance to the Benevolent Fund, but whether either or both of these recommendations were acted upon, did not transpire. The correspondence showed a desire for an enlarged allowance, for a ride to £45, for a district in Scotland or Ireland to, £65; a desire to use the railway instead of keeping and using a horse; a desire for an advance of the yearly allowance; and an advance of £10 to £30 for an outfit on appointment, to be repaid by roundly instalments.

In 1857. No action.

In 1858. The supposed inadequacy of this allowance prompted a writer to suggest an appplication to the Board for an increase, and for a new grant—a subsistence allowance.

In 1859. No action.

In 1860. Complaints alone were penned.

In 1861. The subject was opened by "An Old Ride Officer," who recounted that he had expended £46, 12s. in the purchase of a horse, harness, &c., and that the annual outlay for the keep and repair of his equestrian appointments was £34, 3s. 3d. He asked for an allowance of £30. The utilization of the rail, where the outlay did not exceed the allowance, prompted a suggestion to ask for a rearrangement of official duties, and a scale of travelling allowances, varying from £30, by £10, to £100. These facts, concessions and suggestions induced Riding Supervisors to express a desire for a grant of £30 for horse keep, and £20 for expenses; J. B. for "an adequate daily allowance for his maintenance and that of his horse, when away from his residence;" and One of the Disappointed for an allowance of two shillings per day; and caused Excelsior to urge an immediate application to the Lords of the Treasury. After further expression of opinion, a petition for travelling allowance was forwarded to the Board by the supervisors of Wales Middle Collection—supervisors who were certainly entitled to be heard.

In 1862. The insufficiency of allowances to ride officers and riding supervisors, and the absence of a travelling or subsistence allowance to supervisors, led each of these grades to seek satisfaction. The supervisors.—Guillaume wanted a classification of districts according to the expenditure incurred, while riding supervisor came forward with a scheme—"We want a larger allowance for horse keep, say £40 per annum; if one officer out of residence, £5 extra; if two ditto, £10 extra; if three ditto, £15 extra; if four ditto, £20 extra. This of course will not apply to districts where the supervisor has to remain out of residence during the night." . . . "Let us set about petitioning the Board." These two letters resulted in the preparation and despatch of a petition, signed by only fifty-nine supervisors, to the Lords of Her Majesty's Treasury through the usual channel on the 11th of March, "praying for some allowance on account of their travelling and personal expenses." The receipt of this partially-signed document by the Board was very quickly, but unsatisfactorily, acknowledged by Mr Corbett, who stated, after reviewing the settlement of 1858, that "The Board cannot . . . propose to the Lords of the Treasury to make any alteration in this respect." The movement, however, was of too great importance to the parties principally concerned to be allowed to die out, reasons and suggestions appeared as plentifully as blackberries. Unity would forward "a general grievance petition, which if ineffectual, then agitate for a parliamentary inquiry." No Surrender would again appeal to the Treasury. Cailte suggested that "an account should be kept for twelve months of the expenses incurred, stable, rent, forage, grooming, livery at hotels, and personal expenses there, loss on sale of horses, in short all those things called travelling expenses," and that they should be transmitted to the Board through the collector for the difference to be paid. Excelsior pointed out the additional travelling since the repeal of the paper duty in 1861; a fifth, "Let the railway districts form the first class, give the supervisors their railway fares, and say £10 per annum for subsistence when from home; to those second in order above, sufficient to maintain the horse and a gig, which is now absolutely necessary in every such district, and £20 yearly for subsistence; and to the remainder of the riding districts, forming the third class, sufficient also for the horse and gig, and £30 for subsistence." Surveyors of taxes, it transpired, received liberal allowances. The editor of the *Gazette* argued the claim by observing, each supervisor should be allowed £60 annually; collectors, surveying general examiners, clerks, surveyors of taxes, have an allowance when from home; the Irish constabulary are furnished with a horse and granted an allowance of £50 per annum: that "giving a uniform sum is . . . a very defective expedient. . . . Might not collectors be instructed to make inquiries in connection with the supervisors as to the facilities of transit to and from the residence of their several officers, and from estimates of the weekly expenses incurred in travelling and other ways, taking into account that in the winter season supervisors find it necessary to remain from home at night several times in every few weeks, and that on most days they are absent from their residences varying from eight to sixteen hours? . . . If there be insuperable difficulties . . . we should say that satisfaction would be given if the allowance were raised to £50 per annum, and this condition were annexed that every supervisor should be left to travel in the mode that suited him best."

But it transpired during the expression of these ideas of administration, hope, and encouragement, a second application had been made to the Board, without any better success, and probably not so good as the copy of the curt and decisive reply will substantiate.—"Sir, in reply to your further letter, dated 24th October, the Board desire me to acquaint you that they decline to again bring before the Lords of the Treasury the question of the rates of remuneration for Supervisors of Riding Districts. (Signed) Wm. Corbett"—about December. These two repulses, within a period of nine months, sufficed to silence the pens of the petitioners and their supporter for the remainder of the year. The ride officers did not emulate the zeal of their superiors. They confined their deeds to the expression of suggestive thought—A Victim, "let him perform his business by using what locomotive agencies may best suit him." Sangreen, £30 and the option of keeping would be satisfactory. N. O., that each ride officer should forward a separate petition to the Board, praying the abolition of "the regulation which requires the compulsory keeping of a horse."

In 1863. The discussion of this grievance was resumed in the month of April, by a letter from Reform, who wished for a certain sum to be given, with the option to employ such locomotive agencies as might seem most suitable, which met with an objection from Wilkie, who stated that in some stations a horse was an indispensable. Justice and Sassenach, ride officers, would be satisfied with the annual sum of £30; the riding supervisor expressed a desire for a daily travelling allowance, or £1 per week for horse hire and travelling expenses. A Radical man would abolish the horse allowance. The editor wrote in a spirit of inquisitive surprise—"Do you mean to say that in many cases his unavoidable official expenses as supervisor actually reduce his income below the maximum of the inferior rank from which he was promoted, and in every case make it far less than its nominal amount." Both the riding supervisor and the ride officer appear to have taken a common and equal interest in the correspondence until the end of November, when it ceased.

In 1864. The proceedings of the present year were opened by Scrutator, a supervisor, who addressed the chairman of the Board in the following terms:—"Seek instruction from the humble grades in the service, and do not be satisfied with information after it has been subjected to the filtering process usually adopted in Somerset House." He estimated his horse and travelling expenses at a total of ninety pounds, towards which his country allowed him thirty, and left him to meet the balance of sixty. Delta, Asmodeus, and Novator next addressed the Honourable Commissioners to this effect—that the first would exchange with any division officer, who had attained his maximum, with £5 to boot; that the second, as Jacob Omnium, also a supervisor, could not meet his expenses with eleven and sixpence per week; that the third would have them suspend their judgment on the claims of the examiner, until a general statement of expenses, including those of the ride officer and the riding supervisor, was before them, and that they should set aside the practice of referring such matters to their advisers for report, and examine for themselves the facts and statements, which if declined, their advisers, when directed to report upon them, should be confined to two points; first, whether or not the allowances were sufficient to meet the official expenses of the different ranks; and secondly, if insufficient, and they recommended no alterations, the reasons for not doing so. Diamond observed, in advocating the rescission of the compulsion to keep a horse—"If a horse dies or becomes valueless" the owner has "three outlays—the feeding while sick, the loss of property in the horse, and the expense of working the station," and proposed, in future, where a horse is not kept, the officiator be allowed a portion of the grant. Shear Steel, a supervisor, drew upon his imagination, and promulgated a fictitious "General Order," by which he discontinued the keeping of a horse and the payment of the horse allowance, and substituted an allowance of fourpence per mile for the distance between his residence and that of his officer, and six shillings for every night when absent on official business; the latter, however, not to supersede the allowances granted for sitting expenses, or for travelling beyond the limits of his district. Northumbria sought an allowance of £50 per annum, with a subsistence allowance of eight shillings when absent at night, to either supervisor or examiner. A Three Years' Ride Officer feared the enhanced price of fodder in the "forthcoming winter." Bohemia had lost in five years, as a ride officer, a sum of £70; while Miles-na-Coppalleen avowed that £20 a year was not sufficient to save his owner from being "prosecuted by the Society for the Prevention of Cruelty to Animals." A Worcestershire Ride Officer hoped that a memorial would be prepared in and forwarded from each collection. Progress would have one general petition, to which the signature should be attached by district slips. Fiat Justitia, a ride officer, thought that a ride officer should be selected to receive opinions with a view to the preparation of a comprehensive memorial being drawn out; while S. was persuaded, if a petition authenticated by the particulars of the manifest disadvantages under which the ride officer undoubtedly laboured were properly presented, it would receive due attention, and prove the equity of the request. The stereotyped motto "immediate action" was again sounded on November 12, and within a month a meeting of ride officers and others was held in London on Monday, December 5, when Mr Brosnahan was called to the chair. After he had reviewed the inadequacy of the allowance, and the certainty of official and pecuniary support in the presentation of a petition, and the desirability of a committee being formed, Mr Lumpé moved, and Mr Helm seconded, that the following gentlemen be appointed a committee, with power to add to their number:—Messrs H. Morris, J. S. Houston, A. Innes, R. Bannister, W. Harkness, J. Hall, W. Brosnahan, J. Holmes, J. L. Twynam, T. Lowry. Mr Bannister was appointed treasurer, Mr Brosnahan honorary secretary. Mr Hall then proposed "That the several ride officers and assistants be solicited to contribute a small amount to defray the expenses which may be incurred by the committee in connection with the Horse Allowance Movement," which was seconded by Mr Holmes. It was then arranged that the committee should meet once a week for the despatch of business, and that contributions should be forwarded to the treasurer, and letters to the secretary at 7 Coulston Street, Chelsea, S.W. The fatherly advice of the editor to this committee of inexperienced agitators was, "a respectful tone and a concise statement" on behalf of both ride officer and riding supervisor, and an appeal, if failure be their fate, to the Lords of the Treasury. At the second meeting of the committee on Monday, December 19, Mr J. L. Twynam in the chair, a form of circular, to be forwarded to each ride officer, was submitted, approved, and adopted; and the receipt of several communications was acknowledged, whose facts would be embodied in a "general petition." The treasurer credited three remittances, which gave a total of £6, 9s. 2d. It may be added that this movement, although opened and unenergetically continued by the supervisor, eventually and finally fell under the guidance of the ride officer, who excluded the claims of the supervisor.

In 1865. As both the ride officer and the riding supervisor made separate appeals, the story of each will be separately told. The Horse Allowance Committee, or as designated by the editor, The London Committee of Ride Officers, held a special meeting in Catherine Street, Strand, on Friday, January 13, when Mr E. D. Stanley occupied the chair. It was reported that the whole of the ride officers, with few exceptions, were in favour of a general petition, and that the committee would frame a petition which should embody the suggestions and the statistical information which they had received, and that a printed copy of it, with a blank sheet for signatures, would be despatched to every collection or district, as might be afterwards decided upon, and the signature sheets, when returned, attached to the original petition. These propositions the editor urged it was the duty of the claimants to immediately carry out. Within a month—February—he wrote, "The petition, a copy of which we have before us—fulfils its object so thoroughly, and deals with the whole question in such an able and exhaustive manner, that it leaves us nothing to say except that we cannot peruse it without feeling, as Englishmen who boast of our liberality to those who serve us, a burning sense of shame." On the 6th of March the committee met in Catherine Street, Strand, under the chairmanship of Mr A. Innes, and decided that the petition to which the signatures of "upwards of seven hundred and fifty ride officers had been subscribed, should be presented to the Commissioners on Wednesday the 8th."

The writer of a leading article felt "certain that Justice will at last ascend her throne, which Injustice has so long usurped;" other writers were less sanguine. The Board, however, after reviewing the improvement in the position of the ride officer within the last few years, an improvement computed to be 33 per cent.,—the having to keep a horse on a salary of £97, 10s., until the grant of £20 per annum in 1855; the discontinuance of the superannuation deduction in 1857; the increase of £10 in salary in 1858,—decided, on March 25, that they were "unable to see any sufficient grounds to warrant them in submitting the present application to the favourable consideration of the Treasury." The reply was signed by Mr Sargent, and addressed to Mr H. Morris. The committee, true to the business-like aptitude which it had previously shown, met on March 28, only three days after the date of reply, when Mr J. L. Twynam presided, and it was decided to at once lay the claim before the Lords of her Majesty's Treasury. The promptitude of this act gave general satisfaction to their representees, who to the number of seven hundred and five duly signed the memorial, which was forwarded to their Lordships through the Commissioners on June 12. In the interval between the despatch of the application and the date of the reply, an interval of only eleven days, two able penmen embraced the opportunity to pen a forcible article on the justice of the appeal, and a well-timed and clear exposé of the claim to the chairman of the Board. Their Lordships' reply was transmitted through the Commissioners to Mr H. Morris on June 23, and proved to be an unacceptable answer, which, after the elimination of the official routine, ran thus—"The Lords Commissioners of Her Majesty's Treasury . . . . do not feel warranted in sanctioning any increase to their present allowance." The agitation now apparently subsided until the end of August, when "a strong and vigorous effort to the new Parliament, under the guidance of the committee, found general favour with the claimants who freely expressed their opinions. But the result of this proposition does not fall under the annals of this year. The remittances to the treasurer, with the communications to the secretary, were requested on January 14, to be forwarded to 17 Grove Cottages, Manor Street, Chelsea, S.W. The total remittance was £33, 6s. 3d. This, then, forms story one.

The action of the riding supervisor was less united and more private. Ruricola, one of the earliest writers this year, advocated the payment of the "actual travelling expenses," or an allowance according to "the size of the district:" later writers, threepence for every mile travelled, and in those districts in which the train could be utilised, the purchase of an annual pass. In March a memorial, signed by only thirty-six supervisors, for an increased horse allowance, was transmitted to the Lords of the Treasury through the usual channel, and on the 6th of May Mr Corbett replied on behalf of their Lordships, who, "adverting to the very considerable improvement that had been made during the last ten years in your position and the service, ... would not be warranted in sanctioning any increase to the allowance received by you." This repulse was hopefully reviewed in the following happily-chosen words—"Justice may be opposed and hurled back, as the towering rocks do battle with the waves, but slowly and surely the time must come when the proudest cliff will crumble and give way before the ever-advancing tide." A. B. C. addressed the chairman in the form of an interrogation on the stern logic of hard facts—"Don't you think they want rest and food, and don't you think their masters require a little of the latter before night? Would it be unreasonable to grant them something daily for subsistence under such circumstances." He subsequently suggested a grant of £40 a year. The correspondence now ceased until November, when Perseverance called attention to the fact that a few had determined that if a fair number of the agitants would give in their names, with a small contribution, within eight or ten days to the editor of the Civil Service Gazette, a petition to the Treasury would again be prepared for both horse and travelling allowances.

This, Theophrastus deprecated. He would employ a paid agent, whose duty it would be to transmit a circular to every supervisor, who should be urged to give in his signature. Beyond a few promises given to the proposition of Perseverance, a few letters, and two leading articles, no further effort appears to have been made. This, then, forms story number two.

In 1866. There were still two bands of agitants. The Horse Allowance Committee, whose active and masterly exertions of last year gave an earnest for the present, were found true to the high opinion their confreres had formed of them. Discontent foresaw the value of the sympathy and support of the patron M.P., who might be reached by "the old folks at home." Umbra realised the importance of the statement to members of parliament, and Wilkie the possibility of piercing the proverbial hardheartedness of the Chancellor of the Exchequer, by pointing out the insufficiency of the sum allowed for the keep of the roadster, the slowness of promotion, the possibility and promotive advantage in changing 200 rides into "second class divisions," and the necessity for an annual grant of £36, 10s. The editor, who of course sympathised with the fruitless efforts of the past year, complimented the Committee on their "able pamphlet," which in March was supplemented by the transmission of a petition, signed by 776 ride officers, to the House of Commons. The riding supervisor found an advocate in Drudge, who indited a letter to their honours, in which he narrated the effects of the inadequacy of the sum allowed, and the absence of an order for a travelling and subsistence allowance; in A. B. C., who asked if the movement had been allowed "to die out?" in Aurelian, who would ask for an allowance of £50 for travelling expenses; and in Faithful, who recapitulated the grievances of the grade, and called upon the supervisor and the examiner "to wring out this last tardy act of justice." The quill of the editor of course was not silent. It recorded the actual expense of horse, travelling, and subsistence at a sum varying from £60 to £100 per annum, and placed on record a claim for an average annual allowance of £70. The advocacy of these writers was followed by the presentation to the Treasury of a petition signed by two hundred and eighty supervisors, who asked their lordships not only for an increased allowance for the keep and feed of the steed, but also for a grant for travelling expenses. The application was of course forwarded to their honours, with a letter requesting its transmission to the Cabinet, who replied through the Board by a communication from Mr Corbett, dated June 27, that they could not comply with the prayer of the petition, partly in consequence of the "very considerable improvement that has been made during the last ten years." Again repulsed, again resolved. The next effort, Dictator suggested should be made through the medium of the increase-of pay petition then in active preparation. His idea met with approval, and notably so by the officials in Halifax and Carnarvon collections. No interest was shewn in the movement by letter after the month of October. In 1867. The annalist has but little to record under this long continued and even now unsettled movement, respecting the deeds of the ride officer and the riding supervisor. The lower-grade equestrian appears to have enunciated a new idea in respect to the income-tax. He felt persuaded the income-tax was an unjust levy upon him, seeing that the extra sum expended upon the feed and keep of his steed, over that allowed, reduced his salary below £100; and further, that the Commissioners acted illegally in allowing his rank to deduct £30 from salary and allowance, and understood that several ride officers had resolved to appeal against the assessment. He also thought the Board had taken ample time to consider his claim, and there being no prospect of an increase, that a motion should be brought forward in the House of Commons. The personal interview with the M.P. to insure sufficient support when the motion should be brought forward was not lost sight of. This "most pressing hardship" did not engage particular attention after the month of June, in consequence of its embodiment in the address by the Central Committee. The higher-grade claimant's case was also included. The principal penmen were Briton, Reformer, Old Clo', A Ride Officer, A. B. C., One of the Ride Officer's Committee, J. B., Subscriber, and Cotswold. It was suggested that the balance of the riding supervisors and examiners' horse allowance fund of 1865 should be handed over to the Glasgow Committee. In 1868. The exhaustive statement of departmental claims addressed to their honours in 1867, it has already been observed, included the claims of the "mounted gaugers," yet, notwithstanding the powerful appeal, the desires of the owners of the "gauger's steed" still continued to be recorded, until the issue of the general order of July 17, when fears were expressed that the proposed permissive use of a horse would cause the officials to "become prematurely old by cadging about the country on foot," the department to become a "Department of Tramps," and the horse allowance to become a "bootmaker's allowance." The editor reviewed the "illegal method" of assessing the income-tax of riding supervisors and ride officers: Unity is Strength protested against the indiscreet and selfish application of certain supervisors and officers to the Board for an increased grant of £60 and £30 respectively, while the many penned their several anxieties to induce an early decision on the pending rearrangements. The general order of August 3, by which collectors were authorised to make advances to supervisors and ride officers for the purchase of their horses, gave general satisfaction. In 1869. Hugh Littlejohn observed, prior to the issue of the general order of January 23d, by which those who were required to keep a horse were granted an increase of 50 per cent., that there was now great need for an adequate horse and travelling allowance, considering the frequent visits to each money order office, the collection of the agricultural statistics, and the inquiries respecting dog licences, but that these facts formed "a strange commentary upon the late official avowal that the Board hoped by their future arrangements to enable supervisors and officers to do without horses, and that therefore the necessity for keeping them might be dispensed with." The increase it cannot be recorded, did not give satisfaction: the many were silent; and of the few who were outspoken—Justice considered it only "a sop," another "not fair," a third "a bit of sharp practice," a fourth "a sell," a fifth, that it would not cover expenses, "even when men go about the country on important revenue business, with a meanness which is utterly inconsistent with their station in life, and destructive of every feeling of manliness and self-respect." The enhanced allowances were defined "an infinitesimal instalment of justice:" they were £30 and £45 respectively, with, to those who were not required "to mount," travelling allowances of varied amounts. The rescheming of the stations consequent upon the commutation of the assessed taxes into establishment licences, led the more hopeful to believe that it would afford their honours an opportunity to remove "a glaring evil" by granting the needful "travelling expenses," and thus make "a needy set of officials contented and happy." Three suggestions may be noted: Hugh Littlejohn—that the Board might procure the required season railway tickets at a saving of one-third on the present cost; Kendall—that the distinction of "ride, riding, division, and foot-walk" be discontinued, and the "necessary travelling expenses," be allowed; P. P.—the extension of the period in which to purchase a horse. The correspondence ceased in November.

In 1870. Commencing in January, the nine successive months formed the period in which the dissatisfied recipients of these allowances expressed their sentiments. To particularise two—Porcupine, sarcastically, will those who travel by rail be supplied with a telescope? S., impatiently, "Are riding supervisors ever to receive proper travelling allowances?"

In 1871. The grievance of the inadequate allowance for "gig pitching"—the cause of "plesiosau rusticus" whatever that may mean—and "saddle bumping," found expression in the first proposed Address to the Board by the Inverness Committee, who submitted "that both the fixed limit and the shifting limit should be at once removed and the actual requirements of man and station provided for—subsistence when from home and locomotion." But this address, although subsequently revised and generally approved, was not forwarded to the Board. The individual proposals were, by

John Meanwell, that a servant should be allowed free of licence duty; by Eli-Adepa, that the Government should provide horses, and that those who used them should pay a small percentage on the original outlay; and by N. that the Government should "pay half the sum for a horse, restricting that half to £10."

J. B., an old but not frequent writer, stated, in referring to the origin of the allowances of gig toll, and horse and gig taxes, and for horse keep, that the three first concessions were made on "not more than two applications to the Board by a single individual," and that the last was conceded by the Board and Treasury "on the consideration of one memorial emanating from one person only." The agitation was practically dropped In June.

In 1872. The balance in hand left by the Ride Officers' Committee of 1864—£20, 3s. 6d.—was handed to the Mayo Memorial Fund Committee. An intimation, November, that Commissioners were about to submit to the Treasury a scheme of subsistence allowance to supervisors when absent from home more than eight hours, gave rise to a brief discussion. It ended in discussion, but not in the form—sapid.

In 1873. Nothing to note. In 1874. The horse allowance in its two-fold bearing was laid before the Playfair Commission, but the ride officer feared his class claim had not received sufficient attention, and to satisfy him, Mr Crowe, supervisor, who had an active part in arranging the evidence, wrote to the secretary to the Commission, who replied that the "point" had been so clearly put before the Commission in Mr Westcott's statement, "that further evidence was not required. Mr Westcott was in this case the chosen representative ride officer. The travelling allowance, too, occupied considerable attention, and its inadequacy was also laid before the same Commission. The Board allowed a sum not exceeding sixpence per day to certain London officers who could not reside within the limits of their stations. The actual expense incurred to be paid quarterly. The rumour of 1872 that the Commissioners had recommended the Lords of the Treasury to grant supervisors a subsistence allowance when absent from home in their own districts, was again announced. This claim, similar to the two preceding, was laid before the Playfair Commission. The small grant of three shillings per day to supervisors who granted dog licences at remote places was mentioned. And the examiners in London, on May 5, resolved to petition Her Majesty's Treasury for "an augmentation of subsistence allowance."

A subsistence allowance was granted the supervisor and officer in 1876.[1]

A table in the order of rank:—

Collector.—*See* Sittings.

1688.	2s. in £		on brandy duty collected at outports.
1745.	4d.	„	for each licence signed.
1747.	4d.	„	for each coach receipt.
1780.	5s.	„	for each station collected.
„	5s.	„	for attending a hearing.
1804.	£1 per day		"riding charges."
1830.	10s.	„	in E. } when on the round and at the same
„	8s.	„	in I. } rate for part of a day.
„	8s.	„	in S. to those who were appointed at a reduced salary in five collections. The total, in either collection, not to exceed £50 per annum.
1854.	14s.	„	when on the round for subsistence and locomotion.
„	14s.	„	and night when on revenue business; other
„	8s.	„	if not absent at night, and in both cases, the actual expenses of locomotion.
1857.	14s.	„	when absent at night, } when not on the
„	7s.	„	when only 8 hours. } round, and in either
„	9s. 6d.	„	after 14 days in one place, } case, the actual travelling expenses at first class fares.
„	14s.	„	when on the round for any number of days: no travelling allowance.
„	7s.	„	returning to before, or going from, residence after 1 o'clock.
1876.	16s.	„	travelling and subsistence on the round.
1877.	First-class fare when not on the round.		
„	16s. per day,		} and first-class fare.
„	8s.	„	above 8 hours, }
„	11s.	„	when more than 14 days in same place, }

Inspector—

1854. 14s. per day when officiating on the round, or from resi-

[1] C. S. G. & C.

dence on revenue business, and expenses of locomotion.

1854. 11s. per day for subsistence when in collector's residence.

1876. 16s. „ when travelling.

Supervisor—

1745. 2d. for signing each licence.

1747. 2d. for each coach receipt.

To 1808. 3s. per day } for attending to collect candle duty.

1809. 6s. 6d. „ }

1811. £60 per annum to hop supervisor.

„ £70 „ „

1829. 5s. each I. examiner instructed in brick duty.

1854. 3s. per day at sittings not in residence, and

„ 5s. per day and night.

„ 9s. „ and night when officiating for another supervisor five miles from residence, and in each case actual cost of locomotion.

1842. Assessed taxes on horse and

1854. Tolls, gig, and

1855. £30 per annum for horse keep from Jan. 1, 1856.

1857. 12s. per day when absent at night, } officiating in another

„ 6s. „ when not out at night, } district five miles (in 1877, two miles) from residence, and

„ 8s. 6d. „ after 14 days in one place, and in any of the above three cases, the actual expenses at second-class fares.

„ 12s. „ when absent at night on the round out of residence, and

„ 6s. „ when absent above 8 hours, and not out at night. No travelling allowance in either case.

1804. S. £5 per glass house, provided total not exceed £20 per annum "for extraordinary trouble and expense."

„ S. £16 per annum for horse keep.

1843. 7s. 6d. per day subsistence in travelling to undergo, and while under examination and actual travelling expenses.

1869. £45 per annum for horse keep or for travelling expenses.

1869. 5s. per annum for stationery.

1876. £55 per annum for horse keep.
" £52 " not exceeding for subsistence.

Examiner—

1790. £25 per annum when officiating, "to be charged on the duty which bears the salary."

1796. One day's salary for every 30 miles travelled in going from his division.

1829. 7d. per mile in going to his district; 6d. elsewhere if over 50 miles on revenue business.

1848. 2d class fare.

1854. 3s. per day at sittings not in residence, and 5s. per day and night.

" 9s. per day and night when officiating for another supervisor, 5 miles from residence, and, 6s. per day; and in either case actual cost of locomotion.

1857. 12s. " when absent at night. } Officiating in another district more than 5 miles (1877, 2 miles) from residence, with actual travelling expenses at second class fares.
" 6s. " when not out at night.
" 8s. 6d. " after 14 days in one place.

" 12s. " when absent at night, on round out of residence.

" 6s. " when absent above eight hours and not out at night. No travelling allowance.

1859. Actual expenses in going to district; reasonable expenses of family.

1829. S. £50 per annum when officiating.
1842. £50 " "
1858. £30 " "
1864. £50 " "
1870. £40 " " in footwalk district.
" £60 " " in riding district.

Clerk—

1830. 10s. per day in England, and
8s. " in Ireland when on the round, and at the same rates for parts of a day.

1854. 14s. " on the round for subsistence and locomotion.

1857. 10s. " when absent at night. } When not on the round, and in any case the actual expenses at second class fares.
" 5s. " when not out at night.
" 7s. " after 14 days in one place.

1857 14s. per day on the round, for any number of days.
" 7s. " returning to before, or going from residence, after 1 o'clock; no travelling allowance.

1869. 5s. per annum for stationery.

1876. 16s. per day for travelling and subsistence on the round. £50 and £100 per annum for "duty pay."

1877. 12s. 6d. per day when absent at night.
" 6s. " when absent above 8 hours. } When travelling otherwise than on
" 8s. 6d. " when more than 14 days in one place. } the round and actual expenses at 2d class fares.

Division Officer—

1829. 6d. per mile in going to Chief Office, if over 50 miles.

1857. 10s. per day when absent at night to meet the collector on the round, and
5s. " when not, but absent above eight hours; no travelling allowance.

1869. 5s. per annum for stationery.

1874. 6d. per day to London officers residing out of station.

1877. When specially employed or at sitting out of residence. } same as under clerk, except travelling allowance in latter case, 1877.

Ride Officer—

1829. 6d. per mile in going to division, if over 50 miles.

1842. Assessed taxes on horse, and

1854. Tolls gig and

1855. £20 per annum for horse keep from Jan. 1, 1856.

1856. £20 " to dropped officer if he kept a horse.

1858. 10s. per day when absent at night to meet the collector on the round, and
5s. " when not, but above eight hours; no travelling allowance.

1869. 5s. per annum for stationery.
" £30 " } for horse keep or travelling allowance.
1876. £45 " }
" £19, 10s. per annum, not exceeding for subsistence.

1877. When specially employed, or at sitting out of residence, same as under clerk, except travelling allowance in latter case, 1877.

Officer—

1750. 2d. for each receipt of coach duty.

1804. S. £15 for each glass house.

" 5 per cent. on amount of auction sales discovered.

To 1808. S. 2s. per day } for attending to collect candle duty.
1809. S. 4s. 6d " }

1820. 12s. per day travelling. } for attending prosecutions in
" 12s. " subsistence. } town.

" £50 per annum to "established officer" for double duty.

" 5s. " for serving Writ of Subpæna.

" £2, 2s. for arresting a delinquent.

1829. £1, 10s. for each I. examiner instructed on brick duty.

1834. 5s. per day to Border officer for horse keep.

1843. 6s. " subsistence in travelling to undergo, and while under examination, with cost of travel.

1848. 2d class fare when travelling on revenue business.

1849. 3s. per day to dropped officer, in addition to full salary when he officiated more than 2 miles from residence.

1854. 3s. " when he performed double duty in a division, and
4s. " in a ride, to cover all expenses.

1857. 10s. " when absent at night on special employment. } and actual expenses at second class fares.
" 5s. " when not but more than 8 hours, }
" 7s. " after fourteen days in one place. }

" 3s. " for double duty in division, } and actual cost of travelling, if more
" 4s. " " in ride, } than three miles (in 1877, 2 miles) from residence.

" 7s. " as clerk out of his residence, in addition to actual expenses at second class fares.

" 14s. " on the round (even if in his residence; no travelling allowance.

" Actual travelling at 1st or 2d class fares. } On removal ex-
" Actual subsistence expenses. } on complaint or request.

Officiator—

1804. S. 4d. per mile examiner, officer, expectant, or restored officer.

1811. £80 per annum for doing duty of "surveying officer."

1820. £80 „ to include expectant, dropped assistant, or officer minuted for restoration.

1847. £90 „ employed as a supernumerary.

Supernumerary—

1811. £38 per annum when he officiated for an officer, in addition to salary of £52.

1829. S. £38 „ „ „ „

1829. 6d. per mile in going to his ride, if over 50 miles.

1830. 10s. per day in England, } and at the same rate for part
„ 8s. „ in Scotland, } of a day when on the round.

1839. 13s. „ in U. Kingdom, when on the round.

1846. £38 per annum when officiating.

First Class Assistants—

1829. 6d. per mile in going to his ride if over 50 miles.

1857. 3d. „ on removal, except on complaint or request, if over 5 miles.

Second Class Assistant—

1828. £30 per annum when officiating.

1829. S. £30 „ „

„ 4d. per mile in proceeding to officiate in another collection if over 50 miles.

1834. Horse, used officer's, or was paid by him horse hire.

1854. 2s. per day when officiating in lieu of £30, and £10 horse hire.

1857. 3d. per mile on removal, except on complaint or request, if over 5 miles.

1870. 2s. per day in a division.

„ 3s. „ in a ride.

1876. Subsistence, conditionally.

Permit Writer—

1857. 10s. per day when absent at night.

„ 5s. „ when more than eight hours

„ 7s. „ after 14 days in one place.

When employed out of station, and not officiating for another permit writer, with actual expenses at 2d class fares.

Hop Officer—

1811. £85 per annum.

ALMANACK.

Apart from the occasional incomplete lists of names, with a few other particulars, given in the various handbooks, from Leadbetter's Royal Gauger to Bateman's Manual, no official directory or almanack was issued until 1853. This appeared as a sheet, and contained, with the exception of the names of the Commissioners and of a few of the chiefs of departments, only the names of the surveying general examiners, with their classes, and the names of the collectors, the supervisors, and the clerks, with their respective stations; and was restricted in circulation, for the most part, to the limits of the Chief Office. This sheet is still printed, but with additional facts, under this reservation.

Loftus first published his Inland Revenue Almanack in 1854, in which he gave, in addition to the particulars given in this sheet, the names of the examiners, and the names and stations of all below that rank: he added, in 1855, a list of the superannuation recipients; in 1857, the "companion"—an abstract of station, residence, name, and number; and since then several other useful accompaniments, particularly the marginal notes on points of doubt or difficulty; and, in 1878, he promises in his prospectus "a Summary of the Customs' Laws and Regulations, so far as they relate to, or have any bearing on, the work of the Excise Department," with other new features, at the customary price—not that he has "the slightest wish to depreciate or discourage any man's enterprise."—*See* Ham.

AMALGAMATION.

A term little used until 1855, when certain members of the department began to agitate under *noms de plume*, among whom was

Hugh Littlejohn, for the union of the Customs with the Excise, and an extension of authority to perform duties in connection with the Stamps and Taxes. It is synonymous with the older term Consolidation, which see.

ANNUITIES.

King William the Third gave his royal assent to an Act for levying duties of Excise upon ale and beer, for securing recompence to those who would advance £1,000,000 towards the war against France. This was termed the "Ninepenny Excise," and consisted of an imposition of ninepence per barrel on beer for a period of 99 years from Jan. 25, 1692. By this Act every contributor who advanced £100 was entitled to share in an annuity of £100,000 for his life, and if a contributor or his nominee died, his share was to go to his survivor; or a contributor might, if he shared in the sum, have either a certain annuity of £14 for his £100 during his own life, or the life of any other person whom he might nominate. This was the first Annuity Act, and the receipt having been found insufficient, a second was passed the following year to meet the deficit. Power was afterwards given to commute the life interest into one at the rate of £56 per £100 for a term of 96 years.

The annuitants were advised of the date of payment in 1702, by an announcement in the London Gazette, and were paid at the Exchequer on the production of their "Orders."

ANONYMOUS LETTERS.

It was the practice, from 1698 to 1736, for the Commissioners, in common with other Commissioners, to acknowledge the receipt of anonymous letters, which were often addressed to the Lord High Treasurer, in the London Gazette, and to offer "suitable" or "fitting encouragement" and protection to the unknown writers upon their appearing at the Chief Office and making out their statements, which were usually those of frauds on the revenue, but in two instances an "Expedient for advancing the Revenue." The number seldom exceeded two, and never four, in one year.

ANTI-MARRIAGE ORDINANCE.

Not allowed to marry until he attain the rank of ride officer; this is the sum of a General Order as regards assistants issued in 1852.

The desire to have this rescinded appears to have originated in 1856 with "a White Slave who wants Freedom." It was also advocated in 1857, but was not pressed until 1858. The discussion of "The Marriage Prohibition Order," "Edict," "Anti-Marriage Edict," "The Celibacy Bull," "The Matrimonial Question," was then re-opened by "Gamos," who urged the preparation of petitions to the Board to rescind the "hated order." The aid of poesy was also offered under the title of "To Marry or Not to Marry? That is the Question," in the form of a dialogue of nine stanzas between "a sentimental Expectant of Excise and the Ghost of John Wooden-heart." Petitions were accordingly forwarded from Orkney, Stirling, and Dublin, but as these were unsuccessful, "A Young Friar" appeared on the scene, who appealed to his brother assistants to forward to him to the address of John Campbell, Post Office, Castle St., Edinburgh (till called for), an intimation whether they would vote for the total or partial abolition of the order, or not at all; and promised them that he would intimate the result through the *Civil Service Gazette*. This he did in 1859, having received only five letters—namely, from Elgin, Oxford, Rochester, Stirling, Ware. "John Campbell" next appeared in Glasgow, where on January 24th, 1859, a meeting of first and second-class assistants was convened, and a committee formed, to further the object of the movement. At an adjourned meeting held on February 1st, 1859, a form of petition was adopted, and on the 28th, the completed document despatched to their Honours, to whom others were subsequently sent from Campbelton, Rochester, London South, Elgin, and Oxford; those from Elgin and Oxford being signed by the staff in general. But during the preparation and presentation of these documents, the subject was freely discussed by Agricola, Stoic, A General-Order-made Bachelor, F. C. A., W. H. M., Anti-Tyranny, Luther, and others, and it was not until June 6th, 1859, that "The Order of the

Inland Revenue Friars," so named after the leader—A Young Friar, —received an answer—"To Marry."

Thus ended a movement which had extended over a period of four years. It was closed with "A Yorkshire Man's" Poetical Effusion—

"Thanks, honour'd Sirs! you've sav'd us mighty trouble,
By granting us the right of living double;
But, the rite of marriage, be it understood,
Comes from a higher source, and for our mutual good."[1]

APPOINTMENTS.

It was not until the publication of the *Civil Service Gazette* on January 1st, 1853, that the department, generally, was informed of the movements of its members, and even then but scantily and imperfectly, as only thirty-two were recorded in the first year of its issue. In 1854, appointments included a nomination, an order for instructions, an appointment, a removal, a promotion, an order to officiate, a dismissal. Even these were supplied with considerable irregularity until 1860, and the appointments on reduction were suppressed in 1867. The dates of petition for promotion and of commission were formerly—1856—given, and the announcements were made in 1860 in the order of time, not of rank. The first insertion was that of Mr Colin Campbell, to be collector of Greenock collection, and the total to 1874 exceeded 20,000. Taking an average of twenty years, from 1855 to 1874, the annual is 977; the quarterly, March 31st, 261; June 30th, 231; September 30th, 218; December 31st, 266.

Allied to these is the exchange of appointment or station. Of course down in 1857 little effort was made to effect an exchange, as to that date every officer was removed periodically. From that year and down to 1870, however, the medium of an advertisement in the first instance, was generally employed at an annual average insertion of 42, while from 1871 to 1874, in the *Civilian*, at 153.

[1] C. S. G., 1856-59.

APPRAISER'S LICENCE DUTY.

At first—1806—a stamp duty. A petition was presented to the House of Commons in 1845 to increase the duty, and a bill was brought in and carried the same year, by which the duty was quadrupled. Evasion of duty, however, became so apparent in 1861, that the collection was placed in the hands of the excise branch, and the increased charge which arose by the change induced the authorities to change it into an excise licence duty in 1864. It first included the authority to act as an house agent in 1862. The subjoined table [1] will show the dates of commencement, the variations of rate, the limits of imposition—

Commenced.	Rates.		
	England.	Scotland.	Ireland.
1806, July 5 . . .	6/	6/	—
1815	10/	10/	—
1842, Oct. 10 . . .	10/	10/	10/
1845	£2	£2	£2

AREOMETER.

Similar to the acetometer—a densimeter. This instrument, made of glass, ivory, &c., consisted of a ball with two spindles—the lower, short and circular, with a quicksilver ballast to keep it in an erect position; the upper, long and three-sided, and marked off from 1 to 40 at equal distances, called "degrees." It was about four inches long. Weights were not used. Its figure, the bead not excepted, appears to have been the prototype of the present hydrometer and saccharometer. It was used to show the lightness and heaviness of fluids, and although not used officially, the official mind was drawn to the fact that "if you find that the specific gravity of the whole

[1] C. I. R., 13th v. i. p. 65; v. ii. p. 79.

vessel"—of spirits—"sent you home is different from that parcel which you tried, you may be assured it is some way mixt and adulterated."[1]

ARMORIAL BEARINGS—LICENCE DUTY.

Introduced by Mr Pitt in his budget, on April 25th, 1798.[2] First levied June 24th, 1798, at three rates, then in 1854 at two. Great Britain only.

Year.	Persons charged for any carrriage.	Persons not charged for any carriage but for house and window duties.	Other persons.
1798	£2 2 0	£1 1 0	£0 10 6
1808	2 8 0	1 4 0	0 12 0
	Persons charged for a carriage, £3 10 0.		
1854	£2 12 9		0 13 2
	Painted on carriage.		*Otherwise.*
1870	£2 2 0		£1 1 0

These dutes were first levied as excise licences in 1870. To 1878, the largest number charged was in 1872—

At the higher rate—20,237
" lower " 39,870.

See the Commissioners' First, Fourteenth, and subsequent reports. Numerous cases decided by the Judges will be found in Muir's Stamp and Tax Office Manual.

ARMY AND NAVY PAYMENTS.

These payments are as old as the Excise itself. It will be found

[1] Leadbetter's Royal Gauger. [2] Debrett's Parliamentary Debates.

by going back to the Oxford Excise of 1645, which originated with the necessity for provisioning the garrison of that city, and those in the adjoining counties, that payments were made weekly for the provision of both men and material, and by tracing other authentic documents, that this system of payment for a two-fold purpose was continued down to 1660.[1] Samuel Pepys quaintly wrote in his diary, on January 5th, 1660 (o.s.)—"And so to my office again; where the Excise money was brought, and some of it told out to soldiers till it was dark."

It appears to have been discontinued about this time, though subsequently renewed, but under the character of a disbursement for effective and non-effective services.

The payment to the non-effective men connected with Chelsea, known as the Chelsea Pensioner, is mentioned in the London Gazette of 1760, and confirms the fact of an existing practice: it was consequently not now first introduced. The payment of the Greenwich "Out Pensioner" followed.

Advances or allowances to effective men in active service, or on furlough, were not again made until after 1760. The names under which these have been paid are—

ARMY—Ticket, Pension, Compassionate List, Bounty, Marines.

NAVY—Allotments, Seamen's Wages, Pensions, Compassionate List, Bounty, Half Pay.

And, with respect to the pensioner, the collector formerly received a fee of six, subsequently, three pence for each payment, and the clerk one of three pence for each affidavit.

ARTHUR'S NEW SPIRIT CALCULATOR.

This little 12mo was written in 1829 by E. Arthur, Officer of Excise.

It contains plain rules for reducing and compounding spirits, and for cask gauging; a very, very brief sketch of distillation; the names of the Commissioners, General Surveyors, Surveying General Examiners, and Collectors. It is reviewed by Wm. Townshend, senior, "General Surveyor of the Town Establishment."[2]

[1] Green's State Papers. [2] Eton, Worcester.

ASSAULTS.

The records of the eighteenth century teem with assaults upon officers. They were chiefly inflicted by the numerous lawless, but powerful, smuggling gangs, whose nefarious traffic yielded such large remuneration as to jeopardise even the life itself of those who obstructed their course. Royalty itself frequently proclaimed these ill deeds down to 1781; the Lords of the Treasury also frequently made them known by "Order of Council" down to 1816, and from that date the Commissioners, by advertisement, with in every case the offer of a substantial reward for the apprehension and conviction of the offenders.[1]

The original language will be the best, the most telling.

1714. "By the King, A Proclamation, for the discovering and apprehending of the Persons who Barbarously Wounded and Maimed John Mac-Allen an Officer of Excise in Scotland. George R. Whereas We have Received Information, That upon the Thirtieth Day of November last, between the Hours of Twelve and One in the Morning at Crieff in Perthshire; in that Part of Our Kingdom of Great Britain called Scotland, several Persons in Highland Habits, with their Faces Discoloured and Armed with Sword, Durk, and Pistol, broke into the Lodgings of John Mac-Allen, one of Our Officers of Excise, and Barbarously and Inhumanly Beat, Bruised, and Wounded the said John Mac-Allen in several parts of his Body and Cut off great Part of His Right Ear." The proclamation then announces that £200 will be given for the apprehension of the offenders or any one of them. An accomplice giving information being offered that sum and the pardon of his offence. St. James's, Jan. 15th, 1714-15.[1]

1725. *See* Glasgow Malt Insurrection.

1731. "Whereas the Comrs. of His Majesty's Excise have reported That Thomas Wylde, instructed in the Excise, was on Tenth of November last, in the Night, as he was returning from his country Business of officiating in the Excise, to his Residence at Kintbury, in the County of Wilts, attacked and robbed by Two Foot Pads, of his Money, Horse, Great Coat, and Boots, and was cut, bruised, and beat, in so barbarous a Manner, that he died on the Twelfth of the same Month." In this case His Majesty offered his "most gracious

[1] L. G.

Pardon" to an accomplice, and the Commissioners offered a reward of £50.[1]

1733. "Whereas the Comrs. of Excise have represented, that Samuel Alexander, a Watchman in the Parish of St. Giles's Cripplegate, in the Lordship's Liberty, and the County of Middlesex, having the Seventeenth Instant, about Three a-clock in the Morning, with the Assistance of the Headborough of the Night, and other Watchmen, stopped a Man and a Woman loaded with Run Tea, and having the said Woman in Custody, as soon as the Headborough and other Watchmen were gone to the Watchouse with the said Tea, the said Woman crying out for Assistance, two Men on Horseback, unknown, one on a Chesnut Horse, the other on a Grey Horse, came and not only rescued her, but beat the said Samuel Alexander in so cruel and barbarous a Manner, that his skull was fractured and he died the same Evening." The Commissioners offered a reward of £100.[1]

1737. "Whereas several officers have been assaulted in detecting persons retailing spirituous liquors to discourage such Practices for the future. . . . . Information to be given to Sollicitor, at the Excise Office." Reward £20.[1]

1738. "Whereas Thomas Binham of Rolvenden near Cranbrook, in Kent, did on the 12th of April last, receive a Threatening Letter, requiring him to send Fifty Pounds to a Place therein appointed, And whereas on the 27th of the same Month, two Men, armed with 'Cutlashes' and Pistols came to the said Binham's Lodgings, and demanded the said Fifty Pounds, threatening Vengeance in Case of Refusal; The Comrs. of Excise do hereby give Notice that if any Person will make Discovery of the two Persons aforesaid or any of their Accomplices, so as they may be brought to Justice, they shall receive the Reward of Forty Pounds, to be paid at the Office in the Old Jewry, upon the Conviction of each Offender: One of the said Persons was a well grown Man, about six feet high, of a ruddy Complexion, and a round Visage, about 30 Years of Age, and wore a light coloured Bob Wig; the other a slender Man of low Stature, about Five feet two or three Inches, of a sallow Complexion, wore a Velvet Cap, the Cape of the same buttoned over his Chin, appeared to be upwards of 30 years of Age."[1]

1742. "Whereas John Griffin, Supervisor of Excise at Seven Oaks in the County of Kent, was on the 20th of October last in the

[1] L. G.

Execution of his Duty, assaulted at the House of William Drewry, Victualler, at Kelden, by several Persons unknown, and was grievously beat and abused, insomuch that his Life is in great Danger, from the Wounds he then received: The Comrs. of Excise do hereby give Notice, that if any Person will make Discovery of the Persons concerned in the said Assault, so as they or any of them may be brought to Justice, such Person shall upon Conviction of any of the Offenders, receive the Reward of Two Hundred Pounds, to be paid at their Office in the Old Jewry; and in case any of the Persons concerned will make Discovery of his Accomplices so as they or any of them may be convicted of the Assault he shall receive the Reward as aforesaid."[1]

1743. "Whereas Thomas Skinner of Little Peckham was, on the 17th of October last, arrested upon a Capias by John Rugg, Supervisor of Rochester; and whereas the said Rugg, with two other Persons, his Assistants, being carrying the said Skinner to Maidstone, were assaulted at Barming, about two or three miles from Maidstone, by five Horsemen, armed with Blunderbusses and Pistols, who rescued the said Skinner."[1]

1744. "Whereas William Hird, Officer of Excise at St. Mary Cray, in the County of Kent, was, on the 22nd day of May last, when upon Duty and on Foot, followed by a Person known to be a Smuggler, who, about the middle of Chislehurst Common, knocked him down with his Whip seven or eight Times, and repeated his Blows until the Whip was broke to Pieces, of which Blows the said Officer now lies dangerously ill!"

1763. "Whereas it has been humbly represented to the King that Messrs Crisp and Briggs, Officers of Excise at Faversham, in the County of Kent, having, upon the 7th of August last, observed a Gang of Smugglers of about fifteen in number going over Charing Heath, in the said County, called a Militiaman and two others to their Assistance, and after pursuing for several Miles the Track which the said Gang had gone, they discovered in a Field Sixty-two Bags of Tea, which they immediately secured in a Farm-House; but presently the whole gang of Smugglers came up, and declared they would rescue the goods or die in the Attempt: The Officers of Excise, having determined to defend their Seizure, pressed them to depart; the Smugglers nevertheless attempted to break in the House, which they, in part, effected by forcing out the Bars of the

[1] L. G.

Windows; and they were entering in, threatening, with Oaths and Imprecations, that they would murder the Officers, who were therefore obliged to fire, upon which they were dispersed, and the Officers secured their Seizure."[1]

1768. "Whereas it has been humbly represented to the King that His Majesty's Commrs. of Excise have, by Letters from their Officers at Scarborough and Hull, dated respectively the 9th and 13th inst., August, received an Account of a Murder having been committed on John Smith, late Officer of Excise, who, together with other Officers, had seized a Quantity of Run Goods; and that, after the Seizure and Securing of the said Goods, several Persons, amongst whom were Valentine Bailey of Brockley and Joseph Haines of Hackness, assaulted the said Officer, and some Person deliberately and maliciously presented a Pistol close to the Breast of the said John Smith, killed him on the spot. . . . ."[1]

1769. "Whereas it has been humbly represented to the King, that Mr Dighton, one of His Majesty's Supervisors of Excise at Halifax, in the County of York, was, on the night of the 9th inst., inhumanly shot and murdered within a few yards of his own House, by some malicious Person or Persons unknown. . . . ."[1] Pardon and £100 to an informing accessory. St. James's, Nov. 14, 1769, Weymouth.

1774. "Whereas on Sunday the 10th April inst., about Four o'clock in the Morning, several Persons, armed with large Bludgeons and other offensive Weapons, forced themselves into the House of Samuel Sutton, an Officer of Excise at East Grinstead, and after binding the said Sutton's Hands and Feet, and securing his Maid-Servant, did forcibly take away Four Hundred and twenty-four Pounds weight of Tea which had been condemned by the Judges of the County of Sussex."[1]

1779. "On Wednesday the 7th of April last, about Half-past Four in the Afternoon, as Mr Henry Dent, Collector of Excise, with two other Persons, were on the Road between Northleach and Cirencester, an Attempt was made, as was imagined, to rob them, by several Persons in Disguise, and with Blunderbusses and Cutlasses, who rushed out of a Wood and fired upon them."[1]

1781. "Whereas it has been humbly represented to the King that, on the 28th ult., Christopher Bell, Supervisor of Excise at Saxmundham in Suffolk, assisted by Four Excise Officers, and Twenty

[1] L. G.

Soldiers of the Suffolk Militia, made a Seizure of a considerable Quantity of Rum, Spirits, and Tea; and that in about Ten Minutes after making such Seizure, a large Gang of Ruffians, armed with Bludgeons and loaded Whips, attacked the said Supervisor and Officers, beating them in a most cruel Manner, particularly the Supervisor, whose left arm was thereby fractured in two Places; of which they rescued the said Seizures. . . . ."[1]

1782. "Whereas it has been represented to the Comrs. of Excise, that, in the Night between the 1st and 2nd inst. (March), 14 or 15 Persons came in a Coach, and another Carriage with Fire-arms, and forcibly entered the House of John Lewes, an Officer of Excise at Tooting, whom they used in a very cruel Manner, and at the same Time carried away several Bags of Tea, and 16 Half-Ankers of Geneva."[1]

1782. "Whereas it has been represented to the Comrs. of Excise, that, on the Night of the 28th ult., Thomas Borman, an Officer of Excise at Croydon, was assaulted and cruelly beat by Smugglers, who left him for dead."[1]

1783. "Whereas it has been humbly represented to the King, that, in consequence of an Information of Fifteen Hundred Casks of Smuggled Spirits being harboured in certain Warehouses at Deal, some Officers of Excise proceeded to that Place, attended by a Detachment of about Forty-seven of His Majesty's Troops, under the Command of Captain Pennyman: That on their Arrival at Deal, about Nine o'clock in the Evening of the Eighth day of February last, they found Intelligence had been previously given of their Approach, the Smugglers having prepared to receive them; and they had not been there many Minutes before they were fired upon, apparently by a Body of Persons in one Place, and afterwards from Windows and behind Walls; and that the Troops were prevented from Advancing by Ropes drawn across the Streets; That, having opened the Door of one Storehouse, a Quantity of Brandy, Geneva, and Raw Coffee was seized; the Smugglers continuing to fire on the Revenue Officers and Troops, they retired with what they had seized."[1]

1784. "One Officer was taken from his bed, and in his own house, in the presence of his family, was deliberately murdered."[2]

1784. "Whereas it has been humbly represented to the King, That, about Seven o'clock in the Evening of Tuesday the 30th of

[1] L. G. [2] H. C., Feb. 11, 1784.

November last, Edward Hilborough, who was fined by Two of His Majesty's Justice of the Peace for the County of Wilts in the Penalty of Sixty-five Pounds, for harbouring Seventy-two Gallons of Spirits, came to the House of Mr Robert Mann, Supervisor of Excise at Corsham, in the said County, and paid the said Fine; That, about Eight o'clock the same Evening, a Number of Ruffians came and Knocked softly at the Door of the said Robert Mann, who was standing in the Kitchen with the Division Officer; That, upon the Door being opened, Seven or Eight Men in Disguise entered into the House, all armed with Pistols of various Sizes, and, with horrid Imprecations, demanded the Money to be delivered up immediately, or they would blow out his, the said Supervisor's Brains; and then five of them surrounded him with their Pistols pointed at his Head and Body; That, upon the said Robert Mann asking them what Money they meant, they said, 'The Fine—their own—their own:' That, upon the said Robert Mann's declaring he had it not about him, they obliged him to say where it was; and Four of them forced him upstairs into his Chamber; and upon his taking the said Money out of his Chest, which was in a Purse (?), they pulled the Purse from his Hands, and emptied the Money into one of their Hats, and ran down Stairs, saying to their Companions, 'Here it is—here it is:' That they then left the House, mounted their Horses, and fired many Pistols as they rode along the Street."[1]

1785. "Whereas it has been humbly represented to the King, that, about Twelve o'clock in the Night of the 21st of January last, two men called at the Lodgings of James Ivey and John Thompson, Officers of Excise, at Leatherhead, in Surrey, and under the Pretence that they were the Assistants of another Revenue Officer, and in pursuit of some Smugglers they enticed the said James Ivey out, immediately after which he was surrounded by a large Party of Ruffians, supposed to be Smugglers, who beat him in so cruel a manner as to endanger his Life."[1]

1786. "Whereas it has been humbly represented to the King, that about One o'clock in the Morning of the 16th inst., a great number of unknown Persons, armed with Pistols, surrounded the Lodging-House of Henry Smalldridge, Excise Officer, at Cranborne, in the County of Dorset, which they forcibly entered, and rescued and carried away Twenty-one Casks, containing about a Hundred and ...en Gallons of foreign Spirituous Liquors, which had been

[1] L. G.

seized and deposited there by Mr John Twentyman, Supervisor of Excise at Blandford, in the said County."[1]

1796. "Whereas it has been humbly represented to the King, that on the afternoon of June 11, Mr William Stephens, an Officer of Excise, accompanied by an Expectant, came up with Two Men on Horseback, on the Road between Penryn and Gweek, one of whom had a single Horse, the other Two Ankers, which the Officers supposing to contain smuggled Spirits, attempted to seize, when one of the Offenders immediately cocked his Gun, and presented it at Stephens, swearing with horrid imprecations, that if he attempted to touch it, he would shoot him. That at this time Three more Men had come to the Smugglers' assistance, armed with Bludgeons, which obliged the Officers to desist; and as they were going off, one of the Offenders fired at them, and lodged several Shots in the said Stephens's Hat."[1]

1799. "Whereas it has been humbly represented to His Majesty, that on the 24th of July last, a Smuggling Lugger being observed by some of the Officers of the Revenue, in Cricketh or Kicketh Bay, in the County of Carnarvon, then landing her goods: Richard Bridgwater, Supervisor of Excise, Marcus Williams, Tide-Surveyor of the Customs at Pwllhely, in the said County, together with Two Tide Waiters, and some other Officers in the Service of the Customs, went in a Boat in pursuit of her; that when they came within about Three or Four Hundred Yards of the said Smuggling Vessel (the Custom House Colours being then flying in the Boat), the Officers hailed her, upon which the smuggler asked what Boat it was, and upon being told the King's Boat, they ordered the Officers to keep off, or abide by the Consequence; but being told by the Officers that they should not, the Smugglers immediately fired a Musket, the Ball from which came very near the King's Boat; the Smugglers then fired Eight other Muskets, one of which passed between the Fore and Main-Masts of the King's Boat, and another close behind the Officer, Richard Bridgwater, and upon the Smugglers threatening to drive the Officers into the Water if they did not keep off, they returned without being able to board the said Smuggling Vessel."[1]

1805. A free pardon was offered by His Majesty to any accomplice "or other person" who would discover the offender, who at about 9.30 p.m. on Dec. 12, 1805, fired a loaded pistol through a window at Henry Life, Excise Officer, Hadleigh, Suffolk, and

[1] L. G.

thereby wounded him in the left arm. The reward offered in the case was £500.[1]

1807. "Whereas" .... "a lugger laden with smuggled spirits was chased by the Excise Cutter, 'Lively,' to the shore opposite the town of Folkestone, where the crew board her, but unfortunately in doing so encountered several vollies from the fire-arms of the smugglers and others, His Majesty was pleased to offer a free pardon to an informing accomplice."[1]

1807. "Whereas .... about One o'clock in the Morning of the 7th July last some person unknown, called at the Bed-Chamber Window of Henry Dyer, Officer of Excise, at Parkstone, near Poole, in Dorsetshire, and when it was opened, discharged a Pistol at him, loaded with large Shot or Slugs, which penetrated the glass on all sides."[1]

1808. "Whereas .... about One o'clock in the Morning of the 18th ultimo, Wm. Stockton, John Tucker, William Winn, and Launcelot Thompson, Officers of Excise, with Four Men, acting as their Assistants, after having discovered that the Warehouse at one of the Salt Works at Lawton, in Cheshire, had been clandestinely entered, and a quantity of Salt taken therefrom, for which the Duties had not been paid, and a Portion of which was found upon a Person now in Custody, were violently assaulted by about Twenty Men, and with large Sticks and other Weapons, one of whom directed a Gun at them, and wounded the first of the said Officers with small Shot in Hand, Neck, Shoulder, and Arm."[1]

1816. "Whereas in the night of the 24th ultimo, Mr Andrew Elsworthy Adams, Supervisor of Excise, Battle, together with Wm. Hampton, and Edward Rayner, Excise Officers, after having made a seizure of run goods at St. John's Cross, in the parish of Mountfield, and County of Sussex, were most violently assaulted by five or six men, armed with bludgeons and pikes, and the Supervisor and one of the Officers dangerously wounded."[1]

1816. To avoid assault, states Mr Æneas Coffey: "The parties sometimes having been obliged to enter into terms of Capitulation with the smugglers to surrender their seizures, upon condition of being allowed to depart in safety." He continues: "A number of persons made an attempt between 2 or 3 o'clock in the day to carry him off"—Mr Hendrick, Surveyor of Letterkenny—"from the middle of the town, and had nearly succeeded in their object,

[1] L. G.

but by good fortune, the horse upon which they were attempting to force him, gave one of the ruffians a severe kick, which caused some confusion and delay amongst them, and the approach of some soldiers stationed in the town, prevented them carrying him off; he was, however, most seriously beaten and bruised." In conducting a prosecution in a large room in an inn, the future patentee further continues—"a stone was thrown by some person of nearly three pounds weight, which grazed my forehead, and shattered to pieces the door of a press in the room behind me."

Paul O'Kane, an officer, was banished to an island and barbarously treated, that he might not give evidence.

St. Lawrence, an officer at Cookstown, Tyrone, although guarded by a soldier and his wife, was carried off in a sack.

"In November 1810, while in the act of destroying an unlicensed distillery at Carthage, in the barony of Innishowen, I was attacked by about fifty men, not one of whom, I am sure, ever saw me before; they fractured my skull, left my whole body one mass of contusion, and gave me two bayonet wounds, one of which completely perforated my thigh."

O'Niel, an officer, was shot in the arm while in the middle of a military party, and on another occasion he was nearly killed by a shower of stones in the village of Carn.

The signals to prepare to assault were given by the blowing of horns, firing shots, shooting, and even ringing the church bell, the latter custom occurred in the island and parish of Muff, whose curate observed "it was an ancient custom, which he could not prevent."[1]

1843. Mantraps.—*See* Townland Fines.

1854. A Mr Betty was beaten by a maltster and his servant at Craigue, in return for which they received the intropulsive force of powder and shot.

Mr Vanstone, Supervisor, had his hat knocked to pieces on his head, and Messrs Faith and Cartwright were severely bruised, in arresting a notorious smuggler—John Allen.[2]

1876. James Russ, an officer, was shot at and severely injured at Crofton, near Wakefield, by a man of whom he inquired about a gun licence. Lord Beaconsfield in this case recommended a grant of £300 from the Royal Bounty Fund.[3]

[1] P. Rep., 1816. [2] C. S. G., 1854. [3] Scotsman, 1876, 1878.

ASSESSORS OF EXCISE.

These were persons who were appointed by the Justices of the Peace in 1649, to charge the excise duties on victuals consumed by private families.

ASSISTANT.

A designation older than that of expectant, which, until the introduction of that term, it represented. It is distinctly used in the Letters Patent of May 22, 1707, for the establishment in Scotland, and Highmore thus defines it, 1796, an "Assistant has the like commission as an officer, and by his constitution is an officer; but his not having so much salary as an officer occasions the calling him an assistant." The gentlemen who came under this designation were also called "assistant officers,"[1] "assistants or extraordinary men,"[2] and "occasional, temporary, or extra assistant, not placed on the excise establishment:"[3] the designation was dropped in Scotland in 1815. By Treasury Minute, dated Jan. 13, 1858, it was divided into classes, including First-Class Assistant to represent its old signification, and Second-Class Assistant that of expectant; a dropped assistant—*i.e.* F. C.—being paid as a second, and having prescribed priority of claim to officiate.[4] The Central Committee of 1867 suggested the substitution of Assistant Surveyor.[5]

From 1829 to 1843 the assistant was required, after he had been appointed four months, to petition for promotion to a ride, but since the latter date his advancement has been made unasked in the order of seniority, provided no censure be on record,[6] though the exigencies of the department in 1861 were such as to defer his preferment, and to cause a meeting of some of the sufferers to be held in York, where it was resolved to call upon their rank to memorialise the Board on Feb. 1, 1862. The date of despatch, however, was afterwards fixed for Jan. 20, and, to ensure a general application, it was requested that the name of the station from which the memorial would be sent should appear in the issue of Jan. 1, 1862.[7] Petitions were accordingly forwarded from about fifteen collections, but it is

[1] Leadbetter, 1766. [2] Instructions, 1778. [3] S., 1813. [4] G. I., 1856.
[5] Address. [6] 1863. [7] C. S. G., 1861.

questionable if they were all replied to, or if they served the object in view. The service of the Second-Class had then reached five years.[1]

ASSOCIATION FOR THE REFORM OF EXCISE ABUSES.

This was a society formed about 1847 to obtain the redress of the unequal incidence of duties, the disuse of "useless restrictions" applied in charging the duties, the reform of the system of "distribution of fines," the amendment of the excise laws, &c., &c.

It approached parliament through several members,—notably Joseph Hume,—and commanded the support of no fewer than 11 London, 24 English provincials, 14 Edinburgh and Glasgow, 15 Scotch provincial, and 8 Irish newspapers. The number of petitions presented to parliament through its agency in 1847 was 46.[2] It was also known as the "National Anti-Excise Association." Its office—12 Royal Exchange, Edinburgh.[3]

ATLAS INSURANCE COMPANY.

To meet the long-felt want of some provision for the widow and orphan, an arrangement was made with this company in 1844, by which policies were issued at reduced rates on condition that the premiums were collected for and paid to the company free of expense. This was sanctioned by Board's minute, dated November 6th, 1844. The number of policies in force in 1857 was 1632, amount insured, £330,244; in 1878, 1999, £460,004. *See* Benevolent Fund, under Widows and Orphans' Fund.

AUCTION DUTY.

This branch of the revenue consisted of a duty raised partly by a licence on those who acted as auctioneers, and partly by a poundage on the sales of goods and lands effected by them. The motive for levying this duty was said not to have been a purely financial one. "Auctions," said the noble financier, "had multiplied of late years

[1] C. S. G., 1862, 1863. [2] P. Ret. Public Petitions. [3] The News, S. 1847.

so as to be very mischievous to every fair trader; and in many cases were attended with circumstances of gross fraud and imposture." His Lordship borrowed the idea from Holland.[1] It at first extended to only England and Scotland, but was afterwards imposed in Ireland. The licence duty has varied.

Commenced.	England.		Scotland.	Ireland.	
	London.	County and London Brokers		Dublin, &c.	Elsewhere.
1777 Sept. 29	£1 0 0	£0 5 0	£0 5 0	...	...
1779	1 1 0	0 5 3	0 5 3	...	...
1781	1 2 0	0 5 6	0 5 6	...	...
1783	1 3 0	0 5 9	0 5 9	...	...
1797 May 1 (I.)	...	...	...	1 0 0	1 0 0
1804	0 6 0	0 6 0	0 6 0	...	...
1805	...	...	...	10 10 0	5 0 0
1808	...	...	...	10 0 0	5 5 0
1815	0 12 0	0 12 0	0 12 0	...	...
1825	5 0 0	5 0 0	5 0 0	5 0 0	5 0 0
1840	5 5 0	5 5 0	5 5 0	5 5 0	5 5 0
1846	10 0 0	10 0 0	10 0 0	10 0 0	10 0 0
To 1845 sometimes £25, by £5 licences for selling different articles.					

To 1869 the issue has been—

In	Annual Number.	
	Largest.	Smallest.
England, . .	4400	2415
Scotland, . .	699	324
Ireland, . .	408	204[2]

The poundage duty, of which no account is given in the Commissioners' Report, was recommended to be repealed by the Parnell Committee in 1835;[3] it was repealed by Sir R. Peel in 1845 by a majority of 137 votes—ayes, 167; noes, 30.[4] Petitions were presented to parliament in 1813 and 1816 against sales by auction, and in 1845 against the licence duty, and also for an increased licence duty. The uniform rate of £10 was suggested by the trade, and after a short debate in the House of Commons, carried without a division.[4] Specially prepared instructions were issued in 1825. In 1838, when Dr Bateman published his Auction Laws, the duties were levied under the regulations contained in numerous acts: in 1843, 13; in 1873, 3.

[1] Lord North, H. C., May 14, 1777: Sir R. Peel, Hansard, Feb. 14.
[2] C., 1 and 13 R. [3] Parnell Report, No. 12. [4] Hansard, April 8.

BATEMAN, DR.

This gentleman was appointed from the position of "Chief Clerk" for excise prosecutions to the important office of solicitor in July 1846.[1]

He had previously written two or more works of public utility, as well as the four valuable works which follow, and of which two had passed through two editions, and all had been favourably reviewed by the press. His portrait, engraved on steel by Cochran, from a painting by Burlison, was published in 1846.[2] He retired on a superannuation allowance of £600,[3] and died in 1863.[4]

PUBLICATIONS.

"Bateman's Auction Laws." These were published anonymously in 1838, and, besides the statutes, contained various forms, tables, cases, and directions to auctioneers, useful alike to officer and trader. This work has passed through five editions—the fifth by R. Rouse in 1874.

"Bateman's General Laws of Excise." The second edition was published in 1840. This book contained the statutes at length, mostly in use, and was closely printed for the pocket.

"Bateman's Excise Officer's Manual." A general guide to the officer to the efficient performance of his duties. This manual passed through three editions; the third, with the addition of the principal laws then in force, under the revising hand of J. Bell, S.G.E., 1840, 1852, 1865.

"Bateman's Excise Laws." His greatest work. This, printed in 1843, contained the laws, with historical notes, forms, and cases, in a completed form, and was only superseded in 1873 by a similar issue.

BEAMAGE.[5]

An allowance made on the gross weight in favour of the trader,—the "turn of the scale" having been first taken in favour of the Crown, and an abatement of one or two per cent. then deducted.[6]

[1] Annual Register.
[2] Cock's "Excise Ready Reckoner."
[3] P. P. Superannuation.
[4] P. P. Superannuation, 1864.
[5] P. Rep. Fees, I. 1819.
[6] 1 and 2 Vic. c. 44, sec. 66; 2 and 3 Vict. c. 23, sec. 22.

EART'S WORKS.

"Pocket Diary."—This little diary, five inches by three, compiled by W. Beart, examiner, was issued in only 1867. It contained abstracts of the duties to be paid and to be performed. Published by Loftus, London. "Wine Merchant."—This book was written by the author of the Pocket Diary, but now styled "Sir William Beart, officer of Inland Revenue," a title to which he laid claim: also. Published by Loftus in 1865.

BEER.

This paper, though of considerable length, is but the outline of a great subject, which, for convenience, has been divided as follows—

Term.
Duty.
Exportation.
Importation.
Brewer.
Beer Colour Maker.
Beer Dealer.
Beer Retailer.
Stationery-forms.
Foreign Countries.

TERM.—This—beer—legal generic term has included ale or strong drink, "beere, beare," or weak drink;[1] small beer;[2] strong beer, or that above the value of 16s. per barrel, exclusive of duty;[3] table beer, or that of and under the above-stated value; intermediate beer;[4] spruce beer;[5] vinegar beer;[1] bye-ale;[6] porter.[7] Besides these recognised dutiable distinctions, there were popular ones, such as malt beer,[8] oat beer,[9] molasses beer,[10] young beer,[11] white ale, rumpty-tum,[12] and three threads, a mixture of ale, beer, and twopenny peculiar to London, which being troublesome to draw, one Harwood, a brewer, produced an "entire butt" or "entire," which

[1] Green's State Papers, 12 Car. 2 c. 23.
[2] Scot., 1647; 1670, discontinued; 1802.
[3] Grey's Debates, 1670.
[4] H. C., 1823; L. G., 1824.
[5] 43 Geo. III. c. 69.
[6] Scotch Instructions, 1804.
[7] H. C., April 5, 1816.
[8] 1831.
[9] I., 1808.
[10] 1818.
[11] P. Rep. Beer, 1830.
[12] 1730.

being suited to porters was called "porter." Slang has at least seventeen equivalents for beer included in its vocabulary.[1]

Duty.—Timbs tells us that an "excise" on beer existed as early as 1284: a duty may have been exacted at that date, but not under the name excise. An "excise" duty was suggested on this beverage in 1632, by "a reasonable imposition" on "every ton of drinks or liquor wherein any malt was used, to be paid by all brewers, with the exception of those" "who brewed for their own use, and apothecaries who brewed for physic,"[2] and levied at least as early as 1641;[3] and continued from 1660 down to 1830, when it was repealed by 1 William IV., c. 51.—G.B. Prior to 1660 the brewers who had not paid their duties were twice heard by the Speaker of the House of Commons, who on the first occasion informed them that the House had ordered "That if they pay not their arrears to the Commissioners of Excise by Friday next, that then the respective Summs owing by them to the Commissioners should be distrained for upon their Estate."[4]

The earliest duties appear to have been levied on brewers and housekeepers at the rate of 1s. per barrel, and on the alehouse-keeper and innholder at the rate of 2s. per barrel on strong beer of the value of 8s., on the seller of beer of the value of 6s. per barrel, 6d. per barrel,[5] and on the compounder at so much "by the poll."[6] With the exception of that on the housekeeper, which was discontinued by a resolution of Parliament on December 12, 1651, and printed and publicly distributed on December 17, 1651, the writer cannot trace any change until 1660; the rates were then fixed at 1s. 3d. per barrel of thirty-six gallons on strong, and 3d. per barrel of thirty-two gallons on weak beer, and afterwards doubled by 12 Car. II., c. 24. An allowance of two in twenty-two, and of three in twenty-three barrels respectively, was made to the common brewer to cover waste and encourage truthful entries, which latter were required to be made and discharged weekly and, in the case of the victualler, monthly, under a penalty of double the amount of the duty,[7] until 1802, when those "within the limits of the Chief Office" were allowed to pay roundly.

The London brewers questioned the validity of these rates, abused and threatened the commissioners, and tried by every means to avoid

[1] Slang Dictionary, 1865. [2] Bruce's State Papers [3] Grey's Debates, 1670.
[4] Rushworth's Historical Collections, 1647; Journal of H. C.
[5] P. Ord. 1643. [6] P. Ord. 1646. [7] 12 Car. II., c. 24.

the payment of arrears, which amounted to no less than £296,412, 1s. From this date to 1823 many changes were made in the rates of duty, which were enacted to be levied for certain periods, which varied from one, three, four, sixteen, thirty-two, ninety-five, to ninety-nine years.[1] The duties of 5s. per barrel on ale and 1s. 4d. per barrel on small beer, leviable in 1724, were the aggregate impositions of no fewer than six Acts of Parliament.[2] Changes made after the union of Scotland with England usually operated in that country. Exemption from duty was enjoyed by the University authorities who brewed beer within their own buildings for their own students,[3] and by those who brewed beer to be used in fishing—"no excise to be paid."[4] The duties were not farmed after 1684.

A discriminative drawback was allowed on the stocks on hand on the repeal of the war malt duty in 1816, that brewed from bere in Scotland being in the ratio of two to three.[5]

A new principle of charge was introduced in 1823, by which a quarter of malt was assumed to yield five barrels of beer, which were charged at a uniform rate of 5s. per barrel. That principle has been continued; the assumption only altered, from five to four barrels. The desirability of continuing this duty now engaged public attention, and an unsuccessful effort was made by Mr Maberley in the House of Commons to obtain the appointment of a committee to consider the expediency of commuting the duty to an additional one on malt—ayes 27, noes 119.[6] The following year a further effort was made to readjust the duty, with a like result.[7] Five years afterwards Mr Slaney moved the appointment of a committee to enquire into the "burthens and restrictions" on beer, and the supply of malt liquors to the middle and poorer classes, but this he withdrew.[8] Petitions were also presented to the House of Commons, in which the petitioners complained of the great decrease in the consumption of beer,[9] the absence of a beer duty in Ireland,[10] and prayed for the repeal of the duty.[11] The price and quality of beer formed the subject of inquiry by a Parliamentary Committee in 1818, who reported that the quality of the beer served to the public was due to the power of the brewer, who frequently being the owner of the public-

[1] Green's State Papers, 1670, 1676, 1690, 1692, 1693, 1694, 1697, 1707, 1709, 1710, 1713, 1761, 1802, 1816, 1823. [2] Collection of Statutes, 1724. [3] 1663.
[4] P. Ord. 1644. [5] H. C., April 5, 1816. [6] May 28, 1823.
[7] May 24, 1824. [8] H. C., May 12, 1829. [9] Ireland, 1811.
[10] Scotland, 1829. [11] E., 1802, 1830; S., 1829.

house property, forced any kind of beer he pleased upon the ultimate purchaser. This monopoly was reported upon by another committee, who sat on the same subject in 1830, and who made an eight-and-a-half-pages statement on the probable effects of a "free beer trade," which they recommended and embodied in a Bill to be afterwards noticed. The duty, with the exception of the hereditary duties, long in abeyance, granted to Charles II. and his successors, was immediately afterwards repealed by 1 Will. IV. c. 51, as previously observed. Though this Act did not receive the royal assent until July 16, 1830, and did not take effect until October 10, 1830, so sanguine were the authorities that the measure would pass, that brewers were allowed to brew beer duty-free by permission of the Treasury, as early as the preceding April, on condition that they gave notice to do so, and deposited the whole and kept it in stock, until the date of repeal, in an approved store, to be secured by the revenue official. These regulations were slightly relaxed in favour of the smaller brewers, or those who, from the construction of their premises, were unable to comply with them, in so far as, that the length of the notice was considerably curtailed, and the casks and vats alone were secured by revenue lock. Drawback was allowed on duty-paid beer exported between the date of repeal and April 5, 1831. This repeal occasioned the issue of twelve general orders in 1830, and the reduction of the establishment by two supervisors, one hundred and sixty-seven officers, eight assistants, and four permit writers.[1] The amount of duty repealed was £3,055,000.[2]

The hereditary duties, on the demise of His Majesty King William IV., were charged, as appears to have been customary under similar circumstances, but not paid. In addition to the account taken of the beer brewed since the accession of Her Majesty Queen Victoria, a declaration of the barrels of beer brewed was made by the brewer on the entry paper, from which it was copied, from time to time, and added to the charge already made, until "the pleasure of Parliament" was made known in 1838, when it was cancelled by the authority of an Act of Parliament, in which other provision was made for "the honour and dignity of the Crown."

In Scotland the "ingathering and uplifting" of a duty of 4d. per pint upon "beire" was sanctioned by an Act dated January 31, 1644. The brewer delivered a weekly return of his brewings; the private brewer paid monthly, others weekly. The "maltmen" were required

[1] Rep. Parnell 4th, 1833. [2] C. 13 R.

to keep an account of the names of the buyers and the quantities sold to them, and used by themselves, and deliver a correct account of the same. Millers, too, were enjoined to make a return of the names of the persons for whom they ground malt, and the quantity ground, and to supply these particulars to the excise. Provision was also made for the "far Highlands," by those inhabitants paying the duty to the seller, who gave "a ticket of payment of the excise." Fifteen gallons of ale and twenty gallons of beer were charged on every boll brewed. In 1647 the "brewster" was charged 20s. for every boll of "malt brewen" into ale, and the retailer of beer was empowered to recover this duty by a charge per pint of 2d. on ale or strong beer, and 1d. on small beer, but this was granted for only one year. The duty was farmed in the earlier years of its imposition,[1] and appears to have been levied without intermission down to 1707,[2] when it was re-enacted, with some modifications, in the Act of Union. The same year, on the day of the final dissolution of the Parliament of Scotland,[3] the local authorities at Dundee, Aberdeen, Bo'ness, and Kirkcaldy, were authorised to levy a duty on this commodity in consideration of former privations; and even after the Union[4] a similar special provision was made by Parliament in favour of Dalkeith, where an imposition was permitted for "paving, cleaning, and lighting the streets." This was called "the town's impost."[5]

In Ireland a duty may have been charged earlier than December 25, 1661, as excise duties had been levied for a period of at least six months prior to the Act in which the word excise is first used.[6] At that date, however, the duties were settled on the king and his successors for ever, and among them was this particular duty. The brewer was enjoined to make weekly entries and payments, under a penalty per week of £20 for the first, £40 the second, £60 the third, and the forfeiture of double the value of the beer. The unit of charge was a barrel.[7] The Irish beer duty ceased in 1795, when it was commuted into an additional duty on malt.[8]

Exportation.—The exportation of beer, early allowed on condition that malt sold at 6s. per quarter—3 James I., c. 11—and afterwards on the payment of a Customs discriminative duty[9] has been allowed on the repayment of the duty charged on the beer, less that com-

[1] Acts, 1647, 1661. [2] 1693, 1695, 1696, 1707. [3] March 25, 1707.
[4] 1804. [5] Acts 1695, 1695; S. Instructions 1804. [6] 14 Car. II. c. 1. [7] 1787.
[8] P. Rep., Fees, 1808; H. C., May 24, 1824; C. 1 R. [9] 1660.

puted to be consumed by the ship's crew,[1] on the malt,[2] on the malt and sugar,[3] and on the malt, sugar, and brewing licence—commuted hop duty;[4] except in Scotland, where, in the earliest date of the imposition, no duty was charged on that brewed for this purpose.[5] The duty drawn back was for some time less than that charged by 3d. "per tun for the charges of the officer,"[6] which was deducted by the collector who paid the amount of the debenture.[7] Encouragement to export was given by the payment of a bounty of 1s. per barrel, until about 1830,[8] with the exception of times of "inhansed" prices of corn,[9] which the collector was required to determine by "frequent recourse" to the average price of corn in the London Gazette. The Unions of 1707 and 1800 with Scotland and Ireland necessitated adjustments which were embodied in the respective Articles of Union: in Scotland by reason of the difference in the measures and in the rates of duty, and in Ireland by reason of the absence of a beer duty.[10] On the repeal of the duty, however, in 1830, an allowance was granted at the rate of 5s. per barrel. A barrel was assumed to have been brewed from two bushels of duty-paid malt—an assumption previously employed in 1829—or two bushels four gallons of duty-paid "bear or bigg" malt;[11] and, to meet the requirements of the trade, drawback was also allowed at the rate of 7s. 6d. per barrel, on a declaration being made that three bushels of duty-paid malt,[12] or four bushels of duty-paid bere or bigg malt,[13] had been used. The mere declaration in the case of the higher repayment soon led to a suspicion that the malt had not been exhausted of its wort-yielding properties, but again mashed, and the revenue defrauded, and immediately afterwards to the issue of an order by which a "solemn declaration" that these quantities had been "wholly consumed," or that saccharine matter equal in amount obtainable from these quantities "had been consumed in producing each barrel."[14] To discover an effectual check upon the accuracy of the declaration soon gave rise to an investigation by two able officers of this department, who, in 1847, had the honour to announce the discovery of a process by which they could determine the original specific gravity of the wort of the beer. But this process was not employed "to any considerable extent" until 1851, and then under the authority of the Trea-

[1] 1689. [2] 1830. [3] 1847. [4] 1862. [5] Act Jan. 31, 1644.
[6] 1689. [7] 1701. [8] 1761, 1771, 1803, 1824, L. G. 1824.
[9] 1710. [10] 1829. [11] T. W. Sept. 6, 1831.
[12] T. W. July 7, 1836. [13] T. W. Sept. 19, 1836. [14] 1837.

sury, when the previously noted suspicion was proved to have existed to the extent of no less than 87·7 per cent. of the beer "sampled and examined."[1] This led to a change in the form of the declaration in 1854, from bushels of malt used to the original specific gravity of the worts employed. To this time the brewer and the exporter were unchecked in errors by inadvertence or by wilful fraud. Previously the brewer only made oath, affidavit, or declaration; this was followed by a confirmation by the exporter, who was checked by the officer in so far as "tasting" could do, and which he was ordered to do.[2]

To return. The two previous rates of drawback were retained, and representative specific gravities were fixed at 1054° and 1081° respectively; these, owing to the rapidly increasing exportation, were soon found to be insufficient, and were consequently increased in 1854 by five to seven rates. The scale commenced with a gravity equivalent to one and a half bushels per barrel, and rose by an equivalent to half a bushel up to four and a half bushels per barrel. Prior to this the exporter had been restricted to the exportation of only "strong beer," or its equivalent.[3] In 1861 a scale of greater scope received legislative sanction, by which the exported was permitted to draw back the duty at the rate of 6d. per five degrees from 1040° at 4s. to 1125° to 12s. at 6d. per barrel; increased in 1862, on the commutation of the hop duty, by 3d. per barrel. Immediately the new rates were legalised in 1854, duly-qualified officers were stationed at Liverpool, Bristol, Southampton, Dublin, Belfast, Cork, Glasgow, and Leith, and shortly afterwards at other ports, to examine the samples. In 1874 the number of samples examined exceeded 6000, the barrels of beer represented by them exceeded 313,000, and the percentage of the barrels not entitled to drawback was only 1·78,[4] a striking contrast against 87·7 in 1851.

Importation.—The importation of this beverage has been invariably discouraged, by the exaction of a higher rate of duty, which has varied from three to four times the amount of that on the home-brewed, while that from Scotland and Ireland was charged a countervailing duty, until the assimilation, and afterwards the repeal, of the duty.[5] To quote one instance, "forraine imported beare" in Scotland was charged 00·01·00 per pint, while on the home-produced

[1] C. 1 R. [2] 1770. [3] 1793.
[4] C. 18 R. [5] 1707, 1800, 1803.

only 3d. was leviable.[1] The management of the import duty was transferred to the Customs in 1825.

BREWER.—The "Bruers of Bere, Ale Bruers or Brewers,"[2] "Beere-bruers,"[3] "Brewsters,"[4] pursued the "Mysterie of Brewings,"[3] or "Bruying,"[5] in their "Brewhous,"[6] with little interference, until the imposition of the excise duty. Since then they have been divided, for revenue purposes, into nine classes, and ultimately brought under one generic term—Brewers of Beer for Sale, 1821.

I. The Private Brewer.
II. The Compounder.
III. The Table-Beer Brewer.
IV. The Intermediate Brewer.
V. The Bye-Brewer.
VI. The Spruce-Beer Brewer.
VII. The Retail Brewer.
VIII. The "Usuall"[7] or "Comon Brewer."[8]
IX. The Brewing Victualler.

The private brewer, in all three kingdoms, brewed for the use of only his own family, and paid the ordinary rates of duty.[9] In England, as previously stated, the duty was first discontinued to be levied in 1651, but again levied in 1660, and in 1670, only within the limits of corporations.[10] Always an unpopular mode of levy, the legislature again gave it up, and no effort was made to reintroduce it until 1806, when Lord Henry Petty proposed "a fair and reasonable commutation," to be assessed upon a scale of proportion with the assessed taxes," which in plain terms was a poll-tax, rated according to the size of a man's establishment, with an exemption in favour of the "labouring poor," and those who did not pay assessed taxes. Though the resolution was duty carried, his lordship, after "a mature, deliberate, and even a slow consideration," proposed to defer it "till next year," and in its stead to impose an additional 10 per cent. on the assessed taxes.[11] The next attempt was in 1862, by Mr Gladstone, on moving the commutation of the hop duty, and partook the form of a licence duty, to be charged according to the value of the

[1] Act, Jan. 31, 1644. [2] 23 Hen. VIII. c. 4. [3] 1588.
[4] S. 1647. [5] 22 Hen. VIII. c. 113. [6] 21 Hen. VIII. c. 13.
[7] 12 Chas. II. c. 23. [8] 2 W. & M. sess. 2, c. 10.
[9] E. 1641, P. Q. 1643, S. 1644, I. 1661. [10] Grey's Debates.
[11] Hansard, June 6.

farm or house in which the licencee should reside, and although the principle was accepted, and the resolution passed in a modified form, it was ultimately withdrawn.[1] And a later and less successful effort in 1870, by Colonel Bartellot, in a motion for the commutation of the malt duty.[2]

The compounder,[3] also a private brewer, to avoid the visits of the gauger, agreed to pay a composition of so much per week, which in 1761 was increased from 2s. to 3s. He was at first allowed to lend his utensils upon giving notice,[4] but this permission was afterwards withdrawn, under a penalty of £50.[5] Though brought to account as a beer-duty,[6] it was often referred to in connection with the malt-duty. Repealed in 1783 by a majority of 82 votes; ayes 129, noes 47.[7]

The table-beer brewer, often also the strong beer brewer, as no legal distinction was made until 1784, paid the rate of duty on the class of beer he professed to brew, but was distinguished more particularly by having been restricted to a certain selling price per barrel, which was first fixed by Act of Parliament at a rate exclusive,[8] and afterwards allowed by Treasury Warrant at a rate inclusive, of the duty,[9] and ultimately, by the latter authority, on condition that a certain quantity should be extracted from a given quantity of malt under prescribed regulations. (1816—6½ barrels per quarter; notice to brew and quantity to be brewed; goods be kept until gauged; render account on oath, on paying duty, of malt used and beer produced; brew no party guiles.) These, however, not proving effectual in checking the *guiles*—the sale of more valuable beer under the guise of "table"—their lordships' privilege was withdrawn,[10] and the brewer restricted to the more recent legal rate of 18s. per barrel.[11] Not more than two years elapsed when the fixed rate was relaxed, and others, which were based upon the then current prices of malt and hops, were allowed for periods which varied from six to twelve months each, until the repeal of the duty in 1830.[12] The duty was 2s. per barrel.[13] The fixed licence duty of £1, imposed in 1784 and doubled in 1815, was altered to a limited rateable one in 1825, thus:—

[1] Hansard, May 12. [2] Hansard, March 4. [3] 1660. [4] 1663.
[5] 1682. [6] 1779. [7] H. C., Debrett, June 18.
[8] 22 Geo. III. c. 68 (11s.) [9] 1812 (20s.); 1819 (25s.)
[10] 1821. [11] 59 Geo. III. c. 53. [12] 1823-30. [13] 1830.

Not exceeding 20 barrels brewed,	.	£0	10	0
" 50 "	. .	1	0	0
" 100 "	. .	1	10	0
Exceeding 100 "	. .	2	0	0

The beginner paying the first sum, and at the expiration of his licence, should he have brewed more than twenty barrels, such further sum as, with that already paid, would equal what he should have paid. 5 per cent. was added in 1840. Restricted at first to Great Britain; extended in 1825 to Ireland; repealed 1862.

The intermediate brewer paid the ordinary licence duty, and as the epithet implies, produced a beer of a value between that of table and strong in the proportion of five to five and a-half barrels from a quarter of malt; this was imperative. He made entry and delivered a drawing of his premises, which were not allowed to be situated within one hundred yards of a common brewery, nor within a quarter of a mile of a malt-house; kept an account of the malt received and used; mixed the whole of the wort in the same fermenting tun; declared in a book the quantity and quality of the beer brewed; stored it in casks of not greater capacity than one hundred and eight gallons; sent it out in casks, marked with the figure five, of not smaller content than four, afterwards nine, gallons; paid a duty of 5s. per barrel without any allowance for waste; retailed it at first without further payment, but afterwards on paying a licence duty of £1,[1] and was restricted to a selling price of 33s. per barrel,[2] and as a retailer to 1s. per gallon, for the greater portion of the time during which the duty was levied. The officer took an account of the malt stock roundly, and surveyed in other respects as at a common brewery. Great Britain, 1823. Introduced 4 G. IV. c. 51, discontinued—licence 1825, duty 1830.

The bye-brewer, "By-Brewer," though not by that name, came under the provisions of the Acts of 1660, by which any person might brew and sell small quantities of beer at fairs upon paying the duty before he sold it.[3] In Scotland the privilege was greater, as appears from the directions to supervisors. "You are to go to as many places where fairs, weddings, &c., are kept, as you can, to see if the officers take and enter into their books true accounts of the drink sold on such occasions."[4] In England the people were wont to take

[1] 1825. [2] L. G., 1825. [3] 1740. [4] 1804.

advantage of this exceptional legislation, and applied it to "wakes, revels, and other merry-makings."[1] This class was brought under closer observation in 1826, by being required to make entry of the place of sale, in addition to paying the duty, and was so continued down to the cessation of the duty. The further regulations applicable to brewers were not applicable to this class. He never paid licence duty.[2]

The spruce beer brewer originated about 1811 to imitate "The queen of red or brown beer . . . of Dantzic," commonly called Dantzic spruce, "spruce beer or black beer,"[3] and was at once placed under the regulations applicable to the brewer of strong beer, and on the commutation of the hop duty in 1862, the strong beer licence scale was retained for this class, as only small quantities of, or perhaps no, hops were used.

The retail brewer sold his beer in such small quantities as to disentitle him to the allowances granted to the common brewer, who could not sell less than four and a half gallons at one time. In addition to complying with the ordinary regulations he was required to mash at the least sixteen bushels of malt at one time; brew at the rate of one hundred barrels per annum; pay £2 per annum for his brewing, and £5 per annum for his retail licence, which did not allow the consumption on the premises.[4] There were some few other minor regulations. He was, or rather his premises were, surveyed as those of a victualler. United Kingdom. Introduced 1824, 5 G. IV., c. 54: repealed G. B., 1870; I. 1871. This designation was also applied to those retailers under 1 W. IV., c. 64, who brewed for sale; but the special licence did not, of course, apply.[5]

The common brewer is the only denomination which has remained unchanged in the statute book and official regulations from the earliest time. He has always been subjected to a more or less frequent survey to secure the beer duty, to charge the licence duty, and to prevent the use of forbidden substitutes and adulterants, and he has in many ways attempted to frustrate it. The difficulties which beset the "gagers" on the imposition of the duty soon called for the issue of a Royal Proclamation, threatening severe proceedings against those who should endeavour to brew privately or on a Sunday, or ill-treat or refuse access to those employed by the farmers.[6] These were followed by such frauds as the use of private pipes and utensils,

[1] 1820 [2] 1831 [3] On Beer: Vogel, 1874.
[4] 1830 [5] 1831 [6] Green's State Papers, 1662.

to cope with which notice of erection and entry were required;[1] the declaration of strong as small beer, to check which the officer was required to test the quality[2] by tasting, called "palating;" the private removal of worts, to prevent which the smallest delivery of beer was restricted to four and a half gallons,[3] and a gauge of the goods taken;[4] the mixture of strong with small beer, to meet which the stocks of beer retailers were taken and compared with the quantities brought in by certificate;[5] the use of two-thirds of barley and one-third of malt,[6] to stop which the use of steel rollers[7] or small metal rollers to bruise was recommended[8] and introduced in 1855; the omission to enter the substance employed in brewing, to prevent which a penalty was imposed. These, then, form some of the many difficulties which have beset the path of the officer, and some of the preventive means which he has adopted to remove them.

The visits to the brewery were of course more frequent during the time the duty was charged upon the beer than after its repeal. The brewer having made entry of his premises and utensils, which latter were gauged and tables raised to show the quantity of worts and beer found in them, it was customary for the officer to course the brewery in periods of six hours each in London,[9] and at other places to survey at prescribed times, or, to use the words of a commissioner examined by the Parnell Committee, "Before the repeal of the beer duty the officer surveyed daily, and, if brewing, attended to take a gauge of the first or 'hot wort' within one hour of its leaving the copper; again, in about three hours, to gauge the second wort and take a 'cool gauge' of the first, and so on as often as new worts were run. He was required to take a 'confirming gauge' of the whole when collected in the coolers or backs, and continuing gauging it until it was tunned, when he entered the quantity in the trader's stock. When not brewing, the stock was taken every third day." The trader declared the quantity and quality produced at each guile or brewing. The quality and condition were distinguished by the officer by certain characters, thus—guile of ale, $\overset{-\,\cdot}{a}$ $\overset{-\cdot-\cdot}{a}$ $\overset{--\cdot-\cdot-}{a}$; guile of beer, *h. m. n. bl.*; an entire guile of small beer, $\overset{\cdot}{\overline{\text{VI}}}$ $\overset{\cdot\ \cdot}{\overline{\text{VII}}}$ $\overset{\cdot\ \cdot\ \cdot}{\overline{\text{VII}}}$, &c., to decide the rate of charge. In Scotland other characters were used, but formed in a similar manner. These

[1] 1697. [2] 1696, 1761. [3] 1791. [4] 1807, 1811; S. 1804.
[5] 1761, 1765. [6] 1803. [7] 1831, 1834, Encyclopædia Brit.
[8] P. Rep., Parnell 7th. [9] 1781.

particulars were copied into a "specimen paper" for the trader, and the charges were posted into a "brewery ledger." Allowances, already referred to, were made for waste, and in the case of warm worts "one-tenth part thereof," but instead of deducting the quantity, in the case of that for waste, the rate per barrel was reduced; *e.g.*, in 1761, when it was 8s. per barrel and two and a half were allowed in twenty-three: duty on 23 barrels = 184s., less that on $2\frac{1}{2}$ = 20s. = 164s. ÷ 23 = 7s. $1\frac{1}{2}\frac{1}{16}$d. This mode of abatement was continued till the repeal. The official who may reside in or visit Edinburgh will find, on visiting the interior of the monument erected to, an example of a beer voucher prepared by, Robert Burns.

The survey after the repeal of the duty was less frequent. The object, to quote the same commissioner, was "to check the use of other than legal ingredients, and to assess the rate of the annual licence," and to have machinery in readiness "in the necessity for charging the revised hereditary beer duty immediately on the demise of the Crown until the settlement of the Civil List." To secure this the brewer was required to continue the practice introduced in 1821, of entering the quantity of malt to be mashed and the sugar to be dissolved;[1] and the officer attended the brewery once a day when in residence, and less frequently when out, to copy the quantities into his survey book, upon which, at the close of the year, he estimated the licence duty payable; and occasionally to gauge the drained goods in the mash-tun, which was gauged and tabulated to check the quantity of malt entered, upon which an increase of 20 per cent. was allowed.[2] Everard states that ordinary malt, when the wort shall have passed through it, is more compact by about a sixth part.[3] He of course, in addition to this, had to closely inspect the premises to discover the use of any article which might be employed as a substitute for malt, sugar, or hops, or the practice of private brewing. The daily visit was condemned by the Parnell Committee —"by preventing the use of other ingredients than malt and hops, the survey is inefficacious; and with a view to the licence duty, it is unnecessary . . . . that the survey, with the attendant establishment employed in carrying it into effect, may be wholly discontinued." They recommended "a revision of the whole law relating to brewers . . . . and the re-enactment in a single Act of such provisions as it may be necessary to retain," by which they calculated a saving of £22,000 per annum by the reduction of two hundred

[1] 1812. [2] 1830. [3] Stereometry. 1684.

officers and the cost of stationery. It was, however, modified in 1835 to an "occasional visit," and afterwards, in the same year, to "no longer a period than fourteen days," in 1856 to not greater than seven days, and in 1857 to a period not exceeding fourteen days, with, in every case, a relaxation in the survey of those out of residence.

The licence duty, which now formed the chief object in the survey, was first introduced by Mr Pitt in his budget on June 30, 1784. He proposed to charge a uniform £10, but this he afterwards departed from in favour of a rateable one, which commenced on September 11, 1784, and applied to Great Britain. In 1815 these rates were increased by 50 per cent.; in 1825 the scale was revised in favour of the small brewer, and extended to Ireland, where until this date the licence duty—some time received at the Stamp Office—had been levied according to the locality in which the brewery was situated, irrespective of the quantity of beer brewed; in 1840 increased under the General Percentage Act by 5 per cent.; in 1862 again revised, on the commutation of the hop duty, and based on a constant quantitative, but inconstant fiscal, increment in favour of the large brewer.

An increased licence duty was recommended by the committee previously referred to,[1] and Mr Gladstone, probably not unmindful of this suggestion, proposed, in his maiden budget in 1853, to rectify the scale at the "upper end," and although not then successful, he effected his purpose in 1862, which, the following year, was viewed as a grievance by 1469 signatories, who presented twenty-three petitions against it. He afterwards stated in the House of Commons, on March 24, 1868, that he would support a commutation into an additional duty on malt. This appears to have given encouragement to a party of gentlemen who waited upon the Chancellor of the Exchequer on March 8, 1872, to urge the change or a repeal, and who, with Mr S. Ibbetson, who moved the repeal in the House of Commons on April 24, 1873, not being successful, were followed by two other deputations in March 1874, to again urge the abolition; and these were speciously supported by a patentee who proposed to repeal both the malt and the brewing licence duties, by the introduction of "The Baxter System," or weighing, or "The Bolzano-Reidinger or Bavarian System," or measuring the grain used in brewing by an "automatic machine," constructed on the same prin-

[1] Nineteenth Report.

ciple as the ordinary gas-meter, in which each revolution of the "drum," of known capacity, is registered by an index which points out the quantity passed through. To this "automatic machine" preference has not yet been given. The repeal of the licence duty was proposed in the House of Commons on April 6, 1875—ayes 83, noes 120; the appointment of a committee to consider the licence duty on Feb. 27, 1877, and April 26, 1877; and the repeal again on July 26, 1878, but without the desired result.

The number of "common brewers" in the United Kingdom increased from 28,594 in 1829 to 36,550 in 1830, and steadily, with one exception, up to 49,228 in 1838, after which it began to decrease, until it came down to 25,940 in 1877. The rapid increase being due to the repeal of the duty on beer, and the very sensible reduction since 1862 to the increase of the licence duty.

The brewing victualler,[1] at first distinguished as the victualler, came under different regulations from those applicable to the common brewer, inasmuch as he was not allowed any deduction for waste,[2] his premises were closely surveyed every Saturday night and often on the Sunday, and his stock of beer taken at least three times a week. He was not chargeable with a licence duty until 1824. The fiscal distinction ceased in 1830.

A quarterly return of the number of each kind of brewer, and of the quantity of malt used by each kind, made on the motion of Mr S. Rice in 1831, is still made.

Beer Colour Maker.—The beer colour maker originated in 1811, the same year as that in which the spruce beer brewer appeared, whom he probably assisted. This trader produced his colouring matter from sugar, which he boiled or burned in boilers or pans until it assumed the appearance he desired. It was then removed into vats, tubs, or casks, which were gauged and tabulated, and in which the charge was taken. The duty was returned with that on beer. His premises were entered in the usual manner, and the officer surveyed them when at work every three hours, and when silent twice a day, except in the case of those at a distance, which were visited less frequently. He paid a licence duty, sent out his produce by permit, and his operations were further checked by his stock being taken twice a week. This form of colouring substance, though sometimes substituted by treacle, sugar, or extract of liquorice,

[1] 1761. [2] Leadbetter, 1743.

retained its place until about 1818, when it gradually gave way to "malt very highly dried . . . almost burnt," or "burnt malt, charred, or coloured malt,"[1] or roasted malt.

Beer Dealer, The, was not chargeable with the beer duty, nor did he pay a licence duty until about 1824, but his premises were placed under survey for probably a twofold object—preventing his brewing and selling beer without paying the duty, or receiving that article from any one who had not done so. A dealer in table beer, who did not sell more than one gallon at a time, did not come under this regulation.[2] His premises were surveyed once in ten days,[3] and his stock was frequently balanced by the officer, whose instructions also directed him to see that all was received and delivered by certificate.[4] The licence duty at first, £3, 3s., allowed the sale of any quantity, and on the repeal of the beer-duty and the introduction of the general retail licence, he was permitted, by Treasury Warrant dated September 27, 1830, to retail under that licence, upon complying with its conditions of issue, without extra payment. His sales were ultimately limited to not less than four and a half gallons at a time, but this limitation was removed in 1863, upon paying a dealer's retail licence, provided, or rather on condition that the beer was not consumed on the premises. Both licenses applied to the United Kingdom. To 1875 the largest number of dealers' licenses issued was 6894 in 1875, and of the retail licence 4326 in 1870, not one of the latter having been issued in Scotland. Mr Bruce proposed in 1871 to reduce the rate of the retail licence by one halfpenny, from £1, 2s. 0½d. to £1, 2s.

The Beer Retailer, at first called the "Retayler of beere," or "Spender,"[5] pursued his calling, or the "Utterance of Beere,"[6] or "Retaileing," for very many years without an excise licence; he, however, made a monthly entry of the beer sold, and paid duty upon it, as already shown, and was also required, by a Royal Proclamation dated September 26, 1660, either to give security to pay the duty if he brewed his own beer, or to buy the beer he sold of the common brewer. A century afterwards he was taken under survey to prevent the sale of that which he was suspected of brewing in private, and he was then required to produce a certificate of all that he received, and if an excess were found upon balancing his stock he had to pay the

[1] P. Rep., Molasses, 1831.
[2] 42 Geo. III. c. 38.
[3] 1781.
[4] 1821.
[5] 2 W. & M. c. 3.
[6] 4 Jac. I. c. 14.

duty upon the increase. The certificates were taken up by the officer, who in the case of beer not approved granted a certificate for its return to the brewer.[1] Similar regulations attached until the repeal of the duty. The suggestion to impose a retail licence duty of £1, to be brought into the Exchequer, will be found in Green's State Papers, as early as 1666, but it does not appear to have been adopted, except in part by the Justices of the Peace, who granted "stamped licences," bearing "stamp duties," until 1809, when in Great Britain the publican first paid the imperial two guineas per annum, which was continued for five years, after which it was doubled for two years, after which a distinction was made, with an adjustment in accordance with a petition to Parliament, dated March 2, 1824, according to the rate of the premises, which has been continued, with one exception, introduced in 1863, to prevent the loss of revenue by a person whose house, being rated under £20, obtained a publican's licence at £1, 2s. 0½d. instead of one at £3, 6s. 1¾d., under an Act to be afterwards noticed. In Ireland this class of retailer paid about one guinea until about 1825, when he was charged as in Great Britain. The next form of retailer was that of the intermediate beer, at one guinea per annum, legalised in 1823 at the instance of the Chancellor of the Exchequer, on March 24, 1823. Applicable to Great Britain. Repealed 1830.

Then came the retail brewer, who paid £5 annually to retail. United Kingdom. Introduced 1824. After him appeared the "Tom and Jerry," "cold blood," "Jerry," "Tidley Wink,"[2] or the 1 W. 4 beer retailer, 1830, whose locale was fixed in England and Wales only, the outcome of the generally supposed misuse of the monopoly possessed by the large brewers and victuallers, who, having "invested very large sums in the purchase of public-houses," charged an extravagant price for the article they sold. It was also generally believed that the retailer who occupied the house of a brewer, or "a dependent house," commonly added 22 per cent. of colouring matter to the beer he received to enable him to meet the exorbitant rent charged, while the possessor of a "free house" not being under such a heavy obligation, seldom or never resorted to that practice.[3] This first received the attention of Parliament in 1818, and finally in 1830, when the beer trade was thrown open on the recommendation of a committee who sat on the subject. It is worthy of note that

[1] 1828. [2] H. C., 1865. [3] P. Rep. 1830.

the Surrey Magistrates had petitioned Parliament to authorise the excise to grant a beer licence after the manner in which a tea licence was granted,[1] and that the idea was embodied in the Act referred to. The bill which formed this Act received the support of the then Government, and was carried on the second reading by a majority of 216 votes—ayes, 245; noes, 29;[2] but on the third reading an amendment was proposed, but not carried, to restrict the consumption to the outside of the place of sale.[3] No fewer than 157 petitions were presented against, and 4 in favour of, the measure. The provisions of this Act were soon proved to be too lax. Viscount Melbourne moved and carried a bill in 1831 to limit the hours of sale. Mr Trevor moved in 1832 the prohibition to consume on the premises, and the production of a certificate of character—noes, 111; ayes, 12; the latter Sir E. Knatchbull carried in 1834, and the former Lord Brougham unsuccessfully attempted to do in 1838. Sir J. Packington introduced in 1840 another qualification, which rested on the rate of the premises, and in 1852 he proposed further amendments. A select committee of the House of Lords was appointed in 1849 to consider the operation of the Act, and they reported in 1850 that sufficient vigilance was not exercised by the inferior officers to check the sale of spirits; the improper sale of spirits was well known, as appears by the fact that as early as 1836 no fewer than 174 retailers were convicted of having sold spirits. From the commencement of the operation of the first act down to this time the Houses of Parliament were literally besieged with petitions, in which the petitioners prayed, for the most part, for the repeal or amendment, as embodied in upwards of five hundred and fifty petitions, while a few were presented in which continuance was asked. The publican too petitioned for the diminution of his licence duty in consequence of the retailer selling spirits,[4] and the beer retailer asked to be placed on the same footing as the publican.[5] Advancing to 1860. This retailer memorialised the Chancellor of the Exchequer to place him in a different position, and in the following year Mr Pease inquired if the granting of licences to sell exciseable liquors would be placed under one authority.[6] Next came a deputation to the same high official in 1868, that this retailer's licence should not be renewed; and in 1869, Messrs Ibbetson, Akroyd, and Headlam, with a bill to diminish the number of houses, to increase the police inspection, and

[1] H. C., April 13 1826. [2] Idem., May 4, 1830. [3] Idem., May 21, 1830.
[4] 1833. [5] 1836. [6] H. C., Nov. 28.

to require the production of a magistrate's certificate, which became law. In 1871, Mr Bruce proposed, but without success, to change the rates to one and two guineas respectively. The provisions of the Acts of 1873 and 1874 are familiar.

Only one other form remains to be noticed—the table beer retailer whose licence duty was first levied in 1861 at 5s., and proposed to be repealed in 1871. The production of a magistrate's certificate was rendered obligatory in 1877. The quality of the beer was defined to be that sold at not more than twopence per quart,[1] and afterwards at not more than three half-pence.[2] Chargeable first in Great Britain, then in Ireland.

Forms.—In the year ended March 31, 1872, the Storekeeper General issued upwards of 300,000 forms applicable to this head of duty.[3]

Foreign Countries.—The breviates which follow have been compiled from the replies given by the English representatives in sixteen foreign countries, to a circular addressed to them by Earl Granville on the taxation of beer in 1874.

America—United States.—The brewer here pays a brewing licence chargeable at two rates only—£10 and £20; a stamp tax at the rate of one dollar less 7½ per cent. per 31 gallons, &c., on the beer sold, a stamp being affixed to the cask on removal: he is required to give bond equal to double the probable amount of taxation, and to keep his books in a certain form. The whole of the duty is allowed on exportation. The dealer pays £10, the retailer £4, annually. The beer contains 8 per cent. of alcohol. Private brewing is allowed free of duty.

Austria.—In this country the brewer is required to pay a trade licence; to provide utensils of certain size and proportions; to pay a duty of about 2¼d. per 13 imperial gallons at "per saccharometer degree at 14° Reaumure, and an additional and differential duty "in all towns," with an extra 2s. 2d. on selling to a "retail dealer;" to deposit the amount on giving the 24 hours' notice to brew; to permit the vessels to be gauged and watched; to keep a register of his stock and sales. 23 to 26 lbs. of malt produce 13 gallons specific gravity 1054 deg. 4s. per 13 gallons is allowed on exportation. Private brewing is not practised. A stamp duty is levied on the vendor.

Bavaria.—Here the brewer pays no beer duty, but a trade tax

[1] 1819. [2] 1830. [3] P. P., 1872.

according to the quantity of malt used. He is required, if he make the malt, to provide "The regulation self-acting measuring apparatus, with the Government automatical counter;" to use only malt and hops, and, to insure this, to allow his premises to be inspected. The beer contains from 2½ to 7 per cent. of alcohol. A portion of the duty charged on the malt used in brewing beer is allowed on exportation. The private brewer pays the malt duty. The vendors of beer, except the brewer at his brewery, pay a "trade tax."

Belgium.—Both licence duty and beer duty are paid. The brewing licence duty is determined at the close of the year on the total cubic capacity of the mash tun or vessel which is found by adding as many times as used—the licence duty is therefore variable in so far as each brewer pays according to the number of times he brews—it is divided into sixteen classes, which vary from 9, by variable additions, to 401 francs; no further licence duty is payable except upon retailing. The brewer is required to provide certain utensils; to place over entrance "Brasserie;" to pay a duty of 1 7/10d. per gallon on the capacity of the mash tun or other vessel in which the ground malt or grist is mashed, chargeable every time a new grist is mashed, and payable on the charges for the month, being totalled by one, two, or three instalments within the "terms of credit;" to allow his premises to be inspected during mashing. The duty is returned on beer certified to have been "spoiled or lost." Alcoholic strength 3½ per cent. A portion of the duty is allowed on exportation. Private brewers pay the tax. The vendors pay a licence duty, which is determined by a board of assessors, who ascertain the extent of each tradesman's business. Each then pays one of "66 different rates," according to the rank of the commune in which he resides, after which he may sell any beverage.

Darmstadt.—The brewer here pays the ordinary "trading licence" annually, and £3, £6, or £8 for a "permit" to brew, and if he retail, obtains a "special permission." He is then required to give in eight days before he opens his brewery a duplicate list of the utensils, &c., with their respective capacities, &c.; to use only malt, rice, starch, sugar, syrup, or malt substitutes; to pay 1s. 11d. per 110 lbs. of corn, malt, flour, rice, and starch; 2s. 11d. per 110 lbs. on potato starch and syrup; and 4s. per 110 lbs. on sugar and malt substitutes. Sugar, alone of these, having been previously charged with duty. He formerly paid the duty according to the capacity of the boiling cauldron. He has to pay "before the beer is brewed;"

to give notice of brewing; to comply with the law under a pecuniary penalty for the first offence, and imprisonment for the second; to give 24 hours' notice if he claim a return of duty on spoiled materials. A "quality" of malt "equal to 13·238 per cent." produces a specific gravity of 1054 deg. Alcoholic strength 3·7 per cent. Exportation on full drawback is allowed on giving three days' notice. Private brewing is allowed, provided there be not more than ten persons over fourteen years of age in the house, and the head obtain "a permit." The vendor is required to pay a licence duty and the fixed permit duty if not a brewer.

DENMARK.—Neither growing nor licence duty. "A recent proposal to establish an excise duty on this beverage was at once rejected by the peasant majority in the Lower House of Rijedag."

FRANCE.—Two licences are required by every brewer, viz., the "Patente" and the "License." The former is a tax collected by the "Administration des Contributions Directes;" and the latter is of the nature of an excise duty, and is collected by the "Administration des Contributions Indirectes." The "Patente" is a permission paid by both manufacturer and artisan to exercise his calling, whatever it may be, and its amount differs according to locality and circumstances. In the case of the master brewer in Paris, a fixed duty of rather more than 8d. per 22 gallons on the net capacity of all the boilers used in the brewery is charged, less one-half in the event of only four brewings in the year, and one-fourth in the event of not eight, which is decided on the declaration of the brewer, the records in his books, and the supervision of the assessors. To this is added a duty based on the estimated value of his premises—dwelling and brewing—and plant less a deduction of 5 and 2½ per cent. respectively. To these two are then added "Centimes Additionnels," a municipal tax varying every year, and in each commune, in 1874, 109 per cent. on the patente. The "Licence" amounts to £5, 4s. 2d. This two-fold authority does not permit him to retail. In the case of the man, or labouring brewer, or "brewer á façon,' in Paris a fixed tax of 40 francs plus 5 per cent. on his wages, and in addition the centimes additionnels calculated on the amount of these two sums. The master brewer—he is allowed to use glucose sugar; is charged a duty of 3s. 1½d. per 22 gallons on strong beer, and 1s. 0½d. per 22 gallons on small, which is assessed at the rate of four-fifths of the actual "contents of each boiler, which he has to pay as soon as the manufacture is completed; he has to give notice of the beginning of the process, and lastly of the "barrelling," to enable the "Agents des Contributiones Indirectes" to prevent fraud. Alcoholic strength 7 to 8 per cent. On exportation the duty is repaid; on importation from England, &c., 4s. 9½d. per 22 gallons is payable. The private brewer is under similar obligations, except as to "Licence." Hospital authorities are exempt from all taxes, "except the payment of the duty proportioned to the strength of their home-brewed beer," which duty is determined by two experts, one named by the "excise" ("regie"), the other by the administrators of the hospital. The beer retailer pays a duty based upon the population of the place of sale.

ITALY.—In this peninsula the brewer pays no other licence than the municipal common to every profession and trade. He is not required to make entry of his premises or utensils: he may use what materials he chooses: he is charged a duty of "7 francs per hectolitre," based upon "the presumed quantity to be made, as calculated from the capacity of the boiler, with a deduction of 20 per cent;" but before commencing to brew he has to give twenty-four hours notice, to state the kind and quantity of materials to be used, the number and capacity of the boilers to be employed, the quantity of beer to be brewed, the day and hour of lighting the fire, the day and hour of the termination of boiling and the discharge of the liquor in the cooler, the number and capacity of the coolers, and, indeed, the particulars of all his intended operations. He pays the duty before he commences. All the vessels and utensils, except the fermenting tuns, must be visible: every boiler be of a certain capacity, and walled into the furnace, so that it cannot be enlarged, and that the revenue officer may place his seal upon it. The premises and utensils are open to the inspection of the official, except at night, when the presence of a magistrate, a syndic, or his delegate, is necessary. He is repaid the duty should the process be a failure, and on exportation. Private brewing is not allowed free of duty, but compounding is allowed on making a yearly, half-yearly, quarterly, or monthly payment. The vendor of beer is not licensed.

NETHERLANDS.—In Holland the brewer pays the "Patent" or trading licence, which varies, according to the extent of his business, from 10s. 10d. to £33, 6s. 8d.: in the case of a joint-stock company the patent is granted at the rate of 2 per cent., with 28 per cent., on the amount of the annual dividend paid by the company; and should the beer be sold to be drunk on the premises, a further annual licence is required at a cost of 7s. 6d. He is then required to make a declaration of the plant, premises, and material to be used, and give a new declaration should he alter any utensil. The grist is usually ground malt, but occasionally a mixture of malt and rice meal. He is charged a duty of 1s. 8d. per 22 gallons of the capacity of the mashing utensil on each mashing, or 7d. per ·295 lb. of malt used, and a little less on other materials; he is then taken under survey—he can choose either mode of charge. In either case he is required to make a declaration of brewing twenty-four hours before he commences, and, with other particulars, to declare the mode of charge: the duty is payable on making the declaration to brew, but it may be deferred three months upon giving security, or the charge, if of a certain amount, may be placed to the account of the dealer who buys the beer, upon his giving security. Drawback is allowed on exportation at two rates—in bottles at 1s. 8d. per 22 gallons, otherwise, 1s. 0½d. per 22 gallons; these rates are determined according to a mode of testing by which it can be ascertained if the worts "before fermentation contained not less than nine kilograms of 'Extract' per hectolitre." The private brewer pays on the materials used—the second mode—but no patent. The vendor of beer pays "a trading licence," which varies in amount according to the population of the commune: those who sell by "wholesale in the barrel," 14s. 2d. to £34, 13s. 4d.; those who do not sell more than 44 gallons at a time, 7s. 6d. to £14, 8s. 4d.; "publicans who sell by retail," 7s. 6d. to £26, 13s. 4d.

NORWAY.—Neither brewer nor seller of beer taxed.

PRUSSIA.—A brewing licence is not required, but the brewer has to deliver a notice of his intention to brew: he is not required to provide any particular number or size of utensils: in Alsace the duty is charged according to the size of the "kettle," elsewhere, except Bavaria already described, and Wurtemberg to be noticed, the malt is charged at the rate of about 2s. per cwt., and the duty paid in advance. He is restricted to mashing between 6 o'clock a.m. and 10 o'clock p.m., from October to March, and at other times between 4 o'clock a.m. and ten o'clock p.m., to enable the officer to attend to see the malt weighed: he is also required to keep his books in such a manner that the officer can judge the proportion of produce: he is not allowed to have more malt—ground—after mashing than will be required for the following mashing. The duty is returned in case of loss, and paid back on exportation. Private brewing is allowed free of duty, provided the family consist of "ten grown-up people." Compounding is also allowed.

RUSSIA.—The brewer here has to take out a special patent or licence, the amount of which is decided by a calculation made on the capacity of "the mash-vats and brewing boilers, and according to the number of sanctioned mashes," at "six copecks" per "vedro," or about 2¼d. per 2·707 gallons. But before this is granted he has to deliver a plan and description of the brewery, with a statement of the number of mashes he intends to make per day, and of the period he intends to brew; this done, the "excise inspector" compares it with the plant and premises, and on finding it agree, furnishes him with a note of the "Excise payable by him to the Treasury, for the period of brewing, and on producing a receipt for the amount—which it will have been observed is payable in advance—the officer grants him a licence, which is placed in a conspicuous part of the brewery. Should an interval of more than three days intervene between the brewings, or the brewer not renew his licence, the utensils are then officially sealed. Changes are required to be notified to the Excise. The brewing licence does not authorise the sale by retail. The duty is returned in case of fire, inundation, or other unforeseen cause of loss. The duty is not repaid, even in part, on exportation. Alcoholic strength about 38 per cent. Private brewing is allowed in "earthen vessels and boilers for domestic use" in villages and rural settlements, on condition that no special permanent building be erected, and that the beer be not sold for consumption in other villages, and that the beer in boilers be brewed for the celebration of saints' days, local rural holidays, marriages, and harvest feasts. The vendors of beer are divided into wholesale and retail, and their annual licence duty depends on "class of locality"—the first class is £8, 14s. 2d., the second £4, 15s., the third £2, 7s. 6d.

SAXONY.—Free.

SWEDEN.—No beer duty charged, but a "nykterhets-rattighet" or licence is required.

SWITZERLAND.—Free.

WURTEMBURG.—The brewer in this country is not required to pay a licence duty to brew, but he is required to pay "two florins five kreutzers" per centum, or 3·6d. per 100lbs., less 2 per cent. for waste, on the malt brought to the brewery, which is payable quarterly. He is required to make a declaration of the quantity brought in, and to receive only by fiscal certificate. In case the beer be destroyed the duty is returned. The whole of the duty is returned on exportation; this is determined by the "unexpected attendance" of the officer "at several brewings." 28 to 48 lbs. of malt yield 22 gallons of wort at 1054°. Private brewing is not allowed. The vendor who sells 20 litres, about 4½ gallons or less, is required to pay a life, not annual, licence duty varying from 3 to 120 florins, or from 6s. 1½d. to £12, 5s.[1]

M. Vogel in his statistical sketch on beer: "In turning to the United Kingdom, the evidence must strike us that the breweries there are carried on with a high degree of ability and perfection. The comparatively large quantity of beer and porter exported and used at home is made of worts of high degrees of gravity, and yet we find the average gravity of worts of the total brewings to be not less than 22·25 per cent. below that of Bavaria. This proves superior skill in every single operation, from the moment the barley is put into the steeping-cistern until the beer is sent out for consumption; it proves, besides, that the materials employed must be well chosen and of good quality."[2]

BELL'S COMPENDIUM OF GENERAL ORDERS.

From the year 1700 to 1857 inclusive, with appendices containing copious extracts of the laws, forms, precedents, fees, licence duties, &c., &c., published in 1858 by Loftus, London.

"Bell's Bateman's Manual," 1865, see Dr Bateman.

"Bell and Dwelly's Laws"—see Acts of Parliament.

BILLS OF PARCELS.

These were accepted with tea and coffee instead of the usual permit,[3] until great frauds were discovered, when the commissioners required the production of the "let-pass"—permit.[4]

[1] P. P. 82, 258, 1874.
[2] On Beer, Vogel, 1874.
[3] 1724, 1725.
[4] L. G. 1728.

BLIND HOUSE.

A Gloucestershire term for an unlicensed house, "where tobacco, cider, beer, spirits, and even wines were . . . . consumed in almost fabulous quantities . . . . often patronised by wealthy farmers and others, to whom the illegality of the thing was its most piquant recommendation."[1]

BOARD OF TRADE.

It was during the extensive "running" of the duty on wool that this department appears to have been first suggested to assist this Board, and the suggestion was embodied in a recommendation to the House of Lords in 1831, that the officers should attend the shearing or "pulling" of the wool, see it warehoused, and deliver it only under permit. But probably the first actual aid given was in the suppression of the cattle plague at the various ports on the importation of foreign "beasts." This occurred in 1770, and was continued by subsequent Orders in Council until 1775. The salaries of their inspectors of Corn Returns were first paid in 1828, and the returns first collected in 1842. The greatest service given has been in the collection of agricultural statistics, which commenced in 1866.

BOND.

An obligation entered into with the Crown by both trader and officer, the former for fiscal duties due, the latter for discipline to be observed; also, by the smuggler.

The Trader.—This form originated with the "Oxford Excise" in 1644, when security was exacted for the due payment of the duties on the stocks in hand at the first imposition,[2] and it was general in Scotland in 1669.[3] On the imposition of the duty on malt in 1702, if that duty were not paid within six days security was given to pay it within six months.[4] From that date trade bonds have been

[1] C. S. G., 1865. [2] P. O., Feb. 17, 1644. [3] Parliament S., Dec. 15, 1669. [4] Proc., March 8, 1701, *o.s.*

general, and have been given to ensure—the due payment of duty on the termination of a fixed deferred period, sometimes with and sometimes without interest;[1] the pre-enacted use of a compound in which a dutiable article formed the base, duty-free;[2] the safe removal of a fiscal article into revenue custody, or beyond the leviable limits;[3] the prescribed use of an article liable to duty but made duty-free;[4] the value of a perishable seizure;[5] the prompt payment of penalties.[6]

The penalty of a bond, or extent of pecuniary obligation, has been decided upon different principles. Sometimes the single,[7] at others double[8] and treble,[9] and at another one and a quarter times,[10] the duty based upon a known or possible charge, while in other cases on a probability of evasion.[11] The registration of these securities, for £1000 and upwards, in Great Britain, was formerly made in the Court of Common Pleas,[12] but latterly that has been discontinued, with the exception of those given by Remitters of Revenue and Railway Companies.[13] In Ireland in the Solicitors' Office, Dublin. Those for smaller amounts in Ireland, and all, with the above exceptions in Great Britain, with collectors.[13] The bondsman, with one or two exceptions, paid a stamp duty,[14] 1d. for paper[15] and 8d. for registration.[16]

The sufficiency of the sureties was inquired into annually,[17] and in some instances, if not in all, the obligers had to annually reacknowledge their obligations by their signatures to the original document. This, however, the Parnell Committee of 1835 suggested should be discontinued, and that the plan pursued by the Commissioners of Woods and Forests, of yearly inquiring into the solvency of sureties, should be adopted. "We feel," they stated, "more called upon to direct attention to this point, as it is one upon which we have received numerous representations from various classes of trades, under the control of the Excise, who have strongly urged the inconvenience and hardship of being required thus unnecessarily to renew applications which are seldom willingly complied with."[18] This suggestion

[1] Malt, 1859, 1863; Railway Duty, 1874. [2] Methylated Spirit, 1855.
[3] Sugar, 1855; Spirit, bottled, 1863; Hops, 1785.
[4] Malt Distillery Purposes, 1855. [5] 1830. [6] Beer Retailers, 1830.
[7] Malt, 1702, 1815. [8] Malt, 1830. [9] Hops Exported, 1785.
[10] Malt, 1859. [11] Methylated Spirits, 1872. [12] 1840, 1856.
[13] 1872, 1878. [14] T. W. Jan. 14, 1835. [15] T. W. Aug. 21, 1837.
[16] 1796. [17] 1830. [18] Parnell Committee, 12th Report.

was adopted. Relief was also afforded in 1837, by accepting "Public Stock in the Books of the Bank of England," and Exchequer Bills, deposited in the name of the chairman of the Board, in lieu of the usual bond. These securities were returned to the obligee when the account was passed.[1]

The Officer.—This obligation applied to all three kingdoms, and was given for "good behaviour,"[2] and earliest perhaps in Scotland, where a collector gave security in 1663 not to engage in any trade in which articles subject to the duties of excise or customs were vended,[3] but this has since been enforced by Act of Parliament; though security in the British Guarantee Association of 1848 has been accepted. Returners of revenue money,[4] officers of every grade, within one month or three months of the date of their commission,[5] and even revenue police,[6] once gave bond, in various amounts, for the registration of which they had to pay a fee, which varied from 6s. 6d. to half-a-guinea, with 1s. extra for each obliger above three.[7] The amounts were :—

Collector S. 1804, "sum ordered by Board," with two "cautioners."[8]
 „ I. 1809, variable, £2000 to £10,000.[9]
 „ U. K. 1836, £5000.[2]
Supervisor S. 1804, £500, with two "cautioners."[8]
 „ U. K. 1836, £1000.[2]
Officer S. 1804, £200, with two "cautioners."[8]
 „ U. K. 1836, £200.[2]

There were at this time, 1836, no fewer than 5914 in force.[2] "It appears from the evidence of Mr Thornton," wrote the Parnell Committee in their Twentieth Report, "that bonds for good behaviour have never been put in force. It is a practice that incurs considerable expense which is entirely useless." This observation was not overlooked by Mr Gordon, who proposed in the House of Commons, on April 2, 1841, that these bonds should not be required except from persons in the actual receipt of money. This he carried, and it was embodied in a Bill which received the royal assent on May 20, 1841, but with this proviso, if the Commissioners "shall see fit

[1] 1777. [2] Parnell Com. 20th Rep. [3] Par. Scot., Oct. 8, 1663.
[4] 1764. [5] 1813, 1778. [6] 1847. [7] 1811. [8] Instructions, Scotland.
[9] P. Rep., Irish Accounts.

not to call for the same."[1] Bond with sureties ceased in 1852, on the formation of the Mutual Guarantee Fund, which see. This department first assisted that of the Post Office in the execution of its bonds in 1845.

The Smuggler who had been guilty of offences against the revenue laws and had left the country, was offered pardon, on condition that he would return and enter into a bond with the excise authorities that he would not again engage in smuggling and that he would not leave the country in time of war.[2]

BOOK-KEEPING BY DOUBLE ENTRY.

Although there were "Journal, Entry Book, Cash Book, and Ledger"[3] very early in use, yet this system was not established until 1840. A Parliamentary Committee on Public Accounts, eleven years[4] prior to its introduction, examined several civil service accounts with a view to uniformity of practice, but it remained for the Accountant, who was appointed by the Parnell Committee,[5] to examine the excise system of book-keeping, generally, to suggest its adoption, which was made known to this department in 1839, by the issue of an order to require a competent knowledge of the system by those who acted in the capacity of clerk, supervisor, surveyor, general surveyor, surveying general examiner or collector, and enforced the following year as a qualification for promotion to the rank of supervisor, surveying general examiner or collector. It is also a qualification for a clerkship.[6] It was at the same time ordered to be adopted by thirty-three other departments by Treasury Minute dated January 14, 1840.[7]

BORDER SERVICE.

That portion of the department, consisting of some four "superintendents," and about twenty-five officers, who were specially appointed to exact the differential duty on Scotch spirits which passed the Border, where they were located. Their duty consisted,

[1] 4 V. c. 20, sec. 3. [2] Proc., July 20, 1803. [3] P. O., May 30, 1654.
[4] 1829. [5] Parnell Com., Eleventh Report.
[6] 1857. [7] P. P., 551, 1843; 364, 1844.

in addition to exacting the duty, in riding about day and night to meet people "running spirits into England,"[1] and in the examination of suspected packages, and entailed very great exposure and exertion in its performance. The stocks of spirit traders who were suspected of collusion with smugglers, or "border stocks" as they were termed, were returned monthly or roundly:[2] and intelligent, discreet officers assisted by examining, at the more important railway stations and ports in England, luggage, which, in the case of that brought by rail, had by prearrangement been marked with red labels.[3] The border officer received an allowance of five shillings per day for horse keep,[1] the superintendent a salary of £150, and seven-and-sixpence per day.[4]

This preventive service was discontinued on the repeal of the drawback on malt used in distilling, and the equalization of the spirit duty to that in England in 1855.

BOTTLE DUTY.

"Earthenwares" were subject to excise duty in 1643,[5] and a duty was again imposed on stone and earthenware bottles "from and after" September 29, 1695,[6] and continued until 1698, when the House of Commons resolved to repeal it.[7] If then repealed, it was reimposed: its incidence was examined in 1834, when the cost of collection was shown to be 20 per cent., and the immediate repeal recommended.[8] The gross duty amounted to only £4200: repealed 1834.[9]

BOUGH OR BUSH HOUSE.

A house in England in the front of which a bough or bush was fixed at fair time to indicate the sale of beer, which, under a certain charter, was allowed to be brewed and sold without the payment of excise duty.

BOUNTY.

Bounties have been paid by this department under legal enactment, on exportation on beer,[10] cider, mum,[11] malt,[12] and salt,[13] to

[1] Parnell Committee, Seventh Report, Part I.; Bateman, 1852. [2] 1834.
[3] 1850. [4] C. S. G., 1854. [5] P. O. [6] L. G. [7] January 25, 1698.
[8] P. Rep., 1834. [9] C. 1, R. [10] 1 W. & M., c. 22.
[11] 1761, 43 G. III., c. 69. [12] 31 Geo. III., c. 30. [13] 43 G. III., c. 69.

develope trade: and in Ireland—"bounties"—in the form of an allowance, to distillers, at the rate of 8 per cent. of the duty chargeable on stills of 500 gallons content and upwards, at 16 per cent. on those of 1000 gallons content, "as the collection of the duty was easier," and more exact. No less a sum than £70,000 per annum was saved on the discontinuance of the "bounty" on the smaller, and 8 per cent. on the larger stills.[1] Bounties in general were discontinued in 1830.[2]

BRANDING IRON.

An instrument introduced in 1839 to brand the mould in which bricks were formed, to protect the revenue from loss. The iron seen by the writer consisted of a looped handle and arm, 24 in. by 1 in. long, to which was attached a headpiece, 6 in. by 1½ in., imprinted "EXCISE:" weight, 4 lbs. 14 oz. "3000 lettered branding irons, various," were announced for sale on the disposal of seizures at a three-day sale in April 1846.[3] This number, taken at an average weight, above seen, would represent six and a half tons.

BRIBERY.

The terms bribe and bribery preceded that of collusion in matters excise.

Bribery called for enactment in 1663. £10 was the penalty imposed, or three months' punishment by imprisonment inflicted, on either, or both, the acceptor or offerer. In 1725 it had become more frequent, and the penalty was then raised to £500, but this was special. In 1827 that sum was made general.

Bribery and collusion have not been practised to a serious extent in later times except in Ireland. In England, in early times, the conviction of parties and the escape of the guilty were announced in the London Gazette, No. 4028, 1704; No. 4487, 1708. In Scotland even the Solicitor himself has been tempted with a bribe of £500, with a promise of a like amount a year after.[4] In Ireland it

[1] H. C., May 7, 1806.
[2] Beeton's Universal Information.
[3] L. G.
[4] P. Rep., 1798.

was common and well known, and attributed partly to the low salary paid. Mr Foster, Chancellor of the Irish Exchequer, stated that the spirit duties were not collected in the counties of Donegal, Tyrone, and Cavan, and "As to Dublin, I will not enter into detail of how the distillery stands there, we know it is a common topic of conversation. . . . . I will add one circumstance. . . . . In the books of a distiller there, who became a bankrupt, a charge . . . . of £1200 paid in one year as compliment or contribution to the revenue officers over him."[1] This "relaxed conduct" and "corrupt behaviour" was also referred to in 1808.[2] The following year the Chancellor of the Irish Exchequer proposed to dismiss an officer who had regularly received £20 a week of two distillers, and who was promoted, eighteen months after the discovery, from the situation of surveyor to that of inspector-general; but in this he was not successful by 27 votes—ayes 50, noes 77.[3] He also added, that of thirty-two officers examined by a commission of inquiry, "thirty of them had confessed that they had received similar presents."[4] Collusion has also been associated with seizures, as collusive seizures. There are but few instances of this form of misdeed on record in Great Britain.

BRICK DUTY.

This duty, with which that on tiles was included until repealed in 1833, was levied in the first instance "to provide for the payment of the interest on the heavy debt incurred by the American war, and continued to be levied for a period of sixty-six years.[5] Its imposition was also, however, viewed as "the contrivance of those who wished to multiply officers and extend the influence of the Crown."[6] First fixed at 2s. 6d. per 1000, it was gradually raised to 10s.; and extra large polished bricks were charged at 4s. 10d. per 100, while smaller and cheaper forms were charged at lower rates. A protective duty was levied upon those imported, a return of duty was made upon those exported, and in later times no duty charged on those made for draining purposes.[7] Disputes as to charge were disposed of by sending a sample brick to the Board, who decided the rate.[8]

[1] H. C., March 13, 1805. [2] P. Rep., Sugar, 1808. [3] H. C., May 30, 1809.
[4] P. Rep., Fees, 1807. [5] Bateman's Laws, 1843.
[6] H. C., July 22, 1784. [7] 1828. [8] 1825.

The revenue was protected by branding the interior of the mould "Excise," which of course impressed the brick.[1] This head of duty was reviewed in 1835 by the Parnell Committee in their Eighteenth Report; the number of brickmakers was then 5839, in 1842, 7433. The same committee, in their Nineteenth Report, suggested a graduated scale of licence duties on makers, but this was not legalised. The mode of securing this duty required the maker to make entry of his place of abode, sheds, yards, &c., &c.; the officer to survey, during moulding, once a day, and out of residence as often as he could, and when not moulding once in ten or fourteen days; he had to count the bricks moulded between each visit, allow one in ten for waste, and charge only that number which would produce an exact "integer of duty," ¼d., and carry forward the remainder as "odds;" a specimen was kept in each yard.[2] In 1841 great frauds were committed, and to suppress them he had to survey during moulding, in residence, twice a day, Sunday excepted, and out of residence four times a week. Printed instructions were issued in 1804—Scotland, 1829 and 1842. Except in the statement of duties repealed, expired, or reduced, this duty is not noticed in the Commissioners' Reports.

Public opinion against this impost seems to have been first addressed to Parliament by petition in 1830, and continued yearly, with some variations, until 1849, when a reduction was asked for instead of a repeal, while in the interim returns were made to Parliament.[3] The final effort but one was made by Mr Hume, who moved a drawback on bricks used in building cottages, but this he withdrew.[4] The total repeal was proposed and effected by the Chancellor of Exchequer in his annual financial statement on March 15, 1850. A drawback of 50 per cent. was allowed on the stocks on hand. In only two instances of repeal of excise duties had drawbacks been previously allowed. "The usual course had been to allow some time to elapse before the duty was taken off, in order to enable parties to dispose of their stock; but generally there had been no drawback, and in no case had the full drawback been allowed."[5]

Peculiar to Great Britain. Imposed by Chancellor Pitt in 1784; repealed by Chancellor Wood in 1850.

[1] 1839. [2] 1784. [3] Nos. 82, 397, 1846; No. 168, 1848.
[4] H. C., Feb, 20, 1850. [5] H. C., March 25, 1850.

BROAD ARROW.

A mark used generally by government officials; by this department, specially on the occasion of the detention or seizure of articles capable of impress to signify the claim of the Crown.

BROWN'S SPIRIT PROOFS.

A serviceable book of tables, raised under the immediate check of John Brown the younger, supervisor, Edinburgh, and published at the expense of the Scottish Distillers' Association by Blackwood in 1877.

It applies to only o.p. spirit.

The range is—

From 9 galls. by ¼ galls. to 79·7 at 10·4 to 11·6, and 24·4 to 25·6.
" 80 " 1 " 185 " " "

Then at every tenth of a gallon.

From 25 to 37·9 galls. } at 5·0 to 11·6, and from 20·0 to 25·6.
" 50 to 67·9 " }
" 80 to 155·9 " }

Finally at every whole gallon—

From 80 to 155 galls. from 43·0 to 68·9.
" 80 to 100·9 " 52·0 to 58·0.

Size 13·5 by 7 inches; page 264; stereotyped; price two and a half guineas.

BUDGET.

The introduction of the Budget[1] or Financial[2] Statement to the House of Commons is the occasion usually taken to impose, reimpose, reduce, commute, or repeal excise duties according to the national demand on the one part or to the judgment of the Treasury on the other. An annual statement was not made in the earlier years of the excise; it is now and is looked forward to by the public, and this department in particular, with great interest. It included the fiscal arrangements for Scotland from the date of the Union, but a separate Budget was prepared and produced for Ireland from the

[1] Cobbett, 1772. [2] Hansard, 1865.

Union[1] to 1815.[2] The more sensational statements have been made by Sir R. Walpole,[3] the Hon G. Grenville,[4] Lord North,[5] Mr Pitt,[6] Mr Disraeli,[7] Mr Gladstone,[8] Mr Lowe.[9]

BURNS.

Robert Burns' "order for instructions" is dated March 31, 1788; he was then twenty-nine years of age, and appears to have obtained his nomination through the incidental mention of his desire to Mr A. Wood, his surgeon, who made the request to Mr Commissioner Graham;[10] although Burns himself wrote to the Earl of Glencairn on the subject.[11] The order runs thus:—"To James Findlay, officer, Tarbolton. The Commissioners' order. That you instruct the bearer, Mr Robert Burns, in the art of gauging and practical dry gauging casks and utensils; and that you fit him for surveying victuallers, rectifiers, chandlers, tanners, tawers, maltsters, &c.; and when he has kept books regularly for six weeks at least, and drawn true vouchers and abstracts therefrom (which books, vouchers, and abstracts must be signed by your supervisor and yourself, as well as the said Mr Robert Burns), and sent to the Commissioners at his expense; and when he is furnished with proper instruments, and well instructed and qualified for an officer, then (and not before, at your perils) you and your supervisor are to certify the same to the Board, expressing particularly therein the date of this letter; and that the above Mr Robert Burns hath cleared his quarters, both for lodgings and diet; that he has actually paid each of you for his instructions and examination, and that he has sufficient at the time to purchase a horse for his business. Excise Office. I am your humble servant, A. PEARSON. Edinburgh, 31st March 1788."[12]

Though addressed to an officer at Tarbolton, Ayr, Burns wrote to a friend, "I return to Edinburgh for six weeks' instruction."

His appointment gave birth to these lines:—

> "Och, ho! the day!
> That clarty barn should stain my laurels;
> But—what 'll ye say?
> These moving things, ca'ed wives and weans,
> Wad move the hearts o' stanes!"[13]

[1] Woodfall, 1801. [2] Hansard. [3] 1732, 1733.
[4] Debrett, 1763. [5] Stockdale, 1777. [6] Debrett, 1784, 1787.
[7] Hansard, 1852. [8] Hansard, 1853, 1862.
[9] Hansard, 1871. [10] Dr Currie, 1811. [11] Gall and Inglis.
[12] Cunningham, 1835. [13] Holborn, 1843.

Having received his commission, his convenience was so far studied in 1789, by probably Mr Commissioner Graham, that he was "appointed to an excise division," in the middle of which his house and farm lay, and he then wrote:—"In this I was extremely lucky: without ever having been an expectant, as they call their journeymen excisemen, I was directly planted down to all intents and purposes an officer of excise, there to flourish and bring forth fruit—worthy of repentance." This station seems to have been known as "Dumfries First Itinerancy," a station which embraced a very considerable extent of country, as may be gleaned from his own words:—"For my part, I have galloped over my ten parishes these four days, until this moment that I have just alighted, or rather that my poor jackass-skeleton of a horse has let me down; for the miserable creature has been on his knees half-a-score of times within the last twenty miles, telling me in his own way, 'Behold, am not I thy faithful jade of a horse, on which thou hast ridden these many years?' In short, sir, I have broke my horse's wind, and almost broke my own neck, besides some injuries on a part that shall be nameless, owing to a hard-hearted stone of a saddle."

A severer experience of horsemanship, however, awaited him; he ultimately broke his arm. In the meantime, he had been appointed and promoted, on July 28, 1790, to "Dumfries Third Division, or Footwalk," probably through the influence of Mrs Corbet, whose husband was then a "Supervisor-General of Excise,"[1] and in this station his duties appear to have consisted principally of the survey of tobacco, as it was called the "Tobacco Division." His next appointment was made on April 26, 1792, and must have been at his own request, to Dumfries First Division, which was his last station.

On January 27, 1791, the commissioners ordered Burns's name to be entered on the list for promotion to the rank of supervisor, and his name remained on this list until his death—the word "Dead" being written in the column for the date of promotion. "Again, a register was kept of all censures issued by the board . . . and the absence of Burns's name from the register proves that he was never censured by the Commissioners, not even in the mildest form in which they were in the habit of conveying their displeasure for what they characterised trivial faults. . . . All the officers in Scotland were alphabetically arranged, with a brief statement of the character of

[1] Athenæum, 1874.

each in the margin. A list of this description was made three months after Burns joined the service, and the marginal entry opposite his name is, 'Never tryed, a poet,' with a subsequent interlineation, 'Turns out well.' Three years later a corresponding list was prepared, and the entry in it is 'The poet does pretty well.'" It was in 1792 that Burns was notably indiscreet in connecting himself with the *Gazetteer*, "a violently political newspaper." This gave great offence to the authorities, and the board instructed Mr Collector Mitchel to inquire into his political conduct, and although, as previously shown, he never had a censure recorded against him, he was given to understand that his hope of "getting officially forward" was "blasted." This, however, must have been withdrawn, as "he was acting as a supervisor" in Dumfries "when his last and fatal illness seized him," and had he lived until January 12, 1797,[1] he would have been promoted, in the ordinary course, to the rank of supervisor. His idea of the supervisorship was this (1795):—"The business is an incessant drudgery, and would be nearly a complete bar to every species of literary pursuit."

It was while at Dumfries that the poet-gauger made a poetical defence "'gainst poor excisemen." This was "written on a window at the King's Arms Tavern, Dumfries":—

"Ye men of wit an' wealth, why all this sneering
'Gainst poor excisemen? Give the cause a hearing.
What are your landlords' rent-rolls? Taking ledgers.
What premiers, what? Even monarchs' mighty gaugers.
Nay, what are priests? these seeming godly wise men:
What are they, pray, but spiritual excisemen?"

The first house in which he lived in Dumfries was at Bank Vennel, from here he removed to a small house in a humble street, which has since been called by his name—Burns' Street.

His salary at first was £50, then £75; by "an appointment to an excise division £25 per annum better than the rest;" his "down money" being £70 per annum. But during his illness he wrote, on July 7, 1796, "The deuce of the matter is this, when an exciseman is off duty, his salary is reduced. What way, in the name of thrift, shall I maintain myself and keep a horse in country quarters on £35?" But these straitened circumstances he ceased to endure eleven days afterwards, when he died, having given a period of rather more than eight years' service.

[1] Mr M'Fadzean: Chambers' Journal, 1875.

The necessary sequence to this is the narration of some of the official relics. In Burns's Monument in Edinburgh may be seen a letter written by him in answer to a petition for the remission of a fine: a beer voucher made out by him, "Dumfries Collection, District and 1st Division. Excise, 87th year, 1794. 8th Round Voucher, including 25 May and 5 July:" also the "sword-cane carried by Burns when an exciseman." His commission—"The original document signed and sealed, appointing the poet an exciseman, produced £5, 12s. 6d." at a sale in Wellington Street, London, in 1854[1]: and "the Writing-Table used by Burns when an Exciseman" was offered for sale in George Street, Edinburgh, in 1876.[2] Historical records, too, were shown at a centenary gathering at Dundee—"a leaf from one of his excise-books:" also a letter and an official diary, "in which Burns's name is often mentioned," the latter by Mr Alexander Findlater, who had been his supervisor during the whole of the time Burns held his commission.[3] The following is a copy of a leaf—nine and a half inches long by three and a quarter inches wide—of Burns' diary.

1795. March.			Miles.	Cn. B.	Vr.	Chrs.	Tanrs.	Tawrs.	Maltrs.	Wine.	Spir.	Ted.	Tobco.	Tob, Mrs.	
Lochmaben.	10 m. 10.	Newmains.	8	..	..	..	..	..	1	..	..	..	..	..	In V. Y. a Guage,
John M'Culloch.	&	Residence.	1	..	4	..	1	..	..	1	2	1	2	..	—In Malt a
	pn.	Brinnhill.	3	..	...	..	..	..	1	..	..	..	..	..	Guage. Examined Books and
			12	..	4	..	1	..	2	1	2	1	2	..	nothing to blame.

Then as to the recorded facts of his official intercourse. Burns, Lewars, and other officers were directed to check the smuggling of contraband goods on the coast of Ayr, where "R. B.," discovering a suspicious-looking brig, and seeing that the crew had arms, he despatched Lewars to Dumfries for the dragoons. Between this and his return, Burns had to wait several hours in "a wet salt marsh;" and his patience having become almost exhausted, and made known by a tirade of abuse on Lewars, one of his comrades wished "the devil had him (Lewars) for his pains," and suggested that Burns would do well to indite a song on the "sluggard." The poet then made a few strides among the reeds and shingle, rejoined his party, and chanted, "The Deil's run awa' wi' the Exciseman."

Lewars returned shortly after the bard had delivered this effusion,

[1] C. S. G., 1854. [2] *Scotsman*. [3] C. S. G., 1859.

when Burns, placing himself at the head of the other officers and the guard of dragoons, waded sword in hand to the brig, and was the first to board her. The crew lost heart and submitted, though their number was greater than that of the invading force. The vessel was condemned, with all her arms and stores, and sold by auction the next day at Dumfries—February 27, 1792.

The following is also ascribed to him—a "song written and sung at a general meeting of the excise officers in Scotland:"—

"The de'il cam' fiddling thro' the toun
And danc'd awa' wi' the Exciseman;
And ilk aul' wife cry'd, 'Auld Mahoun,
We wish you luck o' the prize, man.'

Chorus.
"We'll mak' our maut, and brew our drink,
We'll dance and sing and rejoice, man;
And mony thanks to the muckle black de'il
That danc'd awa' wi' the Exciseman.

"There's threesome reels and foursome reels,
There's hornpipes and strathspeys, man;
But the a'e best dance e'er cam' to our lan'
Was the de'il's awa' wi' the Exciseman.
Chorus."[1]

This is probably the song previously referred to.

The following is related of him in connection with a friend, a blacksmith, at Carronbridge, who was suspected of carrying on or conniving at a traffic in liquor, and whose premises were occasionally inspected:—"A man named Matthew Milligan left a considerable quantity of smuggled brandy in a greybeard at the blacksmith's house; it was concealed in a locked press, and the blacksmith and his wife having gone to the shearing on Carronhill, and also dreading a visit from the gaugers, gave the key of the press to Margaret (Mrs Bennett), with strict injunctions that she should on no account give the expected visitors access to the press. Sure enough, in the course of the day Burns and the supervisor arrived, and the latter had evidently got scent of the smuggled brandy, for he plied the girl with questions on the subject, and was particularly desirous to see the inside of the press. In this, it appears, he could not be accommodated; and then he demanded that its contents should be described to him,

[1] Chapman & Lang, 1801,

which was done with considerable facility, but with no mention of the greybeard. Mrs Bennett was accustomed to tell, with considerable humour, how anxious and concerned the poet looked lest the press should be opened. He doubtless guessed what it contained, and knew well how serious a penalty would fall on his friend the blacksmith in the event of the brandy being discovered. 'At one time,' she said, 'he winked hard at me oure the supervisor's shoulder to be sure no let on.' The result was, the supervisor was baffled and the brandy was undetected."[1]

To conclude. Burns—"Aye, Saunders, I did ken that prince o' publicans, Rab Forgie, the honest ale-seller o' the Binnan. He never thought ale any stouter o' a gauger's stick, or brandy any better o' a permit. He was, over and above, nae sma' frien' to free traders. Saunders—that I ken, as I did mony mae in my line o' merchandise (old smuggler); for whan ony o' us war out, gif the water-gleds war on the watch, he aye hoisted a blanket on his yard hedge gif it was day, and at night he set a lunt to a whin 'cow. A bit waff winlestrae thing o' a gauger, I min', ance challenged him when a gin sloop was in the affing, for hoisting his blanket and bleezing his whin. But Rab—who had a breast like a boat-bow an' a arm like a post stoup—tauld him that thae things war his ain, an' he wou'd dae wi' them as he wulled. An', quo' he, gif ye daur to touch my blanket or offer but to spit in my lowe, by a' that's gude, I'll beeze ye in the tane till ye're saft, an' singe ye in the tither till ye're sair. Aye, Rab was the lad for thae lan'-loupers, an' mony a funny sang he had on them. Saunders then sung 'The Gauger,' tune, 'Nancy Dawson:'—

"'The gauger he's gane owre the hill,
Wi' his horn an' his quill,
Will ye wad wi' me a gill,
The gauger he'll come back, man?

'He's houkit thraus o' Irish bags—
He's herrit coves o' brandy cags—
There's hunners 'twixt the Loch an' Largs
Could see him on a rack, man.

'He cost M'Queen a browst o' yill,
He brake Pate Simson's whisky still—
Its awfu' an' unkent the ill
This warlokin has wrought man.

[1] Chambers' Journal, 1875.

'He gars M'Master keep out owre,
He's billy keeps a seventy-four—
He's coft his killing ten times owre!
He'll get what he has cost, man!

'Nae stream can brouk a constant spate—
The dourest things maun ha'e a date—
An' dogs wha ha'e a kintra's hate
Sou'd redd weel wha they bark at.

'Pate Simson he's begun to bann,
An' Patrick has a lang Queen Anne,
Now, Lord ha'e mercy on the man
That Patrick tak's his mark at.'"

"Some time after he was attached to the excise, a smuggler met him one night, while wading by the Nith, and, not aware of who it was, offered to sell him some whiskey he had in concealment. 'You've lighted on a bad merchant,' said the bard, 'I'm Robert Burns the gauger.' The fellow stared, but, with a smuggler's impudence, returned, 'Aye, but you're likewise Robert Burns the poet, an' I mak' sangs too; sae ye'd surely ne'er ruin a brither.' 'Why, friend,' said Burns, 'the poet in me has been sacrificed to the exciseman; so I should like to know what superior right you have to exemption?'"[1]

CALLIPERS.

Instruments used to ascertain the contents of casks by external admeasurement. There are two—the cross callipers consist of two arms of boxwood at right angles to each other, and so fitted, grooved, and marked, as to be adjustable to any dimension within their limit of 59 inches, the cross, or largest or opposite diameter to the bung is taken with them; the bung with the bung rod; the head or smallest diameter is ascertained externally by means of a head rod; with these, and the aid of the slide rule, the mean diameter is found: the long callipers are similarly constructed, with the addition of projecting pieces at either end to enable the dimension to be taken without the interposition of the projecting ends of the staves; the length from head to head, or end to end, is taken by these within a limit of gauge of 66 inches. A deduction is then made to the extent of the thickness of the intervening wood—formerly found

[1] Hew Ainslie, 1822.

by means of a wood-guage--which leaves the approximate internal dimensions, which are equivalent to those of the figure of a cylinder, upon the calculation is based, and the content found, by the manipulation of the slide-rule attached to the head-rod. (See Keene's "Handbook of Gauging," 1868; Maclean's, 1876.) These instruments were early in use at stations at the various ports, but the first observed treatise on them occurs in a book written by one Iley, a gauger and surveyor of excise in London in 1820; then, on the introduction of the Imperial Measure in 1826, of Patent Callipers, Patent Pocket Callipers, and Variety Callipers, by Gutteridge, also a member of this department.

Their use appears to have been very much confined to the port stations until 1833, when the general surveyors and others employed at distilleries and rectifying houses, and country and town examiners, who were not already proficient in the art, were required to attend at the Port of London—the examiners a fortnight—to be instructed by the surveyors and gaugers, who were paid a fee of half-a-guinea by the instructee, who was repaid by the Board, who afterwards paid the fee direct,[1] but ultimately ordered the "pupil gauger" to do. A set of these instruments was immediately afterwards issued to each rectifying-house and distillery station,[2] and continued in use until 1853, when a new principle of computation by the specific weight of the spirit was introduced and applied in charging home-made spirits. They were re-introduced, into the inland stations, in 1870, on the permission to bond foreign wine and spirits.

CANDIDATES.

These aspirants to office obtained their nominations of the Lords of the Treasury, the Commissioners of this department, or the "Dublin County Collector,"[3] between Michaelmas and Lady-Day for many years, but subsequently as vacancies occurred, down to August 31, 1870, by patronage alone; afterwards of the Civil Service Commissioners about twice a-year, on application fourteen days before the date of examination, but on the payment of an examination fee, which has varied from £1[4] to 15s.[5] and again to £1.[6]

[1] 1837. [2] 1838. [3] P. Rep., 1809.
[4] 1871. [5] 1872. [6] 1875.

Under the earlier system it seems to have been customary for the applicant to apply in his own hand-writing, and to enclose certificates of character, age, ability, religion, and family.[1]

A portion of the nominations was always reserved for the Board to dispense to the sons of deserving officers with large families, and the remainder was equally divided between the Treasury and the Commissioners. This mode of distribution continued until the consolidation of the three Boards in 1823, when the Treasury thought it expedient to discontinue a distinction which existed in the other countries, all for Ireland and a portion for Scotland being granted by the Treasury, and to make an arrangement by which each should have a half, and each Commissioner an aliquot part of that half; the Treasury, however, subsequently, on the retirement of a Commissioner, claiming his share. It appears that for several years no nominations were issued, while during the war it was absolutely necessary for the Board to request officers who had eligible sons to ask for nominations for them, as "it was difficult to get men to take the situation."[2] Very different this from the eagerness shown for the appointment on the introduction of the open-to-all system in 1871, when upwards of 1000 applied, and 700 competed for 80 appointments.

Coming, then, to the standards of qualifications and modes of examination:

In 1705 the qualifications were these—age between 21 and 30 years; good writing; arithmetic, first four rules of "vulgar and decimal arithmetick;" ingenuity; health; activity; "sober life and conversation;" in the "communion of the Church of England" or Scotland; "well-affected to the Government;" freedom from debt; not "a larger family than a wife and two children." These were tested by the collector or supervisor, and if approved the candidate wrote out a certificate to that effect, in which he inserted the vocation to which he had been bred, the names of his sureties to answer an obligation of £200 "for the due Execution of his Office," the person by whom he wished to be instructed; it was then signed by the examiner. Below this he wrote out an oath that he had not given any fee to obtain an appointment, and this was signed by a Justice of the Peace.[3]

Less attention having been paid to the examination of character and ability than the Board desired,[4] the subject shortly afterwards

[1] 1705. [2] 1811, P. Rep., 1836. [3] Leadbetter, 1743. [4] S., 1818.

received their Honours' attention; and in 1824 these qualifications were reviewed and amended, in so far as that relating to age was changed from 21 to 30 to 19 to 30, and those relating to ingenuity, sobriety, and communion were entirely omitted, the candidate being allowed to name a place in England or Scotland for instruction.[1] In 1841 also, in so far as that he need not be "well-affected to the present Government." A few years later the attention of Parliament was drawn to the number admitted,[2] and afterwards to the standard of qualifications;[3] and though no change was immediately made, in 1848, "with a view of ensuring educated men," they were again revised as follows:—Age 19 to 25 years; good writing; arithmetic, first four rules of vulgar and decimal fractions; health; activity; good character; dictation, six lines; book-keeping by double entry, vivâ voce; freedom from debt; unmarried and without family, and not to be allowed to marry until the rank of ride officer be attained. The examination by the supervisor now formed the preliminary test, the candidate being required, on the approval of the first certificate, to proceed to the collector's residence with a letter of identity, and undergo a further test in the presence of the collector, a supervisor, and a clerk, who were required to attest his productions with their signatures; or, if in London, in the presence of two Surveying General Examiners, the Accomptant and Comptroller-General, and one of the secrètaries or correspondents. Even these higher qualifications and this stricter mode of examination were soon called in question;[4] and on the appointment of the Civil Service Commissioners in 1855,[5] a correspondence was opened with the Board, which resulted in giving the Commissioners credit for "the care and pains which were taken by them for ascertaining the qualifications of health, character, and intelligence possessed by persons receiving appointments,"[6] and in the issue of reconsidered qualifications. They were these—age between 19 and 25 years; good writing: arithmetic—vulgar and decimal fractions, reduction, proportion, practice, interest; health; activity; good character; dictation; book-keeping by double entry, written; freedom from debt; unmarried and without family, and not to be allowed to marry until the rank of ride officer be attained; the examination papers being prepared by the Civil Service Commissioners, and the examination

[1] S., 1824. [2] P. Ret., 1831. [3] P. Ret., 1843.
[4] C. S. G., 1853, 1854; P. Ret., 1855. [5] May 21.
[6] C. 1, R.: C. S. G., 1856.

conducted by them if in or within forty miles of London, elsewhere in the presence of a collector and a clerk, the preliminary by the supervisor being discontinued.

Punch suggested, "Excisemen to have hydrostatics and chemistry at their fingers' ends."[1] A strict investigation into the age, health, solvency, and occupation followed the issue of this standard;[2] and so strict with respect to age, that the person who compared the certificate with the register of births had to certify—the fact being so—that the entry appeared to have been made "at the time indicated."[3]

In 1866 still higher qualifications were suggested, and in 1868 Sir C. Trevelyan suggested that the Home Civil Service should be thrown open to public competition, which should include soldiers or "time-expired men," of good character, who might be desirous to compete, believing that "there could not be a better training school for the qualities which were more especially required for this class of appointments"—Customs, Inland Revenue, &c.[4] Both of Sir Charles's ideas were adopted. Unlimited open competition, by an Order in Council, dated June 4, 1870; but that which referred to soldiers not without some little patronage. A meeting of military and naval officers was held, under the presidency of Lord Derby, in the United Service Institution in 1871, when Sir Charles attended, and moved that soldiers and sailors who have served their country with credit, and completed a sufficient period of service, and could pass the necessary Civil Service Examination, should have a preference for appointments.[5] His motion was successful, except, perhaps, in regard to preference, and resulted in his model men being allowed to compete, and being "considered to have, on leaving their former service, the same age as when they entered it."[6] The latter idea was further pressed by Sir H. Havelock in 1876,[7] and the subject was investigated and reported upon by a Select Committee of the House of Commons in 1877. The standard for the first open competition on February 22, 1871, was announced on January 21, 1871, the situation at the same time being withdrawn from, but not long afterwards restored to, Schedule A.

Qualifications.—Age between 19 and 22 years on the day of examination;[8] a natural-born subject; give six months' probation before certificate of qualifications be given by Civil Service Commis-

[1] 1856. [2] 1858, C. S. C., 4 R. [3] 1859, 1866. [4] *Times.*
[5] C. [6] C. S. C., Jan. 2, 1872. [7] H. C., Feb. 28.
[8] In 1877, on the first day of the month in which the examination is held. C. S. C., 22 R.

sioners; afterwards given prior to entering on period of probation; the head of the department being satisfied before final appointment; good health and character; not a pupil-teacher or schoolmaster educated at the public expense, except with the consent of the authorities and concurrence of the Treasury: unmarried and without family.

	Marks.	Adopted.[1]	
Handwriting, ...	200	but 300	
Orthography, ...	200	" 300	Dictation, 100
Arithmetic (including vulgar and decimal fractions), . .	200	" 350	
Composition, ...	200	" 200	and Correspondence.

The greater aggregate number "to form the principle of selection."[2]

Other modifications have since been made at different times:—

	1873.	1874.	1875.
Handwriting, ...	300	200	400
Dictation and orthography paper, . .	100	—	—
Orthography, ...	300	200	400
Arithmetic, ...	350	300	400
English composition, ...	200	200	400
Optional.			
Higher arithmetic, including mensuration and square and cube root, ...	—	—	400
Geography, British Isles, ...	—	—	400

In 1873 it was decided to make the examination in future half-yearly, in June and December.[3] In 1874 the examination for the Customs Department was held concurrently with this, the candidate being allowed to state for which department he would be examined, or if for either. In 1875 the qualifications were divided into obligatory and optional, the latter division including, as already shown, mensuration, a subject suggested by "Humanitas," in 1871, and geography, as suggested in Porter's "Inland Revenue Gazetteer," in 1874.

Of the successful candidates in the eight open competitions held between February 22, 1871, and June 12, 1874, for 840 situations, 303 were examined in England, 52 in Scotland, 485 in Ireland;[4] or by percentage, E. 36·07, S. 6·19, I. 57·73. The statistics supplied by the Civil Service Commissioners in their reports are also instructive.

[1] C. S. C., 18 Rep. [2] L. G. [3] C. S. C., April 22, 1873. [4] C. S. G. & C.

Date Dec. 31	Nominees.	Examined	Cancelled.	Passed.	Failed.	Under consideration.	Declined, not healthful, not of age, &c.	Remained to appear.		Report.
1855 . . .	186	120	7	...	...	...	...	59	. . . .	1st
1856 . . .	a682	355	...	328	220	7	79	48	. . . .	2nd
1857 . . .	b994	857	...	504	353	...	143	14	73 honorary additions to I. R. 12 to Excise.	3rd
1858 . . .	200	182	...	111	71	...	23	10	5 honorary additions to I. R.	4th
1859 . . .	156	146	...	107	39	...	7	13	4 " " "	5th
1860 . . .	122	103	...	64	39	...	13	19	1 " " "	6th
1861 . . .	87	89	...	57	32	...	6	11	None	7th
1862 . . .	159	148	...	97	51	...	14	8	None	8th
1863 . . .	108	82	...	55	27	...	12	22	None	9th
1864 . . .	408	332	...	212	120	...	36	62	None	10th
1865 . . .	298	294	...	183	111	...	31	35	None	11th
1866 . . .	348	339	...	216	123	...	16	28	None. The names of all the successful candidates, with the dates of their certificates, from the opening of the Commission to Dec. 31, 1866, are given in this report.	12th
1867 . . .	303	252	...	152	100	...	21	58	. . . .	13th
1868, to June inclusive	179	202	...	127	75	...	17	18		
1868-9 {July 1, 1868, June 30, 1869.}	354	317	...	206	111	...	27	28	. . . .	14th
1869-70 . . .	468 cases dealt with.	409	...	230	179	...	16	53	. . . .	15th
1870-71 . . .	899	704	...	79	c625	...	195	...	. . . .	16th
1871-72 . . .	1319	1100	...	161	939	...	219	...	. . . .	17th
1872-73 . . .	1720	1291	...	200	1091	...	429	...	. . . .	18th
1873 . . .	680	539	...	150	389	...	141	...	. . . .	18th
1874 . . .	1892	1497	...	248	1249	...	395	...	. . . .	19th
1875 . . .	1260	879	...	166	713	...	d381	...	. . . .	20th
	1188	461	...	140	321	...	135	592	. . . .	20th
1876 . . .	1963	985	...	160	825	...	295	683	. . . .	21st
1877 . . .	1892	1000	...	110	890	...	299	593	. . . .	22nd

(a) From commencement on May 21, 1855, to Dec. 31, 1856. (b) Do. to Dec. 31, 1857. (c) Now divided into not competent, 471—and competent, 154; i.e. not needed, though drawn upon in case of ultimate failure, &c. (d) This line includes the examination for the Customs Department: of the passed, 68 were for that service; all entered under the qualifications of 1874.

Pupilage succeeds the successful candidature, dates very far back,[1] and appears to have been entered upon only on the issue of an "Order for instructions," given at the instance of the Board down to 1855, and then at the instance of the Civil Service Commissioners, but always issued by the Board, and which, though usually addressed to the collector of the collection in which the candidate resided, in the case of Burns—which see—was addressed to the instructing officer direct. After, as well as before, the consolidation of the English and Scotch Boards, candidates were permitted to state in their first certificate the place in which they desired to be instructed, but, on condition[2] that when instructed they would return to the collection in which they were first examined; those on the English establishment acquainting the Board at what places they might be found. This privilege of selecting a place for instruction has been continued with perhaps the following exception. It is blue-booked that the Irish candidates were "generally brought over to England for instruction," because of the "greater variety of duties here."[3] This, however, has long been discontinued, though a similar principle was applied within the limits of thirty miles in cases in which one officer could not impart the whole course.[4] Candidates were required to commence their studies within one month of the date of the order. A fee was chargeable at the Treasury in 1831 on "the letters naming persons for instructions."[5]

The periods of instruction have varied not only according to a fixed limit, but also according to the aptitude of the pupil. For a considerable time it seems to have been both in England[6] and Ireland[7] one month; while in Scotland, as early as 1788, six weeks' training was given, a period which has been adopted since 1815—when it was "a month at least" in England—in the sister countries,[8] though on the authority of Sir F. Doyle, Bart., it was "sometimes two months and sometimes four months, the time depending on the abilities of the individual." Some young men having become "very competent in six weeks." The greater period being limited in 1871 to eight weeks.

Pupils in 1703 were not allowed to use revenue stores; all their books and other documents[9] with few exceptions were very probably purchased by them down to 1855, when the instructor's supervisor was ordered to make the necessary purchases and claim the cost

[1] 1703. [2] 1824. [3] P. Rep., 1836. [4] 1848. [5] G. O., 1835; Fees.
[6] 1778. [7] P. Rep., 1789. [8] P. Ret., 1849. [9] S., 1804.

under the head of "Stationery for Pupils;" but this mode of provision was shortly afterwards superseded by the issue of books from the chief office. The various codes of instructions were supplied as early as 1824, though the distillery instructions in England were withheld in 1841. The gauging instruments, hitherto to some a considerable outlay, were also supplied in 1852 free of charge on the completion of instructions[1]—in 1871 in a neat leathern case impressed with the royal arms—but in 1874 under modified regulations.

Official competency having been shown in the preparation of these documents, in the use of these instructions, and in sufficient knowledge of departmental practice, to the satisfaction of the supervisor, a second certificate was prepared, which formerly, on transmission to the chief office, contained a fee of sixpence "under the seal" for the correspondent.[2] The books and other documents were sent to the Board at the pupil's expense.[3] At this stage, too, the pupil was required to take the oaths of allegiance, supremacy, and office; after these the sacrament in the presence of two witnesses, on whom it was not only incumbent to bear testimony to the signatures of the minister and the churchwardens to the certificate, but also to accompany the candidate with it to the Court and witness the administration of the oaths of test and abjuration. The earliest form of the second certificate seen, contained only the certification as to the ability to charge the duties, cast out the gauges, and the likelihood to make a good officer; it was signed by both supervisor and officer.

"THE FORME OF A CERTIFICATE.

"These are to certifye yor Hon^rs^ that Mr A. B. of C. in the County of D, aged — years is instructed pursuant to your Hono^rs^ order bearing date the —— day of —— 1721 and is qualifyed for surveying C.B^rs^ V^rs^ Distillers Malsters—Chandlers &c., that he can cast up Excise and Malt Gages both by Pen and Rule that he hath taken Gages and Stocked for a month in —— Division and entred his Surveys in Books by him prepaired for that purpose and from thence has made true Vouchers and Abstracts, is provided with proper Instrum^ts^ and Instructions and is in every respect well qualifyed for the Employm^t^ of a Gager.

Supervisor.
Officer.

"He proposes for his Securities when Employed A. B. of C. near

[1] S. [2] 1797. [3] 1743.

D. (the next markett Town) in the County of —— Gent., and F. G. of H. near I., in the County of —— Malster."

A more precise form followed in 1804, and embodied :—

The date of the order for instructions.
That he is well skilled in dry gauging.
That he could cast gauges by pen and sliding rule.
That he had surveyed, gauged, and stocked for six weeks, and entered the particulars in books prepared by him.
That he had made true vouchers and abstracts.
That he is in all respects qualified for a gauger's employment.
That he is furnished with proper gauging instruments.
That he had paid for his instructions and examination, and for his board and lodgings during the time of his instruction; and
That he has money sufficient to purchase a horse for his business.

The pupil remaining on survey with his instructor until his services were required. But the supervisor was not to grant this certificate at his "peril" until he had several times surveyed with the candidate —a regulation introduced in 1740. It was then signed by the supervisor, the instructor, and the instructee; by the two former, if inaccurate, under censure of reduction and suspension respectively, and forfeiture of fees.[1] The certification of the ability to purchase a horse was withdrawn in 1824, when a third form was ordered which embraced a detail of the various "traders" he could survey and the fact that he possessed proper instructions. In 1848 a fourth revision was made, with an order to send the certificate through the collector, who was enjoined to also examine the aspirant, and, if qualified, to subscribe the fact and sign the certificate. In 1855 a fifth revision took place; in this no important change is noticeable. In 1871 a sixth revision was carried through. "Second Certificate," and "May it please your Honours" were deleted, and only "Certificate of Instructions" employed, while the facts certified, except that Excise was substituted for Inland Revenue, and the mode of certification, were essentially the same. This revision included an important concession, which allowed the payment of salary at the rate of £60 per annum, from the day, inclusive, on which instruction began.

[1] S., 1804.

The commission, to this date, had been given without further test; now, as previously penned in the earlier part of this paper, a period of probation of six months from the date of the commission was exacted, and until this had been certified the "certificate of qualifications" was withheld by the Civil Service Commissioners, though they soon afterwards granted it on the successful completion of the pupilage, leaving the "final certificate" to be drawn out by the collector.

Remuneration to the instructors for the energy expended in this duty is recorded as early as 1704, and there is little doubt but that it was borne by the recipient of the tuition down to 1856, when a new arrangement was made by which it was paid out of the public purse. The estimates of 1870 *et seq.* show a vote of £700.

CHRONOLOGICAL TABLE OF FEES.

Rank.	Authority and Date.						
	General Letter 1704.	Lead-better. 1743.	Country Instructions. 1778.	London Instructions. 1781.	Scotch Instructions. 1804.	Ireland: Parl. Report. 1807.	Instructions. 1856.
Inspector-General.	...	...	...	...	...	21/	...
Supervisor . . .	20/	20/	20/	...	20/	...	20/
Surveyor or General	...	...	...	10/6	...	...	...
Surveyor	...	...	...	...	...	21/	...
Officer.	40/	...	[1]40/	21/	[1]50/	Chief 21/ Others 10/6	40/

It has been suggested that one or more officers should be retained to instruct, and be granted a fee of £5, and the supervisor a fee of £2;[2] also, that the period should be extended to two months, that the final examination should be defined by a Board's order framed and conducted by a first-class Surveying General Examiner, that the teacher and taught should receive fees in proportion to the number of marks obtained, a given number being reached before the final certificate be granted.[3]

Pupil farming has been defined to be the instruction of pupils by

[1] Half on commencement, half on termination. [2] C. S. G., 1859.

[3] Idem, 1867.

other than the appointed officer, the nominal instructor receiving the fees and handing them over to the actual instructor.[1] Pupils in official slang are termed "pups."[2]

CANDLE DUTY.

"If we light up a candle it is all the same,
Our friend Billy Pitt is with us again."

Royal Library, British Museum.

Imposed in Great Britain on May 1, 1710. The maker of candles was at first restricted to certain statute hours for working, which varied according to the time of the year, and was obliged to make a declaration of the particular number of sticks and hoops, the number of candles to be made on each, and the time of commencing to make them; an entry was made of the places and utensils every six weeks; within the bills of mortality to an official who also administered the "Oaths, and Affirmations for verifying the same." Three commissioners were specially appointed soon after the imposition to manage, and a receiver to receive, these duties with those on paper. To return to the maker: in 1787 he was required to provide covers and fastenings to his utensils, and to give a certain number of hours' notice, which varied according to the situation of the premises, to have them unlocked by the officer. Before this date the officer surveyed the premises in residence once in six hours, when at work, and twice a day when silent; afterwards, daily, and continued to do so, after the repeal of the duty, as a protection to that on soap, until its repeal in 1853. The modes of charge. The number of cubic inches of tallow having been found, were divided by 30·28 the number of cubic inches of tallow in a pound, and the quotient set forward as the charge; or by weight at the rate of 108 lbs. per 112 lbs. found by the factor ·964 itself in turn found thus—112 : 1 :: 108 : ·964.[6] Both modes having been subsequently modified. The duty payable, weekly and roundly, regulated by the place of business, consisted of a levy of one-half penny per pound on tallow, and fourpence per pound on wax candles,[7] and was doubled the following year,[8] and after some few changes in the rates, with the licence duty imposed on the makers and vendors by Mr Pitt in 1784, was repealed

[1] C., 1873. [2] Liverpool. [3] S. 1804. [4] L. G., 1710. [5] Idem, 1714.
[6] Leadbetter's Royal Gauger. [7] 8 Anne, c. 9. [8] 9 Anne, c. 6.

in 1832. These duties were payable on importation, and repayable on exportation, and compounded for with private families at 1s. per head for candles made by them for their own use.

The repeal. A petition was presented to Parliament in 1831, when the repeal of the licence duty was imminent, to continue it, and after it was repealed, the Parnell Committee, who sat in 1836, recommended its reimposition.[1] The abolition of the poundage duty was first moved by Mr Sykes in 1825, but negatived.[2] This motion was followed by the presentation of four petitions for its repeal in 1830, and another in 1831, the unsuccessful proposal of Lord Althorp in 1831 to reduce it, and finally, the adopted proposition of the Chancellor of the Exchequer on July 1, 1831, to repeal it on Jan. 1, 1832. The treasury permitted the manufacture of wax candles, without the payment of duty, after Oct. 10, 1831. Amount of licence duty repealed, £6500; poundage, gross, £477,000, net £470,000.[3]

CANTEEN LICENCE DUTY.

Though at first applied to the sale of beer, spirits, and wine to soldiers in barracks, it was afterwards extended to the Irish Constabulary.[4] In 1845 there were no fewer than 111 in the various barracks in the United Kingdom, and the rents paid to Government varied from £1 to £1343.[5] In 1848 a promise was made to a Colonel Friday, "that on the expiration of the present licences for the sale of spirits in canteens, no spirituous liquors should be afterwards sold in canteens in barracks."[6] This promise was kept; the sale being afterwards restricted to beer and wine at the usual licence rates, except at the higher rate for beer, where spirits are not sold. This licence may be granted at any time of the year.[7] It is not now required at a military canteen conducted on the "regimental system."[8]

CARRIAGE LICENCE DUTY.

The tax on locomotives moved on wheels by animal power dates back to 1747. It was then an assessed tax, and so remained down to 1870, when it was commuted into an excise licence duty, on the

[1] 19 R. [2] H. C., June 7. [3] C. 1 R. [4] 1874. [5] P. Ret., 1846. [6] H. C., Feb. 8. [7] 1863, C. 13 R. [8] 1878.

motion of Mr Lowe in his Budget on April 8, 1869. Between these two dates many fiscal changes were made and proposed.

The principles adopted by the various financiers were these—

The number of wheels.

The formation—number of bodies, kind of spring, no spring at all, diameter of wheel.

The use—hire, sale, stage coaching, common carrying, husbandry.

The number used—a limited progressive duty.

The four-legged power employed—number, height, kind; whether ox or pony.

The weight.

The duty per vehicle too has varied from 2s. 6d. in 1834 to £12 in 1800.[1] Lord Cavendish proposed in 1783 to impose 1s. per wheel on waggons and carts, to assist in preventing the practice of smuggling, then so common and remunerative, by knowing to whom they belonged;[2] and in 1805 the Irish Chancellor of the Exchequer moved a tax on curricles and gigs, and 5s. on each jaunting car,[3] but it does not appear that either of these motions was carried, nor does a carriage licence duty appear to have been charged in Ireland.

The stricter enforcement under the licence system caused several inquiries to be made in the House of Commons as to the legality of some of them.[4] On another occasion a motion to be made for an exemption,[5] and later, a motion for repeal;[6] but both motions were withdrawn.

The result of this increased vigilance was that the total duty increased from—

£430,043 in 1870, to
£525,993 in 1872, to
£529,753 in 1874.[7]

The duty in the first year of which an account can be given, 1792, was £218,205.[8] Upwards of fifty cases decided by the judges will be found in Muir's "Stamp and Tax Office Manual," 1861.[9]

CASES.

"Cases relating to the Duties of Excise, and to the Jurisdiction of

[1] C. 1. & 13 R. [2] May 26. [3] March 13.
[4] May 19; June 22, 1870; July 20, 1871; March 31, 1874. [5] June 20, 1871.
[6] April 1, 1873. [7] C. 14, 15, and 17 R. [8] C. 1 R. [9] Blackwood.

Justices of Peace upon Informations laid before them for Offences against the Laws of Excise: And to the Jurisdiction of the Justices at the Quarter Sessions, relating to Appeals in Cases of the Duty upon Malt," 28 pp. 8vo. London. Name of neither author nor publisher given.

CENSURES.

This generic term includes in the order of severity, or in the language of the *North Briton*, "gradation of censure"—caution, admonition, reprimand, suspension, removal, reduction, and dismissal; and the issue of these respective forms has been made on different principles—life-long (official), brief period, cumulation, degradation.

The caution has partaken of a twofold character—verbal and recorded; three were formerly considered equal to one admonition,[1] while in 1859, unless three "recorded cautions" were issued in one year, the degree of censure attachable to an admonition was not incurred.

The admonition, or "admonishment," was early distinguished as the simple or the sharp "with certification," and issued on the committal of a "trivial fault;"[2] and when six had been certified, as none were "wiped off," a reprimand was registered,[3] but one admonition was not considered a censure on the examination of character for promotion.[4] Later, two were equal to a reprimand;[5] and later still, one remained in force one year, during which a petition for promotion could not be entertained, nor, if issued after recorded, could the petition be considered until the expiration of that period.

The reprimand early signified the mark of disapprobation for the "more serious offence;" this, too, was either simple or sharp "with certification, three being equal to a suspension."[2] Each reprimand delayed promotion six months;[4] three necessitated the presentation of the diary to the Board;[5] later, its force was restricted to two years, with delay in promotion after the manner stated under admonition.

The suspension carried with it loss of salary for such time as the Board thought fit, and two were equal to a discharge.[2] Each suspension retarded promotion twelve months.[4]

The removal, the reduction or "reducement,"[6] or the dismissal or the "discharge" has always been the award of demerit incurred on

[1] 1854. [2] S., 1804. [3] S., 1806. [4] S., 1815. [5] 1830. [6] 1778.

the aggregate of a number of the above censures or on the committal of some almost unpardonable misdeed, though in the case of a discharge a petition for restoration was entertained in 1804, if presented within three months of dismissal, while in 1863 dismissal was not minuted except with the consent of three commissioners.[1] Misdeeds of the deepest dye have been censured by imprisonment or transportation; but these have not been numerous, and have always been adjudged by another authority.[2]

Censures, with the exception of verbal cautions, appear to have been delivered by copy [3] by the collector, who caused the delivery to be noted in the proper diary and the receipt to be acknowledged by the recipient, who inserted his initials, though latterly a written receipt has been given and inserted in the abstract of the diary. A scheme for entering censures was first entered on the back of the abstract of the diary in 1795. In 1839 the issue of more than one censure at the same time occasioned the official character to be specially laid before the Board. In 1863, in the case of assistants under censure, order was given to postpone their promotion for three months to enable the proper collector to report upon their character and conduct. In 1864 order was also made in the case of an officer removing, who may be entitled to an increase of salary, but against whom a censure remained on record, that the particulars of the disapprobative record should be sent to his new collector. In 1804 a somewhat curious custom obtained in Scotland: a copy of a "reducement" or a "discharge" was given to the successor, that he might see the faults for which his predecessor had suffered. In 1848 these extreme punishments were ordered to be carried out immediately.

A departmental register of names, alphabetically arranged, against whom censures were recorded, was in use as early as, if not earlier than, 1740. The character of a discharged officer was not allowed to be given as early as 1732.

CHARACTER DEPARTMENT.

Though not under this identical name has it been known in all three countries, perhaps, but still such a department has existed in them. In Scotland, even in 1707, a clerk of the diaries was appointed,[4] and in the time of Burns reference is made to a character

[1] P. Rep.
[2] 1815, 1834, 1837, 1842, 1844, 1851, 1855.
[3] 1859.
[4] Letters Patent, May 22, 1707.

book. In Ireland in 1807 it consisted of a "principal," an assistant, and a clerk, with a list of sixteen examiners, "many of whom are dead, infirm, and incapable of discharging any duty," yet "short charges" were frequently discovered, but the amounts were seldom recovered. The salary of the "principal" was £300, with about thirty guineas per annum from the sale of old books.[1]

In England as early as 1705 there was a clerk for examining "supervisors' diaries," and about sixteen examiners for examining officers' books.[2] In 1779 there were a clerk and an assistant clerk for examining supervisors' diaries, and a legion of chief and other examiners designated, as was early the custom, by the names of the duties over which they exercised the function of examination. Here, to take a long leap, the idea of a principal and an assistant existed, as in the modern department of 1878, while of course, in this jump, the number of examiners has fluctuated with the exigencies of the service, never, perhaps, greater than in the time of William Pitt. The principalship is now a staff appointment. The hours of attendance in this office in 1844 were from 8 A.M. till 3 P.M.; in 1846 some few remained until 5 P.M. occasionally; in 1850 from 9 A.M. till 4 P.M.; and from December 22, 1851, from 10 A.M. till 4 P.M. The records date back to 1740. The characters of officers from that date to 1871 fill no fewer than 65 folio volumes, and those of supervisors, from 1799 to 1871, 21. A few extracts by Mr Macfadzean, from a character book prepared under the Board of Excise in Scotland, will be interesting:—"For instance, it was recorded of one that 'he was once a good officer, but now tipples;' another was 'a trifling officer—drinks;' whilst a third was put in the pillory as a 'drunken creature.' To these may be added, 'a lazy supervisor, much given to his bottle;' and 'a middling officer, who likes a glass.' The same merciless vein of plain speaking runs through the register on almost every weakness to which flesh is heir. An amiable enthusiast had 'a bee in his bonnet;' and a certain Highlander, who must have been very unlike his kin, had a 'bad moral character.' There was a 'conceited, trifling officer;' another, who was 'slow, needs spurring;' and there was also a 'good officer, but insolent,' as well as a 'gentleman and a scholar.' An Ayrshire gentleman was 'self-opinionative;' whilst an Aberdonian of a practical turn of mind had 'a farm and attended to it more than to the revenue;' and, as if to show that selfishness was not confined to our friends in the north, it was re-

[1] P. Rep. [2] P. Ret.

corded of a Lowlander that he was 'active, and much for his own interests.'

CHARITY FUND.

This fund was raised and applied in all three countries. In Ireland the deduction was made at sixpence in the pound.[1] In 1834 it was customary for an officer who crossed the Channel to have the claim exacted by his new collector.

In Scotland it was founded on the authority of a Treasury Warrant, dated June 19, 1724, by which the commissioners were authorised to deduct threepence in the pound from the salaries of collectors, supervisors, and officers, to form a fund or charity for the relief of the "superannuated or worn-out inferior officers," and such as might be disabled for active service. To 1809,[2] even, such as had been discharged received the charity. The deduction was made quarterly and remitted to the "Bank of Charity," under the management of the Board, who exacted an oath from the applicant that he had served so many years; that he had no estate, employment, or income, of a certain value; that he had not so many hundreds in cash, before he was "put on," or "permitted to partake of the charity." The annuities were variable, and granted on the principle of class or rank.

1743. £25, Collector, E.
1800. £50, " "
1804. £30, " General Supervisor and Surveyor, S.
1743. £20, Supervisor, E.
1800. £35, London Supervisor.
1800. £30, Country " E.
1804. £20, General Examiner, Supervisor, Surveyor, S.
1743. £20, Clerk, E.
1804. £16, Examiner, if 15 years' service, } S.
£12, " " 12 " " } S.
£8, " " 8 " " } S.
1743. £10, Gauger, E.
1800. £22, London Principal.
£17, Others, E.
1804. £12, or £8, dependent upon character and behaviour, S.
1810. £34, Country Officers, E.

[1] P. Rep. Fees, 1809. [2] General Letter.

1800. £15, Assistants, E.
1804. £12, or £8, Assistants, S.

The annuities in Scotland were given only on condition that the collector, supervisor, examiner, or officer and assistant, had not a private income of £30, or £400 in cash, £20 or £300, and £16 or £200 respectively, and were payable half-yearly.[1] The amount annually raised in England was about £1500.[2] The accumulated fund of the Scotch Excise Charity alone, at the time of the transfer, was about £15,000, and the total sum accrued in Great Britain by increase of income over payment to the discontinuance of the deduction on Dec. 10, 1811, and to the transfer to the Consolidated Fund by 52 Geo. III. c. 82 in 1812, was—Customs and Excise Charity and Superannuation Funds—no less than £334,236.[3]

Provision was made in this Act that the Lords of the Treasury, or any three of them, might grant to any officer in England or Scotland, who had been employed seven, but not fewer than ten years, from whose salary deductions had been made for a period of seven years, and who had become incapable, a pension not exceeding one-third of the salary and emoluments of his office. *See* Superannuation.

The estimates show, under the head of Non-effective Charges, the relief afforded by the Irish funds. In 1858 the number was 111, receiving £668; in 1876, 9, £56.

CHECK BOOK.

This book, technically known as "The Check," was the supervisor's general account and survey book for very many years, and each was current one year:[4] a period of six weeks being allowed to complete the transfer of the particulars from book to book,[5] from which it will be inferred the transfer was indeed a task, a task at one time performed by the officer until officially forbidden in 1773.

Its use was continued with probably private murmurs, until a little after the introduction of a class newspaper, when it was publicly and correctly described as the "large quarto volume of obscure names;"[6] "the old-fashioned huge check-book with the hard parchment and millboard covers;"[7] "the brass-mounted

[1] Scotch Instructions, 1804. [2] Royal Gauger, 1740. [3] Lord Naas, 1857.
[4] S., 1804, 1826. [5] 1861. [6] C. S. G., 1856. [7] Idem, 1857.

volume bound in stiff bands and vellum;" the "antiquated, half-useless, and cumbrous quarto;" and when it was suggested that it should be reduced in size;[1] be replaced by one "light and limp;" be used on survey only; be divided into two books—an account-book and a survey book; be abolished.[2] These plaintive and suggestive statements secured the issue of a new book in 1861, and a second new book in 1864, when from ten to twenty accounts were transferred to the "Store and General Register," while its use was discontinued in those collecting districts in which a survey book was required. In 1868 the long lists of traders were transferred to a "Trader's Register," and "The Check" became a completed historical fact on Sept. 30.

CHICORY DUTY.

Foreign chicory appears to have been first chargeable on importation. In 1833, 1834, 1835, customs duties were imposed until they equalled that on colonial coffee, with which it entered into keen competition;[3] but these were soon evaded by the growth and preparation of the root in England, where, in the counties of Essex, Lincoln, Norfolk, Northampton, and York, it became a very profitable production, until an excise duty was levied upon it and its substitutes on—

			£	s.	d.	
	August 28, 1860,	at	0	3	0	per cwt., and
From	March 31, 1861,	„	0	5	6	„
„	June 12, 1861,	„	0	8	6	„
„	April 1, 1862,	„	0	11	0	„
„	January 8, 1863,	„	1	1	9	„
„	April 1, 1864,	„	1	4	3	„
„	May 11, 1872,	„	0	12	1	„

the reduction being due to a reduction, in the same ratio, of the customs import duty on coffee. Every dryer or roaster is required to make entry of his premises for drying and storing to be secured by revenue lock, and is charged according to the actual quantity delivered for consumption, with an allowance of 2 per cent. for waste while in stock. The largest quantity was charged in 1867.[4] Since that date it has been smaller and smaller, owing to the more

[1] Idem, 1857. [2] Idem, 1859. [3] H. C., March 19, 1849. [4] C. 13 R.

successful culture at a smaller cost in Belgium[1] and other continental countries.[2] This article, though chargeable in the United Kingdom, has never been charged except in England, and in 1873 in Yorkshire only.[3]

CHIEF OFFICE.

Known as the "Principal Head Office," the "Grand Office," the "General Office," it has occupied in London, owing to riot, fire, and fitness, several different sites.

The earliest traceable was in Smithfield, and burnt down in a riot in 1646. The next in "Broade Streat," as shown by Fairfax—"Gentlemen, Whereas upon the 8th of December a party of horse and foot came to the Excise Office in Broad Street. . . . Your very assured friend, Fairfax. For my worthy friends the Commissioners of Excise and New Impost." December 8, 1648.[4] Here it was continued until burnt down by the great fire, and then "The Grand Office" was removed to "Southampton-fields, near the House of the Right Honourable the Lord High Treasurer of England," though it appears to have been the intention to have removed it to Bartholomew Lane.[5] As this was only a temporary arrangement, it was afterwards translocated to Aldersgate Street,[6] and shortly afterwards again to Broad Street,[7] where it remained[8] until October 6, 1703, when it was opened in the Old Jewry in Cheapside,[9] where it was kept until the building became too small and dangerous and the lease about to expire,[10] and a successful effort was made to obtain more suitable premises. "On the 17th March (1767) the city members, attended by Mr Dance, the surveyor, waited on the Lords of the Treasury with a plan of the ground on which Gresham College stood, for the purpose of pulling down the old building and erecting an Excise Office in its stead. At a court of common council held on the 22d of May, it was resolved to agree with the proposal of the Government for the purchase." The proposed site was accordingly obtained of the Corporation of London and the Company of Mercers, "for the purchase of the fee-simple in consideration of a perpetual annuity of £500 from Michaelmas day 1768 for ever, quarterly, clear of taxes." The

[1] C. 15 R. [2] C. 18 R. [3] C. 17 R. [4] The Moderate, 1648.
[5] Green's State Papers, 1660, 1666. [6] L. G., 1668.
[7] Idem, 1676. [8] Idem, 1677, 1680, 1697. [9] Idem, 1703.
[10] October 10, 1770.

purchase was confirmed by 8 Geo. III., c. 32. The new building was occupied in 1772, as shown by the London Gazette, by the Commissioners being "At their Court Room, Excise Office, Old Broad Street," though both Haydn and Townsend chronicle that it was built in 1774, and it is thus described by a city historian—"On the east side of this street (Broad Street) stands the Excise Office, a handsome plain stone building of four stories in height, with an entrance through the middle of it into a large yard, in which is another building of brick nearly the size of the principal one. The front building stands on the site of ten alms-houses founded by Sir Thomas Gresham in 1575, and the back one with the yard occupies the space on which Gresham College formerly stood."[1] On this spot it remained until 1852, when Parliamentary powers were procured to effect the sale of the structure and authorise the provision of better accommodation[2] in Somerset House, which, as early as 1775, was vested in His Majesty for the purpose of erecting and establishing certain public offices,"[3] a vote of £10,000 being passed to render Buckingham House convenient for a royal palace in return for His Majesty's palace of Somerset House. This bill was "silently passed."[4] The Old Broad Street office realised £136,044; the preparation of the Somerset House office cost £105,472.[5] Somerset House was first occupied about October 1852, and a new wing added in 1856.

Engravings 1473, 1474, 1520, and 1671 in "Knight's Pictorial History of England" afford views of it at different periods. It is known among the officials as the "Elysian Fields, Strand,"[6] but more familiarly as the cottage or the big house.

The hours of attendance at the chief office were formerly both early and long—from 8 A.M. till noon, from 2 P.M. till 5 P.M.[7]

The chief office in Edinburgh was in the "Cowgate" in 1753,[8] afterwards in Drummond Place[9] and Canongate.

CIDER DUTY.

A duty appears to have been first imposed on "Syder," which included perry, for three years, during the Commonwealth,[10] and

[1] Lambert's History of London; Highmore's Excise Laws; Haydn's Dates, 1866; Townsend's Dates, 1867.

[2] Bills, dated May 20, 1852; Feb. 24, 1853. [3] H. C., April 26, 1775.

[4] H. C., April 28, 1775. [5] P. Ret., 1862. [6] C., 1871.

[7] 12 Charles II., c. 23. [8] Maitland's History of Edinburgh.

[9] Anderson's History of Edinburgh. [10] P. O., 1643.

continued on the restoration of Charles II. down to 1763, when a very animated debate took place in the Houses of Parliament on two propositions—one, to lay an additional duty on the retailer, the other, to lay the aggregate duty on the first buyer; and as these were not accepted, a third, to lay a duty of 4s. per hogshead on the grower. In the course of the discussion Mr Pitt stated his disapproval of the introduction of the excise laws into "the domestic concerns;" "every man's house is his castle;" to which Mr Grenville replied with strong emphasis, "Tell me where you can lay another tax?" and Mr Pitt to that, in a musical tone, "Gentle shepherd, tell me where?" The principal arguments urged in favour of the duty were these—that there had been for many years a considerable duty on malt, which had been lately increased; that the inhabitants of the cider counties, and those who had opportunities of buying immediately of the "grower," drank cider and perry, as the substitute of malt liquor, without paying any duty at all; and that there was a very high tax on beer and a very low one on cider.[1] During the progress of the measure petitions were presented against, and the House of Lords voted upon it, being the first money bill upon which their lordships were ever known to have divided—cons 83, non-cons 49.[2]

The bill passed, under written dissent, in a modified form, in that the duty should be charged on the vendor only. It was always a very distasteful tax; even the commissioners themselves cautioned the officers—whom, it may be remarked, were occasional, and instructed by the established, officers—against "imprudently demanding entrance." The following year a Bill was brought in to reduce the composition duty and extend the period of credit from six weeks to six months;[3] and a motion was subsequently made to repeal the duty; with a result of 264 noes and 115 yeas;[4] while in the interval one of the Sheriffs of London was admitted to the bar of the Commons to present a petition to repeal it,[5] the Devonshire people issued a pamphlet entitled "The Case of the County of Devon . . "[6] and a very able writer produced a paper on "The Right of Appeal to Juries in Causes of Excise asserted," in apprehension of a general excise extending "to every private house," as distinguished from "excise limited to the trader." Petitions were also presented against it in 1766,[7] but its repeal was not effected until the beer duty ceased,

[1] March 8, 1763. [2] March 28, 1763. [3] Feb. 8, 1764.
[4] Feb. 10, 1764. [5] Sept. 23, 1763. [6] L. G., 1763. [7] Cobbett.

and the beer trade was "thrown open," in 1830, and even then in so far only as concerned the reigning monarch, as, the duty being hereditary, it was not an absolute repeal, simply an abeyance or suspension, subject to revival or reimposition on the decease of His Majesty, which occurred in 1837, when an order was issued by the Commissioners to charge it, but on the succeeding day, by order of the Lords of the Treasury, to only charge it until the pleasure of Parliament should be made known. It was not paid.

The duty was fixed in 1660 at fifteenpence per hogshead, increased by addition to addition by seven Acts, to thirty shillings in 1818, payable monthly,[1] at which it appears to have remained until 1826, when it was charged at twopence-halfpenny per gallon.[2] In Scotland a duty of four shillings per hogshead was chargeable, above that paid by the retailer, for one year—1730. Private families were early allowed to compound; in 1764 at half-a-crown a head. And the duty chargeable in London and its vicinity was announced in 1680 to be let to farm.[3] Cider imported from foreign parts was charged in 1660 a crown a tun; in 1724 at £12, 10s., the total imposition of four Acts;[4] in 1818 seventeen guineas per barrel; from Ireland less; into Scotland, ten shillings per barrel for one year—1730. It was also allowed to be exported on the repayment of the duty less threepence per tun for "the officers' charges,"[4] and afterwards on the repayment of the whole duty.[1]

The licence duty payable to retail was for some time the same as that to retail beer;[1] but on the repeal of the duty on cider, a new rate at one guinea was introduced, and increased by five per cent. in 1840. 1900 licences were issued in 1835; 300 in 1864.[5] The amount of duty given up on repeal, £25,000.[2]

CIPHER.

The use of the "Cypher" is traceable in matters excise to 1644, when it was employed very freely, thus, the duty on a "half Bever Hat" was shown—"00· 12·00."[6] It was also in general use in decimal and common notation in 1766, two being used to represent an empty cask (00), one being placed before units, one after when no tenths, and two when under a unit, "when your columns will

[1] Huie's Laws. [2] C. 1 R. [3] L. G. [4] Collection Statutes, Edinburgh. [5] C. 13 R. [6] Act, Scotland.

admit of it; or there is room to alter your true gauge by preponing or postponing any figure:"[1] it was definitely ordered to be used in 1781,[2] the object being to prevent embezzlement and collusion.

CIRCUIT.

A term applied to the geographical extent or round of a commissionership in 1660; also a technical name applied to a portion of a farm.[3]

CIVILIAN.

This weekly paper, established on Saturday, Nov. 27, 1869, by an association, among whom was one member of the Inland Revenue Department, pleads the interests of the Civil Service in general, affords space for the official correspondent and querist, gives the weekly lists of movements in the various departments, and notes the chief features of the week.

With regard to this department in particular, it had received such general support by 1871, as to become a valuable source of information, so that the reader will find it largely quoted from that date throughout this work.

In 1874 it had sufficiently grown in favour to enable the proprietors to state that the outgrowth of necessity demanded that writers should declare that their communications had not been addressed to any other paper.

CIVIL LIST TAX.

A deduction of sixpence in £ on all salaries above £50.[4]

CIVIL SERVICE COMMISSION.

Also called the Playfair Commission.

As early as March 23, 1874, the Chancellor of the Exchequer stated, in reply to Sir J. Lawrence respecting the Civil Service

[1] Leadbetter, 1766. [2] London Instructions, 1781. [3] 16 and 17 Car. II., c. 4.
[4] P. Ret., 1780; Scotch Instructions, 1804.

Writers, that the Treasury hoped to institute an inquiry "also into cognate questions of equal importance to the Civil Service." The cognate questions were three of these four—

1st. The method of selecting civil servants in the first instance.

2d. The principles upon which men should be transferred from office to office, especially in cases where one establishment has been abolished or reduced in numbers, and where there are consequently redundant employés whose services should, if possible, be made available in other departments.

3d. The possibility of grading the Civil Service as a whole, so as to obviate the inconveniences which result from the differences of pay in different departments.

4th. The system under which it is desirable to employ writers or other persons for the discharge of duties of less importance than those usually assigned to established clerks, or duties of a purely temporary character.

The committee consisted of eight gentlemen, and included Dr Lyon Playfair as chairman, and Sir W. H. Stephenson, K.C.B., chairman of this department. The authority of the Treasury is dated April 27, 1874.

This inquiry may be stated to have originated with the "Pro Rata Increase of Salaries Committee," formed in 1872, which see under Salary. The result of the inquiry is embodied in three reports, of which the last affords the chief interest to this department, and further reference will be found in this series of papers.

Punch observed, "What the Civil Service wants is less of Playfair and more of fair play."

CIVIL SERVICE ESTATE AND COLONY, THE.

A projected emigration scheme for needy civil servants, by Charles Edwards of the Inland Revenue. The project was not acted upon.[1]

CIVIL SERVICE GAZETTE.

This "Journal" was first issued on Saturday, January 1, 1853, under the editorship of William Downing Bruce, Esq., of Lincoln's-

[1] C., 1873.

Inn, Barrister-at-Law. Its title so clearly indicates its scope and object that one extract from the prospectus or announcement of its publication will be sufficient:—"It is a fact, though not as yet sufficiently notorious, that the most incapable are promoted through interest, the most able and meritorious neglected from the want of it; the golden sinecures are held by the wealthy, while a miserable stipend is often the sole reward of the toilsome labours of the indigent. . . . . On the grounds, then, with uncompromising boldness, but with due courtesy of language, with no respect of persons, yet without private prejudice, by a wide collation of facts, a fair use of argument, will urge the existing Administration, whether Whig or Tory, the necessity, not of those petty curtailments of salary which, in the words of Macaulay, 'bring on Government the reproach of meanness, without producing any perceptible relief to the finances,' but of such an equitable adjustment of official income and such a wise expenditure of the revenue as may conduce no less to the public interest than to private welfare of the public servant. With these objects in view, the proprietors of the Civil Service Gazette invite the attention of all classes of the community to their projected journal, and earnestly ask the co-operation of that class to whose cause it is especially devoted."

Until the appearance of this issue this department, though it at first supported the paper with some hesitancy, under an impression that such support would be viewed as an act of insubordination, may be considered to have had no special reliable organ through which it could make known its desires: yet so ably, if not at all times discreetly, were the various interests advocated, that the Service at large, in 1855, only two years after its introduction, expressed its sense of appreciation by subscribing for a pictorial mark of esteem to its literary benefactor. The subscription originated with Mr C. P. Measor, who wrote, "The claims of the Civil Service have been so ably advocated by the Civil Service Gazette; its reputation is now firmly established, and it has become the recognised organ of Government officers, as is evidenced by the quotations which are constantly made from its columns in all the leading journals. To the untiring energy and ability of William Downing Bruce, Esq., of Lincoln's-Inn, Barrister-at-law, the success is wholly due," and, observed the editor, "It was suggested in the same circular, that the form of testimonial should be a full-length portrait of Mr Bruce, to be exhibited he Royal Academy, and presented to himself." It is rather remarkable that the task of executing this portrait fell to Mr Walter Measor, the brother of Mr Charles Measor, who is not an artist, but a clerk in the Customs. The portrait was not exhibited, but was, as might be expected, refused admittance into the Academy. . . . . The same artist appears to have been appointed by his brother as the recipient of the moneys accruing from the subscription. And in the latest circular, telling the subscribers the funds are as yet inadequate for the attainment of the object contemplated, Mr Charles P. Measor appends the following—"All communications to be addressed to me as before, No. 2 Great Coram Street, Russell Square, London"—the address of Mr Walter Measor. The doubling of parts by this gentleman, as clerk in the Customs, Portrait Painter, and collector of Mr Charles P. Measor's subscriptions, under favour of Mr Bruce's name, is extraordinary. . . . . We proceed with the statement of facts. In Mr Charles P. Measor's last circular . . . . "statement—

Subscriptions received by Mr Measor . . .	£41	7	0	Artist's account for full length portrait . .	£63	0	0
Ditto by Mr Bruce . .	8	10	0	Frame for ditto . .	12	12	0
Balance due . . .	36	8	5	Printing circulars, &c. .	10	13	5
	£86	5	5		£86	5	5"

Mr Bruce then observed that the amount set down as having been received by him "is over-stated," that "our subscribers will have received a circular from the editor; and after this explanation we trust that they will see that, for the interest of the Civil Service, it is their duty to co-operate with him in punishing persons who have used our name and their money." This article was followed by an exposé of the alleged delinquency of the "self-elected president, treasurer, secretary, and committee, Mr Measor," in which he was charged with an embezzlement to the extent of 30 per cent., and was offered the use of the columns for an exculpatory statement. Mr Measor did not accept this offer, and how this matter of accountancy was settled the columns fail to show, except that a request was made by the editor that Thomas T. Bisgood, Esq., the "treasurer," should be authorised to act. Mr Bruce's successor, for he had now retired from the editorship, wrote a "disclaimer of any participation in the charges made against the Messrs Measor," in which he announced they were inserted in the columns of the *Gazette* without either sanction or knowledge of the proprietors.

The new editor was J. Bolger, Esq., also a barrister-at-law, who, having acquitted himself to the satisfaction of this department in particular, in connection with the successful advocacy of the discontinuance of the periodical removes, and of an increase of salary, was presented in 1858 with a monetary testimonial of £456, under the title of "The Excise Tribute." *See* Salary, 1858.

Not only has the *Civil Service Gazette* been supported by purchase for the use of the officials themselves, but also in times of eager agitation, when a sense of right has underlain the foundation of a movement, copies have been purchased for distribution among those who could aid in obtaining a successful issue. This was known in 1866 and 1872 as the "M.P. Paper Fund."

The hesitancy, to which reference has already been made, is also shown in the correspondence. In 1853 about 13 letters were inserted; in 1854 about 105; in 1855 about 205; in 1869 no fewer than 475. The earliest correspondent appeared under the *nom* Scrutator, and that name was employed down to 1871. Others were:—

A Country Supervisor, . .	1854—1873
Fiat Justitia, ...	1854—1870
Fair Play, ...	1854—1874
Aristides, ...	1854—1873
Nemo, ...	1854—1868
Justice, ...	1854—1866
A. B., ...	1855—1873
Veritas, ...	1855—1871
Observer, ...	1855—1872
Omega, ...	1855—1871
Omicron, ...	1856—1871
Z., ...	1856—1874
Devonian, ...	1856—1867
Harold, ...	1856—1870
Amicus, ...	1857—1867
Beta, ...	1857—1871
J. B., ...	1857—1871

These dates show the periods of their correspondence, though they may extend in some instances later than that shown. Among the later writers may be mentioned:—

Humanitas, ...	1860

Verax, ...	1860
Saxon, ...	1863
Roderick Dru or Dhu, . . .	1863
Littlejohn, ...	1864
Hugh Littlejohn, ...	1867
Cosmopolitan, ...	1866
Fergus, ...	1866
W. E., ...	1867
H. O., ...	1871

The number of *noms de plume* used in 1870 was 249, and the number of letters inserted between 1853 and 1870 exceeded 3900. The amount of "The Excise Tribute," and the continued correspondence by probably the same individuals, show to some extent the value of the paper to this department in the earlier struggles for amelioration, but to a greater extent the numerous extracts which will be found in these papers.

About 1600 queries and replies were inserted down to 1874.

CIVIL SERVICE LIFE-BOAT.

The funds to purchase this life-boat were raised principally through the exertions of Messrs J. A. Dow and A. Goldsmith of the Admiralty in 1866.[1] The boat is named the "Civil Service," and stationed at or near Wexford, and of the 1418 half-crown Civil Service subscribers to the maintenance fund in 1874,[1] 124 belonged to this department.

CLARK'S BRITISH GAUGER.

"The British Gauger or Trader and Officer's Instructor, in the Royal Revenue of the Excise and Customs." In two parts. Part I. contains the "Rules of Vulgar and Decimal Arithmetic, and the whole art of Practical Gauging." Part II., "An Historical and Succinct Account of all the Laws relating to the Excise from the commencement thereof to the present time." By Samuel Clark, who inscribes his book to the "Honourable Commissioners and Governors" of Excise, and subscribes himself, "Their Honours

[1] C. S. G.

most obedient and most dutiful servant." Pages 450. Nourse, London. 1765.

COAL DUTY.

Coal, charcoal, and culm, were articles upon which Excise duties were levied in the seventeenth century.

In Scotland in 1643, an export duty was levied on coal which varied according to the vessel in which it was shipped—home or foreign;[1] in England in 1645, "charcold" was charged by the sack;[2] while both coal and culm were charged in 1695,[3] but all appear to have been repealed before 1784, as Mr Pitt then suggested to make coal a head of duty.[4]

COFFEE DUTY.

At first a licence duty—no person to be "permitted to sell or retaile any coffee, chocolate, sherbett, without Licence first obtained and had by Order of the Generall Session of the Peace . . . or the Chiefe Magistrate of the place . . . nor . . . until Securitie first given by Recognizance or otherwise, For which . . . Twelve pence shall be given and noe more for the payment of the excise:"[5] to the last, with a slight intermission, a licence duty—repealed in 1869. But between these dates. A duty of eighteen pence per liquid gallon, on the quantity sold, was next imposed, and announced to be let to farm in 1680,[6] and levied for some ten years when it proved very troublesome and gave way to a customs per cent. duty on importation, 1690. An "inland duty" was next exacted at so much per pound, and this made known through the medium of the London Gazette, in which the notice occupied rather more than two pages. Roasting houses were provided at the expense of the Crown for roasting berries, and those in London afforded employment to thirty-two persons—officers and others—whose duties consisted in receiving the raw berries to roast at a charge of eight, afterwards four shillings per cwt.[7] Packets of chocolate were impressed with a

[1] Convention of States, Feb. 10.
[2] Oxford, Oct. 11.
[3] 6 & 7 W. & M. c. 18.
[4] H. C., June 30.
[5] 15 C. II. c. 14.
[6] L. G.
[7] L. G., 1724, 1725.

duty stamp;[1] afterwards surmounted with a duty label;[2] cocoa paste packets were stamped; the premises of traders were surveyed;[3] roasting houses were provided in Edinburgh.[4] Drawback was allowed on chocolate on exportation.

This form of the duty attracted the attention of a member of Parliament, who, in 1784,[5] moved that it be commuted into an import duty to be collected by the Customs. His suggestion was acted upon in 1785, and increased by additions at different times;[6] it was re-transferred to the Excise in 1823,[7] and again transferred to the Customs in 1825.[8] The discontinuance of the inland duty and with it the surveillance of this department, for the most part, soon induced persons prompted by a greed of gain to imitate and sophisticate the genuine article by roasting wheat and other substances, and selling them under the name of "breakfast powder,"[9] and by mixing chicory and other substances, in some cases with the approval of the consumer, and selling the mixture as coffee. The wheat-roaster was proceeded against, and he appeared before the Barons of the Exchequer at Westminster to answer a contravention of the law, and ultimately petitioned the House of Commons on the ground of ignorance and poverty, against the penalty imposed.[10] His practice continued a few years,[9] when the House of Lords was asked to legislate on the subject.[11] The adulterator, on the other hand, was less easily detected, seeing that his was a mixture, not a separately-sold rival, and that the trade had been relieved of the obligation to receive into stock by permit,[12] and to permit the officer to inspect.[13] "Chiccoree or succory" was first allowed to be sold as such in 1822,[14] then mixed with coffee in 1840,[15] but the practice became so general, the profits so large, the fraud so great, and the growth of chicory in England so remunerative, that the practice engaged the attention of the consumer, the seller, and Parliament, until a duty was imposed on the home-grown article.

To give a chronological outline of the question:—In 1849 a duty was conditionally suggested on that grown in England.[16] A humourous inch-and-half-square sketch, "Chicory and Chisholm Anstey,"

[1] 1724. [2] 1760. [3] 1822. [4] Scotch Instructions, 1804.
[5] H. C., July 7. [6] 1796, 1803. [7] Order in Council.
[8] Parnell Com., 20th Report. [9] H. L., March 8, 1822; C., 4 R.
[10] Jan. 12, 1820. [11] March 27, 1822. [12] 1828.
[13] 1839. [14] T. W., Dec. 10.
[15] T. W., Aug. 6 and 25. [16] H. C., May 9.

appeared in *Punch*.[1] In 1851 petitions signed by 3682 persons were presented against, and others in favour of, the existing Treasury warrants, and a motion was made to withdraw them, with a result of 89 ayes, 94 noes.[2] In 1852 petitions were again presented to annul the warrants, when it transpired that no fewer than 5000 acres of chicory were under cultivation in England.[3] In 1853 the sale of the mixture was allowed on condition that each packet be labeled "Mixture of Chicory and Coffee."[4] In 1854 petitions were again presented against the adulteration; a Committee of the House of Lords to examine the subject was asked for but not granted.[5] A supervisor inadvertently wrote—"Caution to Grocers. . . . . Mr George So-and-So . . . . has been prosecuted by order of the Commissioners of Inland Revenue, and paid a penalty of £10, for having sold a mixture of chicory and coffee without the requisite label being attached to the package. By Order. . . . . Brentford, May 13, 1854." The reviewer thought it should have "Encouragement to the Fraudulent."[6] In 1858 a report was drawn up on the subject by Professor Graham, Dr Stenhouse, and Mr D. Campbell, and presented to the Commissioners.[7] In 1860, as suggested by the Chancellor of the Exchequer in 1849, an excise duty was imposed on home-grown chicory—*see* Chicory; and, in 1863, on the equalization of the chicory duty to that on coffee, the admixture of chicory with coffee was disregarded by this department. Imposed, 1663; transferred to the Customs, 1825; protected to 1863.

COFFEY'S PATENT STILL.

The inventor was Æneas Coffey, Inspector General of Excise in Ireland, who obtained a patent, No. 5974, dated August 5, 1833,[8] and afterwards became "extensively engaged as a practical distiller on his own account,"[9] though for two years after he had completed the apparatus it remained unused owing to the "exacting character of Mr Stodart."[10] Dawson of Linlithgow, in his "Rambling Recollections of Past Times," writes under 1866, "He"—Dr Liston—"along with Mr Stien, distiller, Kirkliston, invented a still, the

[1] Vol. 16. [2] H. C., June 5. [3] H. L., April 27.
[4] H. C., Feb. 24. [5] H. L., June 23. [6] Chambers' Journal.
[7] Journal Society of Arts. [8] Woodcroft.
[9] P. Rep., Parnell 7th, pt. 2, 1835. [10] P. Rep., Parnell 7th, pt. 1, 1834.

leading principles of which were adopted and patented by one Coffee." The first licence to use this still, for it must be borne in mind that "it was constructed otherwise than according to law," was granted to a distiller in Belfast on January 28, 1833,[1] and from that date down to 1850, when there were about 220 distillers in the United Kingdom,[2] only thirty others had been granted.[1] The regulations under which this and other patent or uncommon stills were first worked are contained in a General Order of 1839.[3] The principle of construction and mode of distillation are given in Loftus's "Inland Revenue Officers' Manual, 1856, and in the "Distillery Instructions," 1871.

COIN.

Owing to the depreciation in the value of silver the "Receivers of the Publick Aids, Taxes, and Revenue," were authorised, in 1698, to allow £1, 1s. 6d. for each guinea tendered,[4] and at a later period probably more than that. As, however, the public did not seem satisfied with this adjustment of value, or were in the habit of "sweating" the guinea, the collectors were instructed, in 1750, not to receive any lighter than 5 dwts. 3 grs., that being the lightest weight taken by "the Bank," the standard being 5 dwts. 9 grs.[5] On the recoinage of 1696, hammered silver was taken at 5s. 8d. per ounce.

With respect to base coin, the collectors were directed to deface them.[6]

Light gold the collectors were ordered, in 1842, to receive at £3, 17s. 10½d. per oz.; in 1843, to cut, deface, and return, agreeably to the Queen's Proclamation;[7] in 1849, to cut, and allow at the rate of 19s. 9d. for a sovereign, and 9s. 10d. for a half sovereign.

COLLECTOR.

This is one of the oldest of the excise designations, though long prior to the establishment of this department there were "Collectours," "coillours: coillo's,"[8] and "Under-Collectours," "south-

[1] P. Ret., 1851. [2] C., 1 R. [3] March 4. [4] L. G., 1698.
[5] Idem., 1750. [6] Hersee, 1777. [7] T. W., Oct. 14, 1843.
[8] Stowe's Annals, 1340; 7 Edw. VII. c. 1; 25 Edw. III. s. 2, c. 6.

coillo's,"[1] employed for a similar purpose to those to be considered. This official designation has been in use since 1621, when it was introduced in connection with an excise duty on wine, peculiar to Edinburgh, and has since been qualified in several ways,—as, general,[2] in contradistinction to particular collector; high,[3] "chiefe" head, in opposition to sub-collector; inland,[4] by way of distinction from port,[5] collector; country collector, to indicate employment in the country as distinct from the town or London establishment;[6] pro,[7] supernumerary,[8] acting, to express a substitute for the fixed or established collector;[9] and collector of Inland Revenue to denote the cumulative character of the office since the addition of the receipt of the stamp and tax duties, in supercession of collector of excise,[10] employed when only excise duties were collected, and since in matters excise pure; while embryo collector has been applied[11] to a hopeful aspirant to the grade, and Receiver suggested by the Central Committee of 1867. The appointment, originally, was direct,[12] or the appointee, in the language of Sir F. Doyle, was "taken from other walks of life,"[13] as exemplified in Ireland down to the Union at least, when the then collector of Dublin was a Member of Parliament; and it is probable the appointee was not required to pass through a number of grades until the office became in some measure administrative as well as collectorial; from that time the "collectorship"[14] has been within the reach of the commissioned officer of the lowest grade who has shown good conduct through the intermediate grades, and given ultimate proof of general ability, subject, of course, to number of vacancies to be filled, and to the approval of the Commissioners. Once attained, it has seldom been quitted, except on retirement, until a new principle of selection for the more important positions in the Chief Office was introduced and adopted in 1876, by which collectors who possessed special merits were made eligible to fill them. The Parnell Committee, too, proposed "one of the assistant commissioners to be selected from among the most experienced and most intelligent collectors,"[13] this, however, has not been adopted.

The duties of the collector at first, as previously stated, confined to the mere receipt and repayment of excise duties, have been ex-

[1] 14 Eliz. c. 8; 25 Edw. III. s. 7. [2] S., 1644. [3] 1 C. II. c. 5. [4] 1781, 1788. [5] 1789. [6] 1811. [7] 1808. [8] 1743, 1778, 1828. [9] 12 V. c. 1. [10] P. O., 1645. [11] 1871. [12] Order in Council, 1645. [13] Parnell Com., 20th Rep. [14] 1663.

tended to the collection of Crown and Quit Rents in Ireland, the stamp and tax duties; to the superintendence of a large staff of officials; to the payment of bounties, army and navy advances, and charity, compensation, superannuation, and commuted pension allowances, and salaries; and to the focalisation of accounts, in general, to about one-ninetieth part of the United Kingdom. Instances of loss by collectors are rare. If poesy may be trusted, under the title of "The crafty Miss, or an Exciseman well fitted," as found in the Roxburghe Ballads, an irrecoverable and unallowable loss of "fourscore pound" was sustained by a collector at Rochester.[2] And in 1774 a collector was relieved by the Treasury from an obligation which he had incurred by advancing a sum of £3600 on Bills of Exchequer drawn by parties who afterwards failed. In Scotland a collector was formerly not allowed to attend a place of worship in which His Majesty was not prayed for.[1]

The value of this official position in earlier times was fixed,[2] in later times variable by various emoluments, and by a division into classes—in 1829 into six, in 1858 into five, in 1870 into three, with an increase in value on each diminution of class—the advance from class to class being dependent on length of service, business aptitude, and official discretion. In Ireland, however, it was far different.[3]

COLLECTOR'S CLERK.

It may be desirable to first trace the efforts to obtain amelioration, and then to give an historical outline of the regulations.

It was not until 1853 that this grade, in common with others, possessed a special medium through which it could represent its desires, nor did it do so then; but in 1854 a desire was expressed that young ride officers should not be selected to fill this office: though the subject generally was more particularly opened with reference to the abolition of fees in 1838, and the transfer of the payment of the Chelsea Pensioner to the Staff Officers in 1846, by which it was stated that this grade had been deprived of an annual sum which had varied from £60 to £100 per clerk. But this was

[1] S., 1804. [2] P. Rep., Public Accounts, 1780; Leadbetter's Royal Gauger.
[3] P. Rep., Irish Accounts, 1809.

not all. A further cause of uneasiness arose in the statement of the fact that the clerks in London had received an increase of salary. The provincial clerks, as might be expected, were soon in communication with each other, and soon afterwards memorialised the Lords of the Treasury for a similar advance. The memorial was signed by eighty-two clerks in England, and duly forwarded to the Board with a request that it might be presented at Whitehall, but instead of this being granted, the memorialists were much surprised by receiving a reply that those who "were not satisfied with clerkships may return to the surveying branch." This occasioned a brief lull, but in 1855 they took up a common cause with others. In 1856 a desire was also expressed for a change of name to that of "Clerk of Inland Revenue"—a desire several times since repeated. Ever watchful for improvement of position, next came, in 1857, to act in the capacity of collector, in his absence, to save expense. In 1858 the claims in general were included in the "Statement" prepared and presented by the Dublin Committee, and the propriety of throwing open the clerkship to assistants was reviewed and conceded, and the necessity for doing so became apparent in 1859 and 1860. In 1861 hope was entertained that the status of the first clerk might be raised to the level of the supervisor, that of the second to that of the examiner. In 1862 fancy fixed upon the designation "First Accountant, Second Accountant," and emulation strove to secure "proper prospects of promotion" for those of distinguished competency. In 1863 the unsettled mind showed itself nearly the whole year. The appointment of the second-class assistant created a source of uneasiness, and the aspirations ran thus—the eligibility for promotion to the office of stamp distributor; the issue of a distinct commission, as "Clerk of Inland Revenue;" equality of pay to each class; the admission of only division officers into "the grade;" the discontinuance of "my clerk;" the liberty to petition for a clerkship of a similar class; and the eligibility for the assistant secretary's office. The correspondence may be stated to have been an improved "pay, prosperity, and position." A petition was accordingly presented on May 30, 1863, with no other result, however, than "the Board could not entertain our petition." The agitation was continued through the whole of 1864, and among the many suggestions made were, the use of "Provincial Clerk," "Accountant;" the less frequent appointment of the first-class assistant; the classification to consist of three classes, as at present, all the first class to be paid alike; the rank of the first class to be equal to that of the supervisor, the second to that of an examiner, the third to that of a division officer; the pay to be £220 by £10 to £250, £170 by £5 to £200, £120 by £5 to £150 respectively; the promotion from class to class in the order of seniority. Immediate action was not taken.

In 1865 the fitful correspondence extended over a period of nine months, in which little was narrated beyond that so frequently and plaintively urged in former years, except, perhaps, by two correspondents. One of these drew attention to the hardship on the return of a clerk on a salary of £140 to a division at a salary of £120; the other would not deprive the collector "of that only bit of patronage which is vested in him," and suggested that "no person should be appointed first clerk unless his period of service had reached from twelve to fifteen years."

In 1866 it was Excelsior who reintroduced the grievance of the grade. "Let a petition," wrote he, "be at once drawn up" and transmitted to Her Majesty's Ministers, and if unsuccessful, then seek the support of the Members of Parliament, and appeal to the House of Commons. This was in February. A goodly number of discussionists, among whom may be mentioned Cato, Tambourie 2, Cedrick, Alarmist, and Aristides, joined the movement, and the editor of the paper urged united action; the result being the transmission of a "General Petition," signed by 110 clerks on August 29, 1866. This fact was announced by advertisement.

In 1867 the claims still remained unconsidered. The question, however, was kept open by Eustace, Oxonian, Z, and others, while Hope offered a series of desirables—promotion by seniority, "character and competency considered;" the selection of only ride officers, the fitness to be tested by an examination in book-keeping, general correspondence, and by the three months' employment; the division into four classes, 30 first, 40 second, 50 third, 76 fourth. Eblana, tired of inaction, recommended the formation of a committee in London, but not in opposition to the central committee,—an idea not adopted.

The claims were ultimately included in the central committee's "address," which precluded particular discussion in 1868, though owing to the prolonged silence occasioned by the importance of that document, it was resumed in 1869, by a rumour that certain gentlemen had presented their claims to the Deputy Chairman of the

Board. In 1870 a general revision was effected. The accidental system of promotion was superseded by the introduction of the principle of seniority, though prior to this a hint was thrown out that the clerkship should be obtainable by open competition.

Satisfaction under these new regulations not having been given, the aim was ably continued in 1871 under the *nom de plume*, Humanitas—a *nom* known in 1860—who proposed to base the classification upon "time, service, and good conduct;" form two classes—the first to be recruited from the second class; the second class to be selected from not below the rank of ride officer of one year's experience, after an examination of his books, and an examination in book-keeping by double entry, English composition, and general revenue law; and have one first class clerk attached to each collection, and of course all other clerks, second class.

In 1872 very little was written. In 1873 it was suggested that the experienced efficient clerk should be eligible to fill future vacancies in the Accomptant and Comptroller-General's office, and to ensure this preferment, it was further suggested in 1874 that the entrance examination should be raised to the standard of Scheme II., then after having been two years in the first class, an applicant should be eligible to compete for an appointment in the previously named office; while those at present in the first class, who might desire to enter the Chief Office, should undergo a similar examination, and one before the Commissioners of Inland Revenue, in revenue accountancy.

But the eye of official advancement was not limited to the entry of these offices alone; it projected an advance "direct to a collectorship," this was designated by Justice "undue exaltation." The claims were afterwards laid before the Playfair Commission by Messrs Hogan and Wenban, and considered and decided by the Treasury on Aug. 31, 1876.[1]

The historical outline of the regulations will show the extent to which these desires have been granted.

The designation at the earliest date at hand was plain "clerk;" then "clerk to collector;"[2] after this "collector's clerk;" in 1854 "established clerk" in contra-distinction, probably, from casual or uncommissioned clerk; the supernumerary was now discontinued and "a second clerk" appointed; in 1858, by a division into numerical sections, as 1st, 2d, 3d clerk, with a varying incremental

[1] C. S. G., 1853—1870; C. S. G. & C.. 1871, *et seq.* [2] P. Rep., 1779.

salary, according to the number employed; in 1870 by a further distinction, as chief with all others divided into classes as first, second, and third class, at fixed incremental salaries, being irrespective of the number employed; in 1876 by the discontinuance of class distinction, the chief becoming "superintending," the first class "chief," all others plain clerk, the initial salary rising by a triennial increment, with, in the case of the superintending and chief clerk, a rate of duty pay to each.

The selection, subject to the approval of the Board, originally lay with the collector who formerly required the services of only one, though in Scotland in 1779, of the thirteen collectors, ten only were granted a clerk each, thus showing that all were not assisted. The collector was at liberty to propose even a near relative, provided he was not under, in England, eighteen, in Scotland, sixteen[1] years of age, and that he accepted the responsibility which might be incurred by "misbehaviour,"[2] but of this he was relieved in 1785 by the rescission of the permission to employ one of near kin. These clerical gentlemen were not allowed to officiate for an officer,[3] nor were they to put an officer to any expense on account of "ordinaries" or "extraordinaries,"[4] but they were required to carry the collector's "portmanteau" in the absence of that official factotum—the supernumerary.[5] They also usually accompanied their collectors on removal to other collections of which the collector informed the Board, but if they did not go, they were not again employed without a second approval.[6] It so happened however, that about this time the qualifications were revised. The vacancy was now enjoined to be first reported, then a "foot walk officer or examiner" to be proposed, and if appointed, to be considered to have equal claim with others to be promoted to the rank of supervisor.[7] In Scotland it was slightly different, though assimilated in 1825. None but "well-qualified practical officers" of three years' experience, who had passed the examination of a "foot walk officer," were to be appointed. A ride officer who preferred this appointment, being allowed to state so in his petition for promotion, but before being appointed to the rank of examiner, being required to "resume his former station . . . . during the space of a complete year, immediately preceding his application for such appointment," and to have his character

[1] 1804. [2] 1703, 1724, 1725, 1762. [3] 1761. [4] 1741. [5] 1778. [6] 1812. [7] 1811.

examined and approved in the usual manner. In 1854 the "surveying officer" became eligible, and, as usual, was proposed by the collector. In 1857, the selection still being made by the collector, the qualifications were three months' officiating in the collector's office, and if satisfactory, a sealed packet containing examination papers on book-keeping by double entry was forwarded to, and the candidate directed to attend upon, a neighbouring collector, who superintended the written examination and transmitted the papers to the authorities who decided "to be, or not to be."

In 1858 the eligible rank was lowered to that of First-Class Assistant, and the examination ordered to precede the probation. In the event of his being desirous to obtain a division, he had to serve twelve months in a ride; and an examinership, to survey two years in a division, with a further period of six months after his application had been recorded. There was now promotion in the clerkship from third to second, from second to first, under the ordinary regulations as to expenses on removal.

In 1870, if not previously in 1863, the eligible rank was lowered to the lowest. The applicant sent his application through the collector to the commissioners, and was allowed to ask for a clerkship in general or in particular; he had to undergo the previously-mentioned test, and give six, instead of three, months' probation, and petition for promotion as in the case of the other ranks.

In 1876 this branch was reconstituted, and placed under the Playfair "Lower Division Scale;" addition to salary being dependent on length of service. A regulation was also introduced in favour of the ride officer, who, on obtaining an appointment, was allowed to retain his previous salary, instead of commencing at the initial salary of his new rank—that being less. *See* Salary.

COMMISSIONERS.

Coeval with the Excise itself. The designation was at first "Commissioners and Governors of the Excise and New Impost,"[1] "Grand Commissioners,"[2] afterwards qualified as the "Chief Commissioners and Governors,"[3] by way of distinction from the "subordinate Commissioner," "Sub-Commissioner,"[4] or "Sub-Comis-

[1] Act 1650. [2] 1660, Green's State Papers.
[3] Royal Proclamation, 1683. [4] 1660.

sioner,"[1] located probably in each county;[2] the "assistant-commissioner" of 1823; the "junior commissioner" of 1848. The commissioners have been selected, with few exceptions, by the Treasury from those outside the department, and appointed by Letters Patent[3] under the Great Seal, and though it may not have been the invariable practice on the addition of other duties in former times, the Letters Patent were revoked by a Warrant passed under the Royal Sign Manual in 1849, when and by which the commissioners were reappointed,[4] to act as a consolidated board. Two exceptions were Thomas Everard and William Jackson; the former was a collector in 1683, a commissioner in 1696; the latter, "a practical officer:"[5] Dr Johnson's "Standish" is of course a figment of fancy.[6] Once appointed, the letters-patent appear to have conferred a life interest on the appointee. There is, however, a record in the Journal of the House of Commons—"Alderman Aitkinson and Mr Pargiter discharged from being Commissioners of Excise,"[7] not that it is supposed that they were discharged in the modern sense of that term. On the Restoration of Charles II. the Commissioners included the Lord Chief Baron—Sir Matthew Hale—two Barons of the Exchequer, the Lord Mayor of London, and two Knights, but they do not appear to have held that position many years. To 1878 the longest tenure of office was 39 years; held by W. Burton. It was the custom on the continuance in office on the reimposition of duties previously enacted to be levied for a certain period, to chronicle the fact in the Journal of the House of Commons,[8] or in the reimposition statute,[9] and on filling up a vacancy to announce the whole of the names of the commissioners.[10] The number has fluctuated with the exigencies of the department, and perhaps the time, as follows—

1660. 13.
1670. 5.
1673. 8.
1677. 9 or 10.
1823. 13.
1832. 9.
1849. 9, then by a diminuendo to
1865 to 5.

[1] 1 W. & M. [2] Act, 1660; T. M., 1671. [3] Royal Proclamation, 1683. [4] P. P., 1849. [5] P. Rep., 1806. [6] Rambler. [7] 1660, 1663. [8] 1646. [9] 12 C. II., cc. 5, 8. [10] 20th Rep.

These numbers may be taken as constant from date to date, with the exception noted; it is apparent that the largest boards were formed on the most important occasions—the Restoration and the Consolidation of the three boards. In Scotland and Ireland the respective boards consisted of five members from the earliest dates at hand down to 1823, when two assistant-commissioners were appointed for each country, and the consolidated board was called the "General Board." The assistant-commissionerships appear to have been dropped in 1829. The Parnell Committee recommended in 1836 that the number should be reduced to three.[1] The total number of commissioners who have sat at the board in England is about 190.

In 1836 the Board performed much clerical duty, such as reading letters, diaries, petitions, &c., but this has fallen into desuetude,[2] very different from the Irish Board in 1814, when one commissioner only attended for some time, and having become tired of the imposition of so much solitary labour, declared that he would resign, as "he accepted the office only because his father told him it was a sinecure."[3]

In 1849 the junior commissioners attended from ten till four, and all enjoyed a vacation of two months in the year, short occasional absences excepted.[4] Four then formed a quorum. The judicial and administrative powers of the commissioners have always been great; in matters of discipline paramount and supreme. From the earliest date,[5] with a slight interruption,[6] the commissioners have been empowered "to nominate, appoint, censure," and "displace all subordinate officers,"[7] with the exception of nomination subsequently shared by the Treasury and ultimately withdrawn.[8] Not confining themselves to the board-room, tours of inspection have been made by the commissioners—"Sometimes a particular commissioner goes into one, two, or more collections, carrying with him three or four examiners; and upon the spot examines into the business of the collectors, supervisors, and officers, and if occasion requires he has them face to face."[9] And in former times it was not an uncommon occurrence for them to attend the Houses of Parliament, thus—in 1696 Thomas Everard and other gentlemen made experiments, in the presence of several members, "to find the true content of the

[1] 20th Rep. [2] P. Rep., 1863. [3] H. C., C. of Irish Excheq., July 1.
[4] T. M.; P. Rep., 1863. [5] 1643. [6] Royal Proc., 1689.
[7] Ratification Scot., 1644. [8] P. Rep., 1836, 1863, 1870.
[9] Higmore's Ex.; C. 1, 2, 9 R.

standard bushel;" in 1729 they were examined "as to the great arrears . . . . standing out;"[1] in 1733, with a view to the better security and improvement of the duties and revenues;[2] in 1743, on the Spirituous Liquors Bill.[3]

They were disqualified from sitting in Parliament by a Bill which passed in 1699, and upon which their Lordships divided—ayes, 70; noes, 23.[4]

Then coming to the pecuniary value to the possessor of this important position, at first in the form of poundage, then by salary.

1643. "Sixpence in every twenty shillings that shall be raised and paid into the Treasurer."[5]
1660 to 1666. Twopence in the pound, and those entrusted with the collection of arrears an extra 2s. in the pound collected.
1666 to 1684. £500.
1684 to 1689. £1,000, Excise and Hearth Money.
1689 to 1717. £800.
1718. £1,000.[6]
1743. £1,000.[7]
1779. £1,000.[8]
1797. £12,250 to 9.[9]
—— £2,000 c., £1,500 d.c., £1,200 others.[10]
1849. £2,000 c., £1,500 d.c., £1,200 others.[10]
1851. £2,000 c., £2,000 d.c.,[10] late £1,500, others £1,200.[11]
1851. £2,500 c., an extra £500.[11]
1869. £2,000 c., £1,600 d.c., £1,200 others.[12]

The Commissioners in Scotland received less—1707, £400;[13] 1753, £500.[14]

A story is told of Sir W. Bucknal, a Commissioner of Excise, who having come to speak with the King, who was in consultation with the Duke of York, imprudently listened to their conversation at the door, where his Grace overheard him, and starting from his seat,

[1] H. C., April 23. [2] Idem, March 14. [3] H. L., Feb. 22.
[4] Idem, April 4. [5] P. O. [6] Beatson's Political Index.
[7] Royal Gauger. [8] P. Rep. [9] P. Rep.
[10] T. M., Dec. 19, 1848, with £2000 to present d.c.
[11] C. 1 R.; T. M., Feb. 7, 1851. [12] Estimates.
[13] Letters Patent. [14] Maitland's Hist. Edinburgh.

rushed out of the room, seized Bucknal, dragged him to the stairs, and kicked him down. It should be added that Sir William, who was an Excise farmer before he became a Commissioner, had often supplied his Majesty with the needful, hence, perhaps, this act of indiscreet familiarity.[1] Sir William must have been a county Commissioner.[2] The royal favour was shown in 1871, when the chairman became Sir W. H. Stephenson, K.C.B.; the deputy-chairman, C. J. Herries, C.B.[3]

The following alphabetical list of Commissioners, from 1660 to 1878, has been prepared from the London Gazette, Beatson's Political Index, and other sources, and includes the names of all appointed for England down to 1823, and for the United Kingdom from that date:—

Adam, Thos.,	1691-1694	Bulstrode, Whitelock,	1710-1715
Ashburnham, Sir D.,	1664-1670	Burrell, Wm.,	1714-1790
Ashburnham, Sir D.,	1678-1689	Burton, Wm.,	1737-1776
Ashurst, Sir H.,	1689-1695	Calvert, Felix,	1683-1688
Ashurst, Sir W.,	1698-1699	Campbell, Alex.,	1807-1832
Ashurst, Sir W.,	1715-1719	Carhampton, J. P.,	1823-1826
Atkins, Sir E.,	1660 ...	Carr, W.,	1698-1699
Backhouse, Jno.,	1823 ...	Carr, W.,	1715-1720
Baggot, Richard,	1765-1774	Caswell, Timothy,	1789-1801
Bende, John,	1679 ...	Cayley, Wm.,	1755-1767
Bennett, Jason,	1823 ...	Cholmondley, G. J.,	1782-1801
Bertie, Hon. C.,	1679-1679	Clark, E.,	1694-1699
Bimon, Geo.,	1660 ...	Claxton, E.,	[4]1643-1646
Bindley, Jno.,	1763-1765	Cocks, Richard,	1699-1702
Birch, Jno.,	1660 ...	Cullam, Th.,	[4]1643-1646
Boulby, Thos.,	1762-1776	Danvers, John,	1694-1698
Bowyer, J. W.,	1750-1780	Danvers, John,	1689-1689
Boys, John,	1703-1706	Dashwood, Sir Sam.,	1689-1696
Brett, Richard,	1673-1673	Davenant, Ch., LL.D.,	1678-1689
Bridges, William,	1684-1684	Davis, Hart,	1824-1850
Brooksbank, Stamp,	1776-1792	Davys, J. D.,	1672-1678
Brougham, John,	1715-1724	Dawkins, R.,	1822-1826
Brown, Sir R.,	1660 ...	Disraeli, Jas.,	1858-1868
Buller, John,	1790-1793	Doyle, Sir F. H., Bart.,	1815-1838

[1] Green's State Papers, 1666.
[2] L. G., 1671.
[3] Idem, 1871.
[4] Perhaps longer.

Doyley, Sir W., .	1660 ...
Duckett, Geo., .	1722-1732
Earle, Augustus, .	1740-1762
Edmonds, S., . .	[1]1643-1646
Edwin, Sir H., .	1689-1691
Elliott, Richard, .	1720-1729
Elves, Sir Jno., .	1677-1679
Evance, Stephen, .	1689-1698
Everard, Thos., .	1696-1699
Eyre, Robert, .	1729-1753
Fane, Sir H., . .	1689-1689
Farrington, Thos., .	1756-1758
Finch, Francis, .	1660 ...
Finch, Francis, .	1674-1677
Fisher, C., . .	1801-1805
Fleming, Wm., .	1698-1710
Foche, John, . .	1689-1698
Foote, T., . .	[1]1643-1646
Forthe, Wm., LL.D.,	1666-1674
Frankland, Thos., .	1689-1689
Frankland, Frederick,	1753-1763
Friend, John, .	1683-1689
Gale, Roger, . .	1715-1735
Garth, Charles, .	1780-1784
Gifford, Sir Wm., .	1710-1710
Goodwin, B., . .	1660 ...
Gordon, Sir A. D., Bart.,	1856-1872
Graham, Richard, .	1684-1689
Graves, Lord, .	1827 ...
Hale, Sir M., .	1660 ...
Haldane, Patrick, .	1724-1727
Hall, Thos., . .	1691-1695
Harrison, Thos., .	1826-1851
Herries, C. J., C. B.,	1842
Hiccocks, Wm., .	1665-1666
Hornby, Nathaniel,	1683-1689
Hornby, Nathaniel,	1691-1694
Howard, F. C., .	1677-1683
Huntingdon, Rob., .	1666-1685
Jackson, Wm., .	[1]1793-1807
James, Sir John, .	1665-1670
James, John, . .	1665-1666
James, John, Jun., .	1666-1683
James, Sir Jno., .	1679-1684
Keith-Falconer, Hon. C. J., . . .	1874
Kendrick, John, .	[1]1643-1646
King, Edward, .	1660 ...
Kingdom, Rich., .	1665-1677
Lancot, John, .	[1]1643-1646
Langham, John, .	1643 ...
Legge, Heneage, .	1776-1782
Lenthall, Thos., .	1660 ...
Lifford, Lord, .	... 1832
Lowndes, Wm., .	1772-1808
Lucas, Anthony, .	1767-1789
Luttrell, Hon. J., .	[1]1785-1807
Maling, C. J., .	1808 ...
Manley, W., . .	1810-1824
Martin, Nath., .	1660 ...
Meadows, Sir P., .	1695-1703
Mellish, Wm., .	1751-1760
Mildmay, Benj., .	1719-1728
Montague, Chris., .	1698-1699
Montague, Chris., .	1706-1735
Montgomery, A., .	1849
Morden, Sir J., .	1689-1691
Morland, Sir S., .	1670 1679
Mortlock, Sir J. C., Bart., . . .	1823-1845
Nicholas, Robert, .	[1]1790-1807
Noell, E., . .	1703-1715
Northcote, W. S., .	1877
Onslow, Foot, .	1694-1710
Orlebar, James, .	1738-1766
Paget, Berkley, .	1826-1842
Papillion, D., . .	1742-1754
Papillion, D., Jun.,	1754-1790

[1] Perhaps longer.

Pargeter,	1660 ...
Parish, Woodbine,	1823-1832
Parry, Francis,	1681-1689
Parry, Francis,	1691-1698
Parry, Francis,	1699-1703
Percy, W. H.,	1828-1849
Phipps, Hon. Edm.,	[1]1792-1807
Phipps, Hon. Aug.,	1823-1828
Plunkett, W.,	1823-1838
Polhill, C.,	1726-1755
Pollexfen, Nich.,	1710-1712
Poole, Henry,	1760-1763
Poole, Sir H.,	1766-1767
Pownall, J.,	1776-1785
Pressly, C.,	1849-1862
Price, John	1712-1715
Prynne, Wm.,	1660 ...
Quarme, G.,	1766-1776
Reveley, H.,	1784-1797
Roberts, H.,	1855-1874
Robertson, Sir T.,	1735-1742
Rushworth, C. P.,	1849-1854
Ryley, Philip,	1699-1715
Scawen, Rob.,	1660 ...
Scott, G. Lewis,	1758-1781
Seymour, Lord G.,	1801-1833
Smith, Jno.,	1698-1710
Southwell, Sir R.,	1671-1681
Spiller, R.	1797-1807
Stephenson, H. F.,	1838-1858
Stephenson, W. H., K.C.B.,	1862-1877
Stonehewer, Richard,	1767-1772
Strong, W.,	[1]1689-1697
Strong, W.,	1699-1714
Thayer, Humphrey,	1732-1738
Thornton, Jno.,	1833-1855
Thynne, H. F.,	1674-1678
Towes, John,	1643 ...
Towle, Jno.,	1726-1750
Townshend, G.,	1699-1726
Townshend, Hon. H.,	1735-1751
Trefusis, Hon. C. R.,	1819-1833
Traunt, P.,	1684-1684
Turner, Sir Christ.,	1660 ...
Vernon, H.,	1660 ...
Vernon, Jas., Junr.,	1710-1726
Vernon, Jas.,	1728-1756
Vernon, H.,	1763-1766
Watson, G.,	[1]1805-1807
West, A. G.,	1872
Whetham, Jno.,	1714-1737
Whish, M.,	[1]1781-1818
Wilcox, Jno., Jun.,	1688-1689
Wilcox, Jno., Jun.,	1691-1694
Wingate, Edw.,	1660-1683
Wiseman, Rob.,	1673-1684
Wood, John,	1833-1856
Wylde, Thos.,	1727-1740
Wyville, Sir M.,	1702-1722

COMMISSIONERS OF APPEAL.

The full designation was "Commissioners for Appeals and Regulating the Excise,"[2] and the duties of the office were "to Hear and Determine Appeals in Cases of Excise"[3] made from the Court of Summary Jurisdiction.[4]

[1] Perhaps longer. [2] R. Proclamation, Dec. 24, 1660. [3] L. G., 1702.
[4] Green's State Papers; L. G., 1702, 1714, 1727, 1734, 1744, 1753, 1800.

Beatson informs us that this Board was first formed in 1662, and consisted of five members at a salary of £200 each, and that the number of its members varied between 1668 and 1679 from seven to eleven, and from the latter date down to 1805, from five to six.[1] Exception, however, must be taken to this historian's first date, as commissioners were appointed to this office during the Commonwealth and were continued in office on the restoration of Charles II.[2] They were appointed by Act of Parliament by name in 1662,[3] and reappointed on the accession to the crown and on the first appointment of a new member, by Royal Proclamation or announcement down to 1800.[4]

Beatson also adds that in Ireland three commissioners were appointed from 1760 down to 1775, and afterwards five down to 1798.[1] In 1833 the English Court was peculiar to London within the limits of the Chief Office, which included 147 parishes and cost £922, 10s. 0d. per annum. The duties were very light, only one case having been heard during the last nine years, and of the nine cases which were lodged during the last twenty years, three were not prosecuted to a hearing and only one reversed. The Parnell Committee recommended the revocation of the Patent,[5] which was ultimately done.[6]

COMMISSIONERS' REPORTS.

The first report of the Commissioners of Inland Revenue, addressed to the Lords of the Treasury and presented to both Houses of Parliament, was made at the close of the civil year 1856; since then, with their Lordships' permission, at the close of each financial year, with one or perhaps two exceptions. It is a valuable one, now out of print. It contains outlines of the various duties, a comparative glance at the establishment on the several consolidations, with other minor details, and an important appendix of about eighty papers, which, among others, contain a long array of accounts of all the duties then being collected for each year since their original imposition, or as near to it as possible, a report on the Laboratory, the origin of the Life Assurance and Benevolent and Mutual

[1] Political Index, 1806. [2] R. Proclamation, Dec. 24, 1660. [3] 12 C. II. c. 8.
[4] Green's State Papers; L. G., 1702, 1714, 1727, 1734, 1744, 1753, 1800.
[5] Third Report. [6] H. C., April 2, 1841.

Guarantee Funds, elaborate abstracts of duties imposed, augmented, reduced, expired, repealed in each year from 1816 to 1856—though the financial year to which the report is brought down is 1855. It should be borne in mind by those reading the comparisons in "measure" that the units of charge were of different cubic content from those adopted in, and employed since 1826.

The arrangement of this report has been observed in most of those subsequently made, with the exception of the Thirteenth, issued in 1870, in which the fiscal and the disciplinary history have been written down to 1869 with very considerable minuteness. The Second and the Fourteenth report each contain the details of two years' management.

Extracts from, and reference to, these reports will appear in this series of papers.

COMMISSIONS.

It is open to question if other than verbal commissions were given to those who were at first—the troublous times—entrusted with charging and collecting the excise duties,[1] though it is on record that they had to appear before the Speaker of the House of Commons to take the oath of office,[2] and that both the earlier and the later commissions, which the writer has seen, contain portions of a Parliamentary Ordinance issued in 1647. In 1660, however, it is distinctly enacted that the Commissioners shall "Constitute under their Hands and Seals such and so many Gagers as they shall find needful," and with the exception of a confusion which arose in 1689 by commissions having been granted by the Crown and Peers as well as by the Commissioners—a confusion to such an extent as to necessitate the issue of a Royal Proclamation to "revoke" those not issued by the Commissioners[3]—commissions have been invariably granted by "major part" of them. The earlier commission, printed and embellished with a vignette of the reigning Sovereign, contained, after the to whom and from whom, the geographical limit, the specific fiscal duties, the "especial Trust and Confidence in the Knowledge, Skill, Industry, Integrity, Fidelity, and Circumspection of . . . . . Gentlemen," the official duties, the right to ask extraneous aid; and formed a lengthy document of nearly 900 words.[4] The seal con-

[1] P. O., Oxford, 1644. [2] P. O. [3] 1689. [4] 1711.

sisted of an embossed crown surmounted with a lion statant, on a slip passed through two slits and secured by wafers. Vellum, 16 by 12 in.[1]

The later commission, copperplate and embellished with a print of the Royal Arms, is less specific, contains no fulsome reference to personal character, but includes the power to act in charging and collecting any of the duties, but more particularly the Excise, under the management of the Commissioners of Inland Revenue, and extends to only about 230 words. In this a footnote includes the right to call in extraneous aid, and the seal consists of a small printed crown. Vellum, 13 by 8 in.[2] A stamp duty of £1, 10s. 0d. formerly attached to it, and was formerly paid by the person in whose favour the document was issued.[3]

Considerable inconvenience was caused by the invalidity which arose on the death or removal of the empowering Commissioner for a period of some thirty-five years, until an Act was passed in the reign of William III. to continue the authority.[4] A greater trouble, however, arose on the Accession to the Crown. This national event was usually followed by the issue of one or more Royal Proclamations to the effect that the officials in commission at the abdication or the demise of the preceding Sovereign should continue in office. The issue commenced on the Accession, or perhaps more correctly the Restoration of Charles II., and was continued down to that of George III., in whose reign a legal enactment appears to have set aside the necessity for any further issue. A limitation to six months in which to renew the commissions was enacted in the reign of William and Mary, but so numerous had the commissioned ranks become on the Accession of George II., that it was found necessary to extend that period by a second Proclamation to nine months, and so much more numerous on the Accession of George III., that the original period was extended, by additions of four months each, by four successive issues, to one year and ten months.[5]

The authority of the Commission having now become co-existent with the tenure of office, advancement, reduction, reinstatement, or

[1] 1834. [2] 1873. [3] 1788, 1789, 1875. [4] 7 & 8 W. III. c. 30.

[5] Charles II. E., Dec. 24, 1660; James II. E., Feb. 16, 1684; James II. S., Feb. 1, 1684; William & Mary, Feb. 14, 1688; Anne E. & I., March 8, 1701; George I. G. B. & I., Aug. 5, 1714, I., Aug. 6, 1714; George II., June 16, 1727; George III., Nov. 10, 1760; G. B. & I., March 20, 1760, June 25, 1761, G. B. & I., Oct. 12, 1761, and Feb. 11, 1761; L. G.

loss of commission alone occasioned a reissue. Promotion from the rank of officer to that of examiner, and from that of supervisor to the next highest rank respectively, necessitated the issue of a larger power; while reduction, reinstatement, or loss of commission required the issue of a smaller or a similar power. Dealing in articles liable to "inland duties," entailed the forfeiture,[1] and suspension, the giving up, of the authority.[2]

Though notice of the loss of the commission was early required to be given,[3] the general unobservance of this regulation resulted in the promulgation of an order in 1818 for collectors to inspect these documents at the next sitting, and annually afterwards at the eighth round sitting, and endorse them in testimony of having done so : the latter has been discontinued.

Commissions issued to those temporarily engaged in charging the duty on hops, were returned annually at the close of the third round,[4] and those taken up casually at the close of the first round, to the Registrar of Securities,[2] the collector making an annual return of the number transmitted.[5] Special commissions were also given to those entrusted with exportation on drawback.[6] Also in 1878 to Dog Inspectors.

Robert Burns' commission was sold in London in 1854 for £5, 12s. 6d.[7]

CONCENTRATED WORT CO.

"In the year 1865 a company was started at Margate for the purpose of making 'Grainstone' or 'Concentrated Wort,' under a patent process, for exportation to India and other warm climates. The idea was to obtain a solid extract of malt and hops, which, being packed in hermetically sealed tins, could be conveyed to any foreign country, and then by simple solution in water and fermentation with yeast, be converted into beer of any desired strength. It was considered by the promoters of the Company that by the saving in freight and land carriage, and by the prevention of loss from leakage, &c., a considerable reduction could be made in the cost of beer in India, so that not only would our troops be supplied with that beverage at a less expense, but it was also hoped that a large demand for it would arise from the natives.

[1] 1726. [2] 1779. [3] 1776. [4] 1795.
[5] 1818, 1827. [6] 1856. [7] C. S. G.

"The Company having applied to be allowed to export the article on drawback, your Lordships authorised us to allow a drawback equivalent to the duties levied on the materials from which it was prepared. The regulations necessary for the protection of the revenue having been prepared, the operations of the Company at the beginning of 1866 became subject to the supervision of our officers, which was continued till the 5th May following, when the manufacture ceased, owing principally to the small demand for the article. The manufacture has, however, been recently resumed.

"During the session of 1866 Legislative sanction was obtained for the allowance of this drawback, and the regulations under which it could be claimed were embodied in the Act 29 & 30 Vict., c. 64."[1]

The Commissioners state in their Fourteenth Report that "About 160 cwts. have been made and exported to India and other hot countries with the view to determine whether the beer prepared from the concentrated wort can favourably compare in price and quality with that exported in the ordinary way from this country."

The point of interest here lies in the fact that John Lammas, gent., and Edm. Everard, Esq., partners in 1710, discovered some such method. A Seasonable Remedy to prevent "Fleet-Beer" frauds by brewing beer after a "more succinct and less cumbersome Way and draw from a clear Malt-Extract" invented by "John Lammas of Waer." Save £282,550 a year: "Whereas after our new Way a fewer Tuns by Seventeen times of our Malt Extract being kept in a far lesser Room and Quantity, under Lock and Key, being taken out every second, third or fourth Day, is mixed and brew'd in any Corner of the Ship in a Wooden Vessel containing a few Hogsheads; mix and stir the Extract or Syrup with the Proportion of Water; then cast in your Yeast; this will make fresh strong Drink for some Hundreds of Men, and it shall be clear, strong and brisk in three or four Days time: and the same method may be repeated as often as you please, during your whole Voyage, tho' it were for three Years. The Quantity of Malt Extract you first took in, will be sufficient, and the Ingredient itself so cleared from all Dregs in its first Preparation, that it will not alter, nor change in a Hundred Years; and therefore the Drink that is made of it will not "turn, nor grow muddy, either in Pease Time nor after Thunder as Beer made after the Old Way usually does": "could sell it to them"--London

[1] C. 13 R.

brewers—"as cheap as they could buy their unwrought Malt." 9½ oz. to make one gallon.[1]

CONSCIENCE MONEY.

An early instance of this mode of payment occurs in the London Gazette of August 15, 1751, in which J. Mingay, Collector of Hull Collection, acknowledges the receipt of "Ten Pounds" sent by a person unknown, but who requested a receipt in this paper. Reference is made to this head of payment in 1871.

CONSOLIDATION.

The saving to be effected by the union of the revenue receiving departments received the attention of the Government, and resulted in the passing of a resolution to appoint "A committee to consider of the putting the Excise and Customs into one receipt," as early as the period embraced between 1650 and 1659,[2] but though thus early conceived, the idea has not hitherto proved feasible except to a small extent; inasmuch as only certain duties have been transferred from the Customs to the Excise, and vice versa, by Mr Pitt,[3] but again transferred from the Excise to the Customs by an Order in Council,[4] and by Viscount Althorp,[5]—with other minor changes not necessary to mention—until 1841 and 1862 when committees were appointed on the subject which will be subsequently noticed.

With the inland departments it has been very different; centralization has been the ruling idea with the successive Governments from that of the Earl of Sutherland in 1718 to that of Earl Russell, who, in 1849, completed the union of the Boards — unless the Post Office be viewed as a revenue department—under the euphonious name of the Board of Inland Revenue; and to show the scope for the early exercise of such an idea, it is only necessary to mention that on the accession of George I. there were then no fewer than nine; these were, Hackney Coaches, Salt Duties, Hides and Taxes, Stamps and Candles, Wine Licences, Excise Appeals, Excise in Scotland, Excise in Ireland, and Excise in England, and

[1] British Museum.
[2] Journals of the House of Commons.
[3] 1784, 1785; P. Rep., 1836.
[4] Feb. 2, 1825.
[5] 1834.

represented an aggregate of fifty commissioners.[1] But the accomplishment has been slow.

Into the three Boards of Stamps, Taxes and Excise have the others been gradually incorporated, and in turn the Stamps with the Taxes in 1833, and again the Stamps and Taxes into the Excise, as already stated in 1849. The Excise itself in the meanwhile having undergone an internal consolidation. There existed in England from nearly the commencement of the imposition itself, a Town and a Country Establishment, whose incorporation though recommended in 1797 by a Select Committee on Accounts and Offices was not effected until many years afterwards. On the motion of the Chancellor of the Exchequer, on March 25, 1823, the Scotch and Irish Boards, termed "Local Boards," were incorporated with the English Board, now termed the "General Board," but the assistant Commissioners for those countries sat in Edinburgh and Dublin until January 1, 1830, when the whole of the administration was transferred to London. Passing over Treasury Letters, dated between 1821 and 1831,[2] the next suggestion appears to have been made by the Parnell Committee in 1835, in their Twelfth Report, in which they state "that the time must be considered approaching when a well-founded recommendation may be offered for the reduction of the number of revenue Boards from three to two, the one to be entrusted as at present with the management and collection of the external or Customs duties; and the other with the management and collection of the internal taxation of every description throughout the kingdom."

This laid in abeyance until 1841,[3] when a Royal Commission was appointed to enquire into the details of the departments of the Customs, Excise, and Stamps and Taxes with a view to "diminishing the expense of them," and to the relief of "the trade and commerce of the country," who having issued two or more reports, and a Treasury Minute having been made upon them,[5] an "Inland Revenue Bill" was brought into the House of Commons, on February 2, 1849, by the Chancellor of the Exchequer, who, having stated that the proposed alteration he had estimated "would effect a saving of between £70,000 and £80,000 to the public without at all diminishing the efficiency of the branches of the public revenue," the measure passed through both Houses with little or no opposition

[1] L. G., 1714. [2] P. Rep., 1836. [3] Nov. 9.
[4] Dec. 29, 1848. [5] C. S. G., 1853, 1855.

and received the Royal Assent on February 27, only twenty-five days after its introduction. But although the superior functions of these departments had become consolidated, the inferior still remained, for the most part, intact, much to the disappointment of those who had expected to receive considerable benefit by the change and who afterwards urged not only a complete discontinuance of the employment of the uncommissioned collector of taxes and others, but also the consolidation of the Customs itself.[1]

Both of these were afterwards attempted. The first in 1862, though the Government hesitated to bring in a Bill, unless it was likely to meet with general assent;[1] it however made an essay in 1864[2] to pass a measure of a partial and permissive character, inasmuch as London was to have been excluded, and the Board to have been authorised to collect the taxes in any county, on declaring their intention to do so, unless more than one-third of the Parliamentary Commissioners protested against it; and though the Government received very considerable support the thrice-amended measure having been four months before the country, and only about 4000 persons having petitioned against it, it was rejected on the final division in the House of Commons on June 20, by only 4 votes—ayes 128, noes 132.[3]

Nearly five years elapsed before any further Parliamentary effort was expended, and this was foreshown on the inquiry of two Members, who subsequently saw the assessed taxes commuted into excise licences through the medium of the financial statement of 1869.[4] The excise and tax branches in Somerset House were consolidated in 1871 but reseparated in 1876.

The second—the consolidation of the Customs and the "Excise." A Select Committee of the House of Commons was appointed in 1862,[5] on the motion of Mr Horsfall, who was appointed chairman, and after whom the committee was called, to consider the practicability and utility of doing so,[6] the Chancellor of the Exchequer observing, however, while assenting to the motion, that "The question of consolidation was not one of principle but one of degree, as they were justified in carrying it to a certain point, but beyond that point it ought not to be carried; and that point would be realised certainly whenever the mind of man would be overstrained by its being carried further, as he thought would be the case in this instance,

[1] H. C., April 3. [2] H. C., Feb. 9. [3] Hansard.
[4] March 5 and 11, 1869. [5] May 7. [6] April 29.

if they were to amalgamate these two departments." This observation was proved on this occasion. The complexity and contrariety of the answers given to the ramified questions, arising out of the simple question at issue entirely baffled the acumen and the official inexperience of the gentlemen appointed to consider it, and they were consequently unable to agree to advise the amalgamation which some of them sought. Beyond a draft report by Mr Horsfall, the only recommendation, bearing directly on the object of the commission, to the effect "that the respective Boards should be directed to continue the system of consolidation and retrenchment, was drawn up by Mr Cardwell who with Mr Bagwell had replaced Mr M. Gibson and Mr Peel, on the motion of Mr Gladstone, much to the objection of Mr Horsfall.[1] The committee therefore presented only the Minutes of Evidence.[2]

No report having been presented, the officials themselves began "to play at administrators." The first of importance to enter the field in 1866 was "C. S."—William Meikle—with "Our Postal and Revenue Establishments,"[3] afterwards called "The Book of Progress,"[4] in which he advocated the utilisation of the Post Office for the receipt and payment of revenue, the sale of stamps and the issue of licences, a thorough consolidation of the Excise and Taxes Branches, and the surveying portions of the Customs and Excise, which advocacy he based upon the evidence taken by the previously-mentioned committee. The second of importance to enter the field in 1867 was "An Economical Reformer," who addressed Lord Stanley through an ably-written pamphlet, in which, among other suggestions made, were these—"merge the office of surveyor and supervisor;" "fuse into one branch the whole collection of the Inland Revenue," and their "internal consolidation once effected . . . the way would be clear for further amalgamation"—the Customs with the Excise.[5] These afforded fine fun in a "great wordy battle," a "wordy war," a "petty paper warfare," under the respective titles of "Rearrangement," "Reconstruction," "Reformation," "Reorganisation," "Revision," "Consolidation," and the "good ship 'Amalgame,'" in which "Mr Meikle and his boys" "Briton," "W.E.," "Cumbrian," "Thistle," and others exchanged a controversial correspondence, extending, in 1869 alone, to upwards of 100

[1] H. C., March 6, 1863. [2] P. Rep., 1863. [3] Pitman, London. [4] C. S. G., 1870. [5] Parkes & Jones, London.

letters, in which "W.E." designated "C.S." "a doctrinaire," his scheme "doctrinaireism;" "Cumbrian" styled "W.E." the "Excise Max-Müller;" and "Thistle" dubbed "Briton's" newly-created official designation--"supervisor—assessing—excising—amalgamated—surveyor—cumulard."[1] Though continued until 1872, the game, like others unskilfully and indiscreetly played, ended in grief.

To return to the constituted authorities.

In 1873 Mr Alderman Lusk was informed that if the consolidation did take place "it would greatly add to the estimates for a long time to come;"[2] a petition was presented from the Liverpool Chamber of Commerce to ask for the change; the Chairmen of the Customs and of the Excise, with Lord Cavendish, were appointed to investigate minor matters, but owing to the retirement of his Lordship in 1874 the committee had not been further engaged in the investigation.[3]

In 1874 Mr W. H. Smith stated on taking the vote for the Inland Revenue Estimates that he thought the proposed amalgamation of the Customs and the Inland Revenue might be advantageously effected in many parts of the country.[4] This probably referred to the bonding warehouses, upon which a question was put by Lord F. Cavendish in the House of Commons on Aug. 2, 1875.

CONSTABLES.

In an imperial document which required the person chargeable with duty to show "a ready and cheerful obedience," the constable was required to assist when it was not shown.[5] This anticipated disobedience occurred to such an extent in 1689—the trader refused to pay, the constable to assist in enforcing payment—that another Royal Proclamation was issued to command the constable to assist,[6] yet in 1725 the same unwillingness existed—"Of late constables and officers of the peace upon request duly made to them have refused, and do refuse"—and necessitated the imposition of a fine of £20 to remove it.

CORN RETURNS.

These returns date back as far as 1687, at the least, perhaps fur-

[1] C. S. G., 1869. [2] H. C., May 12. [3] C.
[4] H. C., June 6. [5] Dec. 17, 1662. [6] Jan. 2; 168⅞.

ther,[1] and were compiled to determine the duties to be exacted on importation and exportation, and to decide when a bounty should be paid; the repeal of the payment of the bounty in 1830 and of the duty on corn in 1849, with the publication of the prices in the various newspapers and special periodicals, has superseded the original object of the compilation. At that date—1687—the Justices of the Peace of the several shires in England were required to appoint two persons to ascertain the quantity of corn sold, compute the average prices, and forward the results to the principal officer of the Customs in the county, but they were guilty of such gross indifference to this, perhaps unremunerative duty, as to be reproved by a Royal Proclamation, which was ordered to be exhibited by the clerk at the Sessions.[2] Though defective, the arrangement probably continued until 1770, when a new and more comprehensive system was introduced under the superintendence of one Wm. Cook, a somewhat significant name, whose duties as comptroller enjoined to publish the weekly average prices in England, Wales, and Scotland in the *London Gazette*, in which the prices in each county of England were separately shown, but grouped into twenty-one inland and nineteen coast counties, while those in Wales were grouped as North and South Wales, and those in Scotland represented as "not compleat."[3] And this system was continued with some few modifications[4] until 1791, when, though each county average was given, the counties were thrown into districts—as the London district, the inland districts, the maritime districts, and Scotland into four districts.[5]

In 1828 there were no fewer than 175 inspectors, of whom 162 were located in England, six in Scotland, and seven in Ireland, at salaries, with the exception of the London inspector at £300, which varied from £30 by 10 to £50, and were paid by the collectors of this department.[6]

The following year 150 inspectorships were placed under the management of the Commissioners; in 1842, 147 more, of which eleven were in Wales and 136 in England; and eighty-five of the offices were in or at public-houses, extending from the "Rising Sun" to the "Half Moon," and another at the "Supervisor's House."[7] These rents were also paid by the collectors, but they were not

[1] Royal Proc., 1667. [2] Idem, 1687. [3] Idem, 1770.
[4] Idem, 1771, 1772, 1790. [5] Idem. [6] T. W. [7] L. G.

chargeable on the department. In no case is extra pay mentioned for these extra-departmental duties. 140 inspectorships were discontinued in 1864, but additions were made to 1865.[1] The space occupied by the insertion of these returns in the paper already mentioned was no less than four pages in 1791, eight from 1843 to 1865, when only the average prices of wheat, barley, and oats were given. "No return. None sold. Inaccurate," were of frequent occurrence. The vigilance, accuracy, and punctuality of this department has been questioned on one or more occasions,[2] though on the whole few marks of displeasure have been made.[3] In Parliament, apart from the Corn Laws, the collection of these returns has seldom enlisted attention—in 1854 permission was given to Mr Bland to bring in a bill to assimilate the mode of collection in Ireland to that in England;[4] and in 1861 a petition, signed by 3850 persons, was presented for an amended system.

COST OF COLLECTION.

The "Charge of the Collection of the Excise," or the cost of collection, early attracted the attention of "disaffected" persons, who took opportunity to declare, during the obstruction and opposition which were made against the proper collection, that half the receipt was "consumed upon officers." This, however, was incorrect, and occasioned the authorities to issue a denial, though partial, to the effect that until that time it "never amounted upon the whole receipt to full two shillings in every twenty shillings," or not 10·0 per cent.[5] It has several times engaged the attention of Parliament, notably so about 1833, 1847, 1862, and on any movement for consolidation, and compared with other departments in the last century has usually been lower. For example, in 1789, on the net, the Land Assessed Taxes, 3·6; Stamps, 5·7; Salt, 8·4; Customs, 8·45; Hackney Coaches, &c., 9·0; Hawkers and Pedlars, 95·45!![6]

The cost in the three countries in 1809 was, on the authority of Mr Wardle, who spoke in the House of Commons and was not contradicted, in England 2·75, in Scotland 6.15, in Ireland 11·6,[7] but whether on the gross or net amount is not stated. And even when shown on the gross or net, it is difficult to conceive that the same

[1] L. G., 1851 to 1865. [2] 1845, 1853, 1859, 1863. [3] C. S. G., 1860.
[4] H. C., May 16. [5] P. O., 1647. [6] P. Rep., 1797. [7] June 19, 1809.

mode of computation has always been adopted; this will appear below, and the various consolidations have made the percentages still less comparable.

		Gross.	Net.	
Excise,	1647	not 10.0	...	"Whole receipt." Parl. Ord.
"	1686	12·7	14·6	Cobbett's Parl. Hist.
"	1688	12·1	13·9	
"	1755	...	5·5	A. Smith.
"	1781	5.6	...	Gross or net not stated. Lord North.
"	1789	5.5	6·4	Parl. Report, 1797.
"	1796	4·6	5·5	
"	1817	5·6	6·0	Gross—exclusive of drawbacks and bounties. Parl. Return, 1858.
"	1827	6·2	6·6	
"	1837	6·7	7·2	
"	1847	6·2	6·7	
"	1857	4·7	...	
Excise, Stamps and Taxes,	1857	3·4	...	
"	1867	3·2	...	"Amount collected." Parl. Ret., 1867.

COURT OF EXCHEQUER.

The proceedings on excise cases in this Court engaged the attention of Parliament in 1819 by a motion being made for a return of the number of excise informations filed during the last seven years, against which the Attorney-General, the Solicitor-General, and the Chancellor of the Exchequer offered a successful resistance by securing a majority of 18 votes—ayes, 54; noes, 72.[1] The petition of a notorious smuggler, who was then in prison in default of the payment of a penalty of £44,450, in which he had been convicted for having sold three chests of Spanish juice to a brewer,[2] together with another petition regarding a less aggravated case, continued to command the attention of Parliament, and to elicit the fact that 700 customs and excise informations were annually filed in this Court.[3] This exposé had the effect of immediately reducing the annual

[1] H. C., March 9, 1819. [2] H. C., March 19, 1819. [3] H. C., June 22, 1819.

average to about 250,[1] while in 1834, of 72 which were filed, only 16 were tried, and since 1843, when a Parliamentary Return was made, the subject has dropped. The Courts of Exchequer in Scotland and Ireland have been, in this respect, seldom mentioned.

These prosecutions were accompanied with very heavy expense, great delays, and even ruinous consequences to the parties against whom they were brought, and induced a Parliamentary Committee who inquired into the subject in 1836 to recommend a "more cheap and expeditious" mode of trial before the local justices, under an impression that "it is by publicity that efficacy is chiefly given to the force of law and to the force of public opinion." The same Committee further observe, "The Commissioners of Excise were formerly in some degree obliged to bring prosecutions in the Exchequer in consequence of a strong leaning against the Excise, which often gave improper protection to delinquents. . . . . The Board is governed in making its decisions whether or not trial shall take place in the Exchequer in some degree by the amounts of the penalties to be recovered. This circumstance affords . . . . inducement . . . . for a revision of all Excise penalties. The peculiarly severe nature of an action in this Exchequer has led to the general habit of making compromises."[2]

COWPOWDER.

A mixture of "vitriol, cocculus indigo, grains of Paradise, Guinea pepper, and other deleterious materials," added to porter by a Canterbury brewer, who was fined for so doing in 1816.[3]

CUNNINGHAME'S IMPERIAL ULLAGER.

A book of rules for ullaging; tables of ullages of casks from four to one hundred and seventy gallons in inches; of differences between the wine gallon and the "old malt bushel" and the imperial measure; of factors, divisors, gauge points; of areas; of duties. This work, "inscribed to Woodbine Parish, Esq., Commissioner of His Majesty's Revenue of Excise in London," by J. Cunninghame, also of the same department, consists of about 350 pages, and was published on the introduction of the Imperial measure,

[1] H. C., Dec. 1, 1826. [2] Parnell, Twentieth Report. [3] H. C., April 3, 1816.

when it ran through a second edition. Entered at Stationers' Hall, 1825. Printed at Stirling.

CUSTOMS AND EXCISE.

The possibility of entirely repealing all duties of Customs and Excise, with suggestions for a plan of Direct Taxation, by John Noble, published in October 1869 by P. S. King, London. The title of a pamphlet of nineteen pages, being the print of a paper prepared for the Social Science Congress held in Bristol.

DALBY'S BOOK OF SONGS.

The composition of J. Dalby, late an officer of this department. Published about 1865.[1]

DARY'S COMPLETE GAUGER.

"The Complete Gauger, in Two Parts, Theoretical and Practical, showing the briefest ways for Gauging all manner of regular Vessels, whether Backs (or Coolers), Tuns, Coppers, and Casks, either whole or the parts, by undeniable Rules of Art. Likewise Tablets of Allowances by Michael Dary, Philomath, heretofore Practical Gauger." Dedicated to the "Farmers and Managers of His Majesties Revenue of Excise," in England, Wales, and Berwick-on-Tweed. Pages 144, 8vo; published 1678.

DEAD WEIGHT.

A slang expression used in 1856 to represent the "check-book, malt stick, slide rule, tape, brass float, diary and case, and ink bottle." "The gross weight of these articles," wrote "A Walking Examiner," "amounts to nearly five lbs., and with them arranged around and about my person with proper respect to its symmetry, have to-day trudged eighteen miles through mud, varying in depth

[1] C. S. G.

from four to eight inches, and in colour from rich brown to any shade of black."[1]

DEBENTURE.

One of the oldest and most important documents in use, a form being embodied in a Parliamentary Ordinance dated May 30, 1654, and its importance being the authority to repay a duty or pay a bounty,[2] but not without, in the case of drawback, an official certification and a trade oath or declaration, though these have been forged for the purpose of obtaining payment,[3] and the penalty attached to doing so in 1798 was equivalent to the guilt of felony, and entailed on the offender "death without benefit of clergy."

The debenture during the earlier imposition of the many indirect duties was prepared in special terms for each duty,[1] since then, in generic as well as specific terms.[4] It carries an *ad valorem* stamp duty payable by the exporter, who also paid for many years a fee of fourpence for its preparation.

DECREET.

A legal term in Scotland for a warrant to recover duty or penalty. (Scotch Instructions 1804).

DEFALCATIONS.

The excise, except in Ireland, compared with the other revenue departments, has suffered little by defalcation.

Starting from 1780 with the evidence of G. L. Scott, Esq., a commissioner, who had acted in that capacity for a period of twenty-two years, affords a view to the effect "that he never heard of a collector being proceeded against for default of payment of money collected by him." Then advancing to 1799, the proceedings of Parliament affirm that in England during the twenty-five years immediately preceding only four defalcations, amounting to £3668, 0s. 3¾d., occurred, of which one amounting to £3600 was written off by the Treasury,

[1] C. S. G., 1856. [2] Postlethwayt, 1766. [3] L. G., 1708. [4] 1856.

indifferent. In this respect it has always applied in a double sense, embracing, as it has, the numerous deeds[1] of the person who kept it, and the misdeeds or "excise sins"[2] of those under his immediate supervision. From the record of each day's deeds—to which the collector formerly added "ex"[3]—with other observations, the collector has written out the supervisor's official character, which has invariably been required to be signed, by each person concerned, in testimony of agreement, or an explanation written in case of dissent. And as to the misdeeds of the subordinates, these the collector has also investigated and explained, and with the supervisor and the person reported, placed his initials under each explanation. The completed document was then transmitted by carrier[4] or other conveyance to the Chief Office, where it was examined by a surveying general examiner and a commissioner, who, in case of demerit, noted the measure of the punishment on the endorsement.[5]

The latter observations apply more particularly to the copy: this was made out monthly,[6] then roundly,[7] and latterly, in the form of an abstract roundly,[8] and afterwards quarterly.[9] In 1848, it was an imposing document of many pages, each fifteen by ten inches, neatly stitched in the "herring-bone" stitch with silk. In this the collector entered his observations on the several reports, in the middle of the page; inserted an account of the supervisor's absence during the year, the number of visits, doubles, and check surveys made in each station; and certified that certain general orders had been read,—and to this portion both supervisor and officers added their initials—that "this diary is a copy of the supervisor's diary book," that the supervisor kept a horse and was "well-mounted," that he exercised "due authority over his officers," that none of the officers brought duty to the sitting, and that they were neither detained longer than business required nor "put to any unnecessary expence." The supervisor certified that the officers had "proper instruments;" reported on the character of the young officers in his district; and inserted an account of his own absence, a scheme of the district, a compare of amounts, in which he showed the "up" or "down,"[3] a table of the time the collector "came in" and "went out" of the district, and a certificate that "The collector collected by Ledger."

It is worthy of remark that, with three exceptions on which other

[1] 1709-1876. [2] 1869. [3] 1761. [4] 1712. [5] 1848. [6] S. 1804. [7] 1854. [8] 1871. [9] Ashby District, 8th Round, 1848.

duties were performed, the "40 miles and traders per day," at four per hour, was sustained throughout the period embraced in the diary under observation: the average daily employment too was twelve and a-half hours. "A reason" was written when no duty was performed.[1]

The diary was in use in Scotland and Ireland[2] long before the consolidation of the respective Boards, but upon that event taking place, the supervisors in North Britain were supplied with specimen diaries compiled under the General Board.[3] New forms were issued in 1829, 1854, and 1868: the sheet diary was discontinued in 1855.

Perhaps no other official book has ever received so many uncomplimentary equivalents—"book of lies,"[4] "badge of distrust,"[5] "impossible diary,"[6] "the terror to evil-doers,"[7] "antiquated humbug," "degrading diary," "Diary Impedimentum,"[7] "relic of barbarous times,"[8] "Daily curse."[9] Even the compilation has been technically termed "padding,"[10] "stuffing,"[11] and this is singularly borne out by an early reproof, of which a copy has fallen into the hands of the writer—"Mr Ord, Supervisor of Pontefract District, Yorkshire. Sir, The Commissioners on their perusal of your 2nd Round Diary, observe that you make use of many affected phrases, and incongruous words, as 'phantation,' 'Preception,' 'Harmony,' 'Scotony,' 'Illegal procedure,' 'prosecuting the Division,' 'Genuine observations,' all which you use in a sense which the words do not naturally bear. I am ordered to acquaint you that if you hereafter continue that affected and school-boy way of writing, and to murder the language in such a manner, you will be discharged for a fool.

"Excise Office, London, EDWARD CLARK."
"18th November 1724.

It was not until 1859, fully a century and a-half after its introduction, that the use, abuse, and disuse of the diary formed the subject of a discussion which has been continued with more or less vigour down to the present time.[12] Notably vigorous was it in 1861, when no fewer than forty letters were written on its merits and demerits, though it remained for the Central Committee of 1867[13] to

[1] Ashby District, 8th Round, 1848. [2] P. Rep., 1808. [3] 1824.
[4] 1870. [5] 1871. [6] 1872. [7] 1861. [8] 1863. [9] 1864. [10] 1868.
[11] 1869. [12] C. S. G., 1859-64, idem, 1868-70, idem et C., 1871-4.
[13] Address.

give greater force to the reasoning for its disuse, and for Fergus in 1868 to apply his masterly quill to point out the principles upon which it seemed to have been based and on which it appeared to be continued.

"The diary," he defined to be "a badge of unworthiness in the man who is required to keep it:" he would have the duties of the district left to his intelligence and personal responsibility; he would have a petition, from each collection, sent to the Board to call up men of "freshness and originality" to devise a new system: he wrote replies in anticipation of objections which might be raised against this "superfluity":[1] he asserted that the lowness of character was "due to the very system which is retained to check it," and that "to impose upon the high-minded and honourable the same penal restrictions and performances" was "unjust and injudicious."

In these desires he was not uniformly supported, and "waving all action which might imply distrust or disrespect of the Commissioners, or which would embarrass the Central Committee," he gave expression to his "manly impulses" in two letters on the "supervisor's work," and the "general interests of the department," which he headed "The Spirit of the Excise." The department he designated "the school of suspicion and snares," and affirmed that the officers were not such "unmitigated reprobates as the existing system was formed to contend with. These letters commanded the approbation of certain correspondents, and it so happened immediately preceded the issue of a general order by which he had the satisfaction of finding an instalment of that freedom conceded, for which he had contended.

The regulations of the "little red book" were further relaxed in 1876.

DIMENSION BOOK.

At first dimensions were entered at the "head of Book."[2] This book was in use as early as 1743[3] at the least, but restricted apparently to the entry of dimensions and areas of vessels which were not required to be tabulated. Oval utensils were represented by a drawing or outline of that figure. The book does not appear to have been kept in use longer than one year. The practice of affix-

[1] Address. [2] Hunt's Practical Gauging. [3] Leadbetter, 1743.

ing the initials on regauging, and the entry of the date and utensil regauged in the front, is old.

DISPLACERS.

These were "invented" by T. Brain, Port Surveyor, London,[1] and introduced in 1853 on a change being made in the mode of charging the duty on spirits delivered from warehouse—the actual quantity in the cask. They are thus described:—"The displacer consists of a set of eight closed tubes joined together by a few links of a chain. Each tube with half the connecting chain will displace, when immersed in a fluid, exactly one pint, and there is a groove round the middle of each tube to indicate half a pint."[2] The limit of displacement is consequently one gallon.

DIVINE SERVICE.

The employés in Scotland in 1804 were strictly enjoined not to attend any place of worship "where his Majesty and the Royal Family are not prayed for as directed by law."[3]

DIVISION OFFICER.

Setting aside such terms as gauger and officer, the earliest equivalent was Foot-Walk officer, and was continued down to 1789, and in Scotland to 1810, when this designation was superseded by that of division officer, which continued unqualified until 1870, when the distinction of senior division officer and junior division officer was introduced and retained till 1876, when reversion was had to division officer. The Central Committee of 1867 suggested the use of second and first class surveyor. In 1847 a division was reached in six years, in 1867 not until ten or twelve, in 1878 ten years.

DOCTOR.

An individual who in Ireland "makes his tour through a certain

[1] C. S. G., 1877. [2] Nov. 4, 1853. [3] Instructions.

class of publicans previous to fairs, races, patrons, or other public assemblages, and doctors their liquor for them, with the stipulation . . . . . that the drink is to be consumed immediately, hence the maddening effect of whisky sold at Irish fairs and other meetings of the peasantry."[1]

DOG LICENCE DUTY.

It was about 1790 that the first mention was made of a tax upon dogs. Mr Martin then suggested, as he had done on a previous occasion, that a tax of one shilling per head should be levied on each dog, to which Mr Pitt replied that "he had heard of an intention to take dogs as a parochial tax and appropriate the produce in aid of the poor rates," and that "whenever any practical plan of that kind should be offered to the House, he would pay it due attention."[2] From this date, however, no further mention appears to have been made until 1796, when the inhabitants of Worcester and Leicester petitioned the House of Commons to adopt the suggestion, and Mr Dent proposed a tax of two shillings and sixpence per dog, except upon those used by blind men, and to give force to his proposition, he stated that no fewer than 1500 sheep had been annually killed by these "confounded curs," and that as many as thirty-three persons had been in one week admitted into the Manchester Infirmary of hydrophobia. In this he was not successful, as the Chancellor of the Exchequer proposed and carried that a tax of three shillings per dog should be paid by those who paid assessed taxes and one shilling by those who did not,[3] but in this even the financier himself was not successful, the Bill having been thrown out on the second reading.[4] But still resolved to impose the tax, he two days afterwards moved that a duty of five shillings be paid on every spaniel, setter, or greyhound kept at an assessed house, and three shillings if kept elsewhere, except where more than one be kept, poor persons being allowed to keep a dog free, if not a greyhound, hound, pointer, setter, or spaniel. This he carried by a majority of 133 votes—ayes 152, noes 29. Here, then, is the origin of the tax, applicable to only Great Britain, and though proposed by the Chancellor of the Irish Exchequer in 1805 to be extended to

[1] Alchymista; C. S. G., 1867.
[2] H. C., Dec. 20, 1690.
[3] H. C., April 5, 1796.
[4] H. C., April 25, 1796.

Ireland,[1] it has, although levied in that country, never been accounted for as an assessed or imperial tax.

In 1831 two petitions were presented to the House of Commons to relieve the shepherd of the tax on his dog, and this relief was subsequently given[2] though afterwards repealed on the change in the form of the tax. This relief has been again and again since sought, but not obtained[3] until 1878, with an exemption in favour of the blind.

The very general belief in 1860 that the tax was largely evaded prompted the suggestion that it should be commuted into an excise licence duty,[4] and six years afterwards, when the cattle plague was supposed to have been spread by wandering, homeless dogs, that the assessed tax should be repealed, and that a five-shilling excise licence duty be imposed in its place.[5] Indeed the Commissioners had drafted a Bill for the purpose as early as June 1866, but as the Government were not then prepared to proceed with the measure,[6] Mr Hunt introduced it, and carried it through Parliament in 1867,[7] and *Punch* caricatured it as "Excisemen going to the Dogs."

The very large increase in the number charged—not forgetting that sheep dogs were previously not assessable—attracted the attention of Parliament,[8] and induced the Commissioners to observe in their Eleventh Report that during the eight months of 1867 upwards of 400,000 more dogs were charged under the new system than in the whole of 1866 under the old system. This great success occasioned a very animated discussion between this section of the department and that of the Taxes, and resulted in several good ideas for the further increase of the charge, such as the following—the holding of sittings by supervisors to grant the licences, the issue of licences at the Post Offices, both of which subsequently received the sanction of the Board.[9] Yet notwithstanding this closer collection and these increased facilities to obtain a licence, a "reproach" has always been cast on the department that very many escaped payment—a reproach which is founded partly on tradition and partly on truth. True, because a wandering cur is ownerless, and consequently unattached to any one on whom liability can be fixed; had a liability

[1] H. C., March 13, 1805. [2] Muir's Stamp and Tax Office Manual.
[3] H. C., April 4, 1872; Deputation to C. of Exc., Oct. 10, 1873; H. C., March 31, 1874. [4] C. S. G., 1860. [5] C. of Exc., March 7, 1866.
[6] H. C., June 20, 1866. [7] H. C., Feb. 16, 20, 1867. [8] P. Ret., 1867.
[9] C. S. G., 1868; A. B., Hugh Littlejohn; Estimates, 1870.

attached as in the case of the former Townland Fines in Ireland, then few would have remained uncharged. This statement is supported by the large capture of wanderers in London in, about, 1868. and in Glasgow in 1877. To remove this slur on the staff, the Commissioners resolved in 1877 to commission suitable persons in 1878 to demand the production of the licence, and failing its production, to report the defaulter, under an agreement for half the penalty recovered. The Commissioners state in their Nineteenth Report that they had also resolved to discontinue the practice of accepting compromise fines, as a rule, as the publicity obtained through the press "has had a very good effect upon the duty," and further, that "We may probably have to propose some measure for delegating to the police authorities some of our powers of instituting proceedings, with a view of obtaining a more thorough collection of the duty and a diminution of the correspondence and registration at this office"—the prosecutions being somewhat "less than one per cent." This power was delegated in 1878.

Among the various changes which have been suggested, since the duty has been collected under the licence system, may be mentioned —the transfer to the police;[1] the extension of the exemption from six to twelve months;[2] the substitution of a discriminating duty;[3] the rigid enforcement of the duty—*i.e.*, "One which permits no unowned, unregistered dogs. Every dog should have a collar with the name of the owner, and the number of the licence."[4]

The rates of duty have varied as follows:—

					Commenced
1796.	3s. to 5s. per dog.	£20 per pack of hounds.			July 5.
1797.	4s. to 6s. „	£24	„	„	
1802.	6s. to 10s. „	£30	„	„	
1806.	10 per cent. added.	„	„	„	
1808.	7s. to 11s. 6d. per dog.	£34	„	„	
1815.	8s. to 20s. „	£36	„	„	
1840.	10 per cent. added.	„	„	„	
1854.	12s. per dog.	£39, 12s. 0d. and £9.			
1867.	7s. „	£23, 2s. 0d. and £5, 5s. 0d.			
1867.	5s. uniformly.[5]				
1878.	7s. 6d., with exemptions.				

[1] C. S. G., 1869. [2] H. C., July 1, 1869. [3] H. C., April 3, 1873.
[4] Contemporary Review, Jan. 1878; Dr Acland on Dog-Poison.
[5] Comrs. Reports.

The gradual numerical increase, since the commutation, is shown below.

440,000 greatest number charged as a tax. Comrs. 19th Report.
1868. 1,465,949 paid for in about 1¼ years. Comrs. 12th Report.

Y.E. March 31.					
1869.	1,068,221,	an incr. of	142·77 °/₀	on old system.	Com. 13th Rep.
1870.	1,140,727,	„	159·25	„	„ 14th „
1871.	. . .	. . .	. . .	. . .	„ 15th „
1872.	1,127,944,	„	156·35	„	„ 15th „
1873.	1,167,189,	„	165·27	„	„ 16th „
1874.	1,238,245,	„	181·41	„	„ 17th „
1875.	1,270,350,	„	188·71	„	„ 18th „
1876.	1,373,936,	„	212·25	„	„ 19th „
1877.	1,399,330,	„	218·02	„	„ 20th „

Tables of cases decided by the Judges will be found in Muir's Manual, already referred to, and in the Board's 11th and 20th Reports.

DOUGARTHY'S GENERAL GAUGER.

"The General Gauger, or the Principles and Practice of Gauging Beer, Wine, and Malt," containing decimal arithmetic, problems in geometry, use of sliding rule, gauging by pen and sliding rule, tables, &c. "The whole laid down more Methodically than any Performance of this Nature yet extant, by Mr John Dougharty, Teacher of the Mathematicks at Worcester." Second edition, 240 pages 8vo. London, 1712.

This book, though not written by an employé, is expressly written for his use, and is dedicated "To the Honourable . . . . Chief Commissioners and Governors for the Management and Receipt of Her Majesty's Revenues of Excise, within the Kingdom of England, &c."

DOUGLAS'S MANUAL

Of Summary Proceedings in Excise Cases, for the Use of Inland Revenue Officers, by Sholto Douglas, Esq., Barrister-at-Law. Printed and published in 1853, by Eyre & Spottiswoode, by order of the Commissioners.

The only other specially-issued manuals, observed by the writer, appeared in 1716, by Ellis, and in 1828 in the form of "Instructions."

DOUGLAS'S TURNSTILE.

A simple, safe, expeditious mode of communicating with duty-free malt kilns and stores without the intervention of revenue lock—save on the regulator—or notice, by means of an ingeniously-contrived circular iron casement, into which are cut two opposite perpendicular openings, through which and a "turnstile" revolving from the centre of the casement, but adjusted by a regulator acted upon by a key, one person may pass at a time in a very perpendicular position, if not too corpulent, the invention of Mr R. M. Douglas, of this department, who had the satisfaction of seeing the first erected at Paisley in 1871, and after a year's trial and some few improvements, which experience showed to be desirable, the further satisfaction of receiving the Board's approval on May 28, 1872, since which it has gradually grown in favour with both the trade and the department, The price in 1877 was about £33. The invention is not patented.

The first attempt of this kind was made by Mr Warner, afterwards of the Stamp Department, Dublin.

DRYDEN, JOHN.

Being in pecuniary difficulties he wrote, in 1683, to Earl Rochester for "some employment in the Customs or Excise that would render his creditors easy." Dryden did not obtain an appointment, but an additional £100 per annum to his laureat pension.

DUTIES.

Fiscal. The generic term is revenue, and has been employed for centuries, but first in connection with the Church, as "revenues" in 10 Richard II., and as "des revenues du droit de la corone Denglet Dre" in 4 Henry IV. c. 4.

It was early applied to the Excise duties, as in the "Cryes of

Westminster" in 1647, and although it is used in the 12 Charles II. c. 23, it was referred to with some little surprise even in 1676 —"The excise, &c., has got the reputation of a Revenue in the King's Speech, and so printed in the King's Speech."[1] Then, again, in 1679, an act was passed "for the Excise to be made a Revenue;"[2] ten years later it was referred to as the "Publique Revenue,"[3] and the following year said Sir J. Lowther, "I move you to settle the Revenue on King William and Queen Mary for their lives;" this invoked the inquiry, "you must tell us what you mean by Revenue, as for the Excise part of it it is hereditary; it was so, and I know not what has made it otherwise."[4] From these statements it will be inferred that the word revenue originally applied to the personal receipts of the Crown.

The specific terms duty, duties—"dutee, dutees," found in use in the time of Henry IV. in an Act respecting feigned suits for the recovery of debts[5]—in the earliest impositions under the name excise were truly specific by reason of their number and distinctive character. This will be seen in the following lists—

Beer, 1s. per barrel of 8s. value.
„ 2s. „ „ „ by innholders.
„ 6d. „ „ „

"Beefs, Muttons, Veals, Porks, Lambs, and other Butchers' Meats," 1s. "on every twenty shillings value of the beast when he is living."

Conies or rabbits, ½d. each.	Mercery ware.
"Currans."	Paper.
"Druggs."	Pepper.
"Earthenwares."	Perry, 1s. per hhd.
Figs.	Pigeons, 1d. per dozen.
Furs.	"Raysins."
Glasses.	Salt.
Grocery ware.	"Saltery wares."
Haberdashery ware.	"Silkes."
Hats.	"Sope."
Lace.	Strong waters.
Leather.	Sugar.
"Linnens."	"Syder," 1s. per hhd.

[1] H. C., March 12, 1676. [2] H. C., May 23, 1679.
[3] 1 W. & M. c. 14. [4] H. C., March 28, 1690. [5] 5 Henry IV. c. 8.

Thread.
Tobacco, 4s. per lb., &c.
Wine, 1d. and 2d. per qt.
Woollen cloth.
"Wyer."[1]

It would appear from Blomefield's "History of Norfolk" that the Magistracy was made use of at this time—"And this year, on Nov. 2, the Excise began; the Excise Office was set up at Mr Alderman Pargeter's house for 6d. a Barrel to be paid for small Beer, and 2s. for Best and all Beer above 6s. a Barrel value."—Norwich.

Again, duties as well "Forreigne as Native"—

Almonds.
"Alum."
"Aniseed," 1s. 9d. per cwt.
Bread, white, 1d. per 1s. value.
Butter, ½d. per lb.
Buttons, gold and silver, 2s. per £. value.
Cheese, ½d. per lb.
Cinnamon, 4d. per lb.
Cloves, 4d. per lb.
Copperas.
"Cotton wooll," 3s per cwt.
Ginger, 5d. per cwt.
Hats.
Hops.
Irish combed wool, 1d. per lb.
Iron, 10s. per ton.
"Licoras," 1s. per cwt.
"Maces," 6d. per lb.
Malt, oaten, 1s. 4d. per qr.
Malt, not oaten, 2s. per qr.
Meat.
Monmouth caps.
Nutmegs, 3d. per lb.
"Oyle," 20s. per ton.
Prunes, 8d. per lb.
Saffron.
Starch.
Stuffs.
Sugar, white, 3d. per lb.
Tin.
Tobacco pipes.
Upholstery.
Wares.
Wood.
Wool, 2s. per lb.[2]

And being pressed for revenue, in addition to these duties, each housekeeper with his family was required to fast once a week, "and to pay what he usually spent at such a meal for the public service."[3] A woman, too, at Henley-upon-Thames, who grumbled at the unwonted taxation, was ordered by the authorities to have her tongue fastened by a nail to the body of a tree by the highway side on a market day, which was accordingly done, and a paper in great letters, setting forth the heinousness of the "fact," fixed to her back to make her the more notorious.[3]

[1] P. O., May 13, Sept. 11, Jan. 9, 1643. [2] P. O., July 6, Feb. 17, 1644.
[3] P. O., March 26, 1644; Lord Clarendon's State Papers, 1646.

In Scotland, too, the duties were over and above the Customs—

Ale or "Beare, 00·00·04" per pint.
„ "00·01·00" „
„ "00·00·06" strong „
Aqua vitæ, 00·02·08" per pint.
Baize, 1s. and 12s. per elne.
Calves, 2s. and 4s. each.
Coal, exported, 6s. and 12s. per £12 value.
Cloth, broad, 6s. and 12s. per elne.
„ cambric, &c., 1s. per 20s. worth.
„ narrow, 2s. per elne.
Goats, 2s. and 4s. each.
Hats, beaver, 24s. each.
„ half do., 12s. „
Kine or bulls, slaughtered—
"00·13·04" to £16 value.
"01·00·00" above.
"02·04·00" when "transported."
Lace, gold and silver, 13s. 4d. per elne.
Lambs and Kids, 2s. each.
Made work, imported, 13s. 4d. per £12.
Plush, 20s. per elne.
"Sattin," 13s. 4d.
Sheep, slaughtered, 2s. and 4s. each.
Silk, imported, 12s. and 24s. per elne.
Silk stuffs, 6s. 8d. and 10s. per elne.
Stirkes, 4s. and 6s. 8d. each.
"Stockins," silk, 13s. 4d. per pair.
Swine, 6s. each.
Tobacco, "00·06·00" per lb.
Wine, French, 1s. 4d. per pint.
„ Spanish, 2s. 8d. „ [1]

And lastly the Oxford Excise—

Apples, 2s. per bushel.
Beans, 1s. per qr.
Brass, 1s. per 20s. worth.
Capons, 2d. each.
Charcoal, 1d. per sack.
Chickens, 3d. per doz.
Ducks, 1d. each.
Faggots, double, 4d. per 100.
Fish, 1d. per 1s. worth.
"Furres," 1s.
Geese, 2d. each.
Hay, 1s. per load.
Hens, 1d. each.
Hen eggs, 4d. per 100.
Hops, 1s. per 20s. worth.
Larks, 1d. per doz.
Leather, etc., 1s. and 1s. 6d.
Mallards, 1d. each.
Oats, 10d. per qr.
Oysters, 4d. per barrell.
Peas, 1s. per qr.
Pears, 3d. per bushel.
Partridges, 2d. each.
Pheasants, 3d. each.
Pewter, 1s. per 20s. worth.
Skins, various.
Snipe, 2d. per doz.
Straw, 6d. per load.
"Sucking Pigge," 2d.
Teal, 6d. per doz.

[1] Act and Ordinance, Jan. 31, 1644.

Turkeys, 3d. each.
Turkey's eggs, 1d. per doz.
Wood, hard, 1s. per load.
Woodcocks, 1d. each.
Wool, 8d. per load.[1]

In this way was the excise revenue at first raised, though not according to what might be paid, but according to a fixed demand per month, hence it has been already shown, under the head Excise, to have been continued from month to month. This is again confirmed in Ayloffe's "Ancient Charters," which, in the case of Scotland, refers to precepts "out of the monethly mayntenance of Excyse," usually collected by so much per county, first for the Army, then for "publick uses;" afterwards by three-monthly sums of £29,331 each, "Scots money," the country being divided into thirty-three districts.[2]

In England, in 1647, the demand was £60,000 per month, the country being divided into seventy districts or collections, from each of which a fixed sum was exacted, which varied from £31, 11s. 6d. in Merioneth to £4763, 1s. 1d. in Norfolk.[3] On Oliver Cromwell uniting England and Scotland into one Commonwealth in 1655, most of the English duties were extended to that country.[4]

The earliest duties to be given up were those on the primary necessaries of life, such as bread, flesh, salt,[5] and gradually the majority of the others, down to the Restoration of Charles II., when in England only those on beer, cider, metheglin, mead, and strong water were retained.

From this date down to 1797 the number of articles or "heads" subject to duty increased to 27, probably the greatest number at any one time chargeable since 1660; and with the growth of the science and art of finance, the duties charged under these, and other heads since imposed, have been divided into various kinds, as indirect, direct, inland, temporary, hereditary, annual, perpetual, growing, licence, per cent., ad valorem, ready money, composition, bye, local, countervailing, import, differential, protective, export, conscience,—all of which will now be briefly noticed.

Indirect Duty—one which is ultimately paid by a second or more remote person; *e.g.*, beer duty added to selling price,[6] malt duty added to selling price, and stipulated quantity of malt given for

[1] "Order," dated Oxford, Oct. 11, 1645.
[2] Scotch Parliament, 1663.
[3] P. O., June 22, 1647.
[4] P. O., May 22, 1655.
[5] P. O., June 11, 1647.
[6] 12 C. II. c. 23.

rent lessened in proportion.[1] In 1869 a paper was prepared for the Social Science Congress in Bristol, in which the writer pointed out "The possibility of entirely Repealing all Duties of Customs and Excise, with suggestions for a plan of Direct Taxation, by John Nolle." Compared with direct, writes Dawes in his "Industrial Life," "comparatively needy persons, ... by smuggling foreign spirits, or by working an illicit still, may hope, if successful in their villany, to gain a prize of many thousand pounds. . . . . In an industrial point of view, then, it seems indisputable that the evils of indirect taxes greatly outweigh those of the direct"—"if successful"!!

Direct Duty—one not recoverable from a second person. Mr Ewart—"That it is expedient that a new direct system of taxation in property should be substituted for the indirect system (the Customs and Excise Duties now in use."[2] Dawes writes here too—"None but the wealthy can possibly practise a fraud to a large amount by evading direct taxes."

Inland Duty as distinguished from the Customs duty on the same article, as tea, coffee, &c.[3]

Temporary Duty.—This distinction was introduced by 12 Charles II. c. 23, which granted duties for the then king's life only, and used in opposition to

Hereditary Duty, or those duties granted by the next chapter to his Majesty, his heirs and successors: the tobacco duty, too, granted under the 14 & 15 Charles II. c. 8, is an hereditary duty. The account of these duties was formerly kept apart,[4] and the distinction obtained in 1736, a motion having been then made to produce an account of the net produce of the hereditary and temporary excise.[5] The hereditary duties in Ireland were "more extensive, not in amount, but in the objects embraced, than the hereditary revenue . . . . in England." The Civil List, in lieu of this revenue, was granted in Ireland in 1793, and in England about the same time.[6]

Annual Duty.—Conspicuous in this list was the malt duty, which was formerly voted annually, but in 1822 made a permanent or

Perpetual Duty, though not in such emphatic language as that

[1] 12 Anne. [2] H. C., May 28, 1847. [3] L. G., 1724.
[4] 12 & 13 W. III. c. 12. [5] H. C., March 8, 1736.
[6] Chancellor Irish Exchequer, H. C., March 12, 1804.

on hops—"continue for ever."[1] Of course the hereditary duties are perpetual, in abeyance.

GROWING DUTY.—This is a term used for the most part by this department, and includes those duties charged in the progress of manufacture, &c. Green, in her "State Papers," in 1665, refers to the "growing excise," and the phrase "to grow due" is used in the 12 & 13 William III. c. 11. Highmore mentions twenty-two heads of duty in 1796, the Parnell Committee[2] twenty-seven articles subject to duty in 1797, but these have been gradually reduced from fifteen in 1833, ten in 1835, to five in 1877. In contradistinction to this is the

LICENCE DUTY—an annual or shorter period payment for permission to act in a defined capacity, to use or sell a certain article, to employ a servant, &c. The licences are divisible into trade and establishment; the duties into "variable" and "invariable,"[3] and charged upon different principles, as, the ad valorem, *e.g.*, rate of house; the progressive, *e.g.*, malt;[4] the discriminative, *e.g.*, retail beer;[5] the conditional, *e.g.*, brewing, refreshment wine; the self-charging, *e.g.*, brewing;[6] the uniform, *e.g.*, dog.

PER CENT. DUTY—a percentage added to an existing duty, as the 5 and 15 per cent. in 1779,[7] and the 5 per cent. in 1781 and 1840.[8]

AD VALOREM DUTY—as paper, "an ad valorem one, estimated by the maker at the price at which he sold his produce;"[9] also indirectly, spirits. *See* Licence Duty.

READY-MONEY DUTY—an old departmental term applied to duties paid without credit.[10]

COMPOSITION DUTY—an old form at first to secure privacy. The Commissioners "to compound and agree" with private persons "for a weekly payment of certaine summe of Money in the Grosse," for the commodities to be used by or spent in their own families.[11] The most remarkable instance is the hereditary composition, in the case of one Forbes, who was allowed to erect a distillery and to make spirits, without limitation, on the payment of a yearly sum "of ffour hundreth merks scots," in consideration of the losses which he had

[1] 1 G. I., sess. 2, c. 2.
[2] Twentieth Report.
[3] Parnell, Nineteenth Report.
[4] W. E. Gladstone, H. C., April 18, 1853.
[5] H. C., April 3, 1873.
[6] P. P., 1835.
[7] H. C., March 12, 16, 1779.
[8] H. C., March 14, 1781; May 1840.
[9] Lord North, H. C., March 19, 1781.
[10] 1782: 12 C. II. c. 23.
[11] P. O., Feb. 17, 1644.

sustained in the support of the State.[1] Other instances may be found in malt in 1713:[2] London publican in 1726; cider in 1764; stage carriage in 1855. The principle was also applied in the case of arrears of duty.[3] The abolition of "composition" was advocated by Mr Gladstone in 1853.[4]

BYE DUTY—one which, owing to the great distance to travel, to charge, or the small amount of duty to be charged, or both, is found impracticable to collect in the usual course; as malt, ale, leather. In Scotland both supervisor and officer were enjoined to attend fairs, weddings, &c., to charge and receive the duties.[5]

LOCAL DUTY, or "town's impost," common in Scotland. A portion of the Excise duties was paid to the Magistrates and Town Council of Edinburgh and other places,[6] and in other instances applied to parochial purposes.[7]

The Town Council of "Air" were authorised by the "Estatis of Parliament" to levy "one merk upon each boll of malt to be ground" at "the milns of Air" for the space of two years, to raise a fund to repair the harbour. It appears that they had previously enjoyed, under the late King, a sanction to levy 20s. Scots "on each boll of malt which was brewen and vended."[8] A somewhat similar concession was made to the inhabitants of Irwin,[8] and a larger one to the people of Aberdeen on malt, ale, and wine; and a like concession to those at Dysart and Culross.[9] An Excise Act was passed in Scotland in 1707 to enable the authorities of Aberdeen, Borrowstounness, Dundee, and Kirkcaldy to make a levy on beer, &c., for local purposes, in consideration of former privations,[10] and after the Union similar exceptional legislation was obtained in 1804 in favour of Dalkeith, and in 1807 in favour of Burntisland and Kinghorn. In Ireland in 1729 the card and dice duties collected in Dublin by this department were applied to the encouragement of navigation.[11]

COUNTERVAILING DUTY. On the cessation of the prohibition and bounties on articles imported from Ireland on Jan. 1, 1801, countervailing duties were, with few exceptions, fixed to continue twenty years: they were also exacted on Scotch and Irish spirits brought into England.[11] A similar duty was also levied on commodities im-

[1] Scotland, Estates of Parliament, 1690.
[2] 12 Anne.
[3] Green's State Papers, 1665; 12 & 13 W. III. c. 11.
[4] H. C., April 18, 1853.
[5] Scotch Instructions, 1804.
[6] Act, July 29, 1644.
[7] Convention of Estates, Jan. 31, 1645.
[8] July 16, 1695.
[9] July 17, 1695.
[10] Estates of Parliament, March 25.
[11] P. Rep., 1809.

ported from the Isle of Man,[1] and is still levied on Channel Islands spirits. "A countervailing duty" is charged on sugar used in brewing.[2]

Import Duty—formerly included three principles—protective, prohibitive, and countervailing, and as such usually higher than that on the same article produced at home—*e.g.*, hops in the ratio of 3 to 1;[3] mum, 3 to 2; spirits, 2 to 1; while malt was seizable.[4] With the exception of Channel Islands spirit, perhaps, import duties are now collected by the Customs on the principles of free trade. The relative duties on foreign to home produce are in the ratios of—Chicory, 13·30d. to 12·1d.; malt, £1, 4s. to £1, 1s. 8d; spirit, 10·5d., 10·2d., to 10·0d.: the extra duty appears to have been imposed to cover the Excise restrictions on the home article.

Differential Duty.—Sir R. Peel, "The great principle of the noble lord, on which the House is to decide to-night, is, whether it be just, with respect to all articles the produce of your colonies, that the same rate of duty should apply as applies to articles the produce of foreign colonies? If that principle be correct, there is an end of your colonial system."[5] An example is found in the import duty on spirits—colonial, 10s. 2d., foreign, 10s. 5d.—difference, 3d.; another in the case of the difference between the duties on spirits in England, Scotland, and Ireland.[6]

Protective Duty.—Though the duty on sugar used in brewing has been shown as a countervailing duty, it is equally so a protective duty to that on malt, with which sugar, in this instance, competes: the chicory duty, too, bears the same relation to that on coffee. "Of all the duties on the Statute Book," observed the Chancellor of the Exchequer in 1851, "protecting duties are undoubtedly the worst. . . . . The protection on coffee is 50 per cent. . . . ."[7] The new term, that is, since free trade principles have been adopted, is "Retaliatory duty."[8]

Export Duty.– Few instances. An early one is found in Scotland on coal,[9] and another on beer used or spent on a voyage.[10] Since the introduction of Free Trade, instead of an export duty, not only is the duty returned, but also an equivalent paid to the producer

[1] T. W., May 14, 1828.
[2] C. of Exc., H. C., July 19, 1850.
[3] 9 Anne c. 12.
[4] Collection of Statutes, Edinburgh, 1724.
[5] H. C., May 13, 1842.
[6] Lord Naas, H. C., May 16, 1851.
[7] H. C., April 4, 1851.
[8] C. of Exc. at Exeter, 1877.
[9] Act and Ordinance, Jan. 31, 1644.
[10] 1 W. & M. c. 22.

of the article for the expense to which he has been put under the excise regulations, though this equivalent is not given in every case.

CONSCIENCE MONEY.—The conscientious payment of an omitted excise duty. Since the transfer of the establishment licence duties it may have been more frequent; it is now brought to account as "Excise."[1] *See* Conscience Money.

DOUBLE and other multiple duty will be presently noticed.

The imposition and modification of duties, as already stated under the paper Excise, have always been authorised—the Commonwealth alone excepted—by the three estates of the realm—the King, the Lords, the Commons—and they will be found both chronologically and historically detailed in the Commissioners' reports. In their first report, printed in 1857, the various changes in the duties which they were then collecting are traced from the earliest dates possible, and each subsequent yearly issue, with the exception of the thirteenth report in which "some retrospective history" is given, indeed, a very valuable contribution, contains a ten-yearly comparison of both quantities and duties, with general observations, but as this series of papers will contain brief outlines of the various duties, no further reference will now be made to them.

Exemption from duty was sanctioned almost as early as the excise itself—"no excise to be paid" on beer and cider used in fishing;[2] "all viveris for wse of the Kingis hous to be free of excyse;"[3] the University of St. Albans and the Mystery of Vintners of the City of London have always been free from the wine licence duty;[4] "all licential books" enacted free from excise duty for seven years to give the advantage of learning.[5] Mr Gladstone advocated "the abolition or almost abolition of exemptions" in 1853.[6] A recent instance of the enactment of this privilege will be found in the establishment licence act of 1869.[7] The transfer of duties from this department appears to have been almost entirely to the customs. Thus, the duties on cocoa nuts, coffee, pepper, foreign spirits, tobacco, and snuff, were handed over in 1825, and that on tea in 1834, all, it will be observed, duties on foreign or imported articles. But with respect to the transfers to this department, the Parnell committee state in their twentieth report, "when Mr Pitt was Prime

[1] 1871. [2] P. O., Feb. 17, 1644. [3] Scotch Act, March 29, 1651.
[4] 12 C. II. c. 25, *et seq.* [5] Scotland, 1669.
[6] H. C., April 18, 1853. [7] 32 & 33 Vict. c. 14.

Minister, he transferred several duties from the customs to the excise, in consequence of the extent to which, at that time, owing to the bad management of the commissioners the customs revenue was defrauded; and latterly, the Government have retransferred several duties from the excise to the customs." Among those to this department may be mentioned—

1719 hide duty from comrs. of taxes.
1798 salt duty from comrs. of salt.
1837 post horse from comrs. of stamps.
1847 railway } from comrs. stamps and taxes.
1847 stage carriage }
1856 racehorse.
1861 stamp licences.
1867 assessed tax-dog.
1870 assessed taxes—horse, carriage, &c.

This leads to the commutation of duties. The first observed mention of this new form of modification is by Mr Gladstone in his first financial statement, when he referred to the "commutation of taxes,"[1] which it has just been shown, was in part effected in 1867 and 1870. An instance of the commutation of an excise duty occurred in 1862, when the hop duty was commuted into a brewing licence duty,[2] and this mode of continuation would seem to have been quite in keeping with the terms of continuance in which this duty—already referred to—was originally granted—"for ever." It was formerly the custom to embody in the act the period during which a duty should be levied, as at first, for one year, as August 1, 1644 until August 1, "in the year of God 1645,"[3] then "one whole yeer longer,"[4] two,[5] three,[6] four,[7] five,[8] sixteen,[9] thirty-two,[10] ninety-six,[11] ninety-nine years,[12] a regnal life,[13] a royal succession.[14] But even under these precise phrases, sometimes a suspension has been authorised, as during a war,[15] or on the agreement to the civil list.[16] The recommencement to levy a duty was formerly called the revival. The most modern mode of continuance is by the Expiring Laws

[1] H. C., April 18, 1853. [2] Mr Gladstone, H. C., April 3, 1862.
[3] Scotch Ratification. [4] P. O., April 8, 1644. [5] P. O., April 25, 1646.
[6] Scotch Convention of Estates, March 7, 1649. [7] 9 Anne c. 12.
[8] Scotland Estates of Parliament, Sept. 6, 1681. [9] 5 & 6 W. & M. c. 7.
[10] 8 Anne c. 7. [11] 5 Anne c. 19. [12] 4 & 5 W. & M. c. 3.
[13] H. C., May 22, 1685. [14] 12 C. II. c. 24. [15] 3 & 4 Anne c. 13.
[16] 11 & 12 W. III. c. 15.

Continuance Acts, as in the case of malt charged by the weight of the grain.

Augmentation—a singular mode of increasing the duties on beer and malt was adopted in 1700; this consisted in requiring obedience in the use of the "ale-quart" instead of the "uncertain measures much less than the standard." This in modern language is termed the augmentation of a duty.[1] The practice observed on the actual addition to a duty has almost invariably been, in later years, to make the charge on the stocks in hand on the day the resolution is passed; it was so in 1854 on the increase of the malt duty;[2] so in 1855 on the additional duty laid on spirits;[3] so in 1863 on the increase in the customs duty on chicory, but in the case of an immediate levy and payment, "on condition, that should the House be pleased not to confirm that resolution the difference of duty paid would be returned."[4] On the reduction of a duty, it has not been necessary to apply a principle so instantaneous in character, seeing that the possessor of the article would benefit more by a larger than a smaller stock. To continue modern instances. In 1852, Mr Disraeli proposed to reduce the duty on malt one-half, on October 10, 1853, and allow repayment to the extent of the stocks then in hand;[5] in 1855 in consequence of the permission to use malt duty free in distillation, the stocks of spirits in the hands of the distillers were taken, and a drawback at so much per gallon was made in the repayment of the duty on the malt, &c., used;[6] and in 1856, on the repeal of the "war malt duty," the same practice was observed. Indeed the practice of the department is based on the principle of give and take, or, to quote the Chancellor of the Exchequer, "that the stock in hand should be subject to the increased duty on the same principle that the stock in hand had the benefit in the case of a reduction of duty."[7] Then with respect to the repeal of a duty, it has already been shown that it was for many years the custom to pre-enact it, *i.e.*, include it in the original enactment, thus in such terms as "cease and determine" or "surcease."[8] It is now usually dependent on the annual estimates.

For the practice on the repeal of a growing duty, see beer duty, &c.

The most general attempt at repeal was made by the least able to do so, in the person of Mr George Potter, who headed a deputation

[1] H. C., April 20, 1855. [2] H. C., May 9, 1854. [3] H. C., April 23, 1855.
[4] Mr Gladstone, H. C., April 30, 1863. [5] H. C., Dec. 3, 1852.
[6] H. C., June 5, 1855. [7] H. C., April 23, 1855. [8] 1647.

to the Chancellor of the Exchequer to urge the repeal of all the excise duties and to suggest an equivalent on "realised property;"[1] a pamphlet on the possibility of the repeal, already mentioned, having been printed in 1869.[2]

The duties, said Mr Pitt, are "computed on the quantities of goods either with respect to gauge, to weight, or to taille," and to these he might have added on other than goods by agreement or composition. The modes of charge exhibit the exactitude of the Excise as a system; they are two—the presumptive, the actual. The presumptive is made while the manufacture is in progress, as in the case of spirits by the attenuation, and in the case of malt by the successive gauges. The actual charge, as in the case of spirits, being the precise quantity delivered. The old mode of ascertaining the amount of duty, though the decimal factor for reducing gross to "neat" was then in use, curiously enough lay in deducting an equivalent to the gross over the net charge from the "integer of duty,"[3] or rate of duty, as shown under Beer on page 81; and in malt, when 4 in 20 bushels were allowed, hence duty 6d. less 1d. of. $\frac{1}{5}$ equalled 4d. 3f. $\frac{1}{5}$ per bushel. "To money" a charge, when the times and the men are considered, must indeed have been an undertaking. But this mode entailed a loss. The fractions of a farthing under a half were disregarded, while those of and above were computed as one farthing. To remedy this Mr Pitt observed that the total excise duty on many articles owing to the various times at which they had been imposed, frequently represented a fraction other than one of the aliquot parts of the current coin of the realm. He then proposed to repeal these inconvenient rates, and impose a single duty of easy calculation. His resolutions relating to both the Customs and the Excise were nearly 3000 in number.

A similar effort was also made in 1803 to raise the duty "when it made a fraction to the next integral sum above it."[5] The cumulative character of the rate of a duty is seen in that on cider in 1724, when it was levied under no fewer than seven Acts of Parliament.[6] The new system of "moneying" malt by first reducing the gross to the net quantity, and then by excluding quantities under five bushels

[1] March 10, 1874. [2] King, London. [3] 1784.
[4] H. C., Feb. 26, 1787. [5] C. of Exc., H. C., June 15, 1803.
[6] Collection of Statutes, Edinburgh, 1724.

has removed the difficulties of calculation and prevented the loss by fractions.

Abatements were always made in cases of loss and overcharge, and latterly in the case of lesser licence permission.

Among those in the case of loss may be mentioned one for the discharge of £21,000 to the farmers of London, Middlesex, and Surrey, in consequence of the loss sustained by the contagion in London,[1] and another for the discharge of "£27,684 out of their rent of the farm in respect of their losses by the plague, and for the moiety of 8d. per gallon on strong water imported"—this was £684 which had been omitted to be charged.[2]

His Majesty foresaw that a smaller receipt would be occasioned by the Plague, and promised an abatement in 1666.[3] So in the case of malt lost or damaged by fire, by shipwreck, or seizure at sea,[4] by unavoidable cause, by "short work,"[5] by defective germination. And so in the case of spirits lost by "conflagration,"[5] by unpreventable escape, &c. All being allowed on the principle that the amount had not been personally received, or that the articles had not been personally consumed. When the duties in Scotland were collected by so much per county per month, it sometimes happened that overcharges arose which were termed in local phraseology the "excressence of the Excyse," and out of which an abatement from the succeeding collection was met.[6] Cobbett refers to claims in his Parliamentary history in 1687 and 1688, and there is no doubt but that they were formerly numerous. Ireland affords a curious claim which arose by computing by the English instead of the Irish currency.[5] By the other and more modern form of "abatement," the lesser licence permission is meant the deduction under the 30 Vict., c. 16—wine licence. A surcharge, though etymologically nearly the same as overcharge, is financially not the same, being an amount due above that first paid by reason of the occupancy of higher-rated premises, the production of a greater or smaller manufacture, &c. Surplusage is an excess of duty above that required; surtax, an equivalent to the Excise restrictions.[7]

Then as to payments. These have been made sometimes on making the charge, sometimes after credit. One of the primitive

[1] T. W., Nov. 21, 1665.
[2] T. W., Sept. 9, 1667.
[3] T. W., Aug. 1, 1666.
[4] 12 Anne.
[5] P. Rep., 1809.
[6] Estates of Parliament, Sept. 9, 1663.
[7] 43 G. III. c. 69, Huie, Malt. C. 19 R.

methods was by a weekly entry of the commodities and payment of the duties upon them before they were consumed,[1] but the first general statutory regulation was that no person should travel further than the nearest market town in the same county on a market day, and that the payment should be made within a week or a month of the date of the entry,[2] and this principle, though much modified, applies now. Persons residing in the more remote places, and paying little duty, were early termed "bye-traders," and as such were allowed to pay their duties to the officer who visited their premises, though not without the written sanction of the collector,[3] nor even then should the duties amount, in Scotland, to more than forty shillings per round per trader,[4] or in England or Wales to one pound or ten shillings respectively, unless the traders were willing to again pay in case of default.[5] Other conditions have also been applied. To take an early instance of a payment in advance—the publican's annual licence duty—one moiety was paid on signing "the permission," the other at the end of six months,[6] and it may be remarked that this principle of prepayment appears to have been applied to the payment of all Excise licences. But "to rebate the time of payment" a discount of 12 per cent. was once allowed.[7] Advances, too, have been made on the duties, though Parliament resolved in 1681 "That whoever shall hereafter cause to be lent by way of advance any money upon the branches of the King's revenue, arising from Customs, Excise . . . . shall be judged a hinderer of the sitting Parliament, and be responsible for the same to Parliament."[8] These were usually made at a percentage, as in 1690, when £250,000 was advanced at 8 per cent. to wage war with France, and other advances were made for the same purpose under the authority of the 4 & 5 W. & M., c. 3, and the 5 & 6 W. & M., cc. 7, 20. They were also made by the farmers,[10] and by a distiller, the writer has been informed, for the Russian war of 1854.[11] For "prompt payment," said Sir Robert Walpole in speaking on the salt duty, "there was always a discount . . . . allowed;"[12] it was also early allowed in Scotland,[13] and in England on hops it amounted to 10 per cent.[14] On the Customs duties, said Lord North, it varies from "2½ to 20

[1] P. O., Feb. 17, 1644. [2] 12 C. II. c. 23.
[3] Scotch Instructions, 1804. [4] 1781, 1829. [5] 1778. [6] 1726.
[7] P. O., 1643. [8] H. C., Jan. 7, 1681. [9] 2 W. & M. c. 3.
[10] Cobbett's Parl. Hist., 1689. [11] Smith, Thames Bank.
[12] H. C., Feb. 9, 1732. [13] Act, Dec. 15, 1669. [14] 9 Anne c. 12.

per cent."[1] To those to whom credit was necessary it was at first given for eight months—one-eighth having been paid monthly,[2] and here is a singular reference to the eighth, which appears to have been observed in allowing a credit of one-eighth of the year, or a round, on giving bond with sureties. The length of credit even in the beginning of the eighteenth century was considerable; thus on salt it was six months,[3] on malt three months,[4] and in 1764 on cider it was six months, but with the changes which have since been made it has been usual to describe it as full,[5] long, short, extended credit, and this last term, though used in 1830, was again introduced by Mr Gladstone in 1863, when he proposed to give further time to pay provided the trader paid a percentage for a period of three months on the amount of the duty deferred.[6]

Into the Exchequer the duties were not at first paid, as the sinews of war were greatly needed by the Army Authorities, to whom the duties were paid direct,[7] though in 1654 it was ordained that every branch of the public revenue should be paid into the "Recipt of the Exchequer," at Westminster, from June 24, 1654.[8] Still it would almost seem that the duties were sometimes paid direct to the Army Authorities as formerly, as Pepys, who was Secretary to the Admiralty in 1660, wrote, "And so to my office again, where the Excise money was brought, and some of it told to soldiers till it was dark." With the restoration of Charles, however, it was enacted that all moneys should be paid into the Exchequer,[9] and though possibly observed, still by an "assignment" on the duties in the county of Leicester;[10] by a Warrant for a monthly payment to be made at Plymouth;[11] by a Warrant to pay £8300 for Secret Service;[12] and by an annual payment of £20,000, in quarterly instalments, for the same service,[13] it would seem that a portion was only "constructively" deposited. And to comply with this enactment the collectors remitted their receipts through approved bankers, who granted bills in favonr of the Receiver-General at so many days' date, as for instance, from Scotland at forty days' date.[14] On the

[1] H. L., March 14, 1781. [2] P. O., 1643. [3] 1707.
[4] 12 Anne. [5] 1807. [6] H. C., Feb. 16, 1863.
[7] Journal of the House of Commons, 1644, 1645. [8] P. O., June 21, 1654.
[9] 12 C. II. c. 23. [10] Green, State Papers, 1660.
[11] May, 1866. [12] Green's State Papers, 1665.
[13] Sir Francis Winnington, Bart., H. C., May 23, 1679.
[14] H. C., June 26, 1821.

Union with that country Lord Henry Petty brought in a bill to provide for the remittance of the Scotch revenue to England, by which collectors were required to send their duties to the local Receiver General, who was also required to deposit half in the Bank of Scotland and half in the Royal Bank, from which he would remit to the Bank of England whenever the total amounted to £5000.[1] The gross receipts were not formerly paid into the Exchequer, as it was usual for the Commissioners not only to discharge the cost of collection, but also to pay hereditary pensions. This very great trust, though previously mentioned in the House of Commons in 1837, appears to have attracted the attention of Dr Bowring ten years later, when he moved that the gross receipt of the revenue should be paid into the Exchequer, and no payment be made except under the express sanction of Parliament. In this the doctor was not successful; he withdrew his motion.[2] It remained for Earl Granville to accomplish this change in 1854 by a Bill which his lordship called the "Public Revenue and Consolidated Fund Charges Bill."[3]

As to the arrears of duty, these were formerly numerous,[4] both by those who could not pay and by those who would not pay, or, "malignants" and "delinquents,"[5] and included what were called the bygone excise,[6] the outstanding excise,[7] and arrears, whether "legally due or not,"[8] or what in modern times are termed uncollected duties, current arrears, and arrears, and were exacted at the very beginning of the system, under a penalty "of treble-value toties, quoties, to be leavied by distresse, and in default, satisfied by imprisonment;"[9] and in other cases four times the value of the duty and "the use of the Commonwealth," though if a sale were effected, which realised more than the amount of the duty, and the expenses incurred in recovering it, the overplus was paid to the defaulter.[9] In Ireland, under the 14 & 15 Charles II. c. 8, a penalty for nonpayment was exacted at £20, £40, and £60, for the first, second, and third week, respectively, with the forfeiture of double the value of the commodities; in England, under 12 Charles II. c. 23, an uniform exaction of double the duty was established, which has been continued down to the present time: both commodities[10] and

[1] H. C., March 19, 1807. [2] H. C., April 29, 1849.
[3] H. L., July 17, 1854. [4] Green's State Papers; Proclamation, Sept. 26, 1660.
[5] Scotland Estates, Parliament, 1646. [6] Idem., Feb. 13, 1661.
[7] Idem., Aug. 25, 1704. [8] 1812. [9] P. O., 1643. [10] 12 Anne.

"utensils" being also since "liable to duties";[1] one exception, however, having been made in a power to compound under the 12 & 13 W. III. c. 11. To show the extent to which this penalty was enforced in 1832, a time when its application was very common, it may be mentioned that no fewer than 501 double duty applications were made. These varied from 7½d. to £298, and although it was awarded in every case, it was not recovered in one instance, nor was the single duty ever lost. Amounts under ten shillings, of which there were many, seem to have been recovered without any charge, those at and above that amount at the uniform increase of 5 per cent.[2] Failing in this mode of recovery, either from the person indebted, or his sureties and their connections, then, as at the very beginning of the system, and as a last resource of satisfaction—imprisonment; the release from which a prayer was presented in 1662, by one who had suffered three years' incarceration.[3] The non-payment of licence duty has been usually enforced by a variable penalty, recoverable out of the offender's goods, or satisfiable by the imprisonment of his person.

ECOCKES'S UNIVERSAL TABLES.

First mentioned as the "Examiner's Pocket Gem," and defined by "W. E." to be two books of tables "to be used in the checking of certain revenue charges made on malt and spirits"—"Universal Tables."[4] To describe, in part, in the author's own words, "Examples. The area of a couch is 16·53, and the dip 11·4. The gauge is found by opening No. 1 book at folio 16, and No. 2 at page 53. The little finger of the left hand on line 11 in column 4 indicates, in No. 1, 182·4, and the forefinger of the same hand, in the corresponding position of No. 2, indicates 6·0, making (mentally) a sum of 188·4, and leaving the right hand free to tick off. And this would also be the charge arising from 1653 gallons of wash which had attenuated 57 degrees (57 × ·2 = 11·4), and the proof gallons 114 bulk gallons at 65·3 per cent overproof. This is simply the product of the factors 1653 and 114, minus the superfluous figures, and is just the same as if we were to multiply separately 16 whole numbers by 114, and 53 hundredths by 114, cross-adding the products to the

[1] 7 & 8 W. & M. c. 30.
[2] P. Rep., 1833.
[3] Green's State Papers.
[4] C. S. G., 1871.

requisite extent only, namely, to the tenth, which is separated from the whole numbers by a line or rule instead of by the customary decimal point." Thus—

No. 1 Book.

16	0	1	2	3	4	*
11	1 76 0	1 77 6	1 79 2	1 80 8	1 82 4	

No. 2 Book.

53	0	1	2	3	4	*
11	5 8	5 8	5 9	5 9	6 0	

* Of course extended to 11·9.[1] This principle of addition of part products will be found under Spirit Duty.

Having myself tested, with the original manuscript, the utility in economising time and labour, my testimony is willingly added to that given by a portion of the examiners in 1871. Mr Ecockes spent ten years in raising these two books of tables. The highness of the estimate for printing, however, precluded the possibility of the publication, if the expenditure were to be met by the sale of the work, as only few copies were ordered,[2] but not daunted by this lack of patronage, the author brought out "Universal Tables:" these were not the whole of those originally intended under that title, simply "Tables for Malt Floors and Areas of Rectangular, Elliptical or Circular Utensils and Incumbrances," with an Appendix on "Gauging"—malts, spirits, casks, and ullaging. Published by the author, price 3s., 1872. And Areas of Circles from the Circumferences, in 1875.

ELLIS'S "INSTRUCTIONS"

For Collectors of Excise in prosecutions before Justices of the Peace for Forfeiture incurred, Offences committed against the Laws relating to the Duties of Excise, and other Duties under the Manage-

[1] Prospectus. [2] C., 1872.

ment of the Commissioners of Excise, with some Observations on several Clauses in the Excise Acts," &c. The author also gives a series of forms and precedents. John Ellis, Excise Office. 1716.

EMBEZZLEMENT.

Personal appropriation of Crown property, whether money,[1] seizures,[2] or stores.

An early instance of the inability to cope with this form of misdeed, by two members of this department, occurred in 1697, when the Receiver-General was sent to the Tower, and Bartholomew Burton to Newgate for embezzling some £7, 12s. which they had obtained by falsely endorsing exchequer bills; and to inflict adequate punishment upon these offenders it became necessary for the House of Commons to specially pass bills to do so; this the House did, but when the measures came before the House of Lords, the votes being equal, the bills were rejected and the prisoners released.[3]

Much more severe was the law on those who, unconnected with office, obtained revenue money by "housebreaking." (See Excise Trial, Edinburgh.) The mere detention of revenue was punished by dismissal and by the exaction of 12 per cent. on the amount detained, and treble the damage to the party aggrieved, under 9 & 10 W. 3, c. 44, probably the first general enactment of this character. In 1809-10 the subject further engaged the attention of the Legislature, and Sir J. Neport brought in "a bill to render the embezzlement of public money by any collector .... felony without benefit of clergy,"[4] so as to have one law "for the rich and the poor," as the principal could not be punished, while the guilty clerk suffered the penalty of death.[5]

The outcome of this effort was the infliction of transportation or the penalty attachable to a misdemeanour, at the discretion of the Court; while making a false statement or return of money, was deemed and adjudged a misdemeanour, punishable by fine and imprisonment.[6] These enactments, with some modifications, have been since embodied in the 7 & 8 Geo. IV. c. 53.

[1] L. G., 1721. [2] 1726. [3] Parliamentary Debates.
[4] H. C., Feb. 17, 1809. [5] H. C., Feb. 15, 1810.
[6] 50 Geo. III. c. 59.

Compared with the large number of employés very few cases have been taken into Court.[1]

EMOLUMENTS.

By the use of "other emoluments" in conjunction with "salary, fees, and," it would seem that fees were formerly considered emoluments:[2] under the income tax regulations will be found "salary, fees, or emoluments."[3] It will be understood in this paper that emoluments other than fees are referred to. They were largest in Ireland. This appears on comparing the result of an inquiry in Ireland in 1809, when it transpired that 865 officers received "other emoluments," which amounted to £4775, or about £5, 10s. each, with that of a similar investigation in England in 1797, when 4649 received £11,908, or about £2, 10s. each.[4]

The subject of emoluments was inquired into by Parliamentary committees in 1797, 1798, 1828, 1830, 1848, 1850,[5] and 1836.

There are now but few, rewards, quit rent, and agricultural statistics, remunerations, duty pay, &c. (See Salary, Fees.)

ENTRY.

It has a three-fold signification. The admittance of an officer into an excise trader's premises as a right established under the 12 Charles 2, c. 23. II. The written return of the amount or quantity of an article made or sold in a given time, as once a week, a month,[6] or six weeks,[7] and in the event of two entries they were termed prime entry, post entry,[8] or the entry of a wrong quantity, short entry, or mis-entry. III. The written or drawn description of a trader's premises; at first in the form of a "notice" of the erection of a utensil or the use of a place,[10] and then gradually extended to an exact description of place, utensil, and purpose to almost every excise trader who, down to Jan. 5, 1828, delivered it to the "office-keeper," but after that date to the officer who surveyed his premises.

[1] 1807, 1815, 1834, 1842, 1844, 1853, 1855, 1873.
[2] P. Rep., 1809.
[3] Muir's Stamp and Tax Office Manual.
[4] P. Rep., 1797.
[5] Lord J. Russell, H. C., April 12, 1850.
[6] 12 C. II. c. 23; 1743 victuallers, distillers, chandlers.
[7] 1743 soapmakers.
[8] 1795.
[9] 1743.
[10] 12 C. II. c. 23; 1729.

To "witness" the making of an entry often sorely tried the attestator's patience, though perhaps he at one time received a fee for doing so;[1] still "Economy," "Hard-up," and others were finally introduced to suggest that a printed form of entry should be legalised,[2] and a "skeleton book" be prepared for its reception.[3]

These suggestions were enacted in the 30 & 31 Vict., c. 90, and acted upon after August 12, 1867, when certain traders were no longer required to make entry. The mark of a person who could not write has always been received, as "William Foulks

ISAAC X BROWN.
his mark,"[4] or . . . . .

"The
Hannah X Dorse,
mark of."[5]

EPITAPHS.

In Alresford Churchyard, Hants.

"Thomas Morgan, gent., died January 8th 1738, aged 76 years.

Near to this place Morgan, surveyor, lies,
Freed from the cares and troubles of Excise.
Now, no Superior power his works inspects,
There no more dread from Supervisor's checks,
For where he's now, he is undoubtedly,
From the reports and from the duty free.
Weep ye his friends, for the departed dust
Was to his King and to his country just,
The integrity he did therein (aford)
D . . . . Omniscient Lord.
Who by one stroke of death displaid His love
And called him to survey the heavens above."

This epitaph is believed by the inhabitants of Alresford to have been composed by Alexander Pope, the poet, who was staying at the Swan hotel at the time Mr Morgan died.

"In Alresford Churchyard, Benjamin Browne, late an Officer in the Excise, born near Penrith, in Cumberland, died May 15, 1750, aged 36 years :—

[1] Ireland. [2] C. S. G., 1857, 1858, 1864, 1865, 1866. [3] Idem., 1866. [4] L. G., 1792. [5] Idem., 1852.

No Supervisor's check he fears,
Now no Commissioners obeys.
He's free from cares, Intreaties, tears,
And all the Heavenly orb surveys."

TEMP. INCERT.

My Gauging-stick is now laid by,
My Sliding Rules neglected lie,
My Box and Tape likewise Brannan's
Must now be put in other hands;
My Brass Plate and Dimension Cane
Myself must never use again;
My Malt-Receiver and My Float
Must never more engage my thought,
My Bottle's broke, my pen wrote out,
My Ink is likewise turned drought;
My Book is closed, my gauge is cast,
And all my work is done at last.

In Lambeth churchyard. "Near this place are the remains of William Bacon of the Salt Office, London, gent., who was killed by thunder and lightning at his window, July 12, 1687, aged 34 years.

By touch etherial in a moment slain,
He felt the pow'r of death, but not its pain.
Swift as the lightning glanc'd, his spirit flew,
And bid this rough, tempestuous world adieu.
Short was his passage to that peaceful shore,
Where storms annoy, and dangers threat, no more.

In Hadleigh churchyard. "Sacred to the memory of Henry Hastings, late officer in the first division of Excise at Hadleigh, in the county of Suffolk. He died April 13th, 1834, aged 81 years. He was officer in the Excise forty years.

And to K. G. ye III. was true in trust,
In hopes to rise amongst the just.
Now here he lies quite free from care,
Until he doth the trumpet hear."

Place not given. "And a smuggler, the sworn foe of all excisemen.

Here I lies
Kill'd by the X I S."[1]

[1] Chambers' Journal, 1873.

ESTABLISHMENT.

That is, the number. Considerable difficulty has been experienced in preparing this paper; first, by the positive absence of information, and, down to a certain date, the scantiness of information; and then, by the perplexity presented, to some extent, in grouping or grading the various titular distinctions.

The earliest detail of the department is preserved in a Blue Book printed in 1705, but this, unfortunately for historical research, contains only the particulars of the London establishment, a note being added, to the effect, that there are no books in the office from which an accurate account can be given of the number of the officers, at this date, in the country establishment.[1] Then with regard to Scotland, it so happens that on the Union of that country with England, Letters Patent were passed to authorise the establishment in that country, but with respect to Ireland, the writer has not succeeded in obtaining an earlier account than that given for 1804.[2] From these sources, the departmental manuals, and the estimates, a table has been raised to show more particularly the number in the several ranks in the out-door branch, and that portion of the in-door which is drawn from the out-door branch of the department.

In all three countries there were distinct town and country establishments—known in England as "The London Establishment," "The Country Establishment;"[1] in Scotland as, "In Edinburgh and Precincts," "The Out-door Establishment;"[3] in Ireland as, "The Dublin City Excise," "The Country Excise."[2]

In connection with this subject are the annual Parliamentary papers, which show the increases and decreases, and the redundancies of employés in the several departments. These returns were probably first made with a view to continuation in 1831, and the largest number on the redundant list, appeared in 1842, in this form, number on the list at the commencement of 1841, 29; died, &c., 59; re-entered, 172; added during the year, 305; number on the list at the close of the year, 103. Redundancies of course arise through the repeal of fiscal duties, the discontinuance of official duties, and the consequent reconstruction of the department, of which an example may be cited in the repeal of the beer duty in 1830.[4] A large reduction also occurred on the repeal of the paper duty in 1861, but since that date there has been, with little exception, a gradual increase.

[1] Parl. Ret., 1705.
[2] Parl. Report, 1809.
[3] Letters Patent, May 22, 1707.
[4] Parnell, 4th Report.

Year.	England. Surveying General Examiners.						Collectors.					Supervisors.		Examiners.	Collectors' Clerks.				Officers.		Ride Officers.	Supernumeraries.	Assistants.	Expectants.	Sur. Gen. Exam.	Collectors.		
1645	...	...	...	...	...	...	1[1]	...	...	...	...	...	...	...	...	...	...	...	...	...	...	...	...	...	...	...		
1705	7[2]	...	...	...	...	...	1[3]	...	...	...	...	17[4]	...	14[5]	...	...	...	...	82[6]	...	...	...	41[7]	...	...	...		
1707	...	...	...	...	...	...	...	...	...	...	...	...	...	...	...	...	...	...	...	...	...	...	...	...	...	10[8]	1	2
1710	...	...	...	...	...	...	...	...	...	...	...	...	...	...	...	...	...	...	...	...	...	...	...	...	...	...		
1725	...	...	...	...	...	...	...	...	...	...	...	...	...	...	...	...	...	...	...	...	...	...	...	...	...	...		
1743	17[14]	...	...	...	...	...	1[3]	...	...	...	...	46[4,15]	...	27[16]	...	...	...	...	26[17]	270[18]	...	...	98[7]	...	...	...		
1743	...	...	...	...	...	...	50[20]	...	...	...	...	190[21]	...	...	22	...	...	...	2700[23]	...	...	...	...	...	...	...		
1766	19[25]	...	...	...	...	...	1[3]	...	...	...	...	61[4,15]	...	29[16]	...	...	...	...	36[17]	293[18]	...	...	106[7]	...	...	...		
1766	...	...	...	...	...	...	50[20]	...	...	...	...	190[21]	...	...	22	...	...	...	2700[23]	...	...	...	...	...	...	...		
1779	22[26]	...	...	...	...	...	2[27]	...	...	...	...	82[4]	...	46[8]	3[28]	...	...	...	91[17]	317[29]	...	...	66[7]	...	1[30]	...		
1779	...	...	...	...	...	...	53	...	...	...	...	272[21]	...	...	54	...	...	...	14[17]	2808[32]	...	52	1	...	2[33]	13		
1779	...	...	...	...	...	...	...	...	...	...	...	42[4]	...	...	...	...	...	...	...	...	...	...	...	...	...	...		
1797	...	...	...	...	...	...	6	...	...	...	...	...	...	...	...	...	...	...	1045[37]	...	...	...	...	...	...	...		
1797	...	...	...	...	...	...	56	...	...	...	...	...	...	...	58	...	...	...	3291[38]	...	...	...	...	...	...	...		
1797	...	...	...	...	...	...	...	...	...	...	...	...	...	24	...	...	...	...	...	...	...	...	...	...	...	...		
1802	20[41]	...	...	...	...	...	...	...	...	...	...	...	...	...	...	...	...	...	...	...	...	...	...	...	...	...		
1804	...	...	...	...	...	...	...	...	...	...	...	...	...	...	...	...	...	...	...	...	...	...	...	...	...	...		
1804	...	...	...	...	...	...	...	...	...	...	...	...	...	...	...	...	...	...	...	...	...	...	...	...	...	...		
1811	30[41]	...	...	...	...	...	...	...	...	...	...	...	...	...	...	...	...	...	...	...	...	...	...	...	...	...		
1811	...	...	...	...	...	...	...	...	...	...	...	...	...	30[41]	...	...	...	...	...	...	...	...	...	...	...	...		
1815	...	...	...	...	...	...	...	...	...	...	...	...	...	40[41]	...	...	...	...	...	...	...	...	...	...	...	...		
1817	3[48]	7	3	9	...	...	...	...	...	...	...	...	...	...	...	...	...	...	...	...	...	...	...	...	...	...		
1821	...	...	...	...	...	...	...	...	...	...	...	...	...	...	...	...	...	...	...	...	...	...	...	...	8[47]	19		
1824	6	13	...	15	...	...	...	...	...	...	...	...	...	...	...	...	...	...	...	...	...	...	...	...	...	...		
1825	6	13	6	25	...	...	...	...	...	...	...	...	...	...	...	...	...	...	...	...	...	...	...	...	...	...		
1828	6	17	6	31	...	...	...	...	...	...	...	...	...	...	...	...	...	...	...	...	...	...	...	...	...	...		
1830	...	...	6	...	...	...	...	...	...	...	...	...	...	68	...	...	...	...	...	...	...	...	...	...	...	...		
1831	...	...	...	...	...	...	...	...	...	...	...	...	...	...	...	...	...	...	...	...	...	...	...	...	...	16		
1833	...	...	...	...	...	...	...	...	...	...	...	...	...	...	...	...	...	...	...	...	...	...	...	...	...	16		
1837	...	...	...	...	...	...	...	...	...	...	...	...	...	...	...	...	...	...	...	...	...	...	...	...	...	...		
1842	...	...	...	...	...	...	...	...	...	...	...	...	...	...	...	...	...	...	...	...	...	...	...	...	...	...		
1843	...	...	...	...	...	...	...	...	...	...	...	...	...	...	...	...	...	...	...	...	...	...	...	...	...	...		
1844	...	...	...	...	...	...	...	...	...	...	...	...	...	...	...	...	...	...	...	...	...	...	...	...	...	...		
1845	...	...	...	...	...	...	...	...	...	...	...	...	...	...	...	...	...	...	...	...	...	...	...	...	...	...		
1846	...	...	...	...	...	...	...	...	...	...	...	...	...	...	...	...	...	...	...	...	...	...	...	...	...	...		
1847	...	...	...	...	...	...	...	...	...	...	...	...	...	...	...	...	...	...	...	...	...	...	...	...	...	...		
1848	...	...	...	...	...	...	...	...	...	...	...	...	...	...	...	...	...	...	...	...	...	...	...	...	...	...		
1849	...	...	...	...	...	...	...	...	...	...	...	...	...	...	...	...	...	...	...	...	...	...	...	...	...	...		
1850	...	...	...	...	...	...	...	...	...	...	...	...	...	...	...	...	...	...	...	...	...	...	...	...	...	...		
1851	...	...	...	...	...	...	...	...	...	...	...	...	...	...	...	...	...	...	...	...	...	...	...	...	...	...		
1852	4	13	4	14	...	...	61	...	...	...	...	295	...	...	72	...	...	...	1883	...	...	...	22	...	...	13		
1855[60]	1[61]	4	16	7[64]	20	...	61[62]	...	...	...	...	283[63]	...	55	75	...	...	...	1731[29]	...	...	55	25	200	...	13		
1856	1	4	16	6[64]	20	...	62	...	...	...	...	288	...	55	128	...	...	...	1768	...	...	...	25	200	...	13		
1857	1	4	16	6[64]	20	...	62	...	...	...	...	289	...	55	128	...	...	...	1743	...	...	...	50	230	...	13		

[1] Oxford excise, "and such as he shall appoint under him." [2] General gauger, chief examiner and
[7] Assistants. [8] Total in "The London Establishment" (Parl. Ret.) [9] Classed according to salary.
added for malt duty. [14] Inspector general, general examiners, chief examiners, general surveyors.
[19] "The London Establishment." [20] Collectors and one supernumerary collector. [21] Supervisors
(Leadbetter, 1743). [25] Inspector general, general inspectors, general examiners, chief examiners, general
general surveyors. [27] London Port and a supernumerary collector. [28] London Port. [30] Officers
[32] "Inferior officers." [33] General supervisors. [34] Including "collecting supervisors." [35] Super
Ret.) [37] "Inferior officials." [38] London and Port. [39] Surveying officers. [40] Count
inspector generals, one inspector. [43] Supernumerary gaugers. [44] Dublin City Excise. [45] Country
[47] General supervisors, general surveyor, general examiner. [48] Comrs. downwards (Edinburgh Almanac)
S., 12 from I. (Parnell, 20th Report). [53] Expectants. [54] Comptroller downwards. [55] Including
[58] According to Dr Bateman. [60] Year ended March 31, estimates. [61] Principal to 71 inc. [62] Every

Scotland: Supervisors	Scotland: Examiners	Scotland: Collectors Clerks	Scotland: Officers	Scotland: Ride Officers	Scotland: Supernumeraries	Scotland: Assistants	Scotland: Expectants	Ireland: Sur. Gen. Exam.	Ireland: Collectors	Ireland: Supervisors	Ireland: Examiners	Ireland: Collectors Clerks	Ireland: Officers	Ireland: Ride Officers	Ireland: Supernumeraries	Ireland: Assistants	Ireland: Expectants	Total
...	...	...	...	...	...	...	...	...	...	...	...	...	...	...	...	...	...	1
...	...	...	...	...	...	...	...	...	...	...	...	...	...	...	...	...	...	228[8]
3	...	...	206[10]	...	11	5	...	...	...	...	...	...	...	...	...	...	...	287[11]
6[11]	...	...	...	...	...	...	...	...	...	...	...	...	...	...	...	...	...	6
...	...	...	101[13]	...	...	...	...	...	...	...	...	...	...	...	...	...	...	101
...	...	...	...	...	...	...	...	...	...	...	...	...	...	...	...	...	...	734[19]
...	...	...	...	...	...	...	...	...	...	...	...	...	...	...	...	...	...	2940[24]
...	...	...	...	...	...	...	...	...	...	...	...	...	...	...	...	...	...	790[19]
...	...	...	...	...	...	...	...	...	...	...	...	...	...	...	...	...	...	2940[24]
6	...	...	41[20]	...	...	3	...	...	...	...	...	...	...	...	...	...	...	1084[31]
36[16]	...	10	404[18]	...	15	...	...	...	...	...	...	...	...	...	...	...	...	3987[36]
...	...	...	...	...	...	...	...	...	...	...	...	...	...	...	...	...	...	42
...	...	...	...	...	...	...	...	...	...	...	...	...	...	...	...	...	...	1051[38]
...	...	...	...	...	...	...	...	...	...	...	...	...	...	...	...	...	...	3405[40]
...	...	...	...	...	...	...	...	...	...	...	...	...	...	...	...	...	...	24
...	...	...	...	...	...	...	...	...	...	...	...	...	...	...	...	...	...	20
...	...	...	...	...	...	...	...	4[42]	1	...	22	...	44[6]	...	10[43]	...	...	164[44]
...	...	...	...	...	...	...	...	...	...	...	...	...	...	...	...	...	...	757[45]
...	...	...	...	...	...	...	...	...	...	...	...	...	...	...	...	...	...	30
...	...	...	...	...	...	...	...	...	...	...	...	...	...	...	...	...	...	30
...	...	...	...	...	...	...	...	...	...	...	...	...	...	...	...	...	...	40
...	...	...	...	...	...	...	...	...	...	...	...	...	...	...	...	...	...	22[41]
73	11	20	603	...	17	...	...	...	...	...	...	...	...	...	...	...	...	860[48]
...	...	...	...	...	...	...	...	...	...	...	...	...	...	...	...	...	...	40[49]
...	...	...	...	...	...	...	...	...	...	...	...	...	...	...	...	...	...	50[50]
...	...	...	...	...	...	...	...	...	...	...	...	...	...	...	...	...	...	60[51]
...	...	...	...	...	...	...	...	...	...	...	...	...	...	...	...	...	...	62[52]
69	...	19	587	...	15	30	205[52]	...	...	...	...	...	...	...	...	...	...	990[54]
74	...	18	704[55]	...	...	...	...	...	...	...	...	...	...	...	...	...	...	1035[56]
...	...	...	...	...	...	...	...	...	...	...	...	...	...	...	...	...	...	5038[57]
...	...	...	...	...	...	...	...	...	...	...	...	...	...	...	...	...	...	6774[58]
...	...	...	...	...	...	...	...	...	...	...	...	...	...	...	...	...	...	6801[58]
...	...	...	...	...	...	...	...	...	...	...	...	...	...	...	...	...	...	6838[58]
...	...	...	...	...	...	...	...	...	...	...	...	...	...	...	...	...	...	6516[58]
...	...	...	...	...	...	...	...	...	...	...	...	...	...	...	...	...	...	6427[58]
...	...	...	...	...	...	...	...	...	...	...	...	...	...	...	...	...	...	6313[58]
...	...	...	...	...	...	...	...	...	...	...	...	...	...	...	...	...	...	6006[58]
...	...	...	...	...	...	...	...	...	...	...	...	...	...	...	...	...	...	5068[58]
...	...	...	...	...	...	...	...	...	...	...	...	...	...	...	...	...	...	5472[58]
...	...	...	...	...	...	...	...	...	...	...	...	...	...	...	...	...	...	5457[58]
77	...	19	551	...	...	..	...	...	16	63	...	21	345	...	...	...	...	3473[58]
78	...	19	499	...	12	106	100	...	16	63	...	...	350	...	...	...	...	5051[71]
78	...	19	509	...	12	106	150	...	16	65	...	33	360	...	...	60	110	5288
80	...	19	540	...	...	150	120	...	16	69	...	33	407	...	...	100	110	5448

general surveyors. [3] Collector at London Port. [4] Surveyors. [5] Examiners. [6] Gaugers.
[10] Gaugers. [11] Comrs. downwards (Letters Patent, May 22, 1707). [12] Added. [13] Gaugers
[14] Port Surveyor. [16] Examiners and assistant examiners. [17] Principal. [18] Officers.
[21] Generally a clerk to each collector. [23] "Common officers." [24] The Country Establishment
surveyors (Leadbetter, 1766). [26] Inspector generals, inspector, chief examiners, general examiners,
[30] General surveyor. [31] The London Establishment, and "In Edinburgh and Precincts."
numeraries and assistants. [36] E.-The Country Establishment; S.-The Out-door Establishment (Parl.
Establishment and Ports (Parl. Ret.) [41] S. G. E. introduced (Parnell, 20th Report). [42] Three
Excise (Parl. Report, 1809). [46] Divided into four classes, June 25, 1817 (Parnell, 20th Report).
[49] Increased August 26, 1824. [50] Do. March 3, 1825. [51] Do. June 30, 1828. [52] 10 from
expectants. [56] All under Comrs. (Parl. Ret.) [57] H. C., June 13, 1837. [58] Parl. Ret., 1852.
class. [63] "Supervisors." [64] Inc. Port Surveyors to 1878. [65] First-class assistants.

England.

Year.	Surveying General Examiners.					Collectors.					Supervisors.		Examiners.	Collectors' Clerks.				Officers.		Ride Officers.	Assistants.	Expectants.	Laboratory.		
1858	1	4	16	7[66]	20	62	...	...	...	...	289	...	55	12	8 ...	...	...	1743	...	...	50	230	...	...	...
1859	1	3	18[66]	19[66]	...	61	...	...	...	...	289	...	50	12	8 ...	...	...	1730	...	...	50[68]	230[68]	...	...	...
1860	1	3	18	18	...	7	16	22	16	...	49[67]	240	50	5	61	61	...	998[68]	...	726	50	230	...	...	...
1861	1	3	18	18	...	7	16	22	16	...	54	235	50	5	61	61	...	1000	...	726	50	230	...	...	...
1862	1	3	18	18	...	7	16	22	16	...	54	235	50	7	61	61	...	999	...	726	50	230	...	...	...
1863	1	3	17	18	...	7	16	22	16	...	51	228	45	7	61	61	...	918	...	686	45	230	...	...	...
1864	1	3	17	18	...	7	16	22	16	...	54	222	45	7	61	61	...	898	...	685	30	230	...	...	...
1865	1	3	16	15	...	7	16	22	17	...	54	222	40	7	61	63	...	899	...	685	30	230	1	1	...
1866	1	3	16	15	...	7	16	22	17	...	54	222	40	8	63	62	...	898	...	685	30	250	1	1	...
1867	1	3	16	15	...	2	5	16	17	...	54	222	40	8	70	64	...	897	...	685	30	255	1	1	...
1868	1	3	16	15	...	1	10	52	...	...	54	222	40	8	72	69	...	897	...	685	42	255	1	...	...
1869	1	3	16	15	...	1	11	52	...	...	56	222	40	11	72	72	...	897	...	685	42	255	1	1	4
1870	1	3	16	15	...	1	11	52	...	...	57	221	40	11	72	73	...	896	...	685	42	300	1	1	5
1871	1	3	15	14	...	1	11	52	...	...	64	227	40	11	72	77	...	916	...	770	59	300	1	1	8
1872	1[69]	3	16	14	...	5	15	44	...	...	64	227	45	5	67	29	65	267[70]	649	770	55	300	1	1	7
1873	1	3	16	14	...	5	15	44	...	...	64	227	45	5	67	29	65	267	649	770	55	300	1	1	7
1874	1	3	16	14	...	5	15	44	...	...	67	227	50	5	67	29	66	283	628	776	58	294	1	1	8
1875	1	3	16	14	...	5	15	44	...	...	65	218	50	5	67	29	67	283	647	772	67	326	1	1	12
1876	1	3	16	14	...	5	15	44	...	...	69	219	50	5	67	31	68	288	640	772	67	299	1	1	13
1877	1	3	16	14	...	6	14	44	...	...	71	219	50	6	68	39	71	287	645	774	70	291	1	1	11
1878	1	3	9	21	...	8	20	36	...	...	60	222	50	6	69	115	...	920	...	782	75	287	1	1	11

[66] Second-class assistants. [67] Distinguished as footwalk and riding. [68] Division and ride officers. [69] "Inspectors of Excise." [70] Seniors to 1877. [71] From this date, downwards, total in department.

…tors.	…tors. (2)	Supervisors	Supervisors (2)	Examiners	Collectors' Clerks	Collectors' Clerks (2)	Collectors' Clerks (3)	Collectors' Clerks (4)	Officers	Officers (2)	Ride Officers	Assistants	Expectants
		SCOTLAND.											
...	...	80	...	...	19	...	...	...	340	...	...	150	120
...	...	80	...	...	19	...	...	...	340	...	...	150	12[illegible]
2	7	26	52	...	2	13	4	...	425	...	115	150	12[illegible]
2	7	28	52	...	2	13	4	...	425	...	115	150	12[illegible]
2	7	26	52	...	2	13	4	...	425	...	100	150	120
4	5	26	50	...	2	13	4	...	395	...	65	140	12[illegible]
4	5	31	48	...	2	13	4	...	381	...	60	115	115
4	5	31	45	...	2	13	4	...	381	...	60	115	115
4	5	31	48	...	2	13	5	...	381	...	60	115	110
4	5	31	48	...	2	13	5	...	367	...	60	115	115
...	...	31	48	...	2	13	5	...	365	...	60	115	115
...	...	31	45	...	2	13	6	...	349	...	76	115	115
...	...	31	48	...	2	13	6	...	349	...	76	115	115
...	...	28	45	...	2	13	6	...	353	...	56	105	113
...	...	28	48	...	2	16	8	18	90	240	86	110	114
...	...	28	45	...	2	16	8	18	90	240	86	110	114
...	...	28	48	...	2	17	9	20	88	246	95	110	114
...	...	28	54	...	2	18	9	20	88	243	105	116	124
...	...	25	53	...	2	15	9	20	78	250	105	117	121
...	...	25	50	...	4	10	14	21	79	254	105	121	126
...	...	25	49	...	4	10	44	...	314	...	103	125	12[illegible]

Collectors	Collectors (2)	Collectors (3)	Collectors (4)	Collectors (5)	Supervisors	Supervisors (2)	Examiners	Collectors' Clerks	Collectors' Clerks (2)	Collectors' Clerks (3)	Collectors' Clerks (4)	Officers	Officers (2)	Ride Officers	Assistants	Expectants	TOTAL
								IRELAND									
15	...	...	...	...	69	...	...	33	...	...	...	407	...	...	100	110	5469
15	...	...	...	...	69	...	...	35	...	...	...	404	...	...	100	110	5445
1	...	2	6	7	11	57	...	3	16	16	...	184	...	220	100	110	5439
1	...	2	6	7	11	57	...	3	16	16	...	174	...	220	100	110	5475
1	...	2	6	7	11	57	...	3	16	16	...	180	...	200	100	110	5412
1	...	2	4	7	10	55	...	3	16	16	...	165	...	175	100	110	5164
1	...	2	4	7	14	50	...	1	4	17	10	155	...	175	70	100	502[illegible]
1	...	2	4	8	13	41	...	1	4	16	15	15[illegible]	...	175	70	100	5019
1	...	2	4	5	13	43	...	1	4	16	15	15[illegible]	...	175	70	85	5025
1	...	2	4	3	11	40	...	1	4	16	15	15[illegible]	...	175	70	80	5036
1	1	12	...	...	11	46	...	1	4	15	14	145	...	175	70	80	5040
1	2	11	...	...	11	46	...	1	4	15	15	145	...	175	70	80	5069
1	2	11	...	...	12	45	...	1	4	15	15	145	...	175	70	80	5127
1	2	11	...	...	12	41	...	1	4	15	16	145	...	175	70	80	5112
1	3	10	...	...	13	40	...	1	16	7	16	34	111	175	70	83	5159
1	3	10	...	...	13	40	...	1	16	7	16	34	111	175	70	83	5190
1	3	10	...	...	13	40	...	1	16	7	16	29	126	172	73	83	5316
1	3	10	...	...	18	40	...	1	16	7	10	29	145	172	77	92	5349
1	3	10	...	...	17	40	...	1	16	9	15	34	145	172	86	11[illegible]	5358
1	3	10	...	...	15	40	...	1	16	9	15	34	149	172	80	101	5424
1	5	8	...	...	17	41	...	1	16	25	...	187	...	173	92	101	5434

ESTIMATES.

In 1837 the attention of Parliament appears to have been first drawn to the fact, that the Commissioners paid their employés without the sanction of that august assembly,[1] and again in 1847 by Dr Bowring, who moved a series of resolutions with respect to the payment of the gross receipts into the Exchequer, and asked why the salaries and pay in other departments "should be annually voted by Parliament; while the salaries of the Officers of the Customs, of the Excise, of the Stamps and Taxes, and of the Post Office never were submitted to Parliament at all until the expenditure had taken place, and Parliamentary inquiry came too late to correct abuse or check extravagance?"[2] He had previously moved similar resolutions, which, like the present, he withdrew. It was not until 1854 that the doctor's desire was realised. Earl Granville then took charge of the "Public Revenue and Consolidated Fund Charges Bill," whose object his lordship stated to be two-fold—to bring in the gross revenue into the Exchequer, and to leave "the expenses of collection to be provided for, as were the expenses of other departments, by the annual vote of Parliament."[3]

The first estimates were accordingly prepared and presented for the year ended March 31, 1855. For several years the estimated expenses were represented under some nineteen sub-heads, but in 1869 these were subdivided, and with others which had arisen in the meantime, amounted to no fewer than thirty, some of which will be noticed in this series of papers. It may be mentioned that the number of individuals, and the amount paid to them, are divided into effective and non-effective charges—the effective will be found referred to under Establishment and Salary; the non-effective under Charity Fund, Superannuation, and Widows and Orphans' Fund.

The amount of each sub-head is compared with that voted in the preceding year, and each has been accounted for, since 1866,[4] at the close of the financial year, when the expenditure is compared with the grant, the variation of surplus or deficit explained, the surplus surrendered, or the deficit requested to be voted, and the extra receipts included. These accounts are prepared under the superintendence of the Accountant and Comptroller General of Inland

[1] Mr Wallace, H. C., June 13, 1837.
[2] H. C., April 29, 1847.
[3] H. L., July 17, 1854.
[4] 29 & 30 Vict. c. 39.

Revenue, and examined under the directions of the Auditor General of Public Accounts, both of whom certify the correctness.

The increases made subsequently to the preparation of the Estimates are under the authority of the Treasury, and embodied in an appendix. This comparison of sums voted and expended is termed the Appropriation Account. The total annual estimate for each year since the estimates were first framed is as follows:—

1855—1,154,594	1863—1,382,274	1871—1,592,751
1856—1,365,950	1864—1,351,771	1872—1,625,625
1857—1,459,207	1865—1,313,467	1873—1,644,308
1858—1,429,133	1866—1,284,157	1874—1,678,236
1859—1,362,258	1867—1,332,707	1875—1,681,013
1860—1,349,864	1868—1,548,124	1876—1,697,172
1861—1,490,813	1869—1,574,210	1877—1,731,304
1862—1,456,485	1870—1,604,616	1878—1,788,850

EVERARD'S STEREOMETRY.

"Stereometry made Easie, or the Description and Use of a New Gauging-Rod or Sliding Rule, by which the Content of any Tun, Copper, Cask, or other Vessel may be readily found, either the whole or in part thereof: The Areas of Circles in Gallons and Barrels found by Inspection only. Also, The Extraction of the Square and Cube-root. Questions concerning Interest and Annuities, and many other Arithmetical Problems, are hereby resolved without Pen or Compasses. To which is added an Appendix containing the Description and Use of another New Rule very useful in gauging of Worts, and resolving Questions in the Mensuration of Solids and Superficies. With a Table of the Areas of Circles and Content of Cylinders in Ale Gallons: Calculated to every tenth part of an Inch, from 12 to 156 Inches Diameter. By Tho. Everard, Philomath, London. Printed by F. Playford, for R. Clavel, at the Peacock, in St Paul's Churchyard, and C. Hussey, at the Flower-de-Luce, in Little Britain. 1684." Dedicated to the Commissioners.

This book passed through at least nine editions. 1st, 1684; 2nd, 1702; 3rd, 1705; 4th, . . .; 5th, 1705; 6th, . . .; 7th, . . .; 8th, 1721; 9th, 1727; the last revised by C. Leadbetter, the author, apparently, of the Royal Gauger.

EXAMINER.

This is an old rank.[1] The designation at first expressed the particular engagement, as examiner of country officers' books,[1] examiner of town officers' books, examiner of London distillery officers' books,[2] but at length assumed plain examiner, and those who, not having been approved and appointed to the rank, though acting in that capacity, were called acting examiners,[3] a term also employed to the examiner,[4] and paid salary as examiner.[5] He is also sometimes called colloquially the sub-supervisor, assistant-supervisor,[6] suffragan-supervisor,[7] deputy-supervisor,[8] expectant-supervisor, probationary-supervisor.[9]

As to the admission to the rank. This was in the earlier days according to seniority and the approval of the survey books,[10] and this probably continued until 1817, when, on a favourable report by the proper collector, the personal examination was conducted by a Surveying General Examiner, who gave in his final report at the end of six months; preference, afterwards, being given to such as by service in two or more parts of the United Kingdom appeared to have embraced the opportunity of qualifying themselves for general service.[11] There were existing, too, at this time several special orders with a view to ensure practical knowledge—these were, instruction in the art of gauging at the Port of London, of which a certificate was required;[12] the ability to perform the import and export duties, and those in the correspondent's office;[13] a knowledge of the survey of the London Distilleries, at each of which three attended per month,[14] a regulation still in force in a modified form —three months in 1854, not more than six in 1872; the mastery of those duties, by Irish Examiners, in which they were uninformed;[11] and competency in the use of the callipers, for which a fortnight was allowed.[15]

That seniority was the first qualification, for many years, will be gleaned from the following regulations—in 1778, nine years' service, the last three in a footwalk[16] or clerkship;[17] in Scotland in 1804

1 P. Rep., 1705. 2 Royal Gauger, 1743. 3 1720.
4 1824, 1870. 5 S., 1804, 1824. 6 C. S. G., 1869.
7 Idem., 1870. 8 Idem., 1874. 9 Salary Statement, 1858; C. 10 R.
10 1810. 11 1829. 12 1815. 13 1817. 14 1818.
15 1833. 16 Instructions. 17 1810, 1829.

seven years, three last in a footwalk; in 1829 nine years, last three in a division; in 1843 seven years, three last in a division or clerkship; in 1845 the collector reporting as to "sufficient health, strength, and activity;" in 1853 seven years' service, the two last in a division. Ineligibility arose in 1815[1] after fifty years of age, and in 1843 any one who deferred his application until upwards of thirty-eight years of age was required to explain the reason for having done so.

No other important general change was made until 1840, when a knowledge of book-keeping by double entry and "grammatical proficiency" were required, but not until the expiration of three months after he had been otherwise approved. This system was revised in 1848 by an arrangement that, after the examination and approval of his performances, as shown by his survey books, he should attend the Chief Office, where he would undergo a test in grammatical proficiency, excise law and practice, handwriting, correspondence, dictation, official calculations, and book-keeping by double entry. Preceded by a preliminary examination before the collector—an examination which has been since discontinued—this system has been continued down to the present time with only few modifications, such as the personal before the book examination, &c.

Copies of the examination papers have been given in the Civil Service Gazette and Civilian since 1873. In Scotland, before the consolidation of the Boards, the candidate had to proceed to Edinburgh "to undergo his trials before the general surveyor, the general examiner, or a general supervisor, with respect to his knowledge of dry gauging casks and utensils, and surveying the several branches of the revenue, who, on being satisfied with the examiner's fitness, gave a certificate of his qualifications for the satisfaction of the Board; but if it so happened after his appointment that he was "not well skilled," he had "to survey" until he became qualified.[2] And the mode of selection in 1815 was this—when an appointment was about to be made, the official character of the three oldest footwalk officers, who had made application and served seven years, was examined, and the one against whom the fewest censures were recorded obtained the nomination, the others losing their claim; but on the next selection a third officer in "Rotation" was added to the two former, and the nomination given, as before, to the one who had

[1] Scotland.

[2] Scotch Instructions, 1804.

the fewest censures, and so on in succession; reference having been made, in every instance, to the collector as to the character of the selected candidate prior to his appointment.

All now proceed, at the expense of the department, except those who may go a second or third time, to Somerset House, "to undergo their trials," and with the exception of those who may reside in the London Collections, usually remain there until the decision is announced—the interval being utilised in the examination of table, dimension, and other books, &c., &c. In 1828 the unsuccessful were not allowed their travelling expenses. The largest number of examinations held in one year, within the writer's observation, was five, in 1869.

A satisfactory result having been obtained, it appears to have been long the practice for the newly-appointed and inexperienced examiner to at once go out to officiate. Otherwise it has long been the custom for each gentleman to proceed to perform the duty of a supervisor in the order in which he had returned from doing so, exception, however, being taken by "the ring," the six senior examiners, who are always the last to leave, and exception again being taken in favour of special aptitude, while an old regulation of 1830 forbade one to officiate where he was last an officer, and an older one of 1817 still requires the collector to report upon the examiner's character on his leaving his collection. His applications to the commissioners were in 1727 required to be sent through the surveying general examiner of that day. He was as early as 1731 and 1759 not allowed to give any official information, nor allowed as early as 1744 to take away any books out of the office without the Board's permission. Reference has already been made to the fact that sometimes several examiners accompanied a commissioner on tours of inspection. This possibly precluded, in some measure, the necessity for the issue of the caution of 1812, that "when travelling" he—examiner—was "not to pay coachmen too liberally."[1] In 1830 he was required to inform the Board one week before he expected to be relieved, when out officiating, and await orders: in 1783 he was required, on his return to the office, to report to his immediate superiors the state of the district.

In this way and under these various regulations, with employment in the office, where in 1817 he was reported upon every three

[1] Bell's Compendium.

months, and instruction in the modes of detecting adulteration in the laboratory,[1] has the variable probationary period of the examiner been filled up, until in possession of "the chair" he has become eligible for appointment to a district,[2] provided well qualified to undertake the survey of every growing duty,[3] but should he object to join his appointment, he was ordered in 1744 to be placed at the bottom of the examiners' list, though this has since been modified by the permission of a system called "begging," by which the appointment is offered to the next eligible in succession down the list, when, should another accept it, the "chairman goes down" and takes his substitute's place. Formerly upon "filling up" a district, the surveying general examiner gave in the character of the ten senior examiners, that the Commissioners might "select" the best qualified. This was prepared from the various reports which were summarised in "a Book."[4]

"Clearing out."—By an order issued in 1811, every examiner was required to produce a copy of certain letters to the "Surveying General Examiner at the time of clearing out to go to his district," a practice which prevailed down to and after the writer's exit. But "clearing out" had for many years a jovial, cheery, aspect in the gift of the supervisor-elect, who provided a supply of wine or other beverage to be quaffed from the office glasses by his lingering colleagues who bade him farewell. The custom in 1870 had, for the most part, fallen into disuse. In 1866 the probationary period was about twelve months; previously about three years. In 1847 a supervisorship was obtained in less than twelve years, in 1867 not under sixteen or eighteen years.[5]

The youngest examiner was formerly called "Boots;" he is now styled "Junior."

It has been suggested that examinations should be held in anticipation of vacancies,[6] and that the newly-appointed examiner should be allowed to gain a little experience in the examination of books before he is ordered to officiate.[7]

EXCHEQUER TALLIES AND BILLS.

A tally was a piece of wood written on two sides with an acquit-

[1] 1855. [2] General Instructions, 1872. [3] Idem., 1856. [4] 1817.
[5] Central Committee's Address. [6] C. S. G., 1873. [7] Idem., 1865.

tance for money received at the Tally Court of the Exchequer by the deputy chamberlain, who clove it asunder and gave one part, called the stock, to the person who paid or lent the money to the Government, and retained the other portion, called the counter-stock or counterfoil, in the Court until called for, and then joined it with the stock.[1] A drawing of this form of receipt will be found in Knight's Pictorial History of England.

It was in this way that advances on excise—both hereditary and temporary—duties were formerly acknowledged at the Exchequer, and it was adopted in the loan of £12,500,000 on the Customs, Excise, and other duties in 1663, when numerous tallies were "struck" in receipt of the respective advances,[2] and it appears by an affidavit made in 1666 that "several constats relating to excise specified, which are wanting, were burnt in the late fire of London, being eighty tallies to the value £136,424, 2s. od. dated from April 24, 1663 to May 26, 1666."[3] The date of repayment of the principal, with the interest accrued, was usually announced in the London Gazette by giving the numbers of the orders and tallies, and at the same time an intimation to the effect that those who failed to apply would not receive any additional interest.[4]

These disbursements were afterwards made by order of "His Majesty's Grand Commissioners of Excise" by this department under similar regulations, in both town and country—"country excise."[5] In 1698 the holders of these pieces of wood were only seven, the pieces only forty-six, the amount due only £3,956, 3s. 5½d.,[6] and in 1703 the Board announced its desire to pay the principal and interest on the "remaining tallies."[7]

Tallies were finally discontinued in the Exchequer in 1834.[8]

The Exchequer Bill succeeded the Exchequer Tally, though both were in circulation at the same time.

These bills appear to have been more generally received in payment of duties in past times than in the present.

They were falsely endorsed to obtain an earlier payment of interest;[9] they were counterfeited to obtain both principal and interest, and in this case by one Wm. Brook of Bewdley, Worcestershire, formerly a "writing master," for whose apprehension the

[1] Beatson's Political Index. [2] Green's State Papers, 1665.
[3] Idem., 1666. [4] L. G., 1666. [5] Idem., 1668, 1669, 1697.
[6] Idem., 1698. [7] Idem., 1703. [8] Imperial Dictionary.
[9] 1697.

Government offered an "encouragement," and to the holders of the original bills, paid the claims due by them[1]; they were also sometimes lost in transmission by post, even to the amount of £1,030, from the intimation of which it is gleanable that they were issued in amount in a multiple of five, as the total consisted in fives, tens, twenties, and one forty; but all were afterwards recovered. They were further, sometimes stolen from the postmen, a case in point being that of 77 amounting to £390 from Diss, between "Rumford and London."[2]

The departmental regulations were codified by Hersee in 1829, and consolidated in a general order in 1872, the rate of interest being now the only variable condition of receipt.

EXCISE AVENUE, COFFEE HOUSE, FLAG, STREET.

This is situated in Queen Square, Bristol, and so called by way of distinction from other avenues leading into the same square, and by reason of the proximity of the Excise Office. The old excise office, supposed to have been built about a hundred years ago, was burnt down in 1831, "the only relic of salvage being an old entry book."

The "Excise Coffee-house, Broad Street, London," probably took its name from its proximity to the Chief Office in that street. Tom Paine addressed a letter from it in 1760 to Oliver Goldsmith respecting the salary movement of that time.[3] The excise maritime flag consisted of a red ground, with a Union Jack which occupied one-fourth of its space at the upper left hand corner, and with a crown supported by a star, containing in its centre E X, which occupied the right hand half.[4]

The street at Kincardine-on-Forth was named by the lord of the Manor, Lord Keith, in 1816, in consequence of several officers living, and the excise office being, in it.

EXCISE COURT

of Summary Jurisdiction. This court was peculiar to London,

[1] L. G., 1698. [2] Idem., 1697. [3] C. S. G., 1872.
[4] Norie's Maritime Flags, 1842.

within the limits of the Chief Office. In Scotland the Commissioners never exercised the power of Summary Jurisdiction, except in the case of offences against the salt laws. The duties of the Commissioners consisted in hearing and determining the applications for penalties, double duty, repayments, and condemnation of seizures (see Seizures). In 1831 the Commissioners heard and determined, with a few exceptions—withdrawals—852 informations and 180 complaints. In 1832, 501 double duty applications—these ranged from so small a sum as seven pence farthing to £298, and although it was awarded in every case, it was not recovered in one instance, nor was the single duty ever lost. Amounts under ten shillings, of which there were many, seem to have been recovered without any charge, those of and above ten shillings at a uniform charge of 5 per cent. The Parnell Committee recommended the abolition of this Court.[1]

The Commissioners heard no fewer than 1200 cases in 1835,[2] but since the Summary Proceedings Bill passed in 1852 to give concurrent jurisdiction, within these limits, to the metropolitan police magistrates,[3] the Commissioners have seldom sat on Excise cases. The last observed case was in 1853, when H. F. Stephenson, A. Montgomery, and C. Pressly, Esqrs., determined an illicit distillation case.[4]

For "Excise Court of Appeal" see "Commissioners of Appeal."

EXCISE PRINTING ESTABLISHMENT.

The Commissioners formerly had an "Excise Printing Establishment," at which they printed all their official documents, but the Parnell Committee recommended in 1836 in their Twentieth Report that it should be at once abolished. The abolition was ordered by Treasury Warrant, dated June 15, 1841.[5]

EXCISE SCHEME.

This was a proposition by Sir R. Walpole, Chancellor of the Exchequer, to place the duties on tobacco and wine conjointly under

[1] Third Report, 1833. [2] Parnell, Twentieth Report, 1836.
[3] 15 & 16 V. c. 61. [4] C. S. G., 1853. [5] P. Ret., 1842.

the Customs and Excise. Hitherto they had been under the Customs only, but it appears that great frauds had been committed for a series of years, which, it was computed, annually amounted to £39,000. Sir Robert's proposal consisted in the erection of warehouses for storing tobacco, the question respecting wine not being discussed, under the care of the excise, the officer having one lock and key, and the depositor another, by whom 4d. per lb. would be paid on delivery. By this it was anticipated about 120 additional officers would be required, at an annual salary of £40 or £50 each, and that the Exchequer would be annually enriched to the extent of £300,000. After a very animated debate, which lasted until two o'clock in the morning, there were on the division for bringing in the Bill 206; against, 205. So much was the scheme thought to be a governmental or political project, that our author has given the names of those members who voted for the motion, and who held any government office—with him a very unusual practice.

On Friday, March 16, the House having again assembled to consider this measure, the Serjeant-at-Arms, as is usual on extraordinary occasions, summoned the whole of the members to attend prayers. On April 11 it was moved that the bill not being within the resolution it should be withdrawn, noes, 232, ayes, 176; afterwards, that it should be read the second time that day seven-night, ayes, 236, noes, 200. It was afterwards moved that the bill should be printed, that each member might have a copy, noes, 128, ayes, 112.

The order of the day having been read for the second reading of this famous bill, the Chancellor of the Exchequer moved that it be read a second time on the 12th June next, which was equivalent to withdrawing the measure; this, perhaps, was occasioned by the tumultuous gathering "in the courts and avenues" of disorderly persons, who, it was thought, had been induced to attend by the common council of the city. These "lovers of liberty" menaced, insulted, and assaulted the members as they left the House, and unquestionably frightened them out of their scheme while in it. In this memorable debate the Chancellor of the Exchequer informed the House that "one Midford, a tobacco merchant, happened to fail when he owed a large sum of money on bond, ... whereupon an extent was issued, ... and the Government got possession of his books, by which a fraud was discovered, in which a piece of paper containing a false weight was artfully pasted over the real weight, to obtain a larger drawback than he was entitled to, because he had to shew his books before he drew back the duty. Before this fraud was discovered he was reckoned as honest a man and as fair a trader as any in the city of London." Mr Alderman Perry asserted that "as to the fraud of 'Socking' (a cant word used for stealing and smuggling it out of the ships after the arrival in the river), I myself (by the permission of the Board) paid an officer a very handsome sum of money, which we all thought his diligence and integrity very well deserved."

The people in the midlands and south of England in particular were very much opposed to Sir Robert's scheme,[1] and numerous declamatory pieces were written and printed,[2] such as,—

The Rise and Fall of the late projected Excise.
A Review of the Excise Scheme.
An Argument against the Excise.
Reflections upon a Pamphlet.
Some Seasonable Animadversions on Excises.
Some Observations on a Paper, intitled the List, that is, of those who voted for and against the Excise Bill.
The Budget Opened, &c.
Englishmen's Eyes Opened; or, All made to see who are not resolved to be blind. Being the Excise Controversy set in a new Light.
A Second Review of the late Excise Scheme.
A Dialogue between Sir Andrew Freeport and Timothy Squat, Esq.
Epigram on the Excise Scheme.

Then coming to the prints and drawings, there is a flood of design, as,—

Excise in Triumph. An engraving printed in blue, and representing a merchant and Sir R. Walpole in the character of an exciseman, with a gauge in his hand and an ink-bottle at his buttonhole, waving his hat and seated astride a barrel, which is drawn by a unicorn with his tail cut and horn broken, on which is mounted a grenadier, and by a lion with his tail cut, wooden shoes upon his feet, and a yoke on his shoulders; over his head is a crow flying, &c. Beneath this is engraved Excise on a hogshead of tobacco.

[1] A Collection of Letters to Members of Parliament, 1733. [2] 1733-4.

The Noble Stand; Or the Glorious CCIIII. Sacred to their Immortal Honour, down to the latest Posterity. A party of men dancing round a May-pole, which is entwined with bunches of graves and leaves of tobacco; at the top of the pole is a label marked "Perry and Barnard," these were the names of the members of Parliament for the city of London who, with 202 others, opposed the "Excise Scheme," and aided in procuring its abandonment.

Excise Sermon. The frontispiece consists of an engraving in red ink, in which Sir R. Walpole is represented coming out of the House of Commons, exclaiming "It must and shall pass." A caution on "The Origin and Essence of a General Excise." "A Sermon Preached on a very Extraordinary Occasion, at a Noted Chapel in Westminster, on Wednesday the 14th of March 1732. By Robert Winer, D.D., pastor of the said chapel. Luke, chapter ii., ver. 1. 'And it came to pass in those days that a Decree went out, that all the world should be Taxed.' The text consists of a mock sermon, followed by an 'Excise Hymn.'"

"Britannia Excisa—Britain Excis'd." A woodcut representing a many-headed dragon harnessed to the chariot of Sir R. Walpole, and with the greater number of jaws devouring bottles, glass, tankards, pipes, sheep, and joints of meat, and decorated with festoons of "coquets and permits."

The London Merchants Triumphant, or Sturdy Beggars and Brave Fellows, being a sketch of the Rejoicings in the City on the Excise Bill being postponed.[1]

The secret of the "Excise Scheme" was perhaps told by the Duke of Argyll eight years afterwards. "My Lords, if that scheme had been contrived for nothing but to prevent smuggling, and had been thought effectual for that end, the very persons that petitioned against it would have petitioned in its favour. Instead of lighting up bonfires at its being rejected, they would have been lighted up on its being passed into law; and instead of ministers and members of Parliament, we should have had thieves and smugglers burnt in effigy in all parts of the kingdom."

[1] Prints and Drawings, British Museum. [2] H. L., 1741.

EXCISE TRIAL, EDINBURGH.

This is a book of 288 pages, with portraits of the two "pannels" by Kay, descriptive of the trial of Wm. Brodie and George Smith, before the High Court of Justiciary in August 1788, for breaking into and robbing the "General Excise Office of Scotland." The money stolen was about £16; the sentence—"to be hanged by the neck, by the hands of the executioner, upon a gibbet, until they be dead." "The crowd of spectators within the street, in view of the place of execution, it has been calculated, could not have been less than 40,000."[1]

EXCISE YACHTS.

Under this name in Scotland in 1779 were known the *Royal Charlotte*, the *Royal George*, and the *Prince of Wales*, vessels fitted out to cruise against smugglers at an annual cost of £684.[2] In 1823 there was a Yacht Department, consisting of an inspector of yachts, a cashier of yachts, and an agent and examinator of yacht accounts, and the vessels had been increased to nine, manned by 281 men and mounted with 72 guns, but by 1831 the number had been reduced to three, by apparently the transfer of the larger portion to the Customs.[3] In 1834 mention is made of only the *Atalanta*, which employed 50 men.[4]

EXCISEABLE LIQUORS (LICENCES) BILL.

This Bill originated with Mr Bruce in 1871, the then Home Secretary. In addition to the revenue it proposed to exact; it also contained regulations for the diminution of the number of houses, the more uniform issue of licence, the better management of houses, the suppression of adulteration, &c. He proposed to consider existing interests, to abolish the table beer licence, to make a distinction between liquors sold in open and closed vessels, to introduce new rates of licence duties, and by doing so, to abolish about four Acts of Parliament, and amend others. The licence to commence

[1] Creech, Edinburgh, 1788.
[2] Parl. Return, 1779.
[3] Edinburgh Almanack, 1821-1831.
[4] Parnell, Seventh Report, Part I., 1834.

on October 1, 1871, in England only. Publican's general licence from £5 to £7; do., limited, variable; beer, £3 to £6; wine, £2 to £5; beer and wine, £4 to £10; inn licences the same as publican's limited licence; eating-house licences the same as publican's limited licence; refreshment house wine licence, £3, 3s. to £5, 5s.; do., limited wine licence, £2, 15s. 8d. to £4, 4s.; railway refreshment rooms licence, £6, one room; £12, two; £17, three; theatre licence, same as publican's general licence; beer shop licence, £1, 1s. to £2, 2s.; spirit dealer's retail licence, £3, 3s; beer dealer's retail licence, £1, 2s.; wine retail licence, £2, 2s. to £3, 3s.; sweets retail licence, £1, 7s. To the present time three distinct methods had been pursued in granting certificates—the magisterial system, the free trade system, the system of popular control. In all cases now proposed, the licences would be preceded by a certificate from the Justices who would be guided by the veto of the rate-payers in each "licensing district," in so far as the power to diminish the number of houses may be concerned, but not the increase of them. The detection of adulteration under the Inland Revenue Chemical Staff.

A monster petition, 900 yards, more than half a mile long, and containing 40,000 signatures against the Bill, was carried to the table by the officers of the House, and presented by Sir T. Bazley on May 2.

The Bill did not pass. House of Commons, April 3—May 4, 1871.

EXCISEMAN, THE,

By Godfrey Grafton, gent. This is the title of one of the eight-page numbers of Kenny Meadows' Heads of the people. It is a description for the most part of the man of the past.[1]

"EXCISE-MEN'S LAMENTATION, THE,"

OR, "THEIR STRANGE CREED AND LETANY."

"O God the Father have mercy upon Us, miserable Excize-men; for we have done those things which we ought not to have done, and left undone those things which we ought to have done, and

[1] Vol. II., 1840.

there is no truth in Us; Lord Pardon all our high, unjust, and illegal proceedings, and deal not with us after our Sins, nor reward Us after our iniquities. And we beseech thee Lord pour thy grace into our hearts, that as we have known Christ thy son's Incarnation by the message of an Angel: so by his cross and passion we may be brought into the glory of his resurrection. But, Lord open thou our hearts, and let our purses shew forth thy praise; and so we may with cheerfulness and alacrity return and give in a most just and due account of all those vast and great sums, which we have wickedly, fraudulently, and deceitfully gained by an unlimited and outstretched Conscience; for we must ingenuously acknowledge and confess, that our carriage and proceedings hath been so high, rigid and harsh both to the Rich and Poor, that with a wet finger we could easily clear and lay up £500 per annum whereas before the blessed Reformation, we were not masters of 50 pence at the year's end: But alas! all those great and ill-gotten Revenues, after some time of Extortion, began to dissolve and melt like snow in warm gleams. Therefore we now earnestly desire to abandon those ways of wickedness; humbly beseeching the Lord to give us hearts to dread him, and for the time to come diligently to live after his Commandments. Yet notwithstanding many there are who still remain rigid and cruel to the Poor; and having lately put in practice their cruell proceedings at Monmouth, the poor people bulky ball'd Time by the forelock, unanimously rose and fell upon the quarters of one Mr Crowe (the Farmer of Excise) beat off his guard, but he himself escaped in his shirt and ran himself in a Tub of Feathers; but all would not save him; for at last he became a Bird in hand, and (contrary to his expectations) set him free with his feathers, who having made him sweare on the Bible, that he should become an honest man, they dismissed him without wounds, but half frighted him out of his wits. . . ." 1652, British Museum.

EXPECTANT.

This designation, introduced between 1779 and 1796, is stated to represent one who "after he is certified for and until he is employed, he is called an Expectant, having to wait till a vacancy happens."[1]

[1] Highmore's Excise Laws; L. G., 1796.

It was used in Scotland,[1] though at one time as "Expectant Officers,"[2] at another, "journeyman exciseman"[3] and its equivalent in Ireland, was probably until the consolidation of the Boards, "Supernumerary Gauger."[4] It was long customary for the supervisor to make a report, on the character of these beginners in his diary,[5] but this was allowed to fall into disuse in 1854. The designation was superseded by that of second class assistant by treasury minute, dated January 13, 1858. Promotion to the next rank has always been by seniority.[6] It has been suggested that the assistant, when unemployed, should be employed by the collector or supervisor.[7]

EXPORTATION.

"Exportation on drawback," by which is understood the return of a duty previously paid on an article afterwards exported, was allowed even during the Commonwealth,[8] and has been continued to be allowed on most of the articles liable to charge,[9] but on different principles, down to the present time, and has formed the subject for special enactment.

The duty drawn back has been sometimes the whole, as in the case of spirits in 1697; sometimes only a portion, as in the case of beer in 1689 and 1761, when, to cover the cost of charging the duty, threepence per tun was retained. At other times it has not been allowed, as in the case of imported mum in 1689, when no portion of the import duty was refunded on exportation. Here appears to be implied an instance of the abuse of repayment, which is not only confirmed by historical records,[10] but also by the introduction of a new system termed "exportation duty-free," exemplified, in 1726, in malt made expressly for exportation without the payment of duty, and in 1855 in spirits and malt made "under bond," with, in a few years afterwards, an adaptation, so far as regards spirits, to the principles of free trade, by the payment of two or three pence per gallon in compensation for the extra cost incurred in the production under fiscal restrictions. Further proof of the abuse of the system of repayment is afforded in 1817, when the Legislature enacted that the

1 1798. 2 1809, 1818. 3 1789. 4 P. Rep., 1807.
5 1819. 6 S., 1815. 7 C. S. G., 1862, 1874.
8 P. O., May 30, 1654. 9 Bateman, 1843.
10 H. C., Feb. 9, 1732.

duty should not be repaid on the exportation of an unmerchantable article.

The frauds committed by admixture, by short weight and measure, by relanding,[1] &c., occasioned the observance of very strict regulations. Even the officer who charged the duty was not permitted to attend the packing and sealing, nor he who saw the packing and sealing to attend the shipping, nor he who saw the shipping to administer the oath that the duty had been paid.[2] The exporter, too, was required to give security in treble the amount of the duty claimed, and wait a month or six weeks before he received the drawback, unless the shipment extended to only the Channel Islands, Isle of Man, or Ireland, then the production of a landing certificate at an earlier date obviated the completion of those periods. The loss of goods on transport, by being taken by an enemy, or by fire, or by shipwreck, on sufficient proof being adduced of the fact, in no way affected the repayment.[3] The exporter was spoken of as one who "drew back the duty."[4] The word drawback, too, was qualified as "countervailing drawback."[5] Allowances were also made on paper,[6] pasteboard,[7] and soap used by manufacturers and as ship's stores.[8]

The officials entrusted with these duties formerly received export commissions,[9] and they were grouped into port stations, notably so in London,[10] where the staff was called the Port Establishment,[11] but by the transfer of duties, both fiscal and official, to the Customs, their numbers have been considerably reduced.

FARMING.

A system of collecting which dates very far back—it may be traced to the reign of William II., 1088,[12] and it is curious to relate that official functions as well as fiscal duties were farmed, for Henry IV. had occasion to forbid the searchers at ports "to let to farm their offices."[13] Indeed it was the ordinary mode of securing the various impositions during the whole of the Restoration.[14]

[1] 1722. [2] 1812. [3] 1801. [4] H. C., June 12, 1733.
[5] Bateman, 1843. [6] 1820, [7] 1830.
[8] 1826, 1847. [9] 1856. [10] P. Ret., 1705. [11] P. Ret., 1779, 1797.
[12] Stow's Annals. [13] c. 21.
[14] Green's State Papers, 1660; L. G., 1665, 1668, 1669, 1676, 1688.

Existing records show it to have been applied to matters of excise in Scotland in 1645, when the commissioners were authorised "to ferme the Excise of the Wine to the Severall Burrows,"[1] and, generally, in that country in 1649 the "Marquis of Argyle" and another having been announced to have taken a "Tak of the Excyse."[2]

In England a Parliamentary Committee was appointed about 1650[3] to consider "as to farming it," and the result of its deliberation appears to have been favourable to the system, seeing that the Commissioners were shortly afterwards empowered to permit "each county to farm the Excise," under the impression that it would be "an advantage to the Revenue and ease to the country for gentlemen to manage the Excise,"[4] though it is questionable if this were realised, as the commissioners were either unable to let the whole of the farms, or, if they did so, the farmers either could not or would not pay the rents, and their honours were consequently ordered to take certain farms under their own immediate management.[3] Green, in her State Papers, informs us that applications for farms were numerous, even females applied, and many of the applicants offered large douceurs to those who were in a position to secure contracts for them, while others sought to obtain them under the plea of privations suffered in the troublous times.[5] In this way were the duties, for the most part, collected down to the Commonwealth,[6] but on the actual accession of Charles II., his Majesty authorised, by his twenty-third Act, the reintroduction of the system, after the duties had been collected for a period of six months, to enable the Lords of the Treasury to ascertain the value of the respective farms, though it would seem that the enactment was not then enforced--his Majesty having addressed the Justices of the Peace on June 28, 1662, to the effect that the people would be better cared for if the farms were let to only those who were recommended by them, and that they would direct those who were desirous to enter into contracts to repair to the Exchequer on August 10, 1662, when they would receive instructions respecting a contract for three years. Hume tells us that £1,000,000 was offered for the Customs and the Excise in 1660, and that it was the greatest sum ever offered. London and its surroundings were let as one farm, but in the country the limits of a county were usually those of a farm, whose rent varied, according to

[1] Act, Jan. 31, 1645. [2] Estaits of Parliament, March 16, 1649.
[3] Journal of House of Commons, 1650-59. [4] Cobbett's Parl. Hist., 1679.
[5] 1660. [6] Hume.

the population, the greater liability to duty, &c. The farmers were mostly men of means, able to advance large sums on account, as they often did,[1] acting even in the capacity of commissioners until they were restrained in 1663,[2] but even these powers, with the exception of the judicial part of hearing and determining offences, owing to their great influence, they regained,[3] and in Scotland even, sitting in Parliament, down to 1705.[4] They soon realised "great estates," and were looked upon by the people as "likely to become the nobility and gentry of England."[5]

The triennial period of lease continued with apparent regularity[6] down to June 24, 1683, when the system was announced, by Royal Proclamation, to be discontinued, though it was proclaimed on Feb. 16, 1684, by a similar State issue, that it would be readopted for the customary term.[7]

The spirit duties were farmed as late as 1796,[8] but the last duty, which was collected under this system, was the post horse, introduced by the Chancellor of the Exchequer of 1787 by a majority of 60 votes—ayes, 116; noes, 56; discontinued in 1836 by the Chancellor of the Exchequer of 1835, who described the system as "That striking remnant of barbarism in legislation."

FEES.

The receipt of fees for small services in England is traceable to 1689. An Act was then passed to forbid the acceptance on "writeing, signing and sealeing Instructions and Orders," except of "their Majestyes."[9] Early thus forbidden by an Act of Parliament, which appears to have been enforced with tolerable strictness, fewer and smaller fees obtained in this country, and with less notice,[10] than in Ireland, where the high rates of the numerous exactions amounted to an annual sum which frequently exceeded the salary paid, and eventually attracted the attention of a member of the House of Commons, who moved the appointment of a committee to enquire into the subject.[11] This committee was engaged in the investigation

[1] Green's State Papers. [2] 15 Car. II. c. 11. [3] 16 & 17 Car. II. c. 24.
[4] Scotch Parliament, July 22, 1705. [5] H. C., Feb. 23, 1670.
[6] L. G., 1667, 1670, 1676, 1677, 1680. [7] L. G.
[8] Parl. Report, Scotch Distilleries, 1799. [9] 1 W. & M. c. 24.
[10] H. C., June 2, 1783. [11] H. C., June 25, 1804.

about two years, and although, as will be presently shown by quotation, the "amount of the fees" was "enormous," the committee observed, "The result of our inquiries on this head impose on us the painful task of stating our conviction that the fees in most cases exceed those acknowledged to us by the officers."[1]

The next inquiry was not made until about 1838, when, owing to the increase in the number of duties, and the attendant increase in the number of fees,[2] another committee was appointed to inquire into and report upon "Fees in Public Offices," and this was the signal for the cessation of the system. With few exceptions, in favour of four London Port officials, who were allowed to continue to enjoy their receipts until the termination of their tenure of office, and of those who filled up pensioners' affidavits, all were deprived of this source of income, except, of course, that portion derived from instruction fees, from and after January 1, 1839,[3] and those who were entitled to claim compensation were granted it by a Treasury Warrant, dated July 20, 1839.

Only three recipients survived in 1868, and the total grant was only £36.[4]

Among the items which formed this source of receipt may be mentioned—

4d. and 6d. for filling up an affidavit.[5]

4d. and 10d. for completing a debenture.[6]

8d. and 2s. 6d. for filling up a bond.[7]

6d. and 1s. to collector, 4d. and 8d. to supervisor, 2d. and 4d. to officer,	per licence, in Scotland, to exert themselves to make "the duties on licences more effectual."[8]
£200 to "Examinator" £150 to "Assistant Examinator"	of Excise for preparing accounts for Parliament.[9]

DISTILLERY FEES—IRELAND.

3d. and 6d. for each permit = £30 a year, but received £70 for that and accommodation, to "full gauger."

2s. 6d. every time still unlocked, for "being set to work."

1 guinea per puncheon of private spirits, and from 20 to 25 sent out per week by one distiller.

[1] Parl. Report, 1807.
[2] 1802, 1804, 1813, 1820, 1822, 1828, 1833.
[3] T. W., Dec. 4, 1838.
[4] Estimates.
[5] 1719.
[6] 1796.
[7] 1796, 1808, 1811, 1814.
[8] Scotch Instructions, 1804.
[9] Hansard, Appendix, 1804.

1½ to 2 guineas per month from each of two distillers.
2 to 3 „ „ for granting permits—by rectifier.
10 to 20 „ „ for a 500 gall. still, } to gauger.
20 „ „ for a 1000 gall. still, }
20 „ „ of each distiller, to surveyor.
20 guineas for gauging or regauging a still; gauged about three times a year, to Inspector General.
20 to 40 guineas "for measurement or readjustment of the body or head of a still at the request of the distiller," to Inspector.[1]

Malt Fees—Ireland.

¼ to ½ of duty evaded on private steepings.
1s. per barrel for granting permits for "pretended removals."
2 guineas, sometimes, for granting a regular permit.
2 to 6 guineas per annum of each maltster, and if cisterns in one house, a double fee. Dublin fees higher than these.
10s. 6d. to clerk on taking out malt licence.
2 guineas per month for granting permits to the Kieve.
5 „ to inspector } on admeasurement of malt house.
5 „ to surveyor }
5 to 10 guineas per month for two houses when at work.[2]

Other Fees—Ireland.

2s. 6d. to 5s. on breaking a hhd. of tobacco.
5s. to 10s. for dimensions and content of tanners' pits.
1 guinea as Christmas box by tobacco manufacturer.
3 to 5 guineas at Christmas of each paper maker.
5 guineas to surveyor } by paper stainer for "not giving much
25 guineas to gauger } trouble."[3]

The total of the authorised fees in all England in 1797 did not exceed £2652,[4] while the total of those received by the "Dublin County Collector" alone, in 1807, amounted to no less than £2112. The annual receipt by the Inspector General varied from £111 to £500; the Surveyor from £7 to £350; the Gauger from £6 to £113. The total of the fees received annually, exclusive of "other emoluments" outside the Dublin boundary, amounted to £27,222; the salaries, to £42,723.

See Allowances, Emoluments, Perquisites, Rewards.

[1] P. Rep., 1807. [2] P. Rep., 1808. [3] P. Rep., 1809. [4] P. Rep., 1797.

FIGGESS'S EXCISE OFFICER'S VADE-MECUM,

or Ready Assistant, pp. 84, 4to, 2s. 6d. Sold by J. Bew, Paternoster Row. It contains simply tables of the rates of duty and "of measures," strictly speaking, an Excise Ready Reckoner. The malt duty table gives the duty to the tenth of a farthing; the table of "Salaries at £48, 2s. 6d. and £86, 12s. 6d. per annum" to the ten-thousandth of a farthing, and contains two columns of computations, one for leap year, one for the common year.[1]

FINANCIAL REFORM ASSOCIATION.

The parent society, formed in Liverpool on April 20, 1848, with Robertson Gladstone president, advocated, among other reforms, "The adoption of a simple and equitable system of direct taxation," —a deadly blow at the excise duties, as shown in the emphatic language of the association itself—"all articles which contribute a large and necessary portion of the food of the community, or minister to the profitable employment of the people."

Though the names of most of the council were withheld, the association had by April 1849 issued some sixteen "Financial Reform Tracts," circulated an address among the tax-payers, prepared a petition to Parliament, secured the services of a lecturer, and obtained no fewer than thirty-six affiliations in the more populous centres in England and Scotland.[2]

FRANCHISE.

The possession of the franchise engaged the attention of Parliament very soon after the Government gave notice of the intention to discontinue the system of farming the excise duties, and the first enactment on the subject appears to have been the Act 3 W. & M., c. 1, which took effect from and after February 1, 1691, and forbade "Supvisors, Gaugers or other Officers" to "pswade . . . or disswade" any elector under penalty of £100 and forfeiture of office, because they had frequently "by threats or pmises soe pvailed upon

[1] In British Museum Library.

[2] 1848-9; Tracts 1 to 16.

severall electors." This was quickly followed by another measure to incapacitate certain civil servants from sitting in Parliament, and it was urged in support of the measure that great carelessness existed in conducting the public business, and if these Crown servants were not allowed to sit in Parliament, that they would devote the whole of their time to their official duties, besides, observed a noble lord, "by a single vote a general excise may be granted and then we are lost." Contents 42, non-contents 40.[1] The first prohibition was revived by the 4 & 5 W. & M., c. 5, and continued by the 5 & 6 W. & M., c. 20. The Commissioners were disqualified from sitting in Parliament in 1699, ayes 70, noes 23.[2]

Somewhat similar regulations were passed in the Scotch Parliament in 1705.[3]

From 1699 to the discussion on Sir R. Walpole's famous Excise Scheme in 1733, the Parliamentary records are comparatively silent on this subject. It was then observed by one of the members that "at his own election, there were many of the voters so free and open as to come to him to tell him, that they would vote for him rather than any other, but that those officers (excise and customs) had threatened to ruin them if they did."[4] Indeed the extension of the excise duties was always viewed from this point with great distrust, and this is shown in a subsequent debate—"The influence which excisemen have or may have upon all borough elections will be very much increased," to which the Chancellor of the Exchequer replied, "they have hitherto generally done their duty with as much credit and good nature as was possible."[5] This distrust was further confirmed in 1770, when Mr Dowdeswell proposed, in a committee of the House of Commons, "That leave be given to bring in a Bill to disqualify certain officers of the excise and customs from voting at elections of members of Parliament." "In the last century," he observed, "the struggle was betwixt the power of the Crown and the liberties of the people. In the present century it was betwixt the influence of the Crown and the independence of the people. . . . This influence has arisen chiefly from the consequences of the three last wars with France . . . the increased taxes which had to be raised to provide for those purposes, had unavoidably drawn on a prodigious increase in the officers who collected them. In King

[1] H. L., 1692. [2] H. L., April 4. 1699. [3] July 22, 1705.
[4] H. C., April 11, 1733. [5] H. C., March 11, 1737.

William's time, the expense of collecting the excise amounted to £100,000 a-year, at present to £300,000." The revenue "is parcelled out in little places to excise . . . officers, who are most of them voters in some city or borough, and who from their situation in life, must be at the command of the Minister . . . every gentleman . . . knows . . . the inconvenience of contending against what is called the 'Court Interest.'" The ministry were surprised by these statements, and observed "that it would be exceedingly cruel to despise so great a number of the people of their franchises, . . . and that if such an act should pass, the . . . excise officers must be made out of lower people than they are at present, as no man of spirit would be content to be despised of so valuable a franchise." It was afterwards stated, "that our ancestors had adopted the principle of the act by enacting that no commissioner of excise . . . should sit in the House of Commons, or ask any person for a vote under a severe penalty, and yet though their franchise was taken away in a much greater degree than was now proposed, yet the Crown found no difficulty in getting gentlemen to accept these offices." Ayes 188, noes 263.[1]

Ten years later petitions were presented from upwards of thirty of the most important centres as well as a number from smaller places, in England and Wales, for an inquiry into the expenditure of the public money, the reduction of the exorbitant salaries, and the abolition of unmerited places,[2] upon which Lord Hilsborough declared, "that it is necessary that the influence of the Crown should be checked for the safety of the constitution." Lord North, the Chancellor of the Exchequer, called "the gentleman in the blue ribbon," replied, that "the influence of the Crown had not been increased of late years, and that any attempt at a diminution of it will be resisted."[3] Mr Dunning asserted and moved "that the influence of the Crown has increased, is increasing and ought to be diminished." This motion was carried by a majority of 18 votes—ayes 233, noes 215—and two others of a similar character, unanimously, "the blue ribbon" gentleman imploring the House not to go on.[4] A bill was accordingly prepared to prevent revenue officers from voting at elections, and upon the second reading, the Lord Advocate "declared he would resist all such bills as long as he had

[1] H. C., Feb. 12, 1770.
[2] H. C., Feb. 8, 11, 1780.
[3] H. C., Feb. 14, 1780.
[4] H. C., April 6, 1780.

a mouth to utter a sentence with, or legs to stand upon, because he considered the bill was an attempt to make a violent alteration in the constitution without having first proved that the constitution wanted alteration." Lord Cavendish said, "did not the learned lord know, did not every man who heard him know, that in truth the revenue officers had no franchise, and it was absolutely impossible for them to give their votes freely, and to the candidate whom they in their consciences approved, without endangering the loss of their places." Mr Rolls added that the revenue officers were under the influence of the Crown, there could be no doubt as his father contested an election with a "Court Candidate," who carried it merely by the great number of revenue officers who had been forced to vote for him. At 1.15 a.m., the House divided, and the numbers were, ayes 195, noes 224, the bill was consequently thrown out.[1]

The next effort was made in 1781 by Mr Crewe, on the motion for the second reading of whose bill, the strangers' gallery was shut during the greater part of the debate. Mr Percival spoke against the measure as one tending to deprive a great and respectable number of the electors of this kingdom of their ancient and inherent franchise. Mr Crespignys mentioned an instance of "a whole body of excisemen resisting bribes and menaces, when thrown out by the Government, to induce them to vote for a man whom they disapproved. These were his constituents, and he had therefore a right to say that they were not dangerous possessors of the right." The bill was not carried, ayes 86, noes 133.[2] Persisting in his purpose, Mr Crewe quoted, on the second reading of his measure in 1782, many cases in which the officers had been allowed to vote for the man of their choice, and others in which they had voted according to their choice in which they had been deprived of their commissions. Earl Nugent stated, "a man who felt like a Briton, would feel it as the pride of his life, that he had a privilege to vote for a representative in Parliament. There were about 40,000 officers employed in the collection of the revenue." Sir P. J. Clerke, to show the necessity of passing the bill, read a letter signed "North" to a person in the borough of Southwark, to whom the votes of all the persons connected with Government were promised. The bill was then read a second time by a majority of 75 votes—ayes 87, noes 12—and having passed through committee, Mr Crewe, accom-

[1] H. C., April 13, 1780. [2] H. C., March 21, 1781. [3] H.C., April 16, 1782.

panied by upwards of 100 members, proceeded with it to the House of Lords, "to show that House how serious they were in the reform."[1] Here it created considerable discussion, the Marquis of Rockingham, observing, "there are no less than 70 boroughs where the election depended chiefly on the votes of revenue officers; the customs alone had 5000 persons belonging to it, besides about 2500 extra tidesmen, &c.; the excise at least 4000 more who are voters." The Lord Chancellor then put the question, when there were contents 34, noncontents 18.[2]

Here then are the main features and facts in connection with the imposition of the electoral disabilities on the members of this department, to whom it was customary for the Board, on an approaching election, to issue a formal caution,[3] and against whom few cases of indiscretion have been proved.[4]

This disfranchisement was borne with personal murmur, there being no special medium through which the disfranchised might co-operate until the establishment of the *Civil Service Gazette* in 1853, when the editor at once threw out, among other watch-words, that of re-enfranchisement. This watch-word remained unheeded until the more pressing needs of the pecuniary status had been relieved, and with little interest,[5] until ten more years had rolled by, when the same quill-driver reopened the question in these denunciative terms—"The time has arrived for repealing an enactment insulting to those concerned and repugnant to common sense,"[6] but even this statement was little heeded,[7] until 1865 when it was early rumoured that the customs were about to agitate for the repeal of the franchise disability, and the editor previously mentioned, wrote, "Few things in this world are more frivolous and inconsistent than the reasons advanced for depriving servants of the Crown of the right of voting. . . . It belongs to a day whose fashions and turn of thought we have discarded, and the sooner it is swept into oblivion the better." This incentive to agitation induced Verax to pen a series of excellent suggestions—"Let a central committee be instantly formed by some of the great departments in London; let the United Civil Service Association for the Franchise be your title and 'equal political rights to all qualified persons' be your motto; let circulars be issued to the entire service, and let a petition to Parlia-

[1] H. C., April 25, 1782. [2] H. L., June 3, 1782.
[3] 1832, 1837, 1841, 1847, 1852, 1857, 1865. [4] 1841, 1842.
[5] C. S. G., 1854, 1855, 1857. [6] Idem., 1863. [7] Idem., 1863, 1864.

ment be prepared for presentation early in the ensuing session; let every member on signing, forward a shilling or more to the treasurer, and ample means would soon be forthcoming to carry on the war, if need be, to the foot of the throne until justice be obtained." Such were the words of this energetic writer, who was followed by "One of the Service," Aristides and others, when the editor proverbially recurred to the subject, in that, "Who would be free, himself must strike the blow." This drew from a correspondent under the somewhat bombastic title of "An Examiner in Science, Metaphysics, and Law," an encouragement to the excise to legal and constitutional agitation, and from Caractacus, that "London ought to lead," while others in the interval between their communications, had severally expressed their opinions. It remained, however, for the editor to again recur to the subject to urge "The Inland Revenue, the Customs, and the Post Office," to united effort, and to assert that the civil servants of the Crown would not be disinterested spectators. He afterwards interrogatively wrote, "But it is surely full time for some positive steps to be taken by themselves, unless they mean to give up the cause without a struggle."[1] Upon this, "A Civil Servant" sought the support of John Bright, M.P., in the removal of "the badge of political servitude." The right honourable gentleman replied on December 29, 1865, three days afterwards, "I think you have a good case, and that there is now no need for the law of which you complain." A provincial civil servant who promised "heart, hand, and purse," inquired, What are the London Civil Servants about? J. B. had determined that unless the movement were immediately taken up the "undervalued minors of the General Post Office would do so." Pro Quæster observed, "a few years ago in one of our colonies . . . the revenue officers there (when appointed by the Home Government) were, by local legislation, actually exempted from taxation, on the ground that they were forbidden to vote." Omega, whose limit of patience had been reached, informed his readers that if the three great departments cannot harmoniously co-operate under one general committee, "the Inland Revenue department will immediately form a separate committee." The editor wrote—"The great question would now seem to be a leader. It is of the first importance that this duty should be entrusted into safe and influential hands. A little indiscretion, a slight excess of

[1] C. S. G., 1865.

zeal, a few trivial blunders, and the first hopes of the service might be wrecked. . . . On all grounds then, of policy, of fitness, and of expediency, the author of the 'Civil Service as a Profession,' is the one to lead the movement for political enfranchisement." This article of 1866, with another of equal merit, and those of last year thoroughly aroused the official mind to its political position and induced a three months' discussion which culminated in a meeting being held on Wednesday, April 4, 1866, at the London Institution, Aldersgate Street, Mr F. J. Scudamore of the General Post Office, in the chair, "for the purpose of obtaining the removal of the civil disqualification under which those employed in the collection, receipt, and management of the public revenues laboured." By name, the Post Office was represented by eleven officials, the Inland Revenue by four, the Customs by five. The chairman opened the meeting with an historical and suasive speech, which was followed by the projected pioneer of the editor, Mr A. Trollope, who delivered a cheerful speech which elicited much applause, and then moved the following resolution—"That as the exercise of the franchise is a privilege, so the prohibition to vote of men otherwise qualified is a stigma and disgrace, and that the civil servants of the Crown employed in the revenue departments feeling the stigma cast on them by their disfranchisement to be unjust, and manifestly impolitic, earnestly desire to obtain the removal of the disability under which they labour." This of course was seconded and carried. Mr Edwin Yates, G.P.O., then read the proposed petition, and moved the second resolution—"That the House of Commons be requested, by petition, to introduce into the Bill now before the House, a clause for the repeal of any acts or parts of acts of Parliament, now in force, which restrain officers of the revenue departments from the free exercise of their electoral rights, and that the petition which has been read to the meeting be hereby adopted." Mr Watts, I.R., seconded the second proposition. It was announced by the chairman that Mr C. Buxton, M.P., had consented to present the petition. Mr Ashburton then proposed the third resolution—"That a committee be formed to secure the presentation of the petition, and to prosecute by the best means in its power the object of this meeting. The editor backed up this decisive step with an argument on the "natural rights of citizenship," and a second argument on "the very smallness of the grievance" rendering "its continuance the less excusable."

Other editorial support was given by the *Times* and the *Inverness Courier*. And the officials in the cities of Bristol and Cork were up and doing. The subject ceased to afford any interest in discussion in June, in consequence, perhaps, of the change in her Majesty's Ministers in July.[1]

In July 1867 the unsuccessful clause moved in the House of Commons on July 4, by Sir H. Verney, ran as follows:—"And when it is no longer expedient under an extended suffrage to withhold the franchise from persons otherwise qualified as electors, on account of their employment in certain departments of the public service: Be it enacted, that the Act of the twenty-second year of George the Third, chapter forty-one, intituled 'An Act for the better securing the Freedom of elections of members to serve in Parliament by disabling certain officers employed in collection of his Majesty's revenues from giving their votes at such elections,' shall be, and the same is hereby repealed." Petitions were presented from Bridgwater, Bristol, Langholm, Sudbury, Wishaw, and Bradford in favour of the motion, which was negatived without a division.[2] Sir Harry was succeeded in 1868 by Mr Monk, the honourable member for Gloucester, who gave notice, in the House of Commons, of his intention to ask leave to bring in a bill to relieve certain revenue officials from the disability to vote for the election of members to serve in Parliament. He was allowed to do so, and the bill was read the first time on March 24. The Derby Inland Revenue Franchise Committee, which will be afterwards noticed, having been formed in the meantime to assist him in bringing it to a successful issue. Mr Monk, on the 10th of June, moved the second reading, which was seconded by Mr Otway, when, contrary to the expectation of the would-be voters, not a voice was raised against it. Indeed, no one sat on the Treasury bench, and only six members on the Ministerial side were present. But on the motion to go into committee, Mr Monk was not so successful, for, after having made a short persuasive speech, Mr Sclater-Booth moved an adjournment, and Mr Ward Hunt, the Chancellor of the Exchequer, admitted that it had been his intention to have opposed the bill on the second reading, but owing to his having been unexpectedly detained that evening, the motion and the reading were over before he had arrived. He now wished Mr Monk to adjourn the discussion on the merits

[1] C. S. G., 1866. [2] Idem., 1867.

and principles of the bill that he might have time to summon his forces against it. Upon this the House divided—ayes, 36; noes, 52—majority for proceeding, 16. Lord E. Trevor next moved the adjournment of the House, and was supported by several members. Mr Bass said "they had now got a good majority," and Mr Monk that "he was determined to bring on the bill to-night." The second division confirmed Mr Bass's opinion, there being a majority of nine for Mr Monk—ayes, 33; noes, 42. The promoter of the measure then adjourned the debate until the 15th, when he asked the First Lord—Mr Disraeli—to appoint a morning sitting for the renewal of the discussion. The Premier fixed the 19th, but when that day came the House was counted out, there being only nineteen members present, although there were upwards of one hundred in the lobbies. This unusual circumstance occasioned some sarcastic remarks between Mr Monk and Mr Disraeli on the 22d, and the postponement of the debate until the 30th. Even on that day a disposition to defeat the measure was apparent. After Mr Hunt had spoken against the bill and Mr Gladstone had made an indecisive speech, Mr Karslake called the attention of those present that there was not a House, but ere the hour-glass had run out the forty were present, the House was "made." At the conclusion of the speech-making there was a majority of 32 for going into committee—ayes, 79; noes, 47.

The bill, which consisted of one clause, barely two lines in length, was read the third time on July 2d. We now come to the House of Lords. On the 13th of July the Marquis of Clanricade, Earl Granville, Lord Dufferin, Earl of Kimberley, and Lord Abinger, having presented petitions in favour of the measure, the latter Lord, in a commendative speech, moved the second reading. His Lordship was immediately followed by the Lord Chancellor, who observed, in the last sentence of an able historical and disciplinary speech, in which he repelled the objections of the Commissioners of Inland Revenue, "With this reservation"—persuasion and dissuasion—"I cheerfully assent to the second reading." Not a dissentient voice was heard. The bill passed through committee without alteration, was read the third time on the 17th, and received the Royal Assent on July 31, 1868, and thus formed the Act 31 & 32 Vict., c. 73, which was afterwards edited by R. Wilkinson, M.A., barrister-at-law.[1]

Not satisfied with this success, Mr Monk gave notice on December

[1] Stevens and Hughes, London.

15, 1868, that he would on an early day move for leave to bring in a bill to enable officials to take part in the election of members, and thus make them politically free.

The Derby Inland Revenue Franchise Committee, already referred to, was formed on March 17, 1868, with Mr J. R. Reed as secretary. The committee at their second meeting prepared an address to the disfranchised departments, and a form of petition to Parliament. Letters from Lord Abinger and Mr Monk to Mr Hogan—Humanitas—were printed to incite energy, and the power of the press secured for the most part in favour of the cause.[1] The Commissioners gave their opinion on the measure, and the officers gave their opinion on the Commissioners. Reports of meetings held at Bristol, Colchester, Elgin, Glasgow, Kettering, and Wexford, in support of the movement were recorded, and among the many petitions which were presented to Parliament to show the desire for the act were upwards of sixty from this department.[2]

Faithful to his promise made in the House of Commons in 1868, Mr Monk, on February 23, 1869, moved for leave to bring in a bill to enable those employed in the collection and management of her Majesty's revenues to take part in the election of members of Parliament. The civil servants employed in the Inland Revenue Department, he had been advised, were politically free by the passing of the Statute Law Revision Act, by which the Act 5 & 6 W. & M., c. 20., s. 48, had been repealed, while those, however, employed in the departments of Customs and Post Office were not allowed "freedom of speech." The bill was then read the first time, and the second reading fixed for March 17.

The Derby Committee, alive to the value of official and general

[1] Daily News, Daily Telegraph, Derby Reporter, Examiner, Irish Times, London Review, Morning Post, Morning Star, North British Mail, Star, Times, Wexford Independent.

[2] Aberdeen, Alloa, Aylesbury, Bedford, Birmingham, Bradford, Bridgewater, Bristol, Carlisle, Chelmsford, Chepstow, Clonmel, Colchester, Cork, Coventry, Derby, Doncaster, Dorchester, Dumfries, Dundee, Edinburgh, Elgin, Exeter, Glasgow, Gloucester, Grantham, Greenock, Hants, Hereford, Hull, Inverness, Irvine, Kidderminster, Kilkenny, Kettering, Leeds, Leicester, Leominster, London, Londonderry, Ludlow, Liverpool, Leith, Maidstone, Monasterevan, Newport, Newport (Salop), Newcastle—U. L., Northampton, North of Ireland, Oban, Padstow, Preston, Sligo, Southampton, Stowmarket, Suffolk, Tiverton, Truro, Wells, Wexford, Ware, Whitchurch—S., Wellington—S., Yeovil.—Civil Service Gazette, 1868.

support to Mr Monk, asked the Revenue Departments to enable him to state "that all the officials desire it, and have petitioned for it to pass." The committee at the same time appended forms of petitions to their memorandum, and the editor added the suasive force of his quill to their directions. Petitions were accordingly prepared and presented on March 12, 15, 16, 1869, and on the day for the second reading, March 17, when Mr Monk rose to move the second reading of the Bill, which he designated "the complement of the Revenue Officers' Disabilities Act, which was passed last session." He considered it "an anomaly that a man should be allowed to record his vote, while, at the same time, his mouth was so effectually closed that he dare not discuss the merits of the rival candidates even with his next door neighbour." Sir H. Verney seconded the motion. Mr Pearse said that he had for several years entertained very strong opinions on the subject, and ultimately moved that it be read that day six months. In this Mr Pearse found a seconder in the Chancellor of the Exchequer, who read extracts from the report of the Commissioners of Inland Revenue of last year, when the advisability of permitting even a simple, unsuasive vote was questioned. He concluded by asking the House not to assent "to a measure whose operation may be so great, while the advantages which it seeks to confer are so infinitesimal." The House shortly afterwards divided, when the Bill was lost by a majority of 119 votes—ayes, 88, noes, 207.

This induced the editor to pen—"We are of opinion that if the Government and those in authority over the officials would show more generosity in their dealings, and more confidence in their subordinates, the required zeal and unimpeachable integrity would be much more likely to be willingly demonstrated than by the pursuit of any other course. . . . . But what we object to is the opposition which Mr Monk has encountered in the unwarrantable assumption which prevailed in all the arguments adduced. The Bill was not compulsory. It did not compel the officials to interfere in electoral matters, to become canvassers, proposers, seconders; it merely proposed that they shall be freed from the numerous and heavy penalties which are now visited on active political partisanship. If the officials possess the judgment and discretion for which they have been so freely credited by the leaders of both parties—and credited, we may remark, with perfect justice—is it not absurd to suppose that they would not be discreet enough to hold aloof from electioneering contests? . . . . Mr Monk has fought well and ably for a great principle; he has been only partially successful, but his name will long continue to be revered by a considerable body of Civil Servants, who will ever regard him with feelings of peculiar gratitude and deep obligation."

After an interval of about four months, the undaunted Parliamentary advocate of this particular claim again reopened the subject by giving notice on Wednesday, August 4, 1869, that on an early day next session he would move the appointment of a select committee to inquire into the necessity for retaining the remaining disabilities; and with this announcement it may be recorded the Parliamentary proceedings terminated.

It now becomes the pleasant duty of the writer to narrate the presentation of tokens of gratitude. On Friday, February 26, 1869, a deputation consisting of ten gentlemen—seven Customs, two Post Office, one Inland Revenue, Mr J. R. Reed—who represented 36,000, waited upon Mr Monk at 2 Buckingham Gate to tender a token in appreciation of his efforts of 1868. "The Address," wrote the editor, "is contained in a magnificent volume, the wording being continued from leaf to leaf, and enclosed in rich illuminated work, which rivals the best illuminations of the middle ages for beauty of workmanship and excellence of design. . . . . The volume is formed of leaves or panels of several sheets of vellum, compressed so as to form a solid surface. The order of the ornament is that commonly known as the Renaissance. . . . . On the first page is the coat of arms of Mr Monk; the second is devoted to the title of the Address, and bears at the top a drawing in distemper of the Houses of Parliament. Following this are four pages which bear the Address in church text, with illuminated initials. The larger space is filled with the richest ornamental work, glowing with gold and colour, but varying in form on each page, and surmounting the text are views of Gloucester Cathedral, Somerset House, the Custom House, and the General Post Office. Two pages more bear the autographs of the Committee.[1] . . . . The body of the volume is of rich blue Levant Morocco, relieved by inlaid margins of white and pale brown, and beautifully tooled in gold." The Address having been read by T. J. Hamel, Esq., Solicitor to the Customs, the

[1] The Inland Revenue—J. R. Reed, W. R. White, J. Steele, J. Fisher, R. Moffatt, P. T. Evans, J. F. Hogan, W. Meikle, J. Murdoch, J. Winter, J. Skinner, J. Mussen, J. J. Lyons.

worthy recipient replied to the effect that he felt highly honoured by the flattering terms of that document. He then gave a brief sketch of the Parliamentary proceedings, in which he noticed the unsuccessful efforts made by Sir H. Verney in 1867, previously narrated, and then observed, coming down to his own direct efforts, "For some weeks after its introduction I received neither petition nor communication respecting it. Then Mr John Reed of Derby came upon the scene. To the efforts of the Derby Committee I believe I was mainly indebted for the passing of the measure. For some weeks Mr Reed was in almost daily communication with me. I shall mention no other name, though during the later stages of the Bill I received valuable assistance from various parts of England, Scotland, and last—certainly not least—of Ireland." The honourable gentleman concluded by stating that "this valued and honourable present—honourable alike to givers and receiver—shall be handed down as an heirloom in my family, precious far above silver and gold. One word in conclusion. I have heard no complaints respecting the re-enfranchised Civil Servants."

The other token of gratitude was handed to Mr Reed for his untiring energy and discreet aid in promoting the repeal of the statutes last year, and his continued assistance in endeavouring to obtain the repeal of the remaining statutes this year. This also was presented by the employés of the Customs, Post Office, and Inland Revenue, and partook of the form of "a handsome gold watch, chain, and appendages, together with a purse of gold." The inner portion of the case of the watch being engraved—"Presented, together with a purse of gold, on the 26th April 1869, to Mr John R. Reed, by his brother officers of the Civil Service, as a token of their appreciation of his successful efforts in assisting them to obtain the franchise." The presentation took place at the Post Office, Derby.[1]

To continue the narration of the efforts in Parliament. Mr Monk, on February 8, 1870, gave notice that on Tuesday the 22d, he would move for a select committee to enquire into the electoral disabilities under which certain Revenue Officers still labour. This, it will be observed, was made for the purpose of affording perfect political freedom. The Government, however, were opposed to it. Accordingly on the 22d, the right honourable gentleman moved—"that a

[1] C. S. G., 1869.

select committee be appointed to enquire and report as to electoral restraints and disabilities affecting the civil servants of the Crown in the several branches of the revenue department, and to consider the expediency of removing them in certain cases." He observed, in the speech by which he prefaced this motion, that the officers of excise, in his opinion, were politically free. "He then stated that the disabling Act of 5 William & Mary, cap. 50, sec. 18, which imposed the minor penalty of £100 on any officer in the excise who presumed to take part in an election, and which disqualified him from ever holding office under the Crown, had been repealed by the Statute Law Revision Act of 1867. The Act of 7 & 8 George IV., c. 53, s. 9, increasing the penalty to £500, was repealed in 1868 by the Act of 32 Victoria, cap. 73, commonly known as the Revenue Officers' Disabilities Removal Act. He submitted to the House that it was a matter of grave public importance that the political status of the Officers in the Revenue Department should be distinctly ascertained, and that no reasonable doubt should be allowed to remain as to whether the disabilities and penalties imposed by the Act of William & Mary, already referred to, had been revived and kept alive by any subsequent Act. He understood that it was alleged by those who advised the Inland Revenue Department that those disabilities and penalties were kept alive by an Act of 55 George III., c. 184, but he entirely dissented from that opinion, believing that the advisers of the officials of the Inland Revenue Department had made a mistake with reference to that Act, which he believed, merely imposed penalties upon the public, upon whom the duties were levied instead of imposing them upon the officers of the revenue. Under these circumstances, he thought he had made out a case at all events for further inquiry." Mr Graves seconded the motion. The Premier thought that the question last year had been "thoroughly sifted and as decisively disposed of, as almost any in the course of the session." He pleaded "sheer weariness," and suggested that the further investigation should rest for a year or two. Sir G. Jenkinson, and Messrs Crawford and R. Gurney, spoke in favour of the inquiry. Mr Monk ultimately acted upon the suggestion of Mr Gladstone, and withdrew the motion. The editor observed on Mr Monk—"He has not been beaten in argument, for on Tuesday evening no argument was used against the motion."[1]

[1] C. S. G., 1870.

The opinion expressed by Mr Monk was confirmed by the Attorney General in 1872—that he "believed that they might now vote, and also interfere in election by canvassing, because the statute which prevented them from doing so had been repealed."[1]

Still persistent, in 1873, Mr Monk gave notice that he would early next session move for leave to bring in a Bill to relieve Revenue Officers from any penalty to which they may be liable for endeavouring to persuade any elector to vote or to refrain from voting, for any person to serve in Parliament.[2]

Not forgetful of his notice he jointly with Mr R. Gurney introduced a "Bill to Relieve Revenue Officers from remaining Electoral Disabilities," which they successfully carried through to the Royal Assent on June 30, 1874. The officers of this department having been declared, by the Attorney-General in 1872, free from any restriction whatever, they did not generally support the bill by petition. The Customs and Post Office departments gave active general support. The Commissioners of Inland Revenue, in common with the heads of the other departments, were requested by the Chancellor of the Exchequer to report upon the measure, and in doing so the Commissioners referred to the satisfactory results of the legislation in 1868, but concluded by observing " . . . since the right of voting can be exercised in full freedom without the right of canvassing, we are at a loss to conjecture by what arguments it can be shown that the benefit which the bill would confer are of such paramount importance as to reduce to comparative insignificance the evils it would create." This report was signed by "W. H. Stephenson, C. J. Herries, Algernon West," and dated April 13, 1874.[3]

The entire political freedom of the revenue officer, by which he was not only entitled to vote but also to "pswade" and "disswade," was accordingly regained in 1874 after a Parliamentary struggle which extended over a period of seven years.

GAME LICENCE DUTY.

Two pence per "peter,"[4] one penny per woodcock, and three pence per pheasant,[5] such were the head-rates at which game first

[1] H. C., April 28, 1872. [2] H. C., June 30, 1873. [3] C. S. G. & C., 1874.
[4] Partridge, Slang Dictionary, 1865. [5] P. O., 1645.

afforded an excise duty, and it does not appear to have done so after the Restoration until 1842.

In 1784 Mr Pitt proposed in his budget of many details a stamp duty on a certificate to kill and keep game in Great Britain,[1] which in a modified form became leviable on October 1, 1784, and on the Union with Ireland in that country on March 25, 1800.[2] From the Commissioners of Stamps to those of Taxes it was transferred, at the instance of Mr S. Perceval, who at the same time took occasion to include woodcock and snipe under game in 1808;[3] in Ireland, from the Commissioners of Stamps to the Commissioners of Excise, in 1842; and in Great Britain, probably on the suggestion of the Commissioners,[4] it was commuted into an Excise licence duty at the instance of Mr Gladstone, who took occasion to include deer under game in 1860.[5] The transfer to this branch of the department was also suggested by a writer in the *Civil Service Gazette* in 1854,[6] and on its being adopted the Board discontinued advertising the names of those who had taken out licences, much to the annoyance of the country newspaper proprietors, who lost some £3000 per annum by the change, and formed a deputation to the chief office to "remonstrate" with their Honours.[7] The duties:—

Date.		Kill.	Keep.	Deal.	
1784.	G.B.	£2 2 0	£0 10 6	...	
1791.	G.B.	3 3 0	1 1 0	...	
1800.	I.	2 2 0	2 2 0[1]	...	
1812.	G.B.	3 13 6	3 13 6[2]	...	
...	...	...	1 5 0[3]	...	
1831.	E.	...	...	£2 0 0	
1840.	G.B.	4 0 10	4 0 10[2]	...	
...	...	...	1 7 6[3]	...	
1840.	E.	...	...	2 4 0	
1860.	U.K.	3 0 0	2 0 0	2 0 0	
...	...	2 0 0	...	...	
...	...	2 0 0	...	...	

[1] In force in Great Britain on paying differential stamp duty.
[2] Not being an assessed servant.
[3] Being an assessed servant.

With respect to the permission to sell and deal in game, the proceedings in Parliament may not be uninstructive. Though not permitted by revenue certificate until 1831, and then only in England,

[1] H. C., June 30, 1784.
[2] C. 1 R.
[3] H. C., April 1, 1808.
[4] C. 1 and 2 R.
[5] H. C., May 24, 1860.
[6] J. B.
[7] C. 5 R.

it in 1827 engaged the attention of the Marquis of Salisbury, who brought in a Bill "to legalise the sale of game, and to do so in the most extended manner, by giving a power to persons qualified by law to kill game, to take out a certificate empowering them to sell game to licensed dealers," the object being to decrease the "crime of poaching," by which the dealers in game had been very much supplied.[1] The measure was lost by three votes.[2] His lordship reintroduced his Bill in 1828, and having moved the third reading, the Earl of Winchelsea moved an amendment which carried 62 votes, while the original motion carried 69 votes.[3] Having originated in the Lords, it was thrown out when it came before the Commons as being a "money bill." This their lordships did not forget; for when the commoners set up their bill, which was to precisely the same effect—to allow small landowners and others, who had been previously debarred the disposal of the game shot on their lands, &c. —it was rejected on the second reading by a majority of 30 votes.[4] No further effort was made until 1831, when Lord Althorp moved, on going into committee on the game laws, "that it is the opinion of this committee that an annual duty of £2 shall be paid for every certificate to empower persons to deal in game," a certificate being granted by the Magistrates at Quarter Sessions. His lordship's motion was agreed to and became law.[5] The assimilation of the duty in the United Kingdom, and the reduction of the duty in Great Britain were effected by that financial assimilator, W. E. Gladstone, in 1860.[6]

As to the collection of the duty the Commissioners state in their First Report, it "is one of those which are considerably evaded;" in their Second Report, it is "the cause of much trouble and correspondence;" in their Eighteenth Report, it is satisfactory as showing "no lack of vigilance," though the high rate of duty "furnishes great temptation to disregard the law;" in their Nineteenth Report, that the Royal Irish Constabulary give effective service, and that they—the Comrs.—receive numerous informations for prosecuting poachers, but very few against offenders of higher rank, and that "some change in system will probably be necessary ere long;" and in their Twentieth Report, that only three licences are paid for each estate of 500 acres and upwards in Great Britain.

[1] H. L., May 23, 1827.
[2] H. L., June 14, 1827.
[3] H. L., May 12, 1828.
[4] H. L., July 5, 1828.
[5] H. C., Aug. 3, 1831.
[6] H. C., May 24, 1860.

In Parliament, since the equalisation of the duty, it has attracted but little attention[1] until Mr Lowe unsuccessfully proposed to substitute a gun licence duty—which see.

Cases decided by the Judges will be found in Woolrych's Game Laws,[2] and in the Commissioners' Third and Fourth Reports: the statistics in their First, Thirteenth, and subsequent Reports; and the finest collection of stuffed specimens of game, in the world, in the British Museum.

GATELY'S INLAND REVENUE OFFICER'S CALCULATOR,

With notes on warehousing transactions, by J. Gately, Officer of Sheffield Third Division, 1878. A small pamphlet of forty pages, price one shilling.

GAUGER, GAUGING, GAUGING APPLIANCES, GAUGING BOOKS.

Le gangeour le Roi, le gangeour, gangeours, gawgear, gawgeable, gawgying, gawgeying, gawinge, gauging, gawged, such were the forms of the word used in the times of Edward I., Richard III., Henry VIII., and Elizabeth, concerning true gauging.[3] The office of gauger was formerly an important and lucrative one. It was first sought after as "Gauger of Excise in London," and five years later in the alternative. Wm. Mar, "For the place of gager of Excise in London in case the late vacancy in that of second clerk of the kitchen granted him by the late king is filled up," and the farmers were under an agreement to allow the Lord High Treasurer and Chancellor of the Exchequer to appoint four gaugers to gauge the beer.[4] These were probably the able artists appointed under 15 Charles II., c. 11, to compute the content of the brewing vessels. The Lord Mayor and brewers of London had in 1704 a "counter gager."[5] There were in the London establishment in 1705 one "general gauger" and 82 "gaugers" proper,[6] and from that date

[1] P. P., 1858, 1862, 1865. [2] 1858.
[3] 22 Hen. VIII., c. 20; 28 Hen. VIII., c. 14; 31 Eliz., c. 8.
[4] Green's State Papers, 1660, 1665, 1666. [5] L. G. [6] P. Ret., 1705.

the art gradually became sufficiently well-known, until 1781, when the able artist was discontinued, and the "general surveyors of brewers" were appointed "General Dry Gagers."

There is a place in Warrington called Gauger's Row, and an excellent story in print of the "Gauger Outwitted," by J. J. Rossiter, in the *Wexford Independent* of 1864.

GAUGING.—It has been shown under "Gauger" that the earliest employés knew little of the "Art of Gauging and practical Dry Gauging Casks and Utensils," as required by Burns. Indeed it never formed an entrance test until a recent period—See Candidates. All down to that period were supposed to master sufficient in practice during their pupilage to qualify them for the office to which they aspired; and it is a fact worthy of note, on the principle that necessity is the mother of invention, that all the minute details of gauging have been published in hand-books prepared by the employés themselves, and very many of the gauging instruments used have also been improved or invented by them.

The most unsatisfactory branch was that of cask gauging—"one of the most difficult parts of the officer's duty . . . . no certain rule." These words were written by Iley, who wrote on the subject, and they are fully supported by the authority of the Scotch Commissioners who directed their officers in cases of a "difference of opinion" when gauging at ports in conjunction with Customs officers, to report their differences "to their superior officers in order that the difference may be amicably settled."[1] The "Four Notions," that is the four varieties were adopted very early, and a very simple mode of ascertaining the capacity of a cask was printed on a half sheet of paper in 1669.[2] Special attention may be drawn to one book on this subject, which exhibits much labour—Cunninghame's "Imperial Ullager." Passing to the act and its recurrence, in general. To carry a brew-house float and compare it every time one met an officer must have been, though partly composed of cork, no light labour, and for the collector to compare every float annually must have been a delightful duty; but such was done.[3] Not only were instruments compared but every effort was made to suppress "stamped gauges,"[4] and what may not be inappropriately termed the "Rule of the Thumb," as exemplified in a blue-book—"We"—

[1] Instructions, 1804.
[2] Gauging Epitomized.
[3] 1778.
[4] Country Instructions, 1778.

Joshua Rogers, an officer, and one of Barclay's men—"were gauging a very large vessel; the man called Bob was assisting; he put his thumb, holding the rule between it and the vessel . . . . and holding up the rule he put his thumb between, making the dimension of the vessel an inch less. . . . . I believe he had a check from the brewer himself for doing it. I said, Bob, how could you serve me so? He said, 'I must do all I can for my master; I am sworn to secrecy.'"[1]

The act of regauging has been performed under different regulations, from the frequent remeasurement of a drip,[2] the remeasurement of a still twice a month,[3] to the less frequent retest of "open utensils" once in a year,[2] two,[4] and four years.[5]

APPLIANCES.—That the staff for very many years "furnished" themselves with these aids in office, there can be no doubt, seeing that as early as 1703[6] the collector was required to report in the supervisor's diary on the very subject, and by several subsequent injunctions the staff were distinctly enjoined to provide them;[7] and that as late as 1830 the provision in one case at least cost £6.[8] The first observed gift is noted under sliding rule, and probably down to the date of the gift to pupils no other instruments were given, though a suggestion was several times made that each station in which they were needed should be supplied with them,[9] a suggestion adopted in 1874. Those purchased by the officers were frequently and long obtained through a person in the "Excise Store Office," one of whom announced in soliciting a continuance of favours, that the manner of supply would be the same as by his predecessors, "from time immemorial."

But with respect to those required at the ports, distilleries,[10] and glass-houses,[11] the Board supplied them on application, formerly[12] through the collector.

The decimal method of notation has obtained in every instance.[13]

The various appliances referred to in this paper are—box and tape, bung rod, callipers, diagonal rule, diameter rod, dimension rod, dipper, dipping rod, float, head rod, interiometer, malt brass plate, malt gauging rod, shoulder rod, sliding rule, spile rod, spit,

[1] P. Rep., Beer, 1819. [2] 1810. [3] 1811. [4] 1804.
[5] 1781. [6] Hersee, 1702; Taylor.
[7] 1778, 1813, 1842; S. 1781, 1804, 1824. [8] C. S. G., 1855.
[9] C. S. G. & C., 1856, 1857, 1873. [10] 1824, 1830; S., 1811.
[11] 1793. [12] 1846. [13] Hunt, 1683; Everard, 1684, *et seq.*

spatula, stave guage, steel ribbon, tickler, vacuity rod, wood guage, yard rule.

I. Box and Tape.—Very early in use were a "Box and Tape" for taking couch and floor-guages of malt,[1] but not very likely was the tape so long, as it is at present 600 or 800 inches. The "tape" was sometimes made of "silk."[2]

Convenient and brief modes of calculation have been devised on this appliance. First may be mentioned a mode based upon logarithms, referred to under "sliding rule." A second based upon the square root of the bushel[3]—thus the square root of the number of cubic inches in a bushel being 47·1, the blank side of the tape opposite 47 inches is marked 1·0 B.; 51, 1·1; 56, 1·2; 61, 1·3; 65, 1·4; 70, 1·5; 75, 1·6; 80, 1·7; 84, 1·8; 89, 1·9; 94, 2·0; and so on.

Then the area of the length multiplied by the area of the breadth and the product by the depth will give the content of the floor, &c., *i.e.*, the respective numbers being multiplied.

A third approximative mode of calculation endorsed on the tape is that based on the areas of straight lines, thus—a straight cubic line of 2218 inches would represent one bushel, hence 221 would represent a tenth of a bushel; then, beginning in this case, with an endorsement of one-tenth of a bushel, we have marked at the back of 221 inches the area ·1; 244, ·11; 266, ·12; 288, ·13; 310, ·14; 332, ·15; 354, ·16; 377, ·17; 399, ·18; 421, ·19; 443, ·2 and so on.

To illustrate by taking one of the easiest and most striking examples: L. 221, B. 221, D. 10·0. Area of 221· × 221· = 22·1 × 10·0 = 221 bushels. A fourth approximative mode, though not marked on either box or tape, is to take 10 per cent. off one dimension, multiply that result by half the second dimension, and that by the depth, *i.e.*, the respective numbers, thus L. 190, B. 90, D. 19·0; 190 − 19 = 171 : 90 ÷ 2 = 45; then 171 × 45 × 19 = 146 bushels.

Bung Rod.—A new one, with the diagonal or content line adjusted to the new standard, was issued in 1826, and improved in 1853 in some minor detail by Mr Brain, port surveyor, London.[4]

Callipers.—See page 109.

Diagonal Rule.—The diagonal rule, formerly used in cask gauging, and now graduated on the malt, bung and spill rods, was

[1] Leadbetter, 1743. [2] Cock. [3] Lindsay, 1801.
[4] C. S. G., 1877.

ordered to be discontinued in 1809 owing to the deception practised by nailing pieces to the heads of the casks, inside.[1] The imperial diagonal line in inches thus—Inches, 28·75 = 54 gallons, will be found in Roose's Ullaging, 1832.

DIAMETER ROD.—Equally a dimension rod, though not of such general application, being usually in two lengths, attached to each other by an open brass cap on the end of each length to allow each to slide over the other, by which the diameter is reached, and the dimension seen at the point where the slider is stopped. In the older diameter rule an area line was graduated under the inch line. These rules are constructed for dimensions varying from 24 to 150 inches and upwards.[2]

DIMENSION ROD.—The old names were "dimension cane" and "sliding cane,"[3] probably in the form described under malt gauging rod, and applicable for the most part to gauging in general. Another but more ingeniously-contrived form consists of a tapering rod 223 inches long, in twelve lengths, with twelve inched and tenthed facets on the first length, into which a brass slider is fixed and connected through a small groove with a circular indicator; which, on the slider being drawn out to the limit of the utensil gauged, rests over the facet proper to the number of the lengths screwed together, and indicates the dimension sought.

DIPPER.—A familiar name[4] applied to a hinged rod, which varies in length from twelve to twenty-four inches, and is used for the most part in floor and kiln gauging at malt-houses. It has a diagonal line for cask gauging up to a content of above thirty gallons, but it has not been supplied by the Board since the issue of the first joint of the malt gauging rod in brass.

DIPPING ROD.—This distinction is usually applied to those in use at distilleries, varying of course in length according to the depth of each vessel. They were long supplied in size one inch by three-eighths of an inch, but they are now uniformly one inch by three quarters of an inch. In consequence of the fraud practised by forcing the rod so as to turn the "pin" down below the bottom of the rod, and thus prevent a correct account being taken, it was ordered in 1840 that these rods should not in future be fixed in utensils. It need scarcely be added that they are now fixed into a brass guide, which is riveted

[1] Hersee. [2] Leadbetter, 1743; Nesbitt & Little, 1832.
[3] Leadbetter, 1743; Lindsay, 1801; Iley, 1820. [4] Cock.

to the vessel, except in some few instances, and occasionally examined.

FLOAT.—The celebrated Beauchamp Hill—see S. G. Examiners—had used a "Top . . . . to ascertain the true dip of the backs while in a state of fermentation . . . . the instrument is formed of a ball fastened to a string, which being immersed in the froth the ball rests on the liquor, and the string shows the depth of the froth."[1] Another device was "a cork plate or plum" for gauging beer when working in the "fatt."[2] A third, an ullage float and block. A fourth, a piece of flat wood fixed at the end of a stick—this was used in gauging starch;[3] but the float proper appears to have been "the rule and cork"[4] made in recent times, with three-quarter inch diameter rod, graduated to not less than half an inch, in lengths of forty and sixty inches each, attached to flat pieces of cork, 8 by 7 by 1 inch, and 7·5 by 5·5 by 1·5 inch each.

HEAD ROD.—This "Head-Stick" is also a sliding rule, 45 inches long, on a large scale, adapted to ascertain the head diameter of a cask up to 76 inches, and to cast out both the content and the ullage of a cask. Except in charging the duties on foreign spirits and wines, it is not now used. A discrepancy between the Excise and the Customs rods was corrected by Mr T. Brain, port-surveyor, London.[5]

INTERIOMETER.—This consisted of two rods in a walking-stick case, and an "angle measure," and was used for ascertaining the interior diameters of casks.[6]

MALT BRASS PLATE.—For taking gauges with accuracy by running the plate down the rod on to the grain, and then holding it firmly against the rod, this has been sometimes screwed to a plain piece of boxwood; sometimes hinged on an eight-inch piece of brass on which and over the hinge a slider, held in position by a spring, secured the plate at a right angle to the piece or handle; it is now screwed on to the fifth joint of the rod.

MALT GAUGING ROD.—The ordinary malt gauging rod has been known by several names, as "a cane or holly-stick, inched and decimally divided,"[7] "malt stick-plain or screw," "screw stick," "couch rod,"[8] "screw rod," "dipping rod,"[9] "malt cane or guaging

[1] P. Rep., 1807.
[2] 1781.
[3] Scotch Instructions, 1804.
[4] London Instructions, 1781; C. S. G., 1877.
[5] C. S. G., 1877.
[6] Gutteridge's Precepts, 1825.
[7] Leadbetter, 1743.
[8] Cock.
[9] Iley, 1820.

rod,"[1] "four foot gauging rod," an arrangement by Mr Brannan or Brenan, some time a collector—"the middle joint is made with a socket to take in and out; so that when each foot is shut (they are made with the common guaging lines on them) they slide one by the side of the other; and it answers every purpose of our sliding rule."[2] The use of the "four-foot" rod for malt gauging was discontinued in 1813. The "Patent Imperial gauging rod" was introduced by Mr Gutteridge, also of this department, in 1825, prior to the introduction of the Imperial measure in 1826—"The best goes into a walking-stick cane, and is ten units in length when connected in the middle by either a screw or hinge joint. It is a decimal graduation, every tenth being figured as well as every unit; thus, ·10, ·20, ·30, and so on up to 1, or unity, called the cubit; then, 1·10, 1·20, &c., up to two units or cubits; and continued in this manner up to the end of 10 cubits."[3]

The "walking-cane containing 36 gauge rod"—the rod in addition to being marked with the diagonal line for cask gauging, was also marked with two other sets of numbers in continuation of the 36 suitable for larger dimensions—first, by unscrewing a small shield cap off the end of the cane, drawing out the rod to the extent of the dimension to be taken, not exceeding 72 inches, and reading the number of inches on the rod at the top of or opening into the cane; then, for greater dimensions up to 120 inches, by screwing on to the end of the cane a brass holder, into which a continuation rod composed of two hinged and marked pieces—also graduated for both malt and cask gauging—were inserted, and proceeding as before. The "walking-cane" with its neatly-fitting screw cap or top, sometimes dyed black,[4] must have been the most genteel arrangement in its day.[5]

In the heavy malting stations, the "steel cistern rod," with brass or other mounting is used, and formerly officers were obliged to provide "iron rods and to use strength to force them to the bottom of cisterns and couches of corn," 1715.

The first joint of the fifty-inch rod, supplied by the Board, is made of brass, and the fifth with a clip is adapted to the "brass plate" or float, and the "malt receiver" or brass receiver for fishing up the barley from the bottom or any other part of the cistern."[6]

[1] 1842. [2] Leadbetter, 1743.
[3] Gutteridge's Precepts, 1825; Ne Plus Ultra, 1828. [4] Cock.
[5] Somerville, 1846. [6] Leadbetter, 1743.

SHOULDER ROD.—At one time known as the "dry inch rule,"[1] but in modern times as the shoulder rod, from the fancied resemblance of the "brass stop" or "top" to a man's shoulder; this instrument is inched and tenthed to usually sixty inches, from the angle formed by the shoulder-piece downwards, and is used in distilleries for ascertaining the dry inches between the "dipping place" or plate and the surface of the wort or wash.

SLIDING RULE.—This very useful invention was adapted to excise requirements about 1683, if not then invented, by Thomas Everard, an officer at Southampton, and usually called Everard's Sliding Rule.[2] "Description and use of another new rule used in gauging of worts, showing, by inspection, how many gallons and hundred parts any small tub will contain at one inch deep (without knowing the diameter . . . . .). The instrument consists of three parts, one fixed (which is 12 inches long), the other two being moveable, may be drawn out till the whole be 36 inches long. . . . . Upon one side . . . . two double lines of numbers A. B. to slide one upon another, by them is performed multiplication, division, rule of three, &c. . . . Upon the other side, ... to square root by inspection, and the areas of circles. Upon another side . . . . a line of inches, and against it three other lines, by which you may find the mean diameter of any cask."[2] Vero, a collector, enlarged the scale; Leadbetter, an officer, made some improvement,[3] and John Lowry and Edmund Hunter invented the gauge points.[4] It was made in lengths, which varied from 6 to 24 inches,[5] and in this form, with some few modifications,[6] continued in use until the introduction of the imperial measure in 1826, when new rules were constructed and issued by the Board—probably the first instance in which an instrument was given to the members of the department.

The form or figure of the rule was not restricted to that of a "parallelopipedon," nor was it always made of boxwood, sometimes of ivory—a very hard injurious material for the eye. It was adapted to slide on a "four foot gauging rod;"[3] on the head diameter rule or rod, in which the slide acted in a two-fold capacity—that of gauge and calculating slide[7]—on a float; a fourth adaptation to the limits of the tape box, described as—"an ingenious device in connection with the line M. D. was adopted some time ago by Mr Morrison,

[1] 1813. [2] Everard, 1684. [3] Leadbetter, 1743.
[4] Bateman, 1840; Nesbitt & Little, 1832. [5] Iley, 1826. [6] 1817.
[7] Leadbetter, 1743; Lindsay, 1801.

supervisor of excise. This line, as well as the lines A and B, was graduated in a circle, so as to fit on to the top of the box in which the measuring tape is usually coiled up; and the line B was made to revolve instead of sliding backwards and forwards. By this method malt arrears could be worked as soon as the dimensions were taken;"[1] the fifth and most remarkable, perhaps, being on a tobacco-box. The principal lines were also "put upon a tobacco-box to slide one by another, as they do upon the rule, but with this considerable advantage, that here the whole of one line is always applied to the whole of another, so that all the questions which may be resolved by these lines on the rule, may be resolved more readily by the said lines on this box."[2] Besides these adaptations, separate "flat" sliding rules were issued with the saccharometer for ascertaining the gravity of wort or wash;[3] with the hydrometer for reducing from one strength to another;[4] with the acetometer for casting out the proof gallons,[5] and lastly for ullaging casks.

Spile Rod.—This rod, as its name indicates, is so small—one quarter of an inch in diameter—as to allow it to pass through an ordinary spile hole, and thus save the time and loss which might be occasioned by drawing the bung. It is usually fifty inches long in ten-inch pieces, and graduated with a diagonal line. The complement formerly consisted of "spile rod, gimlet, and case."[6]

Spit.—A figured instrument formerly used in taking the depths of starch in boxes.[7]

Spatula.—An appliance one inch broad by one-and-a-half inches long, screwed to a long stick, to draw samples of starch from different parts of the utensils—in purpose identical with the malt receiver.[7]

Stave Gauge.—*See* Callipers.

Steel Ribbon.—A recent familiar introduction.[8]

Tickler.—An instrument in general use in past times, for raising the bungs[9] in "stocking,"[10] or taking the stocks of spirits at the various traders.

Vacuity Rod.—Invented in 1853 by Mr T. Brain, port-surveyor, London,[11] to ascertain the space in a cask between the surface of the spirit and the internal edge of the bung stave—the vacuity. It consists of a short rod, inched and tenthed to about twelve inches, set, and secured by a brass pin at either end, into a brass hand-guide

[1] Bateman's Manual, 1840. [2] Everard, 1703. [3] 1816. [4] 1817. [5] 1820. [6] Cock. [7] Scotch Instructions, 1804. [8] 1874. [9] Somerville, 1846. [10] London Instruction, 1781. [11] C. S. G., 1877.

and clip, which, being placed inside the bung-hole on the inner side of the stave, forms a line with it, from which the vacuity is taken by sliding down the rod until the check pin rests on the upper end of the guide.

WOOD GAUGE.—*See* Callipers.

YARD RULE.—A "rule of one yard in length, divided into ten equal parts, and each of those subdivided into ten other equal parts, in order that you may take the dimensions of the goods in yards and hundredth parts of a yard" at calico-printers and paperstainers—so directed the Commissioners in Scotland in 1804.

BOOKS.—The principal gauging books written by members of this department are these—

1678, Dary's.
1683, Hunt's.
1684, 1702, ..., 1703, 1705, ..., ..., 1721, and 1727, Everard's Stereometry.
1704, Tremlett's.
1712, 1739, Dougharty's.
1740, Shirtcliffe's.
......, 1743, 1750, ..., ..., 1766, and 1776, Leadbetter's.
1760, 1765, Clark's.
1765, Moss's.
1801, Lindsay's.
1806, 1819, 1826, 1830, and 1838, Symons's.
1820, Iley's.
1821, Gutteridge's.
1823, Jonas's.
1825, Cunninghame's Imperial Ullager.
1826, 1832, Nesbit and Little's.
1827, Todd's Gentleman's Mathematical Companion.
1827, Gutteridge's Stereometry or Gauging Simplified.
1835, Roose's Complete Guide and Stock Book.
1840, 1852, 1865, Bateman's Excise Officer's Manual.
1841, Todd and Rowlandson's Useful Companion.
1865, Johnston's Inland Revenue Officer's Manual.

GENERAL ORDERS.

These were first referred tó as "Orders and Rules,"[1] afterwards as general letters, bye-laws,[2] regulation orders,[3] familiarly, as generals, and ultimately, in 1824, as general orders; though, in Ireland, reference is made to a "Dublin General Order" in 1794,[4] and in the London Establishment to a "General Order," and an "Index to General Orders" in 1781.[5] Orders of less general application are termed circular letters[6] or circulars.

It was long customary for only one to be issued, addressed "Sir," to each collector, who, roundly acknowledged all received from the accountant, retained the original letter, and caused a copy to be transmitted to each supervisor,[7] who circulated it through his district, and saw that each of his officers copied it,[8] or "such parts" as had "relation" to his duties,[9] in his own handwriting,[10] and even when advantage was taken of the possession of a printed copy to insert it in the order book, the surveying general examiner has been known to draw attention to the fact, that, "the general instructions require the orders to be copied."[11] To copy these documents must have been, sometimes, an irksome task, seeing that in one day[12] four letters were once issued, upon another occasion[13] that one letter alone occupied nineteen foolscap pages, and that the yearly issue once exceeded seventy issues,[14] the largest annual issue ever made. As closely as the writer has been able to estimate, there were issued between 1760 and 1878, including a few circulars in the later years, about 170 on malt, 210 on beer, 350 on spirits, and a total of about 2500.

The person who made the "coppies, coppeis," sometimes mis-"copped, coppid." Here are a few of his slips—"agreeable to president, parson's custody, currant year, wether, wheather, weitther whither, whetether, werther, wheither, wither, wheter, similer, simuler, similier, simeler, similiar, simmiler, hairs and successers, regiment of Calvary."

The syllabification and abbreviations afford fun, and the ff is amusing—proff, thereoff, lawffully, reffering, fforfeiture, fforfeited, ffigures, fframe, ffide, ffront, ffraud.

The phraseology too is not devoid of interest—acquaint you,

[1] Parl. Ordinance, 1654. [2] Hersee. [3] Metheringham.
[4] P. Rep., 1807; Scotland in 1804. [5] London Instructions. [6] 1854.
[7] S., 1804; S., 1810. [8] 1764, 1767. [9] 1770. [10] 1776.
[11] 1847. [12] 1795. [13] 1819. [14] 1822.

notwithstanding, severely censured, incur the displeasure, pain of being suspended, suspension taken off, answer any neglect at their peril, the Board's heavy displeasure, on pain of the Board's severe displeasure, mark of displeasure, on pain of dismissal from the service, forthwith reported to the Board, under colour of such practice, clandestinely, fraudulently removed, good reason to believe, disagreement of moment, the revenue defrauded the fair trader injured, Board's command to acquaint you, commissioners direct you to take notice, by direction of the Board, it is their pleasure that you, herewith you receive the undermentioned, govern yourself accordingly, under existing regulations, the commissioners order, ordered (1725), that the following directions be observed, with the utmost practicable dispatch, that no objection be made on the part of this revenue, that it be revoked, rescinded.

To resume. The privilege of having a printed copy of a long letter, and of a long letter only, was extended to the supervisors in Scotland in 1807, and to the officers in England about 1839, and the guard book {was issued for general use in 1856. The earliest letter in the reprints is dated July 6, 1700, and singular to observe, exhorts one "to be diligent in business,"[1] and it might have been added, fervent in spirit, serving the Commissioners. This leads to the "codification" of the standing orders.

First and foremost stands "The Spirit of the General Letters and Orders," a compilation embracing a period of 128 years—1700-1827—made at the suggestion of "the Parliamentary Commissioners of Inquiry," "after three years of patient research, and no inconsiderable share of labour," by W. Hersee, "accomptant at the chief office for many years." Mr Hersee states in his preface that he projected his plan, twelve years prior to its execution, in consequence of the "great difficulty he had in finding, among a large mass, forming an accumulation of more than a century, the particular document," which he "required," and that he was dissuaded from then entering upon it by the then secretary who considered "that no man would be able to overcome its numerous difficulties." His work is, therefore, very probably, the first of the kind published—it is dated Jany. 30, 1829, pp. 624.[2] This valuable digest was continued in 1834, by G. T. Taylor,[3] also of the chief office, who reprinted the orders from 1828 to 1833, in chronological order, with

[1] Hersee. [2] Clowes, London. [3] Bradbury & Evans, London.

marginal notes and a copious alphabetical index, and continued to publish them annually down to 1850, after which a successor appeared in the person of W. R. Loftus, then an officer of inland revenue, who has reprinted down to 1876, first including the circulars to collectors and supervisors in 1861. William Stones, "officer of excise," compiled an "Index to General Orders, from 1700 to 1847, arranged according to the subjects, which appeared in 1848, and James Bell, examiner, prepared, much after Hersee's model, a "Compendium of General Orders," from the year 1700 to 1857.[1] A further revision has been several times suggested,[2] but it has not been adopted beyond the issue of a "Comprehensive Analytical Index," from 1858 to 1876.[1]

GHOST STORY.

How that a supervisor of excise had been ordered to a town not far from Llanfyllin in Montgomeryshire, that he took "Tee Gwyn," an old mansion, reputedly haunted for the past fifty years; how that he heard footsteps on the staircase, that his hair lifted his hat off his head; how that he set a sand tracing trap, that he discovered some five or six hundred cloven tracks; how that he set six rat traps, that he caught three fine rabbits.[3]

GILT WIRE DUTY.

A growing and a licence duty imposed by Mr Pitt in 1784.[4]

The growing duties of ten pence per ounce on gilt, and seven pence per ounce on silver, wire, with the still higher duties, on these wires, on importation from Ireland, and the licence duty of £2 on the wire drawer, in Great Britain, were doubled in 1805, and the whole, which amounted to a gross annual receipt of £8800, repealed in 1826.[5]

[1] Loftus, London.
[2] C. S. G., 1864, 1870.
[3] Young Ladies Journal, 1868.
[4] H. C., June 30, 1784.
[5] Parnell, 20th Rep.

GLASGOW MALT DUTY INSURRECTION.

"The Malt Tax in North Britain, commencing on the 23d instant (June 1725), the Malsters in and about the City gave ready Admittance to the Officers of Excise, to take an Account of the Stock in Hand. But the Officers who were to do the like at Glasgow, were obliged to send Letters the 21st to the Commissioners of Excise here, acquainting them, that some of the people of that Town had threatened to stone them if they should attempt to visit the Malthouses there. The Commissioners hereupon made Application to Major-General Wade, Commander-in-Chief of His Majesty's Forces in this Part of the Kingdom, who on the 23d sent two Companies to Glasgow, with Orders to assist the Civil Magistrates, as also the Officers of Customs and Excise, in the Execution of their Duty, and to protect them from the Rioters. The Companies marched with great Expedition and arrived there the 24th, between six and seven in the Evening. At their Entrance into the Town, they found a great Mob consisting mostly of Women and Boys, who gave them abusive language, and threw Stones at them as they marched along the Streets, crying, no Malt-Tax. The Officer desired them to forbear, for he intended them no Harm. He applied himself to the Provost, who gave him Billets for Quartering his Men, but told him he could not put him into Possession of the Guard-Room, because it had been locked up, and the Key taken away by the Rabble, when they heard the Soldiers were coming thither. The Officer unwilling to exasperate them by forcing open the Door, ordered the Guard to be kept at a Public House which he hired for that Purpose. About eleven a-clock that Night, several thousands of the Mob got together, and marched towards the House of Mr David Campbell, Representative in Parliament for Glasgow, 'threatening' to plunder it. Upon which Captain Bushel, who commanded the two Companies, sent an Officer to the Provost, letting him know the Mischief they designed to commit, and that he was ready with his Men to assist him in preventing it; but his answer was, that he thought the Number of his Soldiers was too small, and therefore he would not make any Use of them. Thus the Rabble finding no Opposition, nor even the Appearance of a Magistrate to restrain their Fury, with Hatchets and other Instruments forced into the House, and turned out two or three of Mr Campbell's Servants (he with his wife having the day before retired to his Country House), and fell to plundering everything that they could carry away, and destroying what was not portable. This Riot continued till nine the next Morning, when several of the Mob were lying drunk in the House, with the Wine and Liquors they found in the Cellars, but the Magistrates did not get any of them secured. The Officers of Excise during this Time were forced to hide, but some of them being discovered by the Rioters were beaten severely. It was hoped that the Rage of the Mob had been sufficiently gratified in the plundering of Mr Campbell's House, and till three or four in the Afternoon following the Town in Appearance was very quiet, when the Rioters began to meet again, Women or Men in Women's cloaths beating Drums about the Streets to call them together. The Captain of the two Companies, not knowing what their Design might be, ordered the Soldiers to be near the Guard-House, which the Provost had opened for them in the Morning. But the Mob did not long keep their Secret, for they advanced towards the Guard, saying, their next Business was the Soldiers. They gathered from all Quarters of the Town, began to throw Stones at the Soldiers, crying, Drive the Dogs out of Town, we will cut them to Pieces. The Officers told them they did not intend them any Harm, but if they continued to provoke them, they should not be able to refrain from firing at them. They answered, that they durst not fire with Ball, and continued throwing Stones in such Quantities and so large, that they broke some of the Locks of their Pieces, and their Bayonets, and wounded several of the Men. Upon which some of the Men were ordered to fire over their Heads, in hopes to terrify them; but they advancing still upon the Soldiers and throwing Stones in greater Quantities, the Soldiers fired on them and killed three or four, upon which they retired to some Distance. In this short Interval, the Provost sent to the commanding Officer desiring him to save himself and Men, by retreating out of the Town, for the Rioters were collecting all the Arms they had, and if he did not speedily march away there would be a great Deal more Bloodshed. The Captain taking his Advice, immediately marched for Dumbarton, being followed by great Numbers of the Mob, and so closely, that he was forced to fire now and then a Shot to secure his Retreat of the Town. He was followed six Miles by three or four hundred of the Rioters armed, but they durst not come up with him. Captain Bushel has sent an Officer hither, from Dumbarton Castle, to give Major-General Wade this Account of what had passed, and the Major-General has received the like Account by several persons come from Glasgow. The said

Officer relates further, that they miss six of their Men, and that they left their Baggage (which he supposes is plundered) in the town of Glasgow."—Edinburgh, June 26, 1725.[1]

Chalmers in his Caledonia, summarises and completes the narrative of the insurrection in these words, familiar of course to all true Scots—"The malt-tax which had occasioned during the late reign, a motion in Parliament, for the discontinuance of the Union, was extended over Scotland during the present. The consentient voice of every party, and every person, in this country, now concurred in reprobation and resistance of this hated measure.

"It was at Glasgow, a city noted for its loyalty, that an insurrection on the 24th of June 1725, sacked the house of her representative in Parliament and expulsed the king's troops. Every town, and every village, were ready to imitate this example. And the king's servants at length saw with reluctant eyes, that the enlisted passions of a whole people must be respected. . . . General Wade with Duncan Forbes, the king's advocate, marched at the head of an army into Glasgow, where there was none to oppose them. The principal insurgents were arrested, the magistrates of that city were carried prisoners to Edinburgh where they were not long detained. The insurgents were tried before the Court of Justiciary, wherein the Earl of Islay, as Lord Justice General, presided, Sir Walter Pringle, Lord Newhall. . . . and a lawyer of eminence led the court against the Justice General, in support of a mild construction of the law and of a mitigated infliction of punishment. Some of the guilty persons were whipped in Glasgow and some of them were transported to the plantations. By great efforts of management and perseverance, the malt tax was enforced with some mitigation, but a proper respect was henceforth paid to the spirit of the people. The malt tax act, in favour of Scotland, specially directed that, after paying £20,000 to the public, the surplus should be applied towards encouraging her manufactures and commerce."[2]

GLASS DUTY.

September 11, 1643.—This was one of the earliest excise impositions under the term "Glasses," but, in common with very many

[1] L. G., 1725.

[2] Vol. i., pp. 871-2.

others, it was given up on the Restoration of Charles II., and not reimposed until 1695,[1] when three commissioners were specially appointed to manage it with that on bottles "from and after September 29, 1695," when all the makers in England were required by statute to give in an entry of their glass houses.[2] The duty was levied until 1698, when it was reduced one-half,[3] and again repealed in 1699. It was reimposed and extended to Scotland in 1746; extended to Ireland partly in 1797[4] and partly in 1825; a licence duty imposed in 1784; it was modified by reductions and augmentations many times;[5] and finally repealed in 1845, by Sir R. Peel, who stated that it cost no less than 57 per cent. in collection.

Of course, in the period embraced in this rapid review, there were some features of interest. The duty was charged by the cwt. and the foot; the licence duty, originally introduced by Mr Pitt at £10 per house, was afterwards raised to £20 per house, and those who made flint glass paid a further licence duty of £100. Lord Althorp proposed, in his budget in 1831, to reduce the duty by £600,000—this was the first but unsuccessful aim at a repeal:[7] a further indication appeared, in 1832, in the permission to warehouse free of duty; petitions were presented to Parliament, in 1833 and 1835,[8] for the repeal; the Parnell Committee, in 1835, recommended it at "the earliest possible period;"[9] the Chancellor of the Exchequer, in 1844, suggested the repeal of a portion;[10] and petitions were presented, and returns moved for in Parliament[11] until it was repealed,—April 5, 1845.[12]

GLUCOSE.

This glucose or starch sugar, made chiefly from sago or starch, was first manufactured in two establishments in London, about 1864, for the use of the brewer, and classed by the authorities as "British sugar,"[13] or "home-made sugar-starch."[14]

"The term glucose," writes Mr Phillips, "is applied to a descrip-

[1] 6 & 7 W. & M., c. 18. [2] L. G., 1695. [3] H. C., January 25, 1698.
[4] P. Rep., 1809. [5] 1777, 1805, 1809, 1811, 1812, 1814, 1815, 1816, 1817, 1818, 1819, 1825, 1826, 1833, 1835, 1844.
[6] H. C., February 14, 1845. [7] H. C., February 14, 1831.
[8] P. Ret. Public Petitions. [9] 13 Rep. [10] H. C., May 2, 1844.
[11] 1841, 1842, 1844, 1845. [12] 8 Vict., c. 6. [13] C. 9 R.
[14] Idem, 10th.

tion of sugar found in the grape and many other fruits. It is prepared artificially by acting on farinaceous substances, by means of dilute sulphuric acid, at a certain temperature. It is less sweet in taste than ordinary cane and beet sugars, and this may be partially due to the fact that it contains a greater proportion of the elements of water than those sugars.

"A patent has been recently obtained for converting cane into grape sugar or glucose for use in brewing by acting on a solution of cane sugar by means of dilute sulphuric acid. It is made by a Mr Hill at Southampton, and has obtained considerable favour amongst brewers on account of its supposed power of imparting keeping properties to beer." [1]

These two makers ceased working shortly afterwards for about two years,[1] owing either to the small demand, or to the advantages possessed by the foreigner, whose "saccharum" was assessed on a different principle; but, with the high price of malt in 1868,[2] the demand increased, and with a change in the mode of charging the duty, from "its value as a gravity-producing material" to the system adopted by the Customs authorities, according to "its saccharine value," thus placing the home-manufacturer and the foreign producer on the same footing;[3] the manufacture continued to increase down to the date of the repeal of the duty in 1874.[4] This increase was also ascribed by the Commissioners to the comparative absence of the nitrogenous matter so inimical to the keeping quality of beer made from ordinarily low class sugar,[5] though their Honours express an opinion that it is not likely to be used "on a large scale as an economical or desirable substitute for malt." [6]

It was advertised in 1874 as—glucose or grape sugar, an extract from "pure grain," superior both for purity and for richness in saccharine properties, and supplied both as a solid and as a syrup by the Patent Grape Sugar Co. (Limited), Rupert Street, Whitechapel, London. *See* Sugar Duty.

GOLDEN RUMP.

In 1737, a farce entitled the "Golden Rump" was offered to the manager of the theatre in "Lincolns-Inn-Fields," who supposed it

[1] P. Rep. Malt Tax, 1867. [2] C. 12 R. [3] Idem, 13.
[4] Idem, 13 to 18. [5] Idem, 17. [6] Idem, 15.

to be a reflection upon the Government, most likely from their having endeavoured to introduce the vigilance of the excise over the duties on tobacco and wine—golden, and from the fact of their having sat an unusually long time in that session—rump. This play was suppressed by an Act of Parliament, and in the debate upon the bill, the Earl of Chesterfield, who spoke against the measure, supposed "it to be excised; the Lord Chamberlain is to have the honour of being chief gauger, supervisor, commissioner, judge, and jury."—May.

GOULD'S SUNSHINE AND GLOOM.

A tale of modern life, founded on fact, to unveil the virtues and vices of society to the inexperienced and unwary, by William Gould, I.R. Pages 408, 8vo, 1854.[1]

GRASSIE'S LEGENDS

Of the Highlands of Scotland from Oral Tradition, by James Grassie, officer of excise, Inverness. A small 8vo of 104 pages, of purely local interest, inscribed to "Hart Davies, Esquire, Depute-President of the Board of Excise." 1843.[2]

GUN LICENCE DUTY.

Granted at the instance of Mr Lowe in his financial statement of 1870. His proposition lay in the substitution of an uniform licence-duty of £1 on every person who carried a firearm outside the curtilage of his house, in lieu of the existing game licence duties.[3] The object of this new imposition he alleged to be, in addition to being a source of revenue, "to secure the public peace, and diminish the taste for poaching, by placing reasonable restrictions on the use of arms." His proposal did not pass unchallenged. Mr Taylor considered it to be "one more law for the preservation of game;" his

[1] Hodges & Smith, Dublin. [2] Smith, Inverness.
[3] H. C., April 11, 1870.

amendment was lost by 121 votes—41, 162. Mr Muntz moved the omission of the words "to carry," the financier objecting, the motion was withdrawn; he then moved that the duty be ten instead of twenty shillings, the game licence duties remaining, and the Chancellor of the Exchequer assenting, the motion was carried by 57 votes—163, 106. Sir H. Selwin-Ibbetson moved "that for each additional barrel above two an additional five shillings he charged;" rejected. Mr Peel moved "that persons carrying guns on lands in the occupation of the owner should be exempted," carried, ayes 112, noes 90. Mr Henley considered it an "arms act," and inquired "who was to pay for arms, such as muskets, &c., carried in a vessel?" Mr Lowe replied that he "had often heard of a man being a chosen vessel, but never a vessel being termed a man." On the division being taken for the third reading, it was carried by a majority of 129 votes—ayes 179, nos 50.[1] The impost was drafted to operate on April 1, 1870; the bill did not receive the Royal Assent until August 9, 1870. The Commissioners observe in their next annual report, "The measure . . . . . has entailed upon this office a vast amount of correspondence and of prosecutions . . . . . but we may hope that in both cases there will be a diminution when the law is better understood."[2] The yield did not meet the approbation of their Honours, and with respect to Ireland, the inspector of the Royal Irish Constabulary agreed, in 1875, to direct his staff to aid in the suppression of the evasion of the duty.[3] They observe in their next report, that although there is an increase, "It is remarkable, however, that whereas in Scotland the number of licences is almost stationary, and in England has declined, ... in Ireland, the number has increased."

"The substantial explanation of this enormous increase was furnished in our report last year . . . . and the system was fairly started in January 1876. . . . . . We continue to receive the most efficient aid in this respect from the Royal Irish Constabulary, ... and it has been decided that, with the rarest possible exceptions, all cases of breach of the gun licence law in Ireland shall be prosecuted and taken into court."[4]

The legal definition of curtilage may be, to some, serviceable. "Curtilage (*fr.* cour, *Fr.* court; and leagh, *Sax.* place) a court-yard,

[1] H. C., June 23—July 22, 1870. [2] C. 14 R. [3] Idem, 19.
[4] C. 20 R.

backside, or piece of ground lying near and belonging to a dwelling-house; the limit of the premises in which housebreaking can be committed. *See* 24 and 25 Vict. c. 96, s. 53."[1]

The number of licences issued in—

England.	Scotland.	Ireland.	United Kingdom.	Commissioners' Report.
1872—109,863	11,612	3,464	124,939	15th
1873—110,004	11,344	3,403	124,751	16th
1874—116,586	11,872	3,578	132,036	17th
1875—127,671	12,932	3,675	144,278	18th
1876—134,509	13,844	4,253	152,606	19th
1877—130,798	13,983	9,627	154,408	20th
1878—129,635	13,460	9,809	152,904	21st

GUTTERIDGE'S WORKS.

Universal Gauger.—"The Universal Gauger of Great Britain and Ireland and General Spirit Calculator: being a practical system of gauging by pen, sliding-rules, tables, callipers, and logarithms, according to the measures hitherto legally adopted in the British Dominions; and also according to the New Imperial Gallon, as recommended by a select committee of parliament, and containing upwards of forty thousand original calculations on gauging spirits, &c., by William Gutteridge." Pages about 500, 8vo. 1821.

"New Tables of the Weight of Spirits of various Strengths and Temperatures;" these will be noticed under the paper on Spirit Duty. The author describes himself as "Calculator of Tables to Government." Pages 100, 8vo, bound in leather, pocket diary size. 9·5 by 6·3 inches. 1824.

Precepts for an improved system of measuring, gauging, &c. This work was issued on the introduction of the imperial system, and in addition to much then needful information, contains a description of several gauging instruments. Pages 22, 8vo. 1826. *See* Gauging Appliances.

Vade Mecum.—A publication for the use of distillers, rectifiers, spirit-merchants, and revenue officers, but more particularly for the trade, in which numerous rules are given, with examples, for finding

[1] Wharton's Law Lexicon, 1867.

the value in money and alcoholic strength of various mixtures of spirits, or averaging, which the author "believes . . . . originated with himself." A table of duty factors concludes the professional interest in this 64-page 8vo. 1826.

Stereometry or Gauging Simplified, as supplied "by Order of the Honourable Board of Excise." Pages 180, 8vo, bound with the Vade Mecum, 10s. 1827.

NE PLUS ULTRA.—The bombastic title of this book will create great expectations, and indeed, at the time it was published, it no doubt sustained them. The principal features in this work are the table of the strength and weight of spirits, and the long interesting chapter on the hydrometer, both of which will be noticed in the papers on those subjects. This, his apparently last production, is dedicated to his Grace the Duke of Wellington, K.G., First Lord of the Treasury. Pages 160, 8vo, price £1. 1828.

HACKNEY COACH DUTY.

Peculiar to London, Westminster, and the parishes comprised within the Bills of Mortality,[1] in which a duty is stated to have been levied as early as 1662.[2]

The management originally lay with the Lord Mayor and Aldermen, who were authorised to license 400 persons, but, in 1687, it was transferred to five commissioners, who were specially appointed;[2] of whom, three so much misconducted themselves by "receiving bribes and acting arbitrarily," that they were at once removed from office by the decision of Parliament;[3] there were also about ten functionaries besides them. The commissioners received a salary of £200 each.[4] The abolition of this office, recommended in 1797, was subsequently acted upon, in so far as the management of the duties was merged with those under the Commissioners of Hawkers' Duty, whose salaries were fixed at £300 and £400.[5] It was afterwards handed over to the Board of Stamps,[6] and finally to the Commissioners of Excise,[7] under whom the duties ceased to be levied on December 31, 1869.[8]

[1] L. G., 1687. [2] C. 13 R. [3] March 20, 1687-88.
[4] P. Rep., 1779, 1797. [5] H. C., Feb. 2, 1822. [6] P. Rep., 1830.
[7] 10 & 11 V., c. 42. [8] 32 & 33 V., c. 14.

Seldom has a duty fluctuated less—

1774—5s. per week.
1784—10s. „
1832—10s. „ and £5 life licence.
1853—7s. „
1853—6s. „ less Sunday.
1853—20s. annual licence.[1]

There was also a duty of 2s. 6d. per quarter upon hackney chairs, of which there were 400.[2]

A deputation of proprietors waited upon the Chancellor of the Exchequer in 1868 to request the reduction of the duty by one half,[3] and Mr Alderman Laurence moved the total repeal in 1869,[4] and the purpose of his withdrawn motion Mr Lowe included, in the same year, in his financial statement.[5]

HAM'S WORKS.

The Revenue and Mercantile Vade-Mecum. The breviates of the existing regulations on excise duties appear to be more particularly confined to such as might be required on importation or exportation; but the principal point to be noticed here, is, that acknowledgments are specially made to the Chief Inspector and Messrs Weddle, Brain, and Wenban, of this department. By G. D. Ham, of the Customs Department. Published in 1876.[6]

The Revenue and Mercantile Year Book for 1879, as specially published for the inland revenue officer, is an excellent work.

HARD ALE—HERB BEER.

A name applied to "beer in an impure state," sold at about sixpence per quart. On analysis, a pint was found to contain "35 grains of acetic acid;" "the liquor was strong ale that had been spoiled, as it contained six per cent. of alcohol, which was a greater per centage than was discovered in ordinary table beer;" the evi-

[1] C. 13 R. [2] L. G., 1715; P. Rep., 1781. [3] Evening Star.
[4] H. C., March 11, 1869. [5] H. C., April 8, 1869.
[6] Wilson, London.

dence given by the city analyst in Edinburgh at a trial under the Adulteration Act in 1873.[1] It was once made as a regular beverage by adding about two gallons of acid beer or vinegar to good beer.[2]

Herb beer is a cheap beverage also, termed treacle beer, horehound beer made of treacle or syrup, flavoured with herbs, as horehound, &c.

HARDWICKE'S SCIENCE GOSSIP.

The pen-and-ink sketches of the marsh-fly and of a section of the spine of the echinus, are by R. Connor, Esq., of this department, "whose able pencil," writes the editor, "we purpose engaging on other natural history subjects." Nos. 102, 103, 1873.

The same delineator has also exhibited a large number of drawings on the same subject at the Royal, the Quequett, and other microscopical societies, in whose journals his productions have been reviewed in flattering terms.

See Laboratory; Tobacco Duty.

HAWKER'S LICENCE DUTY.

Queen Elizabeth gave her royal assent to a Bill to punish all pedlars and petty chapmen as rogues, vagabonds, and sturdy beggars, but King James II., on ascending the throne, directed, by proclamation, that as the trade had been used "for the Ease and Benefit of Our Loving Subjects dwelling remote from Cities and Market Towns, for that cause the Industrious and Well-disposed Petty Chapman. . . . hath been, in some sort permitted to Travel," though some "Rebels . . . being of no Religion" had "Dispersed, without Inspection, Schismatical and Scandalous Books and Libels," and, that the "Honest" petty chapman may be encouraged "to Travel in his Vocation," there is "no better way to effect the same than by Licensing" upon the applicant producing a certificate of good character, given under the hands of the "Minister and Churchwardens of the Parish" in which he may reside, and entering into bond in a "Penal Sum of Forty Pounds," to continue to be of "Good Behaviour," and "to lodge

[1] Scotsman—Art of Brewing, 1829. [2] C. S. G., 1873.

onely in Inns or Alehouses, and not to travel on Sundays." Officers were appointed and arrangements were made, at the same time, to open twelve offices in different parts of the country, but at a later date, a change fixed the head "office" in London "over against the Upper Pump in Holbourn."[1] These regulations commenced on June 25, 1686,[2] and remained in force until 1697, when the management was transferred to "The Commissioners for Transportation,"[3] who shortly afterwards appointed a cashier in London, and about a dozen riding surveyors for the country, whose duties consisted in riding through the country to grant licences, "to take up" those who traded without licence, and to suppress "illicit hawking," for which they received two pence in £, and a half of every fine,[4] and these duties they performed, for some time, with energy, discovering no few "peddling" with "Foot Licences," razed and adapted to "Horse Licences," and others in which old dates had been blotted out and new ones put in.[5] These mounted surveyors remitted the duties they received, by bill, less their salary; kept a journal which they forwarded to London, monthly; and went up annually in June "to settle their year's account."[6]

Thomas Tomkins, the cashier, unfortunately for the Commissioners, withdrew "himself beyond the seas," leaving their honours liable to a debt to the Crown to such an amount as to induce them to petition the authorities to compound with them or grant such other relief as they "may seem meet;" a prayer, to which Sir Robert Walpole announced his Majesty had been graciously pleased to "assent."[7]

It was suggested that the duty should be transferred from these Commissioners to those of hackney carriages,[8] a suggestion acted upon in 1810; and from these Commissioners to those of stamps,[9] a suggestion acted upon in 1831; by a subsequent enactment it was commuted into an excise licence in 1865.

But the duffer, the swadder, the dudder,[10] early excluded by charter from trading in most towns corporate, gave great offence to the London shopkeepers, who petitioned Parliament to stop his frauds on the "quiet and unwary people," by repealing the Acts,

[1] L. G., 1718. [2] Royal Proc., 1686. [3] L. G., 1697.
[4] L. G., 1703; P. Rep., 1797. [5] L. G., 1704. [6] P. Rep., 1781.
[7] H. C., Feb. 15, 1727. [8] P. Rep., 1797. [9] P. Rep., 1830.
[10] Hawker: Slang Dict., 1865. [11] H. C., June 13, 1785.

and by levying a tax of two shillings a-year on all trades,[1] and though this petition was not then heeded, Mr Pitt eventually imposed a rateable licence on shops at one and two shillings in the £, and at the same time, proposed to repeal the pedlar's licence, as hawking was a "pest to the community and a kind of nursery for inland smuggling"—a proposition which he afterwards departed from, by raising the hawker's licence duty.[2] But both of these duties were repealed four years later on the motions of private members.[3] Petitions have been also since presented to repeal the hawker's licence duty.[4] The duties—

Jan. 24, 1697, E.,	£4 0 0	man;	£4 0 0	each horse.
1785, E.,	8 0 0	„	12 0 0	„
1785, I.,	2 0 0	„	2 0 0	„
1789, E., Aug. 1, 1815, S.,	4 0 0	„	4 0 0	„
1815, I.,	2 2 0	„	2 2 0	„ or servant.
1861, G. B.,	2 0 0	„	4 0 0	„ slightly altered, 1862

1870, G. B., £4, man with a horse, &c., and £4, every other horse.

1870, I., £4, 4s., man with a horse, &c., and £2, 2s., every other horse.

The receipts from this source in Ireland, formerly gave support to the Incorporated Society for English Protestant Schools.[5] The total annual duty has never much exceeded £52,000.[6] The petty chapman was allowed on the first imposition to pay in moieties, equivalent to half-yearly, though if he chose to make "prompt payment," in one sum, he was allowed two shillings;[7] and with respect to the cost of collection, though now very small, it, about a century ago, exceeded 48 per cent. on the gross, and 95 per cent. on the net, receipt—1789.[8]

HEARTH MONEY.

Though levied in England as an "accumulative excise," it does not seem to have been connected with the excise after 1689, yet

[1] H. C., March 19, 1748. [2] H. C., May 9, June 13, 1785. [3] H. C., April 27, 1789. [4] 1813, 1840, 1844. [5] C. 13 R. [6] C. 14 R. [7] 9 Gul. 3, c. 27. [8] P. Rep., 1797.

in Ireland, a form of commission, now before the writer, issued in the reign of George III., authorises the employé in this duty to "search for any goods or commodities exciseable," and in 1809, these employés were included in an excise inquiry, when there were in Dublin 18, and in the other parts of Ireland, 108 supervisors and collectors, who received salaries varying from £60 to £100, and from £40 to £48, a-year, respectively.[1]

HICK'S PATENT APPARATUS,

formerly used, though to a very slight extent, "for collecting and condensing into spirits the vapour arising from bread," known as panary fermentation. It was allowed to be used by Treasury Warrant, dated May 16, 1831, on making entry, paying a distiller's licence, and entering into bond, with one or more sureties, in £500. Printed instructions were issued to officers. It was also called "Hick's oven for the distillation of spirits from bread."[2]

Octavius Smith, of Thames Bank, a distiller, who experimented with the apparatus, found that three bushels of flour yielded from 50 to 70 ounces of proof spirit—a quarter to a third of a gallon; a four-pound loaf, from a half to an ounce of spirit.[3]

HIDE AND SKIN DUTY.

Allied as this duty is to that on leather, with which it was eventually classed, its management was at first placed under Commissioners who were specially appointed,[4] then under six Commissioners of Hides and Affairs of Taxes, certainly an incongruous alliance,[5] and lastly under the Commissioners of Excise.[6]

A duty existed in England in 1645;[7] in Scotland in 1647;[8] it was levied in Ireland in 1794.[9] Even "hare skins" and "rabbit skins" were charged,[10] and the mode of denoting the charge was by impressing a stamp on the hind shank and tail.[11] A motion, in common with that on leather, was made to repeal this duty in 1813; half was

[1] P. Rep., 1809. [2] 1832. [3] P. Rep. Molasses, 1831.
[4] L. G., 1711. [5] Idem., 1714, 1715, 1718. [6] Idem., 1718, 1719.
[7] P. O. [8] Act, March 10, 1647. [9] P. Rep., 1809.
[10] Instructions, 1827. [11] 1820.

repealed in 1822, a portion of the remaining half in 1826,[1] and the remainder, with the licence duties, in 1830.[2] *See* Leather Duty.

HIGHLANDER, THE.

Not in an official sense is "The Highlander Newspaper and Publishing Company (Limited)," Inverness, connected with the department, but as having been established, in 1873, at the instance of an old, able, energetic advocate for the betterment of this department, on his retirement from it—Fergus: John Murdoch.

HOLIDAYS.

These, in 1773, were enjoyed to the extent of fifty-nine days in the year,[3] by the occupants of the Chief Office, and probably granted

[1] C. 1 R. [2] Parnell, 20 Rep.

[3] From "Royal Kalendar," 1773—

Circumcision	Jan.	1	King Geo. III.'s Birthday	June	4
Epiphany	,,	6	Princess Amelia's Birthday	,,	10
Queen Charlotte's Birthday	,,	18	St Barnabas	,,	11
Conversion of St Paul	,,	25	St John, Baptist	,,	24
K. Charles, Mart.	,,	30	Sts Peter and Paul	,,	29
Purification Virgin Mary	Feb.	2	St Swithin	July	15
Valentine's Day	,,	14	Queen of Denmark, "b."	,,	22
Shrove Tuesday	,,	23	St James's	,,	25
Ash Wednesday	,,	24	Lammas Day	Aug.	1
St Matthew's	,,		Prs. Bunfu Birthday	,,	11
St David's	March	1	Prince Wales' Birthday	,,	12
Lady Day	,,	25	St Bartholomew	,,	24
Good Friday	April	9	"London Burnt"	Sept.	2
Easter Monday	,,	12	Holy Rood	,,	14
Easter Tuesday	,,	13	Kings Geo. I. & II.	,,	18
Easter Wednesday	,,	14	St Matthew	,,	21
St George's	,,	23	King Geo. III.; 2 C. Cor.	,,	22
St Mark's	,,	25	St Mic. & Prs. Rs. b.	,,	29
Sts Phil. and Ja.	May	1	St Luke	Oct.	18
Ascension Day	,,	20	King Geo. III. Inaug.	,,	25
King Charles II. Restoration	,,	29	King Geo. III. Procl.	,,	26
Whit. Monday	,,	31	St Simon & St Jude	,,	28
Whit. Tuesday	June	1	All Saints	Nov.	1
Whit. Wednesday	,,	2	All Souls	,,	

partly by statute and partly by usage, similar to those to the Customs, though, in that department, in 1797, they were less numerous, and more were allowed in this than in any other under the Crown.[1] Though comparatively few are now observed, the privilege has been extended to supervisors,[2] and they at first were allowed—the Restoration of Charles II., Queen's Birthday, Queen's Coronation Day, Prince of Wales' Birthday, Good Friday, Christmas Day, but, in 1859, the observance of the Restoration of Charles II., a truly significant one to this department, was discontinued. In 1867 Christmas Day and Good Friday were conceded to officers under certain conditions.[3] With respect to the examiners, who may be in the office, half take the day before, and half the day after those days.

The "Bank Holidays Act, 1871,"[4] in no way affected the holidays kept in this department, but that of 1875[5] discontinued the observance of the anniversaries of Her Majesty's Coronation Day and of His Royal Highness' Birthday, and occasioned an alteration in England and Ireland to Good Friday, Christmas Day, Her Majesty's Birthday, Easter Monday, Whitsun' Monday, first Monday in August, day after Christmas Day, unless Sunday, then the Monday, but no alteration in Scotland—Good Friday, Christmas Day, Her Majesty's Birthday, Her Majesty's Coronation Day, Prince of Wales' Birthday.

The Saturday half-holiday was suggested in 1863,[6] and a memorial was presented to Lord Palmerston in 1864.[6] It was eventually granted under such arrangements as the chiefs in the respective departments might make.[7]

A general fastday was ordered to be observed by the collector, by an issue in 1798, in so far as he was not to collect on that day; and on the local sacramental fast days, in Scotland, the collector, supervisor, and clerk, have for some time been allowed to rest from duty.[8] A subsequent issue includes any fast day.

King William's Birthday	Nov.	4	St Thomas	Dec.	21
Powder Plot	,,	5	Christmas Day	,,	25
Lord Mayor's Day	,,	9	St Stephens	,,	26
Queen Eliz. Acces.	,,	17	St John	,,	27
Duke of Gloster's Birthday	,,	25	Holy Innocents	,,	28
St Andrew	,,	30			

1 P. Rep., 1797. 2 G. I., 1856. 3 Malt Inst. 4 34 Vict., c. 17.
5 38 Vict., c. 13. 6 C. S. G. 7 H. C., July 1, 1867.
8 G. I., 1856.

HOP DUTY.

A pre-Restoration duty, levied in 1645, at 1s. per 20s. worth,[1] but discontinued on or before the Restoration, and not again charged until June 1, 1711,[2] but from then to its commutation and repeal on June 3, 1868. The rates per pound were these—

1711—1d.	1801—$2\frac{1}{2}$d.
1778—1d. and 5 per cent.	1806—2d.
1780—1d. and 10 „	1840—2d. and 5 per cent.
1783—1d. and 15 „	1860— $1\frac{1}{2}$d.[3]
1786—$1\frac{1}{18}$d.	

The Commissions observe, in their first report, it is "of all Excise duties that which is charged with the greatest facility and certainty, with the least amount of interference in trader's operations, and at the lowest cost of collection. . . . . The only difficulty occurs in the collection of the money." No duty, though chargeable, was ever charged in Scotland; it did not extend to Ireland, and in England it was limited, principally, to eleven collections—Canterbury, Essex, Hants, Hereford, Lincoln, Rochester, Salisbury, Stourbridge, Suffolk, Sussex, Woocester.[4] The area of culture, as far as known, varied from 38,000 to 57,000 acres;[3] the planters numbered, in 1858, 6500;[5] the charge, in 1842, was made by 254 temporary officers, at a cost of £3,238;[6] the supervisor, usually an energetic, intelligent officer, receiving, in 1854, an extra allowance at £70 per annum; the cost of collection was about one per cent.;[7] three supervisors were dropped on its repeal.[8]

Punch, who, in few words, puts the exact state of matters, gave, in 1850, a "Conundrum to farmers. Which of the taxes is a perfect robbery? The hop duty, because it is a downright picking of pockets." Though, prior to this date, a motion for its repeal, negatived without a division, had been made in the House of Lords,[9] and numerous returns had been made, and no fewer than 170 petitions for the reduction or the repeal of the duty presented to Parliament, no firm, decisive step appears to have been taken to remove it from the statute book until 1851. The reduction and repeal were then three times moved, and supported by upwards of sixty petitions, but to

[1] P. O., 1644, 1645. [2] L. G., 1711. [3] C. 13 R.
[4] Parnell Sixteenth Report; Bateman, 1843. [5] C. 3 R.
[6] P. Ret., 1842. [7] P. Ret., 1853; C. 1 R. [8] C. 7 R.
[9] H. L., March 20, 1835.

little effect.[1] The following year a deputation waited upon the Prime Minister to urge the same desire, and motions, supported by about sixty petitions, for the same purpose, were made in the House of Commons, much to the same effect.[2]

The incidence of the duty, reported upon favourably than otherwise in 1835,[3] gradually became very serious to those who were immediately liable to it,[4] inasmuch as the system of credit was bad—nine and twelve months,[5] the over production caused sales to be effected at unremunerative prices,[6] credit to be extended at 4 and 5 per cent.,[7] corn and cattle to be sold at 15 per cent. below ordinary prices to meet payments,[8] and, in some cases, even the planters to be planted or "thrust into prison."[9] So severe, indeed, had the incidence of the duty become,[10] that a Parliamentary Committee was appointed to report upon it; yet, although the committee prepared two draft reports, in which an acreage duty was mentioned, neither was adopted, and the committee agreed to only report the minutes of evidence.[11] From this date fewer representations were made to Parliament until 1861, when Mr Dobson moved its consideration on any future remission of taxation, and received poetical support, founded on the precarious bine, from Sir Brook Bridges who distiched—

> "First the flea, next the fly,
> Then the louse, and then I die."

His motion was lost by 92 votes—ayes 110, noes 202.[12]

The idea to be accepted, was given in the *Quarterly Review* of 1861—"an increase of licence duty." It was adopted by Mr Gladstone, who commuted the duty into an additional brewing licence duty at threepence per barrel brewed, basing his estimate on an old supposition[13] that two pounds of hops would be used in brewing every barrel of beer.[14] The repeal was accordingly effected, as previously shown, when half the duty was remitted on the stocks in hand,[15] though the whole duty was charged, on its imposition, on the stocks then on hand.[16]

[1] H. C., May 5, 8, July 29, 1851. [2] H. C., March 23, Dec. 3, 1852. [3] Parnell Sixteenth Report. [4] P. Ret., 1841-1862. [5] C. 1 R. [6] C. 3 R. [7] C. 2, 3, 4, R. [8] Quarterly Review, 1861. [9] H. C., Feb. 17, 1853. [10] H. C., Feb. 17, 1853; May 20, 1855. [11] P. Rep., 1857. [12] H. C., March 5, 1861. [13] 1818. [14] H. C., April 3, 1864. [15] C. 7 R. [16] L. G., 1711.

Mr Gladstone's estimate showed in the year ended March 31, 1863, on comparing the average annual duty, during the ten years preceding the repeal, calculated at three halfpence per pound, with the increase derived from the brewing licence, a loss to the Exchequer of £70,000—£294,534—£224,604.[1]

HORSE LICENCE DUTY.

Ten shillings on every horse on whose harness "a stamp" shall be affixed was Mr Pitt's proposal in 1784,[2] and as it was levied at that date, the duty would seem to have been a stamp-duty,[3] afterwards an assessed tax, and then an excise licence—January 1, 1870. This applied to Great Britain, but it appears that Mr Foster, the Chancellor of the Irish Exchequer, proposed, in 1805, to extend it to that country.[4]

The rates of duty have varied very much—under such decisions as—the purpose for which the horse was used (1784), the number kept (1789), whether horse or mule (1796), the position of the small farmer (1804), the partial use in husbandry, the entire use in husbandry, the height of the animal (1812), the occupation of the person using it (1819-1869), then the exemption on horses used in husbandry (1823), but again chargeable in 1854,[5] and, finally, the uniform licence duty with an exemption in favour of husbandry, &c. (1870).

The horse-dealer, on the imposition of the duty on horses, applied to the Treasury to be exempted from its incidence, and their lordships entertained the application in so far as they substituted a duty upon him instead of his horses. The dealer in London and within the limits of the Bills of Mortality, until 1870, always paid double that exacted of the dealer elsewhere, Scotland included.

The closer collection of the licence duty, consequent on the commutation of 1870, occasioned several inquiries in Parliament as to its legality,[6] and, probably, Mr Laing to move its repeal—a motion which he withdrew.[7] The Parliamentary Committee too, presided over by Earl Rosebery, then sitting on the horse question, recommended that any tax operating as a discouragement on a farmer keeping

[1] P. Ret., 1864. [2] H. C., June 30, 1784. [3] H. C., June 16, 1801.
[4] H. C., March 13, 1805. [5] C. 13 R.
[6] H. C., Feb. 11, March 24, 1870; July 20, 1871; June 8, 1872.
[7] H. C., April 1, 1873.

horses, whether broken or not, should be at once abolished or considerably modified.[1] Their recommendation was more than regarded by Sir Stafford Northcote, Bart., who proposed, in his financial statement of 1874, the repeal of the duty, which took effect from July 1, 1874.[2]

HORSFALL COMMITTEE.

The purpose and result of the appointment of this committee[3] have been noticed under Consolidation. Nominated on May 7, 1862, the committee took evidence, and drafted unadopted reports, until disbanded on July 8, 1863. Their blue book extends to 288 pages[4] of interesting facts and opinions, most of which subsequently appeared in the Civil Service Gazette during the years 1862-64, and the more pertinent portions in Our Postal and Revenue Establishments.

HUNT'S WORKS.

Fall of Tarquin.—"The Fall of Tarquin; a tragedy, by W. H. Gent," in three acts, with prologue and epilogue. The author was a collector of excise. York, 1713.

Practical Gauging.—"Practical Gauging, epitomised with the use and construction of the tables of logarithms. Whereunto is added an abridgment of the Laws of Excise now in force, by William Hunt, student in the mathematics, and one of the general supervisors for the Duty of Excise." This is one of the earliest publications; it contains—"Ordered by the Chief Commissioners and Governors of Excise that the book (entitled Practical Gauging Epitomised) be forthwith printed and published." Dated Ripon, May 10, 1683. Pages about 210, 8vo, with gilt edges. Published at York.

"The Projectors: a comedy as it was intended to be acted at one of the theatres, London," by W. H.—William Hunt, collector. 1737.

[1] P. Rep., 1873. [2] H. C., April 16, 1874. [3] H. C., April 29, 1862.
[4] P. Rep., 1863.

HUSH SHOP.

A house in Lancashire, prior to 1830, in which lawless persons brewed and sold their produce privately to "the very scum and dregs of society,"—the early local name for beerhouse.[1]

HYDROMEL.

An article of similar character to maltheine, which see, but thinner in consistency, and lighter in colour, used in the adulteration of ale.[2] It is the name of a beverage in a foreign country.[3]

HYDROMETER.

"Many other pretty things he shewed me, and did give me a glass bubble to try the strength of liquors with,"—thus wrote Samuel Pepys of "Mr Boyle's hydrometer," as used in the science of alcoholometry in 1668.

There is here the principle, in a rude form, on which the construction of the hydrometer is based—the comparative weight of equal volumes, but, how "proof goods" were determined, will be referred to more particularly under spirit duty.

Clarke's hydrometer was the first to be recognised by the revenue authorities, and though used by them from about 1730, its use was not sanctioned by legal authority until 1788, and even then only until such an investigation could be made, and a satisfactory, uniform standard devised. But the correct action of the instrument being somewhat defeated by sweetened spirit in 1760, the Commissioners ordered the use of "thumb phials," as shown in East's Choice Chips, and the use of "a thermometer, as soon as one can be made." Æneas Coffey, too, suggested a hydrometer for sweetened spirit.[4] The investigation just referred to was entrusted to the "then secretary to the Royal Society, the results of whose labours and researches were put forward with Gilpin's tables in 1794, but no practical measures appear to have been taken in consequence."[5] There were now in use two hydrometers, one for British, and another for foreign

[1] Pacy's Reminiscences. [2] C. S. G., 1868. [3] Morewood, 1838. [4] P. Rep., 1835. [5] Johnston's Handbook.

spirits—the latter termed the "import hydrometer"[1]—in Scotland reference is made, in 1816, to an "export hydrometer;" in Ireland, too, in 1807, that by Spear was used until Clarke's replaced it.[2]

Though dissatisfied with the action of Clarke's instrument, and the subject was referred to Sir C. Blagden,[3] as previously referred to, and the Commissioners advertised for "hydrometers or instruments for ascertaining the strength of spirituous liquors as are now in use, or shall be produced to them . . . . . in order to their making experiments of their accuracy and convenience for use, for the doing of which a proper time will hereafter be appointed;"[4] their Honours were not successful in immediately obtaining a better instrument, as Clarke's was continued from time to time until its use was made perpetual by 41 Geo. III. c. 93. "By 42 Geo. III. c. 97, the Lords of the Treasury were empowered to discontinue the use of Clarke's hydrometer, and to order the use of any other instrument. Clarke's hydrometer, however, remained unsuperseded till the passing of the 56 Geo. III. c. 140, which established the use of Sikes' hydrometer. The operation of the act was to cease on the 1st of August 1818, but when about to expire, it was repealed by 58 Geo. III. c. 28, which directed the continuance of Sikes' hydrometer, and is the act under which that instrument is now used in ascertaining the strengths of spirits." The tables issued in 1816 ranged from a temperature of 30° to 80° F., the indication from 0 by ½ degrees to 100, the strengths from 73·6 o.p. to "100·0" u.p.,[5] but on the "indications" being "divided into five parts instead of halves" in 1818, new tables were calculated by Thomas Soutar. Sikes' instrument was taken into use in England on January 6, 1816; in Scotland on January 6, 1817; in Ireland in 1818.

In 1831 and 1832 the cost of this appliance was moved for by Parliament.[6]

In 1832 the Board "addressed a letter to the Treasury, desiring that a scientific examination might be made of the extent and accuracy of the indications afforded by Sikes' hydrometer, with a view to the improvement of that instrument. . . . . . The Treasury referred the matter for consideration and report to the Royal Society, which willingly formed a committee of its members, and undertook the

[1] 1796, 1800. [2] P. Reps., 1807, 1808, 1809 [3] Gutteridge's Ne Plus Ultra.
[4] Excise Office, London, August 25, 1802, Thomas Burton, L. G.
[5] Brook, London. [6] P. Ret., 1831, 1832.

necessary inquiry." Mr Bates submitted a new hydrometer to the committee, who, after a minute examination, approved it, and with tables "calculated in correspondence with the indication of the proposed hydrometer and the altered standard of proof, and the conclusions generally come to by the Society, after a protracted, patient, and careful investigation, were embodied in a report to the Treasury, drawn up by Professor Faraday."[1]

The last investigation appears to have been completed in 1861 by the Principal of the laboratory. But this was confined to the establishment of "data upon which instruments and tables might be constructed that would furnish . . . . the means of assaying and valuing alcohol of those high strengths which are beyond the range of Sikes' hydrometer."[2] This has not been made publicly known.

To guard against future frauds, the supervisor was ordered, in 1818, to apply for a standard with which he was to examine, once a month, those in use by his officers, noting this performance in his diary; in 1819 he was enjoined to do so once in fourteen days, and note the examination in front of the distillery ledger; the collector, too, was, at the same time, supplied with one with which to compare the supervisor's at each sitting; in 1830 the supervisor was supplied with a reserve on a given scale, according to the number of distilleries in the district; and the officer was allowed a standard. The reserve allowed the supervisor—

If 4	distilleries,	2	hydrometers.
If 5	"	3	"
If 7	"	4	"

If it be permitted to mention Punch's hydrometer, he states "a simple way to detect moisture on the surface of the earth is to wear boots with holes in the soles, or sit upon the ground out of doors for two hours, and then calculate according to the degree of rheumatism to which you will rise."[3] "A cheap hydrometer."

The reader is now referred to a minute popular account of this instrument in Johnston's Handbook; also to Muspratt's Chemistry, article Alcohol; Ure's Dictionary, article Alcoholometry.

[1] Johnston's Handbook. [2] C. 5 R. [3] Punch's Almanack, 1843.

ILEY'S NEW PRACTICAL GAGER.

This treatise by Matthew Iley, many years "a Gager and Surveyor on the London Establishment," was dedicated to his patrons and superiors the Commissioners of Excise. The author informs us that "The chain of connection is never broken by the admission of extraneous matter, nor is the patience wearied by tiresome repetitions, the utmost possible regularity and system being observed throughout the work from beginning to end." This the writer can confirm. His book is divided into fifteen sections, some of which will be noticed elsewhere. The gager in pattens is not unamusing —"Then cause water or other liquor to be admitted to cover the bottom of the cooler, an inch or more in the ebbest part; and chuse a constant dipping place. Next,"—to obtain a mean dip—"put on a pair of pattens and walk over the cooler, taking dips in several parts of it and noting them in a memorandum."

This little 8vo of 464 pages is printed in bold type, and illustrated with excellent wood engravings. Published in 1820.

IMPORTATION.

Attendance was formerly given by members of this department at the various ports,[1] to enforce the observance of the excise laws, which in some instances forbade the importation of articles chargeable with home duties,[2] and in others, exacted higher duties than those levied on the home produce.[3] The excise import duties have been transferred to the Customs.[4] Services were also performed for the Board of Trade, which, with Exportation, see.

INCIDENTS.

The Fund of Incidents in Ireland, was that out of which pensions were paid;[5] the petty incident is a small sum paid for a prescribed purpose.

In connection with the latter form, a grievance long existed of

[1] P. O., Aug. 31, 1644, 1691. [2] 1705. [3] 1803. [4] 1825, 1834.
[5] P. Rep., 1809.

having to make an affidavit—subsequently a declaration—to sums of and above ten shillings,[1] but its public repetition,[2] with an increased expenditure, at length claimed attention, and in 1871, a certificate up to £2 and a declaration above that sum, were substituted. The repayment was originally once a-year,[3] with an advance of £5 to those who had, before the termination of the year, laid out that amount,[4] though in Scotland it was made quarterly,[5] and in England, apparently first in 1871. The Scotch Commissioners too issued a printed "Petty Incident Book," "for the more effectually ensuring a strict compliance with the Instructions," and such a book has since been suggested by "Bow Wow."[6] "Expresses,"—special messengers.

INDIAN FAMINE RELIEF FUND.

This department subscribed to this fund in 1877.

INDICATOR.

Pottinger invented an appliance long before the Messrs Counsel and Norton, to prevent both supply and discharge cocks from being open at the same time, and to register the number of times each was opened—*See* Pottinger.

Firmly fixed in an horizontal position immediately over the supply and discharge cocks of the spirit receiver, the indicator consists of a strong iron plate 20·5 in. by 8·5 in., through which pass some 2 inches, two perpendicular shafts, 4 inches apart, connected with the cocks; on to each shaft and resting on the plate is slid a ratchet wheel, whose motion is confined to one direction by a spring ratchet or detenter, and on to this ratchet wheel a motor index wheel with two arcs and two pins, both ratchet and motor wheels being secured to the shaft with a small wedge; on the side of each shaft, a little above the plane of the motor wheel, is placed a notched brass indicator wheel, numbered from 0 to 11, though serviceable to only 9 by reason of the absence of notches above nine; an index hand

[1] 1705. [2] C. S. G., 1857, 1859, 1861-62, 1870-71. [3] 1713.
[4] 1831. [5] 1804. [6] C. S. G., 1872.

is also fixed into the plate, and with the cover with a glass top and lock fastenings, completes the mechanical contrivance.

Each cock being closed and the indicator wheel set to 0, an arc in each motor wheel is opposite the other; on the lever being applied to the shaft of either cock and moved 90°, the pin in the motor wheel comes into contact with the notch in the indicator wheel and moves it until figure 1 is opposite the index hand, and thus indicates once opened; from this position, the first movement must be to again close the cock by moving the lever onwards other 90°—the indicator wheel still resting with figure 1 opposite the index hand; each arc is now again opposite the other, and either cock may be opened. The chief points of security are the arcs in the motor wheels, and the absence of two notches in each of the indicator wheels.

The makers are Hunter and English, Bow, London. The first indicator was sold to the distiller, at Four Mills Distillery, Bromley, on Sept. 1, 1860, and since that date about ninety others have been sold. A royalty is payable to the inventors, but the careful perusal of Woodcroft has failed to afford the fact that the Indicator is a Patent.

INDOOR WORK.

The times and the men considered, it will not create surprise that the collector was cautioned, in 1781,[1] to report, on this mode of employment, in the supervisor's diary, "without always making use of the same set of words," and required to give the total number of days so shown taken for "indoor business" at the end of the year. The Scotch Commissioners were less exacting in this respect, and enjoined, that the collector should, "instead of tediously particularising the time taken for indoor work, insert only whether more time than is necessary is taken for that purpose."[2] But the moment, so to speak, a special medium afforded easy communication with each other, the supervisor suggested a half-day's holiday per week, or a "ten hours bill."[3] The first concession lay in the permission to take, in riding districts, one day per week during the months of

[1] Instructions. [2] Instructions, 1804. [3] C. S. G., 1854.

June, July, August, and September;[1] those in foot-walk districts soon joined issue with their more fortunate colleagues,[2] and from that date downwards, one day per week, "all the year round,"[3] until conceded in 1868, it never ceased to be requested.[4]

But even now to "note briefly in the diary the nature of the business done," afforded scope for pessimist views, until decided by Mr Secretary A. Y. that "indoor work" alone is sufficient.[5]

It afterwards transpired that the allowance of one day per week for this purpose was originally granted to "J. B." on his "single memorial."[6]

INKHORN.

Thus wrote Boswell of Johnson at Thrale's brewery—"bustling about with an inkhorn and pen in his buttonhole like an exciseman." This form of inkholder consequently preceded the present glass bottle, on which, when the glass duty was levied, many officers were wont to display their ingenuity, as, for instance, on one, in the possession of the writer, about a hundred years old, which is beautifully cut with Scotia's thistle.

Reference is also made to the inkhorn in Patterson's life of Train—"a gang of English surveyors who came down as proud of the inkhorn which hung at their button, as if it had been the insignia of the Order of the Garter."

INLAND BONDING WAREHOUSE.

Though Sir R. Walpole, in his "excise scheme" of 1733, proposed to erect "warehouses for storing tobacco under the care of the excise," the desire to warehouse dutiable commodities under bond, in inland towns, was made to the Treasury about 1836, when a minute, dated Nov. 8, 1836, was issued on the subject, and afterwards ordered to be printed by Parliament in 1837. Eight petitions were presented to Parliament in 1838, fifteen in 1839, twenty-six in 1840, seven in 1841, in favour of it, and twenty-seven, during the same period, against it, while others were presented for particular ware-

[1] 1857. [2] C. S. G., 1857. [3] Idem., 1862.
[4] Idem., 1857-60, 1862-68. [5] Feb. 20, 1870. [6] C. S. G., 1871.

houses, as in Wakefield, Manchester, and for the extension of the suggested system to Ireland.[1] The opposition to the system came from London, Liverpool, Bristol, &c., and certainly, if not all powerful, it was countenanced by the Chancellor of the Exchequer, even many years afterwards, when he stated in reply to an inquiry that it was not the intention of the Government to establish these warehouses in large manufacturing towns.[2] Too powerful were the duty-paying community in the centres of large inland industries to be withheld the privilege possessed by their more fortunately-situated fellow-traders at the ports, &c., and, accordingly, at their own expense, the people at Manchester established "a bonded warehousing place," which, proving a success—the revenue paid in one year being £155,000, at a cost of collection of only ·575 per cent.—induced Mr Hadfield to move the extension of the system, which, being agreed to, he brought in a bill to do so, which was at once read a first time, and, apparently, a last time.[3] This of course was not a purely excise question, but, as such, it received, on the termination of the Horsfall Committee's labours, the consideration of the Chairman of the Board, at whose suggestion[4] Mr Gladstone and two others prepared and passed a measure to permit the deposit of home-made spirits in approved warehouses in inland towns. This gave only partial satisfaction; a question being put at the time by Mr Lygon with respect to including foreign spirits, to which Mr Gladstone replied that "if they were to adopt the principle of making excise warehouses available for foreign spirits, they could not stop there, but must also make them available for tobacco, tea, sugar, and all other duty-paying commodities."[5]

Mr Lygon's idea was adopted in 1869.

INSTRUCTIONS.

The very expression occurs in a Parliamentary Ordinance, dated Feb. 22, 1646, and is there used in precisely the same sense as here.

For many years it was the practice to issue particular instructions separately, as brandy 1723, coffee 1724, candle 1725, plate 1726, malt 1732, sweets 1758, but it eventually changed into the issue of codes, thus, in 1778, Instructions for those in the Country, a quarto

[1] P. Rep., 1833-1852.
[2] H. C., March 28, 1859.
[3] H. C., May 31, 1860.
[4] C. 13 R.
[5] H. C., Feb. 15, March 7, 1864.

of nearly 500 pages; in 1781, Excise Town Instructions, a large quarto of about 760 pages, containing some twenty-eight heads; and, in Scotland, a very large volume of some 940 quarto pages, including about forty-five heads. These codes were signed by the respective Commissioners, and included directions for every grade from the collector downwards, and seem to have been the only codes issued. The term "general," certainly, might have been applied to these quartoes, but it appears to have represented by "excise" as in 1735, 1760, 1766, "excise." A curious custom obtained in 1781, by which the London surveyor "must read, or cause to be read, to all the officers in your division, their instructions once a quarter."

Opportunity was taken in the earlier issues to introduce expressive names, as—under tanner and tawer, Messrs Allum, Hide, Skinner; under brewing victualler, Messrs Early, Backward, Ready, Shiftwell; under rectifier, Messrs Ferment, Strong; under malster, Messrs Watcher, Treadwell; under officer, Messrs Young, Sharpe, Brisk, Careful, Steady; under supervisor, Mr Hawk.[1]

ISLAY.

Islay as it was. "Before the prohibition" of 1796, write the Parliamentary Committee on the Scotch distillery, "Mr Campbell who is proprietor of the greater part of the Island, farmed the Excise revenue for a small sum paid to Government annually. At the time of the prohibition there was a year or two of his lease to run; but he gave it up and aided government essentially to suppress distillation as the law directed. The number of stills which he and the yeomanry took up, was not less, Mr Ross[2] says, than 90, and some of them were above 80 gallons in capacity. After these were taken by Mr Campbell from the distillers and lodged in his own house, the distillers got over from Ireland, tinkers, who fitted up for them cauldrons and boilers as stills; between 90 and 100 of which, some upwards of 100 gallons, were seized by the Excise officers, during the prohibition. After the prohibition was removed, Mr Campbell's lease of the Excise revenue of Islay was not renewed; and the people of the island, finding they were not to get licences for a trifling sum as before, were much displeased and resolved not to take out licences, but they made no resolution not to distil. Mr Ross says,

[1] 1778, 1781, 1827. Collector of Oban.

they are distilling perhaps to a greater extent than ever . . . . but there has not been a licence taken out for distilling spirits, nor has a shilling of Excise revenue been paid in Islay since the prohibition."

ISLE OF MAN.

This islet was given by Henry the Fourth to the Athol family, who received the revenue collected and paid the expenses incurred in it; but George the Third, finding his revenue very much affected by the safe harbour which it afforded the smuggler, one of his Majesty's ministers brought in and carried a bill to purchase it at a cost of £70,000 and an annuity of £2,000, to have the right to exact the duties payable—imperial excise duties are not leviable there.[1] *See* Train's History of the Isle of Man.

Though in the possession of the Athol family, in 1661, Charles the Second granted £100 a year out of the excise for the maintenance of the clergyman, schoolmaster, &c.

JERDAN'S ESSAYS AND LYRICS.

A volume of some 200 pages, containing the productions of Samuel Smiles Jerdan of this department, which he entered in 1869. Died 1878. Elliot, Edinburgh.

JOHNSTON'S WORKS.

Handbook for Officers of Excise: by a Member of the Service. —W. H. Johnston, Supervisor, 1857. This is an excellent publication of only four chapters, but each on a subject, treated in a manner not hitherto given to the department. 1. Composition, Reports, Penmanship, Orthography, Punctuation. 2. Modes of Computation. 3. Valuation of Spirits and Wort, Degrees of Strength and Gravity. 4. Construction of the Revenue Hydrometer and Saccharometer. Loftus: London.

Inland Revenue Officer's Manual.—This is an original work entitled "Loftus's Inland Revenue Officer's Manual," being a guide

[1] H. C., Jan. 21, Feb. 27, March 6, 1765.

to the duties and qualifications of persons employed in the excise surveying department, written and edited by W. H. Johnston, Surveying General Examiner; announced in 1864[1]; published in 1865, by Loftus, London. It contains nine chapters—Taxes, Arithmetic, Principles of Mensuration, Practical Mensuration, Chemistry, Book-Keeping, Abstract of the Principal Excise Laws, Suggestions as to the Reasons of Laws, with an Appendix, Tables and list of Engravings. The position held by the author indicates the character of the production.

JONAS'S WORKS.

DISTILLER'S GUIDE.—This little 12mo of 292 pages published in 1818, being the third edition, not only treats of distilling and rectifying but also of compounding, and will be further referred to under "Spirit Duty. It would be more curious than useful to follow this author through his descriptions of the various beverages,—Plague Water, Surfeit Water, Gout Water, Beauty Water, &c.—Suffice it to state that Peter Jonas was an officer and supervisor for "near thirty years," and that he was the author of an "Abridgement of the Laws of Excise." *See* page 19.

ART OF GAUGING IMPROVED.—"The Theory and Practice of Gauging in the measures of capacity of Great Britain and Ireland; fully illustrated by numerous rules, tables, and examples, and rendered particularly effective by an extensive detail of the legislative regulations, and of the official directions of the Boards of Customs and Excise, in the gauging of glass, sope, malt, beer, spirits and starch: by an account of each particular manufacture; and by numerous exercises, with; with a treatise on cask gauging, in all its departments, as now practised in the port of London, originally written by Peter Jonas, late Supervisor of Excise." A new edition by W. Tate, London, 1823. A special feature in this book is a series of three tables of factors for finding the ullages of Casks. Pages 392, 8vo.

JOURNAL.

An old institution this.[2] New arrangements were issued respecting the "Journal" in 1719 and the form then enjoined obtains, in a

[1] C. S. G. [2] 1702.

slightly modified form, now including the oft-repeated "None else to enter." Privacy was enjoined in 1725 by locking it up in a box; punctuality of entry obtained in 1731, by requiring several officers to enter in the same book; and in the case of the outride officer, who had a journal to himself, by the occasional inspection of an outwalk officer; and facility of access to the supervisor, given in 1778, by the permission to have one key applicable to every journal-box in his district.

LABORATORY.

The father and founder of the laboratory was George Phillips.

On the passing of an Act in 1842 to prohibit the adulteration of tobacco, it became "necessary to find an officer possessing such knowledge of tobacco as to detect on the spot any that might be adulterated, and with such activity and readiness of resource as would ensure a legal proof of the offence. Mr Phillips, who was then a division officer, and had, at his own expense, during leisure hours, acquired a considerable knowledge of chemistry, was selected for this duty, and placed at the head of a Chemical Department, which was then, for the first time, attached to the Inland Revenue Office. In 1846, Mr Phillips, in conjunction with Mr Dobson, made careful experiments to determine the relative values of malt, barley, sugar, &c., to brewers and distillers, the results of which were ordered by the House of Commons to be printed.[1] In the following year, he was again associated with Mr Dobson in a more extensive and difficult series of experiments, with a view to establish a method for ascertaining the original gravities of fermented liquors, the result of which was to give a reliable test for the quantity of malt used in brewing beer, and consequently the proper amount of drawback to be allowed when that article is exported. The services of Messrs Dobson and Phillips on this occasion were recognised on the part of this Board by the award to those gentlemen of a sum of £1000 between them."[2] Mr Phillips shortly afterwards contrived "a very convenient and efficient distilling apparatus" to be used in ascertaining original gravities.[3] The discovery of this method of testing

[1] P. Ret., No. 26, 1847. [2] T. M., May 2, 1874.
[3] Johnston's Manual.

the original gravity of beer was subsequently investigated and confirmed, under the directions of Professors Graham, Hofmann, and Redwood, by Messrs A. Young and C. B. Forsey,[1] and embodied in the Act 19 and 20 V., c. 34.[2]

"In 1854, at the instance of this Board, a very careful and extended research was made with a view to discover some means by which alcohol could be rendered unpotable without at the same time making it poisonous, or unfitting it for use in the arts. In the course of his researches, Mr Phillips was fortunate enough to discover that an admixture with wood naphtha would meet the required conditions; and, after a further investigation by the ablest chemists of the day, Dr Graham and Dr Hofmann, this mixture, under the name of methylated spirit, was legalised as a duty-free spirit, and has proved an immense boon to trades requiring a cheap spirit, besides putting an end to much of the illicit distillation which existed in the large towns."[3]

In the same year, too, he superintended an investigation into "the distinctive character of raw grain and malt," which resulted in the passing of the 19 and 20 V., c. 34, s. 19.[2]

In 1858 and two following years he investigated the "data upon which instruments and tables might be constructed for ascertaining the strength of spirits possessing an alcoholic value beyond that of the strongest spirits to which Sikes's hydrometer and tables are applicable, particularly at high temperatures; and also to give some means by which the true strength of spirits can be readily ascertained from their apparent strength, as shown by the hydrometer and tables;"[4] and, at its close, reported upon the subject, supplying a new hydrometer and tables, which he observed "will, I hope, be found valuable, as they are to my knowledge, trustworthy."[5]

In 1859, the students, who had previously been educated at University College, (which see) were placed under his tuition, and on arriving at this decision the Commissioners stated "We have entire confidence in his ability for this undertaking."[6]

In 1863, "When the present Tobacco Duties Act (26 and 27 Vict., cap. 7), was under the consideration of the Government, Mr Phillips was universally recognized as the person most competent to deal with the subject, and gave very valuable aid in this adjustment

[1] Bell's Bateman. [2] Comrs. First Report. [3] T. M., May 2, 1874.
[4] Comrs. Third Report. [5] Idem., 5th. [6] Idem., 4th.

of the rates of duty and drawback, and in reconciling the tobacco trade to the important changes then made in the law."[1]

But sufficient has now been narrated to show the originality, the personal resource, and indomitable perseverance of the man: it now only remains to note the close of his career. He retired in 1874, at the age of 68, after 47 years' service, of which 32 were spent in the laboratory, on a special superannuation of £750, being the amount of his full salary,[2] granted by Treasury Minute, dated May 2, 1874, in which their Lordships were pleased to notice "the peculiar and exceptional services" which he had rendered.[3] He died January 16, 1877.[4]

Established in Arundel Street, Strand, at the close of 1842, and thence removed to Somerset House in 1859,[5] the laboratory has won a widening reputation, until its authority is now recognised throughout the country.

Its purpose, at first, as already stated, was the suppression of the sophistication of the "weed;" then the protection of the duty on other articles from which the Revenue is drawn; and, then, one by one, protection was afforded to other departments, as the Customs,[6] the merchant Navy,[7] the Board of Trade,[8] the Admiralty,[9] the India Office, the Stationery Office,[10] the Local Government Board, the Foreign Office,[8] while in 1875, the "Sale of Food and Drugs Bill," imposed the honourable task of referee in disputed cases.[9]

It is worthy of remark here, that Mr Phillip's penetrating eye seems to have seen this refereeship, or something akin to it, as early as 1862; as he then observed in his sixth report, "if it be necessary to adopt such an extensive system of analysis to prevent the adulteration of only a few articles of consumption, what must be the magnitude of that system which is designed to suppress the adulteration of all descriptions of food and beverages?"[10] It was actually suggested, in so far as the adulteration of beverages is concerned, by the Government in its Licensing Bill of 1872, that the detection should be entrusted to the experts in this institution; and, the new Principal of the Laboratory was examined by the General-Adultera-

[1] T. M., May 2, 1874.
[2] Superannuation Return.
[3] Comrs. 18 R.
[4] C. S. G., 1877.
[5] Idem., 1859.
[6] Comrs. 8th R.
[7] Idem., 12th R.
[8] Idem., 13th R.
[9] Idem., 19th R.
[10] Idem., 6th R.

tion-Act Committee of the House of Commons, who afterwards proposed to entrust the examination of suspected articles to the laboratory staff.[1]

This necessarily leads to the number of persons employed and the kind of work performed.

The superior and inferior functions were for two years performed by the principal himself, "but," he writes, "as the usefulness of the department became apparent, the business gradually extended so as to embrace the analysis of almost every exciseable commodity, and it became necessary to employ an additional chemist. This arrangement continued until 1852, when, in consequence of a still further and important extension of the business of the department, more assistants were required, from four to six having been employed from that period up to the present time, the latter being now, 1856, fully occupied." But these were only temporary appointments, being made for only two or three years, and it was not until about 1866, when a change was effected, that the appointment became fixed or permanent.[2] *See* column Laboratory in paper, *Establishment.*

Then as to the work performed. First and foremost, perhaps, should be mentioned, certainly from its attractive point of view, "a series of drawings illustrating the distinctive characters of the genuine commodities, and of the adulterants used in their sophistication," by Rochfort Connor, examiner, to whom the Commissioners made an award in appreciation of its excellent execution. This series was afterwards photographed at the expense and for the use of the Kensington Museum.[3] It has since been placed in the Bethnal Green Museum. *See* also Prescott. But not less attractive to the trained microscopic eye are the delicate manipulations of John Brown, ride officer, who "prepared and permanently mounted for microscopical examination upwards of 700 specimens of vegetable substances, including not only those subject to fiscal duties, but also a very large number of others, which, from their being suitable as adulterants, or from their having a bearing more or less on the interests of the revenue, require to be studied."[4]

Leaving the special productions and coming to the ordinary daily engagements, it will be found on perusing the Commissioners,

[1] H. C., May 14, 1874. [2] Comrs. 11th R. [3] Idem., 5th R.
[4] Idem., 8th R.

Reports from the First to the Twentieth, that upwards of 242,000 samples were examined during that period, and in 1860, at an estimated cost of sevenpence per sample, while the miscellaneous samples examined, during the thirty-four years embraced in these reports, included such articles as embrocation,[1] sheepwash,[2] preserved milk,[3] aperitive,[4] "geropiga,"[5] and even the "Angel of Peace."[6]

At the present time the number of samples examined exceeds 14,000 annually. The work done is of a most varied and interesting character, and embraces for the Inland Revenue the examination of all beer and malt exported from London, the suppression of adulteration in tobacco and all dutiable commodities, and the protection of the revenue from licences by the examination of Wines, Sweets, Cordials, &c.; for the Customs, the estimation of drawback on all Tobacco and Snuff exported from the United Kingdom; for the Board of Trade, the testing of all Lime and Lemon Juice used on board the Merchant Navy for the prevention of scurvy; for the India Office, the analysis of about one hundred kinds of articles supplied under contract for military and railway purposes in India; for the Admiralty the examination of Beer for use on board H.M. ships, and of Beer and Wine for hospital use; and finally, many hundreds of samples of a miscellaneous character are analysed for various departmental purposes.

As a training school too it has been remarkably successful. The Commissioners observe in their Second Report—"It has become an essential and prominent part of our system, and we hope to extend the benefits of it by making it a school of chemistry, through which our officers must pass before they become supervisors." This had reference to the fact that the examiners, who at their own request in 1855,[7] had applied to be allowed to attend the laboratory, had been ordered to do so in batches of six, for a period of twenty-eight days, to receive instruction in the more useful scientific checks; and, it may be observed, that down to the issue of their Twentieth Report, upwards of 400 had attended. The Commissioners further state in their Fourth Report, with reference to the opinion already referred to, "Now, however, that our chemical department at this office is so efficient, and that the laboratory is so spacious and complete, we consider that the training of our chemical students can be

[1] Comrs. 3d R. [2] Idem., 6th R. [3] Idem., 16th R.
[4] Idem., 18th R. [5] Idem., 12th R. [6] Idem., 19th R.
[7] Idem., 8th R.

more effectually and more economically conducted under the superintendence of Mr Phillips,"[1] but with the aid of courses of lectures at the Royal College of Chemistry,[2] and a final examination by an impartial examiner.[1] Of the 108 who, from its introduction in 1858, down to the issue of the Board's twentieth annual statement, had completed their course of studies, 89 obtained first, 16, second, and 3, third, class certificates, while five of the first class obtained the maximum number of marks,—even under the searching acumen of Professors Hofmann and Frankland; the former of whom, wrote, in reporting on his second year's examination—"In congratulating you on this remarkable result, allow me to state that during my professional career, I do not remember a similar examination."[3] The Commissioners usually present as a mark of merit, to the most successful, a handsome first-class microscope, and, to the two next, a donation of books or other serviceable gift of the value of £5.

The annual report drawn up by the principal is inserted in the appendix to the Commissioners' Annual Report.

The suite of rooms which constitute the laboratory form one of the best, if not the best, chemical workshop in the kingdom. Here are found balances, microscopes, and other scientific appliances of the finest and most accurate finish, with an excellent scientific library: and here, too, is found perhaps the only sub-department under Government not restricted, except with regard to salary, to a given outlay, or brought specially under the arithmetic of the estimates or its conscience-keeper the appropriation account.

Principals—George Phillips, 1842 to 1874.
James Bell, 1874.

See Adulteration, Establishment, Salary, Tobacco Duty.

LANCASHIRE DISTRESS FUND.

The first mention of a subscription to this fund, which excited so much sympathy in 1862 and 1863, was by "B," who suggested an individual subscription of one day's pay to be paid into and through the Mansion-House Committee. Although not generally complied with, the total amount subscribed by the employés in some twenty

[1] Comrs. 4th R. [2] Idem., 5th & 18th R. [3] Idem., 5th R.
[4] C. S. G., 1862, 1863.

collections, and the staff in the examiners' office, the latter of whom contributed weekly for eleven weeks, was upwards of £238.

LEADBETTER'S ROYAL MANUAL.

Charles Leadbetter, "Many Years a Gauger in the Royal Revenue of Excise," issued in 1743 the second edition of his book, which by 1776 had run through seven editions, and on its first appearance was unquestionably the first comprehensive excise manual. The second edition is divided into two parts. Part one—Decimal Arithmetic, Sliding Rule, Gauging Superficies, Solids, Open Vessels, Cask-Gauging, Gauging Warm Worts, Malt Gauging, Candles, Distillery, Specific Gravity. Part two—Mode of obtaining Employment, Modes of Account and Survey; the Duties of Collectors, Supervisors, and Officers; Instructions respecting Legal Proceedings, the Rise and Progress of the Different Duties, &c., &c. Altogether a bulky 8vo of some 470 pages, containing among other things—"The true reason of my discharge was this. Upon Sunday the 9th of August, Thomas Brooks, officer at Hanley-Arden, came to me at Alchurch very drunk. He said that he and I must change divisions, but brought me no note either from the Collector or Supervisor. For these reasons I told him our sitting was next Tuesday, and then I should have orders from them if it was so. He staid and dined with me, and went home far from being sober, and told his Supervisor, Mr Anthony Gelder, that I refused to remove, which was actually false. Since the undeserved treatment I have met with may possibly be of service to others, I could not but think it proper to make it publick. In witness of the truth hereof I have hitherto put my hand this 24th day of June 1738. Charles Leadbetter."

LEATHER DUTY.

This duty, at first imposed during the Commonwealth,[1] next in the reign of William III.,[2] as an excise duty for three years, to meet certain deficits in other duties, and to pay the annuitants upon the lottery, then again in the reign of Queen Anne[3] for a period of 32

[1] P. O., 1644. [2] April 20, 1697. [3] August 1, 1712.

years,[1] continued to be levied in Great Britain at some fourteen rates per lb., per hide, per skin, per doz. skins, etc., almost without interruption,[3] until 1815. It was then brought under the notice of the House of Commons with a view to the repeal of the additional duty, and the first reading of the bill was carried by 105 to 104 votes,[4] but the second reading was rejected by 125 to 120 votes.[5] It shortly afterwards formed the subject of Parliamentary inquiry[6] and of Parliamentary petition;[7] later of a Parliamentary motion for the total repeal; and lastly, of a Parliamentary motion, supported by petitions, by the Chancellor of the Exchequer, for its total repeal from and after July 5, 1830,[9] when it was repealed, Sir H. Parnell having previously recommended it in his work on Financial Reform, 1830.

In Ireland it was long an annual duty, and the mode of charge was at "2½d. per cubic foot" of the tan-pit, equivalent, to 2½d. per lb.[10]

Mr Pitt introduced a licence duty which in 1818 was on the tanner in London, and within the Bills of Mortality, £10, elsewhere £5, on the hide dresser in oil, and on the currier £4; on the vellum or parchment maker, and on the tawer, £2.[2] *See* Hide Duty.

But the tanning of hides, according to a wit, was not restricted to those formerly borne by animals of four legs—"A tanner near Swaffam in Norfolk invited the supervisor to dine with him, and after pushing the bottle about briskly, the supervisor took his leave; but on passing through the tanyard he unfortunately fell into a vat, and called lustily for the tanner's assistance to get him out, but to no purpose; 'For,' said the tanner, 'if I draw any hides without twelve hours' notice, I shall be exchequered and ruined, but I'll go and inform the exciseman.'"[11]

LEGAL PROCEEDINOS.

These are now usually distinguished as Exchequer Proceedings

[1] 10 Anne, c. 19. [2] Huie, 1818. [3] 1788. [4] H. C., May 18, 1813.
[5] H. C., May 20, 1813. [6] H. C., May 9, 1816.
[7] H. C., March 12, 1818. [8] H. C., May 17, 1824.
[9] H. C., March 15, 1830. [10] H. C., March 2, 1803.
[11] Wit of the World, 1858.

and Summary Proceedings; the former having been for some time the usual mode of recovering fines and forfeitures until by erroneous judgment the latter became general. To be exchequered struck terror into the hearts of the excise-duty-paying people, as shown under "Court of Exchequer."

These legal proceedings, on a change being made in the law in 1814[1], came under the denunciative oratory of Mr Brougham (afterwards Lord Brougham) on his return to the House of Commons as Member for Winchelsea in 1816. He said "the whole dispensing power in all matters relating to a revenue of £43,000,000 was transferred from the permanent, from the unministerial, from the unpolitical hands in which it had until that period been placed, to the hands of the Lords Commissioners of His Majesty's Treasury. The parliamentary history of the summer of 1814, he said may be searched in vain for information respecting the passing of so important a measure. He found on examining the votes of July 19, 1814, that the Bill was proposed after a wearisome debate at 2 o'c. a.m. The House . . . . in which . . . . . there were in all probability not above four present, was entirely taken by surprise. In the course of two or three days the Bill was read a second time; it was speedily committed, and on the 20th July it was read the third time and passed, and on the 30th, after having gone through the House of Lords it received the royal assent . . . . Such was the history of this extraordinary and almost universal change in the administration of the revenue." He then, having given instances in point, moved, certainly that which was equivalent to a vote of censure on the Government, "That the conduct of the Lords Commissioners of His Majesty's Treasury was an unjustifiable exercise of the powers vested in them by law." His charges were rebutted by the Treasury authorities, who commanded, on a vote being taken, on his first resolution, a majority of 76 votes—ayes 48, noes 124.[2]

Twelve years having elapsed, during which a consolidated general regulation act was passed, he was followed by Mr D. Harvey who said in rising in the House of Commons in 1828 to make a motion on the recovery of excise and customs penalties, "it was one of those subjects which abounded in dreary details and cold calculations around which it was impossible to throw the charms of language or the ornaments of eloquence . . . . The resources of the country

[1] 54 Geo. III., c. 171. [2] H. C., April 3, 1816.

were culpably expended in needless prosecutions; that the power of the law officers was unjustly exercised in the prosecution of the innocent, in the oppression of the unintentionally guilty, and in the undue punishment of those who were designedly criminal; that the cause of all this was to be traced to the absence of defined responsibility; and that the effect of the whole was the multiplication of prosecutions, for no other purpose, and producing no other effect than the individual aggrandisement of a few rapacious lawyers." He continued by observing that in the last five years, 1851 prosecutions had been instituted for the recovery of £1,038,709. Of these 911 were excise, and 624 alone successful; but here the honourable gentleman fell into an error, as some were compromised; 940 were customs and 208 alone successful. Of the £1,038,709 sought to be recovered, only £137,826 was received, or two and sixpence in the £, or one-eighth—this calculation too is affected by the compromises. "It appeared, and the House would hear the astounding fact with astonishment and indignation, that after paying £49,597 to that wretched tribe of locusts who paraded the country to fabricate frauds and to entrap the unsuspecting trader, not only was the entire residue absorbed by the rapacious grasp of those who suffer nothing in the shape of money to elude them, but the country was brought in minus, or a debtor to the Crown lawyers in the sum of £28,414." He then moved "that it is expedient that an efficient control should be appointed over the origin and conduct of all proceedings instituted by the Crown for the recovery of penalties under the Customs and Excise Laws." This member was complimented on the clearness and ability of his statement by the Attorney-General who observed that, "The whole of the Acts upon which these penalties were coverable, recognised the existence and reward of informers. The principle of proceeding upon informations of this description was as old as the times of Queen Anne, and had been recognised by every Act passed by the legislature since that period. The revenue could not be protected without it . . . . The local jurisdiction given to magistrates in these cases, was, he contended, a great boon to the public, by the saving of expense which it produced in the attendance of witnesses from the remotest corners of the kingdom at Westminster." His motion was lost by 116 votes—ayes 30, noes 146.[1]

This second defeat closes for the most part the Parliamentary pro-

[1] H. C., May 1, 1828.

ceedings of interest on this subject; only minor charges having since been made,[1] and some few numerical returns of prosecutions and convictions having been ordered.[2]

The rigour of the law was also keenly felt by the issue of extents.

An Extent, writes Highmore, seems to be a paramount process of execution against the land or goods of an immediate debtor to the Crown. An Extent-in-Aid is a process of execution against that debtor's debtor, with a view to render him more able to pay the Crown debts, but it does not extend further than the third person.[3]

It is, of course, exercised in the case of only a large debt. It has, as a grievance, only once perhaps specifically engaged the attention of Parliament, when a motion for a return of Extent issued against Crown debtors was refused as being too personal.[4] Thus, "In the Exchequer. The Queen against George Craven the younger, and Henry Craven. On writ of Extent. To be sold by auction by or before John Clarke, Esq., Collector of Excise for the Leeds Collection," at Tweedale's Hotel, Rochdale, Lancashire, on January 9, 1846, at 6 o'c. p.m., "pursuant to an order of the Court of Exchequer," certain property which Craven the younger had "in the right of his wife, during the joint lives of himself and his wife." Particulars of John Clarke, Esq., and the Board's Solicitor.[5] Again. "For sale, in fee, by auction, under an extent against Mr Thomas Coate, soap-maker, Drayton, before Francis Amey, Esq., Collector of Excise, at the Langport Arms Inn, Langport, on Tuesday, the 28th day of March instant, at 2 o'c. in the afternoon, pursuant to an order of the Court of Exchequer, the following . . . . the property of Mr Thomas Coate. . . . ." This sale comprised eight lots of pasture and arable land, representing 9 a. 2 r. 16 p.[6]

Instructions in conducting Excise Summary Proceedings were issued in 1828, and an enlarged and improved issue was made in 1853.—Douglas's Manual.

There are some few departmental regulations of bygone days perhaps not uninteresting. With respect to the information the department was informed that there had been "Too many instances of late of exhibiting informations which have been very feebly supported by evidence."[7] To amend this it would seem the officers betook themselves to the practice of taking their informers before the magis-

[1] 1835, 1841, 1853, 1874.
[2] 1828, 1831, 1860, 1871.
[3] Highmore's Excise Laws, 1796.
[4] H. C., March 25, 1816.
[5] L. G. 1845.
[6] L. G. 1848.
[7] 1792.

trates to swear to the truth of their allegations—this the officers were cautioned not to do.[1] The collectors too were reproved in that, "The business of exhibiting informations . . . . . has been too frequently left to the care of the supervisor instead of being attended to by the collector in whose particular province it is;"[2] further, that as injunctions have been several times renewed that the collector must attend the hearings "particular notice will be taken of what he alleges (in excuse) he must not expect that trifling excuses will be overlooked or admitted;"[3] but should he not be able to attend that the supervisor must do so;[4] then, that he must be "frugal," not spend more than forty shillings a day, as the excess will be "disallowed";[5] and lastly, to give the exact words, "It seems almost superfluous to add that no additional allowance is made for money given to chamber-maids on any pretence whatever."[6]

Fourteen days' notice was formerly given to the Justices to hear excise cases, and if they refused to act the cases were then heard by the Sub-Commissioners of Excise.[7] This unwillingness, with cases in which erroneous judgments were given, has happened several times. In 1669 the Justices at Salisbury refused to act, either on the evidence of the "sworn gauger" or the statement of the defendant—for this they petitioned "His Majestie's mercy and pardon, ... alledging their said errours proceeded from want of wel understanding the Acts of Excise;" the Lord Keeper of the Great Seal was commanded by his Majesty, to issue in this case, a "Commission of Association" under the Great Seal, to "such Justices of the Peace of the said county . . . to sit," hear, and determine with the Justices of the Corporation.

In 1674 the Mayor and an alderman of the borough of Leicester, gave "an undue judgment," for which "Francis Noble's humbly submitting to his Majestie, and confessing his error, and promising that he would not offend in the like manner for the future, his Majestie was graciously pleased to pardon and dismiss him."[8]

So common, indeed, were these unexemplary acts, occasioned perhaps in part by the merciless exactions of the excise farmers, that his Majesty, with other reasons, found it necessary to proclaim the discontinuance of the farming of the duties, and commanded

[1] 1823. [2] 1722, 1795. [3] 1759, 1789. [4] 1789.
[5] Instructions, 1778. [6] 1822. [7] 12 C. II., cc. 23, 24.
[8] L. G., 1674, Hunt, 1683.

the Justices to assist in the execution of the law.[1] On the accession of William and Mary, too, the Justices refused to act in almost every part of the country, owing in part to the confusion which had arisen among those who had been commissioned by different authorities, and those who had no commission whatever.[2] On the imposition of the malt duty in Scotland in 1713, the Justices in all the counties refused to act in malt cases.[3] Even in 1779 they frequently reduced a penalty incurred by smuggling from £100 to £5.[4]

For a collector to interfere in the election of a Justice was formerly forbidden,[5] but the times have changed; he has since himself become a Justice—J. Cornwall, collector, Edinburgh; L. Counsel, collector, Athlone.[6]

LICENCE DUTY.

Probably the first use of the word licence, in matters excise, occurs in a Scotch Act in 1644, in connection with the issue of a "warrant or licence" with beer for exportation, as beer brewed for that purpose was not then "excised:" in 1660 two Commissioners were specially appointed to issue licences to persons "to utter" wine;[7] in 1663 no person was "permitted to sell or retaile any Coffee, Chocolate, Sherbett, or Tea without Licence . . . ."[8] In 1665, John Lurton, of Worcester, applied to Lord Arlington for a licence to keep a victualling house in Worcester free from excise on any beer or ale that he may sell there;[9] in 1694, certain Commissioners granted licences for Hackney Carriages on £50 being paid "by way of a Fine for such Lycense."[10]

It was not, however, until the close of the American War in 1784 that this form of duty became general in this department. Mr Pitt then proposed some two dozen licence duties, which he carried through the House unchallenged,[11] and which appeared in the Act 24 Geo. III., c. 31, which was quickly followed by others until all were superseded by the Consolidated Act 6 Geo. IV., c. 80.

[1] Procl., June 20, 1683. [2] Pocl., January 2, 1688. [3] P. Rep., 1804.
[4] H. C., 1779. [5] S. Instructions, 1804. [6] C. 1871.
[7] 12 C. II., c. 25. [8] 15 C. II., c. 11. [9] Green's State Papers.
[10] 5 & 6 W. & M., c. 22. [11] H. C., June 30, 1784.

The licence duties in Ireland were long collected by the Stamp authorities, only a portion being paid over by them to the Excise; but in 1815 all were transferred to the Excise.[1] In Scotland it was customary to give the staff fees to make "the duties on licences more effectual."[2] An instance of forging two hawking licences occurred in 1710, for which Andrew Smith was not only fined 6s. 8d. in each case, but also "ordered to stand in the Pillory, viz., once at Charing Cross, and a second time at Tower Hill, and accordingly the said Andrew Smith stood in the Pillory . . . ."[3] It was some such misdeeds as these which led to the inspection of licences by the supervisor. One Denny Sampson, for falsifying the amounts in some licences and pocketing the difference, was in 1842 sentenced to suffer twelve months' hard labour. From this date, though repeatedly urged to be discontinued[4] the inspection was continued until 1866.

It has been suggested that only the facsimile of the Secretary's signature should be attached to licences.[5]

But to examine the system more particularly. The Parnell Committee state: "The licence duty must in our opinion be considered as amongst the least objectionable of the heads of Excise taxation. . . . . Free from those evils . . . . arising from the official interference with the private details of management." The number of distinct heads of licence duty at this date was thirteen—auction, beer, coffee, glass, malt, paper, soap, sweets, tobacco, vinegar, wine, passage vessels. The Committee continue: "We are without information as to the grounds upon which the general distinction . . . . between licences of fixed annual amounts and those at rateable amounts was first adopted, and we are equally unable to state the reason for the special application of the respective principles. . . . ." The "rateable principle" was contemplated by Mr Pitt in 1784, "according to the extent and profit of their respective modes of business." The Committee then state: "There seems to be no reason why, in every case where applicable, the licences payable under the Excise laws should not be calculated upon this principle," and then recommended its adoption under some of the previously-mentioned heads, and its extension, with higher increments, under others, the particulars of which will be found noted elsewhere. They conclude their Nineteenth Report by observing: "We have no hesitation in recommending the enactment of a new comprehensive

[1] P. Rep., 1809; H. C., June 16, 1815. [2] Instructions, 1804.
[3] L. G., 1710. [4] C. S. G., 1859, 1864, 1865. [5] C. S. G., 1868.

statute on the subject of Excise licences at the earliest convenient period;" the assimilation of the laws of Ireland and Great Britain; the discontinuation of the distinction between "wholesale and retail dealers;" the extension of the "rateable principle;" the discontinuance of the certificate of character from publicans; the separation of the police from the revenue regulations; the fixing the "period for the commencement and expiration of licences, with due regard to the customs of tenure in Scotland;" a separate licence for each set of premises.

From this date—1836—until 1868, the licence system does not appear to have been specially laid before Parliament, except in the financial statements; it was now introduced by Mr Marsh, who called attention to "the subject of those licences, which restrict the trade and commerce of the country, with a view to their abolition, and in case of a financial necessity, a transfer of the charges to make or sell any article to a direct tax on the article itself," and moved, "That in the opinion of this House it is desirable that all licences injuriously affecting the industry and commerce of the country should be abolished." The Chancellor of the Exchequer admitted the desirability of dealing with some licences, that there was a difficulty "in imposing a fixed rate of licence," and stated that "trade licences according to the value of the premises" were objectionable. Mr Gladstone observed that "every attempt which he had hitherto made to reduce them to something like order or principle had failed."[1] See Commissioners' Thirteenth Report, Vol. I., "Excise Licences."

The licence list was introduced in 1826 "to facilitate the issuing of licences," and a suggestion was made in 1858[2] that it might be improved by making it both a pay and licence list, a suggestion since adopted. "To keep a register of licences to be digested into columns" appears to have been the initial injunction and issued in 1806: that kept by the officer was discontinued in 1855, that by the supervisor, now termed the "Trade's Register" suggested to be discontinued in 1872.[2]

LINDSAY'S GAUGING.

The full title is "The British Practical Gauging or Trader and

[1] H. C., March 24, 1868. [2] C. S. G.

Officer's Instructor," by John Lindsay, supervisor of excise, aged 70 years, 1801. The book contains a frontispiece in which the author is represented sitting in a high-back chair, quill pen in hand, in front of a table on which are his manuscript and some three books, and a form of inkstand not unfamiliar to the older excise eye. It is "inscribed" to the "Commissioners and Governors of His Majesty's Revenue of Excise in Scotland," and the first information, even before the preface, is a "Receipt for making ink," in which he recommends "aquavitæ" to prevent it from freezing. It is essentially a book on gauging by number, by measure, and by weight, contains much valuable information regarding the local Scotch measures, and at the time of its publication must have been as valuable as it is a painstaking work. Pages 370, 8vo, Oliver, Edinburgh.

LOAN SOCIETIES.

The Board disapprove any connection with these societies, either as members or borrowers, censures having been issued in 1855.[1]

LOFTUS, W. R.

This gentleman was formerly an officer in this department, but on "the London middle-man" ship[2] becoming vacant in or about 1851 he succeeded in obtaining it, and appears to have commenced by reprinting the general orders issued in that year. This publication was followed by the Almanack, and the Tables of Weights of Spirits in 1854, the Hankbook for Officers of Excise in 1858, White's Maltster's Guide in 1860, Johnston's Inland Revenue Officer's Manual in 1865, and several other smaller publications, with at length a launch into business to supply the excise official and trade requisites in general, which he has successfully kept afloat from his start in Pulford Street, Pimlico, afterwards at Edgeware Road, and then in Oxford Street, London. *See* p. 49.

[1] C. S. G. [2] C. S. G., 1866.

LOCKS.

A lock locked by a lock is the earliest form of revenue lock which the writer has seen, and specimens of it may be seen in the Antiquarian Museum, Edinburgh; Sailors' Home Museum, Great Yarmouth; and other museums. That portion of the lock now called the ring or shackle in this case consisted of a strong circular rod fixed firmly to the end of and raised about an inch and a half above the top of the box, with which it ran parallel and extended beyond some two inches. On to this rod, which ran through the staple on the place to be secured, slid a closely-fitting guard which, fitting into the body of the lock, was secured by the bolt in the ordinary manner. Over the keyhole were two guards, the smaller or under one turning upon a pivot covered the keyhole, and carried a fixed staple, on to which the larger and outer guard, with an aperture or hasp moving on a simple hinge, was turned, and then secured by a second lock on the fixed staple. The weight is about three pounds; the key, the model in its wards of those now in use, the date of use about a century ago.

"Lock'd, seal'd, and fastened down" is the phrase of 1768, confirming in some measure the statement; and further confirmation is found in a statement made by the Solicitor General in 1784—"This day convicted some persons who had a house of the first name in the distillery business in Bristol, who had the meanness to pick off the plates of the padlocks put upon the warehouses, which excise officers were authorised to do by law, that the distiller might not be able to work except in the presence of the officers." Fined in the Court of Exchequer.[1]

But embracing the greater security supposed to be afforded by a patent lock the Commissioners have, from time to time, directed new patents to be used. The earliest mentioned is Barron's in 1778, ordered to be used in 1814; Bramah's patent[2] besides Feltham's common lock.[3] Down to 1829 when Gottlieb patented an invention[4] by which he secured the keyhole with a label apparatus, the locks were secured either in a bag, waxed and sealed, or "in the upper part of the circumference of the cylindrical tube and over the upper end of the slider,"[5] also waxed and sealed, a small plumbing iron being supplied to aid in the performance of this adhesive, impressive

[1] H. C., July 12, 1784. [2] No. 1430, 1784. [3] 1818.
[4] No. 5798, June 1, 1829. [5] 1816.

act.[1] Sheets of labels printed in different colours for the different utensils were at once issued, and the officer was required to sign his initials upon each label before he placed it in the apparatus, and to examine it on taking it out to see that it had not been previously removed, &c.; these sheets were superseded in 1853 by books containing one hundred each, and as the spaces between the labels were not then perforated, some sarcastic suggester afterwards hinted the perforation to avoid "going about each with his knife . . . . . like Red Indians with their scalping-knives."[2] But ingenuity prompts ingenuity, and "Go to Bath" is not inappropriate here. It was in this city, in 1833, that this ingenious invention was defeated, by those engaged in the manufacture of a saponaceous article then liable to duty, "by means of a small hole perforated at the bottom or in the side of the lock, through which a strong wire or pin being introduced and pressed against the spring which confines the cover of the key-hole, the spring is released and the cover is opened without injury to the paper label placed within it; . . . . . the hole having been filled up by some soft or yielding substance, resembling in colour the outward appearance of the lock." It was ordered, shortly after this discovery, that locks should be changed from one utensil to another,[3] though curious to relate this was previously forbidden to prevent mistakes by using wrong keys.[4]

Next after Gottlieb's patent came in 1868 one by Tucker and Reeves, a brass lock in which the inside plate of the label box on removing a few screws may be taken out, to remove pieces of paper from the interior.

A more recent familiar patent is that possessing a reversed bolt action, which acts upon a rowel on whose pins, with others on the fixed portion of the lock, the label is placed, and on turning the key to unlock, is torn in a circular direction, and if the rowel be twice turned, a circular piece is torn out. The guard over the key-hole is kept in position by an ingeniously devised spring. The malt cistern lock is so constructed that one key will open any number of them, or in its absence a penny piece, the security being in this case more particularly in the label.

Iron locks were first issued by the Board in 1855, malt cistern in 1865, brass in 1866. The number in use in 1878—iron 4,500, brass 12,000, malt cistern, 1,600; the iron being gradually superseded by the brass lock.

[1] 1819. [2] C. S. G., 1856. [3] 1835. [4] 1817.

The expense of providing this means of security was long wholly or partly incurred by the various traders[1] at 12s and 14s 6d per lock, besides the occasional cost of repairs;[2] the Board in Scotland even suggesting the lockmaker and mender,[3] while at a later date the Commissioners supplied the locks, under similar regulations, direct from the chief office through the supervisor, who received the payment and at the next sitting handed it to his collector, who remitted the receipts, under this head, quarterly, to the Board.[4] On the repeal of a duty the locks and keys belonging to a trader were at once placed in his hands.[5] This two-fold system of supply engaged, in 1853, the attention of the authorities, who now directed a return to be made of all locks "the property of the Crown," not in use,[6] and, in 1855 it was discontinued, all being now supplied at the expense of the board, by a call for a detailed return of "all revenue locks" in hand, the return of all revenue locks not made by Gottlieb, and, by an order for a systematic account to be kept by the store-keeper, the supervisor, and the officer.

In the summer of 1861 an inspector was specially employed to examine all the revenue locks in use in the London distilleries, and subsequently all in use in all the distilleries in the United Kingdom, when nearly 12,000 passed through his hands, those defective being returned to the chief office. He at the same time balanced the stocks and reported upon the subject on leaving each district. His opinion: "Gottlieb's lock—especially the first issue—is a good and useful lock, and in the hands of an intelligent officer who will judiciously change its position from time to time, I apprehend no danger to the Revenue." The time a lock remains in use may be stated to vary from two to twenty-three years.

The construction of, and the security afforded by, the various locks in use, are at the present time engaging the attention of an official possessing technical knowledge of the subject.

LOTTERY.

This was a scheme propounded in the reign of William and Mary to raise an immediate advance of £1,000,000 by £10 per "one Lott or Share" from £100,000 "adventurers," on the security of the salt,

[1] 1774, 1815, 1816, 1855. [2] 1819, 1843. [3] 1811.
[4] 1816, S., 1824, 1835. [5] 1853. [6] S., 1853.

beer, and other duties for a period of sixteen years, during which all were entitled to an annual payment, from the "chance" which varied from £1 to £1,000—annually and the aggregate to £140,000 yearly[1]—probably less expenses. Ten gentlemen "and none others" were appointed by the Treasury to be "the receivers of the moneys to be contributed or advanced," and if the whole were not advanced then a lottery in proportion to the sum contributed.

These gentlemen accordingly announced that the "manner of raising the money in the said Act directed, is: That 100,000 tickets be delivered out at £10 per ticket, which raises that million of money, whereof 97,500 (tho' blanks) are to entitle the numbers against which each is drawn to one pound yearly for sixteen years, which in that time will pay off the full principal money, and better than six per cent. interest for it; and the other 2,500 tickets (which must be called fortunate) and with the 97,500 make up the 100,000 tickets aforesaid, are for the said sixteen years to entitle the number against which they are drawn, to the several benefits hereunto exprest; which, with the benefits allowed to the first and last drawn, makes up £40,000 yearly, which the 2,500 fortunate numbers, with the first and last drawn (among them) will certainly get by this thing. The forty thousand pounds yearly will be divided thus:—To the first number drawn, besides the benefit may come up with it, £150 yearly; 1 ticket yearly £1,000; 9 each £500 yearly; 20 each £100 yearly; 80 each £50 yearly; 90 each £25 yearly; 300 each £25 yearly; 2,000 each £10 yearly; the last ticket drawn, besides the benefit that may come out with it, £100." The drawing to take place at the Guildhall, London, Oct. 8, 1694.[2]

Having apparently succeeded, the plan was again adopted in 1697, when the malt duty was offered as a security;[3] but the original scheme was not successful in so far as it became necessary to make up the deficit by an imposition on another article.[4]

MALE SERVANT LICENCE DUTY.

The citizens of London having offended Henry III., they agreed to pay his Majesty "20,000 markes, for the levying of which fine,"

[1] 5 W. & M., c. 7. [2] L. G. [3] Idem., 1697, 1701; 10 Anne, cc. 18, 19.
[4] 8 & 9 Gul. III., c. 21.

writes Stow, "were taxed as well servants as householders, and manie refused the liberties of the citie to be quit of the charge." The same historian records, under the reign of Henry VI., "That every householder that was alien should pay to the king 13 pence the yeere, and every servant alien six pence."[1] John Evelyn also notes in his diary in 1660, "I paid . . . . 1s. for every servant in my house." This traces the levy down to the Restoration. Not until 1777 does a similar duty appear to have been sanctioned by Royalty. It was then re-imposed and extended to Scotland at the instance of Lord North, as a tax upon "a luxury which rose in proportion to the number kept,"[2] and as it was generally evaded, the collection, at his Lordship's suggestion,[3] was afterwards handed over to the Commissioners of Excise,[4] who directed their officers to attend daily at their respective offices for a stated period, to afford every facility for payment.[5] By them it was probably received until other assessed taxes were imposed. The next date of interest in this duty arose with the proposition made by Mr Pitt in 1785, when he proposed an additional duty on the employer of the male servant, and an entirely new tax on the employer of the maid servant. Curious and jocose were the observations then made on the maid. Honourable gentleman No. 1 would substitute, "a tax on all ladies who are married and put out their children to nurse." No. 2 would exempt wet nurses and dairymaids. No. 3 considered it "a bounty to bachelors." No. 4, "a penalty on propagation." No. 5—

> "Cursed be the taxes, how well soe'er they flow,
> That tend to make one lovely maid my foe;
> Give virtue scandal, innocence a fear,
> Or from the soft-eyed virgin steal a tear!"

The resolution imposing double the duty on a bachelor as compared with a person not a bachelor who kept a maid servant, was carried by a majority of 73 votes—ayes 97, noes 24.[6]

Few taxes have been more frequently changed in amount and incidence than this one,[7] until simplified by Mr Gladstone in 1853.[8] And on its commutation to an excise license duty by Mr Lowe in 1869,[9] the stricter enforcement of payment caused several inquiries

[1] Annals of England, 1266, 1440.
[2] H. C., May 14, 1777.
[3] H. C., April 6, 1781.
[4] L. G., 1781.
[5] 1781.
[6] H. C., May 10, June 8, 1785.
[7] C. 13 R.
[8] H. C., April 18, 1853.
[9] H. C., April 8, 1869.

to be made in Parliament;[1] a deputation on behalf of the hotel keepers to wait upon the Chancellor of the Exchequer to urge him to repeal the duty in so far as they were concerned,[2] and in which they were successful;[3] while a further repeal, made by Sir Stafford Northcote,[4] enabled *Punch* to sarcastically write, "No more Knife-boys."[5]

MALT DUTY.

SYNOPSIS—Introduction; early laws; Commonwealth; duty suggested, considered, imposed; early attempt to levy, and subsequent troubles in Scotland; rates of duty; composition; practice on increase and decrease; quantity made, reasons for little increase; reduction in number of maltsters and malthouses; Parliamentary reports—origin, outlines, outcome; association of maltsters; general laws—utensils, barley book, certificate system, steeping, draining, couch, floor, sprinkling, modes of charge, allowances, survey, instructions, orders, payment, warehousing, loss, fraud, importation, exportation; particular laws—malt charged by weight, malt for distillation, malt for distillation and exportation, malt for feeding animals, germinated grain, roasted malt, bere or bigg malt; license duty; Parliamentary proceedings—motions, questions, deputations, petitions for exemption, commutation, continuance, reduction, repeal from 1802, and their results; publications; technical terms; foreign countries; conclusion. A shorter sermon.

As a branch of industry malting came under royal restriction much earlier than the date of the imposition of the excise duty, but since that date, and more particularly from the beginning of the present century, to nearly the present time, objection has been taken to the duty upon almost every conceivable reason, and though no effort has been spared to obtain its repeal, it still remains on the statute-book, while most of the objections have been met by liberal legislation, by the free importation of foreign grain,[6] and by the gradual passing of the manufacture into fewer hands or into the hands of the capitalist.

Stow states in his "Annals of England," under the year 1315—"The Londoners, considering that wheat made into malt was much

[1] H. C., March 15, 1870, May 15, 1871. [2] 1873. [3] H. C., April 7, 1873. [4] H. C., April 3, 1876. [5] 1876. [6] C. 4th R.

consumed, ordered that from thenceforth it should be made of other graine, the King, according to the Statute of London, sent his writtes through the realm, commanding that from thenceforth no wheat should be made into malt, which, if he had not the sooner caused to be proclaimed, the greatest part of the people should have perished through famine." The sale of other than clean malt was forbidden;[1] the excessive making, first in the county of Kent,[2] then in other places, where the justices required to forbid,[3] but after the imposition of the duty in 1697 it was found necessary to repeal this enactment, as the justices at Quarter Sessions had "taken upon them to make orders to suppresse and restraine maltsters from buying of barley to convert into malt, and from useing and exerciseing the imploy of malting by the space of one yeare," to the lessening of the revenue.[4] But the most important early restrictive legislation was made in 1548-9, in "An Acte for the True Makinge of Maulte." It is here enacted "that they have made the same malte in eighte or nyne dayes wher in deede the same cannot be well and pfeckye made unlesse it have the tyme and space of xxjtie dayes . . . . . and doe slacklye and deceitfullye drye the malte . . . . . for that they wolde have an inordinate encrease . . . . . whereby . . . . . it wil be mustie and full of wevelle. . . . . . For remedye, noe such person, ... from and after the fyrste daye of March next comynge, shall make any barley malte the monethes of June, Julye, and Auguste, onlye excepte, but that the same shall have in the makinge thereof . . . . . in the fatt, flower, stepinge, and suffycient dryenge of the same malte thre wekes at the leste;" and during the excepted period seventeen days.[5] This is an example of the strictures with which the trade was bound at that time, and by the subsequent issue of proclamations, a proof that the provisions of the Act were strictly enforced.[6] The other early Acts are 7 Edward VI., c. 11; 18 Edward VI., c. 9; 27 Elizabeth, c. 14; 35 Elizabeth, c. 7; 39 Elizabeth, c 18; 43 Elizabeth, c. 9; 21 James I., c. 28; 3 Charles I., cc. 4, 5; 6 Charles I., c. 5.

To pass on to the excise duty. The reader who has read this series of papers will have seen under Duties that the first excise charge was made in 1644 at two rates—one and four pence per quarter on oaten malt, and two shillings per quarter on other than

[1] 17 R. II., c. 4. [2] 33 Hen. VI., c. 4. [3] 39 Eliz., c. 16.
[4] 9 W. III., c. 22. [5] 2 & 3 Edw. VI., c. 10. [6] Proc., 1637, 1638.

oaten malt. In common with most of the other duties, this disappeared on the restoration of Charles the Second, nor was it until the "Remonstrance of Edward Stratton, plasterer, St Sepulchre' Parish, London, to the King," in 1666, that its reimposition seems to have been suggested—"Has already brought such remarkable things to perfection, and knows of two or three other ways to raise great sums of money for the King and not prejudice the subject. . . . . . Third, to tax malt, the maltsters being few in number and doing great trades."[1] The plasterer was followed by the politician four years afterwards—"Whatever excise you lay upon malt is an absolute land tax." Col. Birch—" . . . . . . As interest goes up, land goes down, like a pair of scales . . . . . would have some person consult the excisemen what it may bear."[2] It next appeared "in a grand committee on the supply." Mr Sacheverall took the excise to be a land tax, "13d. on every bushel is 6s. 6d. on every hogshead of beer or ale. An acre of corn of three quarters of barley is 20s. 6d. by the excise upon the acre."[3] From this date twenty years appear to have elapsed, and then came "An Essay upon the Excising of Malt," etc., by A. Burnaby of the Middle Temple. The outlines of the essay are these—1st, its universality; 2d, its equality of incidence; 3d, the charge or cost of collection; 4th, the little trouble to the contributors in the collection; 5th, the estimated produce; 6th, the time when it will "be brought into the Exchequer." The presumed objections—1st, "that the tax will fall entirely on one sort of grain, and consequently on one sort of land that bears such grain;" 2d, "the alteration of the coin, the great expense of a great and heavy war, money is become so scarce;" 3d, "It will be a hardship on the brewers to pay the Malt Duty of sevenpence halfpenny per bushel and the Excise Duty too;" 4th, "If neither the maltster nor the brewer will bear the tax, yet the consumptioners will be unequally charged, for those that brew their own drink will not be equally charged with those that buy their drink of the common brewers." The essayist was in favour of the "excising."[4] This, of course, immediately preceded King William's assent to levy it on April 20, 1697.[5] Queen Anne assented to its being levied in Scotland in May 1713,[6] and King George the Third

[1] Green's State Papers.
[2] H. C., Nov. 30, 1670.
[3] H. C., Feb. 27, 1676.
[4] 1696, pages 86, 8vo.
[5] 8 & 9 Wm. III., c. 22.
[6] 12 Anne, c. 2.

The expense of providing this means of security was long wholly or partly incurred by the various traders[1] at 12s and 14s 6d per lock, besides the occasional cost of repairs;[2] the Board in Scotland even suggesting the lockmaker and mender,[3] while at a later date the Commissioners supplied the locks, under similar regulations, direct from the chief office through the supervisor, who received the payment and at the next sitting handed it to his collector, who remitted the receipts, under this head, quarterly, to the Board.[4] On the repeal of a duty the locks and keys belonging to a trader were at once placed in his hands.[5] This two-fold system of supply engaged, in 1853, the attention of the authorities, who now directed a return to be made of all locks "the property of the Crown," not in use,[6] and, in 1855 it was discontinued, all being now supplied at the expense of the board, by a call for a detailed return of "all revenue locks" in hand, the return of all revenue locks not made by Gottlieb, and, by an order for a systematic account to be kept by the store-keeper, the supervisor, and the officer.

In the summer of 1861 an inspector was specially employed to examine all the revenue locks in use in the London distilleries, and subsequently all in use in all the distilleries in the United Kingdom, when nearly 12,000 passed through his hands, those defective being returned to the chief office. He at the same time balanced the stocks and reported upon the subject on leaving each district. His opinion: "Gottlieb's lock—especially the first issue—is a good and useful lock, and in the hands of an intelligent officer who will judiciously change its position from time to time, I apprehend no danger to the Revenue." The time a lock remains in use may be stated to vary from two to twenty-three years.

The construction of, and the security afforded by, the various locks in use, are at the present time engaging the attention of an official possessing technical knowledge of the subject.

LOTTERY.

This was a scheme propounded in the reign of William and Mary to raise an immediate advance of £1,000,000 by £10 per "one Lott or Share" from £100,000 "adventurers," on the security of the salt,

[1] 1774, 1815, 1816, 1855. [2] 1819, 1843. [3] 1811.
[4] 1816, S., 1824, 1835. [5] 1853. [6] S., 1853.

beer, and other duties for a period of sixteen years, during which all were entitled to an annual payment, from the "chance" which varied from £1 to £1,000—annually and the aggregate to £140,000 yearly[1]—probably less expenses. Ten gentlemen "and none others" were appointed by the Treasury to be "the receivers of the moneys to be contributed or advanced," and if the whole were not advanced then a lottery in proportion to the sum contributed.

These gentlemen accordingly announced that the "manner of raising the money in the said Act directed, is: That 100,000 tickets be delivered out at £10 per ticket, which raises that million of money, whereof 97,500 (tho' blanks) are to entitle the numbers against which each is drawn to one pound yearly for sixteen years, which in that time will pay off the full principal money, and better than six per cent. interest for it; and the other 2,500 tickets (which must be called fortunate) and with the 97,500 make up the 100,000 tickets aforesaid, are for the said sixteen years to entitle the number against which they are drawn, to the several benefits hereunto exprest; which, with the benefits allowed to the first and last drawn, makes up £40,000 yearly, which the 2,500 fortunate numbers, with the first and last drawn (among them) will certainly get by this thing. The forty thousand pounds yearly will be divided thus:—To the first number drawn, besides the benefit may come up with it, £150 yearly; 1 ticket yearly £1,000; 9 each £500 yearly; 20 each £100 yearly; 80 each £50 yearly; 90 each £25 yearly; 300 each £25 yearly; 2,000 each £10 yearly; the last ticket drawn, besides the benefit that may come out with it, £100." The drawing to take place at the Guildhall, London, Oct. 8, 1694.[2]

Having apparently succeeded, the plan was again adopted in 1697, when the malt duty was offered as a security;[3] but the original scheme was not successful in so far as it became necessary to make up the deficit by an imposition on another article.[4]

MALE SERVANT LICENCE DUTY.

The citizens of London having offended Henry III., they agreed to pay his Majesty "20,000 markes, for the levying of which fine,"

[1] 5 W. & M., c. 7. [2] L. G. [3] Idem., 1697, 1701; 10 Anne, cc. 18, 19.
[4] 8 & 9 Gul. III., c. 21.

writes Stow, "were taxed as well servants as householders, and manie refused the liberties of the citie to be quit of the charge." The same historian records, under the reign of Henry VI., "That every householder that was alien should pay to the king 13 pence the yeere, and every servant alien six pence."[1] John Evelyn also notes in his diary in 1660, "I paid . . . . 1s. for every servant in my house." This traces the levy down to the Restoration. Not until 1777 does a similar duty appear to have been sanctioned by Royalty. It was then re-imposed and extended to Scotland at the instance of Lord North, as a tax upon "a luxury which rose in proportion to the number kept,"[2] and as it was generally evaded, the collection, at his Lordship's suggestion,[3] was afterwards handed over to the Commissioners of Excise,[4] who directed their officers to attend daily at their respective offices for a stated period, to afford every facility for payment.[5] By them it was probably received until other assessed taxes were imposed. The next date of interest in this duty arose with the proposition made by Mr Pitt in 1785, when he proposed an additional duty on the employer of the male servant, and an entirely new tax on the employer of the maid servant. Curious and jocose were the observations then made on the maid. Honourable gentleman No. 1 would substitute, "a tax on all ladies who are married and put out their children to nurse." No. 2 would exempt wet nurses and dairymaids. No. 3 considered it "a bounty to bachelors." No. 4, "a penalty on propagation." No. 5—

> "Cursed be the taxes, how well soe'er they flow,
> That tend to make one lovely maid my foe;
> Give virtue scandal, innocence a fear,
> Or from the soft-eyed virgin steal a tear!"

The resolution imposing double the duty on a bachelor as compared with a person not a bachelor who kept a maid servant, was carried by a majority of 73 votes—ayes 97, noes 24.[6]

Few taxes have been more frequently changed in amount and incidence than this one,[7] until simplified by Mr Gladstone in 1853.[8] And on its commutation to an excise license duty by Mr Lowe in 1869,[9] the stricter enforcement of payment caused several inquiries

[1] Annals of England, 1266, 1440.
[2] H. C., May 14, 1777.
[3] H. C., April 6, 1781.
[4] L. G., 1781.
[5] 1781.
[6] H. C., May 10, June 8, 1785.
[7] C. 13 R.
[8] H. C., April 18, 1853.
[9] H. C., April 8, 1869.

to be made in Parliament;[1] a deputation on behalf of the hotel keepers to wait upon the Chancellor of the Exchequer to urge him to repeal the duty in so far as they were concerned,[2] and in which they were successful;[3] while a further repeal, made by Sir Stafford Northcote,[4] enabled *Punch* to sarcastically write, "No more Knife-boys."[5]

MALT DUTY.

SYNOPSIS—Introduction; early laws; Commonwealth; duty suggested, considered, imposed; early attempt to levy, and subsequent troubles in Scotland; rates of duty; composition; practice on increase and decrease; quantity made, reasons for little increase; reduction in number of maltsters and malthouses; Parliamentary reports—origin, outlines, outcome; association of maltsters; general laws—utensils, barley book, certificate system, steeping, draining, couch, floor, sprinkling, modes of charge, allowances, survey, instructions, orders, payment, warehousing, loss, fraud, importation, exportation; particular laws—malt charged by weight, malt for distillation, malt for distillation and exportation, malt for feeding animals, germinated grain, roasted malt, bere or bigg malt; license duty; Parliamentary proceedings—motions, questions, deputations, petitions for exemption, commutation, continuance, reduction, repeal from 1802, and their results; publications; technical terms; foreign countries; conclusion. A shorter sermon.

As a branch of industry malting came under royal restriction much earlier than the date of the imposition of the excise duty, but since that date, and more particularly from the beginning of the present century, to nearly the present time, objection has been taken to the duty upon almost every conceivable reason, and though no effort has been spared to obtain its repeal, it still remains on the statute-book, while most of the objections have been met by liberal legislation, by the free importation of foreign grain,[6] and by the gradual passing of the manufacture into fewer hands or into the hands of the capitalist.

Stow states in his "Annals of England," under the year 1315—"The Londoners, considering that wheat made into malt was much

[1] H. C., March 15, 1870, May 15, 1871. [2] 1873. [3] H. C., April 7, 1873. [4] H. C., April 3, 1876. [5] 1876. [6] C. 4th R.

Much has been written in former times respecting the little variation in the quantity of malt made as affected by the excise restrictions.

Quantity charged:—

Year.	Bushels.			
	England.	Scotland.	Ireland.	United Kingdom.
1707	25,002,855	......	......	......
1717	28,859,926	......	......	......
1727	25,401,576	......	......	......
1737	24,491,366	......	......	......
1747	24,886,567	......	......	......
1757	17,640,926	......	......	......
1767	21,894,498	......	......	......
1777	25,814,436	1,812,538	......	......
1787	26,439,578	1,748,273	3,654,028	31,841,879
1797	29,979,110	2,085,672	4,672,989	36,737,771
1807	24,158,843	1,259,298	2,372,293	27,790,434
1817	20,855,566	1,093,678	1,385,486	23,334,730
1827	25,096,337	2,714,073	1,803,091	29,613,501
1837	33,692,357	4,583,446	2,275,347	40,551,149
1847	30,269,965	3,650,445	1,387,405	35,307,815
1857	36,313,926	1,122,303	1,691,159	39,127,388
1867	45,982,399	2,532,047	2,401,382	50,915,828
1877	54,161,922	3,021,891	3,342,869	60,526,682
1878	52,189,941	2,865,846	3,081,409	58,137,196

A very pertinent reply was given to this by the Commissioners in 1835—"Reverting to the subject of the malt duties, we are desirous, in conclusion, of alluding to the fact which has been elsewhere noticed, of the very disproportionate increase of the quantity of malt charged with duty in some of the earlier periods, and at the present time, when the increase of the population and the more general diffusion of wealth are taken into consideration. This circumstance has been frequently, although in our opinion somewhat too readily, ascribed to the effect of fiscal regulations, which are said to have driven many respectable persons from the trade, and to have encouraged the production of an inferior commodity. We are not prepared to assert that the influence of fiscal restrictions, which the proceedings of the trade have rendered necessary for the security of a duty, is to be disregarded in any investigation of the causes which may have led to the comparative diminution of its produce; but it is certain that in the case of malt, many other circumstances have operated in producing that result. It is a well-known fact, that a larger quantity of malt was formerly used in brewing the same quantities of beer, and that modern improvements in machinery, and in other scientific knowledge, have enabled the brewer at once to economize the use of his materials, and to extract their properties in the most successful manner. Besides which, it has been ascertained from detections which have been made by the officers, that raw grain is now, to a certain extent, used in lieu of malt, in the production of beer. In the distilleries the large demand for malt which the increased consumption of spirits would appear to require, is counteracted by the discovery that raw grain of some descriptions will answer the purpose of assisting the process as well as malt; and by the repeal of the law which formerly required that a certain proportion of malt should always be used in the production of corn spirits. In fact, the total quantity does not now amount to 200,000 bushels per annum. But the great counteracting cause is undoubtedly to be found in the extraordinary increase in the consumption of other commodities, which, as it were, come into competition with malt, or the product of malt; and which, upon a little inquiry, will be found fully to account for the proportionate diminution in the use of that article. These commodities are tea and coffee, and foreign and British spirits."[1] The Secretary to the Maltsters' Association also wrote in 1849—"The causes of this apparent anomaly are two-fold: the first is to be found in the excessive duty on Malt. The duty on spirits having been liberally reduced, the retail price has consequently been reduced also. Spirits, as stimulants, are much cheaper to the consumer than the stronger kinds of beer; and beer is drank now generally as a sedative, or as a refreshing beverage, and not as a stimulant, or for purposes of intoxication.

"The second lies in the great improvements introduced into the arts of Brewing and Malting. A far larger volume of extract than formerly is now obtained from an equal quantity of malt. The old system in the breweries was pretty much the same as that still practised in private *families;* and many retail brewers, without dis-

[1] Parnell Rep., 1835.

tinguishing the qualities of their Malt, continued to brew as many barrels from a quarter of malt, not as science would have taught, but custom fancied to be right. In the former of these periods, Stout and Beers of that character were the kinds principally brewed; being about 2½ barrels from every quarter of malt: at the latter periods, and at present, the character of ale and beer mostly in consumption, is of a quality equal to from 3¼ to 4 barrels from every quarter of malt." To which he added the increasing consumption of wine. Among the facts to be borne in mind in comparing the quantities charged with duty are these—to 1826 a smaller bushel; to 1837 a larger allowance; from 1726 to 1865, with little exception, a law to make malt for exportation duty-free; to 1855 an allowance on that used in distillation, and from that date the manufacture for that purpose, &c., duty-free; from 1865 the smaller charge on the lighter barleys; the close competition of sugar with malt, the larger importation of beer, the importation of malt, &c., &c.

The trade too has passed into fewer hands. Reviewing generally, the number may be stated to have gradually become less from the imposition of the licence duty in 1784 from 13,881—Great Britain—until 1826, when by a sudden leap of 3000 it reached 14,806—United Kingdom—the largest number of licences ever issued. It has since that date almost uniformly decreased until in 1878, it is shown 4425 the smallest number ever issued.[1] The number of malthouses has also become less—from 13,947 in 1840 to 9,298 in 1870.[2] That the excise restrictions, estimated by Mr Gladstone to enhance the price of malt by one shilling and nine pence halfpenny per quarter, though not admitted to be so much by the Commissioners,[3] have in some measure produced this result, there can be but little doubt. There were few regulations during the early history of the imposition, but as each successive form of evasion appeared, it became necessary to protect the revenue by suitable enactment; nor was it until the commencement of the nineteenth century that the attention of the Legislature was specifically drawn to these numerous enactments.

To glance then at the Parliamentary Inquiries and reports in the order of time, 1804. This was a committee "appointed to take into consideration what ought to be the difference in the duties upon malt in Scotland," from barley and from bigg as compared

[1] C. 1-20 R. [2] East's Choice Chips. [3] C. 13 R.

with the duty on English barley malt, with a view to relieve the Scotch maltster from a portion of the duty on the grain he malted and which he alleged was inferior in those properties by which good malt could alone be made. The principal witness was an experimental divine who had conducted a series of experiments under the Scotch Board of Excise to test the relative values of barley and bigg, and the conclusions at which he had arrived were these—Scotch bigg and barley to English barley; weak bigg 1 to 3; middling 1 to 2; best 2 to 3; and Scotch barley 3 to 4. The committee whose names are not appended to the report, conclude by suggesting that two-thirds of the duty on barley malt be charged on bigg malt. Report presented and ordered to be printed June 15, 1804. Pages 90. It has been shown in the table of rates of duty that a reduction was made the same year but not to the extent suggested. Dissatisfied with this result the subject was reopened in 1806. Barley and Bere or Bigg. The report of this date is one of a direct experiment under the superintendence of scientific and professional gentlemen and revenue officials by order of the Scotch Board of Excise, who received their authority from the Lords of the Treasury, dated Aug. 4, 1804. The scientific section consisted of Dr Hope, Professor of Chemistry, Dr Coventry, Professor of Agriculture, and Dr Thompson, Lecturer in Chemistry. They at once decided that, to obtain a fair and reliable result, the experiments must be conducted on a scale similar in extent to that in ordinary practice. To do so, "three separate breweries" in different parts of Edinburgh "were fitted up" under the immediate direction of "skilful practical brewers and maltsters," to the satisfaction of the scientific and revenue gentlemen; 718 bolls—538 q. 4 b.—of best, of middling and of inferior English, barley; 700 bolls 2 firlots—525 q. 3 b.—of similar classes of Scotch barley, and 737 bolls, 2 firlots, 3 pecks—553 q. 3 b.—of similar classes of Scotch bear or bigg were ordered to be purchased, and the following gentlemen were directed to make them—John Grant, General Surveyor, "to repair to London by land," to purchase the English barley of the growths of Norfolk, Kent, Essex, and Suffolk, and seal up each bag and then forward it "by water;" James Anderson, Examiner, to purchase the Scotch barley; and Messrs Campbell, General Supervisor, Craigg, Supervisor, and Cossar, Farmer, to purchase the bere or bigg—certainly characteristic caution. The committee observe in writing on the distinctive features—"Bigg grows more rapidly, and in general ripens ten days earlier than Barley, though usually sown more than a week or ten days later. Bigg has been raised from time immemorial in Scotland though not perhaps indigenous. . . . Nothing is more easy than to distinguish Bigg from Barley which is in the straw or ear, but when both are threshed out it is a much more difficult matter. In general the colour of Bigg is darker than that of Barley, it is smaller in size, inferior in weight, its husk is thicker and smoother, and the flour or meal which it yields is generally supposed of a coarse quality. But these differences are liable to considerable variations, in some cases much practice is necessary to distinguish between them. Several samples while under experiment were repeatedly confounded by persons of considerable experience." "Blended bear" is a mixture of barley and bigg. The average weight of these three classes of three different grains.

	Quality.		
	First.	Second.	Third.
English barley, .	50·3	49·9	49·3
Scotch barley, .	51·2	49·7	48·3
Scotch bigg, . .	48·3	47·5	46·1

76 parcels were malted, and the increase of 100 bushels is shown to have been—

	Average Swell.	Least.	Greatest.
English barley, .	124·5	116	138
Scotch barley, .	121·5	115	126
Scotch bigg, . .	117·6	109	123

In the "greatest" and "least" the hours steeped were 52 in the case of the barley, and 40 in the case of the bigg. The increase per cent. of malt on the dry barley, English, 8·0, 2·6, 1·9; Scotch, 5·3, 3·0, 1·9; and on the bigg, 2·1, 1·5, and 6·3. The ages of the floors "in our trials"—longest 20 days, shortest 12 days. So minute were the observations that the balance was used to estimate the weight of "a grain;" the micrometer to ascertain the "shape," length, breadth, and thickness; and the weighing-bottle "the specific gravity." The general conclusion, that "malt made from bigg, the growth of 1804, was eight per cent. less productive than malt made from barley grown in the same year." This was the conclusion of Doctors Hope and Coventry, Dr Thomson asserting in an appendix that it was 14 per cent. inferior. The former decided in this way—bigg 7 per cent. inferior in brewing; extract 9 per cent. inferior in distilling; alcohol, total 16, average 8 per cent.; while the latter entirely omitted the results at the brewery, and included the value of the spirit obtained from the raw grain. The excellent report of these divided doctors occupies 122 pages, but in its entirety 124 folio pages. Indeed so bulky does the manuscript of it appear to have been that the Commissioners in transmitting it to the Treasury subjoin the following:—"P.S.—The report is contained in a box addressed to their Lordships, sent by the mail coach, being too bulky for post." May 17, 1806. Having been received in safety it was ordered to be printed on June 6, 1806. It was not until 1816 that a further reduction was made in the rate of duty. The privilege was extended to Ireland in 1830. "Bear" is used in the South of Scotland, "big" at Aberdeen.[1] Mr Disraeli intended in 1852, on moving a reduction, to have abolished the duty distinction.[2]

1806. *Sprinkling.*—This commission was appointed on the petition of the maltsters of Herts, Cambridge, Essex, Warwick, and other counties, who complained of the operation of the Act 42 Geo. 3, c. 38, by which they were not allowed to sprinkle the grain on the floor until it had been twelve days out of the cistern, nor after it had been removed from kiln. Prior to the passing of this statute there were no restrictions against sprinkling or watering on the floor, neither is it likely there would have been had not the maltsters resorted to that practice to quicken the growth of the plumule in grain which they had improperly taken from the cistern, though reference appears to have been made to the practice by the Commissioners in the *London Gazette* in 1720, when, on referring to the regulation that grain must be wetted only in the cistern, they announce that "if corn making into malt is suffered or made to acrospire, the officers are to take one handful thereof, and if more than one part in fifteen thereof is acrospired, the entire wetting from whence the same shall be taken shall be charged with duty of 6d per bushel without any allowance. . . . ." The maltsters were very much divided in opinion on this subject. Some would not allow sprinkling at all, others would retain the existing regulations, while a third party would relax them; but against this third party was the openly admitted fact, by a maltster, that before the Act in question came into force a practice prevailed of emptying the cistern, in whole or in part, at twenty hours, refilling it, and thus wetting "once by notice once without notice," and of sprinkling the insufficiently steeped grain to supply the needful moisture.

[1] Parl. Rep., 1834. [2] H. C., Dec. 3, 1852.

It now transpired that shortly after the change in the law in 1802, memorials were presented to the Treasury against it, and that these had been referred to the Commissioners of Excise, who stated that prior to the regulation referred to, the practice "was never universal, in some places never existed, in others only partially;" that those who make the best malt do not sprinkle; that sprinkled grain produces "deteriorated" malt, "both in quality and value;" that it affords the best opportunity for lessening the duties and concealing frauds; that sprinkling accelerates germination, gives quantity, and imposes on the purchaser; that the revenue cannot properly be secured if watering be allowed before the expiration of twelve days; that our conclusions are derived from "our most trusty and skilful officers."—Feb. 18, 1803. On this report the Treasury then relied, but now the Commissioners suggested, in reply to their Lordships, on the recommendation of "our experienced officers," "that when any maltster shall uniformly continue the grain under water for the full space of 50 hours," he be allowed to sprinkle "at and after the expiration of eight entire days.—April 19, 1806." And so importunate, though not agreed, were the trade on this point, that they actually obtained permission from the Treasury, dated May 2, 1806 —even apparently while the inquiry was being made—to sprinkle at the end of the ninth day, and to have all pending proceedings, for having previously done so, immediately stayed; while a day later the Commissioners were instructed to prepare a bill to legalise the indulgence, and to order their officers that when they found grain on the floor "illegally wetted" to give immediate notice to the "maltster or his servant," and to make a "memorandum of such suspicion upon the specimen in the malthouse, in order that the maltster may be able to account for such appearance and justify himself from the suspicion by satisfactory proof."—N. Vansittart.

The Parliamentary committee concluded with the opinion and suggestion, "That these Restrictions—contained in the Sprinkling Act, 42 Geo. III., c. 38—were to prevent Frauds upon the Revenue, and that as far as Restrictions can prevent Frauds, the prohibition of watering upon the floor till after the seventh day in the winter months—viz., from the 1st of October to the 1st of May (provided that the Malster during that period be required to steep his malt (!) for not less than forty-eight hours) and till after the fifth day in the summer months—viz., from the 1st of May to the first of October, would equally prevent fraud, and would at the same time afford great relief to the maltsters in the greatest part of England." Pages 90 printed June 17, 1806. There are also two papers printed in 1806 and 1807.

The Treasury concession was legalised by 46 Geo. III., c. 139, but, in consequence of the division of opinion, to remain in operation only one year, at the expiration of which the former law was again enforced until 1829, when the Treasury gave a greater concession by which the grain might be sprinkled at the expiration of eight days, provided all were wetted fifty hours—the advice given by the Board in 1806.

This was enacted on the motion of Mr Dawson,[1] and remained intact until relaxed in 1837 to six days,[2] in 1860 to four days—as suggested by the Parnell Committee in 1835[3] and in 1865 to ninety hours.[4] In an exceptional season a further relaxation has been permitted at the prescribed time, provided the grain be steeped not less than forty hours.[5] The commissioners have since, in an exceptional season, been petitioned to allow sprinkling at the expiration of six days on grain steeped forty hours.[6]

1808. Irish Malt Fees.—These fees have been included in the paper fees and the other points of interest in the present paper. The report, pages 60, printed January 25, 1808.

1821. Additional Duty in Scotland.—The outcome, most likely, of the motion of Mr Weston to repeal the additional duty in Scotland, in which he was not successful by 98 votes—ayes 144, noes 242.[7] Petitions were also presented against the extra duty, and the Chancellor of the Exchequer moved that they be referred to a Select Committee—ayes 56, noes 17.[8] The Committee in consideration of the fact that small distillers used all malt while large distillers a portion of raw grain, recommended that a drawback of one shilling per bushel be paid on that used in distillation, and a reduction of the duty on bigg malt by ninepence per bushel. These conclusions received attention; see the Rates of Duty and Malt Drawback. Pages 90, printed May 31, 1821.

1831. Malt Drawback on Spirits.—Two petitions were presented to Parliament this year for an alteration in the malt drawback on spirits, and one against any alteration. The Commission reported that the existing system of allowing drawback affords great facility

[1] H. C., April 7, 1830; 11 Geo. IV., c. 17. [2] 1 V. c. 49.
[3] Parnell Rep., 1835. [4] 28 & 29 Vic., c. 66. [5] 1860.
[6] C. S. G., 1877. [7] H. C., April 3, 1821. [8] Idem., April 12, 1821.

to commit fraud; and that in reducing or repealing the malt drawback precaution should be taken to prevent the revival of illicit distilation. Pages 178, printed Oct. 4, 1831.

1834-35. GENERAL.—These general reports by the Parnell Committee are unquestionably the most comprehensive and valuable ever written on the malt duty. They will be frequently referred to throughout this paper. *See* Parnell Committee.

1842. EFFECT OF THE REPEAL OF THE MALT DRAWBACK ON SPIRITS IN IRELAND.—This committee was appointed on the motion of the Chancellor of the Exchequer.[1] This report consists of one paragraph, but with the evidence fills 64 pages. June 17, 1842. *See* Malt for Distillation.

1863. "To consider whether, compatibly with the interests of the Revenue, the Laws relating to the Excise Duty upon Malt can be amended so as to operate more advantageously with reference to the cultivation and price of Barley, to the manufacture and price of Malt and Malt Liquor, and to the use of Malt in the feeding of Cattle and Sheep." Nineteen gentlemen were appointed to make this inquiry. Their report—the reappointment of the Committee, pages 2. July 20, 1863.

1865. Experiments undertaken by the Board of Trade to determine the Relative Values of unmalted and malted barley as Food for Stock, by John Bennet Lawes. Pages 82. August 1865. See Malt for Feeding Animals.

1867. The committee of this date was appointed to inquire into the operation of the Malt Tax on the motion of Colonel Barttelot on May 14. The evidence of the then Chairman of the Board, and Mr Carling, is of some official value, especially with respect to those portions on the differential duties on malt and spirit, the drying of swedes and mangel wurtzel, the convictions of maltsters, and cottage malting. The most intelligent and valuable unofficial witness was S. Cayley, Esq., whose evidence is clear, copious, and worthy perusal. The appendix contains copies of memorials received by the Board from maltsters, with the replies given, during the last five years. Unable to complete their inquiry the committee "recommended to the House that the Committee be reappointed in the next session of Parliament." Report and appendix, pages 192. July 25, 1867.

1868. This is the continuation report of that of 1867. To extract

[1] H. C., May 20, 1842.

—"Your committee proceeded to examine several agriculturists of great practical experience, taken, respectively, from all parts of the country. These witnesses appeared to your Committee to be generally of opinion that the effect of the Malt-tax is to interfere with the due rotation of crops, by causing wheat to be sown where barley could otherwise be sown; that it causes inferior barley to be neglected for malting purposes, though it is well known that such barley would make good malt; that it causes the labouring classes to consume an unwholesome kind of beer; that it prevents the farmer giving to their labourers wholesome home-brewed beer; that it prevents, to a great extent, the agricultural labourers brewing beer in their own cottages; that it prevents the farmers making malt on their own premises, as used to be the custom, it having been given in evidence that in the counties of Essex and Cambridge few of the farmhouses were, formerly, without malthouses attached to them. It has been proved to your Committee that malt is valuable for feeding purposes, and that the Excise restrictions, in preventing barley being sprouted for the feeding of horses and cattle, are injurious to agriculturists; that, although some of the witnesses were favourable to the repeal of the tax, they admitted that the trade, as a whole, were opposed to the repeal, on the ground that it would lead to an increase in the number of maltsters, and to the practice of malting by farmers; that the tax compels the maltster to use more capital in his trade, by at least 50 per cent., than would be otherwise required. The Committee feel bound to observe that it is given in evidence that the Revenue officers offer every facility to the maltsters in the conducting of their business." Mr Gurdon of Brantham Court, Suffolk, "has a plan for commuting the malt duty by levying a duty on the malthouse, according to measurement—a plan which certainly appears to have some merit, but upon which your committee are not prepared to express any further opinion, inasmuch as it is novel, and requires to be considered by the officers of Excise." "Two large distillers were examined by your committee, of whom Mr Menzies was anxious that the distillers should be allowed to make beer from some portion of his wort, and that the duty on beer should be charged in the same manner as the drawback is now allowed on exported beer. This witness, with all the large Scotch distillers, presented a memorial to Mr Gladstone to this effect in 1866. But your committee must add that the second witness dissented from this proposition. He also thinks that a reduction of the duty on strong wines would interfere with the spirit duty.

"Your Committee concluded this part of their labours by examining Sir Charles Pressly (formerly Chairman of the Boad of Inland Revenue) and Mr C. B. Forsey (Surveying-General Examiner of Excise). The first of these witnesses stated distinctly that there would be no difficulty in raising a tax from private brewers; and the second could point out no insurmountable difficulty in substituting a brewer's licence instead of the malt tax.

"Your Committee consider that the result of the evidence taken by them is, that the Malt-tax prevents the farmer from cultivating his land to the greatest advantage; that it obstructs him in the use of a valuable article of food for cattle; that, by making it necessary to employ a large additional amount of capital in the important trade of malting and brewing, it has created and tends to foster two large monopolies; and that, by materially increasing the price of beer, it encourages adulteration, and prevents to a great extent the habit of brewing among the labouring people.

"Your Committee, carefully reviewing the whole of the evidence before them, are of opinion that the Malt-tax might be repealed, provided some means for raising the same amount of revenue, if required, be substituted, either in the shape of a brewer's licence or some other form." Dated July 13, 1868.

Of course the intention of an inquiry is to afford relief by suitable enactment. The regulations as previously observed were enacted one by one as occasion required until consolidated by 12 Anne. This was the first consolidated malt Act, and it would seem that no further progress was made in this direction until the reign of George IV. On this intention becoming known to the trade a few of the more energetic maltsters at once repaired to London to obtain every concession they could, and having succeeded in their mission returned quite contented, but to find on the appearance of the Act which applied to the United Kingdom that not a few of the alleged promises of concession had not been kept. This aroused the whole fraternity, who, to the number of 1800, united in forming an Association of Maltsters in the United Kingdom, to consider and obtain the repeal of the objectionable portions of the new law—7 and 8 Geo. IV., c. 52. The Act was certainly very stringent. It was denounced as "one uncouth mass of legislation which shackled and impeded the trade and commerce of the country."[1] M'Culloch stated "it has no fewer than eighty-three clauses; and the regulations embodied in it, though frequently repugnant to common sense, are enforced by 106 penalties, amounting in all to the enormous sum of £13,500. Under such a statute, it was hardly possible for the most honest and cautious maltster to avoid incurring penalties. Such, indeed, is the nature of this Act, that one is almost tempted to believe, in looking into it, that if its framers had any object more than another at heart, it was to condense it into whatever was most contradictory and absurd in the forty-statutes that had previously been passed for the collection of the malt duty and the oppression of the trade. . . . It was not only loudly and universally condemned by the maltsters, but by all the more intelligent officers of excise." It was also reviewed much after the same manner in the *Edinburgh Review*. "It is by courtesy only that it can be called a consolidated Act. It enacts afresh every one of the vexatious restrictions contained in former Acts, and several new ones besides."[2] The maltsters too were wont to say, "The Act of Parliament is the maltster, and not us."[3]

With this "abundance of the law" the Maltsters' Association coped with continuous exertion for a period of three years and finally succeeded, writes Ford, "in obtaining the repeal of no less than nearly two-thirds of the restrictions and penalties by which the trade had been fettered." Of the 83 sections 29 were now repealed.[4] But this was accomplished by at this time "a somewhat novel but effectual mode,"—by the trade electing three of their body to meet a corresponding number of "Surveyors-General of Excise," to prepare a report for the sanction of the Government. There were only two points claimed by the maltsters, which were not, wholly or in part conceded by the Government, and so great was the satisfaction given by the changes in general that until the Coronation of Queen Victoria no further general change was made,[5] nor has there since that date, to the same extent, at one time, except with regard to particular malt laws.

The consideration of the general law would be incomplete without noting the more salient successive changes applicable at the more important points of manufacture and charge.

UTENSILS:—

Cistern: Notice to be given of erection or alteration, 1697; entry

[1] H. C., May 12, 1829. [2] Vol. xlix., page 373. [3] P. Rep., 1835.
[4] H. C., April 7, 1830; 11 Geo. IV., c. 17. [5] 1 V. c. 49.

to be made, 1713; to be so constructed as to admit a regular gauge, and if more than nine feet long a plank to be provided, 1812; to be easily accessible, easily gauged, 1813; to steep above 8 bushels, and to be made at right angles and not exceed certain limitations, 1827.

COUCH FRAME: To be at right angles, three sides permanently constructed, 1827; to be altered only on four days' notice, 1864.

BARLEY BOOK: Introduced in 1808; account of barley in possession required to be delivered to officer annually on July 5, and again after ceasing to work or before commencing to do so; excess exceeding 5 per cent. deemed to be received without entry, deficiency exceeding 5 per cent. deemed to be wetted and deficiency to be charged with malt duty; numerous penalties attached to this institution. The re-enactment of these regulations was strongly condemned by the Maltsters' Association. Equally unacceptable was the certificate system by which the maltster was enjoined to send a certificate with each delivery exceeding four bushels of malt that the duty had been paid, &c.; numerous penalties attached to this series of requirements; discontinued, 1830; partially repealed in 1830, totally in 1837.

STEEPING: 24 hours' notice to wet in towns, 48 elsewhere, between 4 a.m. and 9 p.m., begin within 3 hours or notice void, 1763; I., 1785; 24 hours' notice to wet if surveyed daily, 1763; 24 hours' notice uniformly, 1837; allowed between 8 a.m. and 2 p.m.; empty between 7 a.m. and 4 p.m., 1802; allowed at or before 5 p.m., present season, 1858; allowed between 7 a.m. and 5 p.m., 1860; be continued 40 hours or no allowance owing to short time so kept, not increasing to extent of allowance, 1760; be continued 20 hours, barley sprouted, indulgence, 1800, 1816; if continued 72 hours deemed new corn, charged "with double duty," I., 1806; not to be continued longer than 55 hours, 1812; 75 hours desired by Scotch maltsters; Commissioners granted, 80; Mr Wharton, 65 hours sufficient, longer time enable to twice fill and saturate, H. C., Dec. 11, 1812; be continued 50 hours if to be early sprinkled, T. W., 1829, 1830; 65 hours allowed on giving notice, wetting between 8 p.m. and 11 p.m., and emptying between 1 p.m. and 4 p.m., 1813; duty free continued only 30 hours on notice, 1860; if compressed 2s 6d per bushel, 1710; opinion sufficient proof in 1715; after as shown under couch.

DRAINING.—Allowed once in 40 hours, notice to be given with that to wet, operation be between 8 a.m. and 4 p.m., and grain be

again covered immediately, 1802. Allowed present season provided grain covered 65 hours in the whole, &c., indulgence 1819. Allowed at any time of year, T. W., Oct. 19, 1827, indulgence. Allowed once in 40 hours, on notice, between 8 a.m. and 2 p.m., if grain recovered within one hour, 1830. Allowed between 7 a.m. and 5 p.m., 1861.

COUCH.—In 1781 no fixed form or figure required so long as it could be gauged. Thus the instructions were, if square or oblong, take length and breadth; if a circle, the diameter. To be placed in rectangular form.—*See* Utensils, 1827. To be laid not deeper than 30 inches, 1827, formerly laid "some 60, 70 and more inches deep." —Parl. Report, 1835. So deemed for 30 hours before 1827; may be levelled after gauged, 46888/60, J.

To remain so laid: between March 1 and Dec. 1, 26 hours; other times 30 hours, 1827: year through 26 hours, 1830.

May be broken at expiration of 20 hours:

- before April 1 and Nov. 1, if two gauges taken, and if notice given and grain emptied from cistern between 1 p.m. and 4 p.m., though only one gauge taken, 1849.
- as in 1849, &c.,
  - during present season of 1856, during present season 1857, until further notice, 1858.
- if steeped 60 hours, though emptied before 1 p.m., and though two gauges not taken, if notice given, 1858.
- to be deemed a couch for 24 hours if no gauge taken before, 1860.
- and when out by 10 a.m., two gauges not required after 10 p.m., except once or twice a round, 1861; one gauge only required, 1866.

The Parnell Committee were asked in 1835 to recommend the "breaking" at 20 hours. Couch duty free may be removed on giving notice at expiration of 12 hours, 1860.

COMPRESSION.—At first it was customary, on finding closely-pressed grain, to measure it with a bushel, but to this the trade objected by alleging that it "did damage to the corn," then came the fine "for every bushel of corn steeping or steeped that shall be so pressed, trodden, rammed, or forced." Cases 1715. Compression 5s per bushel in cistern, and now first extended to couch, 1789.

<table>
<tr><td rowspan="4">Compression to the extent of</td><td colspan="2">1 in 20 found by throwing out part and turning o other part, and then levelling. Conclusive · dence—£100, 1801, 1827.</td></tr>
<tr><td colspan="2">6½ in 100 after 12 hours out, found as above, 183</td></tr>
<tr><td>5 in 100 before 8 hours out, 6 in 100 after 8 and before 16 hours, 7 in 100 after 16 hours.</td><td>All the grain havi been thrown ou and returned conclusive evidence;</td></tr>
<tr><td colspan="2">applicable to cistern, 1837.</td></tr>
</table>

The mode of ascertaining the extent of compression adopted in 1829 was by returning the grain into the frame in cones, and this occasioned much litigation. Compression, observe the Commissioners in their First Report, prevailed in the year 1845 to such an extent as to require a vigorous intervention on our part, as it was only by great firmness, and with the support of a well-reasoned judgment of the Court of Exchequer, that we were able to check the growth of this practice." Ford states that in 1846, "more informations were issued against Maltsters, upon the couch question alone than during any five years during the whole of the sixteen years previously." He also adds that an information for illegally compressing the grain in the couch frame, as ascertained by returning it in cones, was dismissed at Croydon on May 30, 1846, and confirmed on appeal. The magistrates who first heard the case paid counsel to support their decision, and those who heard the appeal accompanied their decision by "we do not believe that fraud has either been committed or attempted." The Commissioners ordered in 1849 that, in future, the grain must not be returned in cones, but in the ordinary manner of working. *See* Excise Laws, 1873, p. 273. The Parnell Committee in 1835 were asked to recommend a fine at so much per bushel. The expression "conclusive evidence" has ever been "too much" for the maltster.

FLOORS.—Not more than 5 allowed, including in couch-frame and on kiln, 1812; not more than 6, 1837; be laid in succession, must remain fully 10 days, but if 21, charged on every bushel, I., 1806; an annual return of all above 16 days was formerly made; must remain 7 days, 1855; may be removed to kiln when ready,—indulgence, 1856; must remain 7 days, 1863; may be removed to kiln at 6 days if ready, 1872; duty free earlier. The Commissioners state in their earliest report, to stop the use of raw grain by the malt roaster "An effort to defeat this mode of defrauding the revenue was made

in 1855, by the introduction of a law requiring maltsters to keep grain under process for 168 hours, in order to insure a sufficient amount of germination to make malt readily distinguishable from unmalted grain. But the ingenuity of the malt roaster again baffled us. The maltster who supplied him was instructed to expose the barley to considerable heat on the kiln before it was steeped; its vegetative power was thus destroyed, and at the end of the 168 hours it came forth legally malt, but quite undistinguishable from the raw grain with which it was immediately mixed by the roaster." Failing in this a special provision was made, as noted under roasted malt: gauges were taken in at intervals of 8 or 9 days to 1819, then at intervals of 5 days, sometimes at 2 days, subsequently at intervals of 6 days, except duty-free; a "floor register" existed in 1734; gauges not regularly taken on kiln till 1857.

Sprinkling: *See* under report 1806.

Modes of Charge: "Taken by the Gage according to such Bushell—Winchester—in any cisterne or other in which the grain shall be steeping to be charged as so many Bushells of Malt," 1697: Ireland to 1794 as in England, 12 stones being equal to a barrel, four bushels equal to a barrel, the maltster making a return of all made: "among a variety of subsequent regulations enacted from time to time, the most important was introduced by 34 Geo. III., c. 10, which by imposing a certain and fixed charge upon the maltster, combined a system of assessment with that of survey. This charge was fixed in:—1794 at 12 barrels per 100 square feet of flooring; 1795, 16 do., from September 29 to March 25; 1797, 24 do.; 1805, 64 do., in certain districts; 1805, at 48 barrels per 100 square feet of flooring, in others; 1806, 64 do., in every district, and with as much more malt as should be actually made." But this regulation was modified in so far as "that the maltster should be charged with, and pay duty for, not less than eight months in every year and in every month while he continues working, with eight barrels of malt for every 100 square feet of working or dry floors, with liberty, however, to discontinue work for either a part or the whole of the remainder of the year, at any time after two months from commencement, or one month after any recommencement; that the proper officer of Excise shall return to the collector the monthly charge on the maltster, within 10 days after the expiration of each month; . . . . that the maltster shall be charged at each wetting, with not less than the full content of the cistern" less one-fifth.

The rates per barrel were these:—1785, 2s. 6d.; 1794, 3s. 3d.; 1795, 5s. 3d.; 1799, 6s.; 1800, 6s. 6d.; 1803, 7s. 7d.; 1804, 9s. 9d.; 1806, 10s. 10d. This system ceased in 1827. A new mode is by weight—*see* Malt by Weight. To avoid loss, whole bushels only charged 1854, then highest multiple of 5 bushels 1856. The Committee of 1835 were desired to recommend that entry of each couch charge be made on specimen. Among the modes suggested, that by actual measurement from kiln, on content of cistern, on area of floor: to the first the Board replied that unlike paper "malt could not be enclosed in wrappers, with Excise labels," 1835. The Gurdon system suggested in 1864 lay in a licence duty to be computed according to the superficial measurement of kiln—*see* Bell's Bateman, 1865. The modes of charge in foreign countries will be found at the end of this paper.

ALLOWANCES.—"4 out of 20," "in consideration of the difference between the quantity of such corne when it is wett and swollen, and the quantity thereof when it is converted into dry malt," 1697. 4 in 20 now extended to grain gauged within 48 hours after thrown out of cistern, 1702. 8 in 20 allowed if not yield so great a quantity from the floor as from the fat, 1702. 4 in 20 on grain on floor if gauged within 30 hours after thrown from cistern, 1713. 10 in 20 if gauged on floor, 1713. 10 in 20 after 26 hours out of cistern, 1802. 5 in 20 within 72 hours, 7 in 21 after 72 hours, 10 in 20 after 120 hours after the grain should have been shown out of couch frame; I., 1806. 10 in 20 after 72 hours out of cistern, and to test the propriety a return was ordered for a period stated of the amount of the best couch gauge, amount of the best floor gauge before 72 hours out and then before 96 hours out, with the quantity of barley shown to have been wetted, 1828. 17·5 in 100 on cistern and couch gauge. 1 in 3 before 72, 1 in 2 after 72 hours out, 1830: Ford states. "20 in 100" on cistern being too much, the factor ·82 was suggested to the Chancellor of the Exchequer, but "to our utter surprise" he authorised the factor ·825. An effort has since been made to again obtain the "20 in 100." The Parnell Committee were asked, in 1835, to recommend larger allowances on cistern and couch gauges, and one allowance on floor of "10 in 20." 18·5 in 100 on cistern and couch gauges, 1837. 1 in 2 on floor, 1837. 17 in 100 on cistern and couch gauge of duty free, 1855. 30 in 100 on cistern and couch gauges of rye; C 2, 3 R.

SURVEY.—Officer empowered to enter "House Malthouse" "to

gauge all Cisterns Utting Fatts," and leave a copy of "Return or Report" to Commissioners, 1697. If at night in presence of peace officer, 1713. At night without peace officer, 1802. "Where maltsters steep their barley in ponds or rivers, you must visit them every survey and show their condition as Nil when empty, and hours in when barley is steeping; and in the cistern column instead of a gauge note the number of sacks or bags then steeping," and endeavour to find out steeping places in ponds and rivers, and "cause the maltsters to enter them." Besides couch gauges "take at least two gauges thereof, when it shall be thrown upon the floor, until it is dried off," also frequently gauge "the malt after it is put upon the kiln;" S., 1804. Arrangements were ordered to be made in 1836 for a daily survey to be made on all malthouses in the United Kingdom. The maltsters too have since suggested "one uniform Rule of Survey" on houses in and out of residence, 1845. Precedents and general regulations of survey, *i.e.*, the more important, were issued—1780; 1781, Town; 1804, S.; 1810, G. L.; 1815, G. L.; 1827; 1827, S. and I. Distillery; 1837, G. O.; 1838; 1842; 1842. Roasted, 1859, 1864, 1867, 1871, 1878. The general letters and orders issued between 1760 and 1878 bearing on the subject, generally, exceed 160 in number.

Payment.—Pay within six days or give security to pay within six months was the alternative regulation in 1697. Queen Anne enacted three months, and not sell until the duty be paid—1702—and later that action might be taken to recover the duty within five years—1710. Four months' credit with security was continued by the Georges downwards, apparently until the Parnell Committee wrote: "We also look forward to the discontinuance of the system of giving credit in paying the malt duties, as a measure which, if adopted, would be followed by very good effects." This committee was asked to recommend that which had been previously recommended by a Parliamentary Committee in 1821, the stowing of malt under bond, but this they declined to do. The same idea has been since suggested by the Maltsters' Association to meet the question of "unequal credit," and the association has also suggested a reduction of the period of credit. The Commissioners too, in their First Report, drew attention to the objectionable character of the long period, which Mr Gladstone considered in 1859. He observed:—"In former times it was felt that these questions had an important relation to the system of protection and the independence of the agriculturist upon the price that barley fetched in the market. It was thought, and with some colour of reason, that the system of supplying capital to the man who buys barley from the farmer had a tendency to augment the price of barley to the purchaser. . . . . I do not say that there might not be a further measure in the same direction at a future time, and after matters have been adjusted to the present change . . . . we propose . . . . allowing the maltsters a discount at the rate of 4 per cent. on the payment made under the proposed system. . . . . Of course in future years there would be no operation of discount." The credit was now reduced from 18 to 12 weeks,[1] and the "further measure" introduced the following year when the 12 were reduced to 6 weeks, but in 1863 extended by three months on certain charges on condition that interest, at the rate of 3½ per cent., for three months, be paid on the duty deferred.[2]

LOSS.—It was King William who first sanctioned the repayment of the duty on malt lost by fire or water;[3] and Queen Anne extended the sanction to that on malt taken by the "Enemy" on removal coastwise,[4] the decision being left to the Magistrates at the General Quarter Sessions—"Allowance; Whole Duty; Damage; Value (before damaged)."[5] But since this date a very considerable extension of the principle has been made by allowing the duty on "imperfectly malted grain," on condition that the malt be "mixed with one-tenth of its weight of linseed and be used for cattle food." Upwards of 23,000 bushels were so treated during the period embraced in the Commissioners' Twentieth Report. A return was made to Parliament, in 1840, of the sums repaid on malt damaged by fire between that date and 1827.

FRAUD.—Some of the more general modes of fraud have been already shown, while others are so well known that it is here necessary to point out only a few cases. About 1800, "Men of Straw" or indigent and obscure persons became maltsters, made as much as possible, sold it, and absconded before the pay day, thus evading the due discharge of the debt.[6] About 1812 others made their floors to appear as if in operation twenty or twenty-four days, "the fact being that two operations or steepings had been carried on in the time which was represented as being occupied in one only." These

[1] H. C., July 18, 1859. [2] Idem., Feb. 16, 1863. [3] 13 Wm. III., c. 5.
[4] 4 & 5 Anne, c. 17. [5] 7 Anne, c. 3. [6] Parnell, 15 R.

traders were prosecuted, and on the evidence of experienced maltsters that fourteen days were sufficient, the juries assumed sixteen and made their calculations and gave their verdicts accordingly," "the result of which was a recovery of upwards of £200,000 of evaded duty."[1] In 1845 upwards of 700 bushels of a mixture of malt and grain were seized and offered for sale.[2] In 1857 a continuous fraud on a large scale was discovered by Messrs Adamson and Mason, Surveying General Examiners, and H. E. Richards, Division Officer, to have been "effected by the use of concealed malthouses underneath the entered premises" in Sussex, 3,300 qrs. of malt and 20 qrs. of barley were seized, condemned, and sold, and the offenders were prosecuted for a cumulative penalty of £475,000, of which on request, only £110,000 was awarded, and of which award, by penalties and sale of seizure only £18,383 was recovered.[3] Frauds were formerly very numerous, and the 684 convictions in 1835[4] compared with the 34 convictions in 1855[5] go far to prove the decrease, while the Commissioners state in their Seventh Report "the detections of fraud have not been numerous, and there is no reason to suppose that it prevails to any considerable extent undetected."

Illicit malting though coped with under special enactment may be noticed here. It technically includes conducting the whole process in defiance of the law, usually, now, on a small scale; the grain being placed in a sack or barrel, which is inserted in a bog or drain, then emptied and worked upon a floor and under a bed, and finally, dried upon hair or other cloths, extended upon sticks, over a fire, in a small hut which forms the kiln. 71,000 bushels of this forbidden make were seized in Ireland in 1833, and so general was the practice in that country in 1834 that the Parliamentary Committee who examined the subject made a hasty report, in which they record the opinion that it was due to the repeal of "the old Irish malt law," already noticed, and that "the re-enactment of it would be a proper remedy for the evil."[6]

A fraud was also committed with a substance called essentia bine, "a late invented Liquor or Syrup made from Malt and Water boiled up to the consistency of mellasses, and very much resembling the same," which was put into casks of beer after cleansed.[7] The

[1] Parnell, 15 R. [2] L. G., 1845. [3] C. 2 R. [4] P. Ret.
[5] C. 1 R. [6] Parnell, 10 R. [7] 13 W. III., c. 5.

Young Brewer's Monitor shows it to have been made of "capsicum, coculus indicus, liquorice, and salt of steel."[1] The people in the neighbourhood of the New Forest were wont to use the "golden withy" as a substitute for malt.[2]

IMPORTATION.—The importation of foreign malt was forbidden from the date of the imposition of the malt duty in 1697 to 1860: it then became admissible on the payment of a Customs' duty of 25s. per quarter—which is made up as follows—excise duty 21s. 8½d., corn duty 1s., interest on duty for six months 6d., excise restrictions and licence duty 1s. 9½d. "The allowance on account of excise restrictions," observe the Commissioners, "is no doubt extremely liberal, and it must not be inferred that we admit its correctness."[3] To 1862 none had been imported.[4]

EXPORTATION.—The exportation of malt has always been encouraged, even ground malt at one time,[5] though under different regulations, with the exception of times of scarcity of corn as in 1698, 1710, 1767. The first regulations were simple, the whole duty having been returned,[6] but as time rolled on a difference arose between the trade and the department, inasmuch as the former claimed drawback on the quantity measured for exportation, while the latter alleged the former ran "out their malt into combe" to such a degree as to produce an inordinate increase in bulk, and to render it "worth little more than the drawback paid," much to the discredit of the malt trade abroad and the lessening of the duties at home. It was under these circumstances that an act was passed in 1726 to allow malt to be made free of duty for exportation[7] and that a bill was prepared, though not passed, in 1770, to allow the exportation of "long malt," which it was alleged could not be sold except for that purpose. This act remained in force until repealed and replaced in 1865[8] by an extension of the provisions of the Act of 1855, under which malt was first made free of duty for distilling purposes.

But five years before this change, provision had been made to permit the exportation on drawback of duty paid malt, weighing not less than 39 nor more than 42 lbs. per bushel, less a deduction of 7·5 per cent. "on account of the actual measurement exceeding the gauge according to which the duty was charged."[9] The weight limitation has been since revised and fixed at the extremes of 36 lbs. and

[1] 1824. [2] P. Rep., 1833. [3] C. 4, 5, 13 R. [4] P. Ret.
[5] 1 Anne, stat. 2, c. 3. [6] 1697. [7] 12 Geo. I., c. 4.
[8] 28 & 29 Vic., c. 66. [9] 23 & 24 Vic., c. 113; C. 21 R.

44 lbs. per bushel.[1] This change in the law, though conceded before legalised,[2] made to ease the export market when a demand from abroad could not be met without the surrender of all drawback by the exporter, has been acceptable to the trade, as shown by the fact that in 1874, drawback was paid on upwards of 500,000 bushels.[3] The Commissioners state in their Nineteenth Report that malt "made free of duty for exportation is a business which has never assumed considerable proportions and has not of late materially increased."

To pass on to the consideration of the more specific or particular laws, the result for the most part of the Parliamentary inquiries previously noted.

MALT CHARGED BY WEIGHT.—The examination of the Parliamentary Report on Malt Fees in Ireland, printed in 1808, discloses the fact that David Sherlock "never experienced any inconvenience from being charged by weight, at the rate of four bushels to the barrel, and he has generally found by experience the weights and gauges to correspond." But it is probable that he was not charged in this manner because the malt duty "operated as a prohibition to the sale of light barley for malting purposes."[4] The security afforded to the revenue by locking and labelling the cistern was suggested by W. G. six years before it was adopted.[5] Mr Gladstone explains the principle and expected result of his bill in these words—"A certain weight will be assumed as the average or standard weight of a bushel of barley of such quality as is now ordinarily used for malting. Barley meant for malting will be weighed before steeping by a sample bushel. It will then be gauged as malt in the same manner as now. The whole weight of the parcel will be divided by the standard weight, and the quotient will give the number of bushels to be charged with duty. . . . . According to established rules, when the bulk reached 100 bushels, an allowance was made of 18½ per cent., and that was reckoned decimally—namely, a reduction from 10 to 8·15. . . . By the operation of the present Bill what was done was, that the bulk or 8·1 was multiplied by the weight of barley, and divided by the standard weight (53 lbs.) and the quotient 7·6 would be the amount of the barley to be charged with duty. . . . . . The effect will be to relieve all barleys lighter than the standard," and to afford "a relief

[1] 28 & 29 Vic., c. 66. [2] C. 13 R. [3] C. 17 R. [4] C. 12 R.
[5] C. S. G., 1859.

of from 6 to 7 per cent., varying in proportion to the weight of the barley."[1] The act conferred little benefit during the first year it was in force, owing to the barleys being unusually heavy, but in 1876, the surrender of no less a sum than £43,120, the largest to the date of writing, plainly indicates that the light weight of the home and foreign growths rendered it profitable to work on this system. The extremes of the annual average weight per bushel during this period were 49·6 lbs. and 50·8 lbs., and the estimated relief of 7 per cent. has been very closely afforded. The number of houses worked by weight in 1867 was 575. The operation of this act at first limited to four years, has been since annually continued by the Expiring Laws Continuance Act.

MALT FOR DISTILLATION.—Under this designation an allowance was made upon duty-paid malt used in the distillation of spirits in Scotland and Ireland. The system was first introduced into Scotland in 1821, where private distillation from malt was then general. It was allowed for the purpose of placing the small distiller in a better relative trade position with the large distiller who used a portion of raw grain, of suppressing illicit malting, and of encouraging the use of small licensed stills, the taste of the people being for malt spirit. In Ireland the taste was mixed, and although the same plan was in 1823 extended to that country for the same purpose, it does not seem to have been at the request or desire of either the maker or the consumer, but rather on the part of the Legislature. The allowance was fixed in 1821 at one shilling per bushel, but afterwards modified in the case of bere or bigg.[2] This privilege opened a new avenue to fraud which after the inquiry, noticed in 1831, was so far closed that premises were required to be "entered to make malt to be used in distilling malt spirit only," and the distiller enjoined to place his malt, on the distillery premises, under revenue lock. But this did not remove one important objection to the system, which lay in the fact that the distiller frequently obtained the drawback within ten days after the spirit was made, while he had not paid the malt duty, nor would he have to do so until the expiration of six weeks after it had been charged.[3] Nor did it prevent the substitution of ungerminated or unduty-paid grain for duty paid malt. Fraud being practised in various forms, the Chancellor of the Exchequer

[1] H. C., April 27, June 15, 1865; 28 & 29 Vic., c. 66.
[2] P. Rep., 1821, 1842.
[3] 2 Wm. IV., c. 29.

moved in 1842 the appointment of a committee to examine the question in so far as it related to Ireland, and upon their report, already noticed, the allowance made in that country was at once repeated—5 Vic. sess. 2 c. 15.[1] Advancing to 1852, Mr Disraeli now proposed to deal with it, but owing to the resignation of the Ministry, his proposition was not considered.[2] To Sir G. C. Lewis, Bart., it remained to effectually solve the difficulty—first by repealing the legislative sanction under which the drawback was paid, and by allowing so much per gallon on malt spirit on hand, and then by legalising the manufacture of

MALT DUTY-FREE FOR DISTILLATION [3]—afterward exportation, the provisions of which legislation are well known, though a pun by *Punch* may not be. "The Distiller in Difficulties"—a take-off on the precise directions as to the security of the deposit room and the sack—"Red Tape to the sack—sack to Red Tape."[4] The largest annual make under this Act occurred in 1877, when it exceeded 7,000,000 bushels, of which not quite 60,000 bushels were exported.[5]

MALT FOR FEEDING ANIMALS.—Long was the inability to use malt as a food for cattle free from fiscal exaction a plea against the malt tax. The first attempt to meet this appears to be recorded in the Commissioners' Eighth Report in referring to a proposed mixture of linseed with malt. "The same proposal was made as long ago as 1844, and was submitted, among other questions, to the consideration of Dr Playfair and Dr Graham, who were employed by the Board of Excise upon investigations similar to those now in progress, but their answer was such as, in the state of the law which then existed, discouraged us from any attempt to act upon the suggestion, linseed meal being, according to their opinion, by no means an obstacle to the use of malt for distilling, though it apparently interfered seriously with the employment of it for brewing."[6] In 1845 Mr S. O'Brien took charge of a bill "to allow a drawback on malt used for the feeding of cattle," on which the Chancellor of the Exchequer observed that he "had made several extensive enquiries through the medium of the Excise, and he found that there would be great difficulty in carrying out the provisions of the bill," and on a second endeavour to pass the second reading, Mr Cardwell stated that the provision "to allow the maltster a licence to mix an equal quantity of

[1] H. C., May 9, 20, 1842. [2] H. C., Dec. 3, 1852.
[3] H. C., June 5, 1855. [4] Punch, 1855. [5] C. 20 R. [6] C. 8 R.

oats, barley, pease (crushed or whole) with unground malt or any quantity of these with ground malt, and to sell this mixture to the occupiers of land, with a certificate of the quantity sold," would be no valid security whatever to the excise.[1] From this date, with the exception of two motions, which will be afterwards noticed, though experiments were made by private individuals, on the relative values of barley and malt,[2] the subject remained unnoticed until 1863, when, at the instance of Sir Fitzroy Kelly, it was referred to a select committee.[3] But by this time the objection with regard to distilling had been overcome by the manufacture of malt duty-free, and that with respect to the brewing by a minute investigation of the linseed theory by the Principal of the Laboratory, who gave "convincing evidence [that malt and linseed meal thoroughly and intimately mixed, by being ground up together, could not be profitably used by brewers of beer."[4] The subject thus narrowed became mature for legislation, but prior to detailing the legislation and its result, mention must be made of a series of experiments made by Mr John Bennet Lawes by order of the Board of Trade, to determine the relative feeding powers of these two forms of grain. Mr Lawes first obtained the permission of the Board to carry on a series of experiments on steeped grain under the observation of an officer in one of the maltings belonging to the Messrs Gripper of Hertford. As the experimental process of malting proceeded samples were frequently taken from each of the seventy quarters of grain to be analysed at Rothamsted, Herts, by Mr Lawes and Mr H. Morris, of the Inland Revenue Laboratory, who had been specially sent down by the Principal for that purpose. The conclusion shows that No. 1 barley lost 19 and No. 2 barley 22 per cent. by weight in malting. With the milch cows barley gave the most cream. The barley-fed oxen gave a greater "dead weight" than the malt-fed ones, but the latter yielded a superior meat. With the sheep barley found the most favour. With the pigs those which received a small quantity of malt fed better than those on equal quantities of malt and barley. Mr Lawes' general conclusion is that a given weight of barley will produce more milk and "life-weight," than the amount of malt and malt dust that would be produced from it. May the tabular statements in this document find favour with the fatigued farmers.[2] To return to W. E. Gladstone with his Bill—"that leave be given to

[1] H. C., May 21, 28, 1845. [2] P. Rep., 1866.
[3] H. C., June 23, July 13, 1863. [4] C. 8 R.

bring in a Bill to allow the making of Malt Duty-free to be used in feeding Cattle." This was cheerfully assented to by Sir Anti-Malt Tax Fitzroy Kelly. Col. Barttelot hoped "that it was not brought forward as a substitute for a reduction of the Malt Duty." Mr Bass avowed "If the duty generally were abolished, then the revenue would run no risk, but he was satisfied that if malt were allowed to be dried in this way, however it might be mixed with cattle food the revenue would suffer," and so interested was this large brewer that he conducted the pleasant and gustative experiment of submitting to the members of the House of Commons, a cask of beer brewed from malt and hops, and another brewed from hops, malt and linseed meal, in the proposed proportions, which had been brought into their "kitchen" for that purpose.[1] The bill became law, but limited in its force to five years.[2] It has since the termination of this period been continued annually by the Expiring Laws Continuance Act. The result. Twenty-eight persons the first season made entry of premises, made 10,705 quarters of malt, mixed 8748 quarters, paid duty on another portion, and retained the remainder, upon which the Commissioners observe that it was not likely that a half of these would work on this system next year, not that it would be entirely due to the Excise restrictions.[3] By 1867 only four remained, and of those who had discontinued, one attributed his discontinuance to the want of demand due to the required fineness of the mixture, another to the trouble of proving that the mixture was such as could not be used for brewing purposes, a third to the difficulty of procuring linseed while the others alleged the absence of remunerative demand. The Board now stated "It would appear that the value of malt as food for cattle has been greatly over-rated, and that, though malt might be used with advantage as a condiment . . . . it never can be profitable as a staple article of food."[4] By 1868 one person only remained.[5] By 1870 the manufacture had entirely ceased.[6]

Desirous to afford the agricultural community free experiment with the fiscally-forbidden forms of grain, the Chancellor of the Exchequer further conceded, with a view to close this class claim, the use of

Germinated Grain.—Farmers had been in the habit of steeping grain for their stock as early as 1835, and the Parliamentary Com-

[1] H. C., Feb. 8, 24, 1864. [2] 27 Vic., c. 9. [3] C. 9 R. [4] C. 11 R. [5] C. 12 R. [6] C. 14 R.

mittee who reported upon the malt duty in 1868, came to the conclusion "that the Excise restrictions in preventing barley being sprouted for the feeding of horses and cattle are injurious to the agriculturists." Indeed no plea remained unpleaded to obtain the permission: even the disadvantage (!) of the English, as compared with the foreign farmer, who could use germinated grain and malt, without payment of duty, was not forgotten, by a deputation who, in 1870, waited upon the Chancellor of the Exchequer, who the same year introduced a clause into the Customs and Inland Revenue Bill to comply with the request, subject to certain Excise regulations of an uninterfering character.[1] But as the Act applied only to Great Britain its extension to Ireland has been twice asked and twice refused owing to "the extreme difficulty of controlling it in the more distant parts of the country."[2] "Saccharised grain" is little used.

Roasted Malt.—It was in the year 1818 that the Lords of the Treasury first sanctioned the use of roasted malt to the porter brewer only, and at or about this time that the trade in beer colour-making began to decline. *See* Beer Duty. The regulations under which the roasting was now allowed were similar to other early regulations, very simple, the roaster being required to enter his premises and utensils, an officer to survey them and grant certificates for removal; the brewer to enter a deposit room, to produce each consignment and certificate to the officer who surveyed his premises, to use the malt "in a whole unbruised, unground state, and in his mash tun only;" the officer to register the certificates, and frequently inspect the stock. Within three months of this date every brewer was allowed to use it "provided it be bruised or ground, and be put into the mash tun in the presence of the proper officer." The permission was extended to Scotland and Ireland in 1834. It was long spoken of as coloured, charred, burnt, patent, black, or roasted, or black malt, and in 1869 Prescott writes of roasted and patent as distinct forms—roasted as being prepared from the paler descriptions of malt in a cylinder before a strong fire, until it becomes quite black to give colour to porter. Patent or crystallised malt, as being prepared from inferior grain, copiously watered, germinated the entire, and sometimes more than the entire, length of the grain, slowly dried in an oven, in a wire-covered iron cylinder, in which ample space is left for the free movement of each grain by a rotary

[1] 33 & 34 Vic., c. 32, s. 6. [2] H. C., June 1871; March 1, 1875.

motion, in front of a coke fire placed inside the oven, to be used by brewers in small quantities with ordinary malt. Roasted malt has in some measure superseded blown, brown, or porter malt.[1] The incrustation obtained by roasting afforded a cover for fraud which claimed attention in 1835 by an allegation that much barley and unduty-paid malt passed into the possession of the roaster, and by a suggestion that a strict survey might be of service.[2] It was not, however, until 1842 that a measure was passed imposing a licence-duty on the roaster and the dealer, with a stock account, forbidding in the case of a roaster the receipt of only unroasted malt, and in the case of the dealer only roasted malt, and requiring every delivery to be made by certificate, with other regulations, that the revenue can be considered to have been protected. But the proverbial coach-and-four were driven through this Act of Parliament—" . . . . shall not . . . . receive any corn or grain other than unroasted malt, which shall have been made by an entered and licensed maltster"[3]—the road taken has been shown under Floors. A still severer stricture became necessary in 1856, after which grain not germinated to the extent of 95 per cent. by the prolongation of the plumule by half the length per grain shall be deemed unmalted: while in 1867 it became necessary to enact that grain, though germinated to the legally-required extent, but not "perfectly dried" upon the kiln where made, shall be also deemed unmalted grain. Numerous interesting details regarding the condition of the trade by the Principal of the Laboratory will be found in the Commissioners' Reports. Exportation on drawback was first allowed in 1866. The number of malt roasters and dealers in the United Kingdom in 1877 was 33.[4]

Bere or Bigg Malt.—*See* under Parliamentary Reports.

Licence Duty.—Exigible of every maltster, maltroaster, and dealer in roasted malt, is a licence duty, and formerly of the malt factor was there a similar exaction. Precedence of imposition was taken by Great Britain at the instance of Mr. Pitt in 1784, when he proposed to levy on every maltster a uniform duty of £2,[5] which, though agreed to, was modified to a crown upon the beginner, with a surcharge for every fifty quarters made beyond the first up to the twelfth multiple, the limit of the scale. This continued until 1815, when the rates were increased by one half; and with the exception

[1] P. Rep., 1831, 1835; Art of Brewing, 1829; Ford, 1842. [2] P. Rep., 1835.
[3] 5 Vic., sess. 2, c. 30. [4] C. 20 R. [5] H. C., June 30, 1784.

of an additional 5 per cent. in 1840, with a further exemption in favour of the bye maltster, is the scale in force in 1878. The bye malt licence duty first paid at half a crown by Treasury Warrant, dated December 12, 1826, increased by 5 per cent. in 1840, is an exemption in favour of the occupier of a small portion of land, who makes not more than five quarters of malt of grain grown on that land for his own use. He is grouped and condemned by Ford as belonging to the "liberty-hall class of traders." The provisions of the law were at first not liberal, the licence being applicable only to malthouses which were contiguous,[1] and "only for premises entered at the time" it was taken out,[2] provisions which also entailed a liability to a surcharge. But these have been removed, 1848. In Ireland a different principle existed from 1794 to 1824. Each maltster at first paid a licence duty of £2; in 1798, £10; in 1801, £15 for each house or cistern; in 1806, £30 in Dublin, Cork, Waterford, Limerick, and Belfast, £20 within two miles of Dublin and one of the other cities, £15 in other places; in 1807 increased to guineas, at which the scale stood until assimilated to that of Great Britain in 1824. Each malt factor in 1801 paid £20; in 1807, £21; in 1824, £2, until repealed in 1826. Since 1842 the malt-roaster has paid £20, the dealer £10.[3] The Parnell Committee observe on the maltster's licence—"The present rate of licences are so moderate that we have no doubt that some increase in them would be paid without dissatisfaction, if such increase were accompanied by the diminution of the direct tax on the article, or relief from some of the regulations." The scale proposed by them is ten shillings per 50 quarters up to 500 quarters, and then fifty shillings for each of the two next 50 quarters, thus retaining the payable limit of manufacture to the "exceeding 550 quarters," but raising the limit of licence duty to £10.[4] This has been approved but not adopted by Mr Gladstone.[5]

Parliamentary Proceedings.—So far only occasional reference has been made to the efforts to obtain exemption, commutation, reduction, repeal. These will now be noted in the order of time from the beginning of the present century.

1802. Deputation to the Chancellor of the Exchequer respecting the additional duty; Dec. 4, 1802. This deputation received support by several petitions being presented against the increase.

[1] H. C., July 2, 1822. [2] P. Rep., 1835. [3] C. 1, 13 R.
[4] 19 R. [5] H. C., April 18, 1853.

1804.
1806.
1806. } Previously noted under Parliamentary Inquiries.
1808.
1821.

1823. Motion to inquire into the present mode of taxing malt and beer separately, and whether it would not be expedient to collect the same amount on malt alone—ayes 27, noes 119.[1] It was afterwards stated that, "It had been found very expedient to remove the beer tax in Ireland, and to place the whole duty on malt, for it was very satisfactorily paid, and the trade had been freed from monstrous obstructions."[2]

1829. Motion to inquire into the "burthens and restrictions on the manufacture of malt;" withdrawn.[3] Numerous petitions were presented in 1830-1-2 for the repeal.

1831. Noted under Parliamentary Inquiries.

1833. Motion by Sir W. Ingelby—"That the duty on malt be reduced from 28s. 8d. per qr. to 10s. per qr." A long exciting debate ensued, which terminated in a majority of ten votes for the motion—ayes 162, noes 152.[4] The next day the Chancellor of the Exchequer moved that it is inexpedient either to . . . . or reduce the malt duty; upon which an amendment was moved by Sir William to leave out the word malt. There were then for the amended resolution—ayes 285, noes 131—a majority of 154 votes. Sir William then moved for leave to bring in a bill to reduce the duty—ayes 162, noes 238.[5]

1834. Motion by Sir W. Ingelby that the duty be reduced. He observed on this occasion, in proposing a substitute—"I cannot see why as a man takes out a licence to go to shoot, he should not also take out a licence to go to hell." He then suggested an annual duty of £1000 on each infamous house—ayes, 170, noes 271; majority 101.[6]

1834. Motion by Mr Cobbett—"Resolved that from and after the 6th of October next, all duty upon malt shall cease and determine." Seventeen engaged in the debate—ayes 142, noes 59.[7]

[1] H. C., May 28, 1823.
[2] H. C., March 15, 1824.
[3] H. C., May 12, 1829.
[4] H. C., April 26, 1833.
[5] H. C., April 27, 1833.
[6] H. C., Feb. 27, 1834.
[7] H. C., March 17, 1834.

1835. Motion "Marquess" of Chandos moved the repeal. Twenty-seven members engaged in debate—ayes 192, noes 350.[1]

1835. Lord Teynham moved the repeal; motion negatived without a division.[2]

1835. The Committee of this date were asked to recommend the reduction by one half, and the permission to farmers to make duty free for their servants. Upon which they observe, ". . . . the only ground on which a reduction can be justified, while the present amount of revenue is necessary, is a strong probability that a reduced duty, by means of an increased consumption, yields as great a revenue as that which is obtained from the present duty; but if the importation of foreign barley be permitted, the tendency of a reduced duty to increase the consumption of malt would be counteracted by the price of British barley becoming higher in consequence of the new demand for it, which would arise from the duty having been lowered; and thus . . . . a higher price of barley and a certain loss of revenue;" not recommended. From 1833 to this date 395 petitions were presented for the repeal, the largest number to this time.

1842. Noticed under Parliamentary Inquiries.

1845. Noted under Malt for Feeding Animals.

1848. Deputation to Lord John Russel to urge repeal.[3]

1850. Motion by Mr Cayley—"That leave be given to bring in a Bill to repeal the Malt Tax." In doing so the honourable gentleman made an elaborate speech which fills fourteen pages, and with the speeches of eleven other members, thirty-seven pages of Hansard—ayes 123, noes 247.[4]

1851. Motion by Mr Cayley as above—ayes 122, noes 258.[5]

1851. Motion by Mr Bass—"That on and after the 10th day of October 1852, one half of the malt tax be repealed"—ayes 31, noes 76.[6]

1852. Motion of Mr Disraeli, Chancellor of the Exchequer—"To diminish by one half the amount the present duty on malt." The Prince Consort deliberated with the mover on this proposition.[7] Owing to the immediate resignation of the Ministry this resolution did not pass into law.[8] From 1836 to this date upwards of 1400

[1] H. C., March 10, 1835. [2] H. L., March 10, 1835. [3] Feb. 1848.
[4] H. C., July 5, 1850. [5] H. C., May 8, 1851. [6] H. C., June 17, 1851.
[7] His Life, Vol. II. [8] H. C., Dec. 3, 1852.

petitions containing scores of thousands of signatures, were presented in favour of repeal, while only two or so were presented against it.

1853. Motion by Mr Ball—"That the Farmer may be exempt from the Malt Duty on such quantity of malt as he may require for his own use made from barley of his own growth"—ayes 69, noes, 73.[1]

1853. Motion again made.[2]

1854. Motion by Mr Gladstone to raise duty to 4s. and bere malt to 3s. 1d. This occasioned a very long debate—ayes 224, noes, 143.[3] When the bill came on for the second reading, Mr Cayley moved that it be read six months hence, and made a telling speech on behalf of the grower of barley and the consumer of beer. No fewer than twenty-two other gentlemen joined in the debate, and their speeches unitedly fill thirty-three pages of Hansard. For the second reading—ayes 303, noes 195.[4]

1860. Question—Lord H. Thynne asked the Chancellor of the Exchequer to remit the duty on barley malted for agricultural purposes; No.[5] There were this year presented to Parliament 584 petitions, with 30,795 signatures attached to them, for the reduction or repeal of the duty.

1863. Motion noted under Parliamentary Inquiries.

1864. Motion by Colonel Barttelot that the consideration of the reduction of duty on sugar be postponed "until the House shall have the opportunity of considering the expediency of the reduction of the duty upon malt." The discussion on this motion fills forty-two pages of Hansard. Motion lost by 248 votes.[6]

1864. Motion by Mr Morritt—"That in case of any modification of the Indirect Taxation of this Country, the Excise on Malt requires consideration"—ayes 166, noes 118.[7]

1865. Motion by Sir F. Kelly—"That in any future remission of Indirect Taxation, the House should take into consideration the Duty on Malt with a view to its reduction and ultimate repeal"—ayes 171, noes 251.[8]

1866. Motion by Sir F. Kelly repeated—ayes 150, noes 235.[9]

1867. Motion included under Parliamentary Inquiries.

1867. Deputation from the Central Anti-Malt Tax Association waited upon Mr Disraeli to ask for a Commission of Inquiry.[10]

[1] H. C., June 12, 1853. [2] H. C., Aug. 8, 1853. [3] H. C., May 9, 1854.
[4] H. C., May 15, 1854. [5] H. C., Feb. 24, 1860. [6] H. C., April 14, 1864.
[7] H. C., June 24, 1864. [8] March 7, 1865. [9] H. C., April 18, 1866.
[10] January 15, 1867.

1868. Commutation. Mr Gladstone would support a commutation of brewers' licence duty into an additional duty on malt.[1]

1868. Noted under Parliamentary Inquiries, 1867-8. Between 1864 and this date upwards of 2,400 petitions containing upwards of 255,000 signatures were presented for the repeal, and 25 petitions with 2,347 signatures against it.

1869. Question by Mr M'Combie as to alteration in duty: Chancellor of Exchequer—"Any answer I might give at present would only do injustice to so large a subject."[2]

1869. Question by Sir G. Jenkinson if any relief would be given to the agricultural classes: Chancellor of Exchequer believed the benefit would be divided between the owners of land and consumers of beer, "little or none going to the farmers."[3]

1870. Deputation from the Council of the Central Chamber of Agriculture, representing seventy-two Chambers, waited upon the Chancellor of the Exchequer to ask the repeal. Reasons—because it interferes with the most remunerative rotation of crops, and limits the growth of barley; because it acts as a fine upon high farming; because farmers are deprived of the use of malt and grain as food for animals; because the English farmer is placed at a disadvantage as compared with the foreign farmer, who is free to use germinated grain without payment of duty, and to compete in the meat markets against home produce; because the Malt for Animals Act is inoperative, by reason of the expense; because it does not pay to grow the inferior kinds of barley; because the labouring classes would brew their own beer. Mr Lowe—I must tell you frankly it is simply impossible. All our duties on fermented liquors hang together .... if I could find means of putting the duty at a later stage on beer instead of malt, nothing would give me greater gratification."[4]

1870. Motion by Colonel Barttelot, "That it is expedient that in lieu of the present duties on malt, a reduced charge should be made on the manufactured article beer, as it appears to this House that a licence imposed in the same way as the commuted hop duty should be charged on public brewers and a licence to brew on all private brewers," thus—"If you take 2s 8½d per bushel which was the amount of the malt tax, and double that, you would get 5s 5d per barrel, which with the extra 3d for commuted hop duty, making

[1] H. C., March 24, 1868.
[2] H. C., March 4, 1869.
[3] H. C., Aug. 4, 1869.
[4] March 8, 1870.

5s 8d, would be the charge as brewers' licence." Motion withdrawn. Hansard eighteen pages.[1]

1872. Deputation waited upon the Chancellor of the Exchequer to urge as an alternative, if he could not abolish the brewing licence duty, an additional duty of one shilling per quarter.[2]

1873. Motion.—Notice given by Col. Barttelot that he would a month hence call attention to the incidence of the malt tax.[3]

1873. Deputation of "Working Men" waited upon the right honourable gentleman, the Chancellor of the Exchequer, to ask the repeal.[4]

1873. Council of the Central and Associated Chambers of Agriculture requested an interview with Mr Gladstone, which he declined until after the opening of the new session of Parliament. Reply dated November 7, 1873.

1874. Deputation from the Central Chamber of Agriculture obtain an interview to bespeak the repeal.[5]

1874. Motion by Mr Fielden to reduce the duty; ayes 17, noes 244.[6]

1875. Motion by Sir W. Lawson—"That in the opinion of this House the remission of taxation . . . . on licences for brewers would be suitably met by an equivalent increase in the malt duty." Amendment withdrawn.[7]

1875. Question by Mr Storer: Chancellor of the Exchequer could not adopt any of the foreign modes of taxation, without great loss to the Revenue.[8]

1876. Question by Mr Storer, Will the Chancellor of the Exchequer allow the farmer to use his barley, when malted, free from tax—relieve the cultivation of the soil by some modification or relaxation of the Malt Tax? Ans., Not in the power of the Government to make any proposals other than those already in the statutes.[9]

This concludes the summary of the Parliamentary Proceedings on which the observant reader needs no note, unless it be by *Punch*—"The Agricultural Jeremy Diddler." A cartoon of Mr Gladstone with his cash box and financial statement, and a farmer with his hat in hand. "Malt Tax-Repealer—'You don't happen to have six or seven millions about you, sir?' Gladstone—'Yes, I do—and I mean

[1] H. C., March 4, 1870. [2] March 8, 1872. [3] H. C., Feb. 21, 1873.
[4] January 28, 1873. [5] March 4, 1874. [6] H. C., April 23, 1874.
[7] H. C., May 27, 1875. [8] H. C., April 13, 1875.
[9] H. C., June 16, 1876.

to keep them about me."[1] But the politeness of the nineteenth was preceded by the deception of the eighteenth century :—

> "Some say the exciseman takes more than his due,
> Which makes the poor ale-wife look damnable blue;
> But the brewer he cries, I'll fit them for that,
> As long as fresh water is cheaper than malt."[2]

PUBLICATIONS :—Among the publications of more or less interest bearing on this subject, but not generally known, may be mentioned:—

Appeals in Cases, 1715.

Baxter's Repeal of Malt Tax by substituting a system of weighing or the Bavarian system of measuring, 1874.

Ford's Malting and Brewing, 1849, 1862.

Jules' Malt Tax: Total Repeal.

Levesque's Act of Brewing and Malting, 1836, 1854.

Mas Mault—A ballad, 1810.

Muspratt's Chemistry—Malting Beer, 1854.

Prescott's Strong Drink and Tobacco Smoke—cc. 3, 4, 6, 1869.

Smee's Malt Tax, 1865.

Ure's Dictionary—Malt: Beer.

Usher's Malt Tax and Tillage, 1878.

White's Maltsters' Guide, 1860.

TECHNICAL TERMS.—In prosecuting this research among such a varied and numerous collection of records, as this paper has entailed, many quaint forms have been observed. John Mault, Maltman Barry, men's names; malt, 1644; malte, malts, mault, maulte, maulting, maulter, maulster, malster, malt maker, malt factor, malt meter; dry maltster, barley maltster, oat maltster, maltable barley: fat, using-fat, wetting-vat, malt steeping, steep cistern, swimmings, casting, charge-frame, floored, ploughed :—

> "The maltman here and there doth place,
> And up and down his house doth chase,
> His malt to keep from akerspire,
> And after dries it with soft fire."—1644;

anchor-spire, acre-spire, to acrospire, acrospiring, acre-spired, chip, blade, spear, back spear, spired, plumula, plumulæ, plumule, plume, future stem, vegetative germ, sprout, sprouting, spritting, spring,

[1] Punch, 1865. [2] Tricks in all Trades, 1776.

sweating, come enough, coming heap, running out, graining operation, spring malt long, vegetate the acrospire quite home; dead couch, so called between the sixth and twelfth day, sprinkling not having been allowed before that time; backliers, liebacks, liquored, watered, sprinkled: a short wet, short and long water wettings, run wettings; docking, *i.e.* removing part of a floor to kiln and supplying its place from next oldest, &c.; run part wettings, running steepings, run forward, running the duty: kilne: blowing: pip, endin,' tail, radicle, rootlet, comb, coomb, combing, coming, cumming, uncombed; harped, *i.e.* screened: flints, dried ungrown barley; malted raw grain-grown undried; green, unwrought, working, slack, close, free, close-dried, flint, steely, evil-made, Providence, long-steep, short-steep, long, short spring, sprinkled, perfect, blown, snapped, pale, amber, patent, coloured, brown, burnt, black, roasted, run, ship unduty-paid, unlicensed, and permitted malt, the last a sarcastic term to imply duty not paid: malt syrup, malt extract 1710, extract of malt 1831, malt sacharine, malt lozenges.

FOREIGN COUNTRIES—AMERICA, UNITED STATES.—Beer duty only levied, which see.

AUSTRIA.—As above.

BAVARIA.—A uniform duty is levied on that intended for making beer, barm, spirits or vinegar, for all public and private use at 4s. 2d. per 2·75 bushels in the manner shown under Beer Duty. Maltsters not being brewers, &c., pay an annual licence of three florins for every workman employed. From this it appears the duty is charged by registration on grinding, so that for every other purpose malt is duty free, and if the farmer wish to bruise for cattle food he has to obtain a "polette" or certificate as in other cases.

BELGIUM.—Indirectly. *See* Beer Duty.

DARMSTADT.—A Beer Duty.

DENMARK.—No duty levied either on beer or on malt.

FRANCE.—No duty. No maltsters only, in this country; malt not made for cattle food. *See* Beer Duty.

ITALY.—Malt duty not levied here: import malt chiefly used. *See* Beer Duty.

NETHERLANDS.—No tax levied on malt here, except on its use in brewing and distilling; that used for cattle food quite free. An ordinary trade licence is required for making, which varies from 10s. 10d. to £4, 18s. 4d. per annum, "according to the extent and importance of the malting establishment, and a further yearly licence for grinding which varies from 10s. 10d. to £9, 11s. 8d. for each mill employed for that purpose, and in proportion to the extent of such mill," while for making by joint-stock companies the licence duty "is assessed at the rate of 2 per cent. with 28 per cent. thereupon on the amount of the yearly dividend paid by the company to its shareholders." *See* Beer Duty.

NORWAY.—6s. 3½d. per cwt. on the maker on whose premises an officer stays during the process. He keeps the keys of the premises when malting is going on. "The grain is weighed and assessed as it is carried into the malt room, and the tax must be paid within three months after the assessment. Free disposal, however, over the malt is left to the malster, and no Government certificate accompanies the malt when sold." Farmers are allowed to make for feeding purposes—both two and four-legged animals.

An allowance is made on that used in distillation and the duty is repaid on exportation.

PRUSSIA.—Except in Bavaria, Baden, and Wurtemburg, a uniform duty of about 2s. per cent. is charged on being used in making beer, spirits, or vinegar: the private brewer who has a family of at least ten grown-up persons being free: for all other purposes malt may be made free of duty. *See* Beer Duty.

RUSSIA.—". . . . the preparation of malt is entirely free, and subject to no limitation." *See* Beer Duty.

SAXONY.—"The old malt duties were abolished on the institution of the German braumalzstener."

SWEDEN.—No restriction on maker or malt made.

SWITZERLAND.—On imported malt alone is a duty of "30 centimes per cwt.," exacted in this country.

WURTEMBURG.—In this country a duty is paid, in the manner shown under Beer Duty, on all malt used in preparing beer, brandy or spirit, either for public or private consumption. The tax is not exacted when the malt is employed for other purposes under the control of the proper authorities; it is returned in cases of damage. No restriction attaches to the maker of malt except a removal certificate; the authorities commencing their supervision on arrival at the mill, and continuing it to the place of disposal.

The Parliamentary paper from which these summaries, with those under Beer Duty, which see, have been taken, is probably due to the Malt Duty Repealers, who failing in every home device, sought an idea abroad, and fixed upon the Bavarian system, which, though clearly explained by Baxter in his pamphlet, in common with all other systems, has been pronounced as already stated, impracticable "without greater loss to the Revenue."

A shorter Sermon by Dr Dodd.

The Rev. Dr Dodd, a very worthy minister, who some years ago lived a few miles from Cambridge, and had rendered himself obnoxious to many of the Cantabs, by frequently preaching against drunkenness; several of whom meeting him one day on a journey, determined to make him preach in a hollow tree which was near the road side.

Accordingly, addressing him with great apparent politeness, they asked him if he had not preached much against drunkenness. On his replying in the affirmative, they insisted that he should now preach from a text of their choosing.

In vain did he remonstrate on the unreasonableness of expecting him to give them a discourse without study, and in such a place; they were, however, determined to take no denial, and the word Malt was given him by way of text, on which it is said he immediately delivered the following discourse:—

"Beloved,—Let me crave your attention. I am a little man, come at a short warning, to preach a short sermon, from a small subject, in an unworthy pulpit, to a small congregation.

Beloved, my text is Malt. I cannot divide it into words, it being but one; nor into syllables, it being but one, I must therefore of necessity divide it into letters, which I find to be these four—M, A, L, T.

M, my beloved, is moral;
A, is allegorical;
L, is literal;
T, is theological.

The moral is set forth to teach you, drunkards, good manners, therefore—

M, masters;
A, all of you;
L, listen;
T, to my text.

The allegorical is when one thing is spoken and another meant. The thing spoken of is malt; the thing meant is the juice of malt; which you Cantabs make—

M, your master;
A, your apparel;
L, your liberty; and
T, your trust.

The literal is according to the letter—

M, much;
A, ale;
L, little;
T, trust.

The theological is according to the effects that it works, and these I find to be of two kinds—first, in this world, and, secondly, in the world to come.

The effects that it works in this world, are in some—

M, murder; in others,
A, adultery; in all,
L, looseness of life; and in some
T, treason.

The effects it works in the world to come are—

M, Misery;
A, Anguish;
L, Lamentation;
T, Torment.

So much for my time and text. I shall improve this by way of exhortation—

M, masters;
A, all of you;
L, leave off;
T, tippling.

Or, secondly, by way of excommunication—

M, masters;
A, all of you;
L, look for;
T, torment.

Thirdly, by way of caution, take this—

A drunkard is the annoyance of modesty,
The spoiler of civility,
The destroyer of reason,
The brewer's agent,
The alehouse benefactor,
His wife's sorrow,

His children's trouble,
His own shame,
His neighbour's scoff,
A walking swillbowl,
The picture of a beast, and
The monster of a man."

The Rev. Gentleman concluded his discourse in the usual form; and the young men, pleased with his ingenuity, not only sincerely thanked him, but absolutely profited more by this short, and whimsical sermon, than by many serious discourses they had heard.[1]

MALTHEINE.

A mixture which "contained but little malt, and sometimes, none at all," supplied "to publicans who used it in the adulteration of porter."[2]

MATCH TAX.

The famous proposal in this statement—the financial statement—in regard to the Excise was the "match tax," an idea taken from the Americans—"a halfpenny stamp upon every box containing a hundred;" "a penny stamp upon a box containing 100 wax lights," and "a like penny stamp on every box containing 100 fusees"—estimated revenue £500,000. "I have no particular advice to propose," observed Mr Lowe, "but the motto should be something like this, 'Ex luce lucellum,'" *i.e.*, "Out of a light a tiny gain." The resolution for the imposition of this duty was carried by a majority of 157—ayes 201, noes 44.[3] For the adjournment of the debate,[4] ayes 50, noes 116. For the original resolution 113, against 51, majority 62. The bill was then presented and read the first time. The match-makers and their sympathisers, were now fully alive to the intended imposition and formed a procession, with placards as a mark of their disapprobation, to present a petition to the House of Commons against the proposed duty, but they were stopped by the police who had previously given them notice that

[1] Temperance Orator. [2] C. S. G., 1868. [3] Hansard, 1871.
[4] Mr Dixon.

such a form of presentation was illegal. The Chancellor of the Exchequer withdrew the resolution, April 25.[1] It transpired on the 1st day of May, that stamps had been prepared at a cost of about £1000. Mr Bowring observed in the House of Commons, that this was not "a matchless budget."

A pamphlet, "The Match Tax, A Problem in Finance," written by W. Stanley Jevons, M.A., Professor of Political Economy in Owens College, Manchester, bears the impress of a facsimile of the proposed "match stamp" on the first page. The writer supported the tax. Published by E. Stanford, 6 & 7 Charing Cross, 1871. A humorous poem is also to be found in Jerdan's Essays and Lyrics —"Lucifer Lowe."

MAYO MEMORIAL.

The Mayo Memorial, or in full, "The Civil Service Mayo Memorial Fund." Earl Mayo, when known as Lord Naas, in 1859, obtained the repeal of the superannuation tax on Civil Servants. By his persistence in effecting the repeal of this deduction from salary, of which a lucid historical sketch appeared in the *Morning Advertiser*, his Lordship earned the best thanks of the civil servants; and when it became known that, on February 8, 1872, he was assassinated in India, while acting in the capacity of Governor General, the time, mournful though it was, seemed to have arrived when an expression of those thanks should be made to his widow and orphan survivors. The intention first appeared in the *Daily News* of Tuesday, April 30, 1872, and Lord Henniker soon afterwards informed intending subscribers that their donations would be received at 76 Brook St., London.

The Civil Service Committee was formed on May 15, 1872, and when completed, the Inland Revenue, for this committee, it must be borne in mind, was not a single departmental committee, was represented by the Chief Inspector and twelve other leading members. Lord Henniker stated that one of the late Earl's most cherished desires was to rebuild Palmerstown House; and that the Central Committee was resolved to do so, and, in the event of there being a surplus, to erect a statue to his memory in Westminster Abbey. The subscription list was fixed to have been closed on November 30, but this

[1] Hansard, 1871.

was not done until December 18, 1872, and then only conditionally, when it was agreed that a cheque for £1620 should be at once remitted to the General Committee (*i.e.*, the Central), with an intimation that a small amount then held over, with further expected contributions, would be afterwards remitted. The Storekeeper General acted as treasurer to this department, whose liberality placed his contribution at the head of the list, being more than the Customs, the next largest department. Of the £1697, 5s. 4d. (£1657, 5s. 4d., plus £40 sent direct to the General Committee by the Collector of Dublin Collection) subscribed by the Civil Service, £668, 18s. 8d. was contributed by the Inland Revenue, and seldom or never, did this department contribute so freely and without discussion. The final Civil Service Statement was made on May 9, 1873. The amount received by the General Committee was £9020, but the list remained open until April 30, 1873. The last meeting of the General Committee was held in June, when it was resolved that the total subscription be placed with Messrs Glynn & Co.; that a sum not exceeding £400, be expended on a bust of the late Earl, to include the expenses of fixing in Westminster Abbey or St Paul's Cathedral; that his Royal Highness the Duke of Edinburgh, K.G., Lord Richard Grosvenor, and the Marquis of Drogheda, be the trustees; and that they be satisfied that the remainder be applied to the rebuilding of Palmerstown House. Lady Mayo expressed her thanks by letter to the General Committee, through her three sons —Mayo, George W. Bourke, Charles F. Bourke. The letter was dated "Palmerstown," Sept. 6, 1873.[1]

MEAD: METHEGLIN DUTY.

This beverage first became liable to an Excise duty on the Restoration of Charles II., and its makers on the motion of Mr Pitt in 1784.[2] The duty began at one halfpenny per gallon, payable by the maker, and gradually rose, with the need for the sinews of war, with the wars with France, the war of succession, and other national emergencies, to eighteen pence per gallon, leviable in Great Britain, after the Union, and on importation from Ireland, but at five shillings per gallon from elsewhere. The licence duty, originally

[1] C. S. G., 1872, 1873. [2] H. C., June 30, 1784.

one pound, but increased to two, in 1815, for four years, and the growing duty were repealed in 1834.[1]

MEASURES.

The only measures to be noticed here are the bushel, and the gallon.

THE BUSHEL.—Until the imposition of the duty on malt in England in 1697, the bushel measure was little used as a unit of charge by the Excise. In anticipation of this imposition, however, Mr Thomas Everard, a Commissioner of Excise, with other gentlemen, made experiments in the presence of several members of Parliament in the House of Commons, "to find the true content of the standard bushel." This was called the Winchester Bushel, and was used in Scotland on the imposition of the malt duty there in 1713. The Irish Winchester bushel contained 2178· cubic inches, the English 2150·4 :[2] the Imperial first used, Jan. 1, 1826, 2218·192.[3]

THE GALLON.—In Scotland to the Union in 1707[4] the spirit gallon contained "827·232 solid inches,"[5] afterwards, the same as in England, 231· cubic inches, but this was questioned by a Dr Wybard, and occasioned Messrs Walker and Shales, "two general officers in the Excise," to make an experiment by which it appeared that it contained only 224 cubic inches. This was repeated by Mr Shales at the Guildhall, London, on May 25, 1688, before the Lord Mayor, the Commissioners of Excise, and the Astronomer-Royal, with the same result, though "for several reasons it was at that Time thought convenient to continue the former supposed Content of 231 cubic Inches."[6] On the introduction of the Imperial gallon the Board directed the reduction of wine to the Imperial gallon by dividing the former by 1·24. The Irish gallon contained, in 1778, 217·6 cubic inches, and the factor directed to be used to charge it to an English one, was ·942.[7] The Imperial gallon of 277·274 cubic inches, introduced on January 1, 1826, established uniformly in the United Kingdom.

It may be noted here that no reference is made to these variations in the appendices to the Commissioners' reports.

[1] 4 & 5 W. IV., c. 77. [2] P. Rep., Malt I., 1808. [3] 5 Geo. IV., c. 74.
[4] Scotch Parl., January 16, 1707. [5] Lindsay's Gauging.
[6] Clark's British Gauger. [7] Country Instructions, 1778; P. Rep., 1808.

MEIKLE'S POSTAL AND REVENUE ESTABLISHMENTS.

"Our Postal and Revenue Establishments" considered with a view to utilising the former for the receipt and payment of revenue moneys, the granting of licences and sales of stamps in all provincial towns, and to a thorough consolidation and amalgamation of the surveying branches of these departments. "By a Civil Servant"—Wm. Meikle, supervisor.[1] Pages 600, price 5s. Pitman, London. 1866.

The *Huddersfield Examiner* published an adverse article on this publication, particularly so on the supposed animus shown towards Surveyors of Taxes, which resulted in a defence being offered to the Huddersfield editor, who declined to insert it, but which afterwards appeared in the *Civil Service Gazette.* The *Financial Reformer* favourably reviewed the publication. The discussion between Mr Meikle and the Surveyors not only assumed the form of long letters but also the character of angry ones, and then extended itself to his own fellow employés, who seemed desirous to leave the affairs of administration with their honours and the Lords of the Treasury. The author's detractors were met by Maxwell, who gave an historical outline of the bold and useful services which Mr Meikle had given his colleagues. The next feature was the unproductive sale of the work; which induced Saxon to suggest the individual purchase of a copy, and others to make similar propositions. The liability was stated at £300. "He is one of the veteran champions of Excise Reform," writes the editor, "and even those who do not endorse all his views cannot but admire his unceasing energy, and the great ability with which he advocates them . . . . We are led into these remarks by the receipt of a circular announcing the formation of a committee in Cork to raise subscriptions for the object referred to, and of which Mr Thomas Crabb, Inland Revenue Office, Cork, is treasurer." Fergus followed by observing that "Immediate aid would be double aid." The Central Committee were appealed to by the gentlemen in Cork, but they (C. C.) stated that "the request had been declined for reasons so obvious that they need hardly be stated. The proposal is certainly premature, and otherwise inopportune and infelicitous."

[1] C. S. G., 1867.

This pecuniary testimonial not being generally supported by the department, a meeting was held at Derby on Aug. 12, 1868, to support the munificent desires of their *confrères* in the far-famed city for butter, and this appears to have been the only one. The committee observed on July 27, in making their "final appeal," "of him it may truly be said that he polished departmental ruggedness, and breaking out like a new sun illumined the official mind, dispelled its night of hereditary gloom, and taught it to conquer its own dark and dismal prejudices." The amount subscribed exceeded £39.[1]

"He has lost some £300 by the publication of his book"—writes Humanitas.

The author, known under the *nom de plume* "Hugh Littlejohn," having unfortunately incurred the displeasure of the Commissioners and retired upon a superannuation of £65, it was proposed that this "old, tried, able, and fearless champion of the rights of his colleagues" should receive "the solid good wishes of grateful friends." "He succeeded in many of his efforts on behalf of others; indeed he only failed conspicuously in guarding his own interest." The "initial action" was taken by Fergus on April 6, 1874, by the issue of a circular to the department from which, by the 17th of October, he had received a sum of no less than £161, 2s. 4d.;[2] the ultimate receipt being £161, 6s. 9d.—£1, 17s. 8d. expenses.[3]

METHRINGHAM'S FACILITATOR.

"The Facilitator, or Inland Revenue Officers' Assistant and Ready-Reckoner, being tables to find areas of malt cisterns, couch-frames and kilns, cast floors of malt, and reduce gross bushels of malt to net; to money charges of malt and British spirits (from the smallest fraction of a bushel and gallon); also paper, soap, stage carriage mileage and licences; and an alphabetical list of the licence duties, yearly and quarterly; the gauges of brewer's goods reduced to Q. B. G., and also twenty per cent. added; the bushel divisors multiplied nine times; an easy method to prove multiplication; to find the mean depths of malt floors, mentally; a regulation order respecting suspected couches, &c.; and an explanation of the allowances on malt," by B. Methringham, late Supervisor of Reading

[1] C. S. G., 1868. [2] C. S. G., 1874. [3] Treasurer's Account.

District. A small cloth-bound book of about thirty pages, printed in 1850.

MILITIA.

The staff were formerly[1] liable to serve in the militia, and on the extension of the "Supplementary Militia" regulations to Scotland, the Commissioners made an allowance to an officer who found a substitute,[2] until 1823, when the Lords of the Treasury directed the Commissioners to discountenance the practice. Exemption was obtained by legal enactment in 1827.[3]

MILLS AND KILNS.

Only in Ireland do they come under Excise surveillance. It was in contemplation to so place them as early as 1816; this is stated by the Committee on Illicit Distillation in that year—the survey is a measure which "has been for some time past in the contemplation of Mr Hawthorn, chairman of the Excise Board, that a clause has been prepared under his direction for giving it effect."[4] Afterwards legalised, in 1830 re-enacted, in 1834 exacted under minute regulations, 1853 performed also by Revenue police, the duty has had a demoralising and even ruinous effect upon many young officers. It has been suggested that the survey should be made by the Royal Irish Constabulary:[5] it has also been suggested that the survey should be abolished.[6]

MOLASSES.

The permission to use "Mellasses"[7] in the distillery, with the exception of the times of scarcity of corn,[8] was not granted until some two Parliamentary Committees had enquired into and reported upon the subject,[9] and the distress of the West Indian in 1848,

[1] Leadbetter, 1766. [2] 1798-1810. [3] 7 & 8 Geo. IV., c. 53, s. 11.
[4] P. Rep., 1816. [5] C. S. G., 1853, 1870. [6] C. S. G., 1868, 1869.
[7] 1 W. & M., c. 24. [8] 1799, 1803. [9] P. Rep., 1807, 1831.

induced Lord John Russell to acquiesce,[1] and not in the brewery until 1874.[2]

The inquiry of 1831, at the instance of Mr Poulett Thomson,[3] against which some fifty-four petitions were presented, was restricted to the use of molasses, and among the reasons assigned against it were these—That it would be at the expense of the landed interest at home; that the poor might suffer from an enhanced price; that the rapidity of fermentation endangered the revenue derived from beer; that a solution with water might be added to wort without detection; that the different rates of spirit duty in the different countries raised an almost insuperable difficulty. With respect to the distiller he was allowed a drawback upon the article until 1855, then upon giving bond, he was allowed to remove it from the custody of the Customs into that of the Excise, duty-free, until the repeal of the duty in 1874, when he exercised nearly absolute control over its use; it was now for the first time, that the brewer, who had ceased to pay a beer duty and had become numerically less, was permitted to use it on paying the countervailing duty on sugar. (*See* Sugar Duty.)

It was customary in Edinburgh in 1799 when there were many illicit stills worked in that city on molasses wash, to say on seeing a man exemplify the triumph of matter over mind, that he was "molassed."[4]

MOREWOOD, SAMUEL.

This gentleman wrote—

An Essay on the Inventions and Customs of both Ancients and Moderns in the use of Inebriating Liquors, interspersed with interesting anecdotes illustrative of the manners and habits of the principal nations of the world, with an historical view of the extent and practice of distillation, both in its relation to commerce and as a source of national income, comprising much curious information respecting the application and properties of several parts of the vegetable kingdom, by Samuel Morewood, Surveyor of Excise,

[1] 11 & 12 Vic., c. 100. [2] 37 V., c. 16. [3] H. C., June 30, 1831.
[4] P. Rep., 1831.

London. Dedicated to the Right Hon. Sir Frederick John Robinson, Chancellor of the Exchequer. Longman, London: 1824.

"A Philosophical and Statistical History of the Inventions and Customs of Ancient and Modern Nations in the Manufacture and Use of Inebriating Liquors, with the present practice of distillers in all its varieties . . . . . by Samuel Morewood, Esq., Collector of Excise." Dedicated to Earl Ripon. Pages 746. Longman, London, 1838. This work exhibits very extensive research, no fewer than six hundred authorities being quoted; and as an example of meritorious labour on a particular subject is without an equal in the professional productions of this department.

MOSS'S GAUGING.

"A Treatise of Gauging containing not only what is common on the Subject, but likewise a great Variety of new and interesting Improvements, with the Demonstrations of several very useful and remarkable Properties of Vessels and Instruments, relative to this Art. Illustrated with necessary Examples, and adapted both to the speculative and practical Readers. By Thomas Moss." "Most Humbly Dedicated," "To the Honourable the Commissioners of His Majesty's Revenue of Excise, within the Kingdom of England, &c." Pages 268; published 1765.

MULTUM.

A compound of opium and colouring matter, made into balls, and used as a substitute for malt and hops.[1] Price 5s. per lb.

MUM DUTY.

With the exception of probably the brief period of one year (1813) this was an import duty. It was classed with imported beer, and the duty was first levied at three shillings per barrel, but raised during that exceptional year to one pound five shillings per barrel. Imposed in 1660—though the word mum is not then used—transferred to the Customs in 1825.[2]

[1] P. Rep., 1819. [2] 12 C. II., c. 23; 6 Geo. IV., c. 13.

MUNICIPAL ELECTIONS.

The Lords of the Treasury, by minute, dated August 8, 1807, having expressed their disapproval of this department joining in these local contests, the Commissioners subsequently ordered that, "you, your supervisors and officers are in no manner of way to interfere or meddle with local or municipal Politics in any Borough." This regulation has since fallen into disuse.

MUTUAL GUARANTEE FUND.

This fund was established in 1852 to relieve officers, who were required to give security for the faithful discharge of their duties, from the difficulty which they sometimes experienced in obtaining sureties, and from the obligations under which it was thought they lay to them; and to relieve the Board from the necessity of ascertaining the sufficiency of the sureties, though they were still required to give a personal bond for £1000.

The "paid up Fund" was fixed at £10,000, to be invested in Government Securities, in the name of the Chairman of the Board, under the title of "The Inland Revenue Guarantee Fund," and to be held by the Board for the purpose of making good to the Crown any loss occasioned by the default of any contributor; £500 being kept in a convenient bank to meet repayments on retirement. The contributions by the various grades are these—

A Collector, ...	£50
A S. G. E. now Inspector, . .	30
A Supervisor, ...	10
A Clerk, ...	10

And any other official in such an amount as the Board might determine. These contributions are payable in moieties; the first within three and the last within six months, after appointment, and repayable with interest on retirement.

Each individual, in the event of any claim for loss, and the fund being reduced below the fixed amount, being required to pay his proportion of the sum required to replace the sum withdrawn.[1]

A full cash statement, so far as the writer has observed, has not been issued to the contributors, except in 1857, after the Moah

[1] C. 1 R.

deficit of £4466, 14s. (£5215, 4s.—£748, 10s. the proceeds of effects)[1] towards which each then contributor was called upon to pay in the following proportion—

A Collector, . . .	£7	2	6
A Surveying General Examiner, .	4	5	6
A Supervisor, . . .	1	8	6
A Clerk, . . .	1	8	6

The mode of settlement may be exemplified by one made with a supervisor in 1871—

Deposit, . .				£10	0	0
Interest, . .				3	10	0
				£13	10	0
Proportion of "defalcations,"	£3	12	11			
Paid on account, . .	1	8	6			
				£2	4	5
				£11	5	7

A printed statement of a very partial character, issued in 1873, on the Oding defalcation of £2605, 10s. 2¾d. (£4272, 17s. 2¾d.—£1667, 7s. realised by sale of effects) informed the guarantors that though the fund would not be reduced below £10,000, yet each contribution on being withdrawn would be repaid, less a deduction at the following rates—

A Collector, . . .	£10	11	8
An Inspector, ...	6	7	0
A Supervisor, . . .	2	2	4
A Clerk, . . .	2	2	4[2]

The other claims have been both small in number and amount.[3]

A Secretary, with the exception of a broker, occasionally, appears to have been the only paid employé, and to have been usually selected from the Secretary's office.

NESBIT AND LITTLE'S PRACTICAL GAUGING.

It was on the introduction of the Imperial System in 1826 that a

[1] P. Rep., 1868. [2] Circular, Aug. 18, 1873.
[3] Circular, 1857; P. Ret., 1868.

new edition of this book, with a key in a separate volume, appeared. A subsequent edition is described as—"A Treatise on Practical Gauging, by A. Nesbit, Master of the Commercial and Mathematical Academy, Oxford Street, Manchester, and W. Little, Officer of the Excise. A new edition containing a table of areas calculated for the new Imperial Gallon. Dedicated by permission to the Honourable Commissioners of the Excise." York, 1832.

In addition to the ordinary contents in such a book, it contained a chapter on specific gravity, an abstract of the principal malt acts, an alphabetical list of duties and drawbacks, precedents for making up accounts, and the names of higher functionaries in the "Excise Establishment." Pages about 280, 8vo.

NIGROMALTINE.

"A highly concentrated extract of black malt," prepared by Messrs Bailey & Son, chemical manufacturers, Wolverhampton, in a convenient and very soluble form, to afford brewers the means of adjusting the colour of their worts. Its use is sanctioned by the Board.[1]

OATHS.

Of these there were many—both official and trade. The "solemne Oath" of office was the earliest, and was taken by all subordinate officers before the Speaker of the House of Commons.[2] Next those of Allegiance and Supremacy,[3] and then that of Fees. Of the former writes Lord Clarendon, in his State papers in 1634, "This oath was devised by the State for the better trial how his Majesty's subjects stand affected, in point of their loyalty, and due obedience, as appeareth by the Act 3 Jac. cap. 4, and by his late Majesty's declaration, both in the Book of Admonition to Christian Monasteries, in his proclamation, and by his instruction to the Judges; who have divers times declared at their Assizes, 'That his late Majesty's pleasure was that such as would voluntarily take the said oath should not be molested in their estates for their religion.'"

[1] Brewers' Guardian, 1874. [2] P. O., 1643.
[3] Green's State Papers, 1663; 12 Charles II., c. 23.

After these came those of Test and Abjuration "to prevent the growth of Popery."[1]

There were consequently in all, formerly, six oaths exacted[2] of all below the rank of collector, and with the oath of "Accompt" seven of that rank.[3] In Scotland "The tacksmen or collectors of . . . . . excise" and their "servants" made oath that they would not engage in any trade in which articles, subject to Customs or Excise duties, were vended,[4] and most of the previously-named oaths were renewed by the collector, in that country, on his first assuming that office,[5] and, generally, on the accession to Crown, within six months of that event.[6]

The test oath was partly condemned by the House of Commons in 1787, when, on the motion of Mr Beaufoy, to repeal it, the division which followed showed 100 ayes, against 178 noes.[7] It however was discontinued in 1828, while most of the others were continued down to 1831,[8] when Lord Nugent obtained leave to bring in a bill, which had been prepared by the Boards of Customs and Excise, to abolish some of the numerous oaths required to be taken by the Customs and the Excise: [9] a bill which his Lordship appears to have successfully carried through, as all were now discontinued except those of Allegiance, Office, and Account,[10] and these were, in 1835, changed into declarations.[11]

With respect to the trade oaths and affirmations they were indeed very numerous,[12] having gradually increased with the imposition of new duties, until in one twelvemonths no fewer than 194,612 were taken in this department alone,[9] a frequency of administration which the Legislature thought weakened "the reverence and respect which should attach to such solemn obligations," and led to the repeal of some and to the substitution of the declaration in the place of others, in 1835, as already stated.

Officials were, formerly, specially appointed to administer these oaths and affirmations, and their names were published in the *London Gazette*,[13] and in Scotland the collector received a commission from the Court of Exchequer to authorise him to do so; a duty which he was enjoined to perform "in the most solemn manner,"

[1] L. G., 1704. [2] Leadbetter's Royal Gauger, 1743. [3] L. G., 1696. [4] Oct. 8, 1663.
[5] Scotch Instructions, 1804. [6] H. C., July 4, 1727; Procl., Nov. 13, 1727.
[7] H. C., March 28, 1787. [8] Alcorn's Compendium of Chronology.
[9] H. C., April 13, 1831. [10] 1 & 2 W. IV., c. 4. [11] 5 & 6 W. IV., c. 62.
[12] 9 Anne. [13] 1710.

and then subscribe it "by virtue of a commission from the Court of Exchequer."[1]

OFFENCES.

That his successor may know the misdeeds committed in his station, each officer was enjoined to enter every offence in his General Entry Book as early as 1723, and that the reports of offences might be complete, each supervisor was enjoined to report through his collector "who in conjunction with the Supervisor in whose district the Fraud, &c., was Committed must give the Board a Just Account thereof,"[2] an injunction, with that of quoting the law infringed, and the penalty incurred, set aside in Scotland in 1810.

With the increase of literary ability came the desire from the officer that his report of the discovery of an offence might be sent to their honours, that they may become familiar with the literary attainments of the subordinate section. This was again and again suggested between 1856 and 1862,[3] but not authorised until about 1872.[4]

OFFICE ACCOMMODATION.

In common with other subjects of pressing necessity, on a medium being established through the *Civil Service Gazette*, the extension of the provision and payment of office accommodation by the Board was urged,[5] and those then provided at "public houses" were condemned,[6] yet curious to relate no persistent effort was commenced until 1865, when one "Botrab" reopened the desire by suggesting a revenue office in every town in which there is a revenue officer,[7] and a return was made to Parliament respecting the accommodation provided in Ireland, where, as early as 1807, it was recommended that a "Chamber or Office" should be provided in cities and towns where officers meet.[8] The claim was continued in 1867, by the Central Committee in their Address, under "matters of minor

[1] Scotch Instructions, 1804. [2] 1735. [3] C. S. G., 1856, 1859, 1861, 1862. [4] Instructions. [5] C. S. G., 1854, 1855. [6] Idem., 1858; see Corn Returns. [7] C. S. G., 1865. [8] P. Rep., Fees, 1807.

importance," in which it is stated in referring to the supervisor, in particular, that his house is "daily invaded by miniature mobs of persons of every shade of character and appearance," by which his "privacy is thus invaded, property injured, and domestic comfort impaired." These, with other observations, were supported by a written controversy,[1] until 1871, when the Inverness Committee included the claim in their proposed Address—"We feel that we should have been relieved from the intrusion of having our private apartments turned into public offices, or that we should have been allowed compensation." The subject received little further consideration down to the appointment of the Civil Service Inquiry Commission in 1874.[2]

That an extension has been conceded will appear on comparing the Estimates for rent, repairs, fittings, furniture, fuel, fire insurance, light, &c., for the years ended March 31, 1869 and 1876, which represent, respectively, £34,100 and £42,740. It was formerly the custom to announce the opening of offices in the *London Gazette*,[3] and in some instances to obtain the authority of Parliament to establish them.[4]

OFFICE KEEPER.

This person was formerly an individual of some importance. He was provided with a "proper deputation," upon the delivery of which the collector was enjoined to take his receipt, attested by two witnesses, and by the town crier that he had made known the fact of the appointment to the public, and the "deputation was required to be locked up, except on sitting days, or on any special occasion." This office keeper was also supplied with a commission, and one was appointed in most market towns to receive entries,[5] which unless made with him were illegal.[6] *See* Entry.

OFFICE RECEIPT.

During the recoinage in 1696, it was common to give what were termed office receipts, to persons who chose to pay in their money

[1] C. S. G., 1869, 1870. [2] Idem., 1872. [3] 1686. [4] 1 W. & M., c. 24.
[5] Scotch Instructions, 1804. [6] 1832.

at the Chief Office, with a view to being repaid the same sum by a collector in any part of the country, except in 1702, in the counties of Durham and Northumberland. The plan appears to have originated with a fear, "lest in a time when so Much Money is drawn from the People to be Recoined, they should be deprived of the lawful Money amongst them." The same reasoning was applied to collectors who were required to remit by Bills of Exchange rather than by specie.[1]

OFFICER.

"The designation officer applies equally to all. It should not therefore be applied specially to one rank," wrote the Central Committee, in their address in 1867. This is correct—it is generic, and has long included all under the Commissioners as "officer,"[2] "His Majestie's Officers,"[3] and instead of "Collectors, Surveyors, Gagers, and other Persons,"[4] or "Collector, Supervisor, Gager, or other Officer,"[5] the brief qualified expression, "proper officer,"[6] or "superior officer."[7] The law further defined on the consolidation of 1849 that the old designation "Officer of Excise,"[8] should be replaced, except in certain cases, by Officer of Inland Revenue.[9]

Numerous other distinctions familiarly current need little or no note. These are formed by prefixing the name of the duty charged, the place of survey or duty, and perhaps the most recent introduction is chemical officer. Among the older ones may be mentioned "sworn,"[10] established, or fixed officer, by way of distinction from occasional officer, supernumerary officer; also decayed or charity officer instead of, as now, the superannuated officer.

The reader is now referred to Official Designations.

OFFICIAL DESIGNATIONS.

For some little time those under the rank of collector were called "subservant officers," "under officers,"[11] "servands,"[12] "Excise-

[1] L. G. [2] 12 C. II., c. 23. [3] 6 G. II. [4] 1 W. & M., c. 24.
[5] 5 & 6 W. & M., c. 20. [6] 12 Anne. [7] 23 & 24 Vic., c. 114.
[8] 22 & 23 C. II., c. 13. [9] 12 Vic., c. 1. [10] 1 W. & M., c. 22.
[11] S., 1644; S., 1648. [12] S., 1681.

Men,"[1] "under excisemen,"[2] and it was long common to prefix such words as under, sub, supernumerary, and pro, to the recognised designations. The earliest classified list referred to in these papers was made to Parliament in 1705, and on the Union of Scotland with England, Leadbetter tells us in the Royal Gauger, that one John Downer was "sent down Methodizer of the Excise into Scotland, where he continued near two years; and having faithfully discharged that important Trust with great Judgment and Moderation he returned to London." With the subsequent Union of Ireland and the consequent consolidation of Boards, the official designations are now, with few exceptions, the same as all three countries. These particulars will be found under Candidate, Expectant, Assistant, Supernumerary, Ride Officer, Division Officer, Officer, Gauger, Collector's Clerk, Examiner, Supervisor, Collector, Surveying General Examiner, and Secretary.

OFFICIAL REVIEW.

The title of a weekly newspaper which appeared and disappeared in 1866, but in this brief time advocated the claims of this department to general amelioration.

OFFICIATOR.

The higher ranks have always commanded a more or less experienced "official stop-gap," but in the case of those below that of examiner, persons who had neither commissions nor authorised training were frequently directed to perform their duties, the Board having issued upon one occasion, at the least, an order reproving supervisors and officers for having given such instructions as to qualify them—would-be-officiators—"to become occasional officiators" without their Honour's authority, and cautioning the said officials not to do the like again "upon pain of being discharged."[3] These uninstructed aïdes were engaged when the supernumerary was employed on the round, when no one minuted for restoration was available, or, lastly, when no expectant or dropped assistant was un-

[1] 1647. [2] 1663. [3] 1752.

employed,[1] and they came under the discipline of the diary, and were apparently liable to answer at the "collectorial bar" until their services, on actual survey, were directed to be discontinued.[2]

It is under this official designation that perhaps the only instance of piece-work can be found in the out-door section of the excise branch; and that is, in licence writing, in which each officiator, whether commissioned or otherwise, was required to fill up sixty licences to 1855, and from that date has been required to fill up eighty licences and counterparts to entitle him to a day's pay.[3]

In the case of an officer who performed the duty of another, or double duty, he had to make a special application to the Board through the proper collector at the next sitting for the amount due to him for that service, until 1854, when the collector was authorised to pay him without.[4] The examiner and inspector are entitled to certain allowances when officiating, but a supervisor performing the duty of another supervisor, with his own, is still, strange to state, entitled in many instances to only travelling expenses.

"Jobs" and "officiatings,"[5] paid, were retained by the collector in a list roundly to the board from 1818 to 1849, and with respect to extra duty a duplicate list was sent by him quarterly to 1833.

The supervisor was first enjoined to send a roundly officiating list to the collector, and another list to the accountant in 1828, and that to the collector had to be sent on by him down to 1855. The revised regulations of 1828 were extended to Scotland and Ireland in 1830. The form of list in use in 1878 is the form of list prescribed in 1828.

ORANGE LODGES.

It was in compliance with a request contained in an address of the House of Commons to William IV. that his Majesty consented to use every means "for the effectual discouragement of Orange Lodges and generally of all Political Societies, excluding persons of a different religious faith using secret signs and symbols, and acting by means of associated branches," that the Lords of the Treasury, by a minute dated March 18, 1836, forbade every person in the service of the Crown to join them, and ordered those who had

[1] 1828. [2] 1828, 1854. [3] 1833, 1855. [4] 1778-1854. [5] S., 1804.

done so to withdraw from them, under pain of dismissal, "without hesitation."

ORIGINAL GRAVITY.

The idea of testing the original gravity of wort may be traced back to 1831. Dr Ure who then gave evidence before a Parliamentary Committee,[1] suggested an apparatus, which he stated would not cost more than five shillings, for ascertaining the spirit produced in the wash by attenuation and for checking the declared or original gravity of the wort.

Various suggestions were offered down to 1847, when experiments were made to prove whether the method of partial evaporation, proposed by Mr Peter Stevenson, Philosophical Instrument Maker, in Edinburgh, "is an accurate means of discovering the Original Gravity of Distillers' Wash, Beer, Ale, &c.; as well as the quantity of spirit contained in any unsweetened compound or fermented liquor." Various other methods had been suggested, but all had proved impracticable in consequence of the absence of "one or other of the indispensable requisites, simplicity and accuracy." The present method immediately received attention at the hands of the Honourable Commissioners who directed a series of experiments to be at once made, by their own officers, to test the accuracy of the method and its application to fiscal purposes. But these gave uncorroborative results, and the "whole subject" was then referred to Dr Thomson, of Glasgow, who also arrived at unfavourable conclusions. The discovery of a correct method, however, was of too great importance to be allowed to remain uninvestigated, and accordingly Mr Dobson, S.G.E., and Mr Geo. Phillips, supervisor, were instructed to reopen the scientific pursuit. These gentlemen commenced their labours in the month of February, and after a most patient and laborious investigation, which frequently occasioned their alternate attendance, by day and by night, they successfully concluded, in the month of August, a series of experiments which subsequently formed the data for legislative enactment. The report made by these two gentlemen consists of fifty-two foolscap pages, and is dated, "Excise Office, Aug. 2, 1847."

Accounts of the process will be found in the various handbooks,

[1] Molasses.

published since the discovery, and in the Engineer, of 1857, in two papers contributed by Mr Kay; and other particulars, showing the award to the discoverers and the value of the discovery to the revenue, will be found under Beer Duty and Laboratory—which see.

Dr Ure's two ideas have been accordingly confirmed, though the first idea is not at present in general use—acted upon only in cases of suspicion.

OXYGENATED MURIATIC ACID MAKERS' LICENCE DUTY.

Every person in Great Britain who made oxygenated muriatic acid to be used in bleaching linen, was required to pay an annual licence duty of £5, 5s., to make entry of his premises, to allow the officer to survey, to give bond in double the amount of duty on the salt he might have in his premises free of duty, and to provide the necessary requisites, including "a sufficient and just hydrometer," for ensuring the proper use of the salt, for it was, apparently, for the protection of the salt duty that this licence duty was levied. Imposed 1815,[1] repealed about 1825.[2]

PACEY'S REMINISCENCES OF A GAUGER.

Life jottings of Joseph Pacey, late Collector of Inland Revenue, in support of his son's widow and children. A small book of about 130 pages, published by Tomlinson & Whiles, Newark. Price half-a-crown. 1874.

PAINE, TOM.

This celebrity entered the department in December 1762, but was dismissed in the following terms, by Board's minute, dated August 27, 1765—"Thomas Paine, Officer of Alford Ride, Grantham Collection, having on July 11th stampt his whole Ride, as

[1] 55 G. III., c. 66. [2] 5 G. IV., c. 65.

appears by the specimens not being signed in any part thereof, though proper entry was shown in Journal, and the Victuallers' Stocks drawn down in his books as if the same had been surveyed by him that day, as by William Swallow, Supervisor's letter, of 3d instant, and the Collector's report thereon, also by the said Paine's own confession of the 13th instant, ordered that he be discharged; . . . . ." Paine the following year petitioned to be restored—

LONDON, *July* 3, 1766.

"Honorable Sirs,—In humble obedience to your Honours' letter of discharge, ... I delivered up my commission, and since that time I have given you no trouble. I confess the justice of your Honours' displeasure, and humbly beg leave to add my thanks for the candour and lenity with which you at that unfortunate time indulged me. And though the nature of the report and my own confession cut off all expectations of enjoying your Honours' favour then, yet I humbly hope it has not finally excluded me therefrom, upon which hope I humbly presume to entreat your Honours to restore me. The time I enjoyed my former commission was short and unfortunate—an officer only a single year. No complaint of the least dishonesty or intemperance ever appeared against me; and, if I am so happy as to succeed in this my humble petition, I will endeavour that my future conduct shall as much engage your Honours' approbation as my former has merited your displeasure.—I am, your Honours' Most dutiful humble Servant,

"THOMAS PAINE."

Upon this the Board minuted on July 4, 1766, "To be restored on a proper vacancy." S. T.

In 1772 he wrote "The Case of the Officers of the Excise," of which numerous copies were printed for distribution among members of Parliament, "and the printer complains that he has not yet been paid for printing though much had been contributed and little spent."[1] One of the Commissioners was so struck with the excellence of the style in which the paper was written, that he gave Paine a letter of introduction to Benjamin Franklin.[2]

His biographer informs us "Troubles seldom come alone. He had long been known at Lewes as an officer, inattentive, if not unfaithful." Through his "enterprise on the water and his intrepidity

[1] Oldy's Life of Paine, 1791. [2] Beeton.

on the ice, while watching the smugglers at Lewes he was known to the people by the appellation of 'Commodore.'" "He had sometimes condescended for the purpose of concealment, to drink a bottle with an examiner. But the eagle-eyes of the excise were not to be blinded by bottles. With the watchfulness and jealousy and acuteness which make the excise the cleanest collector at the smallest rate, his supervisor had for some time beheld him dealing as a grocer in exciseable articles, as a grinder of snuff, buying smuggled tobacco; at others conniving in order to conceal himself. He was therefore dismissed from the excise after a dozen years' service in April 1774. He petitioned for restoration; but such was his notoriousness that his patron was unable to protect him."[1]

PAPER DUTY.

It has already been shown under the paper on Duties that an excise duty was levied on paper in England in 1643. A duty was next imposed in England in 1696, and placed under the management of Commissioners other than excise.[2] The excise duty in Great Britain having been first levied after the Restoration, in 1712, and in Ireland in 1798, and continued to be leyied without interruption until repealed in 1861: the licence duty on the maker having been imposed at £2 in 1784, doubled in 1815, 5 per cent. added in 1840, and repealed in 1870:[3] a similar duty of varying amount having also been imposed for some seventeen years on the stainer in Ireland.[4] The rates of duty at one time no fewer than seventy-eight,[5] varied according to size, kind, quality, and commercial value of the fabric: the mode of denoting that the duty had been charged consisted in stamping a peculiarly-designed paper label affixed to the wrapper on each parcel; the amount charged never much exceeded one and a half million.

Down to the year 1830 it was levied with apparently little opposition, but on Sir H. Parnell, Bart., denouncing it in his book on Financial Reform, M'Culloch in his Commercial Dictionary,[6] and Martin in his Taxation of the British Empire,[7] petitions began to be poured into the House of Commons for its repeal, until the incidence of the

[1] Oldy's Life of Paine, 1791. [2] L. G., 1696. [3] H. C., April 11, 1870.
[4] C. 1, 13 R. [5] 1781. [6] 1832. [7] 1833.

duty was referred, in common with every other, to the masterly minds of the Parnell Committee in 1833. Sir Henry and his coadjutors recommended two years afterwards a reduction in the number of the rates of duty, the earlier payment of the duty, the consolidation of the existing laws, the reduction of the penalties and other minor changes,[1] which having been adopted appeared to have appeased the trade until 1845, when petitions were once more presented to Parliament for the abolition of the impost, and returns were ordered by Parliament,[2] at the instance of private members, to apparently assist the agitants in pressing their claim. The repealers commenced in earnest in 1849 by presenting no fewer than twenty-one numerously-signed petitions, after which Mr Milner Gibson presented another, and moved—"That such financial arrangements ought to be made as will enable Parliament to repeal the excise duty on paper," but in this he was not successful by 101 votes—ayes 89, noes 190;[3] he again and again made similar motions with similar results,[4] until, once again, in 1858, he obtained an agreement to—"That the House is of opinion that the maintenance of the Excise on Paper, as a permanent source of revenue, would be impolitic."[5] This was the first sign of unanimity for the repeal, and it so remained until 1860. Mr Gladstone then moved the repeal of the duty. The second reading of his Bill was divided upon in the House of Commons by Sir W. Mills, with a majority of 53 for the original motion—ayes 245, noes 192,[6] and again in the House of Lords, by Lord Monteagle, whose speech fills, with those of the other noble lords, one hundred and six pages of Hansard, with a majority of 89 against the original motion—contents 104, "not contents" 193—as many as 251 noble lords being present in person. This money Bill was accordingly rejected.[7]

Mr Gladstone undeterred by this rejection, included the same resolution in his next financial statement,[8] carried it through both Houses, and, thus, to the satisfaction of the lovers of literature, repealed the duty on October 1, 1861.

"The reductions which the repeal enabled us to make in the establishment," write the Commissioners in their Sixth Report, "were as follows:—

[1] 14 Rep. [2] 1842, 1845, 1849. [3] H. C., April 16, 1850.
[4] H. C., May 12, 1852, ayes 107, noes 195; April 14, 1853, ayes 80, noes 279.
[5] H. C., June 21, 1858. [6] H. C., March 12, 1860.
[7] H. L., May 21, 1860. [8] H. C., April 15, 1861.

6	Foot-walk Supervisors,	£1,470
7	Riding Supervisors,	1,785
130	Division Officers,	17,550
36	Ride Officers,	4,680
2	First Class Assistants,	190
1	Export Surveyor,	350
1	Export Officer,	87
183	Total,	£26,112

"There has been a further annual saving of about £2500 for stationery."

The Paper Hangings Sellers' Licence Duty was peculiar to Ireland—imposed 1805, repealed 1823.[1]

PARNELL COMMITTEE.

Sir Henry Parnell, Bart., M.P., by whose name this committee is usually known, wrote, in 1830, a work "On Financial Reform," which, in 1832, had reached the fourth edition, and in which occurs the following paragraph—"As no inquiry has been made into this department for a great many years, it is impossible to know whether it be well or ill-managed; some circumstances have transpired, particularly with respect to the distilleries, which afford reason to suppose that, if an inquiry were instituted, occasions would be found for making many improvements, and saving a great deal of expense." Sir Henry's idea was accordingly realised—"Treasury Chambers, April 23, 1833.—The King has been pleased by His royal letters patent under the Great Seal, to appoint the Right Honourable Sir Henry Parnell, Bart., Henry Berens, and Henry Lewis Wickham, Esqs., to be His Majesty's Commissioners for enquiring into the department of Excise, and for examining into the whole system of the management and collection of that revenue in all its branches throughout the United Kingdom."[2]

They state the origin of the Royal Commission in these words—"In the case of the Excise, letters, it appears have been written from time to time by the Treasury to the Commissioners, calling upon them to diminish their establishment; and inquiries have

[1] C. 14 R. [2] L. G., 1833.

been instituted in the Treasury with the view of ascertaining the practicability of diminishing it. We here particularly allude to the letters of the Secretary of the Treasury, bearing date 13th August 1821; 11th August 1826; 9th June 1827; 20th February 1830; and 24th December 1831. But we have shown . . . the Treasury failed to attain their object. . . . It was under these circumstances, therefore, that the appointing of a Commission to inquire into the Excise department was the only measure that remained for the Treasury to adopt, in order to arrive at a satisfactory conclusion as to the possibility of effecting those retrenchments or improvements which seemed to be both practicable and expedient."[1]

Proceeding upon this authority, these three Henries at once commenced their inquiry in a most systematic style, and did not complete it until fully three years after the date of their appointment. Their reports were no fewer than twenty in number, and formed the most exhaustive examination into, and report upon, the department, which has ever been made; for which the estimated grant "for their assiduity, care and pains in the execution of the trust reposed in them" was £600.[2]

At the risk of being tedious, they are as follows:—

Résumé.

Report.	Subject.	Pages.	Date.
First,	Tea Permits and Surveys, .	176	July 26, 1833.
Second,	Wine Permits and Surveys, .	86	Sept. 2, 1833.
Third,	Excise Court of Summary Jurisdiction and Court of Appeal, .	70	Sept. 2, 1833.
Fourth,	Survey of Brewers, . . .	46	Dec. 9, 1833.
Fifth,	Stone Bottles and Sweets, .	32	Jan. 20, 1834.
Sixth,	Tobacco and Foreign Spirits, .	144	Feb. 26, 1834.
*Seventh,	Part 1, British Spirits, Manufacture of, ...	458	July 25, 1834.
Eighth,	Starch, ...	82	April 25, 1834.
Ninth,	Vinegar, ...	44	June 18, 1834.
Tenth,	Malt—Ireland, ...	10	July 21, 1834.
Eleventh,	Accounts, ...	224	Dec. 23, 1834.
*Seventh,	Part 2, British Spirits, Disposal of,	136	Feb. 27, 1835.
	Carry forward, . .	1508	

[1] 20 Rep. [2] P. Ret., 1835.

Report.	Subject.	Pages.	Date.
	Brought forward,	1508	
	Digest: Reports 1 to 10,	32	Feb. 27, 1835.
Twelfth,	Auctions,	62	March 20, 1835.
Thirteenth,	Glass,	158	May 16, 1835.
Fourteenth,	Paper,	186	June 30, 1835.
Fifteenth,	Malt—Great Britain,	280	Aug. 27, 1835.
Sixteenth,	Hops,	30	Aug. 31, 1835.
	Digest: Reports 11 to 16,	76	Aug. 31, 1835.
Seventeenth,	Soap,	148	Dec. 16, 1835.
Eighteenth,	Bricks,	30	Feb. 18, 1836.
Nineteenth,	Licences,	138	July 12, 1836.
Twentieth,	Establishment,	464	July 12, 1836.
	Digest: Reports 1 to 20,	258	July 12, 1836.
	Total Pages,	3370	

The comprehensive character will be seen by this brief outline, and again by the digests, the last having been made by a special order of Parliament,[1] and with respect to the contents of the reports these will be found summarised and incorporated in this series of Papers.

A brief History of Excise Management, based on these reports, was prepared and presented to Parliament in 1838.[2]

The numerous minute changes proposed by the Royal Commission were reported upon by the Commissioners in 1837 in a report of 230 pages;[3] again by order of Parliament in 1842,[4] when to the 95 recommendations, 45 replies were given, leaving 50 unnoticed, pages 10;[5] and, lastly, apparently in 1846,[6] while the successive Chancellors of the Exchequer have accepted and adopted the financial proposals.

Mr Disraeli observes in his maiden budget in 1852, in referring to their reports—"Sir Henry Parnell who was at the head of a Royal Commission to inquire into the Excise, and to whose labours we are indebted for some of the most valuable documents in our Parliamentary Library."[7]

[1] Feb. 27, 1836. [2] P. Ret. [3] P. Ret., 1837. [4] Sep. 7, 1841. [5] P. Ret., 1842. [6] P. Ret., 1846. [7] H. C., Dec. 3, 1852.

PARODY.

In a prosecution conducted by the Attorney General against William Hone for writing and publishing a parody on the Athanasian Creed, entitled "The Sinecurist's Creed," the defendant, who was his own counsel, in making his defence, produced an analogous parody, published in "The Foundling Hospital for Wit." It is as follows :—

"Proper Rules and Instructions, without which no person can be an Exciseman.

Quicunque vult

"Whosoever would be an Exciseman, before all things it is necessary that he learns the Art of Arithmetic,

"Which Art, unless he wholly understand, he without doubt can be no Exciseman.

"Now the Art of Arithmetic is this, we know how to multiply and divide. Desunt pauca.

"The 1 is a figure, the 2 a figure, and the 3 a figure.

"The 1 is a number, the 2 a number, and the 3 a number; and yet there are Desunt plurima.

"For like as we are compelled by the Rules of Arithmetic, to acknowledge every figure by itself to have signification and form;

"So we are forbidden, by the rules of right reason, to say, that each of them have three significations or three powers.

"The 2 is of the 1's alone, not abstracted, nor depending, but produced.

"The 3 is of the 1 and 2, not abstracted, nor depending, nor produced, but derived. So there is one figure of 1 Desunt nonnulla.

"He therefore that will be an Exciseman, must thus understand his figures.

"Furthermore, it is necessary to the preservation of his place, that he also believe rightly the authority of his Supervisor.

"For his interest is, that he believes and confesses that his Supervisor, the servant of the Commissioners, is master and man:

"Master of the Exciseman, having power from the Commissioners to inspect his books; and man to the Commissioners, being obliged to return his accounts.

"Perfect master and perfect man, of an unconscionable soul and frail flesh subsisting; equal to Commissioners, as touching the respect which is shewn him by the Excisemen, and inferior to the Commissioners as touching their profit and salary.

"Who, although he be master, and man, is not two, but one Supervisor.

"One, not by confusion of place, but by virtue of his authority; for his seal and sign manual perfect his commission; his gauging the vessels, and inspecting the Exciseman's books, is what makes him Supervisor.

"Who travels through thick and thin, and suffers most from heat and cold, to save us from the addition of taxes, or the deficiency in the funds, by corruption or inadvertency.

"Who thrice in seven days goes his rounds, and once in six weeks meets the collectors, who shall come to judge between the Exciseman and the Victualler.

"At whose coming the Excisemen shall bring in their accounts, and the Victuallers their money.

"And they that have done well by prompt payment, shall be well treated.

"And those that have done ill, by being tardy in their payment, shall be cast into jail; and the Excisemen whose books are blotted, or accounts unjustifiable, shall be turned out of their places.

"These are the rules, which except a man follows, he cannot be an Exciseman.

"Honour to the Commissioners, fatigue to the Supervisor, and bribery to the Exciseman.

"As it was from the beginning, when taxes were first laid upon Malt, is now and ever will be till the debts of the nation are paid. Amen." 1818.

A copy of this is inserted in an old "Area Book" now in Northampton collection.

PASSENGER VESSEL LICENCE DUTY,

Introduced on July 6, 1828, by a special Act of Parliament, to afford passengers an opportunity of purchasing exciseable liquors on board. The licence was at first granted by the Commissioners only, but in 1834, within the limits of the Chief Office, by four persons specially appointed, and in the country by the Collector and the Supervisor. It is exigible in all three countries; and was one pound until 1840, when, by an addition at 5 per cent., it became one guinea, at which it has since stood. The number of licences issued in 1878 was about 440.[1]

PATENT MEDICINE VENDORS' LICENCE DUTY.

Simultaneously with the imposition of the stamp licence duty on the vendors in Great Britain, in 1783, was the imposition of a stamp duty on the articles sold.

Both were levied with apparent uninterruption until 1830. Ten petitions were then presented against them, and in 1844 the incidence again came under consideration by a return being made of the receipts during the ten preceding years. As the collection of the duty could be effected only by instituting a comparatively large number of prosecutions,[2] the stamp licence appears to have been changed into an excise licence in 1864, with a view to a more exact charge—an expectation fully confirmed.[3]

THE RATES OF DUTY.

1783.	London and Edinburgh, £1		Elsewhere,	5s.
1802.	Do.	£2 Cities, &c. 10s.	do.	5s.
1875.	Everywhere, ...			5s.

PATRIOTIC FUND.

The department subscribed to this fund in 1855 £77, 2s. 6d.[4]

PAWNBROKERS' LICENCE DUTY.

The proprietor of the "Lugchovy"[5] (Pawnshop) engaged the attention of Parliament in 1744 and 1745, when strenuous efforts were made to place his business under Magisterial restraint;[6] and he again engaged the attention of that august assembly in 1785, at the

[1] C. 21 R. [2] C. 1 R. [3] C. 13, 18 R. [4] C. S. G., 1855.
[5] Slang Dictionary. [6] H. C., Dec. 4, 1744; Feb. 1, 1745.

instance of Mr Pitt, who proposed that he should pay a stamp licence duty of £10 in London and Edinburgh, and £5 elsewhere, in Great Britain,[1] against the permanent exaction of which he petitioned the following year, the House of Lords, to hear him or his counsel,[2] though without the desired effect.

These rates of duty were increased by one half in 1815, extended to Ireland in 1842, placed under the supervision of the excise in 1861, commuted into excise rates in 1864 and reduced to one rate of £7, 10s. everywhere in 1872. Pawnbroking was examined by a Parliamentary committee in 1871,[3] and their report was referred to a select committee in 1872,[4] when the uniform rate, just noted, was authorised, and a Magistrate's certificate exacted, except in Ireland, of every new beginner.

		Increase per cent.
Duty charged y. e. March 31.	1861—£26,512	
	1862—£27,062	2.66
	1877—£32,520	22.66
	1878—£32,753	23.54[5]

It may not be unserviceable to mention that an unlicensed shop is termed in the language of slang, a "Leaving shop," a "Dolly shop."[6]

PAY LIST.

Before this came into use it was customary to send to the Collector a "Printed Receipt" with the amount payable. The Pay List was introduced in 1833. It is now called the Receipt and Licence List. See page 308.

PECUNIARY EMBARRASSMENT.

An uncongenial subject. It would appear that the frequency of this insolvent position occasioned the issue of general regulations in 1830, by which every one imprisoned for debt, and not able to resume his duties within fourteen days—extended in 1831 to twenty-eight days—was suspended; in 1841, by which every one imprisoned for debt was not allowed to resume business, or to be paid his salary

[1] H. C., May 9, 1785. [2] H. C., May 26, 1786. [3] H. C., Feb. 22, 1871.
[4] H. C., June 17, 1872. [5] C. 1, 13, 20, 21 R. [6] Slang Dictionary.

for the time absent, without the sanction of the Board; in 1848, by which every one who did not produce his schedules within twenty-eight days should be superseded; in 1862, by which every embarrassee should at once inform the Commissioners of his insolvency, under the liability to be dismissed, and that he be at once suspended, and "unless very strong cause be shown to the contrary, within a reasonable time, be superseded." In 1868 it occasioned the issue of a Treasury Minute, dated December 15.

PENSIONS COMMUTATION ACTS.

1869 and 1870. At first these Acts applied only to the Army and Navy and the members of the administrative departments of those combatant forces. It was probably the editor of the *Civilian* who first publicly asked, "What argument can . . . . be urged against the extension of the Act to the rest of the Civil Service?"[1] and who will not aid the promoter in his endeavour to obtain an extension? The promoter was Mr Monk of franchise fame. He gave notice in the House of Commons on April 3, 1871, that he would move its extension, and this he did fifteen days afterwards, when he found a seconder in the person of Mr Alderman Lusk, and a supporter in even the Chancellor of the Exchequer himself, on condition that it be restricted to the abolition of office, as he undoubtedly foresaw the gain which it was alleged would accrue to the Exchequer, as afterwards shown.

Petitions in favour of the measure were presented by this department from Arbroath, Birkenhead, Dalkeith, and Tower Hill. Though desired, the departments in general did not petition, and the Westminster sanction, though obtained as early as June, was secured perhaps principally by the personal interview of, and the issue of circulars to, the members of Parliament, by those materially interested, who formed themselves into a committee about July 1870. Having nearly completed their labours, they were somewhat injudicious in asking for "a subscription sixpence each from members of the Civil Service," towards defraying the expenses incurred, without giving their names or the items of their expenditure, which led to an adverse criticism, in which it was suggested that both the names of

[1] March 1871.

the committee and the details of the outgo should be first given. These were soon supplied. The outlay amounted to £73, 7s. 9d., and the cash statement contained the fact that each member of Parliament had been canvassed by circular three times. Of the £52 odd received by the treasurer towards its discharge, £37, 12s. 3d. was contributed by the Inland Revenue Department.[1]

It was observed of the Government,[2] "we will take power to purchase the retiring allowances of our employés at a price which will enable us to sell them again at considerable profit to the general public." The following Table was prepared to show this:—

Age next Birthday.	Sum offered by Treasury for each Annuity of £100.	Sum required by Government for Annuity of £100.	Amount of Government gain and Annuitant's loss.
25	£1485 3 10	£1926 13 4	£441 9 6
35	1403 8 10	1781 13 4	378 4 6
45	1255 16 8	1552 1 8	296 5 0
55	1030 7 0	1235 16 8	205 9 8

The provisions of the Extension Act, 1871, were announced in the London Gazette.[2] Instructions to persons desirous to commute were issued to Collectors in a circular, dated August 30, 1871, which is contained in the reprint of the General Orders of that year, and the Commutation Board commenced its labours in October 1871. See Civil Service Year Book, 1873-7.

The extent to which the provisions of this commutation have been valued by this department, will be found in the annual superannuation returns to Parliament from 1871 downwards.

PEPPER DUTY.

The duty on pepper was first levied in 1643 (See Duties), again in 1695,[3] and continued until transferred to the Customs in 1825.[4] So zealous were the officers in the discharge of this duty, that it became necessary to caution them not to make any charge "on pepper in pickled state."[5] The dealer in 1823 made entry of his premises, paid a licence duty, similar to the tea dealer, and kept a stock ac-

[1] C., 1871. [2] Aug. 11, 1871. [3] 6 & 7 W. & M., c. 18.
[4] Order in Council, Feb. 2, 1825. [5] 1824.

count, which was checked by the officer. In 1828 the permit and stock account systems were discontinued, and the officer only examined the stock. In 1839 the examination was discontinued. In 1869 the licence duty was repealed.

PERQUISITES.

Both perquisites and gratuities were formerly very freely accepted by this department,[1] often in direct opposition to the desire of the Commissioners, and to such an extent as to have induced Mr Pitt to have moved for a return of them in common with fees.[2]

Among those allowed may be mentioned—

2s. 6d. per ton for burning seized vessels.[3]

6d. in the £ to	£40 to a collector, £30 to a surveyor, £20 to a gauger,	Per annum on foreign wine duty at out-ports.[4]

The proceeds of the sale of the old books, about thirty guineas per annum, to the Principal Examiner in Ireland.[5]

20 galls. spirits at proof,	20 lbs. coffee,		
20	20	to collector, inspector	Or, if quantity insufficient, then a distribution on a proportionate scale, per annum.[6]
15 „ „	10 „	to port and tide surveyor,	
6 „ „	8 „	to warehouse keeper,	
8 „ „	8 „	to port gauger,	
8 „ „	8 „	to import officer,	
8 „ „	8 „	to sample drawer,	

A free house at certain distilleries.

Among those not authorised—from 20 to 52 gallons of spirits per annum, and grazing for a cow and a horse by the Irish distillers.[5]

The acceptance of gratuities has been frequently forbidden,[7] and to impress the injunction on the official mind, the "Meat and Drink" or "Bread and Cheese" letter was read at sittings until a recent date.

See Allowances, Emoluments, Fees, Rewards.

[1] H. C., Feb. 9, 1782. [2] H. C., June 2, 1783. [3] 1771. [4] 1786. [5] P. Rep., 1807. [6] 1822. [7] 1804, 1828, 1833.

PERMITS AND CERTIFICATES

Were preceded in purpose by the "Ticket" or Warrant of 1643,[1] and known in Ireland as the "let-pass."[2]

These documents were introduced on August 2, 1720, by an Act of George the First, whose "revenues" were very "much lessened" by the "clandestine importation" of "strong waters" without the payment of the duty, by persons who at that time were rapidly increasing in both number and wealth, owing to the almost total inability of the officials of that day to summarily cope with their illicit enterprise. They were granted without "fee or reward," to accompany at first only spirits and sweets in quantities of one gallon and upwards, and any quantity respectively, and the terms were used synonymously, unless the "authentick certificate" given by the distiller carried a distinction, though ultimately they were employed to represent two very distinct documents. The announcement of these conditions of removal occupied the whole space of the London Gazette of July 12, 1720.

The evasion of these regulations of course next engaged the attention of these unprincipled persons, who adopted the plan of "drawing" their permits "so low" and of "so mean a quality," that they destroyed them, and then added similar quantities, but of superior quality, to their stocks, and, to such an extent was this practised, that a certificate was required for the removal of even a small bottle of foreign brandy; while the British and foreign spirits were ordered to be kept apart.[3] Another plan, by the tea dealer, who had now come under these regulations, consisted in obtaining a permit for the removal of a portion of his stock, but instead of doing so, he obtained the permitted quantity of the illegal possessor, and removed it direct to his customer. In this he was afterwards checked, first by exacting a written request—required to be kept three years, first in 1796—and secondly, on finding an excess in his stock, by seizing it.[4] This plan was known as a "Dry Permit," and in the case of spirits, generally obtained of a dealer—who had improperly sent out without the required document—to whom the retailer, who had received into stock an equal quantity of unduty-paid spirit, paid a customary fee of half-a-crown or three shillings per gallon.[5] And to avoid the need of a permit altogether, distillers

[1] P. O. [2] 33 Geo. II., c. 10. [3] 1722. [4] 1725. [5] P. Rep., 1835.

used what in their slang were called "Liverpool Jars," which did not contain four gallons, the quantity for which on removal in 1805 the document was required.[1]

Further minor, but in the aggregate important, restrictions, such as the mode of conveyance, a limited time for the removal,[2] were soon added, and then came the employment of the "false permit;"[3] to meet this artful imitation it would appear that "Chief Office" for London, "Excise" for the country, the name of station and officer, the number of certificate and book, and a water-mark were added to the "let-pass;"[4] the detachment from the counterpart made in a "waving line;"[5] the use of stamps to impress "The Buyer's Permit," "The Seller's Permit,"[6]—in Ireland perhaps represented by the "Re-Permit;" the printing of permits in black for British and in red for foreign spirits,[7] in green, brown, pink for other purposes; the impression of an official seal on the back of each permit,[8] while suspicious-looking documents were forwarded to the Permit Examiner, whose office will be afterwards noticed, who, if he agreed with the opinion, forwarded the supposed counterfeit to the proper supervisor for further investigation. The substitution of the excise permit for the distiller's certificate of manufacture was suggested in 1798.[9]

With respect to the removal of private stocks, these let-passes were issued in every market town, upon the owner taking an oath that the duties had been paid,[10] and in London convenience was so far studied by opening four offices for the purpose,[11] while in the case of removal, from Ireland to England or Scotland, a duplicate was sent to the officer of the port at which it was intended to discharge it.[12] In the case of large consignments to one person at the same place by two or more portions at different times on the same day, a permit was granted to accompany each portion,[13] and in the case of a return the quantity was endorsed on the document which was then attached to its counterpart,[14] but latterly on request to the supervisor under modified conditions.[15] The issue of permits to spirit dealers and retailers, and to others for the removal of foreign spirits and tobacco was discontinued in 1848, when the modern certificate, already referred to, was prepared for the use of those traders, and the Customs prepared and issued certificates to the others on the payment of the duties—*see* form in G.O. A shaft, however, has

[1] H. C., March 25, 1805. [2] 1747. [3] 1781, 1783. [4] 1782. [5] 1837. [6] 1784. [7] P. Rep., 1807. [8] S., 1818. [9] P. Rep. [10] 1787. [11] L. G., 1789. [12] 1833. [13] 1826. [14] 1821. [15] 1874.

been sent at this system by "Broad Arrow," who has suggested in lieu of the spirit certificate an adhesive penny stamp, to be called the "spirit removal stamp."[1]

To glance at the legislation. The subject at length became so important as to form a distinct head of enactment under 23 Geo. III., c. 70, amended by subsequent Acts down to the consolidated Act of 2 William IV., c. 16, with, to 1877, some three other amendments.

The office, previously alluded to, consisted in 1779 of a Chief Permit Examiner at a salary of £90, an Examiner at £70, and four assistants at £40 each, whose duties included not only the issue of the books[2] which have varied in size from quarto to folio, and in those forms from 2, 3, 4, 6, 12, to 26 sheets.[1] . . . . but also the receipt of those returned at the expiration of each quarter,[3] or other period[4] as well as the permits taken up after use, but which prior to being returned were arranged and endorsed much after the manner as in 1878.[2] Losses of course being laid before the Board.[5] In accordance with the idea of consolidation this office was merged into that of stores in general, but not, perhaps, until after the system had reached its highest adoption, as it appears that although some had been relieved of the obligation, there were at the time the Parnell Committee wrote their Twentieth Report, no fewer than ten in which a permit or certificate was required to be issued, but in all of which, except that of the distiller, the committee recommended the total abolition.[6] The number of permits issued with spirits alone in 1833 was 1,634,680.[7]

The introduction of this system too, created a class of employés called permit writers, independent of the officers who also performed similar duties in smaller places, but who were often "not at home." The duties of these writers in the cities and larger towns, were, on market days, in particular, very pressing, as not unfrequently there would be a hundred persons waiting for permits at one time; and the hours of attendance in London, though fixed at seven, often exceeded that number, as the "Request Notes upon the file at the expiration of the seven hours shall be cleared off."[8] In Ireland in 1807, there were no permit writers, but in consequence of the abuses practised by the officers in taking fees it was suggested that there

[1] 1821, 1798, 1871, 1835. [2] 1787. [3] 1848. [4] 1864, 1872. [5] 1800, 1832, 1835, 1841. [6] 1836. [7] P. Rep., 1835. [8] 1826.

should be.[1] The salary of this employé was £50 in 1789, increased to about £73 in 1811, to £85 in 1813, with a retrospective payment of the increase for a period of two years,[2] and to £100 in 1858.[3] The permit writer's permission expired in 1860.

PLATE DEALER'S LICENCE DUTY.

Before this form of charge, a duty was levied on wrought plate, at so much per ounce, which commenced in Great Britain in 1720, in Ireland in 1730, and was then placed under the management of the Commissioners of Excise, and collected, in part, by their officers.[4] It was repealed in Great Britain in 1758, when a licence duty was substituted, which was extended to Ireland in 1785. This stamp licence duty was levied by the stamp authorities, until the evasion of it became so apparent, that in 1861 its collection was placed under the supervision of the excise branch, to whom it was finally transferred, in 1864, by commuting it into an excise licence duty.

			Inc. per cent.
Duty received, y. e. March 31, Rates the same.	1861	£20,857.	
	1862	£21,672	3·97.
	1877	£41,280	97·91.
	1878	£42,216	102·46.[5]

An interesting account of this duty will be found in the Commissioners' First Report, and an important Judicial Decision in their twentieth report.

PLAYING CARDS LICENCE DUTY.

The history of the playing card in Imperial records may be traced back to 1631; the King then entered into a "covenant" with the card makers of London that they should bring so many gross—"Twelve dozen Pair to the Gross"—of cards weekly and pay at the rate of eighteen shillings per gross.[6] But to leap to the excise connection.

This department was first entrusted with the collection of the playing card duty in the cities of Dublin and Cork in 1729, not

[1] P. Rep. [2] T. W., July 23, 1813. [3] T. W., Feb. 13, 1858.
[4] L. G., 1720; C. 1 R. [5] C. 1, 13, 20, 21 R. [6] Procl., 1631.

however as an Imperial tax, but as one to encourage inland navigation in that country; it also included visiting cards—the maker taking out a licence once in three years and giving bond in £200.[1] It was not until 1828 that a stamp licence duty was levied in the United Kingdom; this continued down to 1864 when it became an excise licence.[2] The licence duty on the seller was repealed by Mr Lowe in 1870,[3] that on the maker alone remaining. There were in 1878 only 16 makers—15 in England, and 1 in Ireland.[4]

Y. e. March 31, { 1863, duty £805.[2] Increase per cent.
1870, „ £1161.[4]— 44·22.

PORTS.

The attendance at the ports originated with the inland duties on spirit, tea, coffee, &c., over and above the Customs, and in London and some other places it became customary to speak of it as the "Port Establishment." Thus the London Port Establishment, in 1779, consisted of 132 persons—a collector £220, a clerk £70, another £60, a third £50, an inspector £100, a land surveyor £90, an assistant surveyor £60, another £50, 5 tide surveyors £70, 3 port gaugers £65, a warehouse keeper £50, an assistant £40, 2 landwaiters £55, 2 coastwaiters £55, and 110 tidesmen 3s. per diem when on duty.[5] The others were called the "Outports."[6]

The port duties in Scotland were transferred to the Customs authorities in 1830.

PORTER'S WORKS.

The Inland Revenue Directory of Great Britain with an Appendix; compiled by James Porter, Officer of Inland Revenue. "The object of this work," writes the author, "is to supply a want that has been much felt throughout the department in Great Britain in the management of Establishment and other licences." 1871.

The Inland Revenue Gazetteer of Great Britain, compiled from the census population tables, 1872, and the Inland Revenue Schemes 1874, with permission, by James Porter, of the Surveying Branch of

[1] P. Rep., 1809. [2] C. 13 R. [3] H. C., April 11, 1870. [4] C. 21 R. [5] P. Ret., 1779. [6] P. Rep., 1797.

the Inland Revenue. A very carefully prepared work for the same purpose as the Directory.

1700 copies were printed, of which 900 were supplied to subscribers, and the remainder, including a complimentary subscription order of 100, was purchased by the Board. A new edition is contemplated on the completion of the census of 1881. Butler and Tanner: Frome and London.

POST HORSE DUTY.

One penny per mile travelled, or one shilling per horse hired, and a licence duty of five shillings per annum, were the first forms of this, at first, stamp duty. It will be observed that there was an alternative mode of payment given—an unusual condition.

The stamp authorities collected the duty through the agency of their own staff for seven years, when the Chancellor of the Exchequer proposed to let the duty "to farm in like manner as the turnpike tolls were farmed,"[1] for he said "it was a matter of notoriety that the duty in its present mode of collection was most flagrantly evaded, and although every individual who by law was liable did in fact pay it, yet there was a large proportion of that sum which, from the frauds of the collectors, and the collusion between them and the innkeepers, never found its way into the exchequer." Mr Marsham observed that it was "a mode of collecting the public revenue repugnant to the principles and practice of the constitution." The Bill was carried, but not before a division had been taken on each reading, with the following result:—Ayes 76, noes 39; ayes 162, noes 95; ayes 116, noes 56.[2] The Act was made perpetual in 1790.[3]

The Commissioners of Stamps at once proceeded to carry out the provisions of the enactment, and in 1788 advertised the duty to let to farm for a period of two years; and, in 1790, systematically divided the whole of Great Britain into seventeen districts, North Britain forming one, North Wales another, and South Wales a third, and announced the period of let at three years, under which regulations, with little exception, they continued to act down to 1835,

[1] H. C., April 4, 1787. [2] H. C., April 26, May 2, 11, 1787.
[3] H. C., April 23, May 11, 1790.

when, on an exposé being made in the House of Commons, and on the trade presenting some ten petitions to the legislature to repeal the system of farming, the Commissioners advertised the duty to let for a period of one year only.[1] This significant sign of compliance was confirmed by the passing of an Act in 1836 to transfer the collection and management from the stamp to the excise authorities on February 1, 1837.[2] The change was announced in the leading metropolitan and provincial newspapers, toll-bars were erected, and officers were appointed to visit them to take up the hiring tickets, and although an improvement upon the system which it superseded, petitions continued to be presented for the reduction or repeal of the duty, with some three hundred for relief from an alleged blunder,[3] until about 1852, when the postmasters themselves submitted that a licence duty, according to the number of horses and carriages kept, should] be substituted for the unacceptable mileage duty. Mr Gladstone, in his maiden financial statement, accepted the proposal, repealed the duty on the distance driven or ridden, and substituted the suggested licence scale,[4] which remained intact until reduced in 1866,[5] and in that modified form repealed in 1869.[6]

First imposed in Great Britain 1779; farmed from 1787 to 1836; extended to Ireland, licence duty only at first, 1804; commuted 1837; repealed 1869.[7]

POTTINGER'S DISTILLERY APPARATUS.

This was twice reported upon. In the first report, which is simply an account of the apparatus, the Committee state—"Mr Coffey, one of our number, has suggested a different and simpler description of apparatus, to be confined with that affixed by Mr Pottinger to the worm; and we are most sanguine in our expectation that by their united operation the entire revenue can be secured on all spirit made with the . . . utensils."—Custom-House, Dublin, Jan. 6, 1821, pages 4. The second report by J. Taylor, Examiner of Surveyors' Books, and Messrs. D. Logie and Æneas Coffee, Inspectors-General of Excise on experiments with the apparatus at Mr Thompson's

[1] L. G., 1788-1835. [2] H. C., July 8, 1836. [3] H. C., June 10, 1852.
[4] H. C. April 18, 1853. [5] H. C., May 3, 1866. [6] H. C., April 8, 1869.
[7] C. 1, 13, 14 R.

Distillery, Carrickfergus, contains the following:—To "record every part of the distiller's operations from the time he brings his wash into the still-house until he takes the finished spirit out of the receiver" without the agency of the officer who may be in charge of the distillery, and, solely by the action of the machinery, not within the control of either officer or distiller. The vessel employed for measuring the wash "may be called the Wash Measuring Charger." It has a mechanical contrivance by which the charging and discharging cocks cannot be open at the same time, and by which the number of times each is opened is registered. An "over-fall pipe" indicates when it is full. The singling and feints receivers are similarly constructed. The "Spirit Receiver" is connected with a spirit measure which registers the quantity run into it. The head of the still is a tube turning down at an angle of 45° into the worm; the safety-valve is on the arm instead of the breast; there are no other openings in the still except a manhole. A three-way cock is affixed to the end of the worm to convey the spirits, feints, or singlings to their respective receivers; the quality being determined by "Mr Pottinger's hydrometer, which is fixed to the worm close to the cock." These officials then suggest that the utensils be secured by locks whose keys should be kept by the "chief officer of the district, or, if necessary, with the Board in Dublin"—the continuance of the charge on the wash. They consider it will save seven-eighths of the fuel now used, avoid a loss of 8 per cent. on the wash by reason of imperfect distillation, afford a gain of 2 or 3 per cent. in spirit produced by allowing more time for fermentation, wash being often run at 10° to 17° by Dicas, save four-fifths of the labour, discontinue the use of the "disgusting article" soap—a ton being used in a month, in a 300 gallon still—and lessen the cost of the plant in a distillery. The advantage to the revenue they state to be less striking than that to the manufacturer—1s. 2½d. per gallon. The apparatus received their approval. Æneas was the recorder of the experiments which probably gave birth to his patent. Pages 8. The official date is April 16, 1821; the Parliamentary date May 18, 1821.

PRESCOTT'S WORKS.

Tobacco and its Adulterations.—After nine short paragraphs of prefatory observations, H. P. Prescott, Examiner, gives the contents of his book, which he divides into seven chapters:—Introduction; Leaves; Vegetable Cells and Vessels, and their Contents; Anatomy of Plants, &c.; Starches; the Microscope; the History, Use, Cultivation, and Manufacture of Tobacco. The letterpress fills 130 pages. The "illustrations, drawn and etched by H. P. Prescott, of the Inland Revenue Department," are beautifully delineated on forty plates. The book does not appear to have been written for revenue purposes exclusively, the word excise being only once used.[1]

STRONG DRINK AND TOBACCO SMOKE.—"The structure, growth, and use of malt, hops, yeast, and tobacco, with 167 original illustrations, drawn and engraved on steel," by H. P. Prescott, F.L.S., Surveying General Examiner. Like his earlier publication, divided into seven chapters:—Introductory; Materials; How Barley Grows; Structure of Barley and some other Seeds; Hops and Yeast; Malt, Beer, Spirit, Tobacco, and some other Leaves. Under Spirit he gives a simple, clear, description of Coffey's Still. Each of the beautiful plates is described on the opposite page. The author did not live to see his work printed. It is edited by T. H. Huxley.[2]

PRINTED GOODS DUTY.

Imposed by Robert Benson in 1712;[3] raised by W. Pitt in 1784;[4] repealed, except silks, by Viscount Althorp in 1831,[5] when no fewer than fourteen petitions were presented to Parliament to do so. It would seem to have been in connection with this duty that the Commissioners in 1767 allowed the officers to stamp lawns and cambrics at the request and expense of the manufacturers.

The duty in 1803 was charged by the square yard at two rates, seven and three-and-a-half pence respectively, and was returned on exportation.[6] A licence duty of £10 was also imposed on the printer in 1784,[4] subsequently increased to £20,[7] but both growing and licence duties were, on a petition being presented to the House of Commons, repealed, except printed silks repealed in 1826,[8] as previously stated, in 1831.[9]

[1] Voorst, London, 1858. [2] Macmillan, London, 1869. [3] L. G.
[4] H. C., June 30, 1784. [5] Parnell, 20th Report. [6] Consolidated Act.
[7] C. 1 R. [8] 7 & 8 Geo. IV., c. 53. [9] 1 W. IV., sess. 2, c. 17.

The printed silk duty yielded a nett revenue of £19,800; the printed cotton £529,000.[1]

PRISONERS.

"Ashby, a soldier and exciseman under the usurper, was clapped into gaol for saying that the King was as much an usurper as Cromwell."[2] But this is not the class of prisoners to which this paper refers. In 1812 (S) the return was made quarterly for the Treasury, in 1827 monthly in England, half-yearly in Scotland, in 1830 monthly in Scotland, in 1840 a printed form was used, subsequently in each case.

Revenue prisoners were formerly numerous. 1226 smugglers were imprisoned between 1826 and 1833, and in 1833 there were no fewer than 158 incarcerated.[3] In Lifford Gaol, Donegal, alone, in 1843, there were 50.[4] And since that date returns which are designated "in continuation" have been made to Parliament.

East in his Choice Chips refers to an order in which the Commissioners offered a reward of £200 for the recapture of a fugitive who is described as a man "aged about forty-eight years, five foot ten inches high or thereabouts, a little too slender leg'd for his height, of a fair complection, good teeth, large blew eys, and a broad flattish face inclining to be slender rather than fatt. . . . . ."

The estimated allowances for Crown prisoners was in 1855 £2000, in 1875 only £220,[5] in 1878 discontinued.

PROCLAMATIONS.

Long was it customary to announce the imposition of duties, the continuation in office of employés, and sometimes the assaults upon officers, by proclamation. This was continued with marked regularity to the beginning of the present century, but since then the practice has not been closely observed.

PROMOTION.

Promotion, preferment, or advancement, for all of these were in

[1] C. I R. [2] Green's State Papers, 1666. [3] P. Ret., 1833.
[4] H. L., Feb. 28, 1843. [5] Estimates.

considerable distance so great, that many out-ride officers with a family remain as they are from an inability to bear the loss or support the expense." (*See* Removes).

From this date, probably, no general departmental effort was made to compensate for the lack of, or to accelerate promotion until the Dublin Salary Committee of 1858 wrote, in comparing this department with others—"In those, the deficiency of high places is compensated by periodical augmentation of salary, according to servitude, and irrespective of promotion; in this the deficiency remains without any compensation to improve the present condition, or brighten the prospects of the great mass who need not and cannot look to promotion as a means of amelioration."[1] These sentiments were borne out by the Glasgow Central Salary Committee in their Address in 1867, in these words:—"That the existing system of promotion is incommensurate with the needs of the Service." It would introduce a system which would create and sustain merit. The chief defect lay in the fact that of the total of about 3430 in the outdoor section, there were only about 570 appointments above the rank of division, hence only about 2900 cannot make any further real advance, that 5 out of every 6 must remain in a subordinate position, the promotion to which culminates too rapidly. To remedy this, the Committee, among other suggestions, pointed out that the rate of promotion might be improved by an extended classification of stations according to the amount of duty charged, and the method of promotion by a close examination into character, qualifications, and time service, and thus introduce "a system of graduated promotion as will certainly cover the greater part of the official lifetime."

Merit, it has been shown, has been since more generally adopted. The principles and rates of promotion were ably reviewed by "Observer" in the *Civil Service Gazette* of 1871.

QUIT RENTS.

Peculiar to Ireland. The management formerly gave employment to a special staff of six persons who came under the control of the Commissioners.[2] The rents are now taken by the respective

[1] Statement, 1858. [2] P. Rep., 1809.

collectors, who receive remuneration at 2 per cent. on the amount collected, which remuneration is divided between them and their clerks in the ratio of two to one.[1] This emolument varies from £20 to £100 per collection,[2] and in computing the superannuation allowance, the average receipt during the three preceding years is taken, and charged upon the Crown Lands' Revenues' Departments.[3]

RACE-HORSE DUTY.

Originating with Mr Pitt in 1784, and not leviable beyond the limits of Great Britain, at rates which varied from £1, 8s. 9d. to £3, 17s.,[4] it was transferred from the assessed tax to the Excise branch, as an Excise duty, at the instance of Sir G. C. Lewis, Bart., on April 5, 1857,[5] until repealed on the financial proposition of Sir S. Northcote, Bart.,[6] from July 1, 1874.

The Receiver of Race-Horse Duty received a salary of about £440 per annum, and on the discontinuance of his office he was granted a compensation allowance of about £132, 13s. per annum.[7]

RAILWAY DUTY.

This duty, exactable only in Great Britain, was first levied in 1832, at one halfpenny per mile for every four passengers conveyed, and in 1842, on the petition of the parties to Parliament, at 5 per cent. upon the receipts from passengers, the charge being returned by the respective Companies within twenty days after the termination of each month.

It was a Stamp-duty down to October 3, 1847.[8] The Commissioners state that the duty has involved them in much litigation,[9] but that they have been relieved from much responsibility by the appointment of a Committee to report upon the duty.[10] The duty has gradually risen to £741,919.[11]

Mr Laing moved the repeal, at "the earliest opportunity," in

[1] Johnston's Manual, 1865. [2] C. S. G., 1857. [3] 1877. [4] C. 13 R.
[5] H. C., July 9, 1856; March 13, 1857. [6] H. C., April 16, 1874.
[7] Superannuation Ret., 1874. [8] T. W., Aug. 17, 1847.
[9] C. 13, 15, 16, 17 & 18 R. [10] 19 R. [11] 21 R.

1873;[1] a deputation waited upon the Chancellor of the Exchequer to urge the repeal in 1874;[2] a pampnlet, entitled "The Railway Passenger Duty: Its Injustice and Its Repeal," was written in 1874.[3] The Travelling Tax Abolition Committee urged the repeal, while the Railway Companies proposed a commutation.

REFRESHMENT HOUSE LICENCE DUTY.

This two-fold licence—refreshment and wine—was introduced by Mr Gladstone in 1860 to apply at first to only England, but, on request, another bill was brought in to extend it to Ireland. A few notes from Hansard may not be unacceptable. The resolution imposing a half-guinea licence duty on refreshment-house keepers was carried by 173 to 103 votes; but when the guinea resolution came on, it was moved that the duty be a uniform half guinea—for the original clause, 159; against it, 88—majority 71. The Chancellor—"Colonial wines would be classed as Foreign wines." In Committee on the bill, Mr Palk rose and moved, in a somewhat erratic speech, that it be committed that day six months. Mr Packe supported him, but they were not successful, and Mr Palk subsequently withdrew his amendment. An amendment by Mr Gladstone to include British as well as Foreign wines, was agreed to. On the Reputed Quart question, Mr Edwin James observed—"It was already provided for, by an Act of 11 and 12 Victoria, that a reputed quart should be one-sixth of a gallon." Clause 2—"What shall be selling by retail?" The Chancellor—"The intention of the clause was to confine the retail dealer to the sale of one dozen wines at a time to one customer." Clause 4—"What shall be deemed a refreshment house?" The Chancellor—"Now he wished to observe that the clause was limited in two most important particulars. In the first place, the victual or refreshment was to be consumed on the premises; and in the next place, the sale of victuals or refreshments was to constitute the purpose for which the house was kept open, and was not to be accidental, occasional, or secondary." Mr Hardy made a timely suggestion "that all places kept open for refreshments between the hours of ten o'clock at night and 4 o'clock in the morning, should be deemed a refreshment house,"—carried. Clause 5. The Chancellor—"The fact of a

[1] H. C., April 1, 1873. [2] March 17, 1874. [3] Wilson, London.

person holding a wine licence would not disqualify him from holding a beer licence, nor would the holding of a beer licence disqualify him from holding a wine licence." May 10. Clause 21—"What is wine—what spirit?" Mr John Locke—"At present an exciseman calling for brandy, would be in no danger of being served with wine, and *vice versa*." The Customs definition was accepted. Clause 22. The expressions "Foreign wine" and "British wine" were included, because Foreign wine was a dutiable article, but British was not—Mr Gladstone. Clause 35—"The exception in favour of the Corporation of St Albans was inserted, because that body had licensing powers under ancient charter, and which were independent of the ordinary tribunal of the Justice of the Peace. With regard to the Free Vintners, it was certainly one of an anomalous character." May 14. The Committee resumed their labours on May 17, again on the 21st, again on the 24th, and the House passed the third reading on May 25.—House of Commons.

The bill was read a second time in the House of Lords on June 5, and on the third reading it was unsuccessfully opposed by an amendment by Lord Denman by 34 votes—contents 36; not-contents 2. Two written dissents were handed in by Lords Harrington and Denman, and Lords Denman and Dungannon. The occasional refreshment licence of 1864 is granted without payment—*nil*. Except by Mr Bruce, in his Exciseable Liquors (Licences) Bill, and in the motion for a Parliamentary return of the number of houses in places of a population of 30,000, it has but little engaged the attention of Parliament. It never extended to Scotland, and the amount of duty has "greatly disappointed expectation."[2] The number of licences granted in the year ended March 31, 1861, was 4358;[3] in 1878, 9966.[4]

REFRESHMENT ROOM, SOMERSET HOUSE.

It was in 1862 that the first proposal was made to open this place of bibic and comestic accommodation, and though then abandoned awhile, it was renewed in 1863 and carried into effect by an announcement of the opening on January 21, 1864. In 1866 it came to grief by the entrance of an "inhospitable bailiff" in search of a

[1] 1867. [2] C. 5 R. [3] 13 R. [4] 21 R.

"fugitive purveyor," and something similar occurred in 1872 when an effort was made to manage it on the co-operative principle.[1]

REMOVES.

The circumstances under which these were made down to 1798 were promotion, personal request, and displeasure, but from that date down to 1857, with the addition of a periodical remove, which will be further noticed.

Tom Paine tells us—"The pecuniary advantages arising from a foot-walk are so inconsiderable, and the loss of disposing of effects or the charges of removing them to any considerable distance so great that many out-ride officers with a family remain as they are from an inability to bear the loss or support the expense." From this, with the fact that the Commissioners in 1796 had it in contemplation to allow something, it may be inferred that the expenses were not then allowed. With respect to the remove at his own request, the applicant appears to have always borne the expense, and in the case of an exchange, both the parties concerned had to obtain the written consent of the respective collectors, and in one portion of Britain also of their supervisors,[2] before the applications were transmitted to their Honours, under pain of their being rejected, and the applicants incurring the Board's displeasure.[3] No one was allowed to return to his native place, or where he had received his instructions,[4] or to endeavour to obtain a remove through a person unconnected with the department, under a threat that he "shall certainly be discharged."[5] (*See* Censures). It was in 1819 that compliance with an order to remove was first enjoined to be obeyed within three months; in 1823, on the consolidation of the three Boards, that officers were ordered to hold themselves in readiness to proceed to any part of the United Kingdom, as it was "upon these terms alone that they are to be continued in the public service;" and in 1839, that no one promoted from one part of the United Kingdom to another was not allowed to petition for a station out of that part within twelve months after the date of his appointment to it. It was the periodical remove, however, which, above all other

[1] C. S. G. Official Review, C. 1862-72. [2] S., 1804. [3] 1761. [4] 1778.
[5] 1718, 1744.

removes, was the dread of the department. This, though referred to in 1750, originated with Mr Pitt, who caused every surveying officer, not being a supervisor, to be removed every fourth year from one station to another, to avoid that supposed system of barter between a gift-giving trader and a needy officer, which might be transacted at the expense of the revenue. This may be shown on the authority of W. Hetherington, S.G.E. In Suffolk, the first thing a trader says to an officer is—"Come and taste a little of our beer;" and the first toast they give is—"Let us live, and let live."[1] The system was announced in 1794, adopted in 1798, extended to Scotland and Ireland in 1823, period increased to six years in 1856, discontinued in 1857.

But to point out the persistence of the promoters of a proposal to discontinue it.

The Edinburgh Periodical Removes' Abolition Committee, formed in 1852, found a supporter in the editor of the *Civil Service Gazette*, and in the officers at Liverpool, York, Aberdeen, and Glasgow, who sought and obtained the countenance and support of several members of Parliament who drew the attention of the Chancellor of the Exchequer to the financial and domestic importance of the question, and cited an article in *The Times* of December 1834 in support of their application. The then Chairman of the Board being against the movement.

The committee soon opened a correspondence with Joseph Hume, which not being satisfactory was immediately followed by an article from the quill of the editor who reviewed the correspondence, and the less affluent days of the now distinguished financial reformer. The committee were equally unsuccessful in their memorial to the Lords of the Treasury, for, by a Minute dated February 14, 1854, they declined to interfere. Fourteen days after the date of this reply the committee importuned Her Majesty's Ministers by stating the unnecessary delay—frequently four months—in repaying the officers, and the not unfrequent deduction of one-third from the expended amount. In one of the Treasury Minutes reference was made to an existing regulation by which an officer might obtain an advance: this, although conscientiously referred to by the Authorities, was not officially promulgated by general order until some time afterwards—April 1—and occasioned a few pert words from the committee in

[1] P. Rep., 1836.

reply. Not only did they refer to the apparent partiality in the non-issue of an order, but they detailed the vexations incident to the regulation whose abolition they advocated. This communication extended over one and a half pages, was signed by J. Middleton, M.D., John Dalgleish, Robert Spiden, John Stoddart, Archibald Cooper, Walter Henderson (secretary), and dated May 9. The acknowledgment from the Treasury was very short, "have nothing to add to the observations then communicated to you"—May 24, 1854. The energy and determination of this Scotch band of six gentlemen were neither dissipated nor exhausted. They next addressed C. Cowan, Esq., M.P., on the evasive character of the return from the Board of Inland Revenue of the number of officers removed during a period of four years—the average, given, being 224; while in 1834, on the authority of the Parnell Committee, the number was "1271, and the amount of the expenditure incurred in the removal was £5,312 12s 5¾d.". They not only suggested that a second application should be made to the Board for the return, but that they were both ready and willing to petition the House of Commons to order it. The Parliamentary Return gave the average annual expense of all removals, for the past six years, as £2,285.[1]

On January 16, 1855, a deputation from the Edinburgh Committee, consisting of Dr Middleton, Messrs J. Brown, W. Brown, Dalgleish, Stoddart, and Henderson, secretary, waited upon C. Cowan, Esq., M.P., to ask him to present and support a numerously-signed petition to the House of Commons in favour of the abolition. The honourable gentleman complied with the request. Earl Derby too courteously acknowledged the receipt of a memorial. Petitions were also prepared at Gateshead, Liverpool, Margate, Ramsgate, Newcastle-upon-Tyne, and Leith.

On the 31st January the secretary addressed a letter to J. Wood, Esq., on "the glaring inconsistency" of allowing a "bachelor" to remain an extra year, while "those who have families" were removed—in Edinburgh Collection. He was informed on the 8th of February "that the Board beg to decline any further correspondence." He acknowledged this letter, in which he received a copy of a Treasury Minute, dated January 26, 1855, on the salary question, quite ungermane to his subject, and asked the Board to reconsider his communication, but this application was returned to him without any

[1] P. Ret., 1854.

observation whatever. On February 19 he transmitted his rejected letters to the First Lord of the Treasury, pointing out the irrelevancy of the earlier reply and asking his lordship to examine into the disrespect shown towards him, or failing that to return his correspondence, that he might place it in the hands of the committee's representatives in the House of Commons. William Law, on behalf of the Prime Minister, replied that his letters should be laid before the Board of Treasury.

The Edinburgh Committee was re-elected on June 20 and consisted of the following fifteen gentlemen:—John Middleton, Esq., M.D., chairman, John Stoddart, Esq., treasurer, Messrs J. Gordon, T. Monteith, Jas. Wilson, R. Clark, J. D. Niven, A. Cooper, D. Bryce, R. Spiden, R. Rough, D. Small, John Dalgleish, and T. Cairns, and W. Henderson, Esq., secretary. This newly-elected committee resolved to print a pamphlet statement of the grievances, which had been brought before them, "showing the partiality displayed by the Board of Inland Revenue throughout the different collections, contrary to the express declaration of the Lords of the Treasury, of date 14th February 1854."

About this time, an anonymous correspondent, of nearly 50 years' service, under the initials "O. R.," not inaptly interpreted by the indefatigable secretary of the northern metropolis, "Old Routine," challenged a discussion "before a regularly constituted commission," on the desirability of continuing the system of removes so generally denounced, and flattered himself that he would be "supported by every thorough-paced Exciseman, alias, Inland Officer." The committee accepted the invitation, but it is very probable the disputants never met.

The Edinburgh gentlemen announced in their last letter, under the watchword "Perseverance," that Lord Stanley, and Esquires, Ewart, Layard, and Cowan had recommended the preparation of facts for a Parliamentary campaign, and called upon the officers to furnish them with "plain unvarnished tales and real facts." These were of course supplied to them.

Secretary Henderson had by this time won a widening way among those for whose home comfort he had been battling; and, the testimonial subscription suggested in December 1854, was begun early in the year 1855 by two donations. But so timid were the officers, supposed to be in subscribing, by Dr Middleton, that the worthy M.D. treasurer found it necessary to announce that the names of the contributors would not become known to the Board. These being the only amounts acknowledged, a division officer wrote in plaintive terms of the "falling off." And owing to the Bruce Testimonial difficulty—which see—the treasurer had to write again in words of assurance to the subscribers, that the subscription list would not be affected by the Bruce-Measor dispute.

The labours of the Edinburgh Committee were this year crowned with partial success—the extension of the periodical remove from four to six years by the G. O. of January 21, 1856. Secretary Henderson had only four days previously addressed an importunate letter, to the Chancellor of the Exchequer, in which he instanced three cases of expected hardship. Sir Geo. C. Lewis, Bart., acknowledged the receipt on the 21st. And on the 26th, the now victorious secretary congratulated the less-frequently—removable officer; and on the 10th of March, the committee, in the name of the officers, thanked the financier of Her Majesty's coffers, but they did not resign their honorary commission—the abolition. The next appeal was to the House of Commons by petition from Dalkeith and other places; six were presented containing no fewer than 1152 signatures.[1] Then came on Friday, June 13, the tangible expression of gratitude to W. Henderson, Esq., in the shape of "a handsome piece of plate and a purse of money," through the hands of Dr Middleton, in the name of the officers, "in token of their approbation of his valuable services in their cause." The recipient laconically replied that it had been "truly a labour of love." Losing no opportunity which might conduce to the achievement of their purpose, the committee next transmitted a letter of congratulation and appeal to Charles Pressly, Esq., on his appointment to the chairmanship of the Board of Inland Revenue. They urged the abolition of "those antiquated arrangements," and the letter was an undoubted success, the chairman having replied, "that the same shall have my best attention," and on February 12, 1857, sanctioned the total abolition of the system. A few days before the joyful news was received, the secretary was informed on the authority of the Chancellor of the Exchequer, that this system of remove was under the consideration of the Lords of the Treasury, and immediately afterwards, the editor exultingly wrote—"The base and villanous system of 'General Removes' is now an atrocity of the past." "Vindicator" followed—

[1] P. Ret., 1856.

"The winter of their discontent is indeed made glorious summer by the abolition of that hitherto curse of the Service—the General Removes—now for ever abolished." "Thankfulness" came in the rear, exclaiming, how glad he was "to dispense with the assistance of town-crier as also the services of the auctioneer," while the officers in Dublin took advantage of the presence of Charles Pressly, Esq., in that city, to personally thank him for the great boon conferred. But epistolary and verbal expressions of gratitude were soon superseded by a monetary subscription towards a second testimonial to the arduous, indefatigable, and all-victorious secretary, which was kept open until the end of July. That time having arrived, the money aggregated, the form of presentation fixed upon and supplied, the testimonial was presented to Mr Henderson at a supper at the Ship Hotel, East Register Street, Edinburgh, on Friday, October the 2d, in the presence of a goodly assemblage, in which was Donald Ross, Esq., Collector. The picture and purse presentation consisted of a "calotype likeness of that gentleman"—W. Henderson—"with a purse of one hundred sovereigns. . . . . The calotype prepared by Messrs Ross & Thompson, Photographers to the Queen, Princes Street, bears the following inscription—"Presented with a purse of one hundred sovereigns, by the Officers of Inland Revenue, Excise Department, in the United Kingdom, to Mr Walter Henderson, Secretary to the Edinburgh Committee for the Abolition of the Periodical Removal of Excise Officers, as a mark of their esteem and regard, and a memento of their gratitude for his disinterested exertions in bringing to a successful issue, the end which that Committee had in view, whereby a great boon had been conferred on them and their families." A second calotype of the secretary was handed to Dr Middleton, chairman. The amount subscribed £107, 7s.; disbursed—"two calotypes with frames and inscribing £2, 11s.," other expenses and donation £105, 4s. 6d.; deficiency 8s. 6d. Bravo, bravo, Scotia![1]

REVENUE POLICE, IRELAND.

This tale may be told in part by the Parnell Committee. "It may be sufficient to state here that the application of a force of this kind, distinct from, and in addition to, the established officer of excise,

[1] C. S. G., 1853 to 1857.

for the purpose of suppressing illicit distillation, was introduced in the year 1787, at which period a proposal was made by an individual resident in the county of Leitrim, being in the nature of a contract, by which he undertook to keep down illicit distillation in a certain district at a stipulated rate of remuneration. The proposal was accepted under the authority of the Lord Lieutenant, by way of experiment, for one year, and appears to have led to similar contracts with seven other individuals for other parts of the country. No information is produced as to the result of this experiment, or as to the motives or authority under which the contracts were renewed. It appears, however, that the engagements were continued with the original contractors during the whole of their lives, and with others until the service was undertaken in a different form by the department of the Excise in the year 1818, being a period of thirty years from the date of the contract referred to. . . . . . . Whatever may have been the effect of these seven hired parties in the particular districts in which they were employed, it is clear, that neither they, nor any other description of force then employed, were effectual for the general suppression of the evil against which they were directed, since it is well known that during the period above alluded to the practice of illicit distillation prevailed to such a degree as to afford constant employment to the officers of excise, assisted by a large portion of the military, in their attempts to keep it down. The evil consequences to the army from this service . . . and . . . . after various modifications in the mode of their employment, and other abortive expedients had been resorted to, the first attempt at employing an armed force wholly belonging to the excise was made in the year 1818, at the suggestion of Mr Tottenham, an Acting Inspector-General of Excise, Sligo. The suggestion having been communicated to the Government and approved of, arms and accoutrements were issued from the Ordnance at first to the single party originally proposed by Mr Tottenham and subsequently to various other parties in different parts of the country, which were formed on a similar model. The number of the force was 1040: 2 inspectors, 69 lieutenants, 4 supernumerary lieutenants, 70 sergeants, 895 privates. The annual cost, £39,191, 4s 3½d."

The amount of the rewards paid in the year ended January 5, 1822, £243, rose by 1827 to no less than £10,924. The scale of rewards was as follows:—"When effectually destroyed, with the casks, &c., at the place of seizure, for every 100 gallons of potale or worts, 1s; for every gallon of singlings or illicit spirit, 1s; for each vessel containing illicit burned bere or grains not detected in a distillery, with potale, &c., or when a still was at work, 6d; for each barrel of four bushels of malt, net gauge, 1s; when brought to store, for each still, 2s 6d; for each head or worm, 1s 6d; for each barrel of malt, four bushels, net gauge, 4s. Their dress, viz., white cross belts over a green or blue uniform."[1] In 1833 alone they detected 1539 illicit stills, 3300 distilleries, seized 71,782 bushels of malt, 320,813 gallons of wort, and 6944 gallons of spirits.

The force, as already stated, was divided into so many parties thus—in 1826, 32; in 1833, 57; and in 1838, 70. At the time of its discontinuance it cost £63,000 per annum, and consisted of 1131 persons, of whom 591 were received into the constabulary, to whom their duties were transferred at an immediate saving of £43,832, and an eventual saving of £48,450.[2]

The abolition was recommended by the Parnell Committee in 1836,[3] referred to by Mr Gladstone in his maiden financial statement in 1853,[4] and effected, in accordance with his suggestion, in 1857, Mr Bagnell observing that the Government would make a mistake by turning "the Irish Constabulary into a force of excisemen."[5]

REWARDS.

As incentives to the discovery of fraud these have been offered[6] and awarded by the Legislature, the Treasury, and the Commissioners on different principles, as will be gleaned from the following:—

3d and 6d per lb. on illegally imported coffee.[7]

1s 6d and 2s 6d per lb. on tea seized and afterwards destroyed.[8]

3s 1½d to 3s 2½d per lb. on seized tobacco, less 10 per cent. for condemnation charges.[9]

£1	0	0	per cwt. on illegally imported cocoa nuts.[10]
1	2	9	for still head and worm.
0	16	3	still or head; a still and worm.
0	11	4½	a still; a head and worm.
0	5	5	a head or worm.

[1] Seventh Rep., Part 2. [2] C. 2 R. [3] C. 20 R. [4] H. C., April 18, 1853.
[5] H. C., July 24, 1857. [6] L. G., 1706. [7] 1781. [8] 1726, 1763.
[9] 1829. [10] 1731.

1812.	1826.	1829.	
£1 13 0,	£1 2 9,	£1 2 6	per gall. on seized foreign brandy. [1]
1 7 0,	1 2 3,	1 2 6	Geneva. [1]
0 16 10,	0 8 6,	0 8 6	foreign rum. [1]

Whole duty chargeable on spirits seized in Ireland.[2]

£50 for apprehending a smuggler. [3]
£100 if "happen to lose a limb or an eye" in doing so. [3]
£150 to his representatives if he lose his life. [3]
£15 if committed to prison and penalty afterwards paid.[4]
£20 for transferring a convicted smuggler to the navy.[5]

The value of a seizure and the amount of a penalty have also determined the amount of the reward.

$\frac{1}{4}$ of proceeds of fine and forfeiture, necessary charges deducted.[6]
$\frac{1}{3}$ " " " less condemnation charges.[7]
Whole " " " [8]
$\frac{1}{2}$ " " " unless otherwise directed.[9]

The collector or supervisor, on attending a hearing, received one-eighth of the informer's share of the fine, and eight pence per pound of the value of the seizure, for conducting the case, but this was withdrawn in 1815.[10] Two-thirds of the officer's half of the reward for seizing spirits removed coastwise from one part of the United Kingdom to another were payable to the police who assisted him;[11] and in other cases the militia who helped were also rewarded.[12]

Two instances to claims to large awards may be noted in a seizure of Scotch spirits of the value of £5000;[13] and in an extensive malt fraud, in which the cumulative penalties and seizure amounted to £116,000.[14]

The average annual receipt for ten years by the officers in Scotland for seizures alone was £7768.[15] In Ireland it was also large;[16] but the net proceeds from both fines and forfeitures in the United Kingdom in 1866 amounted to only £19,602;[17] and the Parliament-

[1] T. W., Feb. 22, 1812; 6 G. IV., c. 108. [2] T. W., Jan. 22, 1833.
[3] 1736. [4] 1820. [5] 1820, 1822. [6] 12 C. II., cc. 23, 24.
[7] 1726, 1820; 6 G. IV., c. 108. [8] 1 & 2 W. IV., c. 55.
[9] 1745; 18 G. II., c. 26. [10] Scotland. [11] 1847. [12] 1815.
[13] H. C., May 6, 1785. [14] Court of Exchequer, Aug. 24, 1857.
[15] P. Rep., Smuggling, 1784. [16] H. C., May 22, 1816. [17] Estimates.

ary grant for rewards in 1875 was only £10,500, and the expenditure only £9760.[1] The grant has never exceeded £15,000.[2]

Rewards, it will have been observed, were at first granted by Act of Parliament,[3] and occasion afterwards arose for the Legislature to enact that they should be received of only "their Majestyes."[4] In this manner, with little exception, the payment continued down to 1807, when, in consideration of the preconcerted collusive seizures of stills, &c., between the distillers and officers in Ireland, it was suggested that they should be discontinued.[5] This recommendation lay in abeyance, almost unnoticed, until 1834, when a return of the rewards paid to officers was made to Parliament.[6] It afterwards received little attention until 1848, when the suggestion passed in a modified form into law,[7] the Treasury determining the amount of the reward, afterwards delegated to the Commissioners.[8] *See* Allowances, Emoluments, Fees, Perquisites.

RIDE OFFICER.

This designation is traceable to 1683—"Rideing Officer"[9]—though by 1760 a distinction had arisen in the form of "Out-Ride" officer, which however has since yielded in usage to the former. With respect to his promotion to the next grade in 1778 his application was not entertained until after three years' service:[10] in 1804[11] until employed four years, the last in a ride: in 1798 the Board called upon him to petition for a footwalk, owing to the transfer of the salt duty: in 1817, in addition to his petition the collector had to report upon his character as shown during a period of three months: in 1829 his application was not recorded until he had given three years' service from the date of his appointment as an assistant, if in a ride two years: in 1843 not until employed three years, the last in a ride, nor if a censure on record. The practice of examining his survey books is of early origin.

In 1847 a ride was obtained at the end of two years' service; in 1867 not until five. The substitution of the designation "3d Class Surveyor" was suggested in 1867.[12]

[1] Appropriation Account. [2] Estimates. [3] 12 C. II., cc. 23, 24.
[4] 1 W. & M., c. 24. [5] P. Rep., 1807. [6] No. 269, 1834.
[7] 11 & 12 V., c. 121. [8] 1872. [9] Hunt's Practical Gauging.
[10] Instructions. [11] Scotland. [12] Glasgow Central Salary Committee.

The following is a copy of the form of petition used by an applicant in 1846:—

"To the Honble. Commissioners of Excise.

Honble. Sirs, Humbly appealing to your generosity in the advancement of Ride Officers and your encouragement to those endeavouring to gain approbation and confidence. With a view to such, having exerted myself in the three last stations to which I have been appointed, after which the Duties of those having been increased, I humbly pray that your Honours will be pleased to bestow your Favour and Encouragement in my wish to establish a firm and lasting approbation by appointing me to a Footwalk.

With all due Respect,
I am, your Honours'
Humble Servant
R. . . . . G. . . . e
Officer of F. . . . 1st Ride
G. . . . District.
4th Decr. 1846. . . . . Collection."

ROOSE'S WORKS.

COMPLETE GUIDE.—The full title is "The Wine and Brandy Dealers' Guide and Stock Book." It contains "a new and complete Treatise on ullaging made perfectly easy in all its Branches; with short rules illustrated by various examples, marked at length by pen and rule with an Imperial Original Line from half a gallon to three hundred gallons: and rules, with examples, containing all possible cases for charging the spirit duties by the saccharometer: for buying and selling spirits by their strength, for ascertaining the strength, temperature and indication of spirits: raising, reducing, and compounding spirit, wine, medicine from any given to any required strength by pen, rule, and by inspection by extensive New Tables."

The Imperial Diagonal Line for spheroidal casks consists of an ingenious table "by which any person may gauge a cask with a carpenter's rule and walking stick," thus "the diagonal line from the centre of the bunghole to the intersection of the head and staves" from half a gallon to 300 gallons—inches 28·75 = 54: 38·83 = 133.

Dedicated to Collectors and others by Samuel Roose, Officer of Wolverhampton Fourth Division. Whittaker & Co., London, 1835.

Ullaging.—"A New and Complete Treatise on Ullaging" made perfectly easy in all its Branches, with short rules illustrated by a variety of plain and familiar examples both by Pen and Sliding Rule, to which is added an Imperial diagonal line by Samuel Roose, Officer of Ludlow Second Divn.

Dedicated to the Officers of His Majesty's Revenue of Excise. Longmans, London, 1832.

SACCHAROMETER.

This is not such an old instrument as the hydrometer, as it is stated to have been first used by a Mr Richardson, a brewer at Hull, in 1784. John Maitland, General Surveyor of Excise in Scotland, stated, before the Parliamentary Committee on the Scotch Distillery Duties in 1798, that "I am told there is an instrument called a 'saccharinometer' that will ascertain the strength of wort and wash, but of this I have no personal knowledge, having never seen one used," and Mr Graham, Commissioner, and Messrs Bonar and Leven, officers of Excise, report to the same committee, in the following year, "The instrument is in truth a hydrometer for worts. The hydrometer for spirits proves the value by showing their strength or how much lighter they are than water:—That commonly called a saccharometer, proves their value by showing the strength or how much heavier they are than water. . . . . In the two instruments there is great similarity, the latter taking up the check, just as the power of the former ceases to act." These gentlemen then suggest the use of the saccharometer in testing the gravity not as a mode of charge, but as a check upon the substitution of stronger for weaker wort or wash. It was also recommended to be used by a Parliamentary Committee in 1807—"the introduction and constant use of the saccharometer to more effectually prevent the removal of backs"—to this, as of course after this, time, the staff tested "the wash to ascertain if any exchange or change has been made."[1]

It would seem, however, to have remained for Dr Thomson, who, in conjunction with others engaged in the investigation of the relative values of barley and bigg, found the common saccharometer in use to vary so much, as to induce him to construct a saccharometer

[1] P. Rep., July 1807.

to exhibit "the real specific gravity as hydrometers do. In it the zero or beginning of the scale represents the specific gravity of distilled water, which is called one thousand, and each degree is equivalent to $\frac{1}{1000}$ part."[1] Here is the principle of the instrument at present in use, but its adoption has been gradual:—

1806. Authorised to be used in Scotland.[2]
1816. Dr Thomson's model introduced.
1823. Bate's to be used by Treasury Order, Oct. 17, 1823.
1823. Bate's substituted for Allan's in Ireland.[3]
1825. Bate's to be substituted for Allan's in Scotland:[4] but this was not immediately acted upon as will be seen by a B. O. $\frac{445}{58}$ J. May 28, 1858, directing Allan's to be replaced by Bate's on and after July 2, 1858, and the old instruments to be sent to the Collector . . . Edinburgh.
1826. Authorised to be used in England.[5]
1829. Bate's to be used in England.[6]

Dr Ure observes, "Bate's tables have been constructed on a solution of sugar, and with solutions of extract of malt, for they agree sufficiently well with the former, but differ materially from the latter."[7] These tables, apparently first published in 1823, superceded the use of the sliding rule which it had been hitherto customary to issue with the saccharometer.

Used as this instrument has been now for many years to raise a presumptive charge, it has perhaps never since 1805 and 1831, been subjected to further scientific examination; it has seldom been referred to in Parliament:[8] the Commissioners are empowered to authorise the use of any saccharometer which complies with the conditions given in 23 and 24 Vic., c. 114, sec. 72.

The comparison, examination and supply of the instrument noted under Hydrometer apply equally here.

For further information see Muspratt's Chemistry, article Beer; Ure's Dictionary, article Saccharometer; Bate's Tables, and Johnston's Handbook.

[1] P. Rept., 1806. [2] 46 Geo. III., c. 102. [3] B. O., Dublin, Dec. 3. 1823.
[4] B. O., January 1, 1825. [5] 6 Geo. IV., c. 80.
[6] B. O., June 27, 1829; Bateman, 1843; Johnston's Handbook.
[7] P. Rep., 1831. [8] 1831, 1832.

SACRAMENT.

The observance of this church rite by this department originated in 1672 with the Test Act, by which every officer was required to take the sacrament, within three months of his appointment, "to prevent the danger which may happen from Popish recusants." He had also to renew it on a new accession to the throne. It applied to all three countries,[1] and remained for Mr Beaufoy to first endeavour to obtain its repeal, who, in doing so used the following parody on the sacred service:—"All you that are lately appointed to offices under his Majesty, that do truly and earnestly desire your continuance therein, and are in love with the profits thereof; you that are lately become excise officers . . . and have a charitable hope of enriching yourselves with the spoils of the illicit trader, draw near in faith and take the holy sacrament to your comfort, that you may have a legal title to your places."[2] The repeal was effected in 1828.[3] Train tells the following tale:—"Mr A., the parish minister of Cumbrae, was a pusillanimous varlet, having, for several years past, purchased smuggled wine from the sailors of these vessels for sacramental occasions, and that on one occasion his stock was so small that when the vessel happened to be detained beyond her time, the sacrament was postponed until the accustomed supply was obtained from on board."[4]

See Candidates. Oaths.

SALARY.

During the Commonwealth the Commissioners paid their officers "such summes of money" as they thought fit,[5] and on the restoration of Charles, his Majesty proclaimed that "they shall receive from us, during their respective employments, like wages and salaries as hath heretofore used and accustomed."[6] Three years afterwards the subject came under the consideration of the Treasury who issued "warrants for allowing all sums paid the Commissioners of Excise for salaries to the officers of excise,"[7] and from this date it is probable that the Lords of the Treasury have decided the respective

[1] Scotland, Instructions, 1804; Ireland, L. G., 1704. [2] H. C., March 28, 1787.
[3] Alcorn's Compendium of Chronology. [4] Patterson's Memoirs of Train.
[5] P. O., 1644. [6] Procl., 1660. [7] Green's State Papers, 1663.

salaries which have been paid; and no general dissatisfaction would seem to have been expressed until Tom Paine penned, in 1772, "The Case of the Officers of Excise, with Remarks on the Qualifications of Officers, and on the Numerous Evils arising to the Revenue from the Insufficiency of the present Salary; humbly addressed to the Hon. and Right Hon. the Members of both Houses of Parliament." The writer observes in his introduction—"Simple as the subject may appear at first, it is a matter not unworthy a Parliamentary attention. 'Tis a subject interwoven with a variety of reasons from different causes. New matter will arise on every thought. If the poverty of the officers of excise, if the temptations arising from poverty, if the qualifications of persons to be admitted into the employment, if the security of the Revenue itself are matters of any weight, then I am convinced that my voluntary service in this business will produce some good effect or other, either to the better security of Revenue, the relief of officer, or both." On "the state of the salary of the officers of excise," he continues:—"When a year's salary is mentioned in the gross it acquires a degree of consequence from its sound which it would not have if separated into daily payments, and if the charges attending the receiving and other unavoidable expenses were considered, fifty pounds a year, and one shilling and ninepence farthing a day, carry as different degrees of significancy with them as my lord's steward and the steward's labourer, and yet an out-ride officer in the excise, under the name of fifty pounds a year, receives for himself no more than one shilling and ninepence farthing a day. After tax, charity, and sitting expenses are deducted, there remains very little more than forty-six pounds, and the expense of horsekeeping in many places cannot be brought under fourteen pounds a year, besides the purchase at first and the hazard of life, which reduces it to thirty-two pounds per annum, or one shilling and ninepence farthing per day. . . . I have spoken more particularly of the out-rides, as they are by far the most numerous, being in the proportion to the foot-walks, as eight is to five, throughout the kingdom. . . . Were the money in the kingdom to be increased double, the salary would, in value, be advanced by one-half. Every step upwards is a step downwards with them." The author then states the effect of the removal from kith and kin, the sentimental reputation of being an officer, the unwearying devotion to office—"that no set of men under his Majesty earn their salary with any comparison of labour and fatigue with that of the officers of excise. . . . Every year's experience given in the excise is a year's experience lost to trade, and by the time they become wise officers they become foolish workmen." The next chapter contains "Thoughts on the Corruption of Principle and the numerous Evils arising to the Revenue from the too great poverty of the Officers of Excise. . . . If the salary was judged competent an hundred years ago, it cannot be so now." His last chapter contains "Remarks on the Qualifications of Officers. . . . In employments where direct labour is wanting and trust quite out of the question, the service is merely nominal or mechanical. In cutting a river or forming a road, as there is no possibility of fraud, the merit of honesty is but of little weight. Health, strength, and hardiness are the labourer's virtues. But when property depends on the trust, and lies at the discretion of the servant, the judgment of the master takes a different channel, both in the choice and the wages. A known thief may be trusted to gather stones, but a steward ought to be proof against the temptation of uncounted gold. The Excise is so far from being of the nature of the first, that it is all and more than can be put together in the last. 'Tis a place of poverty, of trust, of opportunity, and temptation. A compound of discords, where the more they harmonise, the more they offend. Ruin and reconcilement are produced at once."

The author subsequently wrote to Dr Oliver Goldsmith a letter which very clearly shows the general favour with which the "case" was received:—"Honoured Sir,—Herewith I present you with the case of the officers of Excise. A compliment of this kind from an entire stranger may appear somewhat singular, but the following reasons and information will, I presume, sufficiently apologise. I act myself in the humble station of an officer of excise, though somewhat differently circumstanced to what many of them are, and have been the principal promoter of a plan for applying to Parliament this session for an increase of salary. A petition for this purpose has been circulated through every part of the kingdom, and signed by all the officers therein. A subscription of three shillings per officer is raised, amounting to upwards of five hundred pounds, for supporting the expenses. The Excise officers in all corporate cities and towns have obtained letters of recommendation from the electors to the members in their behalf. Many or most of them have promised their support. The enclosed case we have presented to most of the members, and shall to all before the petition appears in the

House. The memorial before you met with so much approbation while in manuscript, that I was advised to print four thousand copies, three thousand of which were subscribed for by the officers in general, and the remaining one thousand reserved for presents. Since the delivering them, I have received so many letters of thanks and approbation for the performance, that were I not rather singularly modest I should insensibly become a little vain. The literary fame of Dr Goldsmith has induced me to present one to him, such as it is. 'Tis my first and only attempt, and even now I should not have undertaken it had I not been particularly applied to by some of my superiors in office. I have some few questions to trouble Dr Goldsmith with, and should esteem his company for an hour or two to partake of a bottle of wine or anything else, and apologise for this trouble, as a singular favour conferred on his unknown humble servant and admirer, THOMAS PAINE. *P.S.*—Shall take the liberty of waiting on you in a day or two."[1]

1772. Though the result of this movement probably increased the salaries of some it did not stay the desire for further augmentation, as appears by the request of Mr Marsham to read a petition to
1788. Parliament from the "lower grades of excise officers for an increase to their low salaries," to which Mr Pitt replied "the only proper mode of applying to Parliament for an increase of salaries to the excise officers, was by the medium of the Commissioners. . . . . He would never countenance an application to the Legislature by petition from officers themselves."[2] The same desire too is shown
1797. to have existed nine years afterwards by a letter addressed to the collector of Dorset collection—"Sir, the Commissioners being informed that a printed Petition has been circulated through your Collection for obtaining the Signatures of the Officers upon the Round, are very much surprised that considering the Nature and Tendency of that Petition you have not thought it your Duty to make the Matter known to the Board, but since you have not done so, it is their Order that you fail not to apprize all your Officers fully of the Punishment they may incur by being concerned in the said Petition. (Signed) JOHN WILD."

Excise Office, London,
June 9, 1797.

The justice of the claim was eventually conceded. The distillers

[1] C. S. G., 1872. [2] H. C., Feb. 7, 1788.

1799. in Scotland stated "the salaries of the excise officers are . . .
1805. too small:"[1] the Chancellor of the Irish Exchequer observed
" . . . . their salaries are so small . . . . we must raise their salaries liberally, establish gradation in their amount, through which merit and merit alone shall raise the officers. . . . . All the exertions of the superior officers will be inadequate without this measure being
1807. adopted:"[2] the committee on Irish fees wrote in the same
1809. strain: and Mr Huskisson confirmed it on behalf of those in England—"When the present Board of Treasury came into office they found among other legacies . . . . a very detailed report from the Board of Excise of the whole of their establishment. By this document it appeared that the salaries of the excise officers had not been raised for a great number of years, and they were then totally inadequate to their support. The Commissioners of Excise reported in the most forcible terms the absolute necessity of increasing these salaries, as the only means of securing the revenue, by placing the officers above corruption; and that if the augmentation was any longer delayed, a general system of laxity, and a dependence on the parties, whom they were appointed to survey, for loans of money or assistance of some kind, would be the inevitable result. With this representation, in which the Commissioners who made it had no personal interest, as their salaries were not raised, with the example of Ireland, of which we have heard so much lately, before our eyes, with a revenue of £20,000,000 and a system of collection, hitherto remarkable for its regularity and purity, at stake, and with such a forcible appeal from the officers themselves to the justice of the Treasury, could we hesitate in acceding to the proposed augmentation of their salaries? It was granted and though upon an average, it did not exceed £15 to each officer, the aggregate increase of
1820. charge was more than £100,000 a year."[3] This improved position in point of pay Mr Hume in 1820 thought too good, and he moved that as the metallic currency of the country has been restored, the official salaries which have been raised during the dearness of provisions might now be reduced; but in this he was not supported.[4]
1829. The salaries in Scotland and Ireland were, in 1829, revised
1842. and fixed equal to those in England, and those in London, in 1842, on the discontinuance of the London Establishment. Even
1849. after this revision the same financial reformer made a similarly

[1] P. Rep., 1799. [2] H. C., March 13, 1805. [3] H. C., June 19, 1809.
[4] H. C., July 4, 1820.

unsuccessful motion in 1849,[1] though a select committee was sanc-
1850. tioned, in 1850, "to inquire into the salaries and emoluments of offices held during the pleasure of the Crown."[2] But this inquiry if it were made did not affect the out-door employés in this department.

The revision of 1829, from the absence of any evidence to the
1853. contrary, remained unassailed until the establishment of the *Civil Service Gazette* in 1853, since which the salary question has scarcely ceased to be discussed.

1854. On this vital theme the editor of this paper was most pertinent in presenting pictures in point. He discovered an unlucky wight, who by additions to a net salary of £97, 10s had made a total of £101, 6s 8d. "But oh the vanity of sublunary blessings! His extra exertions and extra zeal have brought him under the excruciating income tax screw. He is called upon to pay £4, 4s 5d of that odious double tax, by which his salary and emoluments are reduced to £97, 2s 3d." There were this year some eleven petitions prepared for the Treasury and one forwarded to the House of Commons, but they do not seem to have elicited even an acknowledgment.

1855. The oft-repeated motto, "try, try again," was this year exemplified by the would-be recipients of an augmented income by the lodgment of no fewer than 156 petitions within the doors of the Treasury—and others even by persons not in the department. Of these petitions 109 were forwarded by "officers" and 47 by "collectors' clerks;" and the receipt acknowledged, but the claim not conceded.

1856. Resolved to battle for their rights "a practical executive body" under the noms, An Old Supervisor, Omega, A Division Officer, Justice and Determination, also called the "Address Party," and "Omega & Co.," wrote an address to the Board and another to the department, while a "Guarantee Fund" of £5,000 was proposed to buy out an officer to conduct the movement, but this latter
1857. idea was not acted upon. As Omega and Co.'s addresses were not unanimously accepted the officers in four cities were pointedly reproved for having again petitioned the Lords of the Treasury. But these were not the only nonconformists. There were no fewer than 49 applications sent to the Treasury, probably more, and 11 at least presented to the House of Commons. The

[1] H. C., Feb. 27, 1849. [2] H. C., April 12, 1850.

Commissioners state in their First Report, ". . . . we have already laid before your Lordships our views upon this subject, we need only mention the discontent which prevails among the Excise Officers, as one of those matters which has occupied our most serious attention." Mr Cowan too drew the attention of the House of Commons to the pressing need, when Mr Wilson complained of the similarity in the form of the applications.[1] Upon this becoming known "a full, clear, and matter-of-fact" document was suggested. Omega again introduced his company's plan, obtained general support, and induced the now united mind of the service to collect facts for a Parlia-
1858. mentary campaign. The staff in Dublin accepted the directorate, and prepared an admirable statement for presentation to Members of Parliament and others, and asked for contributions to defray the expenses of printing 10,000 copies. Meetings were now held in many parts of the country, Members of Parliament were solicited to support the claim on its being presented, and even excise traders and others petitioned Parliament in favour of the increase, when Mr Wilson of the Treasury observed that memorials signed by 2,049 officers—27 collectors, 172 supervisors, 38 examiners, 68 clerks, 1179 division officers, 365 ride officers, 23 permit writers, 72 assistants, 105 expectants—had been received during the past year, and that an improved scale of salaries had been transmitted to the Commissioners to frame the estimates upon.[2] This scale the Commissioners state in their Second Report, "will amount in the aggregate to £57,000 in the present year, and when the scheme is in full operation . . . . provision must be made in our estimates for at least £110,000 over and above the expenditure of last year." Gratifying as this announcement was the canvas for support was continued, and 5,000 of the 6,000 copies of the statement were distributed, but shortly after the new scale was officially announced the central committee disbanded, and thus closed the proceedings of a committee whose efforts in hastening the amelioration obtained stand alone in their oneness of design and completeness of arrangement of any departmental committee down to this time. "The author of the draft from which the 'Statement of Claims' was condensed," was John Murdock. The secretary W. Lavender. The central committee fund—received £158, 9s. 4d. : paid £80, 7s. 4½d, printing, posting, &c., £10 "Excise Tribute," £68, 1s. 11½d to the

[1] H. C., July 13, 1857. [2] H. C., Feb. 11, 1858.

Benevolent Fund. Though this concession on the part of the Treasury was viewed by some as only an instalment of justice, it is proper to record that a portion of the recipients transmitted their thanks to their Honours the Commissioners of Inland Revenue and the majority joined in raising "The Excise Tribute" of £456 to J. Boulger, Barrister-at-law, the editor of the *Civil Service Gazette*, for his editorial aid.

1859. From this date down to 1863, every grade, except the clerk, may be stated to have been silenced if not satisfied, but that rank continued its one-grade discussion until 1864, when the claims of the collector to further augmentation were forcibly urged upon that rank, and both, afterwards, separately petitioned for ameliora-
1866. tion—the latter only receiving it. Fergus, alias John Murdock, now asked, "What do the Excise want?" This was the signal for a
1867. new start, and by the beginning of the following year upwards of 100 petitions, containing upwards of 2000 signatures, had been presented to the Treasury and the Board, and a Publication Committee had been formed to prepare a statement of the claims, which it did, under the title of "The Taxes and the Excise Branches of the Inland Revenue, Contrasted. The claims of the Latter to a Similar Treatment with the Former. By one of the Two Hundred organised Excise Committee, 1866." Unsuccessful in this application a Central Committee, composed of the Publication and Glasgow Committees, was formed, and succeeded the Campbeltown Com-
1867. mittee to prosecute the appeal, which it had now become evident would be vigorously supported. All were unanimous in deciding to lay their case before the House of Commons, through the agency of a conference of delegates, who should assemble in London to deliberate upon the best mode of conducting the movement. But ere the delegates had left for Town a Treasury Minute had been issued forbidding officers to use political influence in endeavouring to obtain an increase to their salaries. This meeting was held in Exeter Hall in June, and was numerously attended by gentlemen whose periods of service ranged from six to forty-one years, thus combining the vigour of youth with the experience of age. The condition of the department was discussed from many points, papers were read on the various systems of collection, promotion, &c., deputations were despatched to interview M.P.'s, the power of the press invoked and obtained, and a desire expressed "That a practical inquiry be made into the working of the depart-

ment, that the revenue may be equally assessed, that an increase may be made to the salaries of the officers," &c., &c. A large photograph of a portion of the delegates was taken by the London School of Photography.

The central committee having returned to Glasgow, did not petition the House of Commons for the appointment of a Royal Commission of Inquiry, but chose rather to present an address to the Commissioners to show the desires of the department in detail. This was duly done and acknowledged with the promise "that the Board will not fail to give that attentive consideration . . . . which is due to the importance of the subject, and which the Board will always be ready and willing to afford to any representation . . . . . framed in the tone and spirit which characterise their present appeal." Nov. 23, 1867. Passing over the voluminous correspondence which
1868. was punctually and ably conducted by the secretaries, the Board in 1868 requested an interview with a portion of the committee to confer with them on the numerous subjects contained in their address; and their honours were subsequently pleased to dispense with certain regulations, but regretted that the state of business in the House of Commons had been such as to prevent the introduction of a Bill to change the mode of collecting the self-assessed taxes which had been placed in the hands of the Chancellor of the Exchequer, and by which, when passed, they had hoped to advise a revision of the rates of pay. The committee were severely criticised for their "sleeping policy," and though memoranda were occasionally issued to tell the progress, they were frequently requested to "wake up" and cease "to slumber," and inform their co-memorialists
1869. "in what position our case stands." It was not, however, until the commutation of the assessed taxes into excise licences had
1870. been effected that the Lords of the Treasury sanctioned an increase. Upon this addition the Commissioners state in their Fourteenth Report, "The scale of salaries . . . . causes an immediate additional expenditure of scarcely £20,000 per annum, but gradually rising towards a possible maximum of nearly £50,000." The estimated annual saving by the commutation of taxes was £60,000, showing a net saving of £10,000, plus that in 1867 by the transfer of the dog duty.

Bitter were the words uttered on the manner in which this sum had been apportioned among the various grades, Fergus stating that some 716 would receive "real benefit," while 3141 individuals would receive "little better than blank disappointment." And more bitter still was the invective poured on the committee on the issue of their "Final Report" of 32 pages. The central committee was formed on March 22, 1867, and separated in November 1870, after a duration of rather more than three and a half years, during which it received £1114, 16s 1d, and disbursed £1095, 18s 0d, leaving a balance of £18, 18s 1d in hand Secretaries J. Steele, &c.

A little before the St Mungo Committee had broken up, an "Inverness Committee" was announced to rectify certain alleged misconceptions, and to conduct an "Excise Reform Movement."
1871. Considerable support was shown to "The Effective Central Committee of One"—Fergus—John Murdock—and the Address to the Board received upwards of 2300 signatures, but as their Honours wrote, "The present attempt to renew an agitation in a most objectionable form, for obtaining that which the heads of the department have pronounced to be unreasonable or impracticable appears to be a renunciation of subordination to authority, and cannot be allowed consistently with the maintenance of the supremacy of the Board and the Treasury," the address was not presented, or if so,
1872. not accepted, and "Fergus and Co.," or the "Northern Lights," were twitted with the absence of purpose and determination, but this was scarcely correct—the agitation ceased in deference to official authority. The amount subscribed in aid of these expenses exceeded £317. *See* Testimonials.

Quickly followed the formation of the London Pro Rata Committee, composed of members of the several departments, to put in a plea for a general increase by reason of the increased cost of living which it was shown had risen between 1852 and 1868 on the necessaries of life from 15 to 66 per cent., while the large employers had made advances which varied from 10 to 33 per cent. 3336 names
1873 were attached to the general petition which was duly transmitted to the Commissioners, and by them to the Treasury, where the "general character" of the memorials was considered irregular, each department being required "to prove its own case" by suggesting "reduction or rearrangement." A second memorial, prepared under the hand of Mr Jos. Bell, received 3200 signatures and upwards, and as the Board declined to forward it to the Treasury, it was sent direct, and replied to through the Board, to the effect that their Lordships "must adhere to their former decision." On this becoming known the "senior junior" division officers seceded

from this committee, and at once laid his claim, based on the fact that no fewer than 513 of them had given services varying from twenty-five to thirty years, and had not been bettered one penny by the revision of 1870, before the Commissioners, who replied that they "were not prepared to make a renewed application" on his behalf.

1874. The Pro Rata Committee had now assumed the title of the Consulting Committee, and a Commission of Inquiry was granted under Dr Playfair, after whom it was called, and before whom several of the members of this department were examined. (*See* Civil Service Commission). The other band of agitants pressed their sectional claim, but neither was conceded until the above commission sat, when the Board laid the claims of the examiner and **1876.** the division officer before it.[1] Nor was it until two years after the Commission had issued its reports that these cases, in common with others, were settled, on which the Commissioners were enabled to report—"In the outdoor service . . . . of excise . . . . we have obtained from your Lordships most extensive improvements. We cannot but feel gratified for the attention which your Lordships gave to the statements submitted by us which were closely scrutinised in all their details, but at the same time in the most liberal spirit. It was gratifying to us that our proposals, with but few exceptions, stood the test of the acute examination brought to bear upon them, and that in the result it was admitted, though entailing a large additional expenditure, they were just and reasonable.[2] Great as was the improvement now made, embracing as it did two new allowances of subsistence and duty-pay, one class, however, viewed itself overlooked. The supervisor foresaw this in 1875, and at once endeavoured to obtain a reconsideration of his position as compared with those above and below him in official rank, and **1878.** with those in other departments performing similar duties, but down to 1878, though the most powerful of all pleas, and one laid down as a principle to be acted upon in deciding scales of salaries, "That pay should be apportioned to work, and that for duties similar in kind and responsibility there should be no artificial division into classes carrying different rates of pay," has been urged in his favour, he has not been favoured with an augmentation though it must be acknowledged that he has been favoured with an inter-

[1] C. 17 R. [2] C. 19 R.

view with the chairman of the Board to attain that end, a deputation of six, including the secretary, Mr Crowe, having attended Somerset House on October 23, 1878.

The practice on the issue of a new scale has varied. Sometimes, the payment has been prospective, as in 1870, at others retrospective, as in 1813, when permit writers received a back pay of two years, and in 1858 the whole staff two months.

These salaries were formerly paid out of the duties on which the officers were employed,[1] and the payments were made quarterly down to about 1833,[2] then eight times a year, and a desire for a monthly payment has, since that date, been conceded to certain grades. Deductions were made in 1781 on account of land tax, in 1803 "on the Ratification of a Definitive Treaty of Peace," and to 1857 on account of superannuation which, with Charity Fund, see.

[1] 5 W. & M., c. 7. [2] P. O., 1645; G. I., 1778; G. O., 1833.

TABLE OF SALARIES.

Year.	Surveying General Examiner.	Collector.	Supervisor.	Examiner.	Clerk.	Division.	Ride.	Supernumerary.	Assistant.	Expectant.	Laboratory.
1705	125,80	60	80, 60	100 to 60	...	50	...	...	30[1]	...	... ...
1707 S.	... ...	90 to 65	65, 60	...	...	30	...	25	20[2]	...	... ...
1743	200 to 90	120	90	...	...	50[3]	...	...	...	...	... ...
1779	200 to 100	220	100 to 60	65 to 50	...	60, 52	...	...	40[4]	...	... ...
1779	... ...	120	90 to 80	...	40	60 to 50	...	25	40[5]	...	... ...
1779 S.	190	90	93 to 73	...	...	35, 25	...	25	25[6]	...	... ...
1789	... ...	...	120	95	60 to 40	65	60	...	45	40[7]	... ...
1800 I.	... ...	490[8]	...	...	...	...	...	...	...	...	... ...
1801	... ...	...	140	100	80	80	75	80	60	40[7]	... ...
1802	185[9]	...	...	...	...	...	...	...	...	...	... ...
1806	... ...	...	...	...	...	85	75[1]	...	...	...	... ...
1807	215	...	180, 130	130	120	95	85	90	75	50[1,9]	... ...
1807 I.	150	472[8]	70, 65	...	...	40	...	30	...	...	... ...
1808	... ...	...	...	...	...	...	...	65	65	...	... ...
1809 I.	150, 100, 70	156	100, 70, 65	...	...	40	...	30[10]	...	...	... ...
1811	250	431 to 306	200	...	140	100+10+110	100+10+110	52	85[11]	...	... ...
1812 S.	... ...	...	160	110	100, 85	90	90	90[12]	75[12]	75[12]	... ...
1815	... ...	...	...	...	...	...	...	...	...	50[13]	... ...
1817	1-550, 2-500:	...	...	...	...	...	...	...	...	...	... ...
	1-400, 6-350	...	...	...	...	...	...	...	...	...	... ...
	1-350, 2-300: 9-250[9]	...	...	...	...	...	...	...	...	...	... ...
1821	All increased £50[9]	...	...	...	...	...	...	...	...	...	... ...
1824	3-500 6-350 9-300[9]	...	...	...	...	...	...	...	...	...	... ...
1829 S.	... ...	...	200	150	...	100	...	52	85	50	... ...
1829	1-550 2-500 2-450	2-600 1-550	200	150	...	100	100	52	85	50	... ...
	1 400 16-350 1-350	2-500 14-450	...	...	...	...	...	...	...	...	... ...
	4-300 6-300 14-250	27-400 44-350	...	...	...	...	...	...	...	...	... ...
1854	... ...	...	...	...	110	...	...	...	...	...	... ...
1858	1-600+20° 700	2-650+20° 750	230+5° 250	170	180+5° 220	120+5° 150	110	...	95	60	1-500+10° 600[14]

[1] P. Ret. [2] T. W. [3] Royal Gauger. [4] London Est. [5] Country Est. [6] P. Ret. [7] East's Choice Chips. [8] Dublin. [9] Parnell, 20 R. [10] P. Rep. [11] T. W., Feb. 4, 1811. [12] When employed, T. W., Dec. 14, 1811. [13] When unemployed. [14] T. M., Feb. 13. 1858.

TABLE OF SALARIES—*Continued.*

Year.	Surveying General Examiner.	Collector.	Supervisor.	Examiner.	Clerk.	Division.	Ride.	Supernumerary.	Assistant.	Expectant.	Laboratory.
	3-500+10° 600	8-500+20° 550	210+5° 230	...	140+5° 180	...	...	...	...	...	1-200+10° 300
	1-400	20-450+10° 500	...	...	110+5° 140	...	...	...	...	...	... ...
	15-350	30-400+10° 450	...	...	...	...	...	...	...	...	... ...
	18-300	30-360+10° 400	...	...	...	...	...	...	...	...	... ...
1866	... ...	4-700+20° 800	...	...	...	...	...	...	...	...	... ...
	... ...	12-550+20° 600	...	...	...	...	...	...	...	...	... ...
	... ...	74-400+10° 500	...	...	...	...	...	...	...	...	... ...
1867	... ...	...	...	...	...	...	...	...	...	...	1-600+20° 700
	... ...	...	...	...	...	...	...	...	...	...	1-425+15° 500
	... ...	...	...	...	...	...	...	...	...	...	3-130+10° 250
	... ...	...	...	...	...	...	...	...	...	...	300+15° 400[15]
	... ...	...	...	...	...	...	...	...	...	...	1-120+10° 250
1870	1-800+25° 900	8-700+20° 800	260+10° 300	180	230+10° 280	160+8° 200	110+5° 125	...	95	60	3-260+15° 400[16]
	3-600+20° 650	20-550+20° 600	210+10° 250	...	190+10° 220	130+5° 150	...	...	...	...	2-130+10° 250
	2-450+10° 500	63-450+10° 500	...	...	150+ 5° 180	...	...	...	...	...	... ...
	13-360+10° 400	...	...	...	100+ 5° 140	...	...	...	...	...	... ...
	14-350	...	...	...	...	...	...	...	...	...	... ...
1873	... ...	...	...	...	...	...	...	...	...	...	1-600+20° 700
	... ...	...	...	...	...	...	...	...	...	...	1-425+15° 500
	... ...	...	...	...	...	...	...	...	...	...	4-260+15° 400
	... ...	...	...	...	...	...	...	...	...	...	4-130+10° 250
	... ...	...	...	...	...	...	...	...	...	...	1-110+10° 250
	... ...	...	...	...	...	...	...	...	...	...	1- 70+ 5° 120
	... ...	...	...	...	...	...	...	...	...	...	1- 70+ 5° 105
1876	1-1000	11-700+20° 800	260+10° 300	200	100+15° 200[17]	140+5° 200	115+5° 130	...	95	65	... ...
	3-700+25° 800	30-550+20° 650	230+10° 250	...	...	...	...	...	...	...	... ...
	8-450+20° 650	50-450+10° 500	...	...	...	...	...	...	...	...	... ...
	21-350+10° 400	...	...	...	...	...	...	...	...	...	... ...

[15] After 12 years.

[16] T. M., Aug. 29, 1870.

[17] By triennial increasements with £100 and £50 "duty pay" to superintending and chief clerk respectively.

SALT DUTY.

"The emblem of the nation, so grave and precise,
On the emblem of wisdom have laid an excise;
Pray tell me, grave sparks, and your answer don't smother,
Why one representative taxes another?"[1]

The management of this duty was at first placed under the Commissioners of Excise, and was so continued until 1702, when it was transferred to five Commissioners[2] who were specially appointed under whom it remained, with the exception of a brief inter-imposition of two years, until 1798, when, on the recommendation of a Parliamentary Committee, who sat in 1797, it was retransferred to the Commissioners of Excise, who at the same time appear to have commissioned as many of the salt officers as were found eligible: their duty having consisted in keeping "a score-book" in which the charge was made by the supervisor.[3] Special Commissioners were also appointed for Scotland on May 1, 1714. This special staff consisted, in 1705, in England, of above 340 employés;[4] in 1714 in Scotland, 97;[5] in 1779 in England, 466; in Scotland, 128;[6] in 1797 in England, 464; in Scotland, 459.[7] East gives in his Choice Chips some interesting extracts on the mode of management, &c., in Wales in 1740. The printed collection of salt laws was issued to only the employés.

As to the duty itself: it was first levied as an excise imposition in 1643,[8] and though ordered by Parliament in 1647 "to cease and be no longer paid,"[9] George Williamson, in 1660, offered £100 a year for a farm of the "salt excise" in the county of Cumberland and "a present of £200" to the person who would obtain it for him.[10] It, however, with the better management of public affairs was not levied from that date until 1694,[11] when it became necessary to do so to afford security to those who had advanced money upon a lottery—which see. One of the Articles of the Union with Scotland enjoined that it should not be levied in that country until seven years had elapsed—an injunction just shown to have been strictly observed—May 1. It was next repealed on December 25, 1730. Sir R. Walpole "revived" it in 1732 for, ostensibly, a period of three years in

[1] 1735, King Geo. III., Library British Museum.
[2] L. G.; Beatson's Political Index.
[3] P. Ret., 1781.
[4] P. Ret., 1705.
[5] Idem, 1714.
[6] Idem, 1779.
[7] P. Rep., 1797.
[8] P. O., 1643.
[9] Idem, 1647.
[10] Green's State Papers, 1660.
[11] 5 W. & M., c. 7.

lieu of a land tax, though in doing so he met with much opposition, ayes 225, noes 187:[1] the second reading of his bill having passed on a division with 206 ayes and 180 noes, while in the House of Lords a division was taken at the same stage, with 40 cons. and 25 non-cons.[2] Thus reimposed it was gradually increased,[3] with a further exaction on mineral alkali between 1817 and 1824, until its incidence became so oppressive that even the Chancellor of the Exchequer himself proposed the appointment of a committee to consider the feasibility of substituting another duty.[4] Not fortunate in finding the substitute desired the duty remained unconsidered until 1817, when Mr Calcraft moved for an inquiry into "the great and grievous salt duties," and hoped that, although the committee of 1801 denounced the duty as "detrimental to the public interests in a degree far exceeding the benefit derived from the receipt at the Exchequer," his motion would be attended with a better result—ayes 70, noes 79.[5] Passing over the effort of another honourable member and himself in 1818 and 1819,[6] he next moved for leave to bring in a Bill for the gradual reduction and ultimate repeal by thirds in three years—five shillings per bushel per annum—but in this, although the opinion of Parliament had grown in his favour, he was not successful—ayes 165, noes 169.[7] Followed by a reduction of duty in 1823, and a successor in the person of Mr Wodehouse who exacted a little sympathy from the Chancellor of the Exchequer[8] in 1824, the total repeal was effected in 1825[9] at a gross annual loss to the Exchequer of £389,000.[10]

SEARCH WARRANT.

Though search has been improperly made without a warrant,[11] several houses searched under one warrant,[12] and blank forms signed by Justices and afterwards filled in, to search where the official thought best,[13] the writer has observed only one instance of search questioned in Parliament. This was in 1846. One Joshua Toulmin

1 H. C., Feb. 9, 1732. 2 H. L., Feb. 29, 1732.
3 H. C., June 21, 1767; Feb. 23, 1768; April 25, 1798, &c.
4 H. C., May 15, 1801. 5 H. C., April 25, 1817.
6 H. C., May 22, 1818; March 18, May 13, 1819. 7 H. C., Feb. 28, 1822.
8 H. C., April 6, 1824. 9 5 Geo. IV., c. 65. 10 C. 1 R. 11 1783.
12 1794. 13 1808.

Smith, "a special pleader," residing at "1 Hall Court Temple, London," for the search of whose house for an illicit still, a warrant had been issued, petitioned the House of Lords, through Lord Denman, for the redress of the grievance to which he had been obliged to submit at the hands of an officer who had "treated the females of his family very roughly, and that his wife had never recovered from the shock she received." The Earl of Dalhousie replied by observing that the officer "expressed his regret at having caused any inconvenience, and left the house;" also by observing that, "it happened that in the very same district there had been a house far better in appearance than the one in question, and bearing more the aspect of a gentleman's house, in the drawing-room of which a small still had been found in full operation by the very same officer."[1] Not contented with this explanation, a motion was afterwards made in the House of Commons for a Select Committee to consider the case, and it was defeated by only nine votes—ayes 125; noes 134.[2]

SECRETARY.

An old office. An Act was passed in Scotland as early as June 10, 1648, "anent the Clerkship of Excise," which seems to have been the equivalent at that time for secretary. The Journal of the House of Commons records the appointment of a "Secretary to Commissioners" of Excise,[3] and Green's State Papers confirm that record:—"Excise Commissioners to Sec. Nicholas. Have received a warrant for Capt. Edward Strange to be their Secretary; there has been no such office as a Secretary to the Excise since 1653, only a Registrar, whose laborious duties would not suit a gentleman. Beg that the present Registrar, a man of experience in his duties, . . . may not be removed. Excise Office, Broad S., London, Sept. 6."[4]

The designation registrar was common to many Boards of Commissioners formed after the Excise, but that of secretary in this department, though there may have been an official in that capacity and under that name,[5] was not always subscribed to official documents issued to those outside the chief office. The term correspondent was in use until 1810, when that of secretary was introduced,

[1] H. L., April 6, 1846. [2] H. C., May 14, 1846. [3] 1650-1659.
[4] 1660. [5] Royal Gauger, 1743.

though even down to 1852, and later, there were the northern and the southern correspondents.[1] The Excise secretary has been distinguished as the under secretary,[2] and at a later date as a joint secretary. And from the statement in the Parnell Report,[3] he has not always been selected from the officers "who have gone through the several gradations of office," though that suggestive quotation has since been acted upon. The salary paid to this important official has always been large:—

£300, Secretary and Clerks, Scotland Parl. R. 1707.
£450, Parl. R. 1705.
£450, Royal Gauger 1743.
£865, Secretary and Clerks, Parl. R. 1779.
£800, Under Secretary—Comrs. First Report.
£1500, Secretary, Parl. Paper 1849.
£1200, Parl. Ret. 1863.

Mr Secretary Dobson received a handsome testimonial on his retirement; it consisted of an epergne, a salver, and a tea and coffee service of the value of £610, subscribed by 2489 members of the department; an engraving of the epergne appeared in the *Illustrated London News*.[4] Mr Secretary Corbett was granted a retired allowance equal to his full salary of £1200.[5] These gentlemen passed through the ranks.

Correspondents and Secretaries—

S. Johnson,	From	1718	to 1728	10 years.
C. Wyvill,	"	1729	" 1732	3 "
J. Wyndham,	"	1732	" 1735	3 "
W. Pinney,	"	1736	" 1750	14 "
J. Wardour,	"	1751	" 1751	1 "
R. Noble,	"	1752	" 1758	6 "
M. Lowthian,	"	1758	" 1763	5 "
Joseph Stevens,	"	1763	" 1774	11 "
Bartholomew Sykes,	"	1774	" 1783	9 "
John Collins,	"	1783	" 1785	2 "
Thomas Burton,	"	1785	" 1794	9 "
John Wild,	"	1794	" 1805	11 "
John Storer,	"	1805	" 1809	4 "
William Wardley,	"	1809	" 1823	14 "

[1] Bateman's Manual, 1852. [2] C. 1 R. [3] C. 20 R. [4] Oct. 17, 1863.
[5] Parl. R. Superannuation, 1869.

George Lewis,	.	From 1823	to 1824	1	years.
Thomas Burton,	.	„ 1824	„ 1825	1	„
John Storer, .	.	„ 1825	„ 1827	2	„
Charles Brown,	.	„ 1827	„ 1844	17	„
George Ballard,	.	„ 1844	„ 1853	9	„
Thomas Dobson,	.	„ 1853	„ 1863	10	„
William Corbett,	.	„ 1863	„ 1869	6	„
Adam Young,	.	„ 1869			

SEIZURES.

Down to about 1726 collusive seizures in the country were so common that it became necessary to revise the regulations, in so far as that every seizure was directed to be publicly sold,—but not probably in the case of a dutiable commodity for less than the duty exactable[1]—that one-third only of the net proceeds be given to the informer; that the officer inform his supervisor of the fact within forty-eight hours or lose his reward; and, that those among the officers who dealt in exciseable commodities give up their commissions. But public sales conducted by burning an inch of candle on the completion of which the highest bidder became the purchaser, were made in London as early as 1724. "The Commissioners of His Majesty's Revenue of Excise, design to expose to Sale in their Court-Room at the Excise Office, London, on Wednesday the 20th of this Instant, January, at Three a-Clock in the Afternoon, several Parcels of Bohea and Green Tea, Coffee, and Cocoa Nuts. Printed Allotments of which will be ready to be delivered at the Excise Office and the Goods to be seen any Day at the said Office after the 17th Instant, from One to Four a-Clock in the Afternoon, to the Time of Sale."[2] This is one of the first announcements in the *London Gazette*, and it is worthy of note that the announcements of sales were subsequently made with marked regularity about twice a year, for about three-quarters of a century, though during that period, when smuggling had become a profitable business, five sales were advertised in one year, and two of these were three-day sales. The writer has not traced this mode of publicity later than 1847.[3] But a sale was sometimes not effected, even of a valuable seizure, for it

[1] 1807. [2] January 5, 1724; 1702, 1714, 1720. [3] L. G., 1665-1865.

often happened that the officers were forced to forego their "Find A"[1] or the place of security in which it was stored had to yield to the force of house-breaking appliances. It is recorded that four horses and a quantity of spirits were rescued from a party of officers and others at Bodmin,[2] and on another occasion, that 500 lbs. of tobacco, 1,700 gallons of French Brandy, 200 gallons of Foreign Rum, 1,000 gallons of Foreign Geneva were rescued from the officers at Lennen also in Cornwall.[3] It is also recorded that the Excise Offices at Elgin and Cranborne were broken open and seizures removed by those from whom they had been seized,[4] and that rewards of about one hundred guineas were offered for the discovery of these perpetrators of deeds of force.[5] The appraisement was not usually announced publicly unless of a special character. An instance, however, may be quoted—"At Leith in Scotland 47 ankers or 445 gallons of Foreign Geneva, appraised at 7s per gallon: 553 ankers and 346 half ankers, containing 6,637 gallons and a half of Foreign Geneva, appraised at 6s 9d per gallon: 2 ankers containing 11 gallons of vinegar, appraised at 3s per gallon." Excise Office, Edinburgh, April 25, 1781.[6]

The zeal of the "seizure-maker" is shown in the extent of his deeds[7]—number and value—which upon one occasion extended even to the "poinding" of the painted linen in Theatres, but this had to be given back.[8] A valuable take of spirits estimated at £10,000, was "poinded" on removal from Scotland to England, of which, on condemnation by the Commissioners, the officer was entitled to one-half.[9] Then to instance numbers only, no fewer than 859 stills were seized in Scotland in 1797; 19,067 stills in Ireland in 1811 and two following years; and 804 stills, 25,136 bushels of malt, 122,263 gallons of worts and 624 gallons of spirits, also in Ireland in 1830; then as to the value, His Majesty's share in England for three years ended in 1775 was no less than £24,000, and for the same period ended in 1782, £36,000;[10] in Scotland it varied in ten years from £5,700 to £12,400.[11] From these royal shares may be inferred the officers' shares.

So important had the management of seizures become in 1817 that

[1] Seizure—C. S. G., 1873. [2] L. G., 1797. [3] Idem., 1805.
[4] Idem., 1768-1793. [5] Idem., 1793, 1797. [6] Idem., 1781.
[7] Scotch Instructions, 1804. [8] 1819. [9] H. C., May 6, 1785.
[10] Excise Office, Dec. 4, 1783. [11] 1770-75; 1779-82; Parl. Ret., 1784.

special Instructions on Seizures were issued. The officers in Scotland termed their seizure-register a "Poind Book."

SITTINGS.

Stowe informs us in his Annals of England that Henry VIII. on going to war with France sent commissioners into every shire "with privy instructions how they should proceed in the *sittings*, &c., order the people to bring them to their purpose, which was that the sixth parte of everie mans substance, should be paid in money, or plate to the King without delaie for the furniture of his warre."[1] This proves the antiquity of the "collection-day," and there is no reason to believe but that it has ever been the mode of receipt in this department. There were nine rounds of sittings in the year down to 1759, termed the intermediate round, the half-quarterly round, the half-round collection, the quarterly round, at which the collector was formerly enjoined not "to occasion him"—officer—"to spend above two-and-sixpence;"[2] in the case of dropped officers, not to detain them "at the Sitting in any Way that may subject them to spend Money there,"[3] while in other cases the collector has been reproved that "In numerous instances officers are longer detained at sittings than is actually necessary."[4] These were the jovial days, in which it was necessary to minute even the hours of ingress and egress of the collector himself to and from the seat of sitting, in the supervisor's diary.

The allowances made to those who attended sittings will be found under the paper on that subject. As to the allowance to the publican at whose inn the sitting is held, it is stated to have been first granted under the following circumstances in 1837. "The George was then an old-fashioned hostelry, with many small windows. Byres grudged the window-tax very much. He asked the then collector if he thought he could not get an abatement for the tax on the two small windows that gave light to the excise-room. The result was an application to the Board, when in lieu of an exemption an allowance of five shillings was granted." Going on the rounds or travelling on the round of a prescribed area of country originated in part with the difficulties and expenses experienced by the payer, for whose convenience the sittings

[1] 1527. [2] 1778. [3] 1789. [4] 1825.

were held, but these having partly disappeared with the progress of the people the Parnell Committee were induced in 1836 to write that "There is no reason to apprehend that . . . . inconveniences would arise if the number of rounds were diminished by one-half."[1] This idea though then made, and subsequently repeated,[2] was not adopted until 1871—out of residence. The discontinuance of two of these has been suggested, in Ireland, by Humanitas,[3] as also, the total discontinuance by Sinbad the Super."[4]

SMUGGLING.

For about one-and-a-half centuries[5] the suppression of smuggling engaged the close attention of this department, aided by troops, and the bold, successful and remunerative "runs" were frequently narrated with considerable animation in the Houses of Parliament.

The milder modes of suppression such as prohibiting importation except in certain quantities,[6] the possession of a certificate on the removal of a single bottle of brandy[7] and such like, were soon set aside by the daring bands of men who followed "Black Giles," the smuggler chief, to the number of thirty to eighty at a time, all well mounted and armed, and their horses loaded with 150 to 200 lbs. of "old gown" (smuggled tea), and rode daringly "through the towns in defiance of the King's officers and the dragoons who were sent to assist them."[8] These outlaws were known by various names, as for instance, in Scotland, as "The Cloan Company," "The Mull Company," "The Carrick Company," and consisted of twelve, five, and ten members, habitual smugglers,[9] while those in England who were only occasionally employed received half-a-crown per day, while waiting upon the coast for the landing of the "run goods," and a guinea per day when mounted on horseback with the contraband, and armed and accompanied by bulldogs they rode through the country to assist the "Master in the Private Line"[10] in disposing of his "clandestine or collusive" importation. One clear run in four being considered to pay well, and to obtain this one portion of a party made a sham run to lure away the "Look-out-men" and the

[1] 20 Rep. [2] C. S. G., 1856, 1858, 1864, 1865, 1867. [3] Idem., 1871.
[4] Idem., 1869. [5] 1693-1844. [6] 1693, 1719. [7] 1722.
[8] H. C., March 4, 1779. [9] P. Rep., 1798.
[10] P. Rep., 1798; H. C., Feb. 4, 1734.

"Revenue Sharks," while the other portion smuggled without molestation at another place.[1] Indeed, observes Sir Robert Walpole, "In most of our maritime counties, I do not know but that our military would protect the smugglers instead of bringing them to justice; . . . . and in every county I am convinced the militia would protect the illegal retailer of spirituous liquors, instead of protecting those who serve the public by informing against them." Such is the language of the then Prime Minister.[2]

This statement was made two years after a special act—in the prolonged debate upon which in the House of Lords occurs—"If you intend that any of the officers should dare to do their duty, within some of the counties of England: and this necessity proceeds from the great height smuggling has lately come to, and the vast numbers of men now engaged some way or other in that pernicious trade; insomuch that in some parts of our maritime counties, the whole people of the county are so generally engaged in it, that it is impossible to find a jury that will upon a trial do justice to an officer of the revenue; therefore, unless you agree to this clause, an officer, in any such county, who faithfully performs the duty of his office, must expect to be assaulted, beaten, and bruised, every day of his life; because the people of the county know that he never can recover a verdict against them." Their lordships returned this bill with amendments, which not being heeded, led to a written protest against it, because its provisions were repugnant to the laws and constitution of the kingdom: because it empowered a justice to commit of an intention to smuggle on the evidence of one witness: because the lords' amendments in committee were omitted on the bill being reported. The act contained very stringent regulations, consisted of thirty-eight sections and applied to Great Britain.

Still the "incorrigible" remained unreclaimed by the proffered "grace and clemency," the "unwary" continued to be "seduced," and of course the "wicked practice" prevailed. His Majesty proclaims his willingness to set aside the sentence of the law upon those under sentence and others who had left their country, provided they would enter the navy. God save the King.[3] And this proclamation was afterwards twice repeated,[4] while a Committee of the House of Commons was appointed to investigate the subject;[5] the Isle of

[1] Smugglers and Forresters, 1851. [2] H. C., Feb. 3, 1738.
[3] Proc., May 9, 1744. [4] May 30, 1778; May 3, 1782. [5] 1746.

Man was purchased;[1] numerous smuggling cutters cleared the coast;[2] an Order in Council commanding thirteen smugglers and their accomplices to surrender within forty days was issued;[3] and even the Commissioners admitted that "The evil Practice of Smuggling of late has increased to a pitch of Enormity, and been carried on with a Force and Violence almost without Example in former Times, insomuch that the Revenue Officers can no longer do their duty."[4]

Their Honours statement is borne out by the fact that its purport was included in the Address of Thanks to His Majesty:[5] by Sir Grey Cooper who stated "that on the western coast it was customary when a smuggling cutter hove in sight, for a body of men, sometimes 800 in number, to take charge of the cargo when it was landed; these men had sometimes 40 waggons by which they carried these goods into the country:" and by Lord Cavendish, who observed in moving the appointment of a select committee to enquire into the practice, "The various plans that had been suggested to him he was sure a cart could not contain."[6]

This committee made three reports. It observes in its first report, "If the whole of the information obtained, in addition to the evidence, were to be stated, it would form a detail which might be thought too voluminous, and would open many practices inexpedient to be made public." "The vessels used for smuggling are of various sizes, from 30 to 300 tons, mounting from 6 to 24 guns, and navigated by crews of from 12 to 100 men. The cargoes consist chiefly of tea, spirits, brandy, rum, tobacco stalks, and snuff. The largest of those vessels are capable of bringing in 3,000 half-ankers (about 5 galls. each?) of spirits and 10 or 12 tons of tea. The landing of the cargo is regulated by signals, and secured by large gangs of men, armed chiefly with clubs and heavy whips, generally inflamed with liquor, and assembled in such numbers as to reduce the revenue officers to be quiet spectators of the proceeding: this is very generally the case, except when the revenue officers can obtain a large military force; and even when aid is obtained upon an information, it is generally frustrated; for the scouts placed upon shore give signals to the vessels at sea, which instantly proceed according to the settled signals to some other place of rendezvous, at 15 or 20

[1] 1765. [2] 1764. [3] Nov. 27, 1778. [4] 1781. [5] H. C., Nov. 11, 1783.
[6] H. C., Nov. 21, 1783.

miles distance, and land the cargoes in the night time. The cargo thus delivered is placed in waggons or on horses, being packed and prepared for that purpose in casks and oil-skin bags: it is next either distributed on the coast or parts adjoining for sale and consumption, or brought to the neighbourhood of the metropolis, and into the metropolis, either under the open guard and protection of armed troops of men, or by a fallacious use of permits. The number of large vessels employed in smuggling is 120 besides 200 smaller ones." The Commissioners of Excise believe if smuggling could be stopped, the duties on tea, coffee, brandy, and rum, would amount to £3,000,000 instead of £1,000,000. There are 42 armed revenue cutters in the service of the customs, and 14 under the excise in G. B. "In Scotland it is sometimes the practice for the armed crews of the smuggling vessels to escort the goods into the country, when they apprehend molestation, and they are strong enough to bid defiance to the revenue officers whether on sea or shore. The business is carried on by companies regularly established at different places on the coast, at each of which they pay rents more than the ground will produce; but these lands, upon which they have several houses, are requisite for the accommodation of many dependants and servants (who are necessary for the undertaking), and for the maintenance of carriers and horses, which are seen in waiting, to the amount of 100 or 200 at a time, when vessels are expected."

The House of Commons then went into Committee on these reports. Mr Chancellor Pitt stated tea "to be the staple of smuggling;" that 5,500,000 lbs. of tea are sold annually by the East India Co., but 12,000,000 or 13,000,000 are used. "To meet this evil, the best possible plan was to reduce the duty on tea to such a degree as to take away from the smuggler the temptation to carry on an illegal trade." . . . "It was well-known the price of insurance in so hazardous a trade, and the freight, were about £25 per cent. to the shore, for the inland carriage of it in this kingdom was about £10 per cent. more, and the profit on the whole he would not reckon at more than £5 per cent., so that the £5 per cent. might, upon the whole of the smuggler's capital, be reckoned in the end at £40 per cent. per annum." . . . "It was clear the smuggler must sell at 40 per cent. above the prime cost. Now his plan was to take off the excise duty on tea and impose a custom duty and window tax." Lord Mahon said his Right Hon. friend acted wisely in endeavouring to strike smuggling on the head at one blow, and at this moment his lordship inadvertently hit Mr Pitt, who sat directly beneath him, a blow on the head. The resolution was carried.[1]

Great as this "blow" must have been, the Commissioners again stated, in 1805, that "the pernicious practices of the smuggler have been carried on to an alarming extent, and with unparalleled audacity," and they afterwards enjoined their officers to be vigilant, active, evince the utmost cordiality with the aiding soldier, and zealously co-operate with the customs, suppressing "personal motives or departmental jealousy."[2] The Impress Service Officers were also enjoined to impress every seafaring smuggler possible.[3] The last observed statistics were given for the period 1826-1833. 28 paid the full penalty, 69 paid in part, 596 served in ships, 1226 imprisoned in default, 1029 penalties were remitted, and 158 smugglers were in prison at the date of the return.[4]

A petition was presented to Parliament in 1835 to revise the smuggling laws.

This subject has formed the theme of a three-volume novel, in which c. 6, v. 1, and cc. 9, 10, 12, v. 2, are worth a perusal;[5] and again in Smugglers and Foresters.[6] It has also been written upon by Wilson in his "Tales of the Borders," while Chambers has printed a pithy paper on its droll aspects, with direct reference to the drolleries in the Custom-House Museum, London.[7] It has also been made the source of merriment in song, as—"The Smuggler King," "The Female Smuggler," "Poor Smuggler's Boy," and the source of study in art, as in the painting by Cooper—"Smugglers on the Coast of Sussex, 100 years ago."

The Smuggler or Gauger's Stone, opposite Garscube Toll near the Firhill Iron Works, Glasgow, is this landmark in the form of a large roundish whinstone, of which the story or tradition runs that a smuggler, on being pursued, ran down the Firhill, swam across the Forth and Clyde Canal, and on landing was shot and fell beside this now monument. It was long the habit of the passer-by to throw a stone at it until, "a perfect mound or cairn of stones" was raised, but this has been levelled by the progress of events.

See Assaults. Seizures.

[1] H. C., June 21, 1784. [2] 1807, 1814, 1815, 1816, 1834, 1844. [3] 1807.
[4] P. Ret., 1833. [5] The Highland Smugglers, Bentley, 1832. [6] 1851.
[7] Chambers Journal, 1877.

SOAP DUTY.

Rushworth writes in his "Historical Recollections" under the year 1631—"In order to increase the Crown Revenue by the way of Grants by Letters Patents under the Great Seal of England, the King created a new Corporation within the City of Westminster by the name of the Society of Sopemakers," of whom he continues—"And all sope boilers who will not come into their Corporation, are to be prohibited the trade of sope boilers. And a good Revenue yearly was brought to the King's Exchequer, as is hereafter mentioned, viz., £10,000 by way of advance, and £8 per ton paid also into the Exchequer."[1] Reference is also made to this Corporation by three proclamations of subsequent dates.[2]

Soap first formed an article subject to excise duty in the troublous times in 1643.[3] It next came under tribute in Great Britain in 1712 by 10 Anne c. 19, and the duty appears to have been charged with apparent unconcern by the makers until a proposition was made in the House of Commons in 1778 to allow all goods except linen and woollen goods to be imported from Ireland free of duty, a proposition which the soapmakers petitioned against.[4] At a later period a glass bead having a specific gravity of 1·05 and a thermometer were supplied to those entrusted with charging the duty on soap, to prepare a "liquor," consisting of water and common salt, in which, when at a temperature of 62°, the bead would neither float on the surface nor sink to the bottom, but remain in any part where it might be placed, to form a test for "silicious or earthy matter" in the saponaceous substance. Introduced in 1839, discontinued in 1853. Mr Pitt imposed a two pound licence duty on the maker,[5] which was doubled in 1815, and though afterwards thought by Sir H. Parnell's Committee,[6] and by Mr Gladstone,[7] a fit form of duty to be further increased, Mr Lowe repealed it in 1870.[8] But to return to the growing duty. "We have no wish to burn up our livers; give us clean hands and clean linen, and we leave others to red noses and bloated bodies," said Mr Sykes, on making a motion to repeal it, when the Chancellor of the Exchequer wished to reduce the spirit duty.[9] This aim at abolition was afterwards supported by Sir H. Parnell in his Financial Reform;[10] by Martin in his Taxation of the

[1] January 20, 1631-2. [2] 1632, 1634, 1637. [3] P. O. [4] H. C., May 6, 1778.
[5] H. C., June 30, 1784. [6] Nineteenth Rep., 1836. [7] H. C., April 18, 1853.
[8] H. C., April 11, 1870. [9] H. C., June 7, 1825. [10] 1832.

British Empire:[1] by Porter in his Progress of the Nation;[2] by Punch;[3] by Richard Cobden, who wrote, "What a satire upon our sanitary acts, and all the pompous agitations in favour of baths and wash-houses is the tax upon the necessary elements of cleanliness! Not a word need be said upon it;"[4] by O'Connell, who exclaimed, "I wish to God that their interference in the manufacturing concerns was put an end to for ever!"[5] and by Mr Handley, who prayed, on a suggestion being made, that the duty should be extended to Ireland, that she may "not be polluted by the unhallowed footsteps of a phalanx of a soap-duty-levying excisemen."[6] The Chancellor of the Exchequer admitted that "It is impossible not to be convinced by everything which one sees that the illicit manufacture is at present carried on to a great extent."[7] M'Culloch thought if it could be reduced and an easier mode of charge be devised, it could not then "be found fault with."[8] In common with every other duty it was referred to the Royal Commission appointed in 1833. The cost of collection about this time was 3 per cent.[9] and exchequer prosecutions were numerous.[10]

The next effort to remove it from the statute-book was made by Mr Alderman Thompson, who moved a reduction,[11] which he obtained in 1833. This was soon succeeded by two unsuccessful motions for its repeal by Mr Gillon,[12] but the only statutory alteration effected was a consolidated statute in 1840.

From 1830 to 1845 petitions were most persistently presented for its repeal, notably so in 1838, when no fewer than 104, containing 13,359 signatures, were presented;[13] while from 1830 to 1853 returns of the quantities made and exported, convictions obtained, penalties awarded, and rewards given, were almost continuously made to Parliament. It fell to Mr Gladstone's lot to propose the abolition of this penny and three-half-penny per pound duty in his first financial statement, which, upon becoming known, induced great preparations to be made by the trade to export upon drawback on a large scale, with a view to realise an illegal gain by subsequent importation, an intention which was not realised.[14] Duty was not charged on that placed under revenue security between this date and the date of the

[1] 1833. [2] 1843. [3] 1845. [4] Financial Reform Tract, 1847.
[5] H. C., Feb. 22, 1833. [6] H. C., 1836. [7] H. C., 1834.
[8] Dictionary of Commerce, 1832. [9] Parnell Seventeenth Rep., 183[illegible]
[10] H. C., 1832. [11] Idem. [12] H. C., April 4, 1836; April 3, 18[illegible]
[13] P. Ret. [14] H. C., June 21, 1853.

repeal, July 5, 1853. The gross duty, £1,397,000, drawback £271,000, net £1,126,000, cost £15,000, net final receipt £1,111,000.[1]

A *saponaceous* sentence seems never to have been said on the subject.

SOMERVILLE'S EXCISE READY RECKONER:

"Embracing calculations of the most important excise duties, drawbacks, and allowances, at the various existing rates: the proportionate gallons of proof spirits, corresponding to the beer or bigg malt used: the net bushels of malt, from the cistern or couch bushels: the allowances granted to postmasters: and the proof gallon of spirits, at the various strengths allowed by law. Adapted to all the purposes of excise connected with malting, distilleries, stocking, and warehousing, by John Somerville, officer of excise."

Dunn, Glasgow: pages 46: price 2s.: 1846.

SONGS.

EXCISE.

A NEW BALLAD CALLED A REVIEW OF THE REBELLION.

HE whom the warres leaves worth a grote,
Shall be Delinquent made by Vote,
Are we not like to be bravely reform'd
Who are sure to be so thoroughly warm'd;
Quarterings, Excise, and Taxe,
Expect untill the Axe
And Halter claim by Law their due:
Till then 'tis hard to show,
The ready way to know,
A Rebell from a Subject true.

In black letter.

[1] Mr Gladstone, H. C., April 18, 1853.

THE PENITENT TRAYTOR.

THUS I gain'd much, and by my Money-Pole
And something like Excise, these made whole
My Children Portions too, with much content,
I play'd in State my Act of Parliament.

THE POORE COMMITTEE-MAN'S ACCOMPT,

A voucher by Britannicus, a Ballad in nine verses. Verse three—

THE fifth and twentieth part, Excise, Customs, and Sequestrations;
The King's Revenues too we have, besides the great Taxation;
And that great taxe is monthly laid, upon the associated,
Which comes to three score thousand pounds a month, if rightly stated:
That this is true you need not doubt, examine Mr Needham,
He'll tell you true, and sweare it too, 'tis for the kingdome's freedome.

THE TRUE PROTESTANT'S HUMBLE DESIRES TO THE KING'S MOST EXCELLENT MAJESTY,

WITH "A COMMINATION TO BE CONFIRMED BY A CHORUS OF THE PEOPLE."

The desires extended through 24 verses, each of which commenced "Cursed." Last verse—

CURSED be he that doth not pray,
The Excise may quite be taken away,
And all Traytors to come to decay,
And let all people say, Amen.

IRELAND'S COMPLAINT OF THE ARMIES HYPOCRISIE,

AND ADDENDUM, "NULLA DIES SINE LINEA, OR THE SLIGHTING OF THE WORKS."

THE Excize-man fright quite away,
Butchers you not prize them;
You need not lift sheep or Works,
For fear they should Excise them.

THE EXCISEMAN'S MISTAKE. A NEW SONG.

I KNOW that young folks like to hear a new song,
It's something that's funny, and not very long,
It's of an Exciseman the truth I will tell,
Who one night thought he went down to h—ll.

One night he went for to look for his prey,
He got plenty of smugglers as I heard them say,
In gauging the liquors as I hear them say,
The exciseman got drunk in truth every day.

He got so intoxicated he fell to the ground,
And just like a fat sow he fell to the ground,
Just nigh to a coal pit, the exciseman did lie,
When four or five pitmen did chance to pass by.

Said one to another here is our old friend,
The exciseman that takes all the whiskey and gin,
To give him a fright we think it no crime,
And it happened about the shifting time.

They shouldered him up and hoisted him away,
Like a pedlar's pack hoisted him away,
Into the bucket they handed him down
This jolly exciseman they got under ground.

The exciseman he awoke with terrible fear,
Up starts a pitman what brought you here,
Indeed Mr Devil, I don't very well know,
But I think I am come to the regions below.

What were you when in the world above,
I was an exciseman few did me love,
Indeed Mr Devil the truth to you I will tell,
Since I once got here, I'll be what you will.

Since you are an exciseman here you must remain,
You will never get out of this dark cell again,
The gates they are fast and bind you secure,
All this you must suffer for robbing the poor.

Indeed, Mr Devil, if you'll pity me,
No more I'll keep robbing the poor you shall see,
If you'll look over it as you've done before,
I'll never keep robbing the poor any more.

Come give us your money, and that we demand
Before you can get back to the Christian land,
O yes, Mr Devil, the exciseman did say,
I wish to get back to see light of day.

THE NEW SMALL STILL.—A New Song.

Come all you north country drovers,
And those that deals in red kye;
I set forth the praise of my heifer,
Without ever telling a lie,

A milk that is good for the headache;
They call it the mother o' spleen,
It will cure all female diseases,
So let them never complain.

It will nourish and cherish old women,
And make them look wondrous stout,
And cock up their tail like a mavis,
And so they go cantrin about.
If you take my brawny in winter,
And in a peat-hole let her fall,
She neither will rout nor gravel
Nor in it shall catch no great cauld.

When Judy comes over the *gadger*
She canna weel gang for the milk;
She cocks up her tail in the riggan
You'll find her as soft as silk.
Put her on a fire, you will find her
As hardened as steel,
But clap a hot ingle behind her,
She'll stand as much fire as the deil.

My brawny's not given to jumpin,
Nor neither will she break a dike
There ne'er gled a bull on her hurdies,
Although she is fat and good like.
Her tail is wondrous crooked;
It's three or four times turned round;
She's *free* when the pigeon is helped,
To scatter the rest to the ground.

THE CRAFTY MISS, OR, AN EXCISEMAN WELL FITTED.

Being a true Relation of an Exciseman who lately in the County of Kent, had received the sum of four-score pounds, and lighting into the Company of a Crafty Miss who gave him the Chouse for it all; and riding away with his Gelding, left in the stead a Mare which she had stole; for which Mare he was arraigned, and narrowly escaped the severe penalty of the Law: which may be a sufficient warning to all Excisemen far and near, to amend their lives, to hate a Miss and love their Wives. To the Tune of "Maggie's Jealousie.'

There was an Excise-man so fine, rode into the county of Kent,
And there he received much Coyn, for that very business he went:
He met with a jolly brave Miss, her beauty was fair to behold,
But she gave him a judas Kiss, and shew'd him a trick for his Gold.

She rod on a bonny brave Mare, he rid on a Gelding also;
He whisper'd a word in her ear, straight way to an Inn they did go,
He was of a pretty Condition, he called her the joy of his life,
And then without any suspicion they passed for Husband and Wife.

They set up the Mare and the Gelding, and call'd for a Supper with speed,
Their Wine it was plentily filled in and lovingly then they agreed:
O then they were heartily merry, their joys did begin to abound;
They drank up full brimmers of sherry and the Glass it went merrily round.

He had not the sight of his folly, fond love had so blinded his eyes,
O then he was heartily jolly, he thought he'd gotten a prize,
Then whilst they most lovingly greeted he thought he was certainly blest,
But ne'er was Excise-man so Cheated, O now comes the Cream of the jest.

He pulled out a Purse full of Gold, which he had received for Excise,
And said to his Landlord, behold, keep this till next morning we rise;
His Miss she did call him her Honey, and straight to embracing they fall
But her mind still ran on the Money to give him the Chouse for it all.

And while he was snoring and sleeping, she thought it no time to delay,
But giving the Landlord a Meeting, O thus unto him she did say:
My husband he has not the power to rise, although it be day,
Yet he hath appointed an hour to pay all this money away.

The time doth begin to expire, then prithee now sadlè his Steed,
And Landlord, I do you desire to fetch me the Money with speed:
The Inn-Keeper he did believe it, and fetch her the four-score pound,
And she was as glad to receive it, she neither spar'd horse-flesh nor ground.

But when the Exciseman did waken and found that his Miss she was fled,
And seeing himself thus forsaken, while he had been sleeping a Bed,
O then how he rapped and thunder'd, he was in a Cholerick heat?
His Pockets were pillag'd and plunder'd, he found he had met with a cheat.

The Landlord the Chamber did enter, and bowing himself to the
 ground,
Sir, have you forgot where you sent her to pay in the four-score pound,
The Landlord no sooner had said it but that he was daunted straight-
 way,
But yet for the sake of his Credit, O never a word he would say.

But then he was fretting and petting, he had ne'er a penny of Cole,
His Miss rid away with the Gelding and left him a Mare she had stole;
For which they did soon apprehend him, in sorrow he then did com-
 plain,
For they to a Prison did send him, where did till Sizes remain.

And there he was raigned at the Bar, besides all the Money he lost.
O now you Excisemen beware, you see in your courting your're crost,
The Bill it had like to been found, because he had called for his wife,
It cost him many a pound, and had like to cost him his life.

This was in Rochester City, the truth you may certainly find,
The people afforded no pitty, but said he was served in his kind:
But now the Exciseman is sorry that ever he met with this Jade,
For sure she had learned her Jarry, she lackt but a stock to her Trade.

Printed in Black Letter, Roxburghe Ballads, 1670, Vol. II., Royal Library, British Museum.

THE JOLLY GAUGER.

I AM a jolly Gauger,
And keep a four-foot Rule,
With Colling's Books in Pocket,
New come from Dixon's School.
And a Gauging we will go, we'll go, we'll go,
And a Gauging we will go.

With Colling's Book in Pocket,
And Everard's Rule and Cane,
A sliding Rule for Customers,
And a Conscience void of Stain.
And a Gauging we will go, we'll go, we'll go,
And a Gauging we will go.

When in the Night I ramble,
With Lanthorn in my Hand,
And if in Bed my Landlady,
She'll rise at my Commahd.
And a Gauging we will go, we'll go, we'll go,
And a Gauging we will go.

I hank my Horse still at the Door,
And to the Cellar run,
Where I do gage all empty casks,
As well as those are full.
And a Gauging we will go, we'll go, we'll go,
And a Gauging we will go.

There's Number One holds thirty-six,
And so doth Number Two,
There's Number Four holds forty,
The Fourth's not gauged true.
And a Gauging we will go, we'll go, we'll go.
And a Gauging we will go.

There's Number Five filled up with Small,
As sure as any Thing;
Odsblue, you . . . . it is all Strong,
You must not cheat the King.
And a Gauging we will go, we'll go, we'll go,
And a Gauging we will go.

But in the Item of our Sport,
I wish we had been Wiser,
Just as I at the Window looked
I spy'd the Supervisor.
And a Gauging we will go, we'll go, we'll go,
And a Gauging we will go.

In came the Supervisor,
So pleasantly he looks;
How do you, good Officer?
Pray let me see your Books.
And a Gauging we will go, we'll go, we'll go,
And a Gauging we will go.

But when he looked into them,
He fell into a Rage,
What do you mean you drunken Dog?
Here's neither Stock nor Gauge.
And a Gauging we will go, we'll go, we'll go,
And a Gauging we will go.

For the future I'll admonish you
And take it on my Word,
If ere you do the like again
I'll report you to the Board.
And *no more* a Gauging you'll go, you'll go,
And no more a Gauging you'll go."

—*British Museum.*

NORVAL, OR WHISKY STILLS.

Air—"The Irish Gauger."

My name is Norval, on the Grampian hills,
Fal, lal, la, la, lal, lal, la, &c.
My faither keeps his whiskey stills,
Fal, lal, &c.

His occupation is to shield
His whiskey stills fra the gauger chiels;
And to keep his son at hame as well.
Fal, lal, &c.
And to keep his son at hame as well.
Fal, la, &c.

The moon which shone so bright last night,
Had scarcely set itself—not quite;
When a band of gaugers from the hills
Cam' tumbling down like Jacks and Gills,
And pounced upon our whiskey stills.
Fal, lal, &c.

My faither he was off like a shot,
And said the stills might go to pot:
While I alone withstood the shock,
And tumbled the gaugers o'er the rock,
And made their heads play nick-ety-knock.
Fal, lal, &c.

Full fifty fathoms they fell, I think,
And spattered the rocks all over with ink;
The first he fell down with a thump, thump, thump,
The next he fell down with a dump, dump, dump,
While they all fell together in a clump, clump, clump,
Fal, lal, &c.

THE PRIVATE STILL.

Tune—Original.

An Exciseman once in Dublin,
At the time that I was there,
He fancied that a *private still*,
Was being worked somewhere;
He met me out one morning,
Perhaps he fancied that I knew—
But I didn't—never mind that—
Says he, "Pat how do you do?"

Says I, "I'm very well your honour,
  But allow me for to say,
I don't know you at all, by Jove,"
  "But," says he, "perhaps you may;
I want to find something out,
  Assist me if you will,
Here's fifty pounds if you can tell me,
  Where there's a private still."

"Give me fifty pounds," says I,
  "For upon my soul I can—
I'll keep my word, upon my soul,
  As I'm an Irishman;"
The fifty pounds he then put down,
  I pocketed the fee,
Says I, "Now come along, my boy,
  And straightway follow me."

. . . . . .

. . . . . .

"Half-a-minute more," says I,
  "I'll point him out to you—
"Faith there he is," said I, "old chap,
  Standing 'twixt them two;"
"Who the blazes do you mean?" says he—
  I mean "My brother Bill,"
"Well," says he, "Well," says I—
  "They won't make him a corporal, so he's a
    private still."

The exciseman stamped and said,
  That he would have his money back,
But I jumped in the car myself,
  And off was in a crack;
And the people as he walks along,
  Tho' much against his will,
Shout after him, exciseman,
  Have you found the private still?

THE EXCISEMAN.

To a village that skirted the sea,
  An Exciseman one Midsummer came,
But prudence, between you and me,
  Forbids me to tell you his name.

at this moment his lordship inadvertently hit Mr Pitt, who sat directly beneath him, a blow on the head. The resolution was carried.[1]

Great as this "blow" must have been, the Commissioners again stated, in 1805, that "the pernicious practices of the smuggler have been carried on to an alarming extent, and with unparalleled audacity," and they afterwards enjoined their officers to be vigilant, active, evince the utmost cordiality with the aiding soldier, and zealously co-operate with the customs, suppressing "personal motives or departmental jealousy."[2] The Impress Service Officers were also enjoined to impress every seafaring smuggler possible.[3] The last observed statistics were given for the period 1826-1833. 28 paid the full penalty, 69 paid in part, 596 served in ships, 1226 imprisoned in default, 1029 penalties were remitted, and 158 smugglers were in prison at the date of the return.[4]

A petition was presented to Parliament in 1835 to revise the smuggling laws.

This subject has formed the theme of a three-volume novel, in which c. 6, v. 1, and cc. 9, 10, 12, v. 2, are worth a perusal;[5] and again in Smugglers and Foresters.[6] It has also been written upon by Wilson in his "Tales of the Borders," while Chambers has printed a pithy paper on its droll aspects, with direct reference to the drolleries in the Custom-House Museum, London.[7] It has also been made the source of merriment in song, as—"The Smuggler King," "The Female Smuggler," "Poor Smuggler's Boy," and the source of study in art, as in the painting by Cooper—"Smugglers on the Coast of Sussex, 100 years ago."

The Smuggler or Gauger's Stone, opposite Garscube Toll near the Firhill Iron Works, Glasgow, is this landmark in the form of a large roundish whinstone, of which the story or tradition runs that a smuggler, on being pursued, ran down the Firhill, swam across the Forth and Clyde Canal, and on landing was shot and fell beside this now monument. It was long the habit of the passer-by to throw a stone at it until, "a perfect mound or cairn of stones" was raised, but this has been levelled by the progress of events.

See Assaults. Seizures.

[1] H. C., June 21, 1784. [2] 1807, 1814, 1815, 1816, 1834, 1844. [3] 1807.
[4] P. Ret., 1833. [5] The Highland Smugglers, Bentley, 1832. [6] 1851.
[7] Chambers Journal, 1877.

SOAP DUTY.

Rushworth writes in his "Historical Recollections" under the year 1631—"In order to increase the Crown Revenue by the way of Grants by Letters Patents under the Great Seal of England, the King created a new Corporation within the City of Westminster by the name of the Society of Sopemakers," of whom he continues—"And all sope boilers who will not come into their Corporation, are to be prohibited the trade of sope boilers. And a good Revenue yearly was brought to the King's Exchequer, as is hereafter mentioned, viz., £10,000 by way of advance, and £8 per ton paid also into the Exchequer."[1] Reference is also made to this Corporation by three proclamations of subsequent dates.[2]

Soap first formed an article subject to excise duty in the troublous times in 1643.[3] It next came under tribute in Great Britain in 1712 by 10 Anne c. 19, and the duty appears to have been charged with apparent unconcern by the makers until a proposition was made in the House of Commons in 1778 to allow all goods except linen and woollen goods to be imported from Ireland free of duty, a proposition which the soapmakers petitioned against.[4] At a later period a glass bead having a specific gravity of 1·05 and a thermometer were supplied to those entrusted with charging the duty on soap, to prepare a "liquor," consisting of water and common salt, in which, when at a temperature of 62°, the bead would neither float on the surface nor sink to the bottom, but remain in any part where it might be placed, to form a test for "silicious or earthy matter" in the saponaceous substance. Introduced in 1839, discontinued in 1853. Mr Pitt imposed a two pound licence duty on the maker,[5] which was doubled in 1815, and though afterwards thought by Sir H. Parnell's Committee,[6] and by Mr Gladstone,[7] a fit form of duty to be further increased, Mr Lowe repealed it in 1870.[8] But to return to the growing duty. "We have no wish to burn up our livers; give us clean hands and clean linen, and we leave others to red noses and bloated bodies," said Mr Sykes, on making a motion to repeal it, when the Chancellor of the Exchequer wished to reduce the spirit duty.[9] This aim at abolition was afterwards supported by Sir H. Parnell in his Financial Reform;[10] by Martin in his Taxation of the

[1] January 20, 1631-2. [2] 1632, 1634, 1637. [3] P. O. [4] H. C., May 6, 1778.
[5] H. C., June 30, 1784. [6] Nineteenth Rep., 1836. [7] H. C., April 18, 1853.
[8] H. C., April 11, 1870. [9] H. C., June 7, 1825. [10] 1832.

Little regard was at first paid to the status of the distiller, either with respect to his age, his plant, or his means; as no enactment enforced the regulations on a minor until apparently 1823,[1] nor were his plant officially noted or entered until 1691,[2] nor his means considered until the duty had been considerably raised; though in Ireland as early as 1556, although, before the excise history began, a discrimination existed by which peers and gentlemen of £10 per annum, in land alone, were allowed to distil without the "lord deputie's" licence, as much as was needed for their own use, while others had to obtain that licence.[3] The number of distillers, as just stated, has rapidly declined. In England from 19 in 1804 to 8 in 1869: in Scotland from 329 in 1825 to 110 in 1869: in Ireland from 86 in 1824 to 24 in 1869—the latter date being the latest to which a separate return is shown in the official annual statement. The licence duty which has attached to the distiller since 1748 may be mentioned now. In England to 1751, £5; from 1785 to 1803, ½d. per gallon on the content of the still; from 1804 to 1814, £10; from 1815 to 1825, £20; from 1826, £10, with an addition of 5 per cent. from 1840: in Scotland from 1785 to 1814, ½d. per gallon on the content of the still; from 1815, £10, with the addition of 5 per cent. in 1840: in Ireland, from 1805 to 1814, the spirit licences were granted at the stamp office . . .; from 1825, as in Great Britain. The Parnell Committee recommended, in their nineteenth report, that the licence duty should be regulated according to the amount of duty paid, beginning with £10 when the duty did not exceed £500 per annum, and ending with £75 when it exceeded £20,000.

The use, the number, and the capacity of the utensils long remained undefined, but, at length, in Ireland, a distinction was made between those in the possession of distillers who worked for sale and those in the hands of the distiller for home consumption, the former having been required to use a still of two hundred gallons content, the latter of twelve, sometimes called black pots or alembics.[4] In Scotland it was necessary to only specify the capacity and use of the still.[5] In England to possess and enter a wash still of four hundred gallons content, and a low wine still of a hundred gallons content,[6] but since these dates, though peculiarities are still retained, a general consolidation and assimilation has been made, first in Scotland by

[1] 4 G. IV., c. 94.
[2] 3 & 4 W. & M., c. 15; 2 G. II., c. 17.
[3] 3 & 4 Phil. & Mary, c. 7.
[4] 31 G. II., c. 6.
[5] 3 G. IV., c. 52.
[6] 12 G. III.

the Act 3 G. IV., c. 52, then between Scotland and Ireland by 4 G. IV., c. 94, and lastly in the United Kingdom by 23 and 24 Vict., c. 114.

The materials employed in producing spirit have changed with the progress of the knowledge of distillation, the scarcity of corn, the state of trade. Before the principles of free trade were adopted in this country it was not uncommon for the distillation from corn to be prohibited entirely, by one-half, or by two-thirds, for longer or shorter periods,[1] and public feeling, too, run so high as to petition Parliament,[2] and even upon one occasion to burn down a distillery near Edinburgh,[3] to show the intensity of disapproval of the use of corn in this manner. The stock-feeder, on the other hand, on account of the refuse affording food for cattle, has urged its use, and a Committee of the House of Commons has recommended the speedy withdrawal of a proclamation on that plea.[4] In the reign of William and Mary, the use of "malted corne" was encouraged by the suspension of certain charters and letters patent,[5] and in that of George the Fourth, the use of "corne malted or unmalted" alone was enforced,[6] and the enactment of the right for his successor to prohibit the use by proclamation, when necessary, was passed.[7] The sugar interest endeavoured to suppress the use of corn and substitute that of sugar in 1808,[8] and a bill passed the House of Commons in 1811 to enforce the distillation from barley and sugar, at any time barley sold at 33s. per quarter,[9] but in the House of Lords it was lost by a majority of twenty votes,[10] and a similar desire in favour of the use of sugar was expressed as late as 1847.[11] *See* Sugar Duty. But the consideration of rival materials now forms no part of an official's duty so long as "the gravity of the wort can be ascertained by the saccharometer." Though decayed wines, lees, grounds of beer, cider, honey, perry, and spent wash were formerly used, malt has always held the first place. Barley malt yields from 18 to 19 proof gallons per quarter: malt and grain 20: oats 9 per 140 lbs.: sugar, which will attenuate from 8° to 18° below water, 9 to 12 per 112 lbs.:[12] molasses, 7 to 8 per 112 lbs.:[13] treacle, 6·7 per

[1] 1698, 1757, 1758, 1767, 1797, 1799, 1801, 1813, 1822.
[2] 1802, 1817, 1848. [3] 1784. [4] H. C., March 6, 1800.
[5] 2 W. & M., c. 9. [6] 3 G. IV., c. 52; 6 G. IV., c. 94. [7] 6 G. IV., c. 80.
[8] H. C., May 19, 1808. [9] H. C., March 12, 1811. [10] H. L., May 6, 1811.
[11] H. C., May 17, 1847. [12] P. Rep., 1831; P. Ret., 1847.
[13] P. Ret., 1846.

112 lbs.:[1] "mangel wurzel," 16 per ton:[2] beet root, 18 per ton, Farningham, Kent:[3] bread, see page 276. Besides may be mentioned in the profitable production of inferior spirit, raisins, dates, millet, rice,[4] potatoes,[5] and even sawdust at Queeneville.[6] To realise the utmost produce a patent ferment, consisting of potatoes, honey, and yeast was sometimes used: to impart the peat flavour, essence of peat mixed with the wash: to deprive the "malt of its oil," salt or a mixture of salt and flour: to break down the head on fermentation, butter: to prevent loss by the still "running foul" or over by ebullition, butter or soap.[7]

In no respect have the regulations differed more than in the modes of charge—actual and presumptive—thus, upon the strong-water or aqua vitæ, upon the wash low wines and spirits according to the materials used,[8] upon a presumption that a given quantity of wash or low wines would produce a certain quantity of spirits,[9] upon the capacity of the still and a gallon charge, upon the actual produce, and upon the actual delivery.

The rates are these—

TABLE OF THE RATES OF DUTY PER GALLON.

Year.	England.	Scotland.	Ireland.
1660	2d, 3d, 4d, according to materials.	..	4d.
1690	4d, 8d.	..	..
1691	2d, 4d.	..	..
1707	..	2d, 4d.	..
1709	3d, 6d.	3d, 6d.	..
1715	..	...	7d.
1717	..	..	8d.
1743	3d, 6d, 1s.	3d, 6d, 1s.	..
1746	7½d—1s 3d.	6d, 7½d, 1s.	..
1748	..	4½d—6d—7½d—1s 3d.	..
1752	1s—1s 3d.	..	..
1759	2s 3d—2s 6d.	6d—1s 2d—1s 7½d—1s 2d—1s 7½d.	..
1761	..	1s 2d—1s 4d—1s 7½d—1s 10½d.	10d.
1762	2s 6d—2s 9d.	..	..
1775	..	..	1s 2d.
1779	2s 7½d—2s 10½d.	1s 10½d—2s 1½d.	..
1780	5s 1½d and 5 p. c.	3s 5½d—3s 11½d, and 5 p. c.	..
1781	5s 1½d and 10 p. c.	3s 11½d, and 10 p. c.	..
1783	5s 1½d and 15 p. c,	3s 11½d, and 15 p. c.	..
1785	5s 1½d and 15 p. c.—2s 7½d.	3s 11½d and 15 p. c.—2s 7½d.	1s 1½d.
1786	2s 7½d.	2s 7½d.	

[1] P. Ret., 1847. [2] 1832. [3] 1857. [4] 1856. [5] 1826. [6] 1872.
[7] 1798, 1799, 1818. [8] 1660, 1669, 1746. [9] 1705, 1784, 1808.

TABLE OF THE RATES OF DUTY PER GALLON—*Continued.*

Year.	England.	Scotland.		Ireland.
		Per Gallon of Still Content.		
		Lowland.	*Highland.*	
1787	3s 2d.	1.16.0.	1.4.0.	..
1789	..	3.12.0.	1.4.0.	..
1791	3s 4½d.	..	..	..
1794	3s 4½d—3s 10¾d.	10.16.0¼.	1.16.0.	..
1795	3s 10¾d—4s 4½d.	..	..	1s 5½d.
1796	4s 4½d.	..	..	..
1797	4s 4½d—4s 10½d.	64.16.4, plus 1s 1½d per gallon on the spirits made.	3.0.0, plus 1s 1½d per gallon on 7.16.0½ spirits made.	..
1798	4s 10½d.	..	..	1s 11d.
1799	..	..	..	2s 4½d.
1800	4s 10½ 15/16d—5s 4½ 8/15d.	..	..	..
1801	5s 4½ 8/15d.	..	..	..
1802	..	3s 10½ 60/115d.	3s 4½ 13/18d.	2s 10½d.
1803	5s 4½ 8/15d—8s 0½ 1/15d.	..	..	2s 10½d—3s 6¼d.
1804	8s 0½ 1/15d.	5s 9¾ 3/13d.	5s 0½ 8/13d.	3s 6¼d—4s 1d.
1805	..	..	..	4s 1d.
1807	..	5s 8¾ 1 11/13d.	5s 0½ 8/13—4s 11½ 11/13d.	..
1808	..	..	4s 11½ 11/13d.	..
1810	..	..	..	4s 1d—2s 6½d.
1811	8s 0½ 1/15d—10s 2¾ 7/15d.	5s 8¾ 1 1/3—8s 0½ 10/13d.	4s 11½ 11/13d—6s 7½ ⅜d.	2s 6½d.
1812	10s 2¾ 7/15d.	8s 0½ 10/13.	6s 7½ ⅜d.	2s 6½d—5s 1½d.
1813	..	..	..	5s 1½d—5s 7½d.
1814	..	..	..	5s 7½d.
1815	..	9s 4½ ⅜d.		5s 7½d—6s 1½d.
1816	..	..		6s 1½d—5s 7½d.
1817	..	6s 2d.		5s 7½d.
1819	10s 2¾ 1/15d—11s 8½d.	..		..
1820	11s 8½d.	..		..
1823	..	6s 2d—2s 4¾ 4/13d.		5s 7½d—2s 4¾ 4/13d.
1824	..	2s 4¾ 4/13d.		2s 4¾ 3/13d.
1826	7s.	2s 10d.		2s 10d.
1830	7s—7s 6d.	2s 10d—3s—3s 4d		2s 10d—3s—3s 4d.
1831	7s 6d.	3s 4d.		3s 4d.
1834	..	..		3s 4d—2s 4d.
1835	..	..		2s 4d.
1840	7s 6d—7s 10d.	3s 4d—3s 8d.		2s 4d—2s 8d.
1841	7s 10d.	3s 8d.		2s 8d.
1842	..	..		2s 8d—3s 8d.
1843	..	..		3s 8d—2s 8d.
1844	..	..		2s 8d.
1853	..	3s 8d—4s 8d.		2s 8d—3s 4d.
1855	..	4s 8d—5s 8d—6s.		3s 4d—4s.
Year ended March 31.				
1856	7s 10d—8s	6s—7s 10d—8s.		4s—6s—6s 2d.
1857	8s.	8s.		6s 2d.
1859	..	..		6s 2d—8s.
1860	8s—8s 1d.	8s—8s 1d.		8s.—8s 1d.
1861	8s 1d—10s.	8s 1d—10s.		8s 1d—10s.
1862	10s.	10s.		10s.

The standard strength must have been long unsatisfactory. It would seem to have been early governed by the first or second extraction,[1] by being strong water perfectly made,[2] by the second extraction being proof spirit,[3] which was considered for some time

[1] 1660. [2] 1670. [3] 10 W. III., c. 10.

to be half alcohol and half water.[1] Glass proof, as used by the trade, and considered to be in the ratio to hydrometer proof as 1 to 6,[2] was ascertained by the "Doctor," a mixture of oil of vitriol and oil of almonds, which produced "that sort of bubble which is considered as a proof of the spirit being glass proof."[3] Another test consisted in partially filling "a glass phial and shaking it with your hand; if the blebs, or proof of it, continue a pretty while upon the top or surface . . . . it is then what is called proof goods."[4] A third test lay in deflagration by burning the spirit, which if "after it will no longer burn, the remainder is half as much as the quantity measured out for trial was, then the spirit tried is found to consist of half water and half totally inflammable spirit."[5] Again by explosion, "spirit being poured on a little gunpowder, placed in a dish, and then inflamed, if at the end of the combustion the gunpowder took fire, the spirit was held to be proof, or above proof; but if the gunpowder failed to ignite the spirit was esteemed below proof."[6] A distinction obtained in the singular and the plural of the word; "spiritt" represented single brandy or proof, "spiritts" brandy above proof or double brandy:[7] the expression double spirits,[8] double proof,[9] were also current, and that of "above proofe" was used nearly two centuries ago.[10] In the Emerald Isle the strength for some long time did not enter into fiscal calculations.[11] Among the early standards were 1 to 7 o.p.[8] and 1 to 10 o.p.,[12] by which was understood, in the latter case, that the strength would admit of the addition of a quantity of water equal to one-tenth of the whole mixture to reduce it to proof,[13] "overproof to 10" was an equivalent, and 1 in 10 under proof represented that one gallon of water in ten of such spirit, would have to be taken away to bring it to proof. Though a uniform rate of strength for the United Kingdom was suggested in 1807,[14] it was not sanctioned apparently until 1824, when proof as determined by Sikes' hydrometer formed the standard of charge.[15] *See* page 283. From these facts it will be seen that there is a difficulty in realising even an approximate comparison, between the rates in the preceding table, nor is the difficulty lessened by the system of charge by the content of the still or "still room" and its supposed "doublings,"[11] which prevailed in Scotland. The

[1] 1806. [2] 1798. [3] P. Rep., 1798. [4] 1818. [5] Highmore, 1796. [6] Johnston's Handbook, 1857. [7] 7 & 8 W. III., c. 30; 10 W. III., c. 4, 1733. [8] 1807. [9] 1836. [10] 1 W. & M., c. 24. [11] P. Rep., 1808. [12] 1808 [13] P. Rep., 1809. [14] P. Rep., 1807, 1809. [15] 4 G. IV., c. 94.

art of distillation being supposed to be fully known, this charge was calculated at so much per gallon on the quantity supposed to be distilled annually, exclusive of Sundays: certainly vague, as shown in the case of the distillers in Scotland who were presumed to pay upon a charge at the rate of tenpence per gallon, though in fact it did not amount to one penny, a rate arrived at, in part, by working on a Sunday, for which two distillers near Edinburgh were prosecuted at the instance of the "Kirk of the Parish" and convicted, but still had the "effrontery to continue to work on a Sunday," in spite of the law and a decision against the practice. Thus enabled to import across the Berwick border, much to the disadvantage of the English distiller, the Legislature imposed an import duty,[1] which may be stated to have been continued in force until the equalisation of the duty in both countries. Across the channel in the sister island a bounty of eight per cent. was given to those who used a 500 gallon still, and sixteen per cent. to those who used one of 1000 gallon content, to facilitate the collection of the duty. All, however, under five hundred gallons were subsequently suppressed and the bounty reduced to eight per cent.[2] Another difficulty arose in the thinly-populated portions of Scotland, where down to so late as 1784, owing to the excessive cost of collection, the duties were leased to farm for periods not exceeding three years,[3] and even to 1804, the Commissioners were wont to receive lists of the names of persons recommended by the heritors of the Highland parishes, from which they selected two persons for each parish to supply the parochial consumption from spirits distilled from corn grown in the vicinity. *See* Islay, page 291. But, by lapse of time, the crowning exception is found in the privilege granted to one Forbes of Culloden, Ross. Forbes was one of those who, in the reign of James the Second, stood up in defence of the religion, laws, and liberties of his country, and at very great expense, as well as risk to life and fortune, zealously engaged in promoting the Revolution. His "Brewary of Aquavitæ" having been burnt down, during his absence in Holland, he, on his return, by "supplication" to the Estates of Parliament, was relieved by an act, dated July 30, 1649, "for any levie in all tyme coming" on spirits distilled from the produce of the lands at Ferrintosh, and this continued until 1690, when his successors had to pay a duty of excise of about £22, but after the establishment of a

[1] H. C., Feb. 5, 13, 1788. [2] H. C., May 7, 1806. [3] P. Rep., 1784.

Board of Excise in 1707, frequent representations were made to the Treasury to buy this right, in consideration of the great dissatisfaction it created among the distillers, who manifestly did not complain without cause, as in 1782 the duty paid, as just stated, was £22, while, according to the current rate under ordinary circumstances, £20,000 should have been.[1] A further inequality in the mode of charge lay in the payment of a malt drawback—*see* page 344. The only exceptional legislation in England appears to have been in favour of one or two persons, who were credited with the possession of the secret of making "Geneva to resemble in appearance and flavour Holland Geneva."[2]

Then, more particularly, as to the presumptive system of charge. Based upon experience, one gallon of malt wash was supposed to yield one quarter of a gallon of low wines, and one of low wines, three-fifths of a gallon of proof spirits: one gallon of cider or perry wash, one-fifth of a gallon of low wines, and one gallon of the latter, half a gallon of proof spirits, but these calculations were much below the actual, and as there did not exist at this time, though there formerly did,[3] a comparison with the spirit extracted, the distiller privately introduced large quantities of wash of which no account had been taken.[4] This mode of charge continued until the saccharometer was brought into use, when the presumption was fixed on the number of degrees per one hundred gallons before fermentation,[5] and then upon the attenuation of a given number of degrees, as in the case of sugar wash, upon which the duty was charged for every four degrees decreased in every hundred gallons,[6] and upon malt and grain wash five degrees,—a presumption "generally 8 to 15 per cent. less than the actual produce"[7]—with a comparison with the low wines, less five per cent., and with the actual produce of spirit, the greatest forming the charge, though, if the spirit exceeded by 1·2 proof gallons per 5° attenuated, the distiller was deemed to have an "undue excess," and if it did not yield one gallon, he was charged on the quantity deficient at the expiration of his licence. The annual balance was abolished in 1860. *See* page 379. These stricter regulations, with a notice gravity which admitted of a variation of only three degrees, except in the mash tun and wort underback, with alternate brewing and distilling periods, with the worm

[1] P. Rep., 1784. [2] 1808; P. Rep., 1831. [3] 1706. [4] 1705, 1783.
[5] 3 G. IV., c. 52. [6] 6 G. IV., c. 80. [7] Bell's Manual, 1865.

end secured in "a safe inclosed," provided "upon experiment" it did not "injure the quality of the spirits," and with a stock account, though in an open store, were decided improvements. In the store account no margin was granted for an excess, but one not exceeding three per cent. for a deficiency, if proved not to have arisen through fraud.[1] Reserving the consideration of warehousing for a future page, the next important restrictions applied to delivery, and limited the size of the cask to eighty gallons—since reduced to nine—and the strength of the spirits to 25·0 and 11·0 o.p., and 10·0 u.p., respectively, a range shortly afterwards modified with a margin of six-tenths above and below each strength, and a range which, with amplification, still exists. The deficiency allowed on stock in store was at the same time made discriminative, two per cent. if taken "no further distant" than seven days, and three if it exceeded that period, a sample cock was allowed on the safe, and the charge defined to be less that for exportation.[2] From these enactments, by George the Fourth, which had the merit of giving additional security, removing "many of the trammels," and enabling the Government to raise the duty, to that by Queen Victoria in 1853, few if any important changes were made. The stringency of some of the requirements were slackened, as in the case of shorter notices, of a briefer interval between the final declaration and the commencement to distil, of the removal of the prohibition to mix backs of wash, while greater tension was placed on others, as shown by the requirement of an "apparatus or machine" to prevent the supply and discharge cocks of the spirit receiver from both being open at the same time, by the compulsory requirement to fill the spirit receiver to a depth of fifteen inches, including the power, when under that depth, to add the next tenth above, but with an allowance of one-half per cent. on the quantity, by the spirit store being placed under the officer's keeping, and the spirits, with the exception of one hundred and fifty gallons, being cleared, by payment or otherwise, and the stock taken within six days of the termination of the distilling, with a limit in stock not exceeding one-half per cent. for excess, and one of one per cent. for deficiency, but if the deficiency exceeded three per cent. then no allowance at all; attenuation charges formerly numerous now became less.[3] Attendance was enjoined from 5 A.M. till 8 P.M., except on Sunday, and casks were allowed to be removed either full or on

[1] 4 G. IV., c. 94. [2] 6 G. IV., c. 80. [3] P. Ret., 1831, 1832, 1834.

ullage. But the greatest innovation lay in the ascertainment of the content of the cask by the specific gravity of the spirit, as shown by the hydrometer, deemed "the weight per gallon." This was an old idea now first employed for fiscal purposes. Postlethwayt gives, in his Universal Dictionary of Trade and Commerce, published in 1766, "a table showing, by weight, the quantity of gallons any cask of spirit contains from one gallon to a tun," the standard weight being 7 lbs. 12 oz. Jonas enlarged upon this, in his Distiller's Guide in 1818, by printing sixteen tables of the weight at different strengths, each extending to 252 gallons. Gutteridge, in 1824, published extended tables on data defined in 56 Geo. III. c. 140. They were adapted to six strengths—25·0, 11·0 o.p., proof, 10·0, 17·0, 22·0 u.p.—and four temperatures—35°, 45°, 55°, 65°—and given in "cwts., qrs., lbs., ozs., drs.," up to 200 gallons, but the correction for expansion between any two of the above heats was tedious—"multiply the tabular number of gallons by four times the number of degrees which the spirit exceeds that in the table under use; cut off three figures on the right of the product, then on the left are pints . . . . . which have expanded beyond the tabular quantity," *e.g.*, "table 65° shows 150 galls.; heat 70°, then 150 × 20 = 3(000 pints." In 1828 he improved upon this by the issue of a table which commenced at 30° F., and advanced by one degree to 80° F., commenced with the indication 0, and advanced by a subdivision of two-tenths to 100, and with the corresponding pounds weight, to three places of decimals, per gallon, though he did not give the content in any given weight, only the strength and "equated values." The weight per gallon he showed under the indication. The next observed effort was made by Jos. Harrison, in 1852, by the issue of a table in imperial gallons at 25·0 o.p., proof, and 11·0 o.p., calculated at each degree of temperature from 36° to 70°, in which he, too, showed to the dram! This, then, traces the gradual introduction down to the date at which this principle of measurement was legalised for revenue purposes. Loftus published the first edition of his valuable production in 1854: these tables were computed at the strengths 24·4 to 25·6 and 10·4 to 11·0 o.p., between the temperatures 35° and 70°, and the indications 37·8 to 47·2 and 48·4 to 57·2, with a range of content from 9 by a quarter of a gallon to 80, and then by one gallon to 203 gallons, but with the necessities of the trade these soon proved insufficient, and gave way to more serviceable ones with a range of temperature from 35° to 75°, and of hydrometer indication from 0·0 to 19·0 and 36·6 to 57·2.

Closely connected with the obtainment of the content is that of the proof. Among the earlier compilations may be noticed those by Ashton and Hill. The former computed by part products with two tables—thus 117 gallons at 33·1 o.p.:

First find 117 at 33, . . .	38 galls.	61 cents.	0
Then 117 at 1 by altering decimal place,	0 „	11 „	7
	38 „	72 „	7

"Therefore the charge of overproof" is 38·72 gallons. This dual table ranges from 1 gallon by 1 gallon to 200 gallons, and in strength from 1 to 70·0 o.p., London 1816. Hill raised his in the ordinary manner under the title "Spirit Calculator," and showed the quantity of spirit at proof contained in any quantity, at a strength of 50·0 o.p. by a decrease of ·1 to 17·0 u.p., from 1 gallon to 100 gallons, then by 100 to 1000. Certainly, if correct, a most meritorious book. London, 1849. Those issued by W. R. Loftus in 1874 and J. Brown in 1877 are the most complete within the limits represented: those projected by W. Ecockes in 1871, as shown on page 201, the most comprehensive, the most serviceable, the most ingenious.

The English system of charge was extended to Scotland in 1814, and the distinction of Highland, Intermediate, and Lowland district was discontinued in 1822.[1] Early indications of an equalisation of rates occur on the Union with that country, and again on the termination of the still content rate. The brewing interest in Ireland, being affected by the low rate of duty, were induced in 1811 to petition Parliament to increase it,[2] and shortly after it had been granted the distillers in Dublin, having to compete with an increase in illicit distillation, prayed a reduction which in 1823, it became necessary to make to an extent of more than one-half, a reduction which had a beneficial effect, and which, with a similar change in Scotland, at the same time, placed those countries for the first time on an equality. The rapidly increasing intercourse between all three countries, and a return to three distinct rates, however, rendered the dissimilar duties more and more objectionable and with the more frequent exaction of the differential duty (*see* page 97) led the public, with the Magistrates of Berwick-on-Tweed, to ask Parliament, in 1833 and 1834, to equalise them, and such financial reformers as Parnell and Martin to write—"It is high time to put

[1] 3 G. IV., c. 52. [2] H. C., May 16, 1811.

an end to the different and discriminating duties between England, Scotland, and Ireland." These representations lay unheeded until 1842, when Scotland and Ireland were again placed on the same level, but to continue only one year, during which petitions were presented for a reduction.[1] The increase shown in the table of rates under 1853 was not passed without contention. The members, who represented those countries, gave great opposition to the third reading, by moving, "That the House do now adjourn," no fewer than five times, with the following results, ayes 34, 28, 21, 18; noes 113, 109, 103, 94 respectively, the last motion not having been divided upon.[2] And Lord Monteagle observed in the upper house, "such was the sensitive nature of the spirit duties. . . . . that the quicksilver did not respond more certainly to the heat of the hand applied to the bulb of the barometer than did smuggling follow upon an augmentation of their amount."[3] Lord Naas next suggested a similarity of imposition in the United Kingdom,[4] which received legislative sanction in 1855, so far as England and Scotland were concerned,[5] and in 1858, the United Kingdom, though in the latter assimilation not without an amendment being proposed which resulted in a majority of 192 votes for the original motion—ayes 227, noes 35.[6] According to an early practice[7] the extra duty was charged on the stocks in hand, with an extension to those in the possession of the rectifier, compounder and dealer.

The effect of the augmentation in 1858 seems to have caused at first a small decrease in each division of the United Kingdom, in the number of gallons charged for consumption; the net receipt was highest in 1876, when it exceeded £15,000,000: the consumption of home-made spirits per head of population in 1877, reached in England 0·693, in Scotland 2·005, in Ireland 1·145 gallons.[8] The Commissioners observe, in comparing the results of fiscal changes, between 1852 and 1869, "Among the most important of these must be reckoned the reduction of the duty on foreign spirits and wine in 1860, consequent on the treaty with France. It may also be observed that whilst the duty on British spirits has increased in England since 1852 nearly 27 per cent., in Scotland 172 per cent., and in Ireland 275 per cent.; that on beer (malt) has remained stationary. Under such circumstances it would be natural to expect

[1] 1843. [2] H. C., June 17, 1853. [3] H. L., July 4, 1853.
[4] H. C., April 26, 1855. [5] H. C., April 23, 1855. [6] H. C., April 26, 1858.
[7] 1830. [8] C. 21 R.

that foreign spirits, wine, and beer would to some extent replace British spirits in consumption. The reduction of the duty on tea within the limits of the period under consideration from 2s. 2½d. to 6d. per lb. would have an influence in the same direction. Accordingly, we find that whilst the consumption per head of British spirits has decreased about 32 per cent., that of foreign and colonial spirits has increased 56 per cent.; the decrease in the aggregate of both kinds being 12·5 per cent. At the same time the consumption of foreign wine has increased 116 per cent., beer 32 per cent., tea 77 per cent., and cocoa 55 per cent. . . . These facts, we think, speak conclusively in favour of the increase in the duty on British spirits, which have thus been made to yield a larger revenue. . . . . with a diminished consumption, whilst at the same time an impetus has been given to the substitution of milder stimulants for ardent spirits, which appears likely to be the commencement of a desirable change in the habits of the population.

What, it may be asked, are the comparative rates of taxation to which these articles are subjected? The question has not, so far as we know, been distinctly or properly answered, although on some occasions, comparisons have been made between the alcohol present in beer and spirits respectively, and the tax upon them has been reduced to that standard. Perhaps a more satisfactory method would be to compare such quantities of the articles as would usually be considered equivalents by the consumer. We may suppose, for instance, that a labouring man might hesitate between a pint of beer, a pint of tea, or a glass of gin. Now, the duty on beer being 5s. 9d. per barrel, it follows that the taxation of a pint amounts to one farthing, and supposing (which probably is a large estimate) that a quarter of an ounce of tea is used to produce a pint of the liquid, the tax which it bears is something less than half a farthing. But the glass of gin is burthened with 1½d. as its contribution to the Exchequer (if we suppose that it is retailed at 25·0 under proof); but at all events upwards of 1¼d.; a large per centage on the cost, and five or six times as much as is imposed upon the beer, and twelve times as much as on tea."[1] Other important considerations, with respect to both production and consumption, will be referred to under warehousing, exportation, importation, methylation, retailing.

[1] C. 13 R.

The system of warehousing British spirits, as it exists in 1878, is the gradual development of at least seventy years' experience. Beginning apparently with a permission to warehouse in Ireland free of duty for exportation,[1] the principle of bonding free of duty in general, claimed the attention of a Parliamentary Committee, who sat in 1809, and recommended its adoption. These export spirits were deposited with the Customs until 1812, from this date with the Excise,[2] with whom it was also desired to bond the produce of small stills at the seat of a collection,[3] to afford encouragement to the licensed proprietors of small stills in smuggling districts.[4] In Scotland the same privilege was advocated in 1821,[5] and the distillers' stocks were taken once in thirty days.[6] It was not until 1824 that the distillers, in these portions of the United Kingdom, enjoyed the concession. They were now allowed to do so for exportation, shipping, and home consumption at the strengths of 25·0 and 11·0 o.p. on the payment of one penny per forty gallons per week, and to remove their casks of spirits from one warehouse to another.[7] The distillers in England were given authority in 1826 to warehouse, without payment of duty, for exportation, or for removal to Scotland or Ireland, and under the same act those in the sister countries were allowed to remove from country to country upon payment of the proper duty, or part payment with bond for payment of the remainder within a prescribed time.[8] Under these regulations, for the most part, the trade continued until 1834, when the Parnell Committee reported favourably upon the desire of the distillers in Scotland and Ireland to have the duty assessed upon the "landed quantity," which was equivalent to asking for an allowance for waste. In 1847 and 1848 several applications having been made to Parliament to investigate and alter the system, a "British Spirits Warehousing Bill" was prepared and passed, by which the English distiller was first allowed to deposit in England for consumption, and all were permitted to remove from one part to another for consumption, ships' stores, or exportation, on first paying the duty on all deficiencies which had arisen, and on the spirit removed, being subsequently charged, as if distilled in the country to which it might be sent, with in the case of the distiller in Scotland first repaying the malt drawback of 8d., and 5 per cent. per gallon. General warehouses were now provided in

[1] 46 G. III., c. 88. [2] 52 G. III., c. 30. [3] P. Rep., 1813.
[4] P. Ret., 1816. [5] P. Rep., 1821. [6] 3 G. IV., c. 52.
[7] 4 G. IV., c. 94. [8] 6 G. IV., c. 80

which a transfer was allowed to a purchaser: removal to customs' custody sanctioned: and the rectifier granted, in consequence of the Dutch distiller first warehousing in England, and then exporting to the English Colonies,[1] permission to bond spirits not sweetened for ships' stores or exportation, and be repaid three halfpence per gallon.[2] In committee on this bill, Mr O'Connell moved an instruction to "assimilate the modes of charge in respect to leakage and wastage of colonial and home spirit, *i.e.*, that the account for charge or otherwise shall be taken when sent out of warehouse." On a division having been taken, it was lost by 29 votes—ayes 37, noes 76.[3] This defeat was not allowed to pass unchallenged. Between 1848 and 1850 upwards of eighty petitions were presented, apparently by the Scotch and Irish distillers, with respect to bonding and chiefly for Mr O'Connell's concession. Lord Naas, who represented the distillers in Ireland, now moved for a committee of the whole house, and Lord Stuart, on behalf of the distillers in Scotland, seconded the motion, which was carried by 32 votes—ayes 85, noes 53. The first resolution was with regard to home consumption: it proposed to allow 2 per cent., if not in warehouse more than 3 months, 3 per cent. if more than 3 and not more than 6, 4 per cent. over 6 and not over 12 months, and 1 per cent. for every additional 6 months. Of course on the proof gallons. The second resolution contained similar allowances with respect to ships' stores and exportation. Both were agreed to. On the second reading, the Chancellor of the Exchequer observed, in opposing the bill, "He did not think that the Scotch and Irish distillers had any claim whatever to pay a less amount of duty than they now paid upon their spirits. On the contrary, he thought they ought to pay rather more than less so far as a general policy was concerned, although, for the sake of avoiding illicit distillation, it was found necessary to ask them to pay less duty than the English distillers." He then proposed it be read "upon this day three months"—ayes 195, noes 135. The bill was put off for three months by a majority of 1—ayes 120, noes 121.[4] A greater effort was made to get the principle sanctioned in 1851. Supported by upwards of sixty petitions, his lordship again made a motion, much in accordance with that of last year, and said, "There was a differential duty between colonial and home-made

[1] H. C., June 8, 1848. [2] 11 & 12 V., c. 121. [3] H. C., Aug. 28, 1848.
[4] H. C., June 11, July 4, 8, 1850.

spirits, but it was not made in any degree by way of protection: it was merely laid on as an equivalent, and a very inadequate equivalent, for the restriction and disadvantage under which the home distiller laboured on account of laws enacted for securing the revenue. . . . . . Malt duty 1½d., increased plant 1d., excise restrictions 1d., duty on decreases ½d. = 4d. So this considerable item has dwindled to ½d. on one-eighth of the whole. . . . . It was much to be feared the real objectors to this just demand were the eight English distillers, why? Because they do not want it: they hardly ever bond at all—they sell their spirits hot from the still to the rectifier, and therefore cannot require it. . . . . . If the plan which he desired to see adopted were carried out . . . . it would considerably interfere with their monopoly." The noble lord then referred to 1833, when the differential duty was eighteenpence per gallon, and when two superior officers in this department recommended that the charge should be made on the quantity given out of warehouse. An interesting debate ensued, and on a division being taken, the votes being equal, the speaker gave his vote to the ayes—ayes 160, noes 159. All went well until the second reading, when the distillers of London sent in petitions against it, which were presented to the Chancellor of the Exchequer, who opposed the reading, which was lost by 28 votes—ayes 166, noes 194.[1] The consideration of the claim, if not the justice of it, forced itself upon Mr Gladstone, who stated, in making his first financial statement, "We . . . propose an allowance for waste upon spirits in bond. That allowance for waste will be in Scotland £40,000." In Ireland and England the same, but in the last country, "not for the sake of the English distillers, but for the sake of the Scotch and Irish distillers, with whom it is a great object to bond their spirit here."[2] Reference to the table rates will show that he also took the opportunity of raising the duty at the same time.

The scale of allowances as fixed, in 1853, apparently upon data obtained at the time, has been several times adjusted to meet the requirements which an increasing experience has dictated by closer observation under a higher duty, until superseded by the one now in use, which is not only a liberal scale, but is further enlarged in cases of extraordinary loss with which the Commissioners specially deal. No other change in the mode of charge has ever claimed so much

[1] H. C., May 6, July 9, 1851. [2] H. C., April 18, 1853.

official attention. The immediate result was the opening of numerous warehouses, which, with those previously and subsequently approved, are now divided into six kinds—distillery, distillery bonded, general, crown, bottling, and reducing, from which every facility is given for removal for consumption, from warehouse to warehouse, for exportation, for ships' stores, for methylation, including compounds and liqueurs for certain purposes by rectifiers and compounders, who have been allowed to warehouse on drawback, and for removal to Customs warehouse, and thence for home consumption.[1] In the case of warehousing in vats, a system recommended in 1834,[2] and bottling, special allowances apply.

The facility afforded by bonding, with payment on the quantity delivered, has led to the general practice of storing until fit for consumption.[3] This will be strikingly apparent by the following statistics, which show the proof gallons of British spirits, in round numbers, in bonded store in each year ended March 31—

1868, . .	11,000,000	1874, . .	25,000,000
1869, . .	12,000,000	1875, . .	26,000,000
1870, . .	13,000,000	1876, . .	28,000,000
1871, . .	16,000,000	1877, . .	32,000,000
1872, . .	19,000,000	1878, . .	37,000,000
1873, . .	22,000,000		

On this the Commissioners write—"It is important to notice the production of spirit in excess of the demand for consumption continues with unabated force . . . . In Scotland there is now a sufficient quantity in bond for two years' consumption, while in Ireland it is estimated that there is sufficient for three years."[4]

It has been already mentioned that the system of bonding commenced with spirits which were intended for exportation, though the export trade does not seem to have been important until 1848. The trade from this date gradually grew until 1857, when upwards of 5,000,000 gallons were cleared for this purpose, but since the latter date, it has declined to little more than one million gallons, including spirits compounded by rectifiers, and exported on drawback. The larger quantities were formerly sent to France, Portugal, Turkey, West Coast of Africa, Australia, &c., and to the wine growing countries principally for the fortification of wines. The cheaper production of spirits in Germany is also considered to have reduced the

[1] 27 V., c. 12; C. 8 R. [2] P. Rep., 1834. [3] C. 15 R. [4] C. 21 R.

trade in this country, and this closer competition by the foreigner had, with other considerations, the effect of reducing the estimated increase in the cost of production on account of excise restrictions from 5½d. to 2d. on plain, and 3d. per proof gallon, on compounded spirits, the allowances which are now made to the exporter.

The import duty on foreign spirits was transferred to the Customs by order in Council, dated February 2, 1825. A gradual increase in the importation of foreign and colonial spirits was made until about 1869,[1] when a decrease began which, in 1872, was attributed to the failure of the potato crop in the United Kingdom, and the large importation of potatoes, which, under ordinary circumstances, would have been used on the Continent in the manufacture of plain spirits.[2] In the year ended March 31, 1876, the quantity of foreign and colonial spirits charged for consumption amounted to nearly 12,000,000 gallons,[3] and the consumption is increasing.[4] "German and Russian plain spirits, however, enter into direct competition with home-made spirits in quality and price, and when the price is favourable, supersede them to a large extent in the manufacture of some descriptions of compounded spirit. The price of foreign spirit depends upon the cost of roots from which it is chiefly manufactured, and compared with grain from which the home-made spirit is produced."[5]

The methylation of spirit originated, in 1853, with a gentleman who had obtained a patent for an artificial lubricant, and had applied to the Lords of the Treasury to be allowed to use spirit free of duty, or at a reduced rate. The Commissioners having recommended the application, the principal of the laboratory made an extensive series of experiments with the view to make the spirit unpotable, and ultimately suggested the addition of crude wood naphtha to spirit of wine. The suggestion was referred to Professors Graham, Hofmann, and Redwood, who, having investigated the discovery, reported that a mixture of 10 per cent. of wood naphtha with spirit of wine would effect the twofold object of protecting the revenue and privileging the patentee. The uses to which it might be applied were then thought to be hat-making, varnishing, French polish, lacquering metal, bookbinding, chemical preparations, ethers, choloform, singeing horses, the preservation of objects of natural history, fulminating mercury for percussion caps, lighting, perfumery, and pharmaceutical preparations.[6] The mixture and its use were legalised on October 1,

[1] C. 13, 14 R. [2] C. 18 R. [3] C. 19 R. [4] C. 20 R. [5] C. 21 R.
[6] P. Ret.

1855, and the employment of foreign and colonial rum, and foreign spirits, for the purpose of mixing, under the eye of the Customs, was permitted in 1863 and 1877 respectively, and the exportation of the mixture was allowed by 26 and 27 Vict. c. 102. The quantity made, under the supervision of this department about 1856, was 146,374 gallons, upon which a gradual increase has taken place until 1,373,366 gallons was reached in 1877. Attempts have been made to neutralise the beneficial effects of the mixture by purification to render the spirit potable, but these have not been successful except at a cost too great to be remunerative.[1] Also by saturation with sugar, treacle, &c., then flavouring with a variety of ingredients to conceal the true character, an attempt which, in some parts of the country, became profitable and palatable, until suppressed by the imposition of a moderate fine.[2] An abuse also crept in with those who used finish, but the addition of a little more gum removed this, and a similar improper employment in the preparation of medicine for internal use was checked by the 29 and 30 Vict. c. 64. The laws are embodied in about ten Acts of Parliament. It may be mentioned, to show the efficiency of the wood naphtha or methylic alcohol, that, on a cask being washed ashore in Cornwall in 1876, a dozen fishermen drank freely; five were carried home unconscious, of whom one died almost immediately, and another at night, and the other seven became noisy and riotous, and had to be restrained.[3] A licence duty of ten guineas on the maker was introduced at the time of the mixture, and, in 1861, one of two guineas, and reduced to ten shillings, in 1868, on the retailer: the number of the former has never exceeded fifteen, the number of the latter, in 1878, was no less than 4902. It has been thought that an additional check to the fraudulent use of this spirit might be gained by placing the seller under magisterial, as well as excise, licence.[4]

The business of the rectifier and compounder entails upon this department the duty of protecting the trade and the revenue, by observing that spirits are not illegally obtained or distilled. Among the earliest regulations which brought it under official survey, is that of 1774, by which the stills were required to be placed under the charge of an officer. Concessions have been made to this branch of the spirit industry by permitting warehousing, exportation on drawback, as already stated, sweetening, &c., and a desire has

[1] C. 7 R. [2] C. 10 R. [3] Scotsman. [4] Porter.

been expressed to rectify in bond.[1] The principal official duties are keeping a stock account, making a close survey, and exacting a licence duty, nearly similar to—from the first imposition—that paid by the distillers. The greatest number of rectifiers, to the latest date to which a separate account is given, was licensed in 1869; there were then in England 54, Scotland 7, Ireland 12.

The dealer in spirits was recognised in 1644, but not until 1720 does he appear to have been required to submit his stock and premises to excise inspection. The frequent improper importation of spirits led to this enactment. He was now defined to be one who had a stock of more than sixty-three gallons, and was required to send out a permit with quantities of one gallon and upwards; nor was it until a sensible diminution in smuggling had taken place that these early restrictions were relaxed by discontinuing the stock account, and not requiring the trader to send to the permit writer for a permit,—see page 394: 90,000 dealers and retailers were now relieved from these requirements, and £65,000 per annum were supposed to be saved. There were presented eighteen petitions in favour of, and many against (principally from Scotland) the bill by which this change was effected. The quarterly survey substituted in 1848 was superseded by an annual visit in 1868, since modified. Dealing in bond was allowed until 1860, when those who sold less than one hundred gallons of foreign spirits, in bond, became liable to pay the licence duty. The dealer, not being a retailer, in England paid from 1785 to 1814, £5; from 1815, £10, with 5 per cent. from 1840; in 1848, the "dealer" was granted an additional licence to retail foreign liqueurs at £2, 2s., and in 1862, an additional licence at £3, 3s. to retail in quantities not less than a reputed quart bottle; in Scotland, from 1783 to 1793, £5; from 1794 to 1814 discriminatively as dealer in spirits £5, dealer in aqua vitæ only £3, raised from 1815 to 1825 to £10 and £6 respectively, after that as in England, with the exception of the quart bottle licence; in Ireland there were several distinctions down to 1825, when the duties were assimilated to those of Scotland. The number of dealers in 1778 was E. 7622, S. 467, I. 625.

With the retailer of spirits are classed the spirit grocers in Scotland and Ireland. The year before Queen Anne was crowned, every person was forbidden to sell spirits to be drunk in his house or on

[1] H. C., May 20, 1847.

his premises, without an alehouse license—a condition retained until 1808[1]—and six years after George the First had ascended the throne the retailer came under close survey by entry being made of his premises, and account being taken of his stock—the latter as just stated, being retained until 1848 :—he was not allowed to have more than sixty-three gallons or he became a dealer.[2] The prohibition to sell to be drunk in the house was at once evaded by a practice of selling from a wheelbarrow in the street, a practice which was again and again condemned.[3] The sale of less than one gallon now constituted a retailer who had to pay a licence duty of £20 yearly,[4] but so immoderate had the use of gin become in 1736, even the publicans enticing "their customers with a notice on a board outside the house to the effect—'You may here get drunk for a penny, dead drunk for twopence, and have clean straw for nothing,'"[5] that the Magistrates of Middlesex petitioned the House of Commons to devise a remedy.[6] The licence duty was now raised to £50 with a gallon duty,[7] with a provision that those who happened to incur a fine and refused to pay it, should be whipped.[8] The officers in attempting to charge the duty were frequently ill treated by rioters whom the Commissioners endeavoured to chastise on obtaining conclusive evidence, for which they had to advertise and offer £50.[9] This new law was attended with very unsatisfactory results, and induced the Government in 1743 to prepare a new measure, upon which Smollett writes—"The most severe opposition the new ministry underwent, was in their endeavours to support a Bill, which they had concerted, and which had passed through the House of Commons with great precipitation. It repealed certain duties on spirituous liquors, and licences for retailing these liquors ; and imposed others at an easier rate. When these several duties, amounting almost to a prohibition were imposed, the population of London were sunk into the most brutal degeneracy, by drinking to excess the pernicious spirit called gin, which was sold so cheap that the lowest class of the people could afford to indulge themselves in one continuous state of intoxication, to the destruction of all morality, industry and order. . . . . In order to restrain this evil, which had become intolerable, the Legislature enacted that law which we have already mentioned. But the populace soon broke through all re-

[1] H. C., May 5, 1808. [2] L. G., 1720. [3] 1729, 1733. [4] 2 G. II., c. 17.
[5] Porter's Progress of the People. [6] H. C., Feb. 20, 1736.
[7] H. C., Sept. 29, 1736. [8] 10 G. II., c. 17. [9] L. G., 1737.

straint. Though no licence was obtained, and no duty paid, the liquor continued to be sold in all corners of the streets; informers were intimidated by the threats of the people; and the justices of the peace, either from indolence or corruption, neglected to put the law in execution. The ministers foresaw that a great revenue would accrue to the Crown from a repeal of this Act; and this measure they thought they might the more decently take, as the law had proved ineffectual; for it appeared the consumption of gin had considerably increased every year since these heavy duties were imposed. They therefore pretended that should the price of the liquor be moderately raised, and licences granted at twenty shillings each to the retailers, the lowest class of the people would be debarred the use of it to excess; their morals would of consequence be amended; and a considerable sum of money might be raised for the support of the war by mortgaging the revenue arising from the duty on the licences." Reverting to the proceedings of Parliament—The Lords ordered "that the Commissioners of Excise do attend the House to-morrow upon the second reading the said Bill."[1] Lord Lonsdale, who was the originator of the measure, then "asked several questions of Mr Burton, who appeared, and answered that 9 Geo. 2, which was Sir J. Jekyl's Bill, had been executed so far as the Commissioners of Excise could execute it; about justices of the peace he could say nothing; that the Commissioners appointed supernumerary officers to attend the houses complained of; that never more than three took out licences, and only they were liable to pay the duty of 20s. a gallon; that the care of their officers had no effect; that the lower sort of people in general sell these liquors; some few keep shops without licence, but they are principally sold in private and bye places; that the same care hath been taken by the Commissioners of Excise from the first to the present time."[2] The principles involved in this bill occasioned a long, exciting debate among the Lords, whose speeches with the notes by Smollett so attracted Cobbett's attention as to make his notes extend over twenty-four pages of his Parliamentary History. The Legislature now enacted a uniform payment of one pound, and this principle was retained until 1788, when the rate of the house and premises formed the principle, and this remained, but at various rates till 1835, when a new principle of charge, based on the quantity con-

[1] H. L., Feb. 24, 1743. [2] H. L., Feb. 22, 1743.

sumed, was introduced in apparent agreement with a proposal of the Parnell Committee. This last mode met with the bitter opposition of the retailers, who soon vigorously united in preparing and presenting upwards of five hundred petitions against it, and finally succeeded in obtaining a welcome return to the lowest scale ever sanctioned,[1] and the one which, with the percentage of 1840, at present governs the amount. In Scotland to 1852 the payments have been the same; except in favour of those who retailed "aqua vitæ only" in the Highlands and Lowlands down to 1825; from 1855 a modified scale, to include beer, has been in operation. In Ireland the rates have varied according to place—even to the position of the "public lamps"—to rate to extent of single sale, and finally to rate alone. Unlike the practice in Scotland a distinction has obtained since 1825, in the case of the grocer, who pays on a higher scale for the sale of spirits only, and who in 1812 received certain "bounties" for selling.[2]

A "Pop Shop" was a place where smuggled spirits were sold and consumed.[3] A "Jigger Shop," a house opened for the illegal sale of spirits after the public-houses were closed.[4] A "hold over," a term applied to the magistrates' permission to sell until the certificate can be properly transferred.[5]

The sale by the grocer has been investigated by a Parliamentary Committee, who made a report in 1878.

Illicit distillation or "whiskey spinning," as practised in England down to the discovery of methylating spirit in 1853, generally gave illegal employment to persons, who, surrounded by a considerable population, in a large town the more easily for a time escaped detection. The material which they employed usually consisted of treacle, and from the simple, easy, inexpensive character of the process, with a fair supply of water, enabled them to sell at about a crown per gallon, with a fair remuneration. A detective corps of officers, whose attention was exclusively confined to London, was formed in 1850—see page 173—when, with discoveries in the provinces, 551 detections were made, but since this date the number of detections has decreased until in 1876 only three were reported. The principal locality, now, being the cider districts in the west of England, where a coarse spirit is distilled from cider dregs. In

[1] 1826. [2] 52 G. III., c. 46. [3] P. Rep., 1833. [4] H. C., June 11, 1856. [5] Scotsman.

Scotland in 1823 the forbidden make prevailed to such an extent as to demand a reduction of nearly four shillings in the duty to successfully cope with it. There were at this period no fewer than 14,000 prosecutions instituted for this and illicit malting, but with the assistance of the landlord and the occupier of land, the free use of a mixture of aqua vitæ in the arts and industries, the number has been reduced to two in 1877-8. In Ireland, particularly in the remote or less accessible parts, with an abundant crop of oats, this form of smuggling has always been most practised, and chiefly in the counties of Donegal, Sligo, Galway, and Mayo, and principally to supply the local population, as little is now supposed to be taken into the large towns. Encouragement was given to this contraband traffic by the farmers, who, on selling their corn to a private distiller, generally gave a sum back to meet fines and losses.[1] Probably the most fruitful year in the discovery of illicit distillation happened in 1865, there were now made 3575 detections; in 1874, 731. Upon this subject the Commissioners remark:—"Could we obtain the cordial co-operation of the owners and occupiers of land . . . . as we have in most parts of Scotland, we should have no apprehension of the revival of smuggling to any great extent, even if the price of grain were much lower than at present." The Chancellor of the Irish Exchequer appealed to the country gentlemen in 1813 to afford this aid,[2] and a later incident may perhaps show the propriety of his having done so. It is stated of a reverend gentleman who had been summoned to attend a trial at Derry that he addressed the barrister for the prosecution thus—"You know a revenue oath is of no consequence; you will find I can be of no use to you;" then, turning to the smugglers, who were in great numbers in the court, he said, with the Book in his hand, "Now, boys, you will see how I will switch them for you."[3] Considered with regard to the rate of duty charged being out of all proportion, in all time in this country, the statistics show a great reform, but when it is stated in the words of the Finance Minister of 1811, that "at present only about 6,000,000 gallons paid the duty in Ireland, at a moderate calculation there were 8,000,000 gallons of illicit distillation which paid no duty,"[4] the reform, compared with that will appear still greater. Places, appearances, appliances have each and all conspired

[1] P. Rep., 1808. [2] H. C., June 11, 1813. [3] H. L., June 22, 1843.
[4] H. C., March 19, 1811.

to deceive and deter the detector. In no less a place than Euxton Church vestry and the parson's pantry and coach-house did two officers find an illicit still in 1854; under the Free Tron Church, Edinburgh, in a vault formerly used by the Commercial Bank, was another taken in 1856; a place to "resemble a large heap of stones" has also made "one of the best concealments ever seen"—1855;[1] a brewery has also afforded a cover to carry on illicit distillation on a large scale—1842. Under the firm of "Batley & Co., colour manufacturers and linseed oil merchants," three stills capable of distilling fifty gallons of spirits per day, with one hundred gallons of spirits were seized in 1854; an ingeniously-devised "copper still, placed on iron frames against a wall and heated by means of gas," was discovered, which would produce "every second hour . . . . a gallon of spirit 60 per cent. over proof"—1855. Messrs Carr and Dawson were received by a bull dog on breaking into a house in Leeds—1853; in another case one man has been stationed at a distance of fifty yards from another, in continuation, and in this way conveyed the intelligence of an unwelcome approach, baffled the quickest pedestrian, and enabled the distiller "in the private line" to timely dispose of his plant and produce—1854.[2] A simple appliance—"a tea kettle, a gun barrel, and a barrel of water"—R. Lowe.[2]

Frauds are seldom practised by the licensed distiller, owing to the better adaptation of the laws and regulations, the regard to character by the distiller, and the better position of the officer.

The more important Parliamentary Reports, with some noted under malt duty, are these—

1798. This is an inquiry into the operation or incidence of the licence duty on the capacity of the stills used in the Scotch distilleries, with a view to devise a better mode of charging the duty on "corn spirits." It appears to have originated with the Lords of the Treasury, who addressed a letter to the Commissioners of Excise in Scotland on July 25, 1797, requesting them to obtain certain information from the distillers. The committee were engaged on this inquiry from March 22 to June 11, 1798. Pages 194, large folio.

1799. This is a report in continuation of that printed last year. Unitedly they embrace the most complete historical account of the distilleries, north of the Tweed, to this time. The defects in the systems of licence and survey, separately, are stated to be "incapable

[1] C. S. G. [2] H. C., March 11, 1870.

of being cured:" that the two systems combined with a gallon duty at 2s. 6d. at 1 to 10 o.p. would be advantageous. Pages 394, large folio.

1807. Report on distillery fees. *See* page 231.

1808. A blue book on how far, and under what circumstances, it may be practicable and expedient to confine the distilleries in the United Kingdom, or any part of it, to the use of sugar and molasses. The use of sugar was recommended; the use of molasses, not. Pages 318.

1809. A report appertaining to the drawback and countervailing duties on the importation and exportation of spirits from one part of the United Kingdom to another, and on any alteration which might be necessary in conformity with the Articles of Union. The principal recommendation—that the calculations for drawback and countervailing duty be made on the assumption that the malt used be "one-half of the raw corn or one-third of the whole mixture," and that a uniform strength of 1 to 10 o.p. be employed. Pages 126.

1813. An inquiry into the increase of illicit distillation in Ireland. Page 34.

1816. Two reports on the cause and extent of illicit distillation in Ireland. Pages 4 and 148 respectively.

1821. Copy of the reports made to the Commissioners of Excise in Ireland, by officers appointed to superintend experiments in the process of distillation as carried on at Carrickfergus.

1831. *See* page 329.

1831. A report on how far the use of molasses, the produce of the "West India Colonies," in the distilleries, &c., of the United Kingdom might relieve the colonist, and, at the same time, not prejudicially affect the home interest. A valuable report of 462 pages. *See* page 367.

1834. General report by the Parnell Committee, part 1, British spirits. The evidence contained in this volume was taken in London, Newcastle, Edinburgh, Dundee, Glasgow, Dublin. The first sixteen pages contain an elaborate review of the operation of the laws on the trades subject to them—no bright picture; next, duties on home-made spirits, the various effects of the different rates; distilleries in each country, &c., and finally the suggestion that a "New Distillery Bill" be prepared, containing their recommendations, some of which have been referred to in these pages. Pages 458.

1834. A report on foreign spirits by the same committee. Pages 144.

1835. Another report by the same committee on the disposal of spirits, as the former is on the manufacture. It treats chiefly of the regulations relating to dealing, retailing, rectifying, and compounding. Part 2, pages 136.

1842. *See* pages 330, 344.

1847. A report on production of spirit from molasses by Professor Fownes. Pages 6.

1847. Reports on the use of barley, malt, sugar, and molasses, in breweries and distilleries, by Messrs Dobson and Phillips. Pages 8.

1854. Report, with minutes of evidence, by a select committee of the House of Lords on extending the functions of the constabulary in Ireland to the suppression of illicit distillation. The parliamentary papers printed on this subject between 1731 and 1878, exceed 500.

It was not until the present century that the distillery laws in the three countries can be said to have been compared and consolidated. It began with a consolidated act, in 1823, for Scotland and Ireland, and in 1825 followed one for England, which, with the other, remained in force as general laws for the respective countries, with important additions in 1848, 1853, and 1855, until consolidated for the United Kingdom in 1860. This important act engaged the careful attention of both the trade and the authorities several years, and, with subsequent modifications and additions, is the general law at present in force. The estimated increase in the cost of production, on account of excise restrictions, as already stated, was reduced by this measure from 5½d. to 2d. on plain, and 3d. per gallon on rectified or compounded spirit. The Commissioners report in their second issue—"The bill was originally framed by our solicitor (with a degree of care and labour which deserves our highest commendations) in order that it might form part of the anticipated consolidation of the whole statute law. But as it will probably be some time before the project can be carried into effect, we hope to be able previously to pass an act introducing considerable amendments into our distillery laws, too considerable, probably, to be admitted as a mere consolidation, although, for the most part, acted upon at present, and accepted as law by agreement between us and the distillers. Those portions of the bill which are entirely new are of minor importance, and relate to matters of detail, which were pressed upon our consideration by a deputation from the distillers of the United Kingdom in the early part of last year. It was very gratifying to find both that the demands of these gentlemen were few, and that we were able to promise that almost all of them should be submitted for the sanction of Parliament. Upon the whole, we were able to say, that the vast revenue from spirits has been collected with a degree of ease and regularity which forms a strong contrast to the laborious process by which the more direct imposts are levied."

The bye-laws or general orders issued between 1760 and 1878 are about 350.

Instructions relating to the various divisions of survey and charge have been issued in 1723, 1732, 1778, 1781, 1804 S., 1825, 1826, 1828, 1837, 1840, 1841, 1847, 1848, 1848, 1848, 1853, 1854, 1855, 1856, 1860, 1866, 1866, 1871, 1871.

Among the most curious and useful publications may be mentioned—Jonas, as shown on page 293; Cooper's "Complete Distiller," 1810; Rooney's "Spirit Trader's Guide," 1864; "Distillation of Saccharine, Roots," 1857; "Distiller's Hand-Book of Distilling from Beet Root," &c., 1856; Morewood's Works, as noticed on page 368; Prescott's, as stated on page 402; Johnston's "Hand-Book," 1857, and "Manual," 1865; Bell's "Manual," 1865; "Distillery Instructions," pages 116 to 146, 1871; Ure's "Dictionary," Alcohol, 1867; Muspratt's "Chemistry," Alcohol, a most minute article of 100 pages, with illustrations, 1854.

Jottings from the technology observed in the perusal on this subject:—Nidus, that portion of malt used with grain; setting, in mashing, the "coagulation of the meal into a dense impenetrable mass caused by mashing at too high a temperature;" in filling a back with wort, running at the proper heat; spads the malt, mashes too hot; goods, grist; rob, malt wort boiled down to notice gravity, &c.; lob, a mixture of wort and malt flour to increase the gravity of worts; bub, a mixture to hasten fermentation; browns, treacle; greens, draff; whites, illicit whiskey; draff, "searched grains"; potale, wash; potale, charger, wash charger; sperge, sparge, eperge worts; after worts; raising; flowers, head on fermentation; cutting, switch down the flowers; foxed, tainted wash; corpus mortuum, a mixture of wort in which the yeast has not acted; blinking, souring the wort; primum, wash; singling still, wash still; doubling still, low wines still; ga' or gall, first running, foreshot; faints, feints, after running; organs, feints; singlings, first distillation or low wines; doublings, second distillation or strong spirits; clearie, clearins, spent lees; spent liquor, distilled wash; low wines, first extraction; raw British spirits, second extraction; feints, impure second extraction; British brandy, third extraction, flavoured; rectified British spirits, third extraction, not flavoured; British compounds, third extraction, distilled with seeds, &c.; 43·0 o.p. spirit of wine; plain spirit, mixed with water only, 1834; stained spirit; neutral spirit; raw or gross spirit, corn spirit not consumed until rectified; mixed spirit, compound waters, gin, Geneva, &c.; shamsoo, rice spirit; licit spirit; dulcified spirit, sweetened with water; aqua; aquavitæ, 3 and 4 P. and M. c. 7, 1556; usquebaugh, usquebauh "a literal translation of aqua vitæ, usque beatha or water of life;" O.D.V., eau de vie; robur, spirit free from oil; silent spirit, "very pure, colourless, flavourless," tells no tale from what made; ozone whiskey; Parliament whiskey, legal spirit, also a word of contempt; Parliament brandy, in derision of an act to forbid its make; King's whiskey, legally made; Peel's whiskey, illicit; Farmer's gin; wee still whiskey, illegally made in a small pot; putteen, "whiskey made in a little iron pot," also illicit Irish spirit; jigger, an illicit still without whiskey; mountain dew; landrake dew; native wine, something hard; grog, spirit extracted from the wood of a cask recently emptied, by steaming by hot water, called grogging, cowing, bulling, nursing; Pitlochry, a twit on the substitution of water for whiskey in warehouse.

STAINED PAPER DUTY.

This duty was first charged in Great Britain, then in the United Kingdom, at so much per square yard,[1] and the charge was indicated by the impression of a stamp.[2] Imposed 1712. The licence duty was the same as that on the paper maker, and first imposed at the same time—1784. Both growing and licence duties were repealed on the presentation of nine petitions to Parliament in 1836,[3] probably on the recommendation in their nineteenth report by the Parnell Committee in 1836.[4]

[1] Huie, 1818. [2] L. G., 1716. [3] 6 & 7 W. IV., c. 52. [4] 20 Rep.

STAGE CARRIAGE DUTY.

The management originally placed under the Commissioners of Stamps so remained until 1847, when it was transferred to the Commissioners of Excise.[1]

With respect to the duty which was charged in part as a licence duty and in part as a mileage duty, it appears that though not levied until 1779, Lord North proposed a tax on stage coaches in 1776.[2] The licence duty has varied from a uniform crown, a variable sum according to the carrying capacity of the carriage, to £5, then to three guineas with a variable supplementary duty, after that to half a sovereign, and lastly with an occasional licence duty, which varied according to the number of days it remained in force: the mileage duty raised from one penny, under certain conditions, to fivepence halfpenny per mile was afterwards gradually decreased to one farthing, at which, with the other form of duty, it was repealed by 32 and 33 V., c. 14. The loss to the Exchequer was about £36,000.[3]

The incidence of this head of charge is fully shown in the Commissioners' Thirteenth Report.

It was not until the year 1831 that a desire appears to have been expressed for the repeal, but from that date to 1840, it was general; a petition in 1848 having been presented to the House of Commons to license "omnibus carriages" in Ireland.[4] Motions with a view to the reduction or repeal were made in 1868 and 1869,[5] and the repeal was proposed by Mr Lowe in the House of Commons on April 8, 1869.

STAMP DUTIES.

In common with the custom formerly observed on the creation of a new office, an announcement of the establishment of the "Head Office in Lincoln's Inn," appeared in the *London Gazette* of June 11, 1694. The duties in England were, probably then, certainly in

[1] 10 & 11 V., c. 42. [2] H. C., April 24, 1776. [3] C. 13, 14 R.
[4] P. Ret. [5] H. C., March 24, 1868; March 16, 1869.

1702, placed under the management of five commissioners, at which number it was uniformly continued down to 1806, when it was increased to seven, the salary at first being only £300, but by 1797 £500.

These Commissioners had the immediate supervision of 65 employés in 1705,[1] and 125 in 1779.[2] The duties in Ireland were placed under the Imprest Board until 1786, when six Commissioners were appointed, who in 1790 were reduced by one to five.[3]

These two Boards of Commissioners were consolidated in 1828: this consolidated board was consolidated with the Board of Taxes in 1833, when the services of fifty individuals were discontinued, at an annual saving of £13,342:[4] this consolidated Board was consolidated with the consolidated Board of Excise in 1849.[5]

It is at this point that my own branch becomes interested, in the further adoption of the oft-quoted principle—consolidation. This may be stated to have begun in 1855 by the union of the office of Distributor of Stamps with that of Collector of Excise in Edinburgh, followed in 1860 by a similar arrangement in the sister city of Glasgow,[6] and subsequently down to the issue of the Commissioners' Twenty-first Report by some sixty-three others, at an estimated ultimate annual saving exceeding £26,000,[7] the collector having been granted a special allowance for the performance of the extra duty down to the revision of salaries in 1866. The supervisor and officer have also been entrusted with a similar duty as well as the examination and valuation of the stocks in the possession of distributors: the legal and technical bearings being decided by trained, experienced officials. It has been suggested that postmasters should distribute.[8] Stamp robberies occurred at Manchester in 1866, and at Somerset House[9] about 1877, while defalcations and misappropriations have occurred under the old system at Davenport in 1872, Norwich, and other places.

Rouse published a Manual of the Stamp Duties in 1850, and again in 1853: Muir a Stamp and Tax Office Manual in 1861. The Stamp Laws were consolidated in 1870.[10]

[1] P. Ret., 1705. [2] Idem., 1779. [3] Beatson's Political Index.
[4] P. Ret., 1834. [5] H. C., Feb. 2, 1849. [6] C. 13 R.
[7] C. 17, 18, 19, 20, 21 R. [8] H. C., May 16, 1871. [9] London West.
[10] 33 & 34 V., cc. 97, 98, 99.

STAMPS AND SEALS.

Not a few counterfeit stamps have been devised and detected. The *London Gazette* between 1710 and 1825 supplies numerous instances. In one case it is stated that two culprits having been convicted, "stood in the Pillory at Reading" for their pains: while in another case the discoverer of a similar fraud was rewarded by the Treasury with the "Presentment" to the office of stamper. These stamps were devised to cut, to burn, to ink, an impression, and were sometimes called hammers. The paper stamp was constructed with moveable figures to represent the date, and figures to check, all being moved daily.[1] Some few were stolen or lost.[2]

The seal, employed only with melted wax, invariably contained a device in which the crown occupied a central position, with sometimes the respective national emblem, and around it the word Excise, with other words expressive of the duty charged, and in every case a number.

STARCH DUTY.

It appears that James II. granted a Patent to incorporate the starch makers, and that Charles I. confirmed it, and in addition thereto appointed a surveyor to examine the process of manufacture, who in the event of his discovering any contempt was directed to bring the offender before certain Commissioners, who were also directed should they find exemplary punishment necessary, to take bond of the offender for his timely appearance before the King and the Privy Council in the Star Chamber. His Majesty subsequently entered into a contract with the corporation that they should pay £1500 for the first, £2500 for the second, and £3500 every subsequent year, and, afterwards, issued a Proclamation as to the "well-ordering and making" of the article.[3]

As an excise duty it was first paid in 1644,[4] but lapsed about the Restoration, and was not again paid until 1712,[5] from which date it

[1] S., 1807, 1847. [2] 1833, 1858; S., 1808, 1811.
[3] Rushworth's Historical Collections. [4] P. O., 1644.
[5] 10 Anne, c. 19.

continued until 1834, when with the licence duty at the instance of a Parliamentary Committee, it was repealed.[1] There were at this time in Great Britain thirty-eight manufacturers, who paid an annual licence duty of £5 each, and a total duty—at 3¼d. per lb.—of £117,000 on which the cost of collection reached no less than 25 per cent.[2]

The manufacturer of stone blue was restricted to the use of duty-paid starch and to ensure that he complied with the law he was required to make entry of his premises,[3] and subject his manufactory to a survey which was made three or four times a week.[4] He was allowed to use starch duty-free, shortly before the duty was repealed, upon giving bond to the extent of £300.[5]

It may be added that between the date of the decision to repeal and the date of repeal, the maker was allowed to manufacture duty free upon placing his produce under revenue charge, and that those who had previously received a drawback on starch used in making woven goods were allowed to use this stiffening material on giving bond in £300.[6]

STATION.

Here used in generic sense to include farm, collection, district, division, preventive station, and ride.

England[7] and Scotland[8] and very probably too, Ireland[9] were at first divided into farms which usually included a county, or as enacted in Scotland a "shire;" exceptions were made in the case of England, at Oxford, and once at least when England was let as one farm,[10] and in the cases of London[11] and Edinburgh which were each treated distinctly from the other portions of the counties in which they were situated. England continued apportioned under this name until 1683, when Charles II., for fiscal reasons, issued a Proclamation that it should cease,[10] and upon the rearrangement which followed it would seem that the term collection was introduced.

[1] 4 & 5 W. IV., c. 77. [2] Parnell 8 Rep. [3] 26 Geo. III., c. 51. [4] 1787. [5] 1834. [6] 1834. [7] Green's State Papers, 1664. [8] Scotch Act, 1663. [9] L. G., 1668. [10] Proclamation, June 20, 1683. [11] L. G., 1680.

The limits of a "collexion"[1] appear to have been coextensive with those of a county,[2] though sometimes traversed by more than one collector,[3] and this is also borne out by the fact that the duties were raised by a fixed sum per county, either by an exact levy[4] or by farming,[2] and further proof is also afforded by the names of several collections having been changed, so recently as 1864, from the name of a county to the name of the place which formed the seat of the collection. The number of collections were—

In Eng. in	1743, 49;[5]	in Scotland in	1707, 13;[6]	in Ireland in	1809, 33[7]
" "	1779, 53;	" "	1779, 13;[6]		......
" "	1797, 56;[8]	" "	1833, 16;[9]		......
" "	1838, 56;	" "	1838, 16;	" "	1838, 21[6]
" "	1869, 64;	" "	1869, 13;	" "	1869, 14[8]

The abolition of collections was much discussed in 1872.[9] Collections were not formed in London until after 1836,[10] except one at the Customs House.[11]

The term district never seems to have been so precisely defined in a geographical sense. As used in farming the post horse duties in 1788,[12] it included sometimes several counties; in Ireland it implied a collection, while in that country "survey" was the equivalent for district in England.[7] No date has been observed when the term district was first employed, nor when the distinctions of foot-walk and riding were first used, though the riding district appears to have been for some time distinguished rather by the number of "officers"[13] than by its length and breadth. In 1869 an effort was made to lay it out in entire parishes, and in 1872, the discontinuance of the distinction was advocated.[9]

A division in 1660 included the extent of country over which the sub-commissioner had authority; in 1665 farms were laid out in "Divisions;" in 1690 an Act runs, "officer of Excise for the place or Division;"[14] in Ireland in 1759 and 1809[7] the equivalent was "walk;" in 1757-78 a division—here a generic term—an area not exceeding sixteen miles inclusive, nor exceeding twelve miles exclusive, of cautionary traders, was called a foot walk; in 1781 a

[1] 1 Charles I., c. 5. [2] Green's State Papers, 1663. [3] Idem, 1664.
[4] Scotch Act, 1663. [5] Royal Gauger. [6] P. Ret. [7] P. Rep.
[8] Estimates. [9] P. Rep. [10] P. Rep., 1836. [11] P. Ret., 1705.
[12] L. G. [13] Scotch Instructions, 1804. [14] 2 W. & M., sess. 2, c. 9.
[15] 33 Geo. II., c. 9.

surveyorship was known as a division and divided into "body and outwalk;[1] in 1789 the term division became specific and synonymous with footwalk, and included an extent not exceeding twenty miles inclusive nor twelve miles exclusive; in Scotland in 1804 the term was generic, including both footwalk and ride, the footwalk consisting of not more than sixteen miles including, nor more than twelve miles excluding "cautionaries;" the phrase "itinerant division" apparently including a wider extent of country; in 1810, the word division became specific—the footwalk being called a division.

The preventive station, always of variable extent, has been defined to be one in which there are no "chargeable duties."[2]

Tom Paine refers to the "outride," in his famous "Case," as a station much wider than a division,[3] and this is the only idea to be gathered; in 1778 however, the same station was called a ride and exceeded the limits of the division of that date being divided into so many days' ride, yet the designation outride was not officially discontinued until ten years later when, as in 1778, the same principle was applied to define a ride, but since that date the character of the duties rather than a given distance has determined the extent of this station.

STATIONERY.

50 quills long represented the stationery allowance to an officer; it was this alone, not even the option of a metallic pen, but on the desire being expressed for Loftus's chavasse pen in 1858-9, that black article was supplied in 1860; and on a desire being made known for an allowance of stationery, a pecuniary allowance for stationery, in 1854 downwards to 1869, a crown per annum per station, of whatever rank or number in that rank, was granted in 1869.[4]

STILL LICENCE DUTY.

Two-fold: one on the still-maker, another on the still-user.

The Parliamentary Committee who inquired into the Scotch distillery, in 1799, recommended, to prevent private distillation, that "stillmakers should have and pay for a licence, and the excise

[1] London Instructions. [2] P. Rep., 1834. [3] 1772. [4] C. S. G.

should stamp each still." Their suggestion lay unheeded, except with regard to Ireland, where a licence duty was imposed in 1806, until 1821, when the makers in Scotland and in 1825, in Ireland, were first required to pay a ten-shilling licence duty,[1] which the Parnell Committee considered, owing to its invidious character, objectionable,[2] and Mr Lowe repealed, in 1870.[3] Only eighteen licences were issued in the financial year 1870.[4]

This partial levy also obtained with the licence duty imposed on the chemist, who used a still, as Sir Henry and his two coadjutors observe, "to bring all persons using stills in those parts of the kingdom, where the business of distillation is so generally diffused, under the cognisance of the Excise,"[2] until 1846 when England was included. The number of licences taken out on the first imposition was, in Scotland, in 1821, 27; in Ireland, in 1825, 6; in England, in 1846, 169;[2] while it had risen to, in 1877, in Scotland 110; in Ireland 29; in England 740—the highest number yet issued.[5]

ST ALBANS' WINE CHARTER

"Queen Elizabeth by her charter, dated 7th February 1560, 2 Regni sui, confirmed both the former charters of Edw. VI. and Queen Mary, and upon the petition of Sir Nicholas Bacon, knight, Lord Keeper of the Broad Seal, by her charter, dated at Gorbam, Bury, 24th March anno 1570, 12 regni sui, reciting the grant of the school made by Edw. VI., for the farther relief and maintenance of the master and school, granted that the mayor and burgesses may appoint two discreet and honest inhabitants within the borough, to sell there all manner of wine, and may discharge them, or either of them, from such selling, and appoint other discreet persons, in the place of one or either of them, so often as the mayor and burgesses shall think fit, to sell wine, and shall grant them license by themselves, or assigne in their inns or messauges within the burrough, to keep two wine taverns, so long as they shall please to sell all sorts of wine by any measure, and at any price, to the greatest profit of either of them without any forfeiture; and no other person shall sell any wine within the burrough upon the penalty of £20, so often as he shall do the same; provided if the mayor and burgesses shall not pay to the master of the school the yearly annuity of £20, for his

[1] C. 13 R. [2] Parnell, 19 Rep. [3] H. C., April 11, 1870. [4] C. 14 R. [5] C. 20, 21 R.

maintenance at the Feast of St Michael the Archangel, the birth of our Lord, the Annunciation of the blessed Virgin Mary, and Nativity of St John Baptist, by equal portions, or within one month next after any of the feasts, that then this faculty shall be suspended and cease, until the master of the school shall be fully satisfied of such annuity of twenty pounds, and all the arrearages thereof.

"King James the First by his Charter, dated at Westminster 10 Maii, anno 1605, 3 Regni sui, Aug. and Scot. 43, reciting the several Grants touching the School made by Edward VI. and Queen Elizabeth, and also reciting another Grant, whereas he by Letters Patent dated at Westminster, 18 Decemb. 1606, 4 Regni sui, Aug. and Scot. 44, had granted free liberty to Robert Wooley of this Town, Leonard Wooley his son, and Robert Wooley the younger, another of his Sons, and their Assigns; that Rob. Wooley the elder during his natural Life, Leonard Wooley after the death of Robert his Father, during his natural Life, and Robert Wooley the younger after the death of Robert Wooley the elder, and Leonard Wooley his Son during the life of Robert Wooley the younger, shall have one Tavern or Cellar of Wine within the Burrough of St Alban, in the dwelling house wherein Robert Wooley the elder, Leonard and Robert his Sons, now dwell, or they or their Assigns shall dwell within the Town, and in it may sell and drink by retail by the Gallon, Pottle, Quart, or less or greater Measure, all manner of wholesome Wines at their pleasure, and for such price as the Wine with reasonable profit may be sold without any forfeiture, paying yearly the Mayor and Burgesses to the use of the Free Grammar School, for an augmentation of the Stipend yearly paid to the Master, four Marks at the Annunciation of the blessed Lady the Virgin Mary, the Nativity of St John Baptist, of St Michael the Archangel, and the Birth of Our Lord, by equal portions, during the natural lives of Robert Wooley the elder, Leonard Wooley, and Robert Wooley the younger, and the longer liver of them, and to the intent that the several Rents of £20 and four Marks shall continue hereafter to the Mayor and Burgesses; the King grants to them, that within the Burrough and two miles thereof, there shall be no more than three Wine Taverns for the future; and that after the death of Robert Wooley the elder and his two Sons, and the Surrender, or Forfeiture of their Interests, the Mayor and Burgesses may appoint one discreet and honest person (besides the two persons appointed as aforesaid) to sell all manner of Wines within the

Burrough, and to remove him, and to appoint another in his place, so often as they shall think fit; and that no other person shall sell Wine within the Burrough, or two miles thereof, upon the Penalty of £20, and the Mayor and Burgesses may search any Cellar, House, or Place within the Burrough, or two miles thereof, and if any Wines shall be found there to sell, contrary to this Grant; they may Seize the same, to the use of the King, and imprison the Offender, till he shall be bound to the Mayor and Burgesses, that he will not hereafter sell any Wine within the Burrough or two miles thereof.

"Provided, that if the Mayor and Burgesses shall not yearly pay to the Master of the School the yearly rent or Annuity of Four Marks as aforesaid; this Faculty shall cease, until the Master shall be fully satisfied of the four Marks and all the Arrearages thereof."

Unaffected by 12 C. II., c. 25; 15 Car. II., c. 14, and subsequent acts.

ST KATHERINE'S DISTILLERY.

This distillery was under the sole control of this department for the redistillation of seized spirits. Prior to its establishment condemned spirits were carried in open boats and destroyed in the Thames, but if the intention were known mobs would collect and attempt to rescue them. This practice was therefore discontinued in 1805, when a gentleman named Clarke contracted to redistil the confiscated spirit at one shilling per gallon. A contract of this kind was continued until 1819, when the "St Katherine's Distillery" was erected for the use of the Excise, on premises owned, and formally used for victualling purposes by the Government.

In 1827 a portion of the distillery premises was sold to the St Katherine's Dock Company. The building and plant, which were considered to have been purchased at a high rate, or rather valuation, cost £35,769, and was computed to have stood at a rental of £1920 per annum, which with the working expenses gave an average cost of distillation of 1s. 5d. per proof gallon—7½d. rent and 9½d. working expenses. The gallons produced having been 63,580, the apparent profit per gallon one shilling. Indeed, in such high repute was the redistilled Geneva held, that it frequently sold at 4d. and 5d. per gallon more than that imported directly from Holland. Though recommended to be "permanently discontinued"[1] by the

[1] Parnell, 20 Rep.

Royal Commission of 1836, it appears to have been employed for that purpose as late as 1846, as shown by the advertisement of a sale of 17,000 gallons of Foreign Brandy and 3000 gallons of Geneva at the "Excise Distillery, Saint Catherine's" Docks, London.[1]

SUGAR DUTY.

Except prior to and perhaps during Cromwell's Protectorate,[2] no excise duty was exigible on sugar until the introduction of the manufacture from beet in 1837:[3] it then became necessary to levy a duty on the home-made article in justice to the foreigner whose commodity was assessed by the Customs, and in consideration of the fact that it came into competition with malt, upon which an Excise duty was chargeable. This manufacture appears to have been carried on by one Hercules Bradshaw prior to as well as after the imposition of the duty, and on that plea he twice petitioned Parliament to be relieved from its incidence.[4] Dr Scoffern, too, endeavoured to increase the manufacture by a process which was disapproved by Dr Hofman and others.[5] He was followed by the "Irish Beet Sugar Company," who applied to her Majesty to grant them a charter "for the refining of beetroot sugar,"[6] but after some six years experience the company petitioned for dissolution and "winding-up."[7] Next came Mr Duncan, a London sugar refiner, who established a manufactory at Lavenham, where he continued his industry with varying results down to the date of repeal in 1874.[8] The Principal of the Laboratory, too, published a pamphlet on the manufacture.

The duty, assessed according to the specific gravity of the syrup,[9] though leviable in all three countries, little affected Ireland, and less Scotland, only about a ton having been paid for in the latter country, indeed the Commissioners termed it a nominal duty; it never much exceeded £13,000 per annum.[10]

Scores and scores of petitions were presented to Parliament between 1833 and 1852 respecting the Customs and Excise restrictions: as for instance the refining in bond, the modification, reduc-

[1] L. G., 1846. [2] P. Q., 1643. [3] H. C., June 27, 1837.
[4] P. Rep., 1839, 1840, 1847. [5] P. Ret., 1850.
[6] L. G., 1851; Report, Beet Sugar, Dublin, 1852. [7] P. Ret., 1853; L. G., 1857.
[8] C. R., 13 to 17. [9] 1841. [10] C. 16 R.

tion, equalisation, and repeal of the duty, the permission to use the article in brewing and distilling,[1] and these petitive efforts were continued by memorial[2] and deputation,[3] until all were realised.[4] And the realisation of course includes the use of this saccharine substance in the distillery and brewery, where, with the exception of times of scarcity of corn, and then only for brief periods,[5] or at the distillery under stringent regulations,[6] until 1847 and 1874 respectively, the use was prohibited.[7] As far back as 1806 Lord Temple obtained the appointment of a committee to investigate "the possibility, and if possible . . . . the propriety" of doing so,[8] but as the committee reported unfavourably, the subject then dropped,[9] to be again opened, however, in 1808, at the instance of the Chancellor of the Exchequer,[10] whose object was to confine the distiller to the use of sugar and molasses only; in this case to check the prospective scarcity of corn.[11]

The agriculturists of Essex and Norfolk petitioned against the committee's proposal to act upon the Chancellor's suggestion, while others presented petitions in favour of it: the second reading of the Bill was carried by 51 votes—ayes, 90; noes, 39.[12] But this change in the law in 1847 carried with it several restrictions. The Chancellor stated "that he must have on sugar used in distillation an amount of duty equivalent to the duty paid on malt used in distillation"—*i.e.*, "pay the same duty as spirits made from grain, and also a sum equivalent to the malt duty," to put them on the same footing, or, in other words, an allowance of 1s. 10d. per cwt., after paying the duty of 14s. per cwt.[13] On this principle the use was continued until 1855, when, on the introduction of duty-free malt, the distiller, upon giving bond, was allowed to receive the article duty-free,[14] and this regulation remained in force until the repeal of the sugar duty in 1874.[15] The Chancellor of the Exchequer further observed with respect to the brewing—"The duty payable on a quarter of malt was 21s. 8d. The quantity of sugar supposed to be equivalent to a quarter of malt, for the purposes of brewing was 180lbs.—the duty on which amounted to about 22s. 6d."[13] This calculation was subsequently modified to a mean of 200lbs., deduced from earlier

[1] P. Rep., 1852. [2] 1862. [3] 1874. [4] P. Rep., 1841-3, 1862, 1841-67, et seq.
[5] Distillery, 1808, 1809; Brewery, 1800, 1812. [6] 6 Geo. IV., c. 80.
[7] 10 Vic., c. 6; 37 Vic., c. 16. [8] H. C., Dec. 30, 1806. [9] P. Rep., 1807.
[10] H. C., Feb. 24, 1808. [11] H. C., May 19, 1808. [12] June 3, 1808.
[13] H. C., January 22, 1847. [14] 18 & 19 Vic., c. 94. [15] 37 Vic., c. 16.

inquiries on the subject,[1] and confirmed by experiments specially made Messrs Thomas Dobson, Surveying General Examiner, and George Phillips, Supervisor, who investigated the relative values of "Barley Malt, Sugar, and Molasses," and whose report was afterwards printed as a Parliamentary paper in 1847. On this data the presumption was fixed that a barrel of beer would be produced from every fifty pounds of sugar used, and upon this estimate has the charge for the licence duty been since uniformly made. The duty on the sugar being more than that on its equivalent, no "countervailing duty" was, of course, necessary, but on the Chancellor of the Exchequer proposing a reduction of the duty in 1850, he proposed "to produce such a duty on sugar used in brewing as would render it equivalent to the malt duty," and then moved "That a duty of Excise of 1s. 4d. shall be charged on every hundredweight of sugar used by any brewer of beer for sale."[2] This came into force in 1851,[3] and with the gradual reduction and ultimate repeal of the sugar duty, with a slight modification, in 1867, "that the duty on 210lbs. should be equal to the duty on a quarter of malt,"[4] the countervailing duty has increased to 11s. 6d. per cwt.:[5] the private brewer who may use sugar paying no duty whatever on his beer or on its production.

But with this gradually-growing charge, evasion of duty also gradually grew; and to suppress it, it became necessary to exact a sugar licence duty, and impose the obligation to make entry of premises, in which sugar alone should be kept,[6] with other recent restrictions to defeat the fraud;[7] though since the repeal of the sugar duty the "door open to fraud" has been considerably widened, and only an increased domestic consumption, or failure in production, by which the cost of the article will be raised, will, except cheap malt, lessens its proportions.

See Glucose, page 266: Molasses, page 367.

SUPERANNUATION.

The earliest mode of providing for those who had become disabled for active service, either by age, injury, or malady, appears to

[1] P. Rep., 1831. [2] H. C., July 19, 1850. [3] 13 & 14 Vic., c. 67.
[4] H. C., Feb. 15, 1867. [5] 37 Vic., c. 16. [6] 18 Vic., c. 22.
[7] 33 & 34 Vic., c. 32.

have been either to appoint to sinecure offices or places in which the duties were trifling, or, to oblige the successor to pay the person whom he succeeded a portion of his salary.[1] This mode was continued, with some exceptions,—Charity Fund,—notwithstanding the recommendations of Parliamentary Committees in 1786 and 1797 to establish a system of superannuation, down to 1803. In this year a further step was taken to make provision for the retired servant of the Crown, by the issue of a Treasury Minute, dated August 10, 1803, to the Commissioners of the Customs, who were authorised, on being satisfied of the incapacity, to grant one-third of the "emoluments attached to office;" if the service exceeded ten, and not twenty years, and age not sixty, one-half; or if the service exceeded "twenty years, . . . or having served fifteen years, being more than sixty years of age," two-thirds. In 1808 a committee on public expenditure drew the attention of the House of Commons to the supposed abuse of this power, and the Chancellor of the Exchequer brought in a bill to provide for the excise officers, but he does not appear to have been successful in carrying it through the House. In 1810, however, an act was passed, which, while it corrected certain abuses—such as the employment of a person to fill an active office, while, at the same time, he received a superannuation allowance—and gave power to award the full salary in meritorious cases, it did not specify with sufficient precision the cases in which the allowance should be granted.[1] From this date the rapid growth of the fund may be dated: the amount of the united funds—Customs and Excise—taken by the Government in 1812, when the abatement was discontinued, on condition that the officers of these departments should not be required to pay any further contribution towards their superannuation, being no less than £334,000.[2]

Twelve years having elapsed—1820—the Lords of the Treasury gave notice that a poundage would be deducted from all salaries from and after January 5, 1822, and the following year ratified their notice by a minute dated August 10, 1821. This was the beginning of the "General Superannuation Fund," raised by contributions of 2½ per cent. on salaries under £100, and 5 per cent. on those of and above that amount, under the authority of an act passed at the instance of the Chancellor of the Exchequer in 1822.[3] The redeem-

[1] H. C., 1822. [2] 51 Geo. III., c. 55; 52 Geo. III., cc. 60 & 81; C. S. G., 1874. [3] H. C., March 11.

ing feature in this act was a restitution clause by which the representative, in the case of the death of the contributor, was repaid the amount contributed. But so oppressive was the operation of the statute considered by those who came under its enactments, that they pressed their grievance upon the attention of the House of Commons,[1] and, with the aid of Mr Fowell Buxton, obtained its repeal in 1824.[2] The charge for superannuation was now placed upon the public revenue, and the £90,000 which had been deducted was repaid to the contributors.[3]

The question was reopened by the Chancellor of the Exchequer in 1828, who, on the recommendation of a Committee on Public Income and Expenditure, brought in a bill to reimpose the abatement which was so successfully spoken and petitioned against, that he withdrew the measure until the next session.[4] This withdrawal was not forgotten. In 1829, the Government, by a Treasury Minute, reimposed the poundage exacted in 1822 on all civil servants who entered after August 4, 1829, and as the incidence of the minute was prospective, the commissioned civil servant raised no objection as it did not affect him, and the future entrant, of course, accepted it as a condition on appointment, or, in the language of Lord Naas, it applied to "children unborn."

This minute, with one issued in 1831, to regulate the mode of awarding allowances, was confirmed by Parliament in 1834,[5] and was viewed in the light of an act "to reduce the public expenditure under the guise of a superannuation fund."[3] These words of his lordship were true: it was not until 1848, when the official child had nearly attained his manhood, that an effort was made to convert the abatement into a provident fund by the presentation of Memorial, which, beyond being printed as a Parliamentary Paper,[6] does not seem to have been considered. Though shelved by the Treasury, the subject continued to engage the attention of the parties principally concerned until 1854, they came to the conclusion that the fund was sufficient to meet every claim on retirement, and accordingly urged it upon the Money Minister of the Treasury, who promised that, if on examination it be found correct, he would introduce the matter as a claim of strict justice.[7] This examination was made, and, in 1856, he brought in a bill which approved the scale and sys-

[1] May 13, 1824. [2] June 18. [3] H. C., June 30, 1857. [4] H. C., July 15.
[5] 4 & 5 Wm. IV., c. 24. [6] 1852. [7] H. C., May 5, 1854.

tem of superannuation, and retained the abatement, but the order for the committal of which was discharged on June 18, owing to the great dissent of the civil servants, who, to the number of about 10,000,[1] enrolled their names against it in a petition which was presented by Mr Roebuck, and which, with the bill alluded to, was referred to a Royal Commission appointed to inquire into the existing regulations under which allowances on retirement were granted.[2] The result of the labours of this Commission was issued in a bulky blue book, and that portion of it which contains the evidence of Sir C. Trevelyan, K.C.B., W. H. Stephenson, Esq.—afterwards the chairman of the Inland Revenue, and after that Sir W. H. Stephenson, K.C.B.—and Mr Hobson, is worth a perusal: the first for its historical value, the second for its practical details, the third for its testimony to the hardship of the deduction. The Commission recommended—*1st*, the abolition of the tax without any reduction of salary; *2d*, the continuance of the system of superannuation; *3d*, general retirement at 60, and compulsory at 65; *4th*, gratuities in cases of incapacity when under ten years service; *5th*, compensation to be given for loss of office; *6th*, the regulations to be extended to the employés in the dockyards. The cessation of the tax was suggested to take place on April 1, 1857, on condition that the salaries of the civil servants should be revised with due regard to the amount of the deductions to be remitted, and this was drafted into a bill brought in by the Chancellor of the Exchequer on July 7, but it gave such "universal dissatisfaction that it was withdrawn in deference to the general wish of the House."[3] Had the proposed revision taken place, not only would the salaries have been reduced, but also the awards of superannuation, as they would have been calculated on smaller salaries. "Punch" considered this proposal an "Incivility to Civil Servants."[4]

So dissatisfied indeed were the Civil Servants with the intentions of the Government that no fewer than 448 petitions, signed by 17,497 individuals, were presented to ask for the simple abolition of the tax, and so well founded did the dissatisfaction appear to Lord Naas, that his lordship moved for leave to bring in a Bill to repeal the contribution clause, and observed, in doing so, that the highest public judicial and diplomatic functionaries were in receipt of great

[1] P. Rep., 9791; C. S. G., 10,732. [2] L. G.
[3] Civil Servants' Committee, 1857. [4] 1856.

pensions without deductions: civil servants who received their appointments before August 5, 1829, received liberal superannuations without having paid any deductions, while those who entered after that date paid an annual sum to that fund. Of the 56,740 employés receiving £5,595,000, only 15,311 of those were subject to abatement. "It was calculated that only one in seven of those who paid ever derived any advantage from the fund. . . . . . The tax at present amounted to upwards of £66,000 a year, and the allowances paid were only £11,000. During the twenty-seven years the Act had been in operation, the Civil Servants paid £900,000, of which £80,000 only had been returned to the contributors, in the shape of allowances, leaving a balance of £82,000, which if it had been funded would have amounted to £1,000,000." His Lordship then proposed his short and decisive remedy in a one-clause Bill, which was seconded by Mr Hankey, but objected to by the Chancellor of the Exchequer.[1] His lordship having experienced a little opposition on the order of the day[2] for the second reading, it was postponed until the following Thursday, when Mr Wilson proposed that it be read that day three months. Six other honourable members having spoken, the debate was postponed[3] for six days, and having been resumed and concluded, and a division taken, there were for the original motion 171; against it, 111—majority 60.[4] Owing to the late hour at which the House was asked to go into committee on the Bill, and the unsuccessful efforts of the Chancellor of the Exchequer, Mr Gladstone, and Mr Ayrton, no fewer than three divisions for an adjournment were taken—ayes 18, noes 77; ayes 31, noes 49; ayes 20, noes 55. The measure was consequently reported without amendment, and the House rose at "half after three o'clock."[5] Mr Ayrton stated on the third reading that "he must complain of the undue haste with which the Bill had been pressed forward and the extraordinary zeal which the Civil Servants had exhibited in soliciting honourable members to support it. The measure, in short, was an organised conspiracy on the part of the public servants, was unjust in its provisions, and based on erroneous statements." The House then divided—ayes 91, noes 23.[6] The "zeal" of the outdoor section of this department was ably represented by Mr Cathcart, collector. In the House of Lords, opinion was so unani-

[1] H. C., June 30. [2] July 16. [3] July 23. [4] H. C., July 29. [5] July 30. [6] August 3.

mous on the justice of the measure that the Bill was read the second time without a division.[1] *See* page 362.

Though the contribution clause had been repealed, the Civil Servants were neither silenced nor satisfied. Their next effort was made through Sir Fitzroy Kelly, who inquired respecting the unconsidered portions of the subject, to which the Chancellor of the Exchequer replied in a somewhat airy manner that "he apprehended that the object of the Civil Service had been served in the arrangements made last session for an increase to their salaries by repealing the abatements formerly made under the Superannuation Act. There were he believed some other points that still required to be adjusted, but they had yet to be considered by the Government," and a bill to be prepared with respect to them.[2]

The Chancellor of the Exchequer accordingly obtained leave to bring in a Bill to embody the recommendations of the Select Committee and the Royal Commission.[3] This was twice amended,[4] and although the Government met with some little opposition on some of its clauses, it carried nearly the whole of them, the measure passed the House of Lords without debate, and formed the Act 22 V., c. 26.[5]

From 1853, at the least, the date of the establishment of the *Civil Service Gazette*, to this date the agitation had stood one and alone in the unity of sentiment of the Civil Service, both in its determination and extent: it is probable that every department moved every nerve, both by importuning Members of Parliament, whom they fully informed of the exact bearings of the question, and by using every form of suasion with the press. Letters and leading articles appeared by the hundred to denounce the "Superannuation Abomination,"[6] the "Gigantic Swindle,"[7] the "Superannuation Black Mail,"[8] and fully bore out the expressed intention "to heap repetition on repetition until redress is procured."[6]

From this date—1859—little additional interest was taken in the subject until 1867, when a committee composed of the representatives from various departments reviewed the case of those appointed between 1829 and 1857, and asked for increased pensions for such as might survive superannuation, as apart from the justice of the claim, "The expense to the country of such a concession would be

[1] H. L., Aug. 6. [2] H. C., Feb. 12, 1858. [3] H. C., Feb. 7, 1859.
[4] Nos. 2, 33, 108. [5] H. L., April 19, 1859. [6] C. S. G., 1855.
[7] Times. [8] C. S. G., 1856.

distant, gradual, and evanescent." This request, which embodied the estimate that if the £930,000 deducted between 1829 and 1857, had been funded, it would have been equal to £1,600,000, or equal to an income of £50,000 per annum, was laid before the Lords of the Treasury, but did not receive their Lordships support.[1] Then advancing to 1874 the Chancellor of the Exchequer declined to authorise the Playfair Commission to consider whether alterations might not be advantageously made to facilitate retirement.[2]

The public, too, has also shown concern in the matter of "deferred salaries," that is, on its own behalf. In 1871 Mr Hermon gave notice in the House of Commons that he would move the reduction of the large superannuation and compensation grants:[3] in 1876 the Association for the Reform of Public Finance and Reduction of Taxation,[4] issued a circular to the effect that a Bill would be introduced in the next session of Parliament "to prevent the granting of such allowances in future." The notice to do so was probably given by Mr Boord on April 27, 1877.

This then forms an outline of the successive movements in connection with this important and much-discussed subject. It now only remains to place the different scales in juxtaposition, and note the chief points of interest in the various returns.

For the earliest rates of allowance the reader is referred to head Charity Fund: that is peculiar to this department. The later scales are as follows:—"There are at present three distinct scales of Superannuation Allowance for Officers of the Civil Service, with reference to the dates of their appointments and the number of years employed, respectively, as shown in the annexed table:—

No. 1.

Scale exclusively for officers whose appointments date prior to 5th August 1829.

4 and 5 Wm. IV., c. 24, s. 9.

Years employed.			Proportion of Salary and Emoluments.
10	and under	15	20-60ths.
15	"	20	25-60ths.
20	"	25	30-60ths.
25	"	30	35-60ths.
30	"	35	40-60ths.

[1] C. S. G., 1867. [2] H. C., July 7. [3] June 18. [4] Newcastle.

Years employed.			Proportion of Salary and Emoluments.
35	"	40	45-60ths.
40	"	45	50-60ths.
45	"	50	55-60ths.
50 and upwards			60-60ths.

No. 2.

Scale exclusively for Officers who entered the service after 4th August 1829 and before 19th April 1859.

4 and 5 Wm. IV., c. 24, s. 10.

Years employed.			Proportion of Salary and Emoluments.
10 and under 17			15-60ths.
17	"	24	20-60ths.
24	"	31	25-60ths.
31	"	38	30-60ths.
38	"	45	35-60ths.
45 and upwards			40-60ths.

No. 3.

Scale for Officers generally and exclusively for those who entered the service since 19th April 1859.

22 Vict. c. 26.

Years employed.			Proportion of Salary and Emoluments.
10 and under 11			10-60ths.
11	"	12	11-60ths.
12	"	13	12-60ths.

And in like manner a farther allowance of 1-60th for each additional year of service until the completion of 40 years' service, when 40-60ths may be granted, but no greater allowance for any longer period." The conditions of, and regulations on, retirement in 1865, will be found in Loftus's Inland Revenue Officer's Manual, by Mr W. H. Johnston, by whom the preceding table was raised. The reader is referred to that author's outline, and the Civil Service Year Book, 1873. Duty Pay is an "Emolument of Office." In Ireland the "gaugers" and "surveyors" appear to have received a pension of about three-fourths of their salary out of the fund of "Incidents" with the permission of the Treasury, and one-fourth from the superannuation fund, in all the full amount of salary.[1] The allowance has seldom been refused to a member of this department.[2] "It was the practice," in 1836, "to transmit to the Treasury lists of applicants at different periods, twice a year: but special reports were made on individual cases, whenever the circumstances appeared so urgent as to require a more prompt or particular representation. The decision of the Lords of the Treasury upon these lists and representations, when the claims of the parties" had been "established," was then "communicated in the form of a warrant, authorising the Commissioners to place the individuals on the superannuation list of the department, either temporarily or permanently, according to the circumstances of the annual sums set against their names." Pending inquiries it was the practice, upon application, to make grants to necessitous officers.[3] The Treasury, by minute dated May 24, 1836, decided that the superannuation allowance should commence from the expiration of the limit of payment of salary during illness. In Scotland, the annuity was paid by eight instalments down to 1834, when the quarterly system of payment, prevailing in England, was adopted and continued until 1869, when the roundly payment was established in all three countries.

Coming then to Parliamentary Papers in which there are so many interesting and important facts treasured. The first annual return of allowances was printed in 1833, and referred to allowances in Scotland only, and represented only £280 for this department. The next included those for the United Kingdom, and from 1835 inclusive the returns have included compensation allowances, which, prior to that date, do not appear to have been granted; then from 1872 inclusive, the amounts paid under the Pensions Commutation Act. The number of departments rose from 29 in 1834 to 71 in 1875 The net charge—that is less the total abatement made under 4 & 5 W. 4, c. 24—for both forms of allowance in all the departments rose from £685,678 in 1834 to £725,432 in 1856, while the gross charge —the abatement having been repealed—rose from £803,695 in 1857 to £1,105,681 in 1871, the last being the largest paid down to 1877, excluding, of course, the amount paid under the Pensions Commutation Acts.

To extract the chief features in connection with this department—

[1] P. Rep., 1809. [2] 1854. [3] P. Rep., Parnell 20th.

The total compensation and superannuation allowances which have been paid to this department rose from £121,980 in 1834 to £214,967 in 1855, the highest observed amount.

The average age and period of service on retirement, of the following ranks, in the ten years ended December 31, 1874. Under collector are included surveying general examiners and principal of laboratory: under officer, examiner, division and ride officer, and assistant.

Year.	Collector.			Supervisor.			Collector's Clerk.			Officer.			Total Number.	
		Average.			Average.			Average.			Average.			
	No.	Age on Retirement.	Period of Service.	No.	Age on Retirement.	Period of Service.	No.	Age on Retirement.	Period of Service.	No.	Age on Retirement.	Period of Service.	Superannuated.	Died.
		Y. M.	Y. M.		Y. M.	Y. M.		Y. M.	Y. M.		Y. M.	Y. M.		
1865	4	66·3	42· 1	16	56· 0	33· 6	6	60· 8	37·10	45	54· 5	30·[illegible]	71	85
1866	2	62·0	38· 9	21	55· 1	31·11	5	55· 7	31· 9	66	55· 6	31· 4	94	103
1867	3	66·0	42·10	9	57· 0	33· 5	9	55· 8	32· 8	58	55·11	31· 6	79	105
1868	4	61·9	42· 7	13	56· 3	32· 4	6	55· 4	34· 1	70	54· 3	30· 7	93	117
1869	5	59·8	38· 1	26	55·11	32· 9	3	58· 6	35· 4	66	54· 7	32· 7	100	103
1870	2	69·5	47· 9	10	56· 9	33· 3	7	57· 2	32· 2	69	57· 5	33·[illegible]	84	89
1871	1	63·3	36· 1	7	53· 3	32· 0	3	63·11	38· 2	33	56· 3	32·10	44	92
1872	3	62-5	40· 7	9	57· 2	34· 1	7	57· 3	34· 9	46	56· 1	31· 8	65	93
1873	2	65·3	45· 0	8	56· 4	33· 4	5	61· 7	38· 8	43	54·10	30·11	58	85
1874	6	67·3	45·10	14	59· 6	37· 5	9	58· 7	36· 5	53	58· 9	34· 9	82	83
Average in Decennial Period.	3·2	64.3	42· 3	13·3	56· 4	33· 7	6·0	58· 0	36· 9	54·5	56· 2	31·11	77·0	95·5

In this decennial period no compensation allowances were granted: two officers and one supervisor were reinstated; two received "special allowances" in 1874—a supervisor who had received "severe injury by burning," and the principal of the laboratory who retired on "full pay," and two others, "temporary allowances," in 1869. The annual return to Parliament contains the name, office, salary, age, and cause of retirement, period of service of, and yearly allowance granted to, every individual who has been placed on the list, and the name, office, cause of cessation, and amount ceased of every individual who has been struck off the list, during the year, which, in this return, ends on December 31.

The estimates give, under the head non-effective charges, the statistics of the non-effective staff; they are, as near as can be computed, as follow:—

Year ended March 31.	NUMBER.					
	Surveying General Examiners.	Collectors'	Supervisors.	Collector's Clerks.	Officers.	TOTAL.
1858	5	55	340	47	1166	1613
1859	4	56	331	47	1164	1602
1860	4	56	331	46	1117	1554
1861	3	56	325	43	1064	1491
1862	3	60	326	43	1031	1463
1863	2	56	329	47	1023	1457
1864	2	54	313	46	973	1388
1865	2	41	301	46	933	1323
1866	3	38	294	42	913	1290
1867	3	36	293	44	905	1281
1868	3	35	296	51	1010	1395
1869	3	32	302	52	993	1382
1870	4	32	282	56	989	1363
1871	4	33	279	57	962	1335
1872	3	32	273	50	955	1313
1873	3	31	263	52	925	1274
1874	2	31	253	58	886	1230
1875	2	31	245	55	862	1195
1876	1	34	238	56	852	1181
1877	3	33	247	53	755	1091
1878	2	34	243	54	736	1069

SUPERNUMERARY.

Similar to that of assistant this designation appears in the document for the establishment in Scotland in 1707. It was also in use in Ireland in 1791.[1]

Leadbetter describes the supernumerary in his Royal Gauger of 1743, as "a commissioned Officer who attends on the Collector, carries the Portmantua from Place to Place during the Round;

[1] P. Rep., 1807.

receives Half-pay; and when a Vacancy happens he goes into Business," and in his absence, the instructions of 1718 point out that the clerk was required "to carry the portmanteau, or guard the cash." To perform this duty he was enjoined to provide himself with "a good horse,"[1] and in 1846 he was allowed when on the round the same allowances as those to the collector and the clerk. In officiating he had priority of claim over the assistant,[2] and with respect to his promotion, this depended at first on a vacancy in the collection in which he was employed,[3] but after 1829 it was obtained only on petition after he had been appointed four months though this regulation was withdrawn in 1843; in Scotland he was not promoted to a footwalk until he had been employed in a ride three years.[4]

The designation was discontinued on the introduction of a second clerk in 1854.

SUPERVISOR.

The designation surveyor preceded that of supervisor, to which it was equivalent, though both were afterwards simultaneously in use for many years. "Surveyor" is referred to in the Estates of Parliament in Scotland in 1644, but it was discontinued in that country in 1812: it was in use in Ireland in 1808:[5] it was also in use in England in 1660—"James Bellen. For the office of Surveyor of Excise; is an able accomptant, and lost all his estate for loyalty";[6] and probably last employed in the London Establishment, which was discontinued in 1842. Supervisor is not an Excise-created word. It is found in connection with the Court of Liveries,[6] which the imposition of the Excise duties superseded, but not in use in this department until 1690;[7] in 1691 spelled "supvisor,"[8] and in 1810 it is wittingly written by a wag as "Supersqueesers." It was introduced into Scotland by Letters Patent, dated May 22, 1707, though not brought into general use there until 1812.[9] The division of the rank into riding supervisor and footwalk supervisor is of long standing, and until 1856 implied a sensible difference in the net salary by reason of the horse expenses.

[1] Parnell Report, 1836; Scotch Instructions, 1804. [2] 1828.
[3] Royal Gauger, 1743; S., 1813. [4] 1810. [5] P. Rep.
[6] Green's State Papers. [7] 2 W. & M., c. 3. [8] 3 W. & M., c. 1.
[9] General Letter Linlithgow District.

The duties of the supervisor have always been excessive, and thus writes Burns—"The business is an incessant drudgery, and would be nearly a complete bar to every species of literary pursuit;" and compared with the salary received, the supervisor has been unanimously pronounced the worst-paid official in the Civil Service.

In 1836 the Parnell Committee reported his average daily occupation is fifteen hours, the miles travelled twenty-three;[1] in 1858 the Dublin Committee summed up his duties as "laborious, intricate, responsible, minute, of wide extent; requiring logical and critical acumen, legal skill and tact; and involving expense;"[2] in 1863 the then secretary to the Board gave evidence before the Horsfall Committee to the same effect;[3] and in 1868 the Central Committee gave a clear exposé of his position.[4] Colloquially, too, this is confirmed by the expressions, drudge of drudges, Jacob Omnium,[5] hopeless official drudge,[6] Issachar—the strong ass of the service, hack horse, pack horse,[7] daily trudge and drudge.[8] The officer who usually assists him is termed "cuddie" or "caddie."

Officers were formerly, directly enjoined to report any "neglect or fault" in their supervisors—"do by Letter inform the Board . . . . within six weeks . . . . for that no complt agt Supervisors will be received after that time."[9]

It is probable the collecting supervisor was first appointed on the discontinuance of Argyle North and Caithness Collections.[10]

The supervisor formerly rode armed with a brace of pistols while on the round with the collector.[11]

SUPERVISORS AND EXAMINERS' FUND.

The object of this fund was to promote "the professional welfare of the subscribers thereto, and for rendering special assistance to the families of such in cases of need." The wherewith to be provided by each examiner on "clearing out" by subscribing half a guinea in lieu of maintaining the custom of a parting glass which had prevailed in time past. The six senior examiners, or the "ring," to form the committee of whom three should be a quorum. The senior

[1] Twentieth Report. [2] Statement. [3] Questions, 1600, 1601.
[4] Address. [5] C. S. G., 1864. [6] Idem, 1866. [7] Idem, 1874.
[8] Idem, 1869. [9] G. L., 1718. [10] Bateman, 1852. [11] 1736, 1778.

examiner, treasurer; the junior examiner, secretary. It was further provided that when the sum of five pounds had been subscribed, that it should be deposited in the nearest Post Office Savings' Bank, and that on no account should a sum exceeding five pounds be expended, except on the affirmative decision of the majority of six examiners. The rules concluded with regulation seven, by which "an annual account of proceedings should be published in the *Civil Service Gazette*."

The resolutions, of which the preceding is a breviate, were proposed and seconded, in the Examiners' Office, by Messrs Thomas and Rossiter, in the presence of eight or ten other gentlemen, in March 1866, and it may be recorded ceased to exist on the departure of the signator, Mr Thomas, who had the dissatisfaction to again receive his benevolent subscription in May 1866.

SURVEY.

"Surveu,"—to look over, occurs in II. Henrici IV., c. 6, in connection with the Aulneger, whose duty it was to measure cloth, and if of the required size, to seal it in testimony of the fact.

Ever an important portion of duty, it gradually grew with the increase in the trades which came under excise surveillance, to suppress the illegal act until examined in 1836, when the cautionary survey—the survey on other than growing-duty trades—which was then made on upwards of half a million "traders" was recommended to be abolished.[1] No mode of visit or "view" was then left untried: the "sudden" or "quick return," the "double" and the "check" were alike enjoined, and this frequency of surview with other superhuman requirements no doubt led, in a great measure, to the "feigned" or "stamped survey."[2] Though the system of cautionary survey was partly removed, there remained in 1867, at the time the Central Committee presented their Address to the Commissioners, much excessive surveying, which induced them to state "That a large proportion of the duties enjoined on survey are strictly supernumerary, and therefore useless in reference to the revenue, whatever may be the effect on the officers who are expected to execute them." This respectful representation was admitted and considered by their Honours in 1868.

[1] Parnell, 20 R. [2] 1781.

But there still remained the "Sunday survey" or the "Abominable-compulsory-Sunday-survey-of maltsters-in-residence grievance," or the "Breaking the Lord's Day by Order." With the establishment of the Civil Service Gazette the subject at once engaged the attention of those who suffered most by surveying on the Day of Rest and resulted in their transmitting an application for its abolition to the Board, who, in 1857, acceded in part to the request. It remained a mitigated grievance until 1870.[1] Under the old instructions the officer was enjoined to survey "before or after divine service."[2]

Traders whose operations allow facilities to commit fraud have been long subject to the continuous presence of an officer under the technical term course. And the notices given by them to commence certain operations were enjoined in 1832 to be compared roundly by the supervisor, and a note of its performance to be made in his diary: an order was issued in 1834 to pack them up quarterly, and preserve them for three years—an order extended to Scotland in 1838. "Running notices," by which is meant several given at the same time, were forbidden in 1842, and to "cut out" a notice signifies, in modern times, to declare it void. Double books appear to have been duplicate survey books, by which an opportunity was afforded to present a clear account in the proper survey book, or, sad to relate, lessen a charge.[3]

The use of the word nil is old. "Item est ordenez et assentur g les accompts de nichil en Escheqier soins de tout oustez.—Item, it is ordained and assured, that the Accompts of Nichil in the Exchequer shall be wholly put out."[4] This is the earliest use of the word, in connection with accounts, which this Plain Paper maker has seen. The contracted form nil, from the Latin nihil, has long been in use in this department.[5]

The injunction to make parallel lines dates back to 1741.

It was "to prevent loss by embezzlement" that a register of stores was enjoined to be kept in the general letter book in 1739. A Store and General Register was first enjoined to be kept in every station in 1856, though one was prepared in Scotland as early as 1804.

It is probable the "character" or "mark," termed[6] a hook, was in early use to indicate right or examined:[7] it was distinctly

[1] C. S. G., 1854-1870. [2] 1788. [3] Scotch Instructions, 1804.
[4] 1381; 5 Richard II., c. 13. [5] Leadbetter, 1743. [6] Excise Office Edin. Jan. 29, 1812.
[7] E., 1799.

enjoined to be made by every supervisor in Scotland, "That such examination may appear to have been actually performed" on every gauge[1] and area,[2] and the injunction was twice enforced—S. 1811, 1812—and although the character has been very generally employed, it has been continued through the force of practice rather than by either repeated precedent or direct order. The "black hook"[3] or "bar hook,"[4] or mark of disapprobation made to a minor mistake has been suggested to represent *n* and *r* or not right.

SURVEYING GENERAL EXAMINER.

Long before the introduction of the designation which heads this paper were the equivalents—

Surveyor-General,[5]
Surveyor Itinerant,[5]
General Surveyor,[6]
General Supervisor,
General Examiner,
Inspector,[7]
Inspector-General,[8] in use.

It will be interesting to narrate some few incidents in connection with the earlier as well as the later titles. For the post of surveyor-general, Thomas Hunt put in a plea, that he had "served the late King especially at Salisbury, remained in exile five years, and had his estate seized and forfeited."[5] General Surveyor was in use in both parts of Britain, and in the northern portion it was attainable only by those who had passed through the ranks of expectant, officer, examiner, and supervisor or surveyor, had been employed in a district "at least five years," and had given satisfactory proof of competency, as shown by his books during a twelvemonth. The General Supervisor, too, obtained his position by this experience; the Supervisor was not eligible to occupy the rank of either general supervisor or collector until he had been employed fourteen years, of which five must have been as a "fixed supervisor,"[9] but these

[1] S., 1809. [2] Excise Office Edin. Jan. 29, 1812. [3] C. S. G., 1859.
[4] Idem, 1861. [5] Green's State Papers, 1660.
[6] Parl. Ret., 1705; London Instructions, 1781; Parl. Rep., 1833.
[7] Leadbetter, 1766; I. Parl. Rep., 1808, 1779. [8] London Instructions, 1781.
[9] 1779, 1810.

limits of service were subsequently modified, to ten[1] and two years respectively.[2] He—g. s.—had to provide himself with "two able horses and a respectable servant to ride with your portmanteau, that you may be the better enabled to answer the end of your appointment."[3] The General Examiner in Scotland would appear to have been more particularly employed in superintending the examiners,[4] but in England there was formerly a staff of them, which will be presently referred to.

The terms Inspector and Inspector-General were employed in both England and Ireland,[5] and a curious incident occurred in Parliament in 1809 with reference to the appointee to the Inspector-Generalship in Ireland. The Chancellor of the Irish Exchequer moved that Mr Beauchamp Hill, inspector-general, in consequence of his having confessed "that he had regularly received £20 per week from two distillers," while in a district, and had been alleged to have suppressed the charge of some "15,000 gallons of pot ale" while in a ride, be dismissed—ayes 50, noes 77—a majority of 27 that he remain in office.[6]

General Examiner.—An extract from the evidence given by one who was examined before the House of Commons on the spirit duty, will illustrate the superior intelligence of 1772:—The House then examined Mr Coxsedge on the high price of wheat. Mr Cooper—I think you belong to the Excise Office, Mr Coxsedge; you are what they call one of the Generals of Excise? Mr Coxsedge—I am, your Honour, one of the Generals of the Excise, and have been in office thirty years. Mr Cooper—And pray, sir, what quantity of malt may the distillers, on an average, have used yearly since the year 1738 or 1739? Mr Coxsedge—I am not provided to say; besides, that was before I was in office. Mr Cooper—Then, sir, what might the Excise receive from the distillers? Mr Coxsedge—I can't say, but I'll tell you to-morrow. (A loud laugh through the House.) Mr Cooper—How many bushels of malt, sir, might the distillers, on an average, have used of late years? Mr Coxsedge—Sometimes more, sometimes less; I can't say till I enquire. There be several of us, and I can't tell till I knows what the rest knows. Here the House laughed out, and Mr Coxsedge was ordered

[1] 1815. [2] 1811. [3] Scotch Instructions, 1804.
[4] 1779; Edinburgh Almanack, 1821, 1823.
[5] London Instructions, 1781; P. Rep., 1833. [6] H. C., May 30, 1809.

to withdraw."[1] On the discontinuance of the department of general examiners on July 2, 1802, that of the Surveying General Examiners was formed. This was modified on June 25, 1817, when the services of eight were discontinued, but it was increased by three successive orders to a total of sixty, and again reduced by 1835 to forty-eight, which the Parnell Committee stated "is more numerous and more expensive than is required for the service of the department under a due system of administration and control." "In Scotland," they added, a fact just stated, "each was wont to have a livery servant riding behind him, but this equipage has been discontinued." "We have been given to understand," by several witnesses, "that the object of introducing the practice of sending out in pairs, was to make up cases for Exchequer prosecutions."[2] The expense of this department in 1834 was in salaries £15,900; travelling charges £6494.[3] The Commissioners themselves in 1842 called these officials "Inspecting officers,"[4] and in 1864 came the suggestion to change the designation to Inspector,[5] and in 1867 re-suggested, with an idea that the rank should become permanent London officials, and afterwards embodied in the Central Committee's Address of 1868. A reconstitution under this title was effected in 1871, when it was formed of the members of the Excise and Stamps and Taxes Branches, under the full style of Inspector of Inland Revenue—sub-divided into Chief Inspector, Assistant Inspector, and Inspector; but as this amalgamation bore out the impression formed by the Chancellor of the Exchequer in 1862, "that the question was not one of principle but one of degree, as they were justified in carrying it to a certain point, but beyond that point it ought not to be carried; and that point would be reached certainly whenever the mind of man would be overstrained by its being carried further."[6] Reversion was accordingly had in 1878 to the previously-existing arrangement, and the Excise was separated from, though never practically and fully amalgamated with, the other branch, under the title of Inspector, divided into four sections—Chief Inspector, Superintending-Inspector, Inspector, Assistant Inspector, to the staff section of which eligibility should lie in the principle of selection—without regard to seniority or rank.

The conditions of admission to this rank have varied. No super-

[1] H. C., Nov. 27, 1772. [2] Twentieth Report, 1836. [3] P. Rep., 1842.
[4] C. S. G., 1864. [5] Idem, 1867. [6] H. C., April 29, 1862.

visor in 1778 was promoted to a collectorship until he had been in a district five years; in 1829 he might petition for a surveying-general-examinership if employed three years, and for a collectorship if employed five years; in 1838 he was ineligible unless, as a supervisor, he had surveyed a distillery twelve months; in 1855 these were set aside in favour of an "open competition," an exceptional mode not observed before or since that date. The "Circular to Supervisors" ran thus—"Inland Revenue Office, Somerset House, 1st November 1855.—There being three vacancies in the establishment in Surveying General Examiners, the Board have determined on this occasion to offer the appointment to all Supervisors without reference to their age or length of service. As the Board dispense with the length of service usually required as an evidence of experience and knowledge, they will frame the examination so as to test completely the candidates' qualifications in this respect. Supervisors who desire to offer themselves as candidates must state their intention to the Board on or before the 15th instant. By the Board.—Thos. Dobson."

This of course created a sensation. It was defined "The Examination Hobby" to serve friends.[1] Each examination paper was numbered, and a corresponding number with the candidate's name was inserted in an envelope which was kept sealed until the decision was known; that strict impartiality might be observed in deciding the merits of the respective productions. There were about 105 candidates, and the three successful ones were—Messrs W. D. Richards, C. Boys, and E. Steele.—January 3, 1856.

The ordinary tests were correct dictation, reasons for the laws in force, ability to "draw up a statement on some subject chosen with a view to exhibit his general acquirements,"[2] since slightly modified.[3] Copies of the test papers given in 1864, 1868, 1869, and 1873, will be found in the *Civil Service Gazette* of 1873, and those subsequently given, immediately after the respective examinations. Two examinations were held in 1868. The time in this, for the most part transition rank, in 1877, was not less than six years.

The appointment of a first-class S.G.E. to a first-class collection in 1869 opened a correspondence in which it transpired that it was formerly the custom to look upon first-class collections as the "heir looms" of assistant secretaries and the first-class of this rank.[4]

[1] C. S. G., 1855. [2] G. I., 1856. [3] Idem, 1872. [4] C. S. G., 1869.

It has been suggested that the examinations should be conducted by the Civil Service Commissioners;[1] it has also been suggested that examinations should be held in anticipation of vacancies.[2]

The familiar official synonyms are generals, practical advisers, geniuses of red tape,[3] wire-pullers, dwellers in high places,[4] "ulans,"[5] excise hierarchy,[6] Philistines, freshets—those newly appointed.[7]

SWEETS DUTY.

It was probably the increasing consumption of, and of course the closer competition into which it entered with, exciseable liquors, which led the Legislature to impose an excise duty on gooseberry, elder, currant, grape, birch or cowslip wine as made by infusion with sugar under the name of sweets,[8] or "Sweets or mixt Liquors,"[9] or, more particularly defined as "all liquors made by infusion, fermentation or otherwise, from foreign fruit or sugar, or from fruit or sugar mixed with these materials and commonly made use of for recovering, increasing, or making, of any kind of wine or cyder or of any liquor called wines, are declared to be sweets."[10]

The duty was long levied at thirty-six shillings per barrel upon the maker, and one gathers from Cobbett in his Parliamentary History, under the year 1737, that the duty was so high that it was in the total very small, and extensively evaded. Sir Robert Walpole said, that although he proposed a reduction of duty he expected a larger revenue. He explained the "paradox" by stating that, as the drinking of spirits had been forbidden he expected a large consumption of sweets would be the result; the duty on the sugar formerly used "in the making of punch" would be much greater on the quantity to be used in the manufacture of sweets. Mr Cobbett then informs us "that those who were for the Duty got the better on every division, except one, which was in relation to that clause in the Bill, whereby it is provided, That nothing in that act contained should extend, or be construed to extend, to charge with any duty such wine as the owners or occupiers of British Vineyards should make from the juice of the grapes only growing thereon; for the adding of any such clause, to except such liquors from the duty

[1] C. S. G., 1872. [2] Idem, 1874. [3] Idem, 1868. [4] Idem, 1870. [5] Idem, 1871. [6] Idem, 1873. [7] C. S. G., 1869. [8] 1696-1737. [9] 8 & 9 Gul. III., c. 22. [10] 1699.

on sweets, was opposed by most of the gentlemen, who were favourers of the Duty and Bill." In the animated debate which arose on this proposition is the following—"Can it be supposed that all our gaugers will behave with common decency, when they get into a lonesome house in the country, at a time, when, perhaps, the family are in the fields or haymaking, and no person left at home, but the farmer's wife or his daughter." O Mores! To this the Chancellor of the Exchequer replied that, "they have hitherto generally done their duty with as much credit and good nature as was possible."[1] Cobbett has filled no fewer than fourteen pages of his History with this long and interesting debate. From this time down to the appointment of the oft-quoted Commission in 1833, the duty engaged but little attention, but it was then shown that the manufacture had so declined as to yield only a small receipt at a cost of collection which varied between 15 and 25 per cent. and was consequently repealed in 1834.[2] The duty at sixpence per gallon then amounted to £2700.[3]

In addition to this growing duty a licence duty was imposed, by Mr Pitt on the maker in 1784,[4] and on the retailer about 1791. The licence duty on the maker was extended to Ireland on the Union with that country and that on the retailer six years afterwards. A distinction being made in the case of the maker of mead only who paid but one-fifth of the duty paid by the maker of "other sweets." This trader's licence duty ceased with the growing duty.[3]

SYMONS' GAGER.

"The Practical Gager or the Young Gager's Assistant, containing all the necessary Rules for gaging and fixing the utensils of victuallers, common brewers, distillers, and maltsters, also the method of gaging by equidistant ordinates, inching, and tabulating close casks, &c., instructions for gaging by the Callipers as practised in the Port of London and all the Out-ports, the method of ascertaining the strength of spirituous liquors, and some specimens of vouchers with an appendix containing an abstract of the duties, allowances, bounties, and drawbacks of excise, distinguishing the several Acts of Parlia-

[1] H. C., March 7, 11, 1737. [2] Parnell, 5, 20 Rep. [3] C. I R.
[4] H. C., June 30, 1784.

ment by which they have been respectively granted; besides various other useful tables for computing the said duties, &c. The whole adapted for the use of collectors, supervisors, officers, and clerks of the Excise and Customs as well as for maltsters, distillers, common brewers, victuallers, &c., &c. Dedicated (by permission) to the Honourable Commissioners of Excise, by William Symons, collector of excise"—1819.

This book appears to have been first published in 1807, and being generally acceptable it passed through new editions in 1819, 1826, 1829, and 1838, and J. Bateman, afterwards Dr. Bateman, states in the first edition of his Excise Officer's Manual that, "In undertaking the present work, the author contemplated nothing more than a new edition of Symons' Gauger,"—so popular was Symons.

TABLES.

Curious are some of the tables which have been prepared. Dougharty gives a table to gauge straight lines; the cubic inches in a bushel being then 2150. It commences with the equivalent to ·02 of a bushel, *i.e.* 43 inches, and advances by ·02, with a table of the areas of lines from 1 to 43 inches, from which inter-tabular table the area of any line less than that giving ·02 may be found and added to the nearest area—1 thus line 1,000 inches.

Nearest number	989	area	·46
Difference	11	„	·005116
	1000	„	·465116

Methringham gives the areas of straight lines only from 1 to 1500 inches, while Thomas gives the areas of cubic inches from 2218·192, or 1 bushel, advancing by equivalents of ·01 of a bushel to 110,909·6 cubic inches, or 50 bushels, and Ecockes a table of cubic inches advancing by equivalents to ·1 from ·1 to 520·9 bushels. Todd, the areas of semi-squares in gallons from ·1 of an inch to 1,000 inches as supplied by the Commissioners.—1828.

Everard computed his table of the areas of circles from 40 to 120 inches, those now issued from the Chief Office extend to 400 inches, and contain about 27,000 figures. Loftus's Tables, parts 1 and 2, contain about 625,000 figures: Sikes's Tables, about 105,000; Bates' Tables, about 49,000.

TAXES, ASSESSED.

Commencing with the collection of the coach duty in 1747, that of the servant duty followed in 1781; but not until 1834 does there appear to have been any desire expressed to Parliament to transfer the management to the excise. Six petitions, containing 1088 signatures, respecting the mode of collection were presented in 1837, and a petition for the transfer in 1867.[1] The department itself desired it,[2] and the Local Tax Commissioners failing in some localities, about 1858, to find suitable collectors, the Commissioners appointed them.[3] The attention of the House of Commons was several times drawn to the subject,[4] though with little success until April 8, 1869.—*See* Consolidation, page 161.

TEA DUTY.

Under this title are included a growing duty and a licence duty.

Eighteen pence per gallon on infused tea continued to be levied until 1690,[5] and the duty on tea through many tribulations at rates varying from four to one shilling per pound, until transferred to the Customs in 1834,[6] though in Ireland only transferred from the Customs about 1829.[7] The chief perplexities in the management of this duty were caused by the smuggler, who, owing to the high rates of duty was enabled to obtain large remuneration for his daring, as shown under Smuggling.

The excise restriction by which a permit was enjoined to be taken with every delivery of a certain weight of tea, created quite a sensation among the dealers in London, who petitioned Parliament to relieve them from "the vexatious excise restrictions," and upon its being presented a motion was made to consider it, though lost by 78 votes—noes 233, ayes 155.[8] Nor was the restriction of much value to them. They twice again petitioned the same national assembly to suppress the smuggling of tea, which they alleged to be one-half, and in this they were joined by the dealers resident in the larger

[1] H. C., May 6, 1867. [2] C. S. G., 1854-1868. [3] C. 3 R.
[4] June 22, 1858; Feb. 28, July 6, 1860; March 7, 1861; April 3, 1862; Feb. 8, 1864; April 3, 1865; Feb. 9, 1866; Feb. 26, 1867; March 5, 1869.
[5] 1 W. & M., sess. 2, c. 6. [6] 3 & 4 W. IV., c. 101. [7] H. C., May 8, 1829.
[8] H. C., Feb. 4, 1734.

places on or near the coast from London round to Newcastle.[1] With respect to the system of check, it transpired during the investigation of the Parnell Committee, upon whose recommendation it was discontinued, that there were then 101,687 traders, upon whose premises no fewer than 2,137,424 visits were annually made, to take an account of their stocks. Nor was this the only "humbugging" as they were pleased to call it. They had the inconvenience of sending sometimes two miles for a permit only to find the officer from home, while on a market day, at Exeter, for instance, one hundred persons at a time would be waiting for that document. The officer, on the other hand, complained of the unwillingness shown in his stock-taking; notably, in the city just mentioned. Thus saith John Sayell, in narrating his experience in doing so at a quaker's establishment, where he had a crippled man to help him. On asking his "thouness" for another assistant, "Mr Broad Brim" replied that "he could not hire a person purposely to weigh the stocks", and then told "Crip" that "he need not hurry himself."[2] These counter-complaints terminated in 1836, by the substitution of an inspection of stock once in twenty-eight days,[3] and the substitution terminated on July 5, 1839. Except the twelve-penny licence, noticed under coffee duty, the licence duty commenced in Great Britain and Ireland, July 5, 1780,[4] and terminated July 5, 1869.[5] It yielded in 1869 £76,246.[6]

TESTIMONIALS.

These marks of esteem, since 1854, have exceeded two hundred. They have not always been confined to those who have risen to the higher ranks, but have been given alike to the second class assistant and the Commissioner, nor have they always been gold watches, they have varied from a walking stick, an easy chair, an "elegant phaeton," a life portrait, to the pecuniary tribute of several hundred pounds.

[1] H. C., April 14, 1736; 1779. [2] Parnell, 1 R. [3] Treasury Warrant. [4] C. 1 R. [5] H. C., April 8, 1869. [6] C. 13 R.

	1846.	
Sinton, R., . .	Silver snuff box, engrossed address,	Comber.
	1851.	
Cornwall, J., .	Tea and coffee service, value £200,	Edinburgh.
	1854.	
Fisher, P., .	A purse of sovereigns, . .	Campbelton.
Jarman, J.,	Address on white satin, silver pencil case,	
Bishop, Mr & Mrs,	Melodia Sacra with three sequel volumes,	Londonderry.
French, J.,	Silver tea pot and cream ewer, value £21,	Hull.
	1855.	
Bruce, W. D.,	Life portrait, ...	See page 135.
Cathcart, S., . .	A public dinner, ...	Hereford.
Richards, T.,	A gold watch, ...	Arbroath.
Moffatt, A., . .	A silver salver, value £31, 10s. .	North Shields.
	1856.	
Stewart, A. D., .	Gold pen and pencil case, . .	Montrose.
Damerel, H., .	A farewell address, . . .	Athlone.
Harris, A., .	A farewell address, public, . .	Dunmore.
Ginger, A. H., .	A chaste silver cup, . . .	King's Cliffe.
Flamank, J. G., .	An electro-plated inkstand, .	Newhaven.
Henderson, W.,	A purse of money, a piece of plate,	See page 414.
	1857.	
Henderson, W.,	His portrait and a purse of 100 sovs.	See page 414.
Middleton, D., .	A portrait, ...	See page 414.
Solomon, R., .	Bible and Wesley's Hymns, .	Leominster.
Matthews, W., .	An address and two pieces of plate,	Wexford.
Bowstead, W., .	A massive silver inkstand, . .	Shrewsbury.
Sessions, T., . .	A gold watch and chain, . .	Belfast.
	1858.	
Boulger, J., . .	£456, ...	See page 430.
Armstrong, J. L.,	A gold watch, value £20, . .	Ballymena.
Crowe, T., . .	Address and gold ring, . .	Belfast.
Simpson, G., . .	Address and "a beautiful testimonial,"	Limerick.
	1859.	
Gidley, H. G., .	A gold watch and appendages, .	Easington.
Carter, G., . .	An elegant dressing-case, . .	Waterside.
Bull, E., . . .	A gold watch, etc., value £24, .	Campbelton,
Law, W., . . .	A purse of sovereigns, . .	Glenochil.

	1860.	
Campbell, C.,	A claymore, dirk, skeindu, shoulder-belt, clasps, and shoulder brooch, also a tea and coffee service,	Greenock.
Priest, W. H.,	Macaulay's History of England, 7 vols.	Biggleswade.
Wigglesworth, J.,	Value £41,	
Bright, J.,	Address on white satin : 7 volumes,	Waterford.
Chard, W.,	Electro-plated tea and coffee service, gold pencil-case,	Newland.
	1861.	
Vellacott, Mr,	Chaste gold pencil-case,	Worcester.
Thorn, G.,	Address, timepiece, gold spectacles, preceded by a public tea, 300 present,	Welshpool.
Shacklock, J.,	A silver goblet,	Stourbridge.
Pearce, J.,	A pair of gold spectacles,	Bath.
Cribbes, W.,	A silver flask,	Melrose.
	1862.	
Varley, G.,	Kitto's Cyclopædia of Biblical Literature,	Dartford.
Watson, J.,	An address,	Aberfeldy.
Sparke, W. W.,	A gold albert chain,	Braintree.
Swan, W.,	An easy chair, a gold-mounted walking-stick, gold spectacles, gold watch, etc.,	Glasgow.
M'Lean, L.,	A silver tea kettle and stand,	Windygates.
	1863.	
Mutton, H.,	A gold watch, silver liquor stand, a silver tankard, a snuff box,	Dover.
Hart, A.,	A gold guard, value £4,	Bilston.
Green, T.,	A gold watch and purse of gold,	Tipton.
Dobson, T.,	Secretary, a candelabrum or épergne, a salver and tea and coffee services in solid silver, value £610, by 2489 officers, engraving of gift in *Illustrated London News*, 17th October.	London.
	1864.	
Owens, J.,	A mahogany writing desk,	Bridport.
Pollard, P.,	A silver inkstand and address,	Appledore.
Fincher, H.,	A gold albert and locket,	
Johnson, R.,	100 guineas and a silver tankard,	London.
Hunt, T. H.,	A tea and coffee service,	Leeds.
Winsor, E.,	A large silver goblet,	Newbury.
	1865.	
Robertson, J.,	A gold pencil case,	Warminster.

Bennett, W. H.,	A handsome harmonium, 7 stops,	Dounham Mkt
Green, J., . . .	A silver teapot and cream cover, value £23,	Worcester.
Pacey, J., . . .	A silver cup and stand of bottles,	Leeds.
Moon, J. F., . .	Josephus' works, ...	Blairgowrie.
Watt, A., . . .	De Quincey's works, 15 vols., . .	Auchnacloy.
Shea, J., . . .	A silver inkstand, ...	Aylesbury.
Connacher, P., . .	100 sovereigns, a silver spirit stand: Mrs C., a silver cake basket, a gold brooch, a silver ewer. On his retirement after 47 years' service, without one day's sick or private leave,	Greenock.
Carrig, M., . . .	His full length portrait, by Mayor and others of,	Dudley.
Dodd, E. H., . .	An address by 323 officials, .	London.
Hammond, J., . .	Shakespeare's works, . . .	Bp. Stortford.
Smedley, W., .	A silver cup and inkstand, . .	Birmingham.
Hargreaves, M.,	A silver tea service and an address,	Hull.
Batty, R., . .	A gold watch, ...	Donaghmore.
Geoghegan, A. J.,	A silver épergne, ...	Londonderry.
Smith, F. M., .	A silver teapot, ...	Evesham.
Macfadzean, J., .	A valuable gold chronometer and chain, an address, with cairngorm brooch for Mrs M.,	Elgin.
Bendy, W. T. A.,	An address and electro-plated service,	Liverpool.
Beart, W., . .	A marble timepiece, ...	Windygates.
Brain, T., . .	At a dinner, a scroll of vellum, a silver tea and coffee service, a silver kettle and stand, a binocular microscope, a drawing-room clock, entire value 160 guineas, subscribed by 958 members. The presentation was photographed.	Somerset Ho.

1866.

Marchant, H., .	An address and Bible, . .	Lechlade.
Gould, W., . .	A microscope, ...	Bedford.
Delany, C., . .	A silver tankard, ...	Llangollen.
Varley, G., . .	The Law and the Book, and gold pencil-case,	Dartford.
Hunt, J. S., . .	A gold English lever watch, .	Towyn, N.W.
White, W. R., .	A gold watch and guard, . .	Beith.
Davies, W., . .	A gold watch and chain, a handsome teapot,	Cheltenham.
Owens, J., . .	A silver inkstand, value £12, and address,	Bridport.
Ritchie, J., . .	A tea and coffee service, . .	Derby.
Chambers, W., .	A gold watch, ...	Lichfield.
Cockburn, T., .	Address, gold watch and chain,	Larne.
Hackett, J., . .	A silver snuff-box, . . .	Dublin.
Helm, P., . .	A silver liquor stand, . .	Newburgh.
Stone, H., . .	An illuminated address, . .	Tullow.
Price, J. T., . .	A gold watch and chain, . . .	Defynock.

Fairlie, J., . .	A thermometer in Derbyshire spar,	Wirksworth.
Gillitlie, G. S., .	Group of timepiece and ornaments and address,	Shrewsbury.

1867.

Heppenstall, C.,	A gold albert, a ring, an album, a stick,	...
Mason, G. A., .	"A testimonial in gold," . . .	Leicester.
Hickey, W. R.,	A solid silver claret jug, . .	Wexford.
Campbell, C., .	A gold watch and chain; Mrs C., a brooch,	Greenock.
Weddle, T., . .	A gold chronometer, a silver kettle and ewer,	Portsmouth.
Braby, J., . .	A gold watch, &c., value 35 guineas,	Bridlington.
Townshend, H.,	A silver cup, ...	Pembroke.
Hickling, W., .	A silver cup, ...	Nuneaton.
Crowe, T., . .	A silver salver, ...	Ludlow.
Roles, C., . .	A silver claret jug, ...	Grantown.
Cross, T., . .	A gold albert chain, . . .	Wivelscome.
Donnelly, W., .	A drawing-room clock, . .	Campbeltown
Harris, R., . .	An address and an épergne, .	Cheltenham.
Owens, J., . .	An address and marble timepiece,	Wenlock.
Houston, J. S., .	A gold albert chain; Mrs H., an album,	Stranraer.
Eldred, E., . .	An address and a service of plate,	Dublin.

1868.

Strudwick, F., .	A silver lever watch, . .	Wellington.
King, J., . . .	A silver cup, ...	Alloa.
Ireland, W., . .	An address and purse of gold, .	Oldham.
Ware, W., . .	A silver cup and timepiece, value £23,	Colsterworth.
Meikle, W., . .	£39, ...	See page 366.

1869.

Milmine, J., . .	A gold watch, chain, and timepiece,	Comber.
Longrigg, P., .	A cup and flagon, ...	Paisley.
Macbeth, R., .	A timepiece, ...	Dundee.
Innes, A., . .	A gold watch, ...	Cullen.
Allcorn, A., . .	A tea and coffee service, . .	Bilston.
Reed, J. R., . .	A gold watch, appendages, and purse of gold,	See page 245
Southgate, A., .	An address, a timepiece in gold and enamel, a silver tea service, .	Nottingham.
Bennet, W. H., .	A gold pencil case, ...	Downham.
Owen, R., . .	A silver tea-pot, a liqueur frame,	Llantrissant.
Priest, W. H., .	A gold albert chain, . . .	Nayland.
Flint, J., . . .	"A beautiful bat"—cricket, .	Edmonton.
Valder, J., . .	A drawing-room clock, . .	Aylesbury.
Dore, G., . . .	A tea urn and twelve silver spoons, and a writing desk, . . .	Chittlehampton.
Watts, T., . .	An address in gilt frame, . .	Worcester.
Connor, R., . .	An address and a gold watch, .	Liverpool.
Collins, E., . .	A travelling writing case, . .	Exeter.

	1870.	
Forrister, J., . .	A silver service and a purse of sovereigns	Mauchlin.
Ingleton, . . .	An address and gold watch and chain,	Ballymena.
Jacobs, R. H., .	A purse of sovereigns, . .	Ware.
Oliver, R., . .	An address and a purse of sovereigns,	Exeter.
White, S. E., .	An elegant cup, ...	Hants.
Stone, F. C., . .	A silver salver and claret jug, . .	Brechin.
Weaver, H., . .	20 sovereigns, Matthew Henry's Commentary, a silver service	Tredegar.
Hodgson, W. P.,	An address and gold pencil case, .	Port Ellen.
Evett, G., . .	A gold watch and chain, . .	Somerset Ho.
	1871.	
M'Intyre, D., .	A timepiece, ...	Somerset Ho.
Sanderson, W. J.,	An address and purse of sovereigns,	Lisburn.
Cousins, W. H.,	A valuable épergne, and an address,	Somerset Ho.
Coombor, W., .	A clock and an address, . .	Colchester.
Nicholson, A. W.,	A timepiece, a carbuncle finger ring	Oxford.
Transon, E., .	An address, a timepiece, . .	Hadley.
Potts, W., . .	A diamond ring, . . .	Birmingham.
Mackenzie, W. .	An ormolu timepiece, . .	Kirkliston.
Keay, J., . . .	A marble timepiece, . . .	Coleshill.
Heppenstall, C.,	A timepiece; Mrs H. an album,	Louth.
Flannery, T., .	An inkstand, ...	Letterkenny.
	1872.	
Donohoe, R. J.,	A drawing-room clock, . .	Belfast.
Anderson, R., .	Our Life in the Highlands, . .	York.
Standish, J., . .	A timepiece, ...	Sheffield.
Reed, J. R., . .	An illuminated address, a public dinner	Derby.
Mackay, D., . .	A dressing case and album, . .	Nottingham.
Bartlett, C., . .	A skeleton clock with silver dial and glass	Deddington.
	1873.	
Mayo, Earl, . .	£668, ...	See page 362.
Bell, R., . . .	An address and silver inkstand, .	Port Ellen.
Gale, C., . . .	A silver cup value £10, 10s., and purse of gold	Newark.
Bell, J., . . .	An address, and watch and appendages, value £42	Tower Hill.
Townshend, M.,	A tea and coffee service, &c., .	Cumamman.
Clarkson, F., .	A timepiece; Mrs C. a brooch, .	...
Bayford, J., .	A silver tankard and a meershaum pipe	Swansea.
Thorne, G., . .	An elegant phaeton, specially built,	Stourbridge.
Sneddon, D., .	An address and purse of sovereigns,	...
Horncastle, J. R.,	A costly timepiece, . . .	Plymouth.
Mayo, B., . . .	An address and "testimonial," .	...

Lewis, F. P., .	A purse of 25 sovereigns, . .	Dumfries.
Carling, A., . .	A dressing case and inkstand, .	London.
Murdoch, J., .	An address, a purse of 300 sovereigns, and a silver salver, at a dinner,	Inverness.

1874.

M'Redmond, L.,	An address, ...	Ennis.
Reidy, T., . .	A gold ring, ...	Overton.
Robertson, J., .	A purse of 40 sovereigns, a piece of plate	Alness.
Poole, W., . .	A gold pencil case and inkstand	Orkney.
Young, J. H., .	A gold watch and guard, . .	Maidstone.
Christie, J., . .	A silver snuff box, a purse of sovereigns	Edinburgh.
Norton, F., . .	An inkstand, ...	Bromley.
Farmer, H., . .	A purse of 17 sovereigns, . .	Ellesmere.
Pearson, T., . .	An inkstand, ...	Saffron Walden.
Beavan, J., . .	Chambers' Encyclopædia, . .	Dublin.
Thorburn, J., .	An address, épergne, and clock,	Carlow.
Gamble, J., . .	A timepiece, ...	Bedale.
Campbell, C., .	A silver kettle and stand, and address,	Kingston-on-Thames.
Evans, J. H., .	A purse of sovereigns, &c., .	Maybole.
Webb, W., . .	An address, a gold lever watch, silver salver, &c.	...
Marshall, J., . .	A timepiece ; Mrs M. a card case,	Louth.
Townshend, H.,	A travelling bag and inkstand, .	Coventry.
Thom, J., . . .	20 years collector at Campbelton, a silver tea and coffee service, and a coffee distilling apparatus	Campbelton.
Forth, R., . .	A timepiece, ...	Leicester.
Meikle, W., . .	£160, ...	*See* page 366.

1875.

Kelly, W., . .	A case of silver fish carvers, .	Walsall.
Goodacre, C., .	A timepiece : Mrs G. a cake basket, brooch	Nuneaton.
Eldred, E., . .	An address and "a souvenir,"	Belfast.
Ryan, P. J., . .	A timepiece : Mrs R. a silver cruet-stand	Killinghall.
Chalmers, A., .	A gold watch, value £24, . .	Bathgate.
Peake, J., . .	A gold watch and purse, value £76,	London.
Ridley, A., . .	A drawing-room clock and piece of plate	Glasgow.
Hughes, R., . .	A silver salver, value £31, 10s., .	Llangefni.
Campbell, C., .	A marble and gold timepiece, .	General.
M'Glashan, R., .	A marble timepiece, . . .	Glasgow.
Solomon, W., .	An address, ...	Stafford.

1876.

Hodgson, W. P.,	A gold watch : Mrs H. a percolator,	Bridgend.

Stone, H., . .	A gold watch: Mrs S. jewelry, .	Carlow.
Pape, R., . . .	An address, a silver tea and coffee service, with tray	Lichfield.
Willcocke, J. C.,	A silver cup, ...	Newent.
Chate, F. O., .	A timepiece, a silver fish knife and fork	Ramsbury.
Joliffe, G. J., . .	A gold keyless watch, . .	Liftone.
Lyle, A., . . .	A gold watch, a silver salver, a timepiece, &c.	Campbelton.
O'Meally, J., . .	A gold chain, locket, breastpin, .	Limerick.
Cowie, A., . .	25 years collector at Birmingham. An address and service of plate	Birmingham.
Lees, L. M., . .	£20, ...	Gorey.
Thomas, B. L., .	Barnes's Notes on the Bible, 20 vols.,	Eastwood.
Armstrong, J. N.,	Macaulay, Lamb's works, &c., .	Glasgow.
Philp, A., . . .	An inkstand, a purse of gold, &c.,	Lindley.
Anderson, A. T.,	A diamond pin, gold pencil case, gold-set compass	Dundee.
Turner, W. S., .	An address, ...	Letterkenny.
White, W. R., .	An address and timepiece, . .	Campden.
Nicholson, T., .	Aytoun's Lays, Mrs N. Thomson's Songs	Haddington.

1877.

Hickling, W., .	A silver service in walnut case, a costly clock with ornaments, value £120	Coventry.
Richards, D. W.,	A tea and coffee service, . .	Salisbury.
Shea, J., . . .	An address and silver salver, .	Canterbury.
Price, T., . . .	An address and gold pencil case,	Warminster.
Blair, J., . . .	An address and gold watch and chain,	Waterford.
Knox, Bamford,	Messrs, £8, 11s. 3d. Pro rata salary,	London.
Blofield, J. A., .	Ten volumes by Irish authors, .	Belfast.
Hopper, G., . .	A tea and coffee service, . .	By Supervisors.
Bolger, J., . .	Boydell Shakespeare, . . .	Abergavenny.
Manners, W., . .	An album, ...	Gainsborough
Whitehead, G., .	An address and a gold watch, .	Carlisle.
Henry, J., . . .	A gold watch, ...	Brampton.
Cole, R., . . .	An easy chair, reading lamp, gold spectacles	Bristol.

1878.

Hodge, A. J., .	An address and purse of gold, .	Port Ellen.
Hogan, J. F., .	A "banquet," an address, a silver salver, a purse of two hundred guineas	Dublin.
Offen, S. D. W.,	A timepiece, ...	Peterborough.
Hunt, A., . . .	A half chronometer gold watch, a chain, value 35 guineas: Mrs H. a drawing-room clock	Towyn.

Gott, W., . . .	Portraits in oil of himself and Mrs Gott, and gold spectacles	Glasgow.
Cronin, W., . .	An illuminated address, . .	Nottin
Haslam, W.,. .	A timepiece and purse of gold, £20,	Soham
Moodie, G., . .	A timepiece, a purse of sovereigns: Mrs M. a salver and tea and coffee service, value £200	Ayr.
Sparke, W. W.,	A timepiece, a purse of 100 sovereigns: Mrs S. a gold brooch, a set of wine bottles	Leven.
Baines, T., . .	Address, watch, and appendages, value £20	Leigh.
Westcott, G., .	A gold watch chain, . . .	Birmingham.
Hodgson, W. T.,	A timepiece, ...	Dublin.
Hartrick, G., .	An address, ...	New Ross.
East, R., . . .	A silver salver, ...	Portsmouth.
Lilburn, J., . .	An address, ...	Lurgan.
Guines, J., . .	A marble clock with bronze sphinx,	Portsmouth.
Stephenson, Lady,	Accompanied with an illuminated address, a portrait of her husband, W. H. Stephenson, K.C.B.	Somerset House.

THOMAS'S TABLES.

"An Original Table of Cubic Inches and areas for ascertaining areas and contents in imperial bushels or imperial gallons. Also an improved table for ascertaining the areas of elliptical vessels in imperial gallons. By William Thomas, Supervisor of Inland Revenue, Hadleigh."

This useful issue contains two tables—one by which the areas of rectangular figures may be found by inspection, the cubic inches of the product of the two dimensions being first known; the other, by which the areas of curvilinear figures may be found by the application of a factor to the diameter. Ipswich, 1871. A second edition appeared in 1872.

TOBACCO DUTY.

The cultivation of the tobacco plant in England was first forbidden by James the First, and afterwards by Charles the First, but apparently without effect—M'Culloch's "Dictionary of Commerce" —as several proclamations were issued concerning it.[1] It was also

[1] 1634, 1637, 1639.

prohibited by Act of Parliament on the Restoration of Charles II. for the protection of the colonies or plantations of the kingdom in America, the encouragement and employment of shipping and seamen, and to ensure the Customs "Revenue" on imported "Tobaccho." No one was allowed after January 1, 1660, to "set, plantt, improve, grow, make or cure any Tobaccho" in England, Wales, "Islands" of Guernsey or Jersey, Town of Berwick-upon-Tweed, or in the kingdom of Ireland, under a penalty of forty shillings for every "rodd" or pole, "except in any Phisicke Garden of either University, or in any other private garden for phisicke or surgery only, soe as the quantity soe planted exceed not one halfe of one pole in any one place or garden."[1] But the people in the county of Gloucester, where the "weed" is stated to have been first cultivated in England, and to have always afforded considerable profit, were not to be denied the cultivation except by force. Pepys writes in referring to Kate Joyce in 1667, "she tells me how the Life Guards . . . was sent to Winchcombe (Gloucestershire) to spoil tobacco there, which it seems the people there do plant contrary to law, and have always done, and still been under face and danger of having it spoiled, as it hath been oftentimes, and yet they will continue to plant it." A more stringent enactment was afterwards passed by which the Justices were required to issue warrants to constables, one month before the General Quarter Sessions to ascertain the quantity of tobacco illegally planted, and hand in a presentment at the Sessions that the offenders might be made to comply with the law.[2] The prohibition was extended to Scotland by 22 Geo. III., c. 73, at the instance of Lord Cavendish, after whom "Cavendish tobacco" appears to have been called in facetious commemoration,[3] but by the 19 Geo. III., c. 35, Nicotiana rustica was allowed to be grown in and exported from Ireland into England under the same regulations as those appertaining to plantation tobacco; and this permission remained almost unquestioned down to 1830,[4] when a Parliamentary Committee, appointed probably in consequence of a motion by the Chancellor of the Exchequer to levy a duty of twenty pence per pound on the grower in the United Kingdom,[5]—against which seven petitions were presented—reported upon the question, whether owing to the great smuggling the growth ought to be again prohibited, or a

[1] 12 C. II., c. 34. [2] 22 & 23 C. II., c. 26. [3] H. C., 1782.
[4] H. C., March 26, 1827; March 22, 1830. [5] H. C., April 7, 1830.

duty paid upon it. It now transpired that an Irish acre, which to the English acre is in the ratio of 5 to 8, would yield 1200 lbs. at a cost of about £30, giving a profit of about £70 per acre. There were in 1829 about 458 acres under cultivation in Clonmell, Kilkenny, Naas, Waterford and Wexford collections, and the people appear to have desired to retain the right even though they paid a direct duty either in the form of so much per acre, or so much per pound, but this was not supported by the Committee, who reported, the Irish to be inferior to the American, grown "Fogus,"[1] and that the imposition of a duty would cause smuggling, be expensive, and a loss to the revenue; that the computation of the allowance on exportation would be difficult; that to continue the permission to grow tobacco in Ireland would encourage the native capital and labour at the expense of the revenue; that great smuggling exists, and that it is expedient to prohibit the growth in Ireland from January 1, 1830.[2] Their recommendations were embodied in a Bill brought in by Mr Warburton, and formed the Act 1 and 2 Will. IV., c. 13,[3] upon the continuance of which several questions have since been put in Parliament.[4]

As an Excise duty it has been charged first upon the article and then upon the persons who made and sold it. The duty in Ireland is hereditary.[5] The earliest duty was on that not of English plantation 4s. the pound value, that of English plantation 2s. the pound value, above the Customs duty,[6] while in 1803 it varied from four to thirteen pence per pound weight, and snuff from six to twelve pence per pound weight.[7] It was several times afterwards increased, and ultimately transferred to the Customs in 1825.[8] But prior to this transfer the smuggling had been so very great as to induce Mr Pitt to introduce a "Tobacco Regulation Bill," by which he placed the stocks of the manufacturer and the dealer under the inspection of the Excise, required these traders to make entry of their premises and take out licences. The manufacturer immediately announced his intention "by public advertisement in almost every newspaper" to oppose the bill, and about the same time quietly informed the smugglers "that there must be an end to their connection; for they could receive no more of that article

[1] Tobacco; Slang Dictionary. [2] P. Rep., 1830. [3] H. C., March 10, 1831.
[4] H. C., Feb. 15, 1864; June 29, 1865; March 8, 1870; Aug. 9, 1872; July 20, 1878. [5] 14 & 15 C. II., c. 8. [6] P. O., 1643.
[7] 43 Geo. III., c. 69. [8] Order in Council, Feb. 2, 1825.

from them."[1] William Pitt's bill became law, the Commissioners announced the provisions,[2] and carried them into effect, much to the annoyance of the parties principally concerned. The publican petitioned to be relieved from the licence duty, and the manufacturer petitioned for the Act to be repealed,[3] and disparaging observations were made. The Act is "a heap of contradictions and absurdities thrown together, by some person who could write but could not read. . . . The formation of bills of revenue was much like the process of the manufacture of tobacco. The bills were presented in the stalk or short cut to the boards by some of the chief members; there they were dried, and thence sent to the Treasury mill to be ground and sifted; they received a little infusion in a preliminary and recommendatory speech from one of the great law officers of the Crown, and then an application was made to the House of Commons, as merely for a permit. Such was the usual process, from which who could expect a complete and perfect manufacture?" Mr Sheridan then moved—"That the survey of the Excise is inapplicable to the manufacture of tobacco," but his opinion was not confirmed by a majority of 44 votes—ayes 147, noes 191.[4] The following year no fewer than 156 lots of seized "occabot,"[5] were advertised for sale at the Chief Office, Old Broad Street, irrespective of a second sale, which include some "Hang-bluff."[6]

But the keeping a stock account and the sending out by "let-pass," did not suppress the illicit traffic. Even the Commissioners themselves announced their suspicion by general letter that smuggling was about to be effected,[7] the officers discovered great frauds,[8] others made numerous complaints of adulteration with sugar and treacle,[9] M'Culloch, Parnell, and Martin pointed out the premium offered by the high rate of duty, the Parnell Committee stated, in referring to the regulations, that "the multiplicity and complexity of them . . . . affords . . . . doubt of the practicability of . . . . execution with . . . . punctilious accuracy," and that as a check upon smuggling they were insufficient. The Committee then recommended the abolition of the permit and the survey,[10] which was adopted in 1840, except that the premises of the manufacturer should be examined once in ten days. But this relaxation and a

[1] H. C., June 24, 1789. [2] L. G., 1789. [3] H. C., March 8, 1790.
[4] H. C., April 16, 1790. [5] Tobacco backwards; Slang Dictionary.
[6] Snuff; Slang Dictionary; L. G., 1791. [7] 1821, 1824. [8] 1833.
[9] 1835. [10] Parnell, 6 R.

greater in the law with regard to the process of manufacture,[1] of which the trade took immediate advantage, soon required greater vigilance to secure the revenue and resulted in stricter legislation [2] and closer inspection. An order was at once issued that stocks in residence must be examined daily, those out of residence five times a fortnight, and those in possession of dealers occasionally.[3] The last regulation was rescinded in 1868.

Sophistication had in 1842 in some measure superseded smuggling; it therefore now became necessary to cope with it, and in the person of George Phillips appeared a man able to discover the fraud. But the trade shortly afterwards became so unremunerative by this two-fold illicit traffic and the consequent competition, that a Parliamentary Committee was appointed on March 14, 1844, to enquire into the subject. And in doing so the honourable gentlemen had to pledge their honour to an "Indemnity to Smugglers who speak the Truth," in order to elicit the secrets of their craft, while to test the detection of adulteration by chemical analysis as propounded by the Board, the Committee submitted two series of six samples to the Excise chemists for analyzation, and seven similar samples out of the duplicate of the two series to Dr Ure, but neither the doctor nor his less-privileged fellow analysts gave in satisfactory analyses. Mr Phillips stated that he could rely upon the natural appearance of the leaf under the microscope; in this he was supported by the eminent botanist Lindley. The committee recommended the use of the microscope, and from that date the Inland Revenue Laboratory may be stated to have been firmly established and the trade to have been improved [4] by the closer examination of their premises and stocks by intelligent officers, who made numerous detections and seizures, and supported the prosecutions based upon them.[5]

At the head of the laboratory, as Mr Phillips was down to 1874, he ever took an interest in detailing the facts and figures to show the decreasing adulteration, the increasing consumption, and the consequent efficiency of his system—an efficiency confirmed by the few subsequent minor enactments and by the miscroscopic delineations of plants, made under his superintendence, as well as those by Prescott in his "Tobacco and its Adulterations." Returns

[1] 3 & 4 Vic., c. 18. [2] 5 & 6 Vic., c. 93. [3] 1843. [4] P. Rep., 1844.
[5] C. I R.

relating to the subject of seizures, adulterations, prosecutions, &c., have been made to Parliament since 1846.

Until 1878 the trade has scarcely moved in matters fiscal, and not then entirely excise. It then, affected by the recent increase of the Customs duty, met in London, and, among other decisions to which it came, decided to ask the Chancellor of the Exchequer to appoint a committee to consider "the laws affecting the trade generally."[1]

One aspect of the question requires amplification—the licence duty.

Charles the First, by the proclamations issued during his reign regarding "the unordered retailing of tobacco,"[2] and the "abusive venting of tobacco," by which "men and women" used it "to satisfie an inordinate appetite,"[3] appears to have exacted a royalty upon the "retailing," by empowering Commissioners "for licensing retailers of tobacco" whom his Majesty had afterwards reason to proclaim had "forborn to make payment of their rent."[4] Falling into disuse, as it probably shortly after this date did, no further exaction on the sale of the article appears to have been made until Mr Pitt, in 1789, proposed his annual licence duty on both the manufacturer and the dealer.[5] The former paid, in England and Scotland, the following year, for it then first came into force, as a beginner, £2, and if his manufacture exceeded 20,000 lbs., then, with nearly uniform progression, £1 per 10,000 lbs. in excess to a limit of £20. This scale, augmented by one-half in 1815, remained unchanged down to 1825. In Ireland, commencing in 1790, as in Great Britain, the licence duty was uniformly £12: this continued until 1793, when the payment was made at per table—£8 for one table, and, then advancing by £4 per table to £20, the extreme limit of exaction: these rates were increased to guineas—or 5 per cent.—in 1808, at which they remained unchanged also down to 1825. Upon the consolidation of the licence laws, in 1826,[6] the rates were revised, and made uniform in all three countries. The beginner now paid £5, and if his manufacture exceeded 20,000 lbs. then, with uniform progression, £5 per 20,000 to £30, the limit of the scale to which 5 per cent. was added in 1840.[7] The committee who examined this scale, in 1836, recommended a new one, which commenced at £5, and rose by £5 per 20,000 lbs. manufactured—except the second

[1] July 31, 1878. [2] October 13, 1633. [3] March 13, 1633.
[4] Proc., August 11, 1639; August 19, 1639. [5] H. C., July 8, 1789.
[6] 6 Geo. IV., c. 80. [7] C. I R.

increment—to £50:[1] a recommendation which does not seem to have been since noticed, except by Mr Gladstone, who, however, while he approved, did not enact it.[2] The latter, that is the dealer, paid a discriminative licence duty. He who dealt in London paid a crown; he who did so in the country half a crown; and in Scotland "rates of duty same as in England." These rates were doubled in 1815, and at those augmented sums they continued down to 1825. In Ireland the wholesale merchant, not being an importer, paid £1 until 1806, when he paid £10, increased by 5 per cent. in 1808, at which increased rate it remained until the previously-observed consolidation and assimilation, when it was fixed at five shillings, increased by 5 per cent. in 1840,[3] at which it has since stood. The committee of 1836 also made a recommendation here based upon the quantity sold—not exceeding 25 lbs. 5s.; 100 lbs. 21s.; 200 lbs. 42s.; 300 lbs. 63s.; 500 lbs. 84s.; exceeding 500 lbs. 105s.[1] Mr Gladstone here, too, approved, but did not legislate:[2] he introduced the great licence in 1864.[4] The tobacco dealer, who is also a spirit retailer, is not required to obtain a special licence to sell at fairs and races.[5]

Among the books, not mentioned, bearing upon the subject may be noted—Steinmetz on Tobacco; its history, cultivation, manufacture, adulteration; Bentley, London: Prescott's Strong Drink and Tobacco Smoke: the Seven Sisters of Sleep; Blackwood, London: Abridgments of specifications relating to the preparation and use of Tobacco, 1721-1866; Eyre and Spottiswoode. The Tobacco Trade Review.—This monthly contains a series of papers on tobacco adulteration, the joint production of R. Connor, Esq., of this department, and J. F. Tape, Esq., with a series of six plates delineating leaf and starch structure, from the able pencil of the former gentleman. Vol. I., Nos. 7 to 12. 1868.

See pages 220, 273, 294.

TODD'S SEMISQUARES.

Thomas Todd, an officer at Liverpool, demonstrated the truth and exemplified the utility of a table of the area of semisquares in

[1] Parnell, 19 R. [2] H. C., April 18, 1853. [3] C. 1 R.
[4] Occasional; H. C., April 7, 1864. [5] T. W., Sept. 22, 1829.

the "Gentleman's Mathematical Companion," in 1827, and the Board printed them in 1828. *See* Tables.

TODD AND ROWLANDSON'S

"The Gaugers' Useful Companion, or a supplement to all former treatises on gauging, containing upwards of thirty arithmetical and mathematical tables, original and selected: with the application of the latter to the purpose of practical guaging in all its branches, by which the operations are simplified and contracted to a degree never before exhibited. . . . By Thomas Todd and Matthew Rowlandson, officers of Excise." Manchester, 1841.

TOWNLAND FINES.

Peculiar to Ireland, and leviable on the "Vicinage where the offence is committed."[1] Under this system of recovering penalties, it happened more than once that when the trade of hiring out a still had failed, or a still had been worn out, that the still was laid in a plantation, by a person who afterwards informed the officer who then made the discovery, obtained a conviction, and gave the informer a portion of his reward. While in 1817 there were in the whole of Ireland, except Donegal, 593 townland fines levied, in that county alone no fewer than 619 were imposed, and so persistent were the people in their illicit practices, that one "Lucius Carey had actually imported mantraps, with the avowed intention of catching any revenue officer that might come near them."[2] Lord Mount-Charles also stated that there were no fewer than "300 townlands' fines trials" at the Donegal assizes, and that application had been made for a grant to enlarge the county in consequence of the numbers confined from the inability to pay the fines."[3] Parliament was also petitioned for relief by those who suffered by them.[4] The Parliamentary history of this mode of punishment appears to be this—"These townland fines were enacted by the Irish Parliament for the prevention of smuggling so long back as 1783, and continued with various modifications until the year 1803, when they were, for the first time

[1] P. Rep., 1816. [2] H. C., May 30, 1818. [3] H. C., April 30, 1819. [4] H. C., May 7, 1819.

since the Union, noticed and amended. In 1810, on the proposition of the then Chancellor of the Irish Exchequer (Mr A. Pole), Parliament suspended their operations for two years, and in the year 1812 repealed them." Increased illicit distillation, however, immediately followed, and petitions were sent to Parliament to re-enact them—an admirable one being sent from Belfast. A committee was accordingly appointed to investigate the subject, and it recommended the reintroduction of the system, which shortly afterwards was again legalised, and "special collectors of still fines were appointed," to do what the High Constable of Donegal could, or would not do. In 1818, a motion to bring in a bill to repeal them was negatived without a division,[1] but the hardship of the incidence of the fines having been shown in a case of a farmer who had been deprived of "three horses and four cows which were collusively sold among the officers for £3,"[2] with other instances of "rapine and plunder," the Chancellor of the Exchequer brought in a bill to limit the continuance of the "Townland Fines Act" where the police were employed; to levy a fine only where a still may be found complete, not as heretofore, where only a part was found; to pay one half of the expense incurred by the employment of the police; to bar the infliction of fines after three years.[3] Further change appears to have been made in 1820,[4] and by 1831 the laws for the suppression of illicit trading in this country had become so numerous and complicated that a Consolidated Act was passed, which came into force on December 2, 1831—1 & 2 Wm. IV., c. 55—and which has been amended by five subsequent Acts.

TRAIN, JOSEPH.

Joseph Train, F.S.A. Scot., was a supervisor of excise at Cupar-Fife, Queensferry, Falkirk, from which he was removed on censure to Wigtown, from which, at his own request, he removed to Dumfries, from which he was removed by reduction, but after an interval of some six months reinstated in Castle Douglas District, where he appears to have superannuated. He died in 1852. But it is not in his official movements the interest lies. He was intimately associated with Sir W. Scott, to whom he contributed the principal inci-

[1] H. C., May 30, 1818. [2] H. C., May 7, 1819. [3] H. C., May 20, 1819.
[4] H. C., June 7, 1820.

dents in "Old Mortality," in which his contributions are acknowledged; he also assisted Chalmers in his "Caledonia," and Strickland in her "Lives of the Queens of Scotland." He himself wrote a volume entitled, "Poetical Reveries," in 1806; a "History of the Isle of Man," in 1845; "The Buchanites from First to Last," in 1846, besides some minor pieces, including an Essay, "showing the defects and abuses of the Excise Statutes, and pointing out how those defects might be remedied," this he forwarded through his friend Sir Walter to the Lords of the Treasury, with whom the author of the Waverley Novels endeavoured to create an impression in Train's favour. He was regarded "as one who had dared to think sometimes of other things than Excise business," and he commanded the esteem of the community in general, as the following incident, which happened while he was an officer, will show—"One day, having no official duty to perform, he set out across the hills to where a Highland Gathering was that day to be held. This was what Joseph most of all things wished to see, ... he did not reach the gathering, for coming suddenly on a deep glen, which lay along his track, he espied a gang of smugglers who were busily pursuing their nefarious operations in the dell below. On perceiving the gauger they made directly for where he was. Judging their intentions towards him would be of no peaceful nature, he took to his heels in a homeward direction, but he was soon overtaken; some of them were for administering condign punishment on the spot, but others, who had previously been in his power, and had experienced kind treatment at his hands, would not allow him to be injured, so he was marched down to the bottom of the glen where two stills were at work. He was placed between two of the party, who were armed—the one with a Queen Anne, which he took care to load with great formality in his presence, the other with a rusty claymore, which they said had killed several king's men on the haughs of Cromdale. There he was detained until the whole contents of the stills were wrought off. This done and the spirits and utensils removed, he was set at liberty, so late in the evening, that it was with considerable difficulty he reached Balnaguard."[1] This incident is most certainly doubly significant—neither gathering nor still—"Not for Joe."

[1] Patterson's Memoir of Joseph Train, 1857.

TRIAL BY JURY.

"The Right of Appeal to Juries in Causes of Excise, asserted." This is the title of a very ably-written pamphlet "to point out the indispensable necessity of asserting this right now, by explaining the particular power of juries to protect us against the pernicious effects or the farther extension, of a new insidious and unconstitutional mode of excise, lately introduced into the cider counties."[1]

This mode of trial was also advocated by Mr Beaufoy in 1785,[2] and became legal, as shown by Lord Loughborough, who stated that, "It was always a maxim with the jury, in cases of excise, to examine whether the officer had behaved rudely or not in the execution of his office, upon an information when it was wrong. If his conduct was insolent, and exceeded his authority, they punished him by damages accordingly."[3]

UNIVERSITY COLLEGE.

John Wood, Esq., chairman of the Board of Excise, was elected a member of the Council of University College in 1836, and continued to act in that capacity until his death in 1857, but, during the last eleven years, as chairman of that committee.[4] It was probably through his connection with this institution in London, and on the need of scientific knowledge becoming apparent in this department, that young officers were selected to study within its halls, with a view to the application of their acquired knowledge to the protection of the revenue. The first four to enter upon this course of study were Messrs Phillips, Drinkwater, Bainbridge, and M'Culloch, in 1844; the number being increased in 1845 to sixteen, at which, with little variation, it was continued, at a cost, exclusive of maintenance, down to 1854, of about £96 per student. Each remained, on an average, about two sessions,[5] until 1859, after which no further excise matriculations were entered on the register of this University. *See* Laboratory.

It is probable that about one hundred gentlemen passed through this collegiate course, and some of them became so distinguished as to command the award, in the same session, of two gold medals given for excellence in analytical and in theoretical chemistry.[6]

[1] 1764. [2] H. C., May 6, 1785. [3] H. L., June 22, 1786.
[4] C. S. G., 1857. [5] P. Ret., 1855. [6] 1858.

The examination papers prepared for candidates, in 1857, were these—two days. First day—Quest. 1. State generally the duties of an excise officer? Q. 2. Have you any, and what, knowledge of chemistry? Q. 3. State the restrictions you consider most calculated to secure the malt duty? Q. 4. Describe the method now adopted by this revenue to ascertain the content of casks of spirits, and the principle upon which it is founded. Q. 5. What is meant by a rectangular vessel, and what is understood by the term area, applied to a cistern or couch-frame? and show the area of a cistern of the following dimensions, L. 427·7. B. 82·4? Q. 6. Describe the construction and mode of action of the common lifting pump.

Second day—Quest. 7. Describe the construction of the barometer, and the principle upon which it is considered to work, and its uses. Q. 8. State from what countries we receive the following articles—tea, coffee, sugar, cotton, wool, silk, palm oil, quicksilver, gutta percha, oranges, tobacco. Q. 9. If a ream of paper be weighed in a false balance, in the one scale 17 lbs., and in the other 10 lbs., what is the real weight? Q. 10. Give the derivation and meaning of the following words—geometry, hexagon, decimal, equilateral, geography, hemisphere, probation, granivorous, geology, alphabet, nomination, rectilinear, photography, hydrogen, locomotive, postscript, philosophy, cyclopædia, horticulture, manufacture. Aug. 20 and 21.

Open as this system of partial tuition was to the angry discussion of the unsuccessful aspirant, it soon formed the field for a fierce paper war, on a medium being established, through the columns of the *Civil Service Gazette*; although the attention of Parliament had been previously drawn to the system by Mr Bright, and some reference had been made to it in the *Times* and *Morning Advertiser*. It was facetiously designated "The University Mania," the "Chemical Education Scheme," the "University Pets," the "College and other Chemical Hobbies," the "Pet Scheme,"[1] "King Wood and his . . . . . . ," an "Aristocracy in the Excise," the "Wooden Hobby Horse,"[2] and the discussion partook of the character of "Experience and Ability *v.* College Lore," "Favouritism *v.* Seniority and Merit."[1]

Drawing for once upon his own observation, the writer has no hesitation in stating, that whatever may have been the attendant jealousies and preferences which the privilege introduced, it has

[1] C. S. G., 1854. [2] Idem, 1856.

[illegible] MAKER'S LICENCE DUTY.

[illegible] licence duty [illegible] repealed [illegible]

[illegible] radical [illegible] and [illegible] the Re[illegible] was raised [illegible] eight shillings [illegible] more than [illegible] upon [illegible] 1844 [illegible] first [illegible] Great Britain [illegible] 1826 [illegible] was first charged [illegible] G R [illegible] growing duty was [illegible] 1834 [illegible] twenty-eight [illegible] where the stock was [illegible] one [illegible] The [illegible] were discontinued [illegible] considerably [illegible]

[illegible]

[illegible] of the United [illegible] the Ampt[illegible] Parnell [illegible] Parnell [illegible]

Museum, Edinburgh. Sets were also supplied to supervisors in 1815—"A Case of Sealed Weights"—as also in 1826. Those issued in 1707 and 1826 are in the cup shape, each fitting into the other, and the latter set ranges, by a multiple of two, from one quarter of an ounce to sixty-four ounces.

WHITE'S MALTSTER'S GUIDE.

"The Maltster's Guide, being a history of the Art of Malting from the earliest ages, also a description of the various systems of malting, &c., &c., the construction of malt-houses, and an abstract of the whole of the Malt Laws. By Edward Skeate White," Supervisor of Inland Revenue. Loftus, London, 1860.

This book exhibits considerable research, and contains much useful information.

WIDOWS AND ORPHANS' FUND.

Provision for the widow and the orphan engaged the attention of this department as early as 1748, at the least, and originated with the North Briton, who established a compulsory fund, and whose committee continued to enrol members down to 1835, when the funds were transferred to the Government. Various unsuccessful efforts were afterwards made, down to 1845, when an optional fund was formed, and though of some service to the department, it proved, in a few years, to be not generally acceptable, and this unacceptability induced an agitation for a change in its constitution, or for the formation of a new one, neither of which endeavours has yet been accomplished—1878, though the Lords of the Treasury have sometimes, in special cases, sanctioned a provision. Outlines of these two funds and the efforts to form new ones will now be given.

"The Excise Incorporation of Scotland"—probably the outcome of a four years' agitation.[1]

This was a fund raised, under the authority of a Royal Charter, dated July 14, 1748, by the compulsory contributions of its members until 1805, when larger payments were exacted under the authority of an Act of Parliament,[2] to provide annuities for the widow and the

[1] C., 1872. [2] 45 G. III., c. 3.

orphan. The first authority patented "a perpetual Endurance of Succession," and divided the department into the three classes, who yearly during life, paid, in eight equal instalments, £3, 4s., £2, 8s., and £1, 12s. respectively, for which the widow became entitled to an annuity of £16, £12, and £8 respectively, payable quarterly, during her "natural life" and viduity, or, in case of no widow, but children, then to the children, until the youngest attained the age of twelve years, or in case of a widow and children, and the widow died or re-married before the youngest attained the prescribed age, then to the children, until the youngest reached that age. The second authority continued the three classes, raised the payments to £7, 10s., £5, 12s. 6d., and £3, 15s., and the annuities to £32, £24, and £16 respectively; increased the duration of payment to the child to the age of sixteen; and gave the original contributor the option of acceding to its provisions. Small additional contributions were paid on a second or subsequent marriage, and the difference in the rate on the promotion of a member from a lower to a higher class was exacted. Provision was also made that in the event of the fund being more than equal to meet the annuities, the latter should be increased by one half, but not more, and if then a surplus, it should be applied to lessen the rates, or in such other manner as the majority of the contributors should decide. This anticipative legislation was needed. The annuities to the relicts of both acceders and non-acceders were actually raised to that extent £48, £36, £24: £24, £18, £12—while the benefit to the child was extended till the attainment of his eighteenth year.[1]

But arrangements were made, in 1833, to transfer these ample funds to the Consolidated Fund, and to discontinue the enrolment of new members after January 5, 1833,[2] under the plea that the management of the revenue of the excise had been placed in the hands of one general board of commissioners for the United Kingdom, and that, as the officers would be liable to removal to any part, the exigencies of the service, and the discontinuance of the chief office in Edinburgh, would not allow the officials to meet to manage the fund—it had, therefore, become expedient to abolish it. Members, however, were enrolled until January 5, 1835, when the funds, which exceeded £54,000, were to be realised and carried[3] to the "Consolidated Duties of Excise," into which the then members contributions were afterwards carried, and out of which, under the

[1] 5 & 6 W. IV., c. 72. [2] Scotland G. O. [3] P. P., 1836, 1838.

head of "incidents," the then and future annuities were to be paid: the number of contributors at the time of the repeal was, under the Royal Charter, or "Non-acceders," 1 first, 7 second, and 17 third class; under the Act or "Contributors' Acceders," 30 first, 119 second, 555 third class.[1] The books and other documents were removed from Edinburgh to London, and the commissioners were authorised to act in the interests of the expiring corporation, until the death of the last contributor, or until the payment of the last annuity, whichever might be the later.

The gradually-decreasing payments appear in the Estimates under the head of non-effective charges: they are, with another head not specially defined, whether gratuitous or by purchase, as follow—

Year ending March 31.	Incorporation of Scotland.		"Pensions to Widows and Orphans."	
	No.	Amount.	No.	Amount.
1858	263	6900	80	1368
1859	258	6800	79	1340
1860	264	7006	78	1336
1861	267	7042	76	1321
1862	269	7090	69	1203
1863	268	7060	68	1193
1864	225	6300	68	1190
1865	225	5700	68	1190
1866	222	5700	50	1100
1867	223	5800	48	1000
1868	200	5500	53	1050
1869	200.	5500	44	665
1870	192	5106	44	620
1871	188	5046	37	544
1872	181	4866	37	544
1873	177	4706	39	536
1874	166	4530	38	504
1875	165	4482	34	502
1876	158	4326	30	458
1877	146	4044	25	420
1878	137	3768	14	269

The further usefulness of this fund, then, being restricted by legal enactment to its present recipients and the future relicts of its present contributors, an effort was at once made to establish a new fund.

[1] 5 & 6 W. IV., c. 72.

The Commissioners, at the instance of the officers who forwarded petitions, addressed the Lords of the Treasury on May 18, 1835, with a view to obtain assistance in its formation, and their Lordships made the following minute, 9938, on July 30, 1835, "There is no subject to which My Lords will more readily turn their attention, or view in a more favourable light, than any proposal which may contribute to the comfort of the officers under their superintendence, or which may facilitate their securing a provision for their families. There are two objections, however, which will prevent the Board from taking any immediate steps on this subject.

"*1st.* The whole of the Excise Establishment has been referred by My Lords, to the Commission of Excise Inquiry, and it will be extremely difficult to make any satisfactory arrangements until My Lords have before them the recommendation of that Commission.

2d. "The advanced state of the present session, and the pressure of the business now in progress will not allow sufficient time for taking any final measure on the subject; not only would the procuring the necessary information, and the preparation of the requisite table occupy more time than My Lords apprehend now is likely to remain, but as any plan which they might propose would be for the purpose of giving general satisfaction to the officers themselves, My Lords consider it would be advisable, that before any scheme were finally adopted, there should be an opportunity of making it generally known through the department, and receiving any observations and suggestions which might be made by the parties interested in the subject." This minute was transmitted to the Commissioners on August 1, 1835, with a request that their Lordships' opinions might be made generally known throughout the department, and the encouraging promise "that My Lords will after the prorogation of Parliament proceed to take the subject into their attentive and favourable consideration, and to enquire how far it will be possible to meet the wishes expressed in the numerous applications before them."

But this request of their Lordships was not transmitted by the Board to the Department until December 12, 1835—an interval of four months.[1] In 1836, the endeavour was continued, and no fewer than 4208 officers declared in favour, and 437 against, the establishment of a society which should apply to the United Kingdom; but, notwithstanding this emphatic vote in favour of compulsory provi-

[1] G. O., 1835.

sion, the project fell to the ground,[1] unless the Old Store Fund mentioned in 1843,[2] and out of which annuities were paid to the widows of deceased officers, but which lapsed on remarriage, was the result of the movement.[3] In 1855, it amounted to £8000. This fund was handed over to the committee of the Excise Benevolent, which, named the Inland Revenue Benevolent Fund in 1849, was established in 1845 in connection with the Atlas Assurance Company, to provide annuities for the widows and orphans of those who chose to insure in this office, and assign the bonuses on their policies to this fund, and to assist superannuated members of seven years' standing in paying their premiums. The fund has been sustained—1st, by voluntary contributions; 2d, by grants from the Board; 3d, by a percentage given by the Atlas Company, on the premiums paid by the members; 4th, by an annual donation from the Atlas Company; 5th, by bonuses on policies of deceased members, which bonuses had been applied to the fund.[3]

In the year ended July 5, 1878, the amount paid to widows was £3375, to orphans £33, to superannuated members £196, and the amount of the funds standing to the credit of the widows, orphans, and superannuated members' fund was £20,346. The superannuated members received assistance at the rate of 12½ per cent. on the amount of their premiums.[4]

The annuity to the widow was at first granted at the rate of five per cent. on the amount of the policy of her deceased husband, until the actuary recommended it to be reduced to four per cent., and then to three per cent. This unsatisfactory state of the fund induced the officials in Wales West Collection in 1858 to petition their Honours for a closer inspection of the management, and for the appointment of a competent person to act for widows. It did not transpire if the commissioners moved in the matter. Neither did it appear if the appeal for a full attendance at the next quarterly meeting on July 10 was successful, but it did appear that an influential meeting was held at Somerset House on August 10, when several resolutions were passed with a view to improve the fund.

In 1861 the rate was increased to three and a-half per cent.,[3] and since that date to four per cent., to the widow not more than ten years younger than her deceased husband; and lowered to three per cent to the widow more than ten, but less than fifteen years, and to two per cent. to the widow of and above fifteen years younger.

[1] C., 1872. [2] G. O. [3] C. S. G., 1862. [4] Committee's Report, 1878.

These benefits were extended in 1849, on the consolidation of the Stamps and the Taxes with the Excise, to all in the department. Inland Revenue Benevolent Fund in Aid was established in 1858, as its name implies, "For the purpose of aiding the objects of the Benevolent Fund, by granting additional annuities to the widow and orphan of contributors" who chose to pay an annual subscription of five shillings per £100 assured in addition to their premiums. The other sources of support have been, voluntary contributions, donations, fines, and interest on stock deposited. In the year ended June 30, 1878, the additional aid given to widows through this auxiliary fund was £407.[1] The committee of management consists of all who have insured to the extent of £300. The benefits of these funds, then, are obtainable only through the medium of the Atlas Assurance Office.

The "distinctive features" of these funds were plainly given in the "Civilian" in December 1871. All have been constantly advertised since 1862. Printed reports were first issued quarterly, then half-yearly, and in 1873 yearly. These, with any further information, are supplied through any supervisor. Brief as this outline must be, reference must be made to the honorary secretary, who from the commencement of the funds took great interest in their adequacy and proper appropriation; see under "Testimonials" 1865. Brain.

Then to glance at the other forms of relief proposed but not realised—in 1846 "The Civil Service Provident Fund:" the formation of this fund first received consideration in 1846; in 1848, Lord John Russell was memorialised;[2] in 1852, Mr Fitzroy presented a petition to the House of Commons, praying for the appropriation of the superannuation assessments to this fund, upon the principle of life assurance, without detriment to the superannuation allowance, and Dr Farr assisted the committee by preparing life and other valuable tables, which were submitted to the Government. Of the 46 departments in London and Dublin, 42 returned in favour of the application, and of the 3582 contributors in these 42 departments, 3196—1958 married, 1238 single—signed the memorial; in 1858, a letter signed by the representatives of 22 departments, among whom was one belonging to this, was despatched from the Audit Office on December 7, to the Chancellor of the Exchequer, to ask for the establishment of the fund,[3] which, however, the Government declined to form.[4] Then to resume the glance.

[1] Committee's Report, 1878. [2] P. P., 1852. [3] C. S. G.; P. P., 1855.
[4] C. S. G., 1854.

In 1854, "The Civil Service Fund:"[1] in 1856, "The Civil Service Orphan Asylum:"[2] in 1858, a "Home for Widows of the Civil Service," and a "National Civil Service Orphan Institution:"[3] in 1862, a "General Provident Scheme:"[4] in 1863, a "Widows and Orphans' Fund."[5] in 1864, a fund established by Act of Parliament:[6] in 1868, a "Civil Servants' Widows' Fund:"[7] in 1874, a "Civil Service Benevolent Society:"[8] and in the House of Commons, a motion by Mr B. Cochrane, on April 18—"That, in the opinion of this House, the alleged grievances of the widows and orphans of those Civil Servants of the Crown, who die in the service of their country, are worthy of the consideration of Her Majesty's Government." He did not press his motion, and the Chancellor of the Exchequer replied, "A Royal Commission had fully inquired in the matter some years ago, and had reported in favour of the continuance of the present system of remuneration. It was quite competent for civil servants, like other people, to make an assurance of their lives for the benefits of their widows and families, if they were married men. If they made deductions from their salaries for the purpose of making such provision, it would be an injustice to the unmarried men, and also to those who were married but had no families. The proper system, as it appeared to him, was to pay their men fairly and liberally for the work required of them, and leave them to make what provision they thought right for those they left behind them."

But to return to my own department in particular. The Benevolent Fund, established and managed on economical principles, soon failed to prove generally acceptable, and as such to prompt the suggestion of a new fund, in 1856. A meeting was also held in Dublin about 1858, to consider the practicability of forming a fund similar to the old Scotch Incorporation previously noted;[9] and owing to the numerous "Strong Appeals,"[10] various suggestions were made down to 1871, when the collector and the whole of the staff in Derby Collection, with Mr J. Skinner, as secretary, formed themselves, after a preliminary meeting in November, into a working committee to establish a fund, the support of which they proposed should be compulsory with future entrants, optional with those already in commission, and that the minimum annuity should be £40, with gratuities

[1] C. S. G., 1854. [2] Idem, 1856. [3] Idem, 1858. [4] P. P., 1852.
[5] Idem, 1863. [6] Idem, 1864. [7] Idem, 1868. [8] Idem, 1874
[9] Idem, 1860. [10] Idem, 1856 to 1870.

to children under the age of thirteen.[1] The next important step taken by the committee was on May 1, 1872, when a circular was issued to obtain the opinion of the department, in a catechetical form, to enable them to place the desires of their fellow-officials in a brief report.[2] This having been obtained, a report was at once drawn up and distributed, and commenced with a statement, to the effect that meetings had been held, with more or less formality, at seventy different places throughout the United Kingdom, and that, in round numbers, 1500 had expressed a desire for the establishment of the fund, while only eleven had stated that they were adverse to the movement. The committee then proceed with the resolutions passed and the suggestions received. The resolutions were five. 1. That, in the meantime, the establishment of the contemplated fund should be in connection with the Inland Revenue Department only. 2. That the allowance to a widow be not less than thirty pounds per annum. 3. That children shall not participate in the benefits of the fund during the life-time of their mother; but, in the case of their mother's death, remarriage, lunacy, or misconduct, provision be made for their enjoying a sum not exceeding the mother's allowance, divided by scale fixed according to their number. 4. That the allowance to a child cease on its attaining the age of seventeen, except in the case of severe mental or bodily infirmity. 5. That the amount of the annuity shall depend upon the amount of the annual premium paid. The suggestions were—that the sympathy and co-operation of the Commissioners should be enlisted: that the proposed fund should be managed after the manner of "The Scotch Incorporation of Excise Officers' Fund:" that, to the 180 representatives nominated by the 77 collections, or some portion of them, must the movement be now committed, but that, for the present, communications and suggestions, as to the best steps to be taken, as for instance, whether or not it is desirable to send a small deputation, or a memorial to the Board; to take opinion of actuary; to consult the committee of the Benevolent Fund; or any proposition deemed serviceable may be sent with as little delay as possible to the Hon. Secretary at Derby.

It is recorded that meetings were held in Glasgow, Tower Hill, Alloa, Campbelton, and Waterford, at which the resolutions and suggestions contained in the report were discussed, and a general con-

[1] P. P., 1871. [2] C., 1872.

clusion come to that an actuary should be consulted. To this the Derby Committee gave effect, and announced on September 14, that his report might be expected in the course of a few weeks. The actuary's report is dated December 1872. At the outset the actuary stated, that he approached the subject with some diffidence, "partly because so many minds of different shades of opinion, and possessing different directions of personal interest, have to be consulted and satisfied, and partly because of the novel nature of some of the elements, which should form part of the risk and consequently of the contribution necessary to cover that risk, without any basis of past experience on which to form the probabilities in regard to the future." He then suggested as the basis of the fund—1st, That the scheme be based upon the supposition that a rate of three per cent. interest will be realised upon the investments. 2d, That the contributions in other respects be based upon data which shall not show "what may be termed cheap rates, but rather that they be full and safe without being superfluous." 3d, That the means for defraying the expenses of management be drawn from two sources—"1. directly, from a uniform payment by each member and each annuitant for each contribution paid or each annuity drawn; 2. indirectly, from the excess of the interest over the rate of three per cent." Minor suggestions—that the expenses of each year be paid each year, not out of the annuity paid, but by an individual rate of at the most not more than two shillings each: that a small "entry money," of five shillings for each £10 annuity, be charged to cover stamp duty and medical fees: that future entrants be compelled to join: that the contributions cease on retirement, and thus so far incorporate that branch of the Benevolent Fund in Aid which renders assistance to superannuated members in the payment of their contributions: that all members on a first marriage pay a sum of £1, 1s. for each £10 annuity, and double these sums on a second marriage: that a member dying and bringing a claim on the fund before he has paid ten years' contributions, the annuity should suffer abatement for such term as shall complete that number of contributions.

On these data, in regard to the future members of the service compelled to join the scheme, and assuming the age to be 21, &c., the actuary calculated that—To provide an annuity of £10 to each member, whether resulting from a first or subsequent marriage, with continuation to his orphan family until the youngest shall attain the age of seventeen; and to assure the sum of £6, 13s. 4d. (=2-3rds.

do. of annuity) payable on death of member, would require an annual subscription of—

£2, 6s. 5d. payable during the entire lifetime of the member.
£2, 7s. 8d. „ until age 70 is attained.
£2, 9s. od. „ „ 65 „
£2, 10s. 8d. „ „ 60 „

To meet the case of the already-commissioned officer, *i.e.*, to give him the option of joining the fund, upon paying during his entire lifetime after entry, the actuary proposed—

Ages.		Annual payment for annuity of £10 to wife after husband's death, and for assurance of £6, 13s. 4d. on death of husband.	Annual payment for annuity of £10 to wife after husband's death, with continuance of annuity to orphan family until the age of 17, and for assurance of £6, 13s. 4d. on death of husband.
Husband.	Wife.		
30	25	£2 18 7	£3 6 11
35	30	3 3 3	3 9 3
40	35	3 8 6	3 17 9
45	40	3 14 7	4 3 6

These were the salient points in his report. The actuary was James Meikle, Edinburgh. The only action, recorded to have taken place on this report, this year, was at Alloa on December 18, when it was resolved "That the Derby Committee be desired to communicate with the committee of the Benevolent Fund, and submit to its members the actuary's report and other information bearing upon the movement, with a request that the last-named committee will be pleased to consider the practicability of establishing for the service a widows and orphans' fund, independent of life assurance." Apart from a meeting held at Tower Hill, London, on the 11th January 1873, at which the Derby Committee were requested to lay the desires of the department, with the actuary's report, before the committee of the Inland Revenue Benevolent Fund, with a view to giving practical effect to them, and two encouraging leading articles from the pen of the editor of the Civil Service Gazette, no further steps were taken to promote the establishment of this fund—to use the language of a correspondent, a "total apathy rested upon the service."

The cash statement showed that of the total amount given to defray expenses—£62, 4s. 6d.—£34, 1s. 1d. was collected in England, £20, 17s. 11d. in Scotland, and £7, 5s. 6d. in Ireland, and that after every claim had been discharged, a balance of £31, 13s. 11½d. remained in the hands of the treasurer. This document is dated December 1873.

The last effort was made by a committee formed in Bristol in 1877. Having carefully ascertained the opinion of the department, they came to the following resolution—"That the committee, having considered the response to their appeal of the 4th October last, they are not warranted in pressing their proposals, but they are persuaded that compulsory life assurance is imperatively called for, and that the Honourable Board be requested to take such steps as may be necessary, that all persons entering the excise branch of the service shall be required to effect an assurance upon their lives within three months of being placed on the establishment"—May 20, 1878. A memorial in accordance with this resolution was duly despatched to the Commissioners, who replied that they no power to make life assurance compulsory.

WINE DUTY.

"Off the customs and exsyis of the soume of four pundis vsuall money of Scotland of ilk Tune of wyne," to be paid to the authorities in Edinburgh.[1] This shows the wine duties to have been one of the very earliest of the excise duties, and the following that it appears to have been continued. The Commissioners were authorised "to ferme the Excise of the Wine to the severall Burrows;"[2] and this they did "Sir William Dick for ane 3 year tak of the Excise on Wines."[3] This refers to Scotland. In England, in 1643, the duty was paid at so much per "tunne" on importation, and again by the retailer at twopence per quart,[4] at which it would seem to have remained until 1648, when it was continued for 3 years.[5]

Charles the Second, in 1660, retained wine as a dutiable, not, however, as an exciseable article, and exacted a licence duty (with an exemption in favour of the Universities, the Borough of St Albans, and of the Mystery of Vintners in the city of London),[6] and, in 1663,

[1] Act, Aug. 4, 1621. [2] Act, January 31, 1645. [3] Act, May 9, 1648.
[4] P. O., 1643. [5] P. O., 1648. [6] 12 Charles II., c. 25.

assigned the revenue derived from it to his "Royal Highness the Duke of Yorke and the heires males of his body,"[1] an assignment afterwards commuted for £24,000.[2] Ten Commissioners were appointed, in 1660, "to license" persons to "utter by retaile" at "a yearly rent" to be agreed upon for a term of twenty-one years, to be paid half-yearly, and not a little trouble did they experience. The duty was not paid with promptitude, threats were issued, farming was tried and discontinued, country agents were appointed, the issue of "Labitats" was threatened until 1758, when the management was placed under the Commissioners of Stamps,[3] under whom it appears to have remained until about 1790, when it was transferred to the Commissioners of Excise.

But, in this period of 160 years, a growing duty had been again exacted upon wine,[4] and again as an excise duty relinquished, and again as an excise duty reimposed by taking a part of the customs duty in order to bring the trade under excise survey, stock, and permit, to suppress the smuggling which, in 1786, had become so common. The wine trade became alarmed at the resolution, and petitioned Parliament to hear them, or their counsel, on the measure, but to little effect, as the bill was carried by a majority of 84 votes.[5] An addition of 167 officers was needed to carry out the regulation, which remained intact until 1825, when the duty was re-transferred to the customs.[6] The discontinuance of the survey, stock, and permit, was recommended in 1833,[7] and adopted, except with regard to those who also sold spirits, in 1835. A drawback was allowed on certain wines in 1860 in accordance with a pre-arrangement.[8]

With respect to the licence duty. Different rates were exigible in all three countries down to the consolidation of the licence laws in 1820.[9] The rates then fixed at £10 the dealer, £4, 4s. the retailer having a beer but not a spirit licence, and £2, 2s. the retailer having a beer and a spirit licence, with the addition of 5 per cent., in 1840, still remain. It has been suggested that the distinction in the case of the retailer should be discontinued.[10] Wine was first bonded in excise warehouse in 1869.

See Excise Scheme; Refreshment House Licence; St Albans' Wine Charter.

[1] 15 Charles II., c. 14. [2] 1 James II., c. 21.
[3] L. G., 1665-1743; Beatson's Political Index. [4] 10 Anne, c. 19.
[5] H. C., May 5, 25, 26, 1786. [6] Order in Council, Feb. 2, 1825.
[7] Parnell, 2 R. [8] T. W., July 8, 1843. [9] C. 1 R. [10] Parnell, 19 R.

ZENAS'S PROMOTION REGISTER.

"Inland Revenue Promotion Register of Clerks, Division and Ride Officers, and table showing the value of licences in general use, with a full index to stations by Zenas." Douglas, Bangor, 1872.

Most of the facts which form this issue were collected by the author during a period of about eighteen months. About 700 copies were sold.

Zenas *alias* E. Owen, ride officer.[1]

[1] C. S. G., 1871-1873.

CORRECTIONS AND ADDITIONS.

Page 29, line 24, *for* "an increased allowance was made in 1869," *read* increased allowances were made in 1869 and 1876.

" 45, *for* "1829 S," *read* 1812 S.

" 52, *after* "December 31st, 266," *read*—Lists of appointments were first issued by the Board on March 3, 1877.

" 67, *read* rate of licence under Dublin, 1805, £10, 1808, £10, 10s.

" 81, line 16, *read* revived *for* revised.

" 84, line 21, *cancel* "Both licences applied to the United Kingdom," and line 24, *cancel* "not one of the latter having been issued in Scotland."

" 102, line 21, *read* pages.

" 111, line 21, *read* qualification.

" 127, line 22, *for* 1876, 9, £36, *read* 1878, 3, £14.

" 141, line 17, *for* 1858, *read* 1852, and after reference 7, at bottom of page, insert 1858.

" 189, line 5, *read* Noble.

" 210, year 1867, under collectors, *read* 2, 5, 16, 22, 17.

" 223, line 4, *read* grapes.

" 223, bottom line, add reference number 2,

" 253, last line, *read* spile-rod.

" 290, line 2, after Ireland, insert A Parliamentary Committee reported on this subject in 1840.

" 300, *read* Royal Gauger.

" 345, line 4, *read* repealed *for* repeated.

" 356, line 28, *read* uting *for* using.

" 372, line 4, nigromaltine, insert not between "is sanctioned."

" 377, line 11, *read* in *for* "as."

Inland Revenue Building Society, incorporated under the Building Societies Act, 1874. Established in 1877, under the mutual benefit principle, to enable members of the Inland Revenue and their friends to acquire freehold, copyhold, or leasehold property, it has so far proved a success. Somerset House, London.

INDEX.

TURNBULL AND SPEARS, PRINTERS, EDINBURGH.

LaVergne, TN USA
29 November 2010
206676LV00004B/179/P

9 781146 989640